Fundamentals
Software Engineering

Comprehensive insights into SDLC design quality and AI/ML in software

2nd Edition

Dr. Hitesh Mohapatra

Dr. Amiya Kumar Rath

www.bpbonline.com

Second Revised and Updated Edition 2025

First Edition 2020

ISBN: 978-93-6589-338-0

LIMITS OF LIABILITY AND DISCLAIMER OF WARRANTY

The information contained in this book is true and correct to the best of author's and publisher's knowledge. The author has made every effort to ensure the accuracy of these publications, but the publisher cannot be held responsible for any loss or damage arising from any information in this book.

All trademarks referred to in the book are acknowledged as properties of their respective owners but BPB Publications cannot guarantee the accuracy of this information.

Dedicated to

Beloved parents
and
Dear students

About the Authors

- **Dr. Hitesh Mohapatra** received his B.E. degree in Information Technology from **Biju Patnaik University of Technology (BPUT)**, Odisha, in 2006, and the MTech. degree in CSE from **Odisha University of Technology and Research (OUTR)** University, Odisha in 2009. He received his Ph.D. in Computer Science & Engineering in 2021 from Veer Surendra Sai University of Technology (VSSUT), Burla, India. He has contributed 50+ SCI and Scopus-indexed research articles, and has authored two books on software engineering and C programming, respectively. He has 15 years of teaching experience both in industry and academia. He has served the research community in various capacities like session chair, technical chair, keynote speaker, etc. His research interests include wireless sensor networks, smart cities, smart grids, and smart water. Currently, he is working as an Associate Professor at the School of Computer Engineering, KIIT Deemed to be University, Bhubaneswar, and Odisha.
- **Dr. Amiya Kumar Rath** received his B.E. degree in computer from Dr. Babasaheb Ambedkar Marathwada University, Aurangabad, in 1990, his M.B.A. degree in systems management from Shivaji University in 1993, the MTech. degree in computer science from Utkal University in 2001, and the Ph.D. degree in computer science from Utkal University in 2005, with a focus on embedded systems. He is currently a Professor at the Department of Computer Science and Engineering, Veer Surendra Sai University of Technology, Burla, India. He has contributed over 100 research-level papers to many national and international journals and conferences. He has published seven books by reputed publishers. His research interests include embedded systems, ad hoc networks, sensor networks, power minimization, evolutionary computation, and data mining. He was deputed as an adviser to the **National Assessment and Accreditation Council (NAAC)**, Bangalore, India, from 2019 to 2023. Currently, he is working as Vice Chancellor for **Biju Patnaik University of Technology (BPUT)**, Rourkela, Odisha, from 2023 up to 2028.

Acknowledgements

With the release of this second edition of *Fundamentals of Software Engineering*, we take this opportunity to express our heartfelt gratitude to everyone who has supported and inspired us throughout this journey.

First and foremost, we would like to thank our parents and families for their continued encouragement and unwavering belief in us. Their support has been the foundation of our work, both during the first edition and now as we present this updated volume.

We are deeply grateful to the readers, students, and educators who engaged with the first edition. Your feedback, suggestions, and thoughtful critiques have been instrumental in helping us refine and improve the content. Many of the enhancements in this edition are a direct result of your insights and experiences.

We also extend our sincere thanks to the academic community and our peers, whose discussions and collaboration have enriched our understanding of software engineering. The evolving nature of this field demands continuous learning, and we are fortunate to be part of a network that fosters that growth.

Our appreciation goes once again to the team at BPB Publications for their ongoing support, flexibility, and commitment to quality. Their cooperation allowed us the necessary time and space to revise and expand the material for this edition carefully. Given the dynamic scope of software engineering, this continued partnership has been key to maintaining the clarity and relevance of the book.

Finally, we are grateful to everyone who has been part of this journey - seen and unseen. Your encouragement and contributions, no matter how big or small, have helped bring this second edition to life.

Preface

In today's rapidly evolving digital landscape, the demands on software professionals are higher than ever. Software engineering has grown beyond traditional methodologies, integrating advanced technologies like artificial intelligence, machine learning, and data-driven development. As professionals, it is crucial to stay ahead of these changes and continuously adapt to new practices, tools, and techniques. This book is a comprehensive resource designed to bridge the gap between conventional software engineering and cutting-edge advancements.

Whether you are a beginner taking your first steps into the world of software development or a seasoned professional looking to update your skills, this book offers something for everyone. By blending foundational knowledge with modern innovations, the goal is to provide a clear, structured pathway for learning and applying key software engineering concepts. Through this journey, readers will explore everything from core principles such as the **software development life cycle** (**SDLC**) and agile methodologies to more advanced topics like machine learning, AI-driven development, and large language models (LLM) architecture.

This book has been crafted to not only equip readers with the theoretical knowledge needed to understand software engineering but also with the practical insights required to excel in real-world applications. We hope it serves as a valuable companion for software engineers, project managers, and IT professionals alike, empowering them to develop efficient, scalable, and future-proof software solutions in an ever-evolving field.

Thank you for embarking on this journey, we wish you great success in your software engineering endeavors.

Chapter 1: Concepts of Software Engineering – The objective of software engineering is to understand the user conceptual model and develop a better specification, to improve design languages and reusable code, to use participatory design and interactive debugging, and to provide a specification of interface and mock-up to confirm the specifications. This chapter discusses the concepts of software engineering, demonstrating the software development process during system development.

Chapter 2: Modeling Software Development Life Cycle – Application software, when it becomes large and complex, requires looking into different aspects like readability, reliability, security, reparability or maintainability, and usability. For analysts, designers, and developers involved in the process of software development, it becomes important to break down the tasks into clear-cut phases of development and assign them to various development groups. On completion of certain tasks, the next task can only be taken. Therefore, a structured development process needs to be adopted. In this chapter, a number of software development models are discussed, along with the advantages and disadvantages of each. A software developer will be introduced to the concept of reliability, performance, safety, and security being used in a life cycle model and understand the activities that are involved in a software development process. The developer will have a clear idea of which model is most suitable to meet his requirements.

Chapter 3: Software Requirement Analysis and Specification – This chapter covers the goals and objectives of the system, emphasizing the need for high-quality requirement specifications. It details system interfaces, information flow, structure definitions, diagrams, and major functions. Design constraints, technological risks, and alternative requirements are evaluated. Inconsistencies and module redundancy are examined, and system validation is performed. Tools and techniques for requirement determination are explored, including computing support, joint application design, prototyping, and appropriate elicitation methods.

Chapter 4: Software Project Management Framework – Project management involves planning, organizing, and managing resources to achieve specific goals. It is related to program management but differs in scope. A project is a temporary endeavor with a defined beginning and end, constrained by time, funding, or deliverables, aimed at achieving beneficial change or added value. Unlike ongoing business operations, projects require distinct technical skills and separate management approaches.

Chapter 5: Project Scheduling Through PERT or CPM – The objective of this chapter is to provide a comprehensive understanding of project management techniques used to plan, schedule, and control complex projects. By exploring **Program Evaluation Review Technique (PERT)** and **critical path method (CPM)**, this chapter aims to equip readers with the knowledge to effectively allocate resources, estimate project timelines, and manage uncertainties. Through detailed explanations and examples, the chapter guides professionals in identifying critical tasks, optimizing project duration, and ensuring timely project completion while minimizing costs and risks.

Chapter 6: Software Project Analysis and Design – During the analysis and design of a project, the designer must know what the software product will do and how the software accomplishes the task. These are laid down in the software specification requirement in the form of design-to-specification, and software function and performance specification. At this stage, the software documentation and requirement specification must be complete.

The objective is to meet the need for a good specification and meticulously usage of the specification requirement at each level of software development. The objective of this chapter is to describe the analysis and design requirements, identify and classify the design levels, describe the need to design a database, and coordinate and correlate all the steps of the design process.

Chapter 7: Object Oriented Analysis and Design – The main objective of this chapter is to introduce the object-oriented methodologies and their applications in the software design process. The OO terminologies, concepts and principles underlying the OO approach are discussed. The process of object identifications and class identifications are introduced in this chapter. You will also learn analysis and design activities are blended in the OO approach. The techniques and associated notations are incorporated into a standard object-oriented language called Unified Modelling Language. The various static and dynamic models are described using UML with examples.

Chapter 8: Use Case Diagram – The objective of this chapter is to provide a comprehensive understanding of how these diagrams model the interactions between users (actors) and a system. Use case diagrams are essential for visualizing system behavior, capturing functional requirements, and identifying the roles of users within the system. This chapter aims to equip readers with the knowledge to create and interpret use case diagrams, ensuring they can effectively define system functionality and user interactions. By the end of the chapter, readers will be able to use these diagrams to enhance communication between stakeholders and improve the overall design process.

Chapter 9: Designing Interfaces and Dialogues and Database Design – This chapter covers system interface and dialogue design, focusing on information input, display sequences, and user-computer interaction. It outlines interface and dialogue design rules, navigation between forms and reports, and deliverables. Data requirements are described using interfaces, databases, forms, and reports. Entity-relationship diagrams and graphical notations are introduced for conceptual data modeling. Logical data modeling is explored for structuring data with minimal redundancy and stability over time. The chapter also discusses relational databases, principles of relational data models, and their connection to entity-relationship models to reflect actual data requirements in forms and reports.

Chapter 10: Coding and Debugging – Programming is a sequence of statements, called code, which can be executed by a computer. Coding is translating the detailed design of the product into a series of statements. The design specifications are translated into codes in the design phase. The objective of this chapter is to provide a guideline for programmers who can write programming statements with clarity, efficiency, and low cost. The code can further be tested easily and implemented quickly. What are the selection criteria for a suitable programming language, what are the style rules to produce a good code, and what are the types of languages suitable for writing a program are the main objectives of this chapter.

Chapter 11: Software Testing – The objective of system testing is to identify and remove software defects, ensuring error-free operation under specified conditions. Effective testing is crucial for system success, as inadequate testing can lead to long-term problems, with errors becoming more complex over time. Testing early in the process reduces costs by preventing issues later. Additionally, system testing serves as a user-oriented validation tool, ensuring the software meets user needs. This chapter outlines testing dynamics, key terminologies, strategies, techniques, and tools used in testing, emphasizing the importance of test planning and different types of testing in system development.

Chapter 12: System Implementation and Maintenance – The objective of this chapter is to identify the software development tasks required for the implementation and maintenance of a software system, to describe the steps for implementation and maintenance of the system, to identify the factors that influence the implementation and maintenance process, and to build up the guidelines for carrying out the implementation and maintenance procedures. This chapter deals with both system implementation and maintenance separately.

Chapter 13: Reliability – The objective of this chapter is to emphasize why reliability is required while developing a software package used by the public. Also, it introduces the need for reliability for the developers to apply the concept for a smooth running of the product. The developer should have a sound knowledge of similar terms like quality, reliability, maintainability, availability, etc. The chapter identifies and describes the important properties of good reliability models for software measurement. Developing a software reliability model will help to predict software products to run faultlessly and to use the models in test planning and software design.

Chapter 14: Software Quality – Software quality can be understood in various ways depending on factors such as the person involved, the context, and the type of software system in question. A clearer approach is to define the characteristics of high-quality software. This module aims to describe software quality by outlining the expected properties of superior software. To achieve this, it is essential to consider the perspectives and expectations of users, as well as those involved in the development, management, marketing, and maintenance of the software. Additionally, individual characteristics associated with quality and their interrelationships must be examined, with a focus on the critical aspect of functional correctness.

Chapter 15: CASE Studies and Reusability – A good workshop for any craftsperson, including software engineers, requires useful tools, an organized layout, and skilled usage. Software engineers need diverse tools and an efficient workspace. Software development requires an engineering discipline, focusing on common techniques, standard methodologies, and automated tools. The use of automated tools in information system development led to computer-aided software engineering.

Chapter 16: Recent Trends and Developments in Software Engineering – Advances in sensors, wireless communications, and mobile devices have enabled ubiquitous software applications that adapt to user contexts. Context-aware applications are widely used in e-commerce, e-learning, and e-healthcare. Capturing and processing contextual information is challenging, requiring new techniques as traditional tools fall short. Barry Boehm highlighted key trends in software engineering, including software-system integration, user-centered design, security, rapid changes, globalization, and legacy system integration. These trends demand new skills and approaches.

Chapter 17: Artificial Intelligence Integration with SDLC – This chapter explores the transformative impact of artificial intelligence on the software development life cycle. As software development processes grow more complex and demand greater efficiency, AI emerges as a pivotal technology that enhances various stages of the SDLC. This chapter provides an in-depth analysis of how AI is integrated into each phase of the SDLC—from requirement gathering and analysis to design, coding, testing, deployment, and maintenance.

Chapter 18: Integration of Machine Learning in SDLC Process – It outlines how ML can enhance various phases of the SDLC, from requirements gathering to deployment and maintenance. The introduction also discusses the growing relevance of ML in software engineering and the benefits of incorporating intelligent models to automate and optimize SDLC processes.

Chapter 19: Unlocking the LLM for SDLC Model – It provides an overview of how LLMs, like GPT-4 and similar advanced models, can be leveraged to optimize various stages of SDLC. The chapter emphasizes the importance of integrating LLMs to automate repetitive tasks, enhance decision-making, and improve software quality.

Chapter 20: Model Questions with Answers – Model questions with answers with few solved papers.

Code Bundle and Coloured Images

Please follow the link to download the
Code Bundle and the ***Coloured Images*** of the book:

https://rebrand.ly/emhnf75

The code bundle for the book is also hosted on GitHub at **https://github.com/bpbpublications/Fundamentals-of-Software-Engineering-2nd-Edition**. In case there's an update to the code, it will be updated on the existing GitHub repository.

We have code bundles from our rich catalogue of books and videos available at **https://github.com/bpbpublications**. Check them out!

Errata

We take immense pride in our work at BPB Publications and follow best practices to ensure the accuracy of our content to provide with an indulging reading experience to our subscribers. Our readers are our mirrors, and we use their inputs to reflect and improve upon human errors, if any, that may have occurred during the publishing processes involved. To let us maintain the quality and help us reach out to any readers who might be having difficulties due to any unforeseen errors, please write to us at :

errata@bpbonline.com

Your support, suggestions and feedbacks are highly appreciated by the BPB Publications' Family.

Piracy

If you come across any illegal copies of our works in any form on the internet, we would be grateful if you would provide us with the location address or website name. Please contact us at **business@bpbonline.com** with a link to the material.

If you are interested in becoming an author

If there is a topic that you have expertise in, and you are interested in either writing or contributing to a book, please visit **www.bpbonline.com**. We have worked with thousands of developers and tech professionals, just like you, to help them share their insights with the global tech community. You can make a general application, apply for a specific hot topic that we are recruiting an author for, or submit your own idea.

Reviews

Please leave a review. Once you have read and used this book, why not leave a review on the site that you purchased it from? Potential readers can then see and use your unbiased opinion to make purchase decisions. We at BPB can understand what you think about our products, and our authors can see your feedback on their book. Thank you!

For more information about BPB, please visit **www.bpbonline.com**.

Join our book's Discord space

Join the book's Discord Workspace for Latest updates, Offers, Tech happenings around the world, New Release and Sessions with the Authors:

https://discord.bpbonline.com

Table of Contents

CHAPTER 1
Concepts of Software Engineering

Introduction

Software engineering (SE) is a pragmatic discipline that is based on computer science to provide scientific foundations in the same way that traditional engineering disciplines such as electrical engineering and chemical engineering rely on physics and chemistry. Software engineering, being a labor-intensive activity, requires both technical skill and management control. Management science provides the foundation for software project management. Computing systems must be developed and maintained on time and within cost estimates. Software engineering activities occur within an organizational context, and a high degree of communication is required among customers, managers, software engineers, hardware engineers, and other technocrats. There are various methodologies for the development of software engineering projects depending on their size. The fundamental principle for managing the complexity is to decompose an extensive system into smaller, more manageable subunits with well-defined interfaces. The approach of divide and conquer is routinely used in the engineering discipline. In software engineering, the units of decomposition are called **modules**. The modules are not disjointed. The development process begins with a definition of system needs and ends with a product that is supposed to perform specific tasks with a required degree of precision and accuracy within a predefined time length. The success of the system lies with the system development team, the involvement of users from the beginning, commitment and cooperation from both the management groups.

Structure

In this chapter, we are going to discuss:

- Definition
- Evolution and impact of SE
- Software engineering
- Importance of SW project construction
- System analysis and design

Objectives

The primary goal of software engineering is to improve the quality of software products and increase the productivity and job satisfaction of software engineers. Software engineering is a new discipline, distinct from but based on the foundations of computer science, management science, economics, communication skills, and the engineering approach to problem-solving.

Definition

Software engineering is the application of a systematic, disciplined, and quantifiable approach to the development, operation, and maintenance of software. It encompasses techniques and procedures, often regulated by a software development process, to improve the reliability and maintainability of the software system. The effort is necessitated by the potential complexity of those systems, which may contain millions of lines of code.

According to *Boehm*, software engineering involves *the practical application of scientific knowledge to the design and construction of computer programs and associated documentation required to develop, operate, and maintain them*. The definition covers biological, financial, manufacturing, medical, legal, government, and many other systems.

The term software engineering was popularized by *F. L. Bauer*, during the NATO Software Engineering Conference in 1968. The discipline of software engineering includes knowledge, tools, and methods for software requirements, software design, software construction, software testing, and software maintenance tasks. Software engineering is related to the disciplines of computer science, computer engineering, management, mathematics, project management, quality management, software ergonomics, and system engineering.

Evolution and impact of software engineering

During the past few decades, significant advances have occurred in all areas of software engineering. Analysis techniques for determining software requirements have been developed. Methodical approaches to software design have developed and design notations have proliferated. Implementation techniques have been improved, and new programming languages have been developed. Software validation techniques have been examined, and quality assurance procedures have been instituted. **Computer-aided software engineering (CASE)** tools are developed and deployed during the development process. Formal techniques for verifying software properties have evolved, and software maintenance procedures have been interpreted to mean that the problems of SE have been solved. The level of SE is indicative of the vast number of problems to be solved.

Software engineering process

The process of software engineering is the structure of the development of a software product. There are different models of software process (software lifecycle) used in different organizations and industries.

Software engineering

The field of software engineering is concerned with the study of complex systems. The complex system is composed of many components with complex relationships. It is essential to make various modules or components and link them together to represent complex systems. The term engineering encompasses the use of certain principles and building the software methodically. To apply the principles, the software engineer should be equipped with appropriate methods and specific techniques that will help to incorporate the desired properties into the process and product. Sometimes, the methods and techniques are packaged to form a methodology. The purpose of the methodology is to promote a certain approach to solving a problem.

Levels of software process

Three levels of software process are identified for its projects. These levels balance the different needs of different types of projects. Scaling the process to the project is vital to its success. Too much process can be as problematic as too little. Too much process can slow down a purely R&D exploration, and too little process can slow down a large development project with hard deliverables. The levels are briefly identified as follows:

- **Level 1:** R&D
    - No software products delivered, pure research
    - Minimal software process
- **Level 2:** Research project
    - Larger development team, informal software releases
    - Moderate software process
- **Level 3:** Delivered system
    - The large software development team, formal software releases
    - More formal software process

The software process and software engineering practices have become more formalized and more structured as the project proceeded through different levels.

A set of software engineering best practices is implemented in three software process levels. These include source code control, neat code builds, writing reusable code, using different team models, commitment to deadlines, design and code reviews, risk management, bug tracking, software metrics, **software configuration management** (**SCM**), and requirements management.

SCM is a step up in formality and reproducibility from source code control and includes controlling and versioning of software releases.

Importance of SW project construction

At one time, software development and coding were thought to be the same. As distinct activities in the software development life cycle have been identified, some of the best minds in the field have spent their time analyzing and debating methods of project management, requirements, design, and testing. The rush to study these newly identified areas has left code construction as the ignorant cousin of software development.

Discussions about construction have also been hobbled by the suggestion that treating construction as a distinct software development activity implies that construction must also be treated as a distinct phase. Software activities and phases do not have to be set up in any relationship to each other, and it is useful to discuss the activity of construction, regardless of whether other software activities are performed in phases, in iterations, or in some other way.

Typically, construction makes up about 80 percent of the effort on small projects and 50 percent on medium projects. Construction accounts for about 75 percent of the errors on small projects and 50 to 75 percent on medium and large projects. Any activity that accounts for 50 to 75 percent of the errors presents a clear opportunity for improvement.

The irony of the shift in focus away from construction is that construction is the only activity that is guaranteed to be done. Requirements can be assumed rather than developed, architecture can be shortchanged rather than designed, and testing can be abbreviated or skipped rather than fully planned and executed. But, if there is going to be a program, then there must be construction, and that makes construction a uniquely fruitful area in which to improve development practices.

Problems in system development

Many problems are encountered during a system development process. Before the system is launched, it is abandoned. The reasons for a system failure could be from either side of the development house or the user. An experienced developer having foresightedness can apprehend a problem much earlier and can take remedial action before it surfaced during development. The developer and the user should work in groups so that they understand each other's problems and solve them amicably. In developing a large and complex software project, many problems are associated as follows:

- **Time schedule overlap:** Sometimes, a large project becomes very much time-consuming. There may be a drastic change in the system that has been desired at the beginning. The originally designed concepts to solve the scope of the project are no longer valid during development. It causes a time delay in delivering the system. The user may lose interest in further developing the project to implement.
- **User interface**: The man-machine interaction is sometimes not considered initially surfaced in the course of development. This causes further additions of controls and displays. New hardware and software are felt necessary to be included later.
- **Test and integration:** Often, the project finds deficiencies during testing and integration of the software project. The inadequate parts are included in the latter part of the development process. This happens due to inadequate thoughts being given at the initial stage.
- **Maintenance problem:** Many problems surfaced at this phase after handing over the system to the client. The user intends to include many additions and changes to the system when he operates independently. The developer allows the user to handle the system and takes the modification activity as the user experiences many technological, functional, and performance problems. Therefore, at the time of implementation, a warranty period is considered to set the teething problems right by the developer without any additional cost encountered by the user.

Solutions to the problems

The problems faced at a later stage can be avoided if proper analysis and design are done initially. This may avoid unnecessary cost escalation during the development process. Some of the possible solutions are discussed as follows:

- **Time schedule overlap:** The problem can be prevented by postponing the technology decisions for as long as possible or reducing the system development cycle time. Since the financial impact is to be ascertained initially, detailed analysis and design are made early in the development process. The detailed cost estimates are made based on the analysis and design. Technology decisions are taken on maturity issues. It is better to use the available software and hardware so that the development time cycle can be reduced. A phased development approach is a better solution. The system is analyzed, designed, developed, tested, and implemented in segments. Any problem encountered in a segment can be settled immediately by referring to the previous phase.
- **User interface:** Associate the users in the development process who will be finally using the system. Take their views to simplify the system operation. Many interface activities can be simplified and streamlined during the development process.
- **Test and integration:** Define a comprehensive test program. Assign to a member of the system team having good testing experience. Include a member from the

user side during the acceptance test. Obtain agreement from the user step by step after module testing, integration testing, and system testing.

- **Maintenance problem:** Design the system to accommodate the changes at a later stage. The changes may include additional hardware to increase accuracy and speed and changes in the software to increase the computing power. Have proper documentation of the system so that it can be referred for making a change at a later stage during its life cycle.

Qualities of the software

Higher the quality of a software product and process, the software produces more serviceability, less problematic, and longer life. The user wants the software product to be reliable, efficient, and easy to use. At the same time, the software producer wants the product to be verifiable, maintainable, portable, and extensible. The external qualities are visible to the users of the system, whereas the internal qualities concern the developers. The qualities of the software product are closely associated. Some of the software qualities are tabulated in *Table 1.1*:

Quality	Description
Correctness	The specification of the system meets the desired goal.
Reliability	Least error in software and dependable.
Robustness	Software or hardware sustainability under abnormal conditions.
Usability	Software friendliness during user interface.
Performance	Better usability of the system with optimum utilization of resources.
Productivity	Quality of the software production process with efficiency and performance.
Verifiability	Ability to verify the correctness or performance of the software system.
Maintainability	Ease to modify the system and put it into use without much distress.
Repairability	Correcting the defects of the software with reasonable effort and time.
Evolvability	Modifiable over time to provide new functionality over the existing.
Reusability	Usage of new components along with the existing software.
Understandability	Making the software less complex and easy to understand by others.
Portability	The system adapts to any kind of environment for better usage.
Interoperability	The ability of the system to coexist and cooperate with other systems.
Timeliness	After processing the software, the ability to deliver the product on time.
Visibility	Documenting all the steps and current status available to others.

Table 1.1: *Software qualities*

System analysis and design

The development of a good system needs proper system analysis and design. The objective of an analysis is to find the customer requirements, to create a base to develop software, and to define various requirements which are to be developed subsequently. A good system analyst can break up the system into various modules for development and integrate them finally into a flawless workable product.

A system engineer or a system analyst performs the following technical tasks:

- Analyze the existing system and make a requirement list by discussing the users.
- Prepare a conceptual (logical) design for the system based on the requirements.
- Establish the boundaries of the system to use the inputs, outputs, and interfaces.
- Define the functions to be performed and the parameters to measure performance.
- Find out the internal structures of the system and their dependencies.
- Prepare mathematical models to support the evaluation of system performance.
- Make alternative solutions and their weighted evaluation to choose the best.
- Decompose the system into various logical sub-systems to be integrated later.
- Participate in system development, testing, integration, and implementation.
- Associate with the users, developers, and management for steering the project.
- Work as a change agent and catalyst for process development.
- Act as a leader in all the phases during the system development.
- Prepare the project plan and schedule for phase-wise project completion.
- Determine the system's reliability, availability, and quality.
- Prepare system development a cost estimates and perform cost-benefit analysis.

System analysis

System analysis is the process of gathering and interpreting the facts, solving the problem, and using the information to recommend improvements to the system. System analysis involves the study of an application area to fully understand the problem being posed. This study includes interviews, observations, hands-on experience, consultations, and many other forms of data gathering. Activities are focused on developing a comprehensive knowledge of the existing system, its strengths and weaknesses, and the underlying reasons for the need to restructure, replace, or automate the existing system. The analyst produces a problem statement as a result of this activity.

A system analyst is a designated person who is responsible for studying and designing a system. A system analyst has many roles to play as an investigator, planner, designer, modulator, communicator, implementor, trainer, change agent, architect, psychologist, salesperson, motivator, politician, conflict resolution, persuader, and imposer. An efficient system analyst can take the entire responsibility to take up the software project from initiation to implementation. A successful analyst can dream of a successful software project.

The analyst, during system analysis, has to carry out the following tasks:

- Understand the existing system, its merits, and demerits.
- Planning the new application or modification of the existing one.
- Scheduling the activities to be performed during the development.
- Consider alternative candidate solutions.
- Emphasize the re-engineering process and method study.
- Carry out operations like backup procedures, audits, quality checks, and security procedures.
- Lay down the plans and cost reduction activities.
- Give importance to system enhancement and recycling.

System architecture and design

The system design involves the development of a structure or architecture of the system. The design is an ongoing process from the stage of inception. The system design begins with **what is to be built** and with **how it is to be built**. The involvement of the software engineer begins with attending meetings with the users, reading preliminary documents, and participating in system-level reviews and walkthroughs. This helps the software engineer to gain a deeper understanding of the system. He has to prepare the process modeling that focuses on the design of the software resources, that is, the programs and procedures needed by the proposed system. It concentrates on developing detailed specifications for the program modules, with specifications and procedures needed to meet user interface and data design specifications. The software engineer should be well versed in the application area. With his knowledge, various software functions and specifications can be designed. The system and sub-system performance requirements can be ascertained by the software engineer. The software engineer can participate in system architecture development.

Conclusion

Software engineering brings the logical concept of a system into an operational physical system by converting the dreams into a stream. A well experienced and committed software engineer is very much required who works as a driving force in the development team. The system should be implemented well in time and fulfill user requirements. The system should give visible benefits that can be accepted by the user. To have a long life, the software product should have proper quality and reliability. The system should be easy to understand and change, so that it can be maintained effectively for sustained use.

In the next chapter, we will discuss the various **software development life cycles (SDLC)**, examining their distinct phases, methodologies, and key properties. This discussion will provide deeper insight into how different SDLC models support diverse project requirements and how they can be tailored to enhance project success.

Exercises

To solidify your understanding of the concepts covered in this chapter, try the following exercises.

Multiple choice questions

1. **What is a key goal when creating a user conceptual model in software development?**
   a. To speed up coding
   b. To develop a better specification based on user needs
   c. To optimize system performance
   d. To simplify debugging
2. **Which of the following is a benefit of reusable code in software development?**
   a. Reduces system testing requirements
   b. Speeds up user interface design
   c. Improves maintainability and efficiency in future projects
   d. Increases manual coding efforts
3. **Participatory design focuses on:**
   a. Involving users in the design process to ensure the system meets their needs
   b. Reducing project costs
   c. Streamlining project timelines
   d. Optimizing database design
4. **What is the purpose of a software mockup during the development process?**
   a. To train users on system functionality
   b. To confirm that the system specification aligns with user requirements
   c. To test system security
   d. To automate code generation
5. **How has the evolution of software engineering (SE. impacted system development?**
   a. It has slowed down the software development process
   b. It introduced more complexity without benefits

c. It improved collaboration, productivity, and software quality
d. It led to a decline in reusable code practices

Short answer questions

1. Define software engineering and explain its role in system development.
2. How can design languages contribute to creating reusable code? Provide an example.
3. Describe how participatory design improves the software development process. Why is it important for user satisfaction?
4. Explain the importance of software project construction in ensuring project success. What are the key components involved?
5. Define system? What are the characteristics of a system?
6. Explain briefly the functions of the following business sub-systems. (Production, Finance, Personnel).

Essay questions

1. Discuss the software engineering process and its importance during the system development life cycle. Provide examples of how a well-structured process can improve the quality and reliability of software systems.
2. Analyze how system analysis and design contribute to the overall success of a software project. Include a discussion of how mockups and specifications help confirm user requirements.
3. Evaluate the impact of evolving software engineering practices on modern software development. How has the evolution of SE improved collaboration and system design processes?
4. What are the advantages of involving a software engineer or a system analyst in software development?
5. What are the problems encountered during system development?
6. In your view, what is system-level architecture?
7. Do you think a successful system analyst must be an experienced programmer? Give reasons for your answer.
8. What are the qualities necessary to incorporate during the development of software?
9. Describe the tasks of a system analyst during a software development process?

Multiple choice answers

1. b
2. c
3. a
4. b
5. c

CHAPTER 2

Modeling Software Development Life Cycle

Introduction

Modeling the **software development life cycle (SDLC)** is about understanding the process of creating software, from the initial idea to the finished product. It involves a series of steps that help teams plan, build, test, and deploy software in a structured and efficient way. By modeling these stages, teams can visualize the entire process, anticipate potential challenges, and ensure that each phase, whether it is design, coding, or maintenance, aligns with the overall goals. It is a way to keep the development organized and on track, ensuring the final product meets both technical and user needs effectively.

Structure

In this chapter, we are going to discuss the following topics:

- System analysis and design
- Overview of SDLC
- Types of SDLC models

Objectives

When application software becomes large and complex, there is a need to look into different aspects like readability, reliability, security, repairability or maintainability, and usability. Many analysts, designers, and developers get involved in the process of software development. It becomes essential to break down the tasks into clear-cut phases of development and assign them to various development groups. There is a dependency among the phases. On completion of specific tasks, the next task can only be taken up. Therefore, a structured development process needs to be adopted.

System analysis and design

Information is power. An organization having all the information is considered to be more pragmatic. To make the information available, a computerized system is developed, which not only provides information but also helps the management to make decisions quickly. It is an organizational improvement process. The analysis and design of an information system are based on the objectives, structures, and processes that help to exploit the information technology to the advantage.

Data and process

An information system consists of data, data flow, and processing logic. Data are raw facts that describe an entity (for example, people, place, or an object). The data from the system produces **information**. The relationships among the data are described using various techniques. **Data flows** are the groups of data that move and flow in a system, including the source and destination. **Processing logic** describes the steps in the transformation of data. The steps are triggered by calling certain events.

Process oriented approach

The importance is given to the process where the emphasis is given to flow, use, and data transformation. When and how the data moves from source to destination, through intermediate steps, is tracked. The processes of using the data and transforming the data into information are considered. This approach takes care of the sequence of the processes. The data files are used when they are required by the process. Several data files are created for different applications. It causes duplication of data in various files. The same data element in different files must be changed or updated during the process. It becomes more cumbersome to have specialized data files. The same data elements in different files have different names. The standardization of data for the organization is felt necessary since the data plays a vital role in the process.

Data oriented approach

More focus is given to **data** than the **processes**. Many techniques are used to simplify the data and their related problems, like data redundancy, data indexing, and establishing their relationships. The data model describes the rules and policies of a business organization. A systematic data organization is becoming more essential. The **process** may change from time to time, but the **data** remains the same for the organization. Data files are becoming larger and more complex day by day. Therefore, more care is given to data and data normalization rather than the process. In this approach, the process and data are handled separately. Data handling software is available to handle the queries more efficiently. A **database** is used for every software application system. The database can be used by many application systems simultaneously. Designing a database becomes important and can be used by different applications. A **data repository** can be used for the current and future systems without causing problems in changing the data. Many organizations maintain a central database for various applications.

Types of systems and system developments

The users are many in an organization with their respective usage. With a broad range of people and interests, different types of information systems are required to be developed. The people who are directly or indirectly associated with an information system are system managers, system analysts, programmers, end users, auditors, business managers, heads of the organization, and support technicians. There are different classes of information systems that can be used effectively by different people.

Transaction processing system

A **transaction processing system (TPS)** is a set of information that processes the data transaction in a database system that monitors transaction programs. The essence of a transaction program is that it manages data that must be left in a consistent state. For example, if an electronic payment is made, the amount must be either withdrawn from one account and added to the other, or none. In case of a failure preventing transaction completion, the partially executed transaction must be rolled back by the TPS. While this type of integrity must also be provided for batch transaction processing, it is particularly important for online processing. For example, if an airline seat reservation system is accessed by multiple operators, after an empty seat inquiry, the seat reservation data must be locked until the reservation is made. Otherwise, another user may get the impression a seat is still free while it is actually being booked at the time. Without proper transaction monitoring, double bookings may occur. Other transaction monitor functions include deadlock detection and resolution, and transaction logging (in **journals**) for **forward recovery** in case of massive failures. The features are as follows:

- **Rapid response**: Fast performance with rapid response time is critical. Businesses cannot afford to have customers waiting for a TPS to respond. The turnaround time from the input of the transaction to the production of the output must be a few seconds or less.
- **Reliability**: Many organizations rely heavily on their TPS; a breakdown will disrupt operations or even stop the business. For a TPS to be effective, its failure rate must be very low. If a TPS does fail, then quick and accurate recovery must be possible. This makes well–designed backup and recovery procedures essential.

- **Inflexibility**: A TPS wants every transaction to be processed in the same way regardless of the user, the customer, or the time of the day. If a TPS were flexible, there would be too many opportunities for non-standard operations. For example, a commercial airline needs to consistently accept airline reservations from a range of travel agents, accepting different transaction data from different travel agents would be a problem.
- **Controlled processing**: The processing in a TPS must support an organization's operations. For example, if an organization allocates roles and responsibilities to particular employees, then the TPS should enforce and maintain this requirement.

Management information system

A **management information system** (**MIS**) is a subset of the overall internal controls of a business covering the application of people, documents, technologies, and procedures by management accountants to solve business problems such as costing a product, service, or a business-wide strategy. MISs are distinct from regular information systems in that they are used to analyze other information systems applied to operational activities in the organization. Academically, the term is commonly used to refer to the group of information management methods tied to the automation or support of human decision making. For example, DSS, expert systems, and executive information systems.

MIS combines technology with business to get people the information they need to do their jobs better, faster, and smarter. MIS often requires data from several TPSs. Information is the lifeblood of all organizations. MIS professionals work as systems analysts, project managers, systems administrators, etc., communicating directly with staff and management across the organization.

An MIS is a planned system of collecting, processing, storing, and disseminating data in the form of information needed to carry out the functions of management. In a way, it is a documented report of the activities that were planned and executed. The terms MIS and information system are often confused. Information systems include systems that are not intended for decision making. The area of study called MIS is sometimes referred to, in a restrictive sense, as information technology management. That area of study should not be confused with computer science. IT service management is a practitioner-focused discipline. MIS also has some differences with **enterprise resource planning (ERP)** as ERP incorporates elements that are not necessarily focused on decision support.

Decision support system

Decision support systems (DSS) are a specific class of computerized information systems that support business and organizational decision-making activities. A properly designed DSS is an interactive software-based system intended to help decision-makers compile useful information from raw data, documents, personal knowledge, and business models to identify and solve problems and make decisions.

Typical information that a decision support application might gather, and present would be as follows:

- An inventory of all of your current information assets (including legacy and relational data sources, cubes, data warehouses, and data marts)
- Comparative sales figures between one week and the next
- Projected revenue figures based on new product sales assumptions

Beginning in about 1990, data warehousing and **online analytical processing (OLAP)** began broadening the realm of DSS. As the turn of the millennium approached, new Web-based analytical applications were introduced. DSS belongs to an environment with multidisciplinary foundations, including (but not exclusively) database research, artificial intelligence, human-computer interaction, simulation methods, software engineering, and telecommunications.

The advent of better and better reporting technologies has seen DSS start to emerge as a critical component of management design. Examples of this can be seen in the intense amount of discussion of DSS in the education environment.

A **passive DSS** is a system that aids the process of decision making, but that cannot bring out explicit decision suggestions or solutions. An **active DSS** can bring out such decision suggestions or solutions. A **cooperative DSS** allows the decision-maker (or its advisor) to modify, complete, or refine the decision suggestions provided by the system, before sending them back to the system for validation. The system again improves, completes, and refines the suggestions of the decision-maker and sends them back to her for validation. The whole process then starts again, until a consolidated solution is generated.

Expert system

An expert system is a software that attempts to reproduce the performance of one or more human experts, most commonly in a specific problem domain, and is a traditional application and subfield of artificial intelligence. A wide variety of methods can be used to simulate the performance of the expert. However, common to most or all are the creation of a so-called knowledgebase which uses some knowledge representation formalism to capture the **subject matter experts (SME)** knowledge and a process of gathering that knowledge from the SME and codifying it according to the formalism, which is called knowledge engineering. Expert systems may or may not have learning components. However, a third common element is that once the system is developed, it is proven by being placed in the same real-world problem-solving situation as the human SME, typically as an aid to human workers or a supplement to some information system. Problem-solving is accomplished by applying specific knowledge rather than a specific technique. This is a key idea in expert systems technology. It reflects the belief that human experts do not process their knowledge differently from others but possess different knowledge. With this philosophy, when one finds that their expert system does not produce the desired results, work begins to expand the knowledge base, not to re-program the procedures.

There are various expert systems in which a rule-base and an inference engine cooperate to simulate the reasoning process that a human expert pursues in analyzing a problem and arriving at a conclusion. In these systems, to simulate the human reasoning process, a vast amount of knowledge needs to be stored in the knowledge base. Generally, the knowledge base of such an expert system consisted of a relatively large number of **if-then** types of statements that were interrelated in a manner that, in theory, at least, resembled the sequence of mental steps involved in the human reasoning process. It is because of the need for large storage capacities and related programs to store the rule-base, that most expert systems have, in the past, been run only on large information handling systems. Recently, the storage capacity of personal computers has increased to a point where it is becoming possible to consider running some types of simple expert systems on personal computers.

In some applications of expert systems, the nature of the application and the amount of stored information necessary to simulate the human reasoning process for that application is just too vast to store in the active memory of a computer. In other applications of expert systems, the nature of the application is such that not all of the information is always needed in the reasoning process. An example of this latter type of application, would be the use of an expert system to diagnose a data processing system comprising many separate components, some of which are optional. When that type of expert system employs a single integrated rule-base to diagnose the minimum system configuration of the data processing system, much of the rule-base is not required since many of the components, which are optional units of the system, will not be present in the system.

Overview of system development life cycle

The **systems development life cycle (SDLC)** is a conceptual model used in project management that describes the stages involved in an information system development project, from an initial feasibility study through maintenance of the completed application. Various SDLC methodologies have been developed to guide the processes involved, including the waterfall model (the original SDLC method), **rapid application development (RAD)**, **joint application development (JAD)**, the fountain model, and the spiral model. Mostly, several models are combined into some sort of hybrid methodology. Documentation is crucial regardless of the type of model chosen or devised for any application and is usually done in parallel with the development process. Some methods work better for specific types of projects, but in the final analysis, the most important factor for the success of a project may be how closely a plan was followed. *Figure 2.1* is the classic waterfall model methodology, which is the first SDLC method and it describes the various phases involved in development.

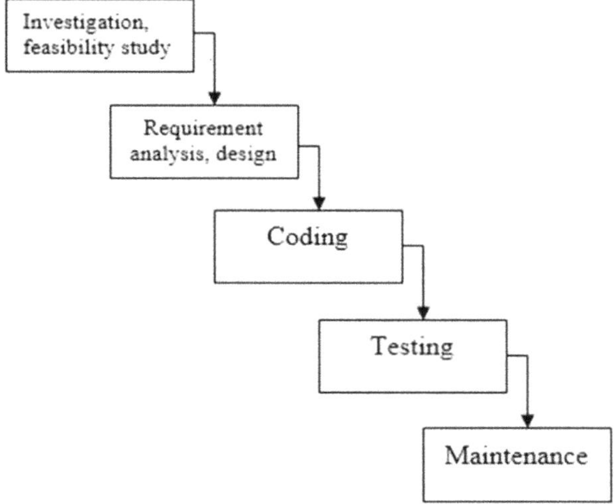

Figure 2.1: *Classic waterfall model*

Brief description of different phases

The SDLC refers to a structured process used in software development to ensure the production of high-quality, reliable software systems. It is a systematic approach that divides the development process into distinct phases, each addressing specific aspects of the project. These phases typically include planning, requirements gathering, design, implementation, testing, deployment, and maintenance. By following these phases, development teams can manage the complexity of software projects, minimize risks, and deliver solutions that meet user needs. SDLC provides a framework that enhances collaboration, improves project control, and ensures software quality at each stage.

Brief descriptions of each phase and their utilities are outlined in the following section. These phases are used for the development of a software system irrespective of the different models discussed in this section.

Feasibility study

The feasibility study is used to determine if the project should get the go-ahead after analyzing the business problems and opportunities. If the project is to proceed, the feasibility study will produce a project plan and budget estimates for the future stages of development. Conduct a study to determine whether a new or improved information system is needed. Develop a project management plan and obtain management approval.

During the feasibility study, the problem or opportunity definition is crystallized. The aspects of the problem are determined to be included in the system. The cost-benefits are estimated accurately, and a formal proposal is made on the nature and scope of the problem solution.

The feasibility study includes the following:

- Statement of problem
- Summary of findings and recommendations
- Details of findings (methods, procedures, output reports, file structure, cost, and benefit analysis)
- Recommendations and conclusions (personal assignment, costs, project schedule, and target dates)

Requirement analysis and design

This stage includes a detailed study of the business needs of the organization. Options for changing the business process may be considered. Analysis gathers the requirements for the system. Analyze in detail the information needs of end-users, the organizational environment, and any system presently used. Develop the logical input, processing, output, storage, and control requirements of a system that can meet the needs of the users. Develop specifications for the hardware (machines and media), software (programs and procedures), people (specialists and end-users), data resources, and information products that will satisfy the information needs of end-users.

The design focuses on a high-level design, such as what programs are needed and how they are going to interact, low-level design (how the individual programs are going to work), interface design (what the interfaces are going to look like), and data design (what data will be required). During these phases, the software's overall structure is defined. Analysis and design are very crucial in the whole development cycle. Any glitch in the design phase could be very expensive to solve in the later stage of software development, and much care is taken during this phase. The logical system of the product is developed in this phase.

Coding

In this phase, the designs are translated into code. Computer programs are written using a conventional programming language or an application generator. Programming tools like compilers, interpreters, and debuggers are used to generate the code. Different high-level programming languages like C, C++, Pascal, and Java are used for coding. Concerning the type of application, the right programming language is chosen.

Testing

In this phase, the system is tested along with the coding. Normally, programs are written as a series of individual modules, and these are subject to a separate and detailed test. The system is then tested as a whole. The separate modules are brought together and tested as a complete system. The system is tested to ensure that interfaces between modules work (integration testing), that the system works on the intended platform and with the expected volume of data (volume testing), and that the system does what the user requires (acceptance or beta testing).

Maintenance

Use a post-implementation review process to monitor, evaluate, and modify the system as needed. Before handing over the software to the user, the necessary training and documentation are provided. Inevitably, the system will need maintenance. The software will change once it is delivered to the customer. There are many reasons for the change. The change could happen because of some unexpected input values into the system. Also, the changes in the system could directly affect the software operations. The software should be developed to accommodate changes that could happen during the post-implementation period.

Types of SDCL models

As a product development life cycle, from its inception to maturity, the software product also passes through different phases. The phases are from the investigation stage to the maintenance phase through which the sequence of operations is carried out by proving different resources. As per the size of the system, its complexity, and the user requirement, various development models are used.

Developing computer software can be a complicated process, and in the last 25 years, researchers have identified numerous distinct activities that go into software development.

They include the following:

- Problem definition
- Requirements development
- Construction planning
- Software architecture or high-level design
- Detailed design
- Coding and debugging
- Unit testing
- Integration testing
- Integration
- System testing
- Corrective maintenance

All these activities are not very specifically shown while discussing various models. However, all these are considered more or less while developing the software using different models.

Iterative waterfall model

This is the **classical** model of system development. An alternative name for this model is a one-shot approach. As can be seen from *Figure 2.2*, there is a sequence of activities working from top to bottom. The figure shows some arrows pointing upwards and backward. This indicates that a later stage might reveal the need for some extra work at an earlier stage, but this should be the exception rather than the rule. After all, the flow of a waterfall should be downwards with the possibility of just a little splashing back. The limited scope for iteration is, in fact, one of the strengths of this process model. With a large project, you want to avoid having to go back and rework tasks that you thought had been completed.

In software engineering, reopening previously completed tasks disrupts timelines and delays promised completion dates. This typically occurs due to undetected defects, requirement changes, or miscommunication, leading to rework in phases like design or testing. The result is project delays, increased costs, and reduced stakeholder confidence, making effective planning, testing, and communication crucial to prevent such setbacks. They are as follow:

- **Feasibility study**: It is the initial study before the system analysis and design starts. Many feasibility studies are disillusioning for both users and analysts. The feasibility study is to serve as a decision document to answer three key questions. Is there a new and better way to do the job that will benefit the user? What are the costs and benefits of the alternatives? What is recommended? Three key considerations are involved in the feasibility analysis, such as economic, technical, and behavioral. The feasibility report is generally prepared by a senior person who has a sound knowledge of the system and organization. Depending on the results of the initial investigation, the survey is expanded to a detailed feasibility study. The study summarizes what is known and what is going to be done. It consists of the following:
  - Statement of the problem
  - Summary of findings and recommendations
  - Details of findings
  - Recommendations and conclusions
- **Requirement analysis and definition:** The system's services, constraints, and goals are established by consultation with system users. They are then defined in detail and serve as a system specification. The analysis is a detailed study of the various operations performed by a system and their relationships within and outside of the system. The solution to this phase is what must be done to solve the problem. In this phase, the system boundaries are determined. Data flow diagrams, entity-relationship diagrams, interviews, on-site observations, and questionnaires are used. Once the analysis is complete, the system analyst has a firm understanding of what is to be done in the next phase.

- **System and software design:** The systems design process partitions the requirements to either hardware or software systems. It established the overall system architecture. Software design involves identifying and describing the fundamental software system abstractions and their relationships. This phase is the most creative and challenging phase of the system life cycle. Interface for input and output of data and data processing are designed and tested to meet the system objective along with documentation. Information on personnel, money, hardware, software, facilities, and their estimated cost must be available.

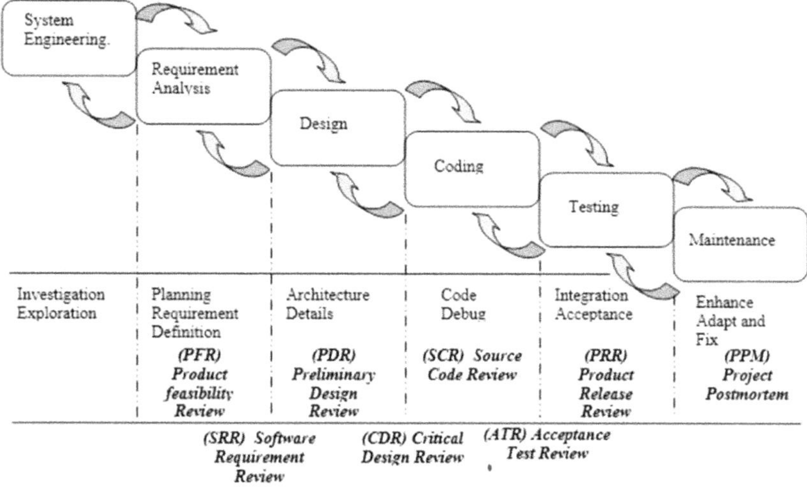

Figure 2.2: *Waterfall model-a traditional approach*

- **Coding**: In many organizations, separate groups of programmers do the programming. Each programmer is assigned one or more modules for coding. The analyst or the designer will integrate the program modules and integrate them at a later stage.
- **Implementation and unit testing**: During this stage, the software design is realized as a set of programs or program units. Unit testing involves verifying that each unit meets its specifications. It is primarily concerned with user training, site preparation, and file conversion. Linking to remote sites and terminals, establishing a telecommunication network, and testing are included. All the manuals are handed over to the users at the time of system implementation.
- **Integration and system testing**: The individual program units or programs are integrated and tested as a complete system to ensure that the software requirements have been met. System testing checks the readiness and accuracy of the system. After testing, the software system is delivered to the customer.
- **Operation and maintenance**: Normally, this is the longest life-cycle phase. The system is installed and put into practical use. The user staff is adjusted to the changes created by the candidate system. Maintenance involves correcting errors that were

not discovered in earlier stages of the life cycle, improving the implementation of system units, and enhancing the system's services as new requirements are discovered. The importance of maintenance is to continue to bring the new system to standards.

We contend that there is nothing intrinsically wrong with the waterfall approach, even though more recent writers have suggested different models. Ideally, the project manager strives for. The waterfall approach allows project completion times to be forecasted with more confidence than is the case with some more iterative approaches, and this allows projects to be controlled effectively. When there is uncertainty on the system implementation, this flexible and iterative method is very much desired.

V process model

Figure 2.3 gives a diagrammatic representation of this model. This is an elaboration of the waterfall model and stresses the necessity for validation activities that match the activities, which create the products of the project.

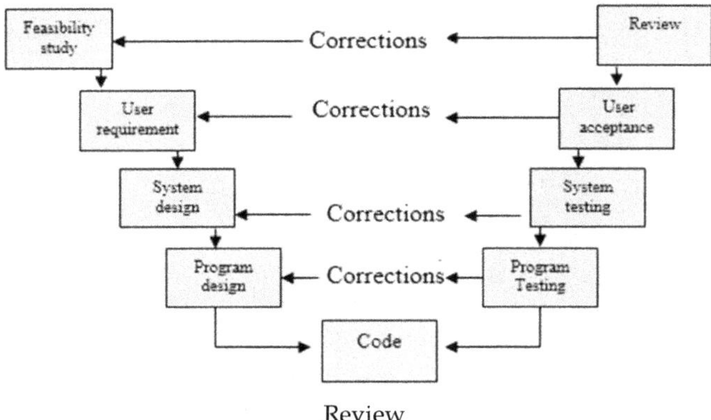

***Figure 2.3:** V-process model*

The V-process model can be seen as expanding the testing activity in the waterfall model. Each step has a matching validation process that can, where defects are found, cause a loop back to the corresponding development stage and a reworking of the succeeding steps. Ideally, this feedback should only occur where a discrepancy has been found between what was specified by a particular activity and what was implemented in the next lower activity on the descent of the V loop. For example, the system designer might have written that a calculation is carried out in a certain way. The person who structured the software that fulfilled this design might have misunderstood what was required. At the system testing stage, the system designer would carry out checks that ensure that the software is doing what was specified in the design document and would discover the program designer's misreading of that document. Only corrections should be fed back, not the system designer's second thought, otherwise, the project would be slipping into an evolutionary prototyping approach.

Spiral model

This is another way of looking at the basic waterfall model shown in *Figure 2.4*. In the waterfall model, there is a possible escape at the end of any of the activities in the sequence. A feasibility study might decide that the implementation of a proposed system would be beneficial. The management, therefore, authorizes work on the detailed collection and analysis of user requirements. Some analysis, for instance, the interviewing of users, might already have taken place at the feasibility stage, but a more thorough investigation is now launched. This might reveal that the costs of implementing the system would be higher than originally estimated and lead managers to decide to abandon the project.

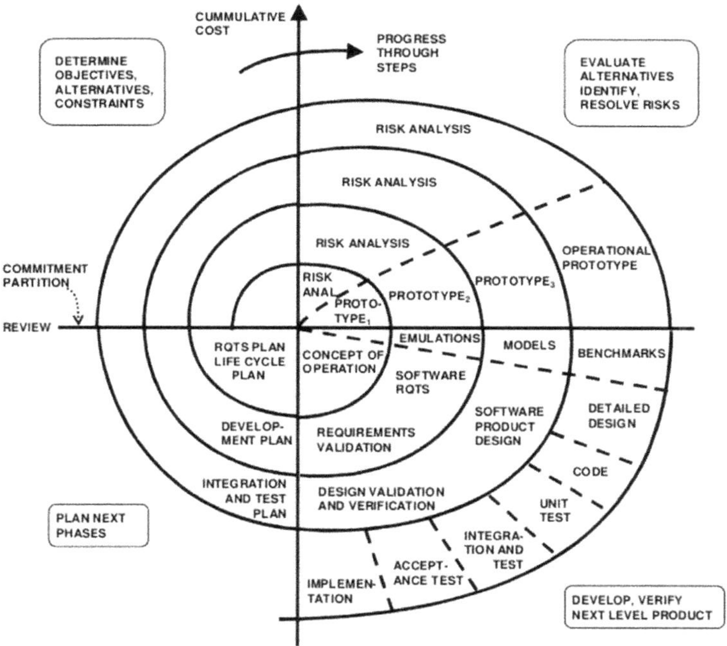

Figure 2.4: A spiral model

A greater level of detail is considered at each stage of the project and a greater degree of confidence about the probability of success for the project should be justified. This can be portrayed as a loop or a spiral where the system to be implemented is considered in more and more detail in each sweep, and an evaluation process is undertaken before the next iteration is embarked upon. The figure above illustrates how the **Structured Systems Analysis and Design Method (SSADM)** can be interpreted in such a way.

Software prototyping

Before starting the actual development, a working prototype of the system should first be built, as in *Figure 2.5*. This is a working model that is functionally equivalent to a subset of the product. The prototype is a toy implementation of a system having limited functional capabilities, low reliability, and inefficient performance. The model is illustrated to the customers along with input data formats, messages, reports, and interactive dialogs. The technical issues associated with the product are critically examined. The issues like the response time of a hardware controller, the efficiency of sorting algorithms, etc., are discussed. Since it is not possible to get the right one for the first time, we must be ready to throw away the first product to develop a good product.

The next step is to start with an approximate requirement and carry out a quick design. The model is built using several shortcuts, which may involve inefficient, inaccurate, or dummy functions. The dummy function may be using a table look-up rather than performing the actual computations. Then, the developed prototype is submitted to the customer for further evaluation. Based on the user feedback, requirements are refined. This cycle continues until the user approves the prototype. The actual system is developed using the classical waterfall approach.

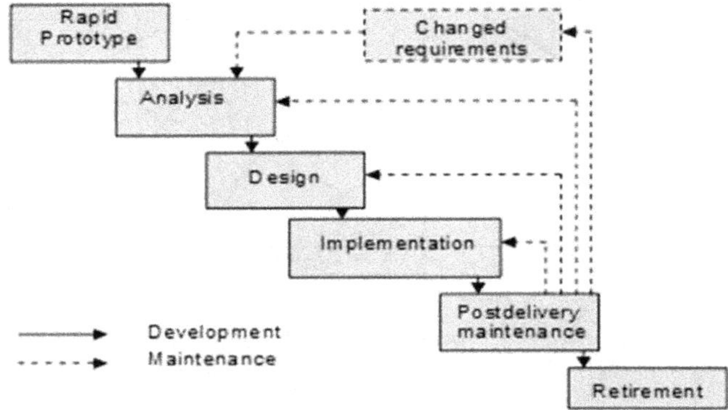

Figure 2.5: *A prototype model*

In this model, the requirement analysis and specification phase is becoming redundant. The final working prototype, after incorporating the user feedback, serves as an animated requirement specification. Even though the construction of a working prototype model involves additional costs, the overall development cost will be lower for the systems with unclear user requirements and unresolved technical issues. Using the prototype approach, many user requirements get properly defined, and technical issues are resolved through these, which would appear as change requests, resulting in massive redesign costs.

Prototypes can be classified as throw-away, evolutionary, or incremental. They are described as follows:

- **Throw-away prototypes** are used only to test out some ideas and are then discarded when the development of an operational system is commenced. The prototype could be developed using a different software environment where machine efficiency is important or even on a different hardware platform.
- **Evolutionary prototypes** are developed and modified until it is finally in a state where they can become operational systems. In this case, the standards that are used to develop the software have to be carefully considered.

- **Incremental prototypes** are strictly not prototyping. The operational system is developed and implemented in small stages so that the feedback from the earlier stages can influence the development of the later stages. This can be termed as learning by doing. When we have just done something for the first time, we can usually look back and see where we have made mistakes. This will improve communication, user involvement, consistency and completeness of a specification. This will reduce the need for documentation and maintenance costs.

Incremental approach

The approach involves (advocated by *Tom Gilb*–published by *Addison-Wesley* in 1988) breaking the system down into small components that are then implemented and delivered in sequence. Each component that is delivered must give some benefit to the user. *Figure 2.6* gives a general idea of the approach.

The feedback from early increments can influence the later stages. The possibility of changes in requirements is not very high, as with large monolithic projects, because of the shorter period between the design of a component and its delivery. Users get benefits earlier than with a conventional approach. Early delivery of some useful components improves cash flow because you get some return on investments early. Smaller sub-projects are easier to control and manage. **Gold plating**, the requesting of features that are unnecessary and not used, should be less as users will know that they get more than one opportunity to make their requirements known. If a feature is not in the current increment, then it can be included in the next.

On the other hand, the disadvantages are **software breakage**, that is, later increments might require the earlier increments to be modified. Developers might be more productive working on one large system than on a series of smaller ones.

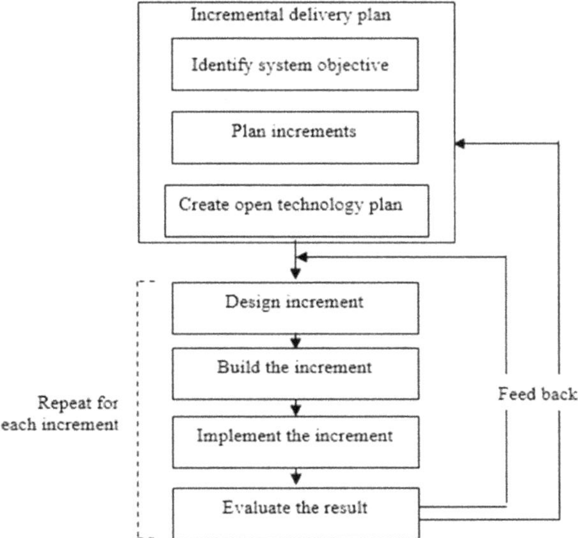

***Figure 2.6:** Incremental model*

Evolutionary model

An evolutionary model, see *Figure 2.7*, is developed with successive versions. The system is broken down into several modules, which can be incrementally implemented and delivered to the customers. First, develop the core modules of the system. The initial product skeleton is refined into increasing levels of capability by adding new functionalities in successive versions, which can perform some useful work. This becomes a new version being enhanced over the old one. Many organizations use a combination of iterative and incremental developments. A new release may include new functionality, which may be a modified version of the current one. Initially, the first version was developed as A. More functionality was added to A. The new version became a larger one consisting of both A and B. Similarly, C was added to the previous one, making a new version having more capabilities than its predecessors.

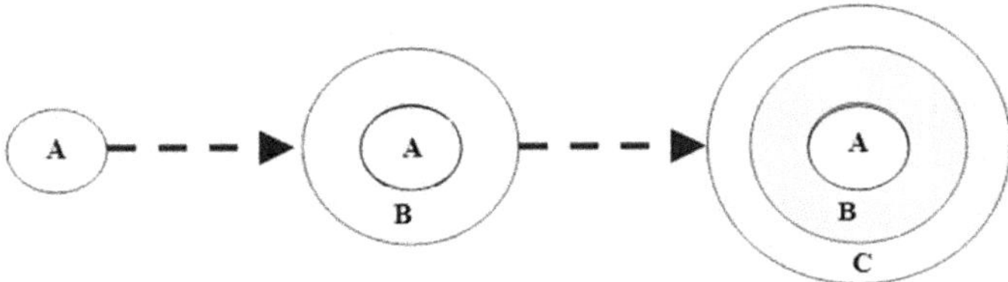

Figure 2.7: *Evolutionary models*

The following are the advantages:

- In this model development process, the users get a chance to experiment with a partially developed system much before the full working version is released. This helps in finding the exact user requirements before the full working system is developed.
- The core modules get tested in this model, which reduces the chance of errors in the final product.
- The advantages of an evolutionary model with iteration are the possibility of starting training on an earlier release, taking the customer feedback into account.
- The frequent releases allow developers to fix unanticipated problems quickly.

The following are the disadvantages:

- The model is often difficult to subdivide problems into functional units, which can be incrementally implemented and delivered.
- The evolutionary model is useful for very large problems where it is easier to find modules for incremental implementation.

Importance of metaphors

The history of science is full of discoveries based on exploiting the power of metaphors. Metaphors contribute to a greater understanding of software-development issues in the same way that they contribute to a greater understanding of scientific questions. In his 1973 Turing Award lecture, *Charles Bachman* described the change from the prevailing earth-centered view of the universe to a sun-centered view. Ptolemy's earth-centered model lasted without serious challenge for 1400 years. Then, in 1543, *Copernicus* introduced a heliocentric theory, the idea that the sun, rather than the earth, was the center of the universe. This change in mental models led ultimately to the discovery of new planets, the reclassification of the moon as a satellite rather than a planet, and a different understanding of humankind's place in the universe.

Bachman compared the Ptolemaic-to-Copernican change in astronomy to the change in computer programming in the early 1970s. When Bachman made the comparison in 1973, data processing was changing from a computer-centered view of information systems to a database-centered view. *Bachman* pointed out that the ancients of data processing wanted to view all data as a sequential stream of cards flowing through a computer (the computer-centered view). The change was to focus on a pool of data on which the computer happened to act (a database-oriented view).

Today it is difficult to imagine anyone's thinking that the sun moves around the earth. Similarly, it is difficult to imagine anyone's thinking that all data could be viewed as a sequential stream of cards. In both cases, once the old theory has been discarded, it seems incredible that anyone ever believed it at all. More, people who believed the old theory thought the new theory was just as ridiculous then as you think the old theory is now. A software metaphor is more like a searchlight than a roadmap.

Conclusion

In this chapter, we have discussed various models for software development and introduced you to information systems analysis and design to be adopted for a complex system in an organization. The difference between process-oriented design and data-oriented design has been discussed. Process orientation focuses on what the system is supposed to do. The data orientation focuses on the data the system needs to operate. Process orientation provides a less stable design than data orientation as the business processes change faster than the data change. In process orientation, data files are designed for a specific application, but in data orientation, the data files are designed for the whole organization with control of data redundancy. The various people in the organization who are involved in system development are system analysts, programmers, information system managers, important end-users, software testing, and quality control personnel, telecommunication engineers, software experts, and system auditors. Different kinds of systems are developed, like transaction processing, MISs, DSS, and expert systems. Various system development models are discussed with their respective phases in a life cycle. The merits and demerits of each type of model are also discussed.

In the next chapter, *Software Requirement Analysis and Specification*, the readers will learn how to systematically gather, analyze, and document software requirements to ensure a clear understanding between stakeholders and developers. This chapter will cover key concepts such as functional and non-functional requirements, requirement elicitation techniques, use case modeling, and the importance of well-defined software specifications. By mastering these principles, students will be better equipped to translate business needs into precise, actionable requirements that drive successful software development.

Exercises

To solidify your understanding of the concepts covered in this chapter, try the following exercises.

Multiple choice questions

1. **The next major step before system design and after the feasibility study.**
   a. Analysis activity
   b. Equipment selection
   c. Implementation activity
   d. None of these
2. **The first step in SDLC is**
   a. Preliminary investigation and analysis
   b. System design
   c. Database design
   d. None of these
3. **In a passenger seat reservation system, which of the following is most critical?**
   a. Ease of program
   b. Response time
   c. GUI
   d. None of these
4. **The detailed study or investigation of the present system is frequently referred to as:**
   a. System planning
   b. Feasibility study
   c. System analysis
   d. None of these
5. **The present trend in the data processing system is**
   a. Distributed processing

b. Remote processing
c. Real-time processing
d. None of these

6. **The system development phase associated with the creation of test data is**
   a. System analysis
   b. Physical system
   c. System acceptance
   d. Logical design

7. **Prototype is a**
   a. Mini model of the existing system
   b. Mini model of the proposed system
   c. Working model of the existing system
   d. None of the above

Short answer question

1. How does a phased life cycle model assist software management?
2. What are the two required characteristics of a milestone?
3. For each of the following documents, indicate in which phase(s) of the software life cycle it is produced: final user manual, architectural design, SQA plan, module specification, source code, statement of work, test plan, preliminary user manual, detailed design, cost estimate, project plan, test report, documentation.
   a. Final user manual in the implementation phase
   b. Architectural design in the design phase
   c. SQA plan Project in the planning phase
   d. Module specification in the Design phase
   e. Source code in the implementation phase
   f. Statement of work in the feasibility phase
   g. Test plan in the requirements phase
   h. Preliminary user manual in the requirements phase
   i. Detailed design in the Design phase
   j. Cost estimate in Project planning phase
   k. Project plan in Project planning phase
   l. Test report in Testing phase
   m. Documentation in the Implementation phase

4. Order the following tasks in terms of the waterfall model: acceptance testing, project planning, unit testing, requirements review, cost estimating, high-level design, market analysis, low-level design, systems testing, design review, implementation, requirement specification.
   a. Market analysis
   b. Project planning, cost estimating, requirement specification (may be done concurrently)
   c. Requirements review
   d. High-level design
   e. Low-level design
   f. Design review
   g. Implementation
   h. Unit testing
   i. Systems testing
   j. Acceptance testing

Essay questions

1. Contrast process-oriented and data-oriented approaches to system analysis and design. How are these complimentary but not competing for system development?
2. Why is it important to use system analysis and design methodologies while building a system? Why not just build the system in whatever way seems to be quick and easy? What value is added by using a system engineering approach?
3. List and explain the different phases in the system development life cycle.
4. What is prototyping? Explain.
5. What is the system development life cycle? Explain the first three phases of SDLC.

Multiple choice answer

1. a
2. a
3. b
4. b
5. a
6. c
7. b

CHAPTER 3

Software Requirement Analysis and Specification

Introduction

Software requirement analysis and specification is a critical phase in the software development process that focuses on understanding and defining the needs and expectations of the users and stakeholders. This phase involves gathering, analyzing, and documenting the functional and non-functional requirements that the software must fulfill. Effective requirement analysis ensures that the software system being developed meets the intended purpose, aligns with business objectives, and satisfies user needs. It also helps in identifying potential risks, ambiguities, and conflicts in the requirements early in the project. The specification serves as a blueprint, detailing how the software should behave and the constraints it must operate under. Clear and concise documentation at this stage is crucial for communication between development teams, stakeholders, and clients, ensuring that everyone has a common understanding of the system's goals and functionalities. Ultimately, accurate requirement analysis and specification help avoid costly errors, rework, and project delays, leading to a more successful software development lifecycle.

Structure

In this chapter, we are going to discuss the following topics:

- Introduction to software requirements
- Software requirement definition

- Software requirement specification
- Software requirement collection
- Modern methods for system requirements
- Radical methods for the system requirement
- Software requirement classification
- Software requirement analysis
- Software requirement documentation

Objectives

In this chapter, we are going to discuss the need for high-quality specifications and the important role played by the requirement specifications at all levels of the software system development process, the main and all-important interfaces to all system elements, the information flow and the structure definitions, the basic diagrams, and the major functions. We will also discuss the realistic design constraints, the technological risks of system development, the alternative software requirements, the existence of inconsistencies, the module redundancy, and the validation of the system is performed. You will learn about various tools and techniques for determining the system requirement, and also how joint application design and prototyping is used to ascertain the system requirement.

Introduction to software requirement

A system analyst must understand the information domain, before building a software product. They should know the required functions, behavior, performance, and interfaces to be used in the software. The requirements for the system and software are documented and reviewed with the customer for further analysis.

Conceptually, requirement analysis includes the following three types of activity:

- **Eliciting requirements**: The task of communicating with customers and users to determine what their requirements are. This is sometimes also called requirements gathering.
- **Analyzing requirements**: Determining whether the stated requirements are unclear, incomplete, ambiguous, or contradictory, and then resolving these issues.
- **Recording requirements**: Requirements might be documented in various forms, such as natural-language documents, use cases, user stories, or process specifications.

Requirements analysis can be a long process during which many delicate psychological skills are involved. New systems change the environment and relationships between concerned people, take into account all their needs and ensure they understand the implications of the new systems. Analysts can employ several techniques to elicit the requirements from the customer. This includes holding interviews, holding focus groups, and creating requirements lists. More modern techniques include prototyping, and use cases. Where necessary, the analyst will employ a combination of these methods to establish the exact requirements of the stakeholders, so that a system that meets the business needs is produced.

The success of software development is directly related to the following:

- Level of detail in which the team activities are recorded
- Quality of the software specification
- Integrity of the software specification
- Accuracy of the software specification
- Established development processes
- Rigor with which the established process is followed
- Quality and number of reviews and audits
- Accuracy of the models used to estimate software attributes
- Effectiveness of the test and integration plan, specification, and test data
- Level of preparation for system maintenance

Seven of the ten items are directly related to specification.

Requirement engineering

Systematic requirements analysis is also known as **requirements engineering**. It is sometimes referred to loosely by names such as requirements gathering, requirements capture, or **requirements specification**. The term requirements analysis can also be applied specifically to the analysis, as opposed to elicitation or documentation of the requirements.

Requirement engineering is a sub-discipline of systems engineering and software engineering that is concerned with determining the goals, functions, and constraints of hardware and software systems. In some life cycle models, the requirement engineering process begins with a feasibility study activity, which leads to a feasibility report. If the feasibility study suggests that the product should be developed, then requirement analysis can begin. If requirement analysis precedes feasibility studies, which may foster outside the box thinking, then feasibility should be determined before requirements are finalized.

Software requirements specification

A **software requirements specification (SRS)** is a complete description of the behavior of the system to be developed. It includes a set of use cases that describe all of the interactions that the users will have with the software. Use cases are also known as functional requirements. Besides use cases, the SRS also contains nonfunctional (or supplementary) requirements. Non-functional requirements are requirements that impose constraints on the design or implementation (such as performance requirements, quality standards, or design constraints). The requirements for software development are shown in *Figure 3.1:*

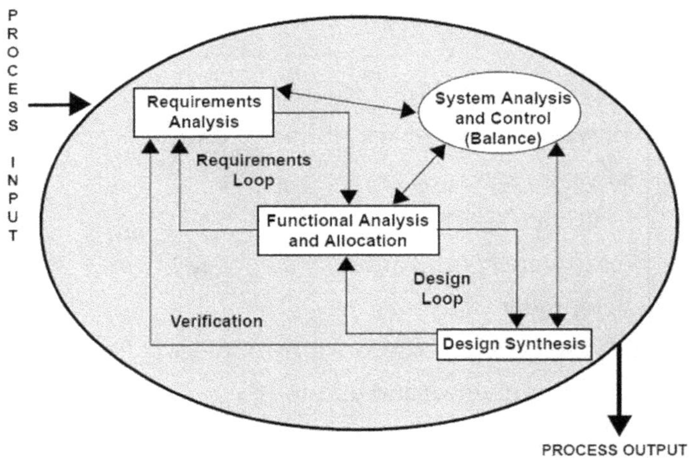

***Figure 3.1:** Requirements in software development*

Software requirement definition

There are two phases in the analysis phase. They are planning and software requirement definition. The outcome of planning is the system definition, the project plan, and the preliminary user's manual. The outcome of the software requirements definition activity is recorded in the software specification. The technical requirements for the software product are specified completely and concisely in an unambiguous manner. Depending on the size and complexity of the problem, the size of the document varies.

Software requirement

A SRS is a complete description of the behavior of the system to be developed. It includes a set of use cases that describe all of the interactions that the users will have with the software. Use cases are also known as functional requirements. In addition, to use cases, the SRS also contains nonfunctional (or supplementary) requirements. Non-functional requirements are requirements that impose constraints on the design or implementation (such as performance requirements, quality standards, or design constraints).

The format of a requirement specification is presented in *Table 3.1:*

Section 1	Product overview and summary
Section 2	Development. Operating and maintenance environment
Section 3	External interfaces and data flow

Section 4	Functional requirements
Section 5	Performance requirements
Section 6	Exception handling
Section 7	Early subsets and implementation priorities
Section 8	Foreseeable modifications and enhancements
Section 9	Acceptable criteria
Section 10	Design hints and guidelines
Section 11	Cross-reference index
Section 12	Glossary of items

***Table 3.1:** Format of a software requirement specification*

Sections 1 and 2 of the requirements documents present an overview of product features and summarize the processing environments for the development operation and maintenance of the product. This information is an elaboration on the software product characteristics contained in the system definition and the preliminary user manual.

External interfaces such as user displays and report formats, a summary of user commands and report options, data flow figures, and a data dictionary are included in external interfaces and data flow. High-level data flow diagrams and data dictionaries are derived. Data flow diagrams specify data sources and data sinks, data store transformations.

Software requirement collection

Gathering system requirements is like conducting an investigation. A good system analyst should have the following characteristics for the required determination. These characteristics include:

- **Impertinence**: You should question everything. You need to ask such questions as, are all transactions processed the same way?
- **Impartiality**: Your role is to find the best solution to a business problem or opportunity. For example, to find a way to justify the purchase of new hardware.
- **Relaxed constraints:** Assume anything is possible and eliminate the infeasible. For example, do not accept this statement such as, **We have always done it that way, so we have to continue the practice**.
- **Attention to detail**: Every fact must fit with every other fact. One element out of place means that the ultimate system will fail at some time.
- **Reframing**: Analysis is a creative process. You must look at the organization in new ways and find a better way of the work process.

The **deliverables** for requirement determination are as follows:

- Information collected from conversations with or observations of users: interview transcripts, questionnaire responses, notes from observation, and meeting minutes.
- In existing written information, the business mission and strategy statements, sample business forms and reports and computer display, procedure manuals, job descriptions, training manuals, flowcharts and documentation of existing systems, and consultant reports.
- In computer-based information, the results from joint application design sessions, transcripts or files from Group Support System sessions, **Computer-Aided Software Engineering** (**CASE**) repository contents and reports of existing systems, and display and reports from system prototypes.

Traditional methods for system requirements

The basic requirement in system analysis is to collect information on the existing procedure and to propose an improved system. The best practice is to talk to the people who have been involved in the existing system in various capacities and seek their suggestions on constraints being faced and opportunities that can be availed.

Interviewing and listening

This is one of the primary ways of gathering information. Spend a lot of time interviewing people about their work, the information they use, the type of information processing, and their suggestions for overcoming the constraints. The stakeholders may be interviewed to understand the organizational direction, vision, mission, policies, and expectations. Gather facts and opinions. Observe body language, emotions, and other signs of what people want and how they assess the present situation. You need to decide what mix and sequence of open-ended and close-ended questions you will ask. Open-ended questions are used for which there are no precise answers. It helps in surfacing the unknown information. Close-ended questions are yes or no, true or false, and multiple-choice type.

Questionnaires

Since interviews are time-consuming and expensive, a limited number of questions need to be framed. It helps in gathering information from many people in a short time. Choose a representative sample of people who will be your questionnaire respondent. The difficult part is to design a questionnaire that can cover your total requirements. This includes only close-ended questions.

There are other methods of information gathering like group discussion, brainstorming, and directly observing people at the site. All the facts and findings need to be documented properly and analyzed which need to be placed before the management before proceeding further.

Modern methods for system requirements

There are more other techniques through which the information on the current system and the new system can be gathered. **joint application development (JAD)**, **Group Support Systems (GSS)**, CASE tools, and prototyping are some of the modern methods used for information gathering.

Joint application development

This is a structured process in which the users, managers, and analysts work together in the design and development of a software application through successive collaborative workshops called the **JAD session**. The objective of JAD is to bring the key users, managers, and system analysts involved in the current system to gather information and discuss the business needs. The group defines the new system requirements, designs a solution, and monitors the project till completion.

The typical participants in a **JAD** are:

- **JAD session leader** organizes and runs the JAD. He has sound knowledge of group management, facilitation of sessions, and system analysis. The JAD leader sets the agenda and ensures it is met. They remain neutral on issues and do not contribute ideas and opinions. They keep the group on the agenda and resolve conflicts and disagreements.
- The **key users** of the system are vital participants in a JAD. They have a clear understanding of what it means to use the system daily.
- **Managers** of the workgroups who use the system provide insight into the new organizational directions, motivations in the impact of the system, and support for requirements determined in the JAD.
- A JAD must be sponsored by someone at a relatively high level who can meet the expenses. The **sponsor** usually attends the meeting at the beginning or at the end.
- Members of the system analysis team attend the JAD, although their actual participation may be limited. **System analysts** are there to learn from the users and managers.
- A **scribe** takes notes during the JAD sessions. This is done on a computer using a word processor and CASE tools for diagrams.
- **IS staff** such as programmers, database analysts, IS planners, and data center personnel may attend to learn from the discussion and possibly to contribute their ideas on the technical issues of the proposed system and on technical limitations of the current system.

The advantages of JAD are as follows:

- It brings people together, working in business organizations and IT professionals in a highly focused workshop.

- JAD eliminates many of the problems associated with the traditional meeting. JAD turns a meeting into a workshop.
- They are less frequent, more structured, and more productive.
- The JAD approach leads to faster development and greater client satisfaction due to client involvement.
- It improves the quality of the final product by focusing on the development life-cycle by reducing the errors that are expensive to correct at a later stage.
- JAD may be costly but highly effective.

CASE tools in JAD

The CASE tools most useful to analyze during a JAD are those referred to as upper CASE, as they are applied to the early phases of the system development life cycle. These include planning tools, diagramming tools, and prototyping tools such as computer display and report generation. Running a CASE tool during a JAD allows analysts to enter system models directly into a CASE tool, providing consistency and reliability in the joint model-building process. The CASE tool captures system requirements in a more flexible and useful way than a scribe or analyst takes notes.

GSS with JAD

Since JAD is a structured group process, it can benefit from the same computer-based support that can be applied to any group process. GSS can be used to support group meetings. In JAD meetings, there is not enough time for each member to contribute, or some people dominate the meeting when others do not get a chance to speak. Some people are afraid to speak before a group meeting where they might be criticized, or some are not willing to challenge what their bosses have told them. JAD suffers from these types of problems in the meeting. GSSs have been designed specifically to help alleviate some of the problems with group meetings. To provide the same chance to everybody in the meeting, group members type their comments into the computer rather than speak them. No one knows who has typed what. It provides a chance to criticize your boss. The whole process also takes less time instead of waiting for anyone to complete it first.

Prototyping for the system requirement

Prototypes are required in the analysis phase because users may not be sure what functions the computer could perform, or how one would use computers. Prototyping is an iterative process. A rudimentary version of an information system is built with the help of analysts and users. This is again rebuilt with the users' feedback. The prototyping can augment the requirement determination process. To gather an initial basic set of requirements, there is a need to interview users and collect information. Prototyping will allow converting quickly the basic requirements into a working, though a limited, version of the desired information system. The prototype will then be viewed and tested by the user. If necessary, redesign the prototype to incorporate the suggested changes. Prototyping is possible with several **Fourth-generation languages (4GLs)** and with CASE tools.

Development of a prototype is quite useful, especially in the following situations:

- Where the user is unable to specify the requirements in advance.
- Users can not visualize the desired system they want. The new users do not have any idea of what a system would look like.
- When the environment is new and not fully understood by the user or the analyst.

Radical methods for system requirements

In some organizations, management is looking for new ways to perform the current task other than the above two methods. These new ways may be radically different from how things are done now, expecting better payoffs. The new method that has replaced the current one is referred to as **business process reengineering (BPR)**. BPR occurs in a top-down manner, beginning with the identification of major business objectives and goals and culminating with a much more detailed specification of tasks that define a specific business process.

BPR is an iterative process. A changing business environment is adopted to achieve the goals and processes. This model defines the following six activities:

- **Business definition:** The business goals are defined with the following guidelines:
    - Cost reduction
    - Time reduction
    - Quality improvement, and manpower development and
    - Empowerment

  Goals may be defined for a specific component of the business.
- **Process identification**: To achieve the goals, the critical processes are identified and prioritized by importance and need for change.
- **Process evaluation**: The existing process is analyzed in detail and measured. The tasks of the process are identified. The costs and time consumed by individual process tasks are considered.
- **Process specification and design**: Use cases are prepared for each process with outcomes to a customer. With the specification of the process, a set of tasks is designed.
- **Prototyping**: A redesigned business process is prototyped before it is fully integrated into the business. The activity tests the process to allow further refinement.
- **Refinement and instantiation**: Based on the feedback of the prototype, the business process is refined and then instantiated within a business system.

BPR can be effective if the people are motivated and trained, who understand that this process is a **continuous** activity. When the information system is integrated with the business process, the result of BPR is expected.

Principles of re-engineering

There are seven principles of reengineering suggested by *Michael Hammer* and *James Champy* to streamline the work process and achieve significant levels of improvement in quality, time management, and cost. They are as follows:

- Organize around outcomes and costs.
- Identify all the processes in an organization and prioritize them in order of redesign urgency.
- Integrate information processing work into the real work that produces the information.
- Treat geographically dispersed resources as though they were centralized.
- Link parallel activities in workflow instead of just integrating their results.
- Put the decision point where the work is performed and build control into the process.
- Capture information once and at the source.

Software requirement classification

Requirements are categorized in several ways. The following are common categorizations of requirements that relate to technical management.

- **Customer requirements**: Statements of fact and assumptions that define the expectations of the system in terms of mission objectives, environment, constraints, and **Meas**.
- **Measures of Effectiveness and Suitability (MOE/MOS)**. The customers are those that perform the eight primary functions of systems engineering, with special emphasis on the operator as the key customer. Operational requirements will define the basic need and, at a minimum, answer the questions posed in the following listing:
    - **Operational distribution or deployment**: Where will the system be used?
    - **Mission profile or scenario:** How will the system accomplish its mission objective?
    - **Performance and related parameters:** What are the critical system parameters to accomplish the mission?
    - **Utilization environments**: How are the various system components to be used?

- **Effectiveness requirements**: How effective or efficient must the system be in performing its mission?
- **Operational life cycle:** How long will the system be in use by the user?
- **Environment**: What environments will the system be expected to operate effectively?

Functional requirements

Functional requirements define the specific behaviors or functions a system must perform to meet user needs or achieve its objectives. These requirements outline what actions the system must take under certain conditions, focusing on the tasks or activities that need to be executed. They form the foundation for system design and are crucial for ensuring that the system operates as intended. During functional requirements analysis, these high-level functions are broken down into more detailed components, enabling developers to design and implement solutions that address each requirement effectively. This process ensures the system's functionality aligns with the project's goals.

Performance requirements

The extent to which a mission or function must be executed is generally measured in terms of quantity, quality, coverage, timeliness, or readiness. During requirements analysis, performance (how well does it have to be done) requirements will be interactively developed across all identified functions based on system life cycle factors and characterized in terms of the degree of certainty in their estimate, the degree of criticality to the system success, and their relationship to other requirements.

Design requirements

Design requirements are detailed specifications that define how products or systems are to be built, coded, or procured. These requirements serve as the blueprint for development, providing precise instructions on how to achieve the desired functionality and performance. For physical products, design requirements often include **build to** guidelines, indicating the materials, dimensions, and construction methods. For software, **code to** requirements specify the programming standards, algorithms, and implementation details. In cases where procurement is involved, **buy to** requirements outline the criteria for purchasing pre-existing components or systems. Additionally, for processes, the design requirements provide the **how to execute** instructions, offering clear guidance on the correct methods, procedures, and technical documentation, such as technical data packages and manuals, needed to ensure successful execution. These requirements are essential for ensuring that all aspects of the design are understood, implemented correctly, and meet the intended specifications.

Derived requirements

Derived requirements are those that are not explicitly stated but are implied or inferred from higher-level requirements. These requirements emerge during the design or development process as a result of translating broader objectives into specific technical needs. For instance, if a system requires long-range performance or high speed, this may naturally lead to a derived requirement for reducing the system's weight. Derived requirements play a crucial role in shaping the design, ensuring that the system meets overarching goals while also addressing more detailed technical challenges. These requirements must be carefully analyzed and integrated to maintain coherence with the original high-level requirements and ensure the system's overall performance and feasibility.

Allocated requirements

This is a requirement that is established by dividing or otherwise allocating a high-level requirement into multiple lower-level requirements. For example, a 100kg item that consists of two subsystems might result in weight requirements of 70kg and 30kg for the two lower-level items.

Software requirement analysis

Systematic requirements analysis is also known as **requirements engineering**. It is sometimes referred to loosely by names such as requirements gathering, requirements capture, or requirements specification. The term requirements analysis can also be applied specifically to the analysis proper, as opposed to elicitation or documentation of the requirements, for instance.

Requirement engineering is a sub-discipline of systems engineering and software engineering, that is, concerned with determining the goals, functions, and constraints of hardware and software systems. In some life cycle models, the requirement engineering process begins with a feasibility study activity, which leads to a feasibility report. If the feasibility study suggests that the product should be developed, then requirement analysis can begin. If requirement analysis precedes feasibility studies, which may foster outside the box thinking, then feasibility should be determined before requirements are finalized.

Requirements analysis in systems engineering and software engineering encompasses those tasks that go into determining the needs or conditions to meet for a new or altered product, taking account of the possibly conflicting requirements of the various stakeholders, such as beneficiaries or users.

Requirements analysis is critical to the success of a development project. Requirements must be actionable, measurable, testable, related to identified business needs or opportunities, and defined to a level of detail enough for system design.

Software requirement documentation

Requirements documentation is the description of what a software does or shall do. It is used throughout development to communicate what the software does or shall do. It is also used as an agreement or as the foundation for agreement on what the software shall do. Requirements are produced and consumed by everyone involved in the production of software: end-users, customers, product managers, project managers, sales, marketing, software architects, usability experts, interaction designers, developers, and testers, to name a few. Thus, requirements documentation has many different purposes.

The variation and complexity of requirements documentation make it a proven challenge. Requirements may be implicit and hard to uncover. It is difficult to know exactly how much documentation is needed and how much can be left to the architecture and design documentation, and it is difficult to know how to document requirements considering the variety of people who shall read and use the documentation. Thus, requirements documentation is often incomplete (or non-existent). Without proper documentation of requirements, software changes become more difficult and, therefore, more error-prone (decreased software quality) and time-consuming (expensive).

The need for requirements documentation is typically related to the complexity of the product, the impact of the product, and the life expectancy of the software. If the software is very complex or developed by many people (for example, mobile phone software), requirements can help to better communicate what to achieve. If the software is safety-critical and can harm human life (for example, nuclear power systems and medical equipment), more formal requirements documentation is often required. If the software is expected to live for only a month or two (for example, very small mobile phone applications developed specifically for a certain campaign), very little requirements documentation may be needed. If the software is a first release that is later built upon, requirements documentation is very helpful when managing the change of the software and verifying that nothing has been broken in the software when it is modified.

Traditionally, requirements are specified in requirements documents (for example, using word processing applications and spreadsheet applications). To manage the increased complexity and changing nature of requirements documentation (and software documentation in general), database-centric systems and special-purpose requirements management tools are advocated.

Architecture or design documentation

Architecture documentation is a special breed of design documents. In a way, architecture documents are the third derivative of the code (design documents being the second derivative, and code documents being the first). Very little in the architecture documents is specific to the code itself. These documents do not describe how to program a routine, or even why that routine exists in the form that it does, but instead merely lays out the general requirements that would motivate the existence of such a routine. A good architecture document is short on details but thick on explanation. It may suggest approaches for lower-level design but leave the actual exploration and trade studies to other documents.

Another breed of design docs is the comparison document or trade study. This would often take the form of a white paper. It focuses on one specific aspect of the system and suggests alternate approaches. It could be at the user interface, code, design, or even architectural level. It will outline what the situation is, describe one or more alternatives, and enumerate the pros and cons of each. A good trade study document is heavy on research, expresses its idea clearly, and, most importantly, is impartial. It should honestly and clearly explain the costs of whatever solution it offers as best. The objective of a trade study is to devise the best solution rather than to push a particular point of view. It is perfectly acceptable to state no conclusion or to conclude that none of the alternatives are sufficiently better than the baseline to warrant a change. It should be approached as a scientific endeavor, not as a marketing technique.

A very important part of the design document in enterprise software development is the **database design document (DDD)**. It contains conceptual, logical, and physical design elements. DDD includes the formal information that the people who interact with the database need. The purpose of preparing the DDD is to create a common source to be used by all players within the scene. The potential users are as follows:

- Database designer
- Database developer
- Database administrator
- Application designer
- Application developer

When talking about relational database systems, the document should include the following parts:

- Entity-relationship schema, including the following information and their clear definitions:
    - Entity sets and their attributes
    - Relationships and their attributes
    - Candidate keys for each entity set
    - Attribute and tuple-based constraints
- Relational schema, including the following information:
    - Tables, attributes, and their properties
    - Views
    - Constraints such as primary keys, foreign keys
    - The cardinality of referential constraints

- Cascading policy for referential constraints
- Primary keys

It is very important to include all the information that is to be used by all actors in the scene. It is also very important to update the documents as any change occurs in the database as well.

Technical documentation

This is what most programmers mean when using the term software documentation. When creating software, code alone is insufficient. There must be some text along with it to describe various aspects of its intended operation. The code documents need to be thorough, but not so verbose that it becomes difficult to maintain them. Several how-to and overview documents are found specific to the software application or software product being documented by **application programming interface (API)** writers. This documentation may be used by developers, testers, and also the end customers or clients using this software application. Today, we see a lot of high-end applications in the fields of power, energy, transportation, networks, aerospace, safety, security, industrial automation, and a variety of other domains. Technical documentation has become important within such organizations as the basic and advanced level of information may change over time with architecture changes. Hence, technical documentation has gained a lot of importance in recent times, especially in the software field.

Often, tools such as Doxygen, NDoc, Javadoc, Eiffel Studio, Sandcastle, ROBODoc, POD, TwinText, or Universal Report can be used to auto-generate the code documents, that is, they extract the comments and software contracts, where available, from the source code and create reference manuals in such forms as text or **hyper text markup language (HTML)** files. Code documents are often organized into a reference guide style, allowing a programmer to quickly look up an arbitrary function or class.

Many programmers like the idea of auto-generating documentation for various reasons. For example, because it is extracted from the source code itself, the programmer can write it while referring to his code and can use the same tools he used to create the source code to make the documentation. This makes it much easier to keep the documentation up to date.

Elucidative programming is the result of practical applications of literate programming in real programming contexts. The elucidative paradigm proposes that source code and documentation be stored separately. Often, software developers need to be able to create and access information that is not going to be part of the source file itself. Such annotations are usually part of many software development activities, such as code walks and porting, where third party source code is analyzed functionally.

User documentation

Unlike code documents, user documents are usually far more diverse concerning the source code of the program, and, instead, simply describe how it is used.

In the case of a software library, the code documents and user documents could be effectively equivalent and are worth conjoining, but for a general application, this is not often true. On the other hand, the Lisp machine grew out of a tradition in which every piece of code had an attached documentation string. In combination with strong search capabilities (based on a Unix-like apropos command) and online sources, Lisp users could look up documentation prepared by these API writers and paste the associated function directly into their code. This level of ease of use is unheard of in putatively more modern systems.

Typically, the user documentation describes each feature of the program and assists the user in realizing these features. A good user document can also go so far as to provide thorough troubleshooting assistance. It is very important for user documents not to be confusing and for them to be up to date. User documents need not be organized in any particular way, but they need to have a thorough index. Consistency and simplicity are also very valuable. User documentation is considered to constitute a contract specifying what the software will do. API writers are very well accomplished in writing good user documents as they are well aware of the software architecture and programming techniques used.

There are three broad ways in which user documentation can be organized. They are as follows:

- **Tutorial**: A tutorial approach is considered the most useful for a new user, in which they are guided through each step of accomplishing particular tasks.
- **Thematic**: A thematic approach, where chapters or sections concentrate on one particular area of interest, is of more general use to an intermediate user. Some authors prefer to convey their ideas through a knowledge-based article to facilitate their needs. This approach is usually practiced in a dynamic industry, such as the information technology, where the user population is largely correlated with the troubleshooting demands.
- **List of reference:** The final type of organizing principle is one in which commands or tasks are simply listed alphabetically or logically grouped, often via cross-referenced indexes. This latter approach is of greater use to advanced users who know exactly what sort of information they are looking for.

A common complaint among users regarding software documentation is that only one of these three approaches was taken to the near exclusion of the other two. It is common to limit provided software documentation for personal computers to online help that gives only reference information on commands or menu items. The job of tutoring new users or helping more experienced users get the most out of a program is left to private publishers, who are often given significant assistance by the software developer.

Conclusion

There are three sub-phases in the system analysis phase of the system development life cycle. They are requirement determination, requirement structuring, and alternative generation of choice. In requirement, determination covers the gathering of information on the existing system, and then the need to replace the system is analyzed. The traditional sources of information are gathered through interviews, questionnaires, observation, and group discussions. Formulating questions in questionnaires, preparing an agenda in a group discussion, and preparing relevant questions in an interview must be very precise to avoid ambiguity so that a proper response is obtained. The results of all methods should be compared and normalized. JAD begins with an idea of a group interview and adds structure. The JAD group includes a session leader, a scribe, key users, managers, a sponsor, and the system analyst. The JAD session is held off-site and may last for a week or so. It has been discussed how the information system can support the requirement analysis using CASE tools and prototyping. In prototyping, the user and the analyst work together to determine the requirements. This continues by revising the model till it meets the user requirements. BPR is an approach used to change the process radically using the new information requirements by changing traditional business rules. This would help to form a base guideline for further analysis and design.

In the next chapter, readers will explore the Software Project Management Framework, which serves as a structured approach to managing software development projects effectively. This framework includes the processes, tools, techniques, and methodologies that help project managers plan, execute, and monitor software projects from initiation to completion. It addresses key areas such as project planning, scope management, scheduling, resource allocation, risk management, quality assurance, and communication among stakeholders. By understanding the Software Project Management Framework, readers will gain insights into how to ensure successful project delivery, meet deadlines, and achieve business objectives while adhering to quality standards.

Exercises

To solidify your understanding of the concepts covered in this chapter, try the following exercises.

Multiple choice questions

1. **What is the primary goal of software requirement analysis?**
    a. To design the system architecture
    b. To gather and define what the users need from the system
    c. To implement the software
    d. To test the software

2. **Which of the following is NOT a type of software requirement?**
   a. Functional requirements
   b. Non-functional requirements
   c. System requirements
   d. Hardware requirements

3. **In software requirement specification (SRS), functional requirements describe:**
   a. The internal architecture of the system
   b. The operations, inputs, and outputs of the system
   c. The testing strategy
   d. The user interface design

4. **Which of the following is an example of a non-functional requirement?**
   a. The system must allow users to log in
   b. The system should respond to requests within 2 seconds
   c. The system must allow the user to generate a report
   d. The system should allow password recovery

5. **What is a common technique used in requirement elicitation?**
   a. Coding
   b. Prototyping
   c. Unit testing
   d. Documentation

6. **Which document serves as a bridge between client needs and the development team in software engineering?**
   a. Source Code Document
   b. Test Plan
   c. **Software requirement specification** (SRS)
   d. User Manual

7. **What is the purpose of requirement validation?**
   a. To gather more requirements
   b. To ensure the requirements are feasible and meet stakeholders' needs
   c. To develop the system
   d. To test the software functionality

8. **Which model helps in understanding and documenting requirements by showing the system from an external user's perspective?**
   a. **Data Flow Diagram (DFD)**
   b. Use Case Model
   c. **Entity-Relationship Model (ERM)**
   d. Class Diagram

Short answer questions

1. What are the attributes of a good SRS document?
2. What is requirement engineering?
3. What are the activities of the specification phase of clean room technology?
4. What is requirement management?
5. Name different components of requirement analysis.
6. What are the objectives of system analysis?
7. Name some interface requirements.
8. Name some functional requirements.
9. What is requirement analysis? Name five areas of requirement analysis.
10. Name three types of requirements.

Essay questions

1. What are the attributes of a good SRS document?
2. Define the following terms.
3. Describe four traditional techniques for collecting information during analysis. When might one be better than another?
4. What is JAD? How is it better than traditional information-gathering technique? What are its weaknesses?
5. How can CASE tools be used to support requirement determination? Which types of CASE tools are appropriate for use during requirement determination?
6. Describe how prototyping can be used during requirements determination. How it is better or worse than traditional methods?
7. What do you mean by business process reengineering? What are the principles of reengineering?
8. Explain any three fact gathering techniques in detail.

Multiple choice answers

1. b
2. d
3. b
4. b
5. b
6. c
7. b
8. b

Join our book's Discord space

Join the book's Discord Workspace for Latest updates, Offers, Tech happenings around the world, New Release and Sessions with the Authors:

https://discord.bpbonline.com

CHAPTER 4
Software Project Management Framework

Introduction

The **Software Project Management Framework** is a structured approach designed to manage and guide software development projects from initiation to completion. It encompasses a set of practices, tools, methodologies, and techniques aimed at ensuring that projects are completed on time, within scope, and within budget, while meeting quality standards. This framework helps project managers plan, execute, monitor, and control every phase of the project lifecycle, from defining project goals to delivering the final product. Key aspects of the framework include scope management, time scheduling, resource allocation, risk assessment, and stakeholder communication. By implementing this framework, organizations can improve project efficiency, minimize risks, and ensure successful software delivery.

Structure

In this chapter, we are going to discuss the following topics:

- Project definition
- Project management
- Cost management

Objectives

Project management is the discipline of planning, organizing, and managing resources to bring about the successful completion of specific project goals and objectives. It is often closely related to and sometimes conflated with program management.

A **project** is a temporary endeavor, having a defined beginning and end (usually constrained by date, but can be by funding or deliverables), undertaken to meet particular goals and objectives, usually to bring about beneficial change or added value. The temporary nature of projects stands in contrast to business as usual, which is repetitive, permanent, or semi-permanent functional work to produce products or services. In practice, the management of these two systems is often found to be quite different, and as such, requires the development of distinct technical skills and the adoption of separate management.

Project definition

A **project** is a multitask job with due consideration of performance, cost, time, and scope requirements and is done only once. It has a definite starting and ending time with budgets and costs having clearly defined scope or magnitude of work to be done.

There is a need to optimize the project resources considering the complexity of the business, time, and resources at least cost.

Project management

Project management is the application of knowledge, skills, tools, and techniques to project activities to meet project requirements. Project management is accomplished through the application and integration of the project management processes of initiating, planning, executing, monitoring and controlling, and closing. The project manager is the person responsible for accomplishing the project objectives.

This does not mean that the knowledge, skills, and processes described should always be applied uniformly to all projects. The project manager, in collaboration with the project team, is always responsible for determining what processes are appropriate, and the appropriate degree of rigor for each process, for any given project.

Managing a project includes the following:

- Identifying requirements
- Establishing clear and achievable objectives
- Balancing the competing demands for quality, scope, time, and cost
- Adapting the specifications, plans, and approach to the different concerns and expectations of the various stakeholders

Project managers often talk of a **triple constraint**, that is, project scope, time, and cost in managing competing project requirements. Project quality is affected by balancing these three factors. High-quality projects deliver the required product, service, or result within scope, on time, and within budget. The relationship among these factors is such that if any one of the three factors changes, at least one other factor is likely to be affected. Project managers also manage projects in response to uncertainty.

Scope management

Project scope management describes the processes involved in ascertaining that the project includes all the work required, and only the work required, to complete the project successfully. It consists of the scope planning, scope definition, creating the **work breakdown structure (WBS)**, scope verification, and scope control project management processes.

- **Control**: Controlling changes to the project scope.

  These processes interact with each other and with processes in the other knowledge areas as well. Each process can involve effort from one or more persons or groups of persons, based on the needs of the project. Each process occurs, at least once, in every project and occurs in one or more project phases if the project is divided into phases.

  In the project context, the term scope can refer to:

  - **Product scope**: The features and functions that characterize a product, service, or result.
  - **Project scope**: The work that needs to be accomplished to deliver a product, service, or result with the specified features and functions.

Scope planning

Defining and managing the project scope influences the project's overall success. Each project requires a careful balance of tools, data sources, methodologies, processes, procedures, and other factors to ensure that the effort expended on scoping activities is commensurate with the project's size, complexity, and importance. The prerequisites of the project can be represented as:

- **Inputs**:
  - Enterprise environmental factors
  - Organizational project assets
  - Project charter
  - Preliminary project scope statement
  - Project management plan

- **Outputs**:
  - Project scope management plan
- **Tools and techniques**:
  - Expert judgment
  - Templates, forms, standards

Scope definition

The preparation of a detailed project scope statement is critical to project success and builds upon the major deliverables, assumptions, and constraints that are documented during project initiation in the preliminary project scope statement. During planning, the project scope is defined and described with greater specificity because more information about the project is known. Stakeholder needs, wants, and expectations are analyzed and converted into requirements. The points given in the following are the details of the scope definition:

- **Inputs**:
  - Organizational project assets
  - Project charter
  - Preliminary project scope statement
  - Project management plan
  - Approved change requests
- **Outputs**:
  - Project scope statement
  - Requested changes
  - Project scope management plan (updates)
- **Tools and techniques**:
  - Project identification
  - Alternatives identification
  - Expert judgment
  - Stakeholder analysis

Create work breakdown structure

The WBS is a deliverable-oriented hierarchical decomposition of the work to be executed by the project team, to accomplish the project objectives and create the required deliverables. The WBS organizes and defines the total scope of the project. The WBS subdivides the project work into smaller, more manageable pieces of work, with each descending level of the WBS representing an increasingly detailed definition of the project work. The planned work contained within the lowest-level WBS components, which are called work packages, can be scheduled, cost estimated, monitored, and controlled. The following points describe the details of the scope of work breakdown structure:

- **Inputs**:
  - Organizational process assets
  - Project scope statement
  - Project scope management plan
  - Approved change requests
- **Outputs**:
  - Project scope statement (updates)
  - Work breakdown
  - WBS dictionary
  - Scope baseline
  - Project scope management plan
  - Requested changes
- **Tools and techniques**:
  - Work breakdown structure templates
  - Decomposition

Scope verification

Scope verification is the process of obtaining the stakeholders' formal acceptance of the completed project scope and associated deliverables. Verifying the project scope includes reviewing deliverables to ensure that each is completed satisfactorily. If the project is terminated early, the project scope verification process should establish and document the level and extent of completion. Scope verification differs from quality control in that scope verification is primarily concerned with acceptance of the deliverables, while quality control is primarily concerned with meeting the quality requirements specified for the deliverables. **Quality control** is generally performed before scope verification, but these two processes can be performed in parallel. The following points describe the details of the scope verification:

- **Inputs**:
  - Project scope statement
  - WBS dictionary
  - Project scope management plan
  - Deliverables

- **Outputs**:
  - Accepted deliverable
  - Requested changes
  - Recommended corrective actions
- **Tools and techniques**:
  - Inspection

Scope control

Project scope control is concerned with influencing the factors that create project scope changes and controlling the impact of those changes. Scope control assures all requested changes and recommended corrective actions are processed through the project's integrated change control process. Project scope control is also used to manage the actual changes when they occur and is integrated with the other control processes. Uncontrolled changes are often referred to as project scope creep. The details of the scope control are as follows:

- **Inputs**:
  - Project scope statement
  - WBS
  - WBS dictionary
  - Project scope management plan
  - Performance report
  - Approved project requests
  - Work performance
- **Outputs**:
  - Project scope statement
  - WBS
  - WBS dictionary
  - Scope baseline
  - Requested changes
  - Recommended corrective action
  - Organizational project asset
  - Project management
- **Tools and techniques**:
  - Change control system

- Variance analysis
- Re-planning
- Configuration management system

Time management

Project time management describes the processes concerning the timely completion of the project. It consists of the activity definition, activity sequencing, activity resource estimating, activity duration estimating, schedule development, and schedule control project management processes.

Project time management includes the processes required to accomplish timely completion of the project. *Figure 4.1* provides an overview of the project time management processes, and *Figure 4.2* provides a process flow diagram of those processes and their inputs, outputs, and other related knowledge area processes. The project time management processes include the following:

- **Activity definition**: Identifying the specific scheduled activities that need to be performed to produce the various project deliverables.
- **Activity sequencing**: Identifying and documenting dependencies among scheduled activities.
- **Activity resource estimating**: Estimating the type and quantities of resources required to perform each scheduled activity.
- **Activity duration estimating**: Estimating the number of work periods that will be needed to complete individual scheduled activities.
- **Schedule development**: Analyzing activity sequences, durations, resource requirements, and schedule constraints to create the project schedule.
- **Schedule control**: Controlling changes to the project schedule.

These processes interact with each other and with processes in the other knowledge areas as well. Each process can involve effort from one or more persons or groups of persons, based on the needs of the project. Each process occurs at least once in every project and occurs in one or more project phases, if the project is divided into phases. Although the processes are presented here as discrete components with well-defined interfaces, in practice, they can overlap and interact.

Activity definition

Defining the scheduled activities involves identifying and documenting the work that is planned to be performed. The activity definition process will identify the deliverables at the lowest level in the WBS, which is called the work package. Project work packages are planned (decomposed) into smaller components called schedule activities to provide a basis for estimating, scheduling, executing, monitoring, and controlling the project work.

The following points give details:

- **Inputs**:
  - Enterprise environmental factors
  - Organizational project asset
  - Project scope statement
  - Work breakdown structure
  - WBS dictionary
  - Project management plan
- **Outputs**:
  - Activity list
  - Activity attributes
  - Milestone list
  - Requested changes
- **Tools and techniques**:
  - Decomposition
  - Templates
  - Rolling wave planning
  - Expert judgment
  - Planning component

Activity sequencing

Activity sequencing involves identifying and documenting the logical relationships among scheduled activities. Schedule activities can be logically sequenced with proper precedence relationships, as well as leads and lags to support the later development of a realistic and achievable project schedule. Sequencing can be performed by using project management software or by using manual techniques. Manual and automated techniques can also be used in combination. The details of input, tools, techniques and output are shown in the following:

- **Inputs**:
  - Project scope statement
  - Activity list
  - Activity attributes
  - Milestone list
  - Approved change request

- **Outputs**:
  - Project schedule network diagrams
  - Activity list (updates)
  - Activity attributes (updates)
  - Requested changes
- **Tools and techniques**:
  - **Project diagramming method (PDM)**
  - **Arrow diagramming method (ADM)**
  - Schedule network templates
  - Dependency determination
  - Applying leads and lags

Activity resource estimation

Estimating schedule resources involves determining what resources (persons, equipment, or material), what quantities of each resource will be used, and when each resource will be available to perform project activities. The activity resource estimating process is closely coordinated with the cost estimating process. Following are the examples:

- A construction project team will need to be familiar with local building codes.
- An automotive design team will need to be familiar with the latest in automated assembly techniques.

The details of input, tools, techniques and output are shown in the following:

- **Inputs**:
  - Enterprising environmental factors
  - Organizing process assets
  - Activity list
  - Activity attributes
  - Resource availability
  - Resource availability
  - Project management plan
- **Outputs**:
  - Activity resource requirements
  - Activity attributes (updates)
  - Resource breakdown structure

- Resource calendar (updates)
- Requested changes

- **Tools and techniques**:
  - Expert judgment
  - Alternatives analysis
  - Published estimating data
  - Project management software
  - Bottom-up estimating

Precedence diagramming method

Precedence diagramming method (PDM) is a method of constructing a project schedule network diagram that uses boxes or rectangles, referred to as nodes, to represent activities, and connects them with arrows that show the dependencies. *Figure 4.1* shows, a simple project schedule network diagram drawn using PDM. This technique is also called **activity-on-node (AON)** and is the method used by most project management software packages.

PDM includes the following four types of dependencies or precedence relationships:

- **Finish-to-Start (FS)**: The initiation of the successor activity depends upon the completion of the predecessor activity.
- **Finish-to-Finish (FF):** The completion of the successor activity depends upon the completion of the predecessor activity.
- **Start-to-Start (SS):** The initiation of the successor activity depends upon the initiation of the predecessor activity.
- **Start-to-Finish (SF):** The completion of the successor activity depends upon the initiation of the predecessor activity.

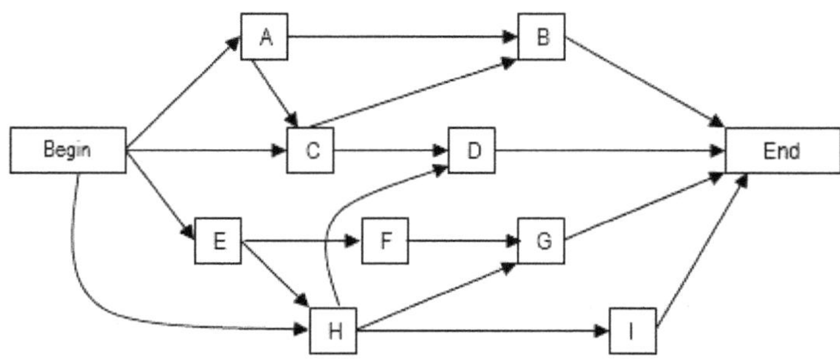

9 Activities, 18 Logic dependencies

***Figure 4.1:** Precedence diagram method*

In PDM, finish-to-start is the most commonly used type of precedence relationship. Start-to-finish relationships are rarely used.

Arrow diagram method

Arrow diagram method (ADM) is a method of constructing a project schedule network diagram that uses arrows to represent activities and connects them at nodes to show their dependencies. *Figure 4.2* shows a simple network logic diagram drawn using ADM. This technique is also called **activity-on-arrow (AOA)**, and although less prevalent than PDM, it is still used in teaching schedule network theory and in some application areas.

ADM uses only finish-to-start dependencies and can require the use of **dummy** relationships called dummy activities, which are shown as dashed lines, to define all logical relationships correctly. Since dummy activities are not actual scheduled activities (they have no work content), they are given a zero-value duration for schedule network analysis purposes. For example, in *Figure 4.2,* schedule activity **H** is dependent upon the completion of scheduled activities **A** and **F**, in addition to the completion of scheduled activity **G**.

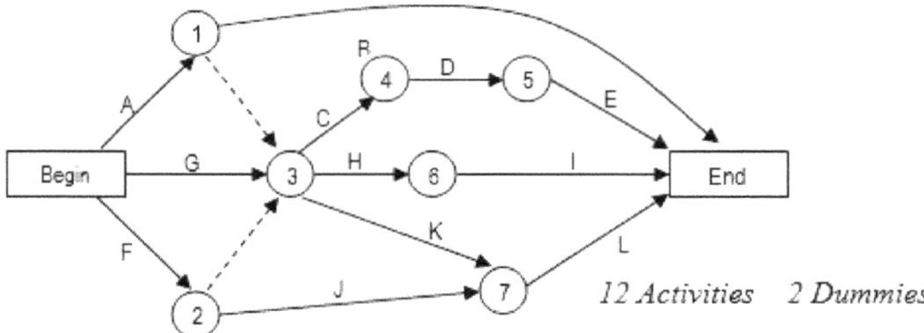

Figure 4.2: Arrow diagram method

Activity duration estimating

The process of estimating scheduled activity durations uses information on the scheduled activity scope of work, required resource types, estimated resource quantities, and resource calendars with resource availabilities. The inputs for the estimates of scheduled activity duration originate from the person or group on the project team who is most familiar with the nature of the work content in the specific scheduled activity. The duration estimate is progressively elaborated, and the process considers the quality and availability of the input data. For example, as the project engineering and design work evolves, more detailed and precise data is available, and the accuracy of the duration estimates improves. Thus, the duration estimate can be assumed to be progressively more accurate and of better quality.

Cost management

Project cost management describes the processes involved in planning, estimating, budgeting, and controlling costs so that the project is completed within the approved budget. It consists of cost estimating, cost budgeting, and cost control project management processes.

The cost of the project depends upon the size of the code in terms of the number of source instructions or the number of function points. The process through which the development takes place also adds to the cost. It takes care of avoiding non-value adding activities such as rework, delays, and communication overhead. The capabilities and productivity of the persons engaged in the project have an impact on the cost of the project. The required quality for the product features, performance, reliability, and adaptability must be decided to control the cost.

It provides a process flow view of these processes and their inputs, outputs, and other related knowledge area processes.

- **Cost estimating**: Developing an approximation of the costs of the resources needed to complete project activities.
- **Cost budgeting**: Aggregating the estimated costs of individual activities or work packages to establish a cost baseline.
- **Cost control:** Influencing the factors that create cost variances and controlling changes to the project budget.

Project cost management is primarily concerned with the cost of the resources needed to complete scheduled activities. However, project cost management should also consider the effect of project decisions on the cost of using, maintaining, and supporting the product, service, or result of the project. The broader view of project cost management is often called life-cycle costing. Life-cycle costing, together with value engineering techniques, can improve decision-making and is used to reduce cost and execution time and to improve the quality and performance of the project deliverable.

Software measurement

Measurement is a standard practice in engineering and management, too. We believe that measurement increases the depth of our understanding, and we express a normal impulse to try to measure what we do or seek to do [Stan Rifkin]. How to measure the business value of the software to be constructed is a concern typically found in business data processing. Since we do not know how to measure the value of what we are producing, a number of surrogates are created, such as **Lines of Code (LoC)**, functional size, functional points, etc.

Empirical cost estimation

Expert judgment, a qualitative approach is adopted for cost estimation of a project. A group of experts is responsible for giving their individual views through their past experience on a similar project and predicting the cost estimation of the target project. Any variation of the target project in comparison to the previous one is adjusted by increasing or decreasing the cost. Experts give different cost estimates on the same project. The final figure has to be reconciled, and the experts have to arrive at a consensus without having a group meeting in order to avoid undesirable side effects. A technique called the **Delphi technique** was adopted here. In this technique, all the experts work separately. Each one will produce their own estimates and rationale for the estimate. These estimates and rationales are distributed to all experts, who now produce a second estimate. The process of estimation and distribution continues until the experts agree on an acceptable tolerance.

Heuristic cost estimation

The **Constructive Cost Estimation Model (COCOMO)** was first developed by *Barry W. Boehm* in 1981 as a model for cost estimating effort, cost, the requirement of manpower, and schedule for software projects. It was established on a study of 63 projects, each having 2,000 to 10,000 LOC and programming language from assembly to `PL/1`. This was called COCOMO 81, the basic model. It is good for quick, early, rough order magnitude estimates of software cost, but its accuracy is limited due to its lack of factors to account for the difference in project attributes (cost drivers). In 1997, COCOMO II was developed and finally came into force in 2001. This intermediate model is better suited for estimating modern software development projects. It provides more support for the modern software development process and an updated project database. The detailed COCOMO additionally accounts for the influence of individual project phases. The three types of COCOMO models consisting of a hierarchy with detailed and accurate forms are in use.

It is a static, single-valued model that computes software development effort and cost as a function of program size expressed in estimated LoC. **COCOMO** applies to three classes of software projects:

- The equation of the basic model is as follows:

  $$E = a.S^b.M(x)$$

  Where the following:

  - **M(x):** adjustment multiplier
  - **E**: Person-months of effort
  - **S**: Thousands of lines of delivered instructions (KSDI)
  - **a and b**: adjustment factors

- The schedule time of development is given by:

  $$T = c.E^d$$

  Where the following:

  - **E:** Development effort in person months
  - **T**: Time for development in months
  - **a, b, c, and d**: Parameters are determined by model and development mode

Three classes of software products are considered in COCOMO. They are as follows:

- **Organic**: Used for relatively small groups with a familiar environment and well-understood application programs.

- **Semidetached**: Used when there is a mix of experience in the project team and a less familiar environment. It is more convenient for the new text editor or statistical software development.
- **Embedded**: Used when the project is strongly coupled with complex hardware and stringent regulations in operating procedures, for example, the development of new operating system software.

Following is a COCOMO problem:

- Two software managers separately estimated a given project to be of 10,000 and 15,000 LoC, respectively. Bring out the Effort and Schedule time implications of their estimation using COCOMO. For the effort estimation, use a coefficient value of 3.2 and an exponent value of 1.05. For the schedule time estimation, the similar values are 2.5 and 0.38, respectively. Assume all adjustment multipliers to be equal to unity.

Following is the answer:

- All adjustment multipliers are equal to unity.
  - **Effort estimation:** $E = 3.2 * S1.^{06}$ (E in person months, S in **Kilo Delivered Source Instructions (KDSI)**)
  - **The schedule time of development estimation**: $T = 2.5 * E0.^{38}$
- T is time for development in months.
- Line of code estimations are below 50 KSDI. We can assume the given project to be an organic one.
- Now, for 10,000 LoC:
  - $S = 10\ KSDI$
  - Effort $E = 3.2 * 10^{1.06} = 35.90$ person months
  - Schedule time $T = 2.5 * 35.90^{0.38} = 9.75$ months
- For 15,000 LoC:
  - $S = 15$ KSDI
  - Effort $E = 3.2 * 15^{1.06} = 54.96$ person months
  - Schedule time $T = 2.5 * 54.96^{0.38} = 11.46$ months

Basic constructive cost estimation model

The basic **COCOMO** model computes software development effort as a function of program size expressed in estimated LoC. **Effort (E)** is in person-months and **Time (T)** is the development time in chronological months. **Kilo Lines of Code (KLOC)** is the estimated number of delivered thousand LoC for the project. The **coefficients** of a and c and the **exponents** of b and d are given in the following *Table 4.1*:

Effort $E = a*(KLOC)^b$

Time $T = c*(E)^d$

Software Project	a	b	c	d
Organic	2.40	1.05	2.50	0.38
Semi-detached	3.00	1.12	2.50	0.35
Embedded	3.60	1.20	2.50	0.32

Table 4.1: *Basic model parameters*

Following is the basic COCOMO problem:

- For a project, the LOC estimate is 33,200 lines to be developed. Use *Table 4.1*, where the project is assumed to be organic. Calculate the effort and schedule time required for the project.

Following is the answer:

- Effort $E = 2.4\ (KLOC)^{1.05}$
  - $= 2.4\ (33.2)^{1.05}$
  - $= 95$ person months
- Project duration $T = 2.5\ E^{0.35}$
  - $= 2.5\ (95)^{0.35}$
  - $= 12.3$ months

The project duration time will help the analyst determine the recommended number of software professionals, N, to be deployed.

$$N = E/T = 95/12.3 \approx 8\ people$$

Intermediate constructive cost estimation model

The basic model is extended to consider a set of cost-driver attributes that can be grouped into four major categories: product attributes, hardware attributes, personnel attributes, and project attributes. Each of the 15 attributes in these categories is rated on a six-point scale ranging from very low to extra high (in importance or value). Based on the rating, an effort multiplier is determined. The product of all effort multiplier results in an **effort adjustment factor (EAF)**. The typical values for EAF range from 0.9 to 1.4. The effort, in this case, will vary, but the time will not vary.

$$E = a*(KLOC)^b * EAF$$

and, $T = c*(E)^d$

The value of a and b will change, as shown in *Table 4.2*. The value of c and d will remain the same:

Software project	a	B
Organic	3.2	1.05
Semi-detached	3.0	1.12
Embedded	2.8	1.20

Table 4.2: Intermediate model

Effort adjustment factors

The EAF is calculated using 15 cost drivers. The cost drivers are grouped into four categories. Each cost driver is rated on a six-point scale ranging from low to high importance. Based on the rating, an effort multiplier is determined using *Table 4.3*. The product of all effort multiplier is the EAF:

Code	Description	RATING					
		Very low	Low	Nominal	High	Very high	Extra high
Product							
RELY	Required software reliability	0.75	0.88	1.00	1.15	1.40	-
DATA	Size of application database	-	0.94	1.00	1.08	1.16	-
CPLX	Complexity of product	0.70	0.85	1.00	1.15	1.30	1.65
Hardware							
TIME	Execution time constraint	-	-	1.00	1.11	1.30	1.66
STOR	Main storage constraint	-	-	1.00	1.06	1.21	1.56
VIRT	Virtual machine volatility	-	0.87	1.00	1.15	1.30	-
TURN	Computer turn-around time	-	0.87	1.00	1.07	1.15	-
Personal							
ACAP	Analyst capability	1.46	1.19	1.00	0.86	0.71	-
AEXP	Applications experience	1.29	1.13	1.00	0.91	0.82	-
PCAP	Programmer capability	1.42	1.17	1.00	0.86	0.70	-
VEXP	Virtual machine experience	1.21	1.10	1.00	0.90	-	-
LEXP	Language experience	1.14	1.07	1.00	0.95	-	-

Code	Description	RATING					
		Very low	Low	Nominal	High	Very high	Extra high
Project							
MODP	Modern programming practice	1.24	1.10	1.00	0.91	0.82	-
TOOL	Software tools	1.24	1.10	1.00	0.91	0.83	-
SCED	Development schedule	1.23	1.08	1.00	1.04	1.10	-

Table 4.3: *Software development effort multipliers*

Advanced constructive cost estimation model

The **advanced COCOMO model** computes effort as a function of program size and a set of cost drivers, weighted according to each phase of the software life cycle. The advanced model applies the intermediate model at the component level, and then a phase-based approach is used to consolidate the estimate. It is usually complex to carry out the cost estimation.

The four phases used in the detailed COCOMO model are the following:

- **Requirement Planning and Product Design (RPD)**
- **Detailed Design (DD)**
- **Code and Unit Test (CUT)**
- **Integration and Testing (IT)**

Each cost driver is broken down by phase, as shown in the example shown in *Table 4.4*:

Cost Driver Rating	RPD	DD	CUT	IT
ACAP Very Low	1.80	1.35	1.35	1.50
Low	0.85	0.85	0.85	1.20
Nominal	1.00	1.00	1.00	1.00
High	0.75	0.90	0.90	0.85
Very High	0.55	0.75	0.75	0.70

Table 4.4: *Analyst capability effort multiplier for detailed COCOMO*

The overall project estimates made for each module by combining all the subsystems. Using the detailed cost drivers, an estimate is determined for each phase of the lifecycle.

Analytical cost estimation

In the last three decades, many quantitative software cost estimation models have been developed. They range from empirical models such as **Boehm's COCOMO models** to analytical models. An empirical model uses data from previous projects to evaluate the current project and derives the basic formulae from analysis of the particular database available. An analytical model, on the other hand, uses formulae based on global assumptions, such as the rate at which developer solve problems and the number of problems available.

Halstead software science method

Halstead proposed the code length and volume metrics. Code length is used to measure the source code program length and is defined as follows:

$$N = N1 + N2$$

Where, $N1$ is the total number of operator occurrences, and

$N2$ is the total number of operand occurrences.

The volume corresponds to the amount of required storage space and is defined as:

$$V = N \log(n1 + n2)$$

Where, $N1$ is the number of distinct operators, and $N2$ is the number of distinct operands that appear in a program. There have been some disagreements over the underlying theory that supports the software science approach. This measurement has received decreasing support in recent years.

SLIM

Putnam developed a constrained model called **SLIM** to be applied to projects exceeding 70,000 LoC. **Putnam's model** assumes that effort for software projects is distributed similarly to a collection of Rayleigh curves. Putnam suggests that staffing rises smoothly during the project and then drops sharply during acceptance testing. The SLIM model is expressed as two equations describing the relation between the development effort and the schedule. The first equation, called the software equation, states that development effort is proportional to the fourth power of development time. The second equation, the manpower-buildup equation, states that the effort is proportional to the cube of the development time.

- **The Norden-Rayleigh curve**: The Norden-Rayleigh curve represents manpower as a function of time. SLIM uses separate Rayleigh curves for design and code, test and validation, maintenance, and management. A Rayleigh curve is shown in *Figure 4.3:*

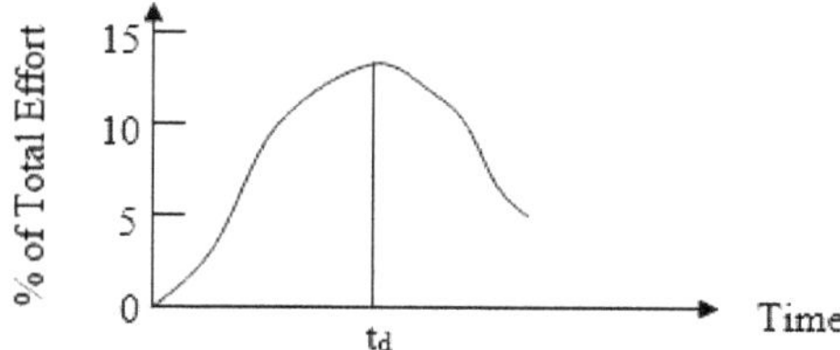

Figure 4.3: Rayleigh curve

- **The software equation**

  Putnam used some empirical observations about productivity levels to derive the software equation from the basic Rayleigh curve formula. The software equation is expressed as:

  Size $L = C.K^{1/3}.t_d^{4/3}$

  Where:

  - L = Delivered lines of code
  - K = Effort in person-years
  - t_d = Development time in years
  - C = Software development environment
  - C = 2000 (poor), C = 8000 (good), C = 11000 (excellent)

  From the above equation $L^3 = C^3.K.t_d^4$

  Hence, $K.\ t_d^4 = (L/C)^3$

  = Constant for a given software project

  Thus, Effort in person-years, $K\ \alpha\ (1/t_d^4)$, that is, $K1/K2 = t_{d2}^{4}/t_d^4$

  The following is effect of the schedule change

- **Putnam model:**

  Effort in person-years, $K\ \alpha\ (1/t_d^4)$

  where, t_d = Development time in years

- **Jensen model:**

  Effort in person-years, $K\ \alpha\ (1/t_d^2)$

  where, t_d = Development time in years

  Putnam's model is more pessimistic while the Jensen model returns a more optimistic schedule. Although $K.t_d^4 = constant$, it does not mean that we can vary td as much as we like. In reality, td can only be varied between 80 percent and 120 percent of its original value. Thus, for the 10-month project, the schedule can only become between 8 and 12 months but neither below 8 months nor above 10 months.

Following is an example:

Schedule change:

- Original effort = 36.9 person-month
- Development time = 9.85 months

New effort for project completion in 8 months:

According to Putnam model:

- New effort = $36.9 * (9.85/8)^4$ = 84.8 person-months
- = 2.3 times more

According to Jensen's model:

- New effort = $36.9 * (9.85/8)^2$ = 55.9 person-months
- = 1.5 times more

- **The manpower-buildup equation:** To allow effort estimation, Putnam introduced the manpower-buildup equation:

$$D = E/t^3$$

Where:

- D is a constant called manpower acceleration.
- E is the total project effort in years, and
- T is the elapsed time to delivery in years

Human resource management

Project human resource management describes the processes that organize and manage the project team. It consists of human resource planning, acquire project team, develop project team, and manage project team project management processes.

Communication management

Project communications management describes the processes concerning the timely and appropriate generation, collection, dissemination, storage, and ultimate disposition of project information. It consists of communications planning, information distribution, performance reporting, and managing stakeholders' project management processes.

Risk management

Project risk management describes the processes concerned with conducting risk management on a project. It consists of risk management planning, risk identification, qualitative risk analysis, quantitative risk analysis, risk response planning, and risk monitoring and control project management processes. In general, software engineers do nothing about risks until something goes wrong. They get into action to correct the problem rapidly.

Project risks cause problems to project plans like schedule slips and increases in cost. Risk identification is essential to avoid and control. There are some predictable risks in the following generic categories:

- **Product size:** Risks associated with the size of the software.
- **Business impact:** Risks associated with constraints imposed by management.
- **Customer characteristics**: Risks associated with the customer and the developer's ability to communicate promptly.
- **Process identification**: Risks associated with the degree to which the software process has been defined and followed.
- **Development environment**: Risks associated with the availability and quality of tools to be used to build the product.
- **Technology to be built**: Risks associated with the complexity of the system to be built and the newness of the technology to be used in the system.
- **Staff size and experience**: Risks associated with the overall technical and project experience of the software engineers.

An effective strategy should be made for risk avoidance, risk monitoring, and contingency planning. This is achieved by developing a plan for risk mitigation and monitoring the activities of the project manager. A **Risk Mitigation, Monitoring, and Management plan (RMMM plan)** can be organized.

Project planning

Project planning is an aspect of project management that focuses a lot on project integration. The project plan reflects the current status of all project activities and is used to monitor and control the project. The project planning tasks ensure that various elements of the project are coordinated and, therefore, guide the project execution.

Project planning helps in the following:

- Facilitating communication
- Monitoring or measuring the project progress, and
- Provides overall documentation of assumptions or planning decisions

The project planning phases can be broadly classified as follows:

- Development of the project plan
- Execution of the project plan
- Change control and corrective actions

Project planning is an ongoing effort throughout the project lifecycle.

If you fail to plan, you plan to fail.

Project planning is crucial to the success of the project. Careful planning right from the beginning of the project can help to avoid costly mistakes. It assures that the project execution will accomplish its goals on schedule and within budget.

Steps in project planning

Project planning spans across the various aspects of the project. Generally, project planning is a process of estimating, scheduling, and assigning the project's resources to deliver an end product of suitable quality. However, it is much more as it can assume a very strategic role, which can determine the success of the project. A project plan is one of the crucial steps in project planning in general.

Typically, project planning can include the following types of planning:

- **Project scope definition and scope planning:** In this step, we document the project work that would help us achieve the project goal. We document the assumptions, constraints, user expectations, business requirements, technical requirements, project deliverables, project objectives, and everything that defines the final product requirements. This is the foundation for successful project completion.
- **Quality planning:** The relevant quality standards are determined for the project. This is an important aspect of project planning. Based on the inputs captured in the previous steps, such as the project scope, requirements, deliverables, etc., various factors influencing the quality of the final product are determined. The processes required to deliver the product as promised and as per the standards are defined.
- **Project activity definition and activity sequencing:** In this step, we define all the specific activities that must be performed to deliver the product by producing various product deliverables. The project activity sequencing identifies the interdependence of all the activities defined.
- **Time, effort, and resource estimation:** Once the scope, activities, and activity interdependence are clearly defined and documented, the next crucial step is to determine the effort required to complete each of the activities. The effort can be calculated using one of the many techniques available such as function points, LoC, complexity of code, benchmarks, etc. This step estimates and documents the time, effort, and resources required for each activity.
- **Risk factors identification:** Expecting the unexpected and facing it. It is important to identify and document the risk factors associated with the project based on the assumptions, constraints, user expectations, specific circumstances, etc.
- **Schedule development:** The schedule for the project can be arrived at based on the activities, interdependence, and effort required for each of them. The schedule may influence the cost estimates, the cost-benefit analysis, and so on.

Project scheduling is one of the most important tasks of project planning and the most difficult tasks. In very large projects, several teams may work on developing the project. They may work on it in parallel. However, their work may be interdependent. Again, various factors may impact the successful scheduling of a project. Popular tools can be used for creating and reporting schedules such as Gantt charts.

- **Cost estimation and budgeting:** Based on the information collected in all the previous steps it is possible to estimate the cost involved in executing and implementing the project. A cost-benefit analysis can be arrived at for the project. Based on the cost estimates, the budget allocation is done for the project.
- **Organizational and resource planning:** Based on the activities identified, schedule and budget allocation resource types and resources are identified. One of the primary goals of resource planning is to ensure that the project should run efficiently. This can only be achieved by keeping all the project resources fully utilized as possible. The success depends on the accuracy in predicting the resource demands that will be placed on the project. Resource planning is an iterative process and necessary to optimize the use of resources throughout the project life cycle thus making the project execution more efficient. There are various types of resources like equipment, personnel, facilities, money, etc.
- **Risk management planning:** Risk management is a process of identifying, analyzing, and responding to risk. Based on the risk factors identified a risk resolution plan is created. The plan analyses each of the risk factors and their impact on the project. The possible responses for each of them can be planned. Throughout the project's lifetime, these risk factors are monitored and acted upon as necessary.
- **Project plan development and execution:** Project plan development uses the inputs gathered from all the other planning processes, such as scope definition, activity identification, activity sequencing, quality management planning, etc. A detailed work break-down structure comprising all the activities identified is used. The tasks are scheduled based on the inputs captured in the steps previously described. The project plan documents all the assumptions, activities, schedules, timelines, and drives the project.

  Each of the project tasks and activities are periodically monitored. The team and the stakeholders are informed of the progress. This serves as an excellent communication mechanism. Any delays are analyzed, and the project plan may be adjusted accordingly.
- **Performance reporting:** As described above, the progress of each of the tasks or activities described in the project plan is monitored. The progress is compared with the schedule and timelines documented in the project plan. Various techniques are used to measure and report the project performance, such as **earned value management (EVM)**. A wide variety of tools can be used to report the performance

of the project, such as **program evaluation and review technique (PERT)** charts, Gantt charts, logical bar charts, histograms, pie charts, etc.

- **Planning change management:** Analysis of project performance can necessitate that certain aspects of the project be changed. The requests for changes need to be analyzed carefully, and their impact on the project should be studied. Considering all these aspects, the project plan may be modified to accommodate this request for change. Change management is also necessary to accommodate the implementation of the project currently under development in the production environment. When the new product is implemented in the production environment, it should not negatively impact the environment or the performance of other applications that share the same hosting environment.
- **Project rollout planning:** In enterprise environments, the success of the project depends a great deal on the success of its rollout and implementation. Whenever a project is rolled out, it may affect the technical systems, business systems, and sometimes even the way business is run. For an application to be successfully implemented, not only the technical environment should be ready, but the users should accept it and use it effectively. For this to happen, the users may need to be trained on the new system. All this requires planning.

Project size estimates

Accurately estimating the project size, cost, effort, and time for development are the biggest challenges for the software industry nowadays. It is important to accurately estimate the project size for the further estimation of project cost and schedule.

The initial project size estimates are made from the system requirements, and further, estimation can be carried out through various techniques. Those are the following:

- LoC or Kloc
- Function point analysis
- Feature point analysis

LOC or KLOC

Each source line acts as one loc irrespective of the number of instructions used in that source line. For N number of source lines, it becomes **N-Line of Code (NLOC).**

When, $N = 1,000$, it becomes KLOC.

Function point analysis

The empirical estimation is done based on countable measures of the software information domain. Some adjustments are made depending on the complexity of the software. The functionality cannot be measured directly. This is derived indirectly using other direct measures called function points. The function points are collected by the core team on the discussion at the client site. The function points are categorized into the following:

- **External Inputs (EI)** to the application given by the users (data).
- **External Outputs (EO)** from the application (reports, screen, message, etc.).
- Number of **External enQueries (EQ)** by the users of the software as a combination of input requests and output retrievals.
- The number of master **Internal Logical Files (ILF)** would be maintained and updated by the application.
- Number of **External Interface Files (EIF)** of other applications

Function points are computed by using *Table 4.5,* where counts are provided.

$$Function\ Point\ (FP) = Count\text{-}total * [0.65 + (0.01 * sum\ (F_j))]$$

The F_j *(j = 1 to 14)* are complexity adjustment values based on the questions. Each one is expressed on a scale from 0 to 5, depending on their influence on the development process:

- **0**: No influence
- **1**: Incidental
- **2**: Moderate
- **3**: Average
- **4**: Significant
- **5**: Essential

Computable Measure	**Multipliers**		
	Simple	**Average**	**Complex**
External Inputs (EI)	3	4	6
External Outputs (EO)	4	5	7
No. of **External enQuiries (EQ)**	3	4	6
No. of master **Internal Logical Files (ILF)**	7	10	15
No. of **External Interface Files (EIF)**	5	7	10

Table 4.5: *Function point computation*

Following are the complexity adjustment values:

- Does the system require reliable backup and recovery?
- Are data communications required?
- Are there distributed processing functions?
- Is performance critical?
- Will the system run in an existing heavily utilized operational environment?

- Does the system require on-line data entry?
- Does the on-line data entry require the input transaction to be built over multiple screens or operations?
- Are the master files updated on-line?
- Are the inputs, outputs, files, or inquiries complex?
- Is the internal processing complex?
- Is the code designed to be reusable?
- Are conversions and installation included in the design?
- Is the system designed for multiple installations in different organizations?
- Is the application designed to facilitate change and ease of use by the users?

Following the example:

Compute the function point value for a software project with the following details:

- **user inputs**: 12,
- **number of files**: 6,
- **user outputs**: 25,
- **external interfaces**: 4,
- **inquiries**: 10,
- **number of algorithms**: 8

Assume the multipliers are average and all the complexity adjustment factors are at their moderate to average values. Multiplier= 1.

Computable Measure	Countable measure values	Multipliers at average	Count = measure * multiplier
External Inputs (EI)	12	4	48
External Outputs (EO)	25	5	125
No. of **External enQuiries (EQ)**	10	4	40
No. of master **Internal Logical Files (ILF)**	6	10	60
No. of **External Interface Files (EIF)**	4	7	28
Count-Total			**301**

Table 4.6: *Function point calculation*

$$Function\ Point\ (FP) = Count\text{-}total * [0.65 + (0.01 * sum\ (F_j))]$$

$14\ F_j$ – each assumes a value of 2.5 in case the influence is moderate to average.

Hence, $sum\ (F_j) = 14 * 2.5 = 35$

Thus, $FP = 301 * (0.65 + (0.01 * 35)) = 301$

Number of algorithms is not relevant here.

Equivalent line of coding of function point

Depending on the programming language, there is a relationship between LOC and function points. This is used to implement the software and the quality of design. *Table 4.7* provides a rough estimate of the average number of LOCs required to build one FP in different programming languages.

Language	Equivalent LOC of FP
C	130
COBOL	110
JAVA	55
C++/Turbo PASCAL	50
Visual BASIC	30
Access/Excel	10-40

Table 4.7: *Equivalent LOC of FP*

Following is an example:

The FP of a software product is 270.

Assuming C++ environment, $LOC = 270 * 50 = 13500 = 13.5\ KLOC$

Using COCOMO (basic, organic):

Effort $E = 2.4 * (13.5) * 1.05 = 36.9$ person-months (P-M)

Development Time $D = 2.5 * (36.9) * 0.38 = 9.85$ months (M)

Compare this with $E_{FP} = 270/7 = 38.6$ person-month (assuming 7 FP/P-M)

Development Time $D = 9.85\ M \approx 10\ M$

Hence, software engineers required = 36.9/10 ≈ 4

If one engineer costs Rs. 50,000 per month

Project cost = Rs. 50,000 * 10 * 4 = Rs. 20,00,000

The estimates give a constant number of software engineers, meaning a uniform distribution of effort throughout the project period. However, in reality, the software development effort is not uniform. Rather, it follows a Rayleigh distribution in *Figure 4.3*.

Projects as proxies

An alternative proxy is the **Object line of Code (OLC)**. The idea, here, is that there is a relationship between the size of the code when written as messages to objects and the final code size. The link between the two is made by estimating the size of the objects. Humphrey shows, in his book, a good regression line between OLC and LOC.

The size of an object can be estimated in terms of the number of methods that are required to implement the object and an estimate of the category of the object. The following *Table 4.8*, taken from Humphrey's book, shows a collection of estimates of object size in LOC per method. Your lineage may be different.

Category	Very Small	Small	Medium	Large	Very Large
Calculation	2.34	5.13	11.25	24.66	54.04
Data	2.60	4.79	8.84	16.31	30.09
I/O	9.01	12.06	16.15	21.62	30.09
Logic	7.55	10.98	15.98	23.25	33.83
Set-Up	3.88	5.04	6.56	8.53	11.09
Text	3.75	8.00	17.07	36.41	77.66

Table 4.8: *C++ object size in LOC per method.*

It highlights the process requires that we design the system before you estimate its size. The process can be considerably improved by using statistical methods to track the accuracy of your estimates.

Feature point analysis

A superset of function points called feature points was introduced in **1986** by Jones in an attempt to improve the accuracy of estimates for real-time, operating systems, embedded, communications, and process control software systems *(Garmus 1996)*. Feature points introduce a new parameter (algorithms) to the five standard function point parameters. Algorithms are assigned a default weight of three and logical files are reduced to seven (from ten), which has the effect of reducing the significance of data storage and grouping more prevalent in **MIS** applications.

Jones (1995) found that when feature points are used in classical MIS applications, the results are often similar, except in the case where MIS applications are severely dominated by files. For a telephone-switching project, the Feature Point estimate was notably higher due to the high algorithmic complexity.

Feature points must be counted like the function points. They are a superset of the latter. This prompted Jones to introduce ten rules specifically identifying exactly under what conditions an algorithm exists. Further research is underway to develop a more rigorous taxonomy and weighing scale for algorithms.

Mythical man month

Cost varies as the product of men and months. Therefore, man-month as a unit for measuring the size of the job is a dangerous and deceptive myth *(Fred Brooks)*. Why is software project disaster so common? The answer is estimation techniques are poor and assume things will go well. The estimation techniques fallaciously confuse effort with progress, hiding the assumption that men and months are interchangeable. When the schedule slippage is recognized, the natural response is to add manpower, which is like dousing a fire with gasoline.

Mostly, all the programmers are optimistic. The first false assumption is that all will go well or each task takes only as long as it ought to take. The programmer should consider the larger probabilities without using fuzzy milestones (get true status). In many cases, the process is sequential in nature, which will take the basic minimum time. Do not try to reduce it further. The bearing of a child takes nine months, no matter how many women are assigned. Testing is the most unpredictable and unscheduled part of the process. Therefore, allocate more test times and understand the task dependencies.

It is a misconception that adding more people will complete the job early. To calculate, how long does a twelve-month project take? One person will take twelve months. Suppose two persons take seven months, which adds two man-months extra. If three persons take five months, that adds three man-months extra. There is no linear relationship between man and time. The myth of additional manpower relies on hunches and guesses, which invites gutless estimation. Brooks's law states that *adding manpower to a late project makes it later*.

Conclusion

The Software Project Management Framework is essential for managing software projects, ensuring alignment with objectives through a structured approach. It helps oversee the entire project lifecycle, balancing time, cost, and quality to meet business and user needs. The framework aids in risk management by identifying potential issues early, reducing delays and budget overruns. It also promotes effective resource allocation, scheduling, and communication, ensuring all team members understand their roles. Ultimately, this framework ensures timely, budget-conscious, high-quality project delivery, fostering efficient project outcomes in a fast-evolving tech environment.

In the next chapter, we will explore **Project Scheduling through PERT or CPM**. This chapter will delve into how these two powerful techniques, **Program Evaluation Review Technique (PERT)** and **critical path method (CPM)**, can help in planning and managing project schedules effectively. You will learn how to estimate task durations, identify the critical path, and optimize the allocation of resources to ensure timely project completion.

By understanding these methods, you will gain valuable insights into minimizing project delays and managing dependencies, ensuring smoother execution of complex software projects.

Exercises

To solidify your understanding of the concepts covered in this chapter, try the following exercises.

Multiple choice questions

1. **Which of the following is NOT a key component of the Software Project Management Framework?**
   a. Scope management
   b. Resource allocation
   c. Stakeholder ignorance
   d. Risk management
2. **The primary objective of the Software Project Management Framework is to:**
   a. Deliver projects on time, within budget, and with low-quality standards.
   b. Ensure the project scope is undefined.
   c. Complete projects with a balance between time, cost, and quality.
   d. Prevent communication between stakeholders and project teams.
3. **Risk management in the Software Project Management Framework involves:**
   a. Ignoring potential issues until they arise.
   b. Identifying and mitigating risks early in the project lifecycle.
   c. Allocating unlimited resources to solve every problem.
   d. Focusing only on project timelines.
4. **Which phase of the Software Project Management Framework focuses on defining project deliverables and setting the project timeline?**
   a. Execution
   b. Planning
   c. Initiation
   d. Closure

5. **In the Software Project Management Framework, what is the purpose of stakeholder communication?**
   a. To report only after project completion.
   b. To ensure all parties are aware of the project's progress, risks, and changes.
   c. To allocate all project resources to stakeholders.
   d. To create conflicts between project teams.

Short questions

1. Define the Software Project Management Framework and explain its primary purpose.
2. What are the main phases of the Software Project Management Framework?
3. How does a project manager balance the constraints of time, cost, and quality within the framework?
4. Why is risk management important in software project management, and how does the framework address it?
5. What role does communication play in the Software Project Management Framework?
6. Explain the importance of scope management in software project planning.
7. How does resource allocation affect the success of a software project?
8. Describe how a project manager can use the Software Project Management Framework to monitor and control a project.
9. What are some of the common risks that software projects face, and how can the framework help mitigate them?
10. Discuss the importance of stakeholder involvement in the Software Project Management Framework.

Essay questions

1. Describe the process of project initiation and planning within the Software Project Management Framework. What key activities are performed during these phases?
2. Explain how the Software Project Management Framework helps in ensuring project deliverables meet the required quality standards.
3. Discuss how time management and scheduling are handled in the Software Project Management Framework. How can project managers ensure deadlines are met?
4. What are the major challenges a project manager may face while implementing the Software Project Management Framework? How can they overcome these challenges?

5. In the context of the Software Project Management Framework, explain the importance of tracking project progress and performance through **Key Performance Indicators (KPIs)**.

Multiple choice answers

1. c
2. c
3. b
4. b
5. b

Join our book's Discord space

Join the book's Discord Workspace for Latest updates, Offers, Tech happenings around the world, New Release and Sessions with the Authors:

https://discord.bpbonline.com

Chapter 5
Project Scheduling Through PERT or CPM

Introduction

Effective project scheduling is crucial for managing time, resources, and costs in any project. Two of the most widely used techniques for project planning and control are **Program Evaluation and Review Technique (PERT)** and **critical path method (CPM)**. Both methods provide a systematic approach to defining tasks, estimating timelines, and identifying critical paths that directly impact project completion. While PERT focuses on handling uncertainty in project activities through probabilistic time estimates, CPM emphasizes a more deterministic approach, ideal for projects with well-defined activities and timeframes. Understanding these methodologies allows project managers to optimize schedules, minimize delays, and ensure efficient resource allocation.

Structure

In this chapter, we will be discussing the following topics:

- Origin and use of PERT
- Origin and use of CPM
- Application of PERT and CPM
- Solution by network analysis
- Critical path method

- Time cost curve
- Program evaluation and review technique
- Mathematical programming method
- Gantt chart

Objectives

Many times, a big project consists of a large number of activities that pose complex problems in planning, scheduling, and control, especially when the project activities have to be performed in a specified technological sequence. With the help of PERT and CPM, the project manager can plan the project ahead of time and foresee possible sources of troubles and delays in completion, schedule the project activities, at the appropriate times, to confirm the proper job sequence, so that the project is completed as soon as possible and coordinate and control the project activities so as to stay on schedule in completing the project.

Thus, both PERT and CPM are aided in efficient project management. They differ in their approach to the problem and solution techniques. The nature of the project generally dictates the proper technique to be used.

Origin and use of PERT

PERT was developed in the U.S. Navy during the late 1950s to accelerate the development of the **Polaris Fleet Ballistic Missile**. The development of the weapon involved the coordination of the work of thousands of private contractors and other government agencies. The coordination by PERT was so successful that the entire project was completed two years ahead of schedule. This has resulted in further application of PERT in other weapon development programs in the Navy, Air Force, and Army. Nowadays, it is extensively used in industries and other service organizations as well.

PERT incorporates uncertainties in activity times in its analysis. It determines the probability of completing various stages of the project by specified deadlines. It also calculates the expected time to complete the project. The PERT analysis identifies various bottlenecks in a project. It identifies the activities that have a high potential for causing delays in completing the project on schedule. It helps to take necessary preventive measures to reduce possible delays. This is because of its ability to handle uncertainty in job times, PERT is mostly used in research and development projects.

Origin and use of CPM

CPM closely resembles PERT in many aspects but was developed independently by *E.I. du Pont de Nemours Company*. Both PERT and CPM techniques were developed simultaneously. The major difference is that CPM does not incorporate uncertainties in job times. Instead, it assumes that activity times are proportional to the number of resources allocated to them, and by changing the level of resources, the activity times and the project completion time can be varied. Thus, CPM assumes prior experience with similar projects from which the relationships between resources and job times are available. CPM then evaluates the trade-off between project costs and project completion time. CPM is mostly used in construction projects where there is prior experience in handling similar projects.

Application of PERT and CPM

A partial list of applications of PERT and CPM techniques in project management is as follows:

- Development of large integrated software projects.
- Installation of computer hardware, networking, and hardware procurement.
- Construction projects (for example, buildings, highways, bridges, and houses).
- Preparation of bids and proposals for large projects.
- Maintenance planning of oil refineries, ship repairs, and other large operations.
- Manufacture and assembly of large items such as airplanes, ships, and computers.
- Development of new weapons systems, space missions, and new manufactured products.
- Simple projects such as home remodeling, moving into a new house, home cleaning, and painting.

Project network

Analysis by PERT/CPM techniques uses the network formulation to represent the project activities and their ordering relations. The explanation was given, in *Chapter 4, Software Project Management Framework,* the construction of a project network is done as follows:

- Arcs in the network represent individual jobs in the project.
- Nodes represent specific points in time, which mark the completion of one or more jobs in the project.
- Direction on the arc is used to represent the job sequence. It is assumed that any job directed toward a node must be completed before any job directed away from that node can begin.

Mathematical programming method

Given that the project must be completed by time T, we want to determine how the project activities are to be expedited such that the total cost of crashing is minimized. The problem can be formulated as an LP problem as follows:

- **Model-I:**

$$Min\ Z = \sum_{(i,j)} Cij(kij - tij)$$

Subject to

$$t_j - t_i \geq t_{ij}$$

$$\ell_{ij} - t_i \leq k_{ij}$$

$$t_n - t_1 \leq T$$

$$t_i \geq 0 \quad \textit{for all i=1, 2,.......n}$$

Where:

- o $\mathbf{k_{ij}}$: The normal completion time of the *job(i,j)* if no additional resources are assigned
- o $\boldsymbol{\ell_{ij}}$: crash completion time with the maximum amount of resources
- o $\mathbf{C_{ij}}$: the unit cost of shortening the duration of the *job(i,j)*
- o $\mathbf{t_{ij}}$: the completion time of the *job (i,j)*, which is an unknown variable between ℓ_{ij} and k_{ij}
- o $\mathbf{C_{ij}(k_{ij}\text{-}t_{ij})}$: Cost of crashing

- **Model-II:** Suppose, an additional budget of B(money) is available for crashing the project activities. We want to determine how these additional resources may be allocated in the best possible manner so as to minimize the project completion time.

$$Min.\ Z=tn-t1$$

$$S.t.\ tj\text{-}ti \geq tij \textit{ for all jobs(i,j)}$$

$$\ell_{ij} \leq t_{ij} \leq k_{ij} \textit{ for all jobs(i,j)}$$

$$\sum_{i,j} C_{ij}(k_{ij} - t_{ij}) \leq B$$

$$ti,j \geq 0 \textit{ for all i=1,2,......n}$$

The solution gives the least project duration that can be achieved by additional budget B, the activities to be crashed, and their durations.

- **Model-III:**

Let:

$$T^* = \textit{optimal length of the project}$$

$$F = \frac{Indirect\ cost(OH)}{Per\ unit\ time}\ \alpha\ project\ duration$$

$$F(tn\text{-}t1) = \text{Indirect cost},$$

$$tn\text{-}t1 = \text{unknown length of project}$$

$$\sum_{(i,j)}^{n} C_{ij}(k_{ij} - t_{ij}) = \text{Direct cost}$$

t_{ij} = *unknown length of job(i,j) i.e., the completion time of job(i,j)*

Minimize the total cost.

$$Min\, Z = F(t_n - t_1) + \sum_{(i,j)}^{n} C_{ij}(k_{ij} - t_{ij})$$

Subject to $tj - ti \geq tij$ *for all jobs (i,j)*

$\ell ij \leq tij \leq kij$ *for all jobs (i,j)*

$ti \geq 0$ *for all* $i=1,2,\ldots\ldots n$

Diagram representation

Following are the examples of diagram representation:

- **Example 1:** Consider seven jobs A, B, C, D, E, F, and G with the following job sequence:
  - o Job A precedes B and C
  - o Jobs C and D precede E
  - o Job B precedes D
  - o Job E and F precede G

  The project network is shown in *Figure 5.1:*

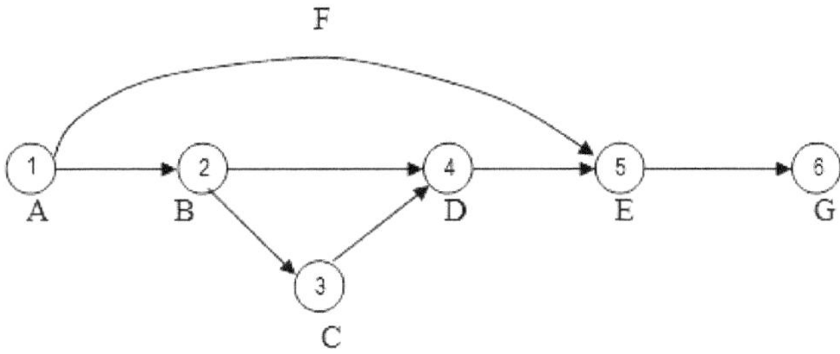

***Figure 5.1:** Network diagram*

In the network, every *arc (i, j)* represents a specific job in the project. Node 1 represents the start, and node 6 denotes the completion of the project. The intermediate nodes represent the completion of various stages of the project. The nodes of the project network are called events.

An event is a specific point in time that marks the completion of one or more activities, well recognizable in the project.

- **Example 2:** Consider a project with five jobs A, B, C, D, and E with the following job sequence:
  - Job A precedes C and D
  - Job B precedes D
  - Job C and D precede E

The completion times for A, B, C, D, and E are 3, 1, 4, 2, and 5 days respectively.

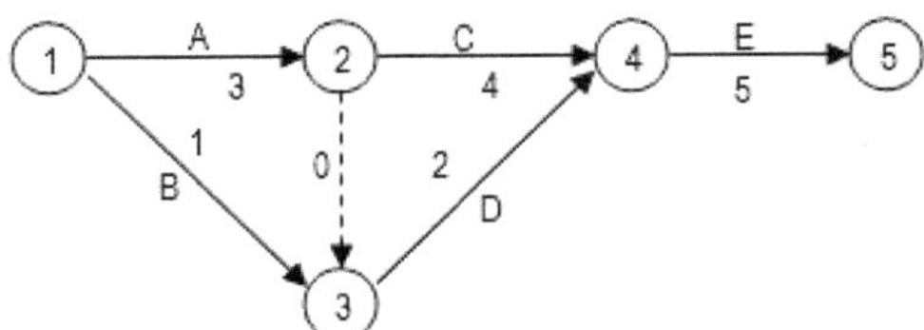

Figure 5.2: Network diagram with times

In the above figure, *arc (2, 3)* represents a **dummy job** that does not exist in reality in the project. It is necessary so as to avoid ambiguity in the job sequence. The completion time of the dummy job is always 0, and it is added to the project network whenever we want to avoid an *arc (i, j)* representing more than one job in the project. Event 3 represents the completion of job B and the dummy job. Since the dummy job is completed as soon as A is completed, event 3, in essence, marks the completion of jobs A and B.

Critical path

A path in the project network connecting the starting event (node) and the ending event such that it passes through the critical jobs is called a **critical path**. It is shown in *Figure 5.3:*

Figure 5.3: Critical path

It can be shown that finding a critical path in a project network is equivalent to finding the longest path in the network.

Solution by network analysis

The **earliest time** of node j, denoted by *Uj*, is the earliest time at which event *j* can occur. We know that event *j* can occur as soon as all the jobs (arcs) directed towards node *j* are completed. In the following *Figure 5.4*, event *j* occurs as soon as jobs A, B, and C are completed:

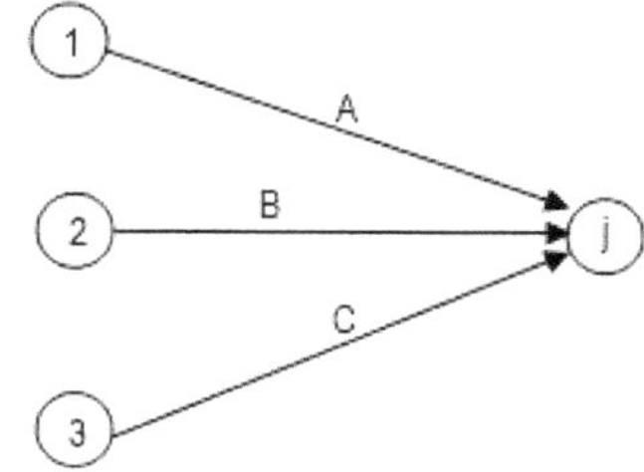

Figure 5.4: *Activities joining into a node*

The earliest time of node j is then given by

$$Uj = max\ (U1 + t1j,\ U2 + t2j,\ U3 + t3j)$$

Where, $t1j$, $t2j$, and $t3j$ are completion times of A, B, and C.

The general formula for calculating Uj is:

$$Uj = maxi\ (Ui + tij)$$

Where, the index I ranges over all nodes for which $arc(i, j)$ exists and t_{ij} is the completion time of the job represented by an $arc\ (i, j)$. *Figure 5.5* shows an example of a project network

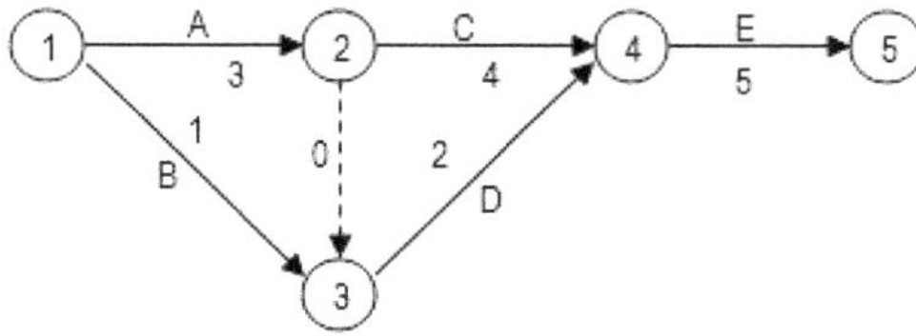

Figure 5.5: *Example of a project network*

For the above network, the U_j are calculated as follows:

- Set $U1 = 0$
- Then, $U2 = U1 + t12 = 3$
- $U3 = max\ [(U2 + t23), (U1 + t13)]$
- $= max\ (3, 1) = 3$
- $U4 = max\ [(U2 + t24), (U3 + t34)]$
- $= max\ (7, 5) = 7$
- $U5 = U4 + t45 = 12$

Hence, the minimum duration of the project is 12 days from the start. We need to calculate the latest time of an event. The latest time of node i, denoted by Vi, is the latest time at which event i can occur without delaying the completion of the project beyond its earliest time. The following figure shows activities emerging from a node:

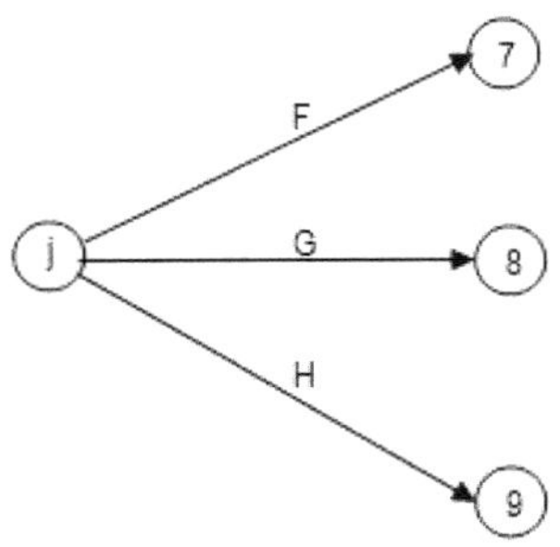

Figure 5.6: Activities emerging from a node

The project will not be delayed if the three jobs, *F*, *G*, and *H*, are completed by *V7*, *V8*, and *V9*, respectively.

$$Vi = min\ [(V7 - ti7), (V8 - ti8), V9 - ti9)]$$

Hence, the general formula to calculate *Vi* becomes:

$$Vi = minj\ (Vj - tij)$$

Set the latest time of the last event equal to its earliest time and work backward.

Thus,

- $V5 - t45 = 12$
- $V4 = V5 - t45 = 7$
- $V3 = V4 - t34 = 5$
- $V2 = min\ [(V4 - t24), (V3 - t23)]$
- $= min\ (3, 5) = 3$
- $V1 = min\ [(V2 - t12), (V3 - t13)]$
- $= min\ (0, 4) = 0$

The difference between the latest time and the earliest time of an event is called a **slack time** of that event. The slack time denotes how much delay can be tolerated in reaching that event without delaying the project completion date (called **float**).

For the project network shown in *Table 5.1*, the slack times of events 1, 2, 3, 4, and 5 are given by 0, 0, 2, 0, and 0 respectively. Those events that have zero slack times are the critical events, where every care must be taken to stay on schedule if the project is to be completed on time. The critical jobs are the arcs (jobs) in the critical path having zero slack time.

The critical path is 1, 2, 3, 4

The jobs are A, C, and E

Events	Earliest Time		Latest Time	Slack Time	Remarks
1	0		0	0	Critical
2	3		3	0	Critical
3	3		5	2	Non-Critical
4	7		7	0	Critical
5	12		12	0	Critical

Table 5.1: *Results of network analysis*

To prepare a project schedule in terms of the activities, it is essential to have the starting time and the ending time of all jobs. From the event times it is possible to get the following information on each one of the activities in the project:

- The earliest starting time
- The latest starting time
- The earliest finishing time
- The latest finishing time
- The slack time (float)

The above figure represents the following:

- **Ui**: The earliest occurrence time of event *i*
- **Vj**: The latest occurrence time of event *j*
- **Tij**: The completion time of job *J*
- **Vj-tij**: Latest starting time of job *J*
- **Ui + tij**: Earliest completion time of job *J*
- **Vj-Ui**: Maximum time available for job *J*
- **Vj-Ui-tij:** The slack time of job *J* (maximum delay in completion)
- **Vj-Ui = tij**: If job *J* is critical

Table 5.2 shows a schedule of a network:

Job	Expected Duration (days)	Earliest Start	Latest Start	Earliest Finish	Latest Finish	Slack Time (Max.delay)	Remarks
A	3	0	0	3	3	0	Critical
B	1	0	4	1	5	4	Non-critical
C	4	3	3	7	7	0	Critical
D	2	3	5	5	7	2	Non-critical
E	5	7	7	12	12	0	Critical

Table 5.2: *Schedule of the network*

Critical path method

The basic assumption in CPM is that the activity times are proportional to the level of resources allocated to them. By assigning additional resources (capital, people, materials, and machines) to an activity, its duration can be reduced to a certain extent. Shortening the duration of an activity is known as **crashing** in the CPM technology. The additional cost incurred in reducing the activity time is called **crashing cost**.

For critical path analysis, it is assumed that every job has a normal completion time (maximum time) if no additional resources were assigned, and a crash completion time (minimum time) with the maximum amount of resources. The project management problem is to be crashed that will minimize the total cost of the project.

Following is an example of enumerative method:

Consider a software project of 8 jobs analysis-module-1 and **system requirement study (SRS)-1**, analysis-module-2, **system requirement study (SRS)**-2, GUI design, GUI coding and unit testing-1, **database (DB)** design, DB coding and unit testing, and integration and system testing. Two groups of professionals are deployed to develop the system. The required time for each activity and the precedence of activities are given in *Table 5.3*:

Job	Job Description	Predecessor	Normal Time (days)	Crash Time (days)	Cost of Crashing (100 Rs)
A	Analysis-1 and SRS-1	-	10	7	4
B	Analysis-2	-	5	4	2
C	SRS-2	B	3	2	2
D	GUI Design	A, C	4	3	3
E	DB Design	A, C	5	3	3
F	GUI Coding and Unit Testing	D	6	3	5
G	DB Coding and Unit Testing	E	5	2	1
H	Integration and System Testing	F, G	5	4	4

Table 5.3: *Activity and precedence of the project work with crashing*

Given **overhead (OH)** cost as Rs. 500 per day, we want to determine the optimal duration of the project in terms of both the crashing and overhead costs and to develop an optimal project schedule.

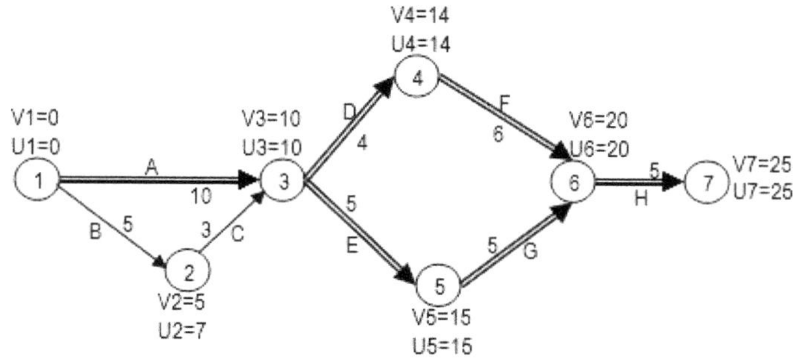

Figure 5.7: *Network of software project with activities*

Table 5.4 outlines the key details of each job in the project using the CPM. Jobs marked as critical, such as *A, D, E, F, G,* and *H,* have zero slack time, meaning any delay will impact the overall project timeline. Non-critical jobs, like *B* and *C,* have slack time, allowing some flexibility without affecting the project's completion.

Job	Expected Duration	Earliest Start	Latest Start	Earliest Finish	Latest Finish	Slack Time (Max.delay)	Remarks
A	10	0	0	10	10	0	Critical
B	5	0	2	5	7	2	Non-critical
C	3	5	7	8	10	3	Non-critical
D	4	10	10	14	14	0	Critical
E	5	10	10	15	15	0	Critical
F	6	14	14	20	20	0	Critical
G	5	15	15	20	20	0	Critical
H	5	20	20	25	25	0	Critical

Table 5.4: *The computation of software project*

If all the jobs are done at their normal times, the project duration (length of the longest path) is 25 days. Hence, under a no crashing schedule:

A, D, F, H= 25 days

Or, A, E, G, H= 25 days

Total cost= Overhead costs + Crashing costs

= Rs. 500 (25) + 0 = Rs. 12,500

If all jobs are crashed, as per *Figure 5.8*, the new critical duration is 17 days:

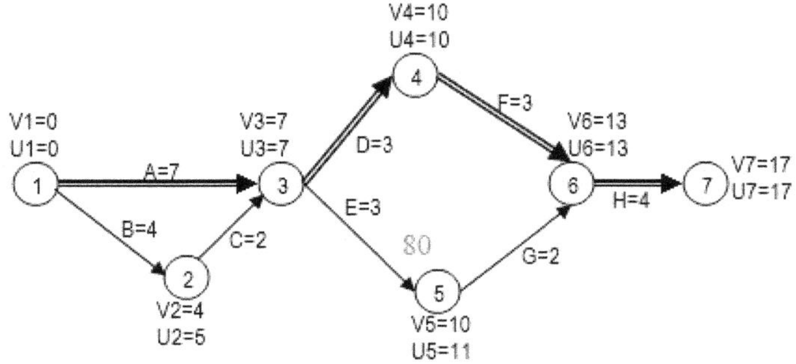

Figure 5.8: *The network of software project with crashed activities*

(A=7) + (D=3) + (F=3) + (H=4) = 17 days critical duration

Total cost = Rs. 500 (17) + cost of the critical path length

+ Rs. 400 (10-7)	*cost of activity A/day*
+ Rs. 200 (5-4)	*cost of activity B/day*
+ Rs. 200 (3-2)	*cost of activity C/day*
+ Rs. 300 (4-3)	*cost of activity D/day*
+ Rs. 300 (5-3)	*cost of activity E/day*
+ Rs. 500 (6-3)	*cost of activity F/day*
+ Rs. 100 (5-2)	*cost of activity G/day*
+ Rs. 400 (5-4)	*cost of activity H/day*

Rs. 13,200

It is not advisable to crash all the activities at random, paying such a big cost. Moreover, the critical path is changed. An economic consideration has to be given which will not further increase the cost. We have to explore the critical activities, the duration of which can further be reduced without increasing the total cost. Therefore, the objective is to determine the optimal duration of jobs that will minimize the total cost. Let us consider the two critical paths of 25 days each for finding the scope of cost reduction. This is shown in *Figure 5.9*:

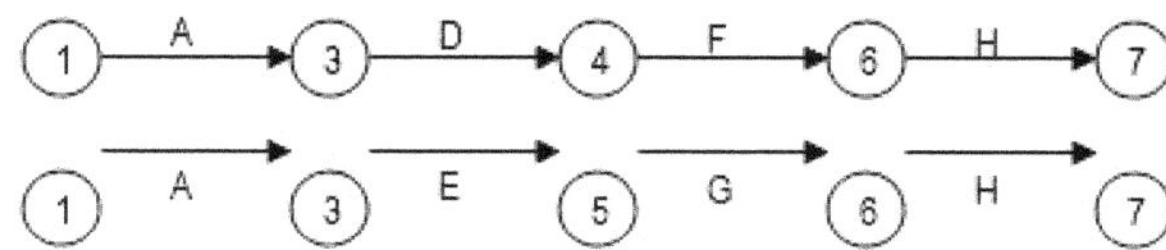

Figure 5.9: *Scope of cost reduction*

The total cost of the project under normal time = *Rs. 12,500*

Consider the critical path to reduce the duration.

Activity *H* can be crashed by 1 day at a cost of Rs. 400

Due to the reduction in *OH* cost of Rs. 500

Saving Rs. 100

The total project cost was reduced from Rs. 12,500 to (500 X 24 days) Rs. 12,200

Activity A can be crashed by 2 days (originally 10 days). More than this, both B and C will be critical since the sum of both activities will be *5+3 = 8* days.

Crashing cost = 200 X 4 = Rs. 800

Reduction of OH cost = 200 X 5 = Rs. 1000

Total savings = Rs. 200

The total project cost will further come down from Rs. 12,500 to Rs. 12,200.

To reduce the project duration by one more day, we must crash job *A* by 1 day and either *B* or C by 1 day. The total cost of crashing *A* and *B* is Rs. 600, which is more than the savings on *OH* costs. Similarly, crashing *A* and C activities is not economical.

Now, consider the critical jobs *D, E, F,* and *G*. Since, we have parallel critical paths between nodes 3 and 6, we have to crash one job in the path between 3 and 6 as shown in *Figure 5.10(a)* and one job in path as shown in *Figure 5.10(b)* to reduce the project length. We must try four different combinations, as given in *Table 5.5*:

Figure 5.10(a) *Figure 5.10(b)*

Table 5.5 presents the alternative combinations of activity cost:

Jobs	Increase in Crashing cost	Decrease in OH cost	Net change in Total cost
D and E	300 + 300 = Rs. 600	Rs. 500	Increase by Rs. 100
D and G	300 + 100 = Rs. 400	Rs. 500	Decrease by Rs. 100
F and E	500 + 300 = Rs. 800	Rs. 500	Increase by Rs. 100
F and G	500 + 100 = Rs. 600	Rs. 500	Increase by Rs. 100

***Table 5.5:** Alternative combinations of activities*

Only a combination of *D* and *G* is economical when we crash both jobs, *D* and *G*, by one day. The total project cost is reduced from Rs. 12,200 to Rs. 12,100. No further crashing is economical. Hence, the optimal schedule is as follows:

- Crash job A to 8 days
- Crash job D to 3 days
- Crash job G to 4 days
- Crash job H to 4 days

Jobs *B, C, E,* and *F* are completed in normal time. The optimal length of the project is 21 days. The activity-wise schedule is shown in *Figure 5.11*. The minimum project cost is Rs. 12,100.

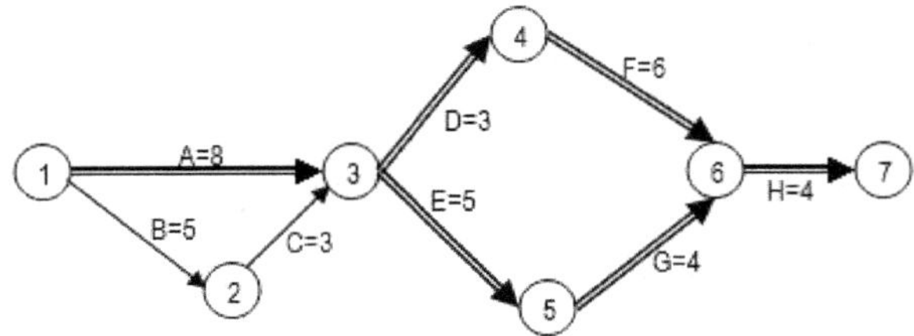

Figure 5.11: *The optimal network after crashing of events*

Time cost curve

CPM places equal emphasis on time and cost. This is done by constructing a time-cost curve for each activity, as shown in *Figure 5.12*. This curve plots the relationship between the budgeted direct cost for the activity and its resulting duration time. The plot is normally based on two points, the manual and the crash. The normal point gives the cost and time involved when the activity is performed in the normal way without any extra cost.

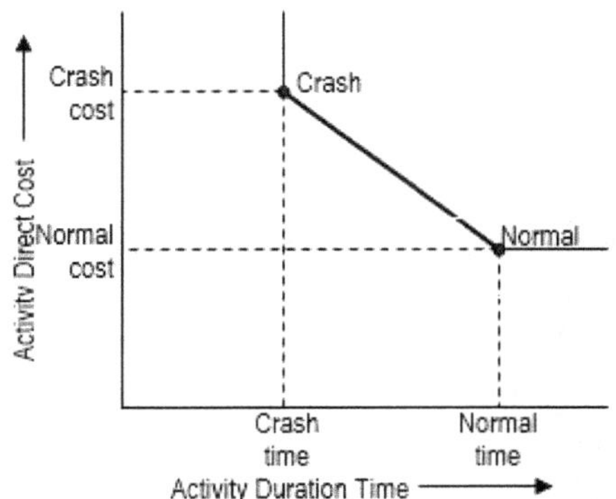

Figure 5.12: *Budgeted cost with time duration*

The crash point gives the time and cost when the activity is performed on a crash basis, that is, it is fully expedited with no cost spared to reduce the duration time as much as possible. As an approximation, it is then assumed that all intermediate time-cost tradeoffs are also possible and that they lie on the line segment between these two points.

The basic objective of CPM is to determine just which time-cost trade-off should be used for each activity to meet the scheduled project completion time at minimum cost.

Figure 5.13 gives a typical plot of the direct (activity) costs against the project duration.

- T_{max} = The project duration with all jobs in their normal time.
- T_{min} = The project duration with all jobs reduced to their crash time.

The cost function is called a piecewise linear function.

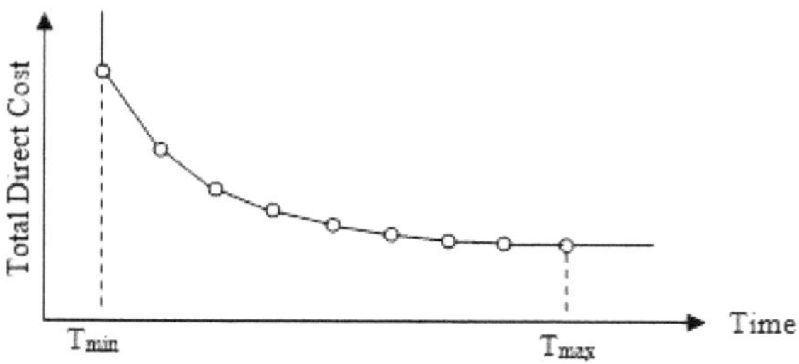

***Figure 5.13:** Time cost curve*

Figure 5.13 shows the direct cost of completing the project activities increases when the project duration is reduced. The indirect costs discussed earlier were reduced with a reduction in project duration. Hence, it will be of interest to study how the total cost (*direct + indirect cost*) varies with the project duration. For various project lengths, the indirect cost is added to the direct cost, and a plot of points is obtained to get a relationship between the project length and the total project cost. *Figure 5.14* is a U-shaped curve called a project **cost curve**.

With the help of this curve, a project manager can select the optimal project duration (T^*) that will minimize the total costs. Corresponding to the optimal value of T, the project manager can determine the optimal durations of all the jobs, the cost of crashing, and the critical path.

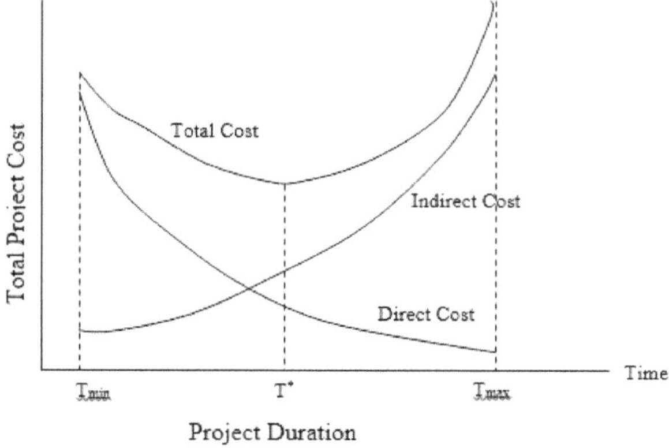

***Figure 5.14:** Optimal project duration with costs*

From this information, the optimal project schedule can be prepared.

Program evaluation and review technique

PERT is a variation on critical path analysis that takes a slightly more skeptical view of time estimates made for each project stage. This technique is used to find the probability of completion of a project before it is taken up, where the individual task completion time is not clearly known. Therefore, three types of time estimates are considered. To use it, estimate the shortest possible time each activity will take (pessimistic time), the most likely length of time for completion of the task, and the longest time (optimistic time) that might be taken if the activity takes longer than expected. The characteristic of this type of project is considered a **Beta distribution**, which has an unimodal asymmetric distribution and finite non-negative endpoint elements. *Figure 5.15* represents a Beta distribution:

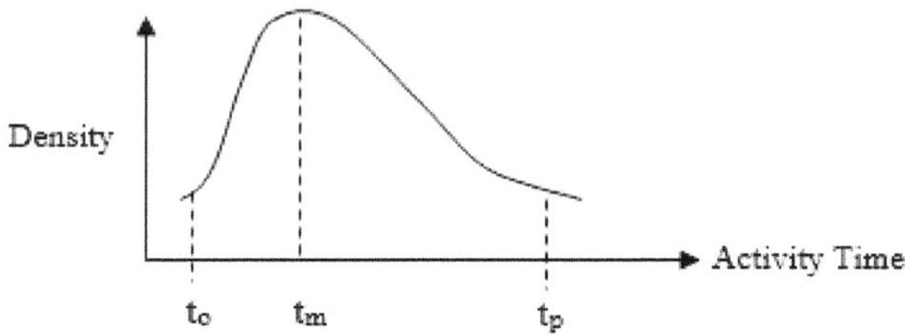

***Figure 5.15:** Beta distribution*

Use the following formula to calculate the time to use for each project stage:

- Expected time = $T_e = (t_o + 4\ t_m + t_p)/6$
- Variance = $V_e = \{(t_p - t_o)/6\ \}2$
- Where, t_o = Optimistic time
- t_m = Most likely time
- t_p = Pessimistic time

This helps to bias time estimates away from the unrealistically short time-scales normally assumed.

For example, consider a project consisting of 9 jobs (*A, B, ...I*) with the following relations and time estimates:

Job	Predecessor	Optimistic Time(a)	Most probable Time(n)	Pessimistic Time (b)
A	--	2	5	8
B	A	6	9	12
C	A	6	7	8
D	B, C	1	4	7
E	A	8	8	8

Job	Predecessor	Optimistic Time(a)	Most probable Time(n)	Pessimistic Time (b)
F	D, E	5	14	17
G	C	3	12	21
H	F, G	3	6	9
I	H	5	8	11

***Table 5.6:** Activity wise times in the network*

Figure. 5.16 presents the PERT chart diagram:

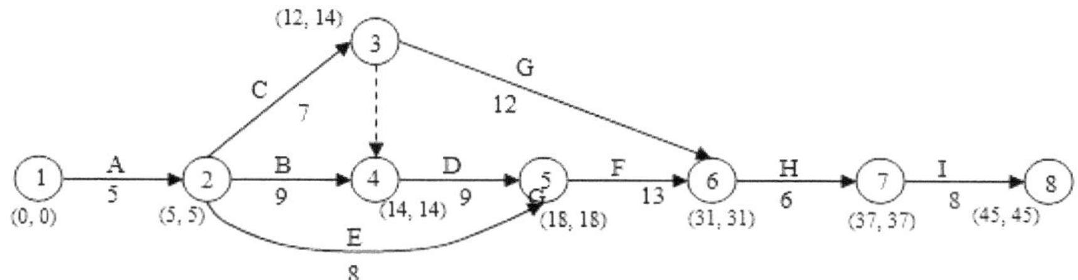

***Figure 5.16:** Network events with earliest and latest time*

Table 5.7 represents the time computation of each activity:

Job	Average time	Standard deviation	Variance
A	5	1	1
B	9	1	1
C	7	1/3	1/9
D	4	1	1
E	8	0	0
F	13	2	4
G	12	3	9
H	6	1	1
I	8	1	1

***Table 5.7:** Time computation of each activity*

First, we compute the average time from the three times given in *Table 5.6* and the variance for each one of the jobs. They are tabulated in *Table 5.7*. *Figure 5.16* gives the project network, where the numbers on the arcs indicate the average job times. Using the average job times, the earliest and latest times of each event are calculated.

The critical path is found as 1→2→4→5→6→7→8.

Let T denote the project duration. Then, the expected length of the project is:

- $E(T)$ = sum of the expected times of jobs A, B, D, F, H, and I
- $= 5 + 9 + 4 + 13 + 6 + 8 = 45$ *days.*

The variance of the project duration is:

- $V(T)$ = Sum of the variance of jobs A, B, D, F, H, and I
- $= 1 + 1 + 1 + 1 + 1 + 1 + 1 + 1 + 1 = 9$

The standard deviation of the project duration is:

- $\sigma(T) = \sqrt{V(T)} = 3$

For example, on the optimum duration and the minimum duration cost.

Table 5.8 shows jobs, their normal time and cost, and crash time and cost for a project.

Job	Normal Time(days)	Cost (Rs.)	Crash Time (days)	Crash Cost (Rs.)
(1-2)	6	1400	4	1900
(1-3)	8	2000	5	2800
(2-3)	4	1100	2	1500
(2-4)	3	800	2	1400
(3-4)	Dummy	-	-	
(3-5)	6	900	3	1600
(4-6)	10	2500	6	3500
(5-6)	3	500	2	800

Table 5.8: *Activity wise values of the network*

The indirect cost for the project is Rs. 300 per day.

1. Draw the network of the project
2. What is the normal duration cost of the project?
3. If all activities are crashed, what will be the project duration and its costs?
4. Find the optimum duration and minimum project cost.
   a. Network is shown in *Figure 5.17*.
   b. Assuming that all activities occur at normal times, the critical path calculations are shown in the figure under normal conditions. The critical path is 1→ 2→3 →4 →6. The duration of the project is 20 days and its associated (normal) cost is Rs. 9200.

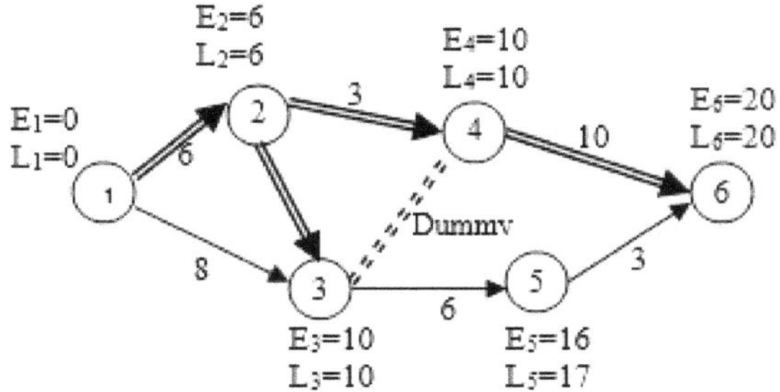

Figure 5.17: *Critical network path*

c. Now compute the different minimum cost schedules that can occur between normal and crash times, mainly depending on the cost time slopes for the different activities. To calculate these, use the formula:

$$\textit{Cost Slope} = \frac{\text{Crash cost - Normal cost}}{\text{Normal time - Crash time'}}$$

These slopes are summarized in the following tabular form:

Activity	(1-2)	(1-3)	(1-3)	(2-4)	(3-5)	(4-6)	(5-6)
Slope	250	267	200	600	233	250	300

Following are the reason:

1. This is because the present schedule involves more time. The schedule is reduced by crashing some of the activities. As the activities lying on the critical path control the duration of the project, therefore the duration of some activities lying on the critical path is reduced.

   Start reducing the duration of that activity, which involves a minimum cost slope. As the activity (2-3) has the minimum cost slope, the duration of this activity is reduced from 4 to 2 days resulting additional cost of *Rs. 2 x 200 = Rs. 400*. But this activity should be shortened only by one day, since path 1→2 →4→6 becomes a parallel critical path. So, the revised schedule corresponds to 19 days with a cost of *Rs. (9200 + 200) = Rs. 9400*.

2. Now, it is evident that the activities (1-2) and (4-6) among the remaining activities lying on the critical paths have the least slope. Therefore, either (1-2) or (4-6) can be compressed only for days. This is due to the fact that 1 →3 →5 →6, 1→2 →3 →4→6, and 1 →2 →4 →6, becomes three parallel critical paths. So three alterative choices are given as follows:

   - Compress (1-2) by 2-days at a cost of Rs. 250.
   - Compress (4-<)) by 2-days at a cost of Rs. 250.
   - Compress (1-2) and (4-6) by 1 -day at a cost of Rs. 250 each.

The additional cost thus will be *Rs. 2 x 250 = Rs.500*. Thus a 17 days least cost schedule is obtained with a cost of *Rs. (9400 + 500) = Rs.9900*.

- To determine the optimum schedule, compute the total cost by adding, the indirect corresponding to each schedule to the cost of crashing (slope). The optimum schedule (duration) is then obtained, for which the total cost is the least. Required calculations are put in the following table:

Normal Project Length(days)	Crashing time and cost (days/Rs)	Indirect cost @Rs.300	Total cost (Rs.)
20		20x300	600
19	1 x200 = 200	19x 300	5900
18	1x250 = 250	18x300	5650
17	1x250 = 250	17x300	5350
16	1x200 + 1x600 + 1x233 =1033	16x300	5833

***Table 5.9:** Cost computation*

For example, for the project, find the earliest and latest expected times for each event and also the critical path in the network. This is shown in *Figure 5.18*:

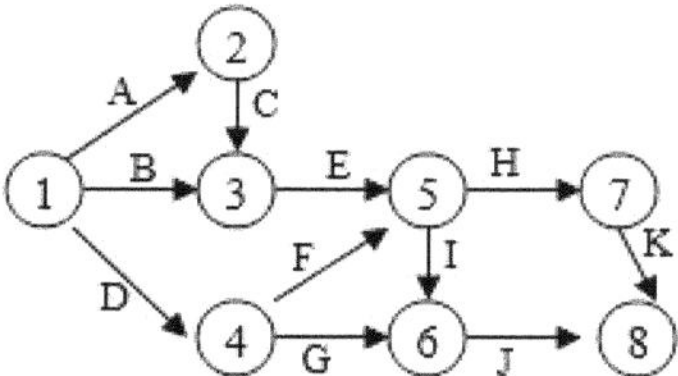

***Figure 5.18:** Critical path network*

Task	A	B	C	D	E	F	G	H	I	J	K
Last Time	4	5	8	2	4	6	8	5	3	5	6
Greatest Time	8	10	12	7	10	15	16	9	7	11	13
Most likely time	5	7	11	3	7	9	12	6	5	8	9

***Table 5.10:** Activity wise times*

Task	Last time a	Greatest time B	Most likely time m	Expected time (a+b+4m)/6
A	4	8	5	5.33
B	5	10	7	7.17
C	8	12	11	10.66
D	2	7	3	3.50

Task	Last time a	Greatest time B	Most likely time m	Expected time (a+b+4m)/6
E	4	10	7	7.00
F	6	15	9	9.50
G	8	16	12	12.00
H	5	9	6	6.33
I	3	7	5	5.00
J	5	11	8	8.00
K	6	13	9	9.17

***Table 5.11:** Expected time computations*

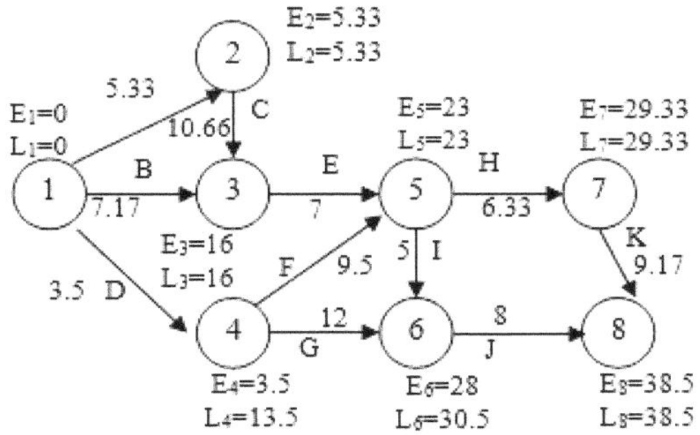

***Figure 5.19:** Network Diagram*

Task	Expected Time(t_a)	Start		Finish		Total Float
		Earliest	Latest	Earliest	Latest	
A	5.33	0.00	0.00	5.33	5.33	0.00
B	7.17	0.00	8.81	7.17	16.00	8.81
C	10.70	5.33	5.33	16.00	16.00	0.00
D	3.50	0.00	10.00	3.50	13.50	10.00
E	7.00	16.00	16.00	23.00	23.00	0.00
F	9.50	3.50	13.50	13.00	23.00	10.00
G	12.00	3.50	18.50	15.50	30.50	15.00
H	6.33	23.00	23.00	29.33	29.33	0.00
I	5.00	23.00	25.50	28.00	30.50	2.50
J	8.00	28.00	30.50	36.00	38.50	2.50
K	9.17	29.33	29.33	31.50	38.50	0.00

Critical path is A→ C→ E→ H→K.

Table 5.12: *Computation of float time for each activity*

For example, a project is represented by the network shown in *Figure 5.20* and has the following data:

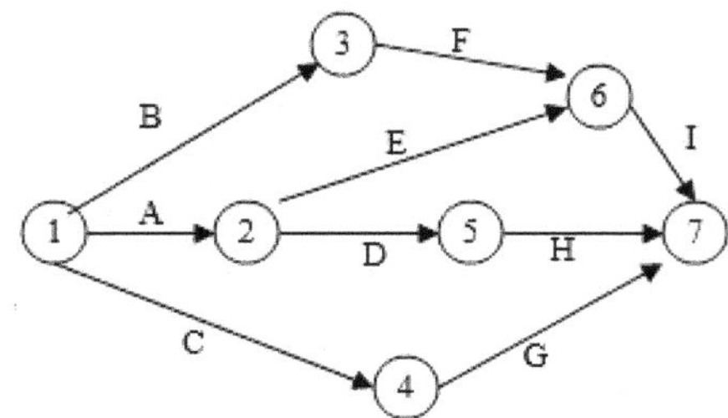

Figure 5.20: Project network diagram

Task	A	B	C	D	E	F	G	H	I
Leal time	5	18	26	16	15	6	7	7	3
Greatest time	10	22	40	20	25	12	12	9	5
Most likely time	8	20	33	18	20	9	10	8	4

Table 5.13: *Activity wise times*

Example 5.1

Determine the following:

- Expected task time and its variance
- The earliest and latest expected times to reach each node
- The critical path, and
- The probability of node occurring at the proposed completion date if the original contract time of completing the project is 41.5 weeks
- Proceeding as in the above example, we obtain the *Table 4.13*.

  to - Optimistic time — *tm* – Most likely time

  tp - Pessimistic time — *te* - Expected time

  Ei – Early start time of ith node — *Li* – Late finish time of ith node

Activity	t_o	t_p	t_m	t_e	σ^2
(1-2)	5	10	8	7.8	0.69
(1-3)	18	22	20	20.0	0.44
(1-4)	26	40	33	33.0	5.43
(2-5)	16	20	18	18.0	0.44
(2-6)	15	25	20	20.0	2.78

Activity	t_o	t_p	t_m	t_e	σ^2
(3-6)	6	12	9	9.0	1.00
(4-7)	7	12	10	9.8	0.69
(5-7)	7	9	8	8.0	0.11
(6-7)	3	5	4	4.0	0.11

Table 5.14: *Variance computation*

- Proceeding exactly as in above example, find earliest times in usual notations.

  $E_1=0, E_2= 0 + 7.8, E_3= 0 + 20 = 20, E_4= 0 + 33 = 33, E_5= 7.8+ 18=25.8,$

  $E_6 = max\ [7.8 + 20, 20+ 9]= 29, E_7 = max\ [33+ 9.8,25.8+ 8, 29+4] = 42.8$

Moving backwards, calculate the latest times as before,

$L_7 = 42.8, L_6= 42.8 - 4 = 38.8, L_5= 42.8 - 8 = 34.3, L_4 = 42.8 - 9.8 = 33,$

$L_3= 38.8 - 9 = 29.8$

$L_2 = min[34.8\text{-}18, 38.8\text{-}20] = 16.8, L_1=min\ (16.8 -7.8.\ 29.8\text{-}20, 33\text{-}33] =0$

To find the critical path, calculate slack time by taking difference between the earliest expected times and latest allowable times. Calculations are given in the *Table 5.15* and critical path is shown by double line in the *Figure 5.21*:

Node (i)	t_e	E_i	L_i	Slack	σ^2_i
2	7.80	7.8	16.8	9.0	0.69
3	20.0	20.0	29.8	9.8	0.44
4	33.0	33.0	33.0	0.0	5.42
5	18.0	25.8	34.8	9.0	1.13
6	9.0	29.0	38.8	9.6	1.44
7	9.8	42.8	42.8	0.0	6.12

Table 5.15: *Computation of slack time*

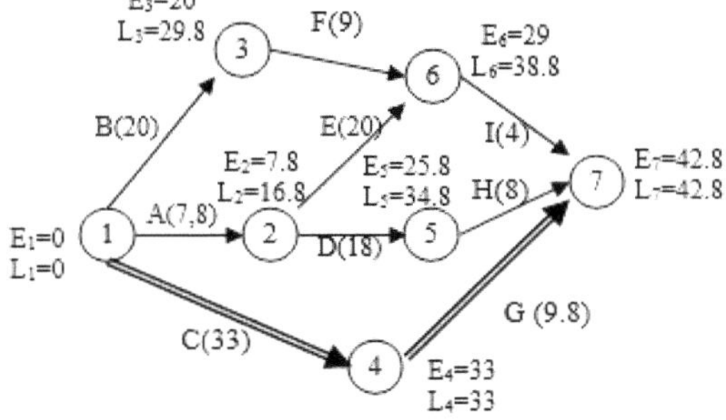

Figure 5.21: *Critical path of the network*

- The scheduled time of completing the project is 41.5 weeks. Therefore, the distance in standard it deviations, that schedule time from earliest expected times *Et* is given by:

$$D_i = \frac{ST_i - E_i}{\sqrt{(Var(i)]}} = \frac{41.5 - 42.8}{\sqrt{(6.12)}} = -0.52 \text{ where, ST denotes the schedule time}$$

Therefore, $P(Z \geq -0.52) = 1 - P(Z \leq 0.52] = 1 - 0.70 = 0.30$ (from Normal Table) which is the area under the standard normal curve bounded by ordinates at $x = 0$, and $x = 0.52$.

From this, it is concluded that if the project is performed 100 times under the same conditions, there will be 30 chances when this job would take 41.5 weeks or less to complete it.

Mathematical programming method

Given that the project must be completed by time *T*, we want to determine how the project activities are to be expedited such that the total cost of crashing is minimized. The problem can be formulated as an LP problem as follows:

- **Model-I:**

$$Min\ Z = \sum\nolimits_{(i,j)} C_{ij}(K_{ij} - t_{ij})$$

Subject to

$$t_j - t_i \geq t_{ij}$$

$$\ell_j - t_i \leq k_{ij}$$

$$t_n - t_1 \leq T$$

$$t_i \geq 0 \quad \textit{for all } i=1,2,\ldots\ldots.n$$

Where:

  - K_{ij}: The normal completion time of the *job (i,j)* if no additional resources are assigned.
  - ℓ_{ij}: Crash completion time with the maximum amount of resources.
  - C_{ij}: Unit cost of shortening the duration of the *job (i,j)*.
  - $T_{i,j}(K_{ij}-t_{ij})$: Cost of crashing.

- **Model-II:** Suppose, an additional budget of *B* (money) is available for crashing the project activities. We want to determine how these additional resources may be allocated in the best possible manner to minimize the project completion time.

$$Min \quad Z = t_n - t_1$$

$$S.t. \quad t_j - t_i \geq t_{ij} \quad \text{for all jobs}(i, j)$$

$$\ell_{ij} \leq t_{ij} \leq k_{ij} \quad \text{for all jobs } (i, j)$$

$$\sum_{i,j} C_{ij}(K_{ij} - t_{ij}) \leq B$$

$$Ti,j \geq 0 \quad \text{for all } i = 1, 2, \ldots\ldots n$$

The solution gives the least project duration that can be achieved by additional budget *B*, the activities to be crashed and their durations.

- **Model-III:**

  Let *T* --optimal length of the project*

$$F = \frac{Indirect\ cost(off)}{Per\ unit\ time} \alpha\ project\ duration$$

$F(t_n-t_1)$ = Indirect cost, t_n-t_1= unknown length of project.

$$\sum_{(i,j)}^{n} C_{ij}(K_{ij} - t_{ij}) = Direct\ cost$$

t_{ij}—unknown length of job (i, j) that is, the completion time of job(i, j)

Minimize the total cost.

$$Min\,Z = f(t_n - t_1) + \sum_{(i,j)}^{n} C_{ij}(K_{ij} - t_{ij})$$

$$s.t. \ t_j - t_i \geq t_{ij} \text{ for all jobs } (i, j)$$

$$\ell ij \leq tij \leq kij \text{ for all jobs } (i, j)$$

$$t_i \geq 0 \text{ for all } i = 1, 2, \ldots\ldots n$$

In the previous example (*Chapter 4: Software Project Management Framework*)

- **Duration of project:** *t7-t1*
- **Overhead cost:** *5(t7-t1)*
- **Cost of crashing A:** *4(10-t1,3)*
- **B:** *2(5-t_1,2)*

Following is the **linear programming (LP)** formulation:

$Min\ Z = 5(t_7-t_1) + 4(10-t_{13}) + 2(5-t_{12}) + 2(3-t_{23}) + 3(4-t_{34}) + 3(5-t_{35}) + 5(6-t_{46}) + 1(5-t_{56}) + 4(5-t_{67})$

S.t.

$$t3-t1 \geq t13 \quad 7 \leq t13 \leq 10$$

$$t2-t1 \geq t12 \quad 4 \leq t12 \leq 5$$

$t3-t2 \geq t23 \quad 2 \leq t23 \leq 3$

$t4-t3 \geq t34 \quad 3 \leq t34 \leq 4$

$t5-t3 \geq t35 \quad 3 \leq t35 \leq 5$

$t6-t4 \geq t46 \quad 3 \leq t46 \leq 6$

$t6-t5 \geq t56 \quad 2 \leq t56 \leq 5$

$t7-t6 \geq t67 \quad 4 \leq t67 \leq 5 \quad t1, t2, \ldots \quad \ldots\ldots t7 \geq 0$

The above LP has 15 decision variables. Setting *t=0*, an optimal solution is found by the simplex method as:

$t_2=5, t_3=8, t_4=11, t_5=13, t_6=17, t_7=21, t_{13}=8, t_{12}=5, t_{23}=3, t_{34}=3, t_{35}=5, t_{46}=6, t_{56}=4, t_{67}=4$

The optimal project length=21 days and minimum cost of project = $121. Job A crashed by 2 days, and jobs D, G, and H each crashed by 1 day.

Gantt chart

This technique of using a special type of bars representing activities was developed by Henry Gantt and named as Gantt chart. The Gantt chart is also known as the **timeline chart**. It is useful and used to allocate resources to various activities. The resources are manpower, computer hardware, workspace, etc. Each bar, an activity, is drawn against a timeline. The shaded part of the bar is the estimated time and the white part of the bar is called the **slack time** by which the activity has to finish. Therefore, the shaded part can be shifted, if necessary, to any part to the extent of the white bar limitation. This allows the project manager to allocate resources suitably by shifting the activity on the timeline without affecting other activities. Many activities can start concurrently. *Figure 5.22* shows the activities to be carried out on a timeline.

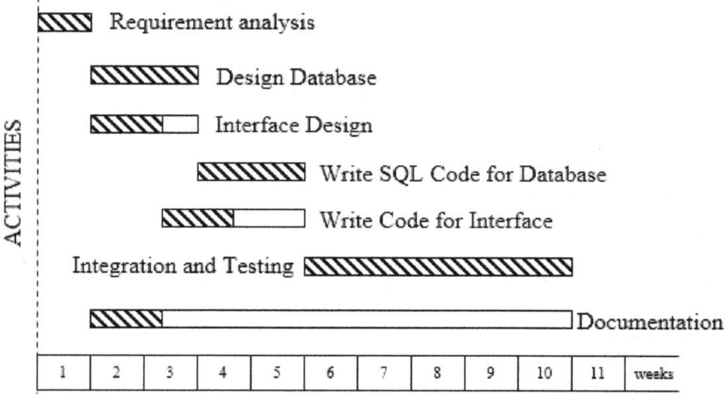

***Figure 5.22:** Gantt chart for software development*

Conclusion

To improve the software process, the managers and the practitioners need to do proper planning, tracking, and control of the software project. The software project, the process, and the software product are to be judiciously measured, which will help the management determine the requirement of resources. A function point is required to measure the problem's complexity. The size of the problem is assessed through a line of code to measure the man month or effort requirement. The planner plays a great role in estimating project duration, effort, and resource requirements. Scheduling a project, combined with estimation and risk analysis, becomes a road map for the project manager. In scheduling, the process is decomposed into various tasks along with their precedence. The tasks are critically examined after obtaining the project's critical path. The necessary resource allocation is done to further reduce the individual task completion times which helps in reducing the project cost.

In the next chapter, the readers will explore the fundamental principles of analyzing software requirements and designing efficient system architectures. They will learn how to translate business needs into well-structured software solutions using methodologies like UML, data flow diagrams, and entity-relationship models. This chapter will also cover key design principles, including modularity, scalability, and maintainability, ensuring that students develop a strong foundation for building robust and efficient software systems.

Exercises

To solidify your understanding of the concepts covered in this chapter, try the following exercises.

Multiple choice questions

1. **Which of the following is a key difference between PERT and CPM?**
   a. PERT is used for projects with well-defined activities, while CPM is used for uncertain projects.
   b. PERT uses probabilistic time estimates, while CPM uses deterministic time estimates.
   c. CPM is designed for uncertain projects, while PERT is for routine projects.
   d. Both PERT and CPM use probabilistic time estimates.
2. **In PERT, which of the following is used to calculate expected time for an activity?**
   a. Optimistic, pessimistic, and most likely times
   b. Only the optimistic time

   c. The critical path time
   d. Only the pessimistic time

3. **What is the critical path in CPM?**
   a. The shortest path through the project
   b. The path with the most uncertain tasks
   c. The path with the least slack or float
   d. The longest path through the project network

4. **What is slack in the context of CPM scheduling?**
   a. The total duration of a project
   b. The time a task can be delayed without delaying the overall project
   c. The difference between optimistic and pessimistic times
   d. The buffer time allocated for project risks

5. **Which of the following is true for both PERT and CPM?**
   a. Both methods account for project uncertainties equally.
   b. Both methods are used to identify the critical path.
   c. Neither method can handle large projects.
   d. Both methods ignore resource allocation.

6. **In a PERT network, the probability of completing a project within a given time can be determined using which distribution?**
   a. Poisson distribution
   b. Normal distribution
   c. Exponential distribution
   d. Binomial distribution

7. **What is the purpose of crashing in the CPM technique?**
   a. To identify critical activities
   b. To reduce the project duration by allocating additional resources
   c. To delay non-critical activities
   d. To calculate slack time

8. **Which of the following best describes event in a PERT chart?**
   a. A milestone that represents the completion of an activity
   b. The start of the project

c. A delay in project activities
d. The critical path activity

9. **In CPM, if a project has a float time of zero, what does it imply?**
   a. The project can be delayed without affecting the completion date.
   b. The activity is on the critical path.
   c. The project is ahead of schedule.
   d. The activity is not part of the critical path.
10. **Which of the following is NOT a step in the PERT process?**
    a. Defining activities
    b. Estimating activity times
    c. Determining the probability of project completion
    d. Allocating resources to tasks

Short questions

1. What is software project planning?
2. What is software project tracking (PT)?
3. What is intergroup coordination (IC)?
4. Name three generic project team organizations.
5. Define a DD type team organization.
6. Define a CD type team organization.
7. Define a CC type team organization.
8. What are the characteristics of a DD team structure?
9. What are the characteristics of a CD team structure?
10. What are the characteristics of a CC team structure?
11. Name a few project coordination techniques.
12. What is the objective of project planning?
13. What resources are needed for software development?
14. Name the different types of projects.
15. Name two project scheduling tools.
16. What activities are involved in project planning?
17. What are the different ways of tracking the schedule of the project?
18. List the main components of a software project plan.
19. What specific questions should a project plan consider?

20. Name some important reviews.
21. What is the role of a project manager?
22. What is the role of a software engineer?
23. What the role of a senior manager?
24. List the activities those are carried out during software project management.
25. Name three points that a project planner must estimate before a project begins.
26. What is a timeline chart?
27. What is risk management?
28. Why is there pressure to do risk management more systematically?
29. What will risk management do for my business?
30. What are the categories of a project estimation technique?
31. What are the steps involved in structured project management?
32. List the main applications of function points.
33. Compare function points with the measure of lines of code.
34. What do function points measure?
35. What are the drawbacks of function points?
36. State the productivity equation.

$$\text{Pr}\,oductivity = \frac{size}{effort}$$

37. Is the software quality measure 'number of faults per thousand lines of code' a useful one?

Essay questions

1. Discuss the benefits of network technique in project planning and control.
2. What is the total time required to complete the project? (based on normal time)
3. A small software project is composed of seven activities whose time estimates are listed in the following table. Activities are identified by their beginning (i) and ending (j) node members.
4. Draw the project network and identify all paths through it.
5. Find the expected duration and variance for each activity.
6. Calculate early and late occurrence times for each node. What is the expected project length?
7. Calculate the total slack for each activity.
8. Draw the project network.
9. Calculate the length and variance of the critical path.

10. What is the approximate probability that jobs on the critical path will be completed by the due date of 41 days?
11. What is the approximate probability that jobs on the next most critical path will be completed by the same due date?
12. What is your estimate of the probability that the entire project will be completed by the due date? Explain.
13. To develop a software project, what are different types of COCOMO estimation models are used? Give suitable examples of software product development projects belonging to each of the types.
14. What do you mean by a project? How do you manage a project?
15. What is project scope? Why is it necessary while developing a project?
16. What is the importance of activity sequencing? What are the tools and techniques are used?
17. For the cost drivers to be multiplied together the underlying assumption is that they must be independent of each other, does this sound reasonable?
18. If all cost drivers were at minimum value, what would be the product of the cost drivers?
19. If all cost drivers were at maximum value, what would be the product of the cost drivers?
20. Based on the results to the two questions above, what is the ratio between maximum and minimum possible predicted effort?
21. Does the possible range from maximum to minimum effort seem reasonable?
22. COCOMO starts from estimate of size, subjective assessment of 15 (independent?) cost drivers (with values - on potentially a 6-point scale - based on 60+ datasets), to estimate effort. How much confidence should you have in the final estimate?
23. Discuss Putnam's model in contrast to Jensen model to estimate effort requirement in software project development.
24. While developing a software product what are risk factors one has to consider?
25. Explain what is a project plan?
26. What do you mean by size of a project? Discuss on size estimation.
27. As the manager of a software project to develop a product for business application, if you estimate the effort required for completion of the project to be 100 man-months, can you complete the project by deploying 100 software professionals for a period of one month? Justify your answer.

    (Hint: A women takes 9 months to produce a baby. Can 9 women produce the baby in one month time?)

28. You are developing a software product in the organic mode. You have estimated the size of the product to be about 2,00,000 lines of code. Compute the nominal effort and the development time of the product.
29. What are the normal project length and its minimum project length?
30. Determine the minimum crashing cost of schedules ranging from normal length down to, and including, the minimum length schedule. That is, if L = length of normal schedule, find the cost of schedules which are L, L-1, L-2, and so on, days long.
31. Overhead costs total $60 per day. What is the optimum length schedule in terms of both crashing and overhead costs? List the scheduled duration of each job for your solution.

Multiple choice answers

1. b
2. a
3. d
4. b
5. b
6. b
7. b
8. a
9. b
10. d

CHAPTER 6
Software Project Analysis and Design

Introduction

The analysis and design concepts provide the software developer with a foundation from which more sophisticated methods can be applied. There are several concepts that have evolved in association with analysis and design. Abstraction is the process of generalization by reducing the information content of a concept or an observable phenomenon, retaining only the relevant details for a particular purpose. Complementary to this, refinement involves elaboration, where a hierarchy is developed by decomposing a macroscopic function statement stepwise until programming language statements are reached. In each step, instructions are further broken down into more detailed components. Modularity plays a crucial role in software architecture by dividing it into distinct components called modules, ensuring better organization and maintainability. Software architecture itself refers to the overall structure of the software, providing conceptual integrity and yielding the highest return on investment in terms of quality, schedule, and cost. Within software architecture, control hierarchy represents the organization of program components and their levels of control. Structural partitioning allows program structure division both horizontally and vertically, where horizontal partitions define separate branches of the modular hierarchy for different program functions, and vertical partitioning ensures control and work distribution from top to bottom. Data structure is essential for representing logical relationships among individual data elements, while software procedure focuses on processing each module independently. Additionally, information hiding ensures that modules are designed such that their internal details remain inaccessible to other modules unless explicitly required, thereby enhancing security and maintainability.

Structure

- Design consideration
- Levels of design
- Software design methodologies
- Coupling and cohesion
- Software design approach
- Software specification tools
- Data flow-oriented design
- Case studies

Objectives

During the analysis and design of a project, the designer must know what the software product will do and how the software accomplishes the task. These are laid down in the **software specification requirement (SRS)** in the form of design-to-specification, and software function and performance specification. At this stage, the software documentation and requirement specification must be complete. The objective is to meet the need for a good specification and meticulously usage of the specification requirement at each level of software development. The objective of this chapter is to describe the analysis and design requirements, identify and classify the design levels, describe the need to design a database, and coordinate and correlate all the steps of the design process.

Design considerations

There are many aspects to consider in the design of a piece of software. The importance of each should reflect the goals the software is trying to achieve. Some of these aspects are as follows:

- **Compatibility**: The software can operate with other products that are designed for interoperability with another product. For example, a piece of software may be backward-compatible with an older version of itself.
- **Extensibility:** New capabilities can be added to the software without major changes to the underlying architecture.
- **Testability**: In a good design, every requirement is testable. A design that cannot be tested against its requirements is not an acceptable design.
- **Fault-tolerance**: The software is resistant and able to recover from component failure.

- **Maintainability**: The software can be restored to a specified condition within a specified period. For example, antivirus software may include the ability to periodically receive virus definition updates to maintain the software's effectiveness.
- **Structure**: A good design presents a hierarchical structure that makes logical use of control policies among components.
- **Modularity**: The resulting software comprises well-defined, independent components. That leads to better maintainability. The components could then be implemented and tested in isolation before being integrated to form a desired software system. This allows the division of work in a software development project.
- **Discreteness**: A good design separates data, procedures (functions), and timing considerations to the extent possible. Although separated, these three design considerations cannot be completely isolated.
- **Packaging**: Printed material such as the box and manuals should match the style designated for the target market and should enhance usability. All compatibility information should be visible on the outside of the package. All components required for use should be included in the package or specified as a requirement on the outside of the package.
- **Reliability**: The software can perform a required function under stated conditions for a specified period.
- **Reusability**: The modular components designed should capture the essence of the functionality expected out of them and no more or less. This single-minded purpose renders the components reusable wherever there are similar needs in other designs.
- **Robustness**: The software can operate under stress or tolerate unpredictable or invalid input. For example, it can be designed with resilience to low memory conditions.
- **Security**: The software can withstand hostile acts and influences.
- **Usability**: The software user interface must be intuitive (and often aesthetically pleasing) to its target user or audience. Default values for the parameters must be chosen so that they are a good choice for the majority of the users. In many cases, online help should be included and also carefully designed.
- **Documentation**: A good design always comes with a set of well-written documents. An excellent design without good quality documentation becomes a poor design.

Levels of design

A design process proceeds through a series of discrete levels. Each design level begins with a set of requirements as input and produces some form of realization as its output.

The output or realization for one design level is the input or set requirements for the next design level, as in *Figure 6.1*. Realization means the development of a solution to the problem taken in the requirements at each design level.

The first design level, after analysis of input requirements, is a partition or decomposition of stated requirements. Further, it continues to the next level until it produces results in the form of a specific physical realization in hardware or software. This process leads to an architecture for that design level. The design progresses from top to down. The top-level architecture is system architecture. The software architecture is a detailed extension of the system architecture. The system architecture can provide guidance in developing a software structure.

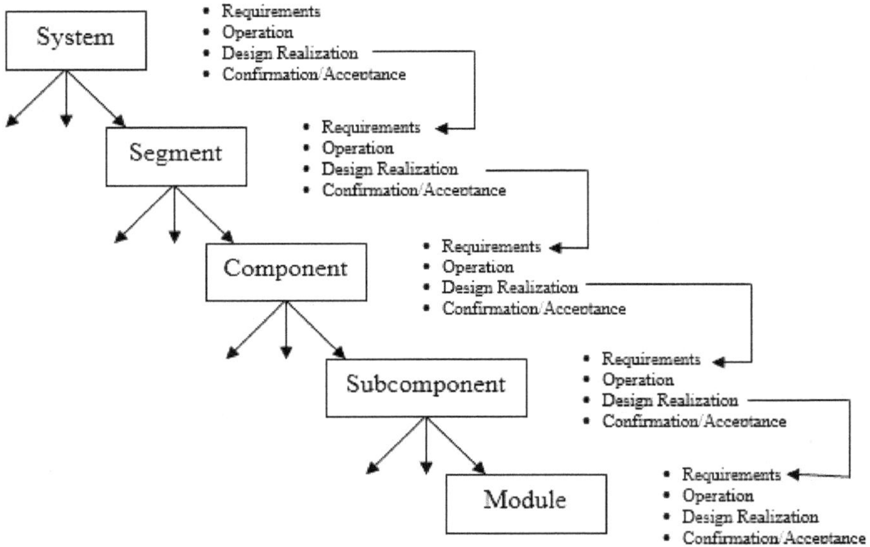

Figure 6.1: *Design levels*

Following are the levels of designs:

- **Level 1: Software system**

  The first level is the entire system. Some programmers jump right from the system level into designing classes, but it is usually beneficial to think through higher-level combinations of classes, such as subsystems or packages.

- **Level 2: Division into subsystems or packages**

  The main product of design at this level is the identification of all major subsystems. The subsystems can be a big-database, user interface, business logic, command interpreter, report engine, and so on. The major design activity at this level is deciding how to partition the program into major subsystems and defining how each subsystem is allowed to use each other subsystems.

- **Level 3: Division into classes**

  Design at this level includes identifying all classes or components in the system. For example, a database-interface subsystem might be further partitioned into data access classes and persistence framework classes, as well as database metadata. A subsystem might be divided into classes, and it implies that the other subsystems are also decomposed into classes.

- **Level 4: Division into routines**

  Design at this level includes dividing each class into routines. The class interface defined at *Level 3* will define some of the routines. Design at *Level 4* will detail the class's private routines. When you examine the details of the routines inside a class, you can see that many routines are simple boxes, but a few are composed of hierarchically organized routines, which require still more design. This level of decomposition and design is often left up to the individual programmer, and it is needed on any project that takes more than a few hours. It does not need to be done formally, but it at least needs to be done mentally.

- **Level 5: Internal routine design**

  Design at the routine level consists of laying out the detailed functionality of the individual routines, that is, modules. Internal routine design is typically left to the individual programmer working on an individual routine. The design consists of activities such as writing pseudo-code, looking up algorithms in reference books, deciding how to organize the paragraphs of code in a routine, and writing programming-language code. This level of design is always done, though sometimes it is done unconsciously and poorly rather than consciously and well.

Low level design versus high level design

In defensive programming, the use of iterative design writing in pseudo-code is a low-level design that helps in preventing defects. One can review the detailed design without examining the source code. The low-level design helps in reviewing the system easier, faster, and at a reduced cost. Making changes at the low-level design stage is easy and further refinement at high-level design is less time-consuming. Successive refinement at small steps allows checking the design as we drive it to lower levels of detail. The top-down incremental integration allows beginning coding before the low-level designs are complete. Hence, the top-down approach usually involves disadvantages, in spite of advantages, to handle buggy interfaces or performance problems before the end of the project.

The software architecture is the high-level part of software design that holds the most detailed parts of the design. The architecture is described in a single document referred to as the top-level design. A high-level design refers to design constraints that apply at the sub-system or multiple class levels. In high-level design, one needs to be careful to handle invalid parameters in a consistent way throughout the program. It causes robustness and correctness. The high-level design should indicate the inputs to and outputs from the routine. The pre-condition and the post-condition are guaranteed while passing through the routines. The system performance goal is achieved through high-level design. It avoids wasting time scrapping incremental improvements. Big optimization comes from high-level design.

The software needs to be validated rather than proven, which means it is tested and developed iteratively until it answers the question correctly. Software is a heuristic process that needs iterative revisions and improvements. Both high-level and low-level design attempts should be repeated. A first attempt might produce a solution that works, but it might not be the best solution. Taking several repeated and different approaches, it produces insight into the software problem.

Software design methodologies

Design is the initial step in the development of an engineering product. This is initiated only after the clear exposition of the expected product function. The design of a software system and its components should follow an orderly sequence of steps. A creative process is generally not structured and predictable. In a thought-provoking creative design process, the ideas and concepts are continually challenged the current design baseline. The designer's aims are to develop a model or abstraction of the product based on experience, heuristics, formal synthesis, and realization of techniques, or by following some fundamental design principles. Some design elements are intrinsic to any of the methodologies available today. The idea of top-down design and a step-wise refinement makes the design implicit. Nowadays, there is a phase shift from the function-oriented approach towards the object-oriented approach. The SRS is made using functions and performance formats.

Function oriented design

The function-oriented design emerged from a popular structure paradigm. The theory of modularity or functionality underwent steady progress during the 1970s and the 1980s. When the software product became larger, it was extremely difficult to handle a single monolithic block of code for debugging and maintenance. It was virtually difficult to understand the program written by another programmer. The solution was to break the product into smaller pieces called functions, procedures, or modules. Every functionality of the product is given a name that is easy to develop or modify. These are a set of contiguous program statements having a name so that other parts of the system can invoke it. Each function can have its user interface and database. The principle of divide and conquer holds well during the design phase by having smaller independent blocks of code to suit a specific function. Testing and integrating functions is also easy.

Object oriented design

Object-oriented design is different than conventional. There are many benefits available in object-oriented design. These are simplifications of requirements, ease of design, and faster implementation. The benefits are achieved by modeling the problem domain with objects that represent the important entities, encapsulating the functions with data, reusing the objects within a project and between projects, and having a solution that is much closer ideally to the problem. In object-oriented design, there is only one kind of module, that is, abstract data type module. Using object-oriented design terminology, we call such modules as classes. A class exports the operations that may be used to manipulate its instances. Such operations are defined by procedures, usually called methods in object-oriented terminology.

Coupling and cohesion

In software engineering, coupling and cohesion are two fundamental concepts that describe the relationships and dependencies between different modules or components of a software system. Coupling refers to the degree of interdependence between software modules, indicating how closely connected they are. Lower coupling is desirable as it promotes modularity, making the system easier to maintain, test, and extend. Cohesion, on the other hand, measures how well the tasks within a single module relate to each other. High cohesion means that a module performs a single, well-defined function, improving code clarity and reusability. Together, coupling and cohesion are key principles for designing robust, maintainable, and efficient software systems, as they promote modularity and a clear separation of concerns.

Cohesion

The extent to which all instructions in a module are related to a single function is called **cohesion**. In a cohesive module, all of the instructions in the module pertain to performing a single, unified task. Try to maximize cohesion in modules. Maximally cohesive modules also tend to be the most loosely coupled. Achieve high levels of cohesion in system design, helping in minimizing coupling. If a module is designed to perform one and only one function, then it does not need to know about the interior workings of other modules. The cohesive module only needs to take the data it is passed, act on it, and pass its output on to its super-ordinate module. The seven types of cohesion are as follows:

- **Functional cohesion:** It is the most desirable type in that all instructions contained in the module pertain to a single function or task. Many times, the name of a module will indicate that it is functionally cohesive, for example, maintaining the proper temperature for the steel furnace, calculating the interest rate, or selecting a supplier.
- **Sequential cohesion:** The instructions inside the sequential cohesive modules are related to each other through the data that is input rather than through the

task being performed. The first instruction acts on the data that are passed in, and the second instruction uses the output of first instruction then becomes input for the third instruction, and so on. The sequence or the ordering of events is very important.

Following is an example:

```
CUT DOWN TREE
CUT TREE INTO PLANKS
PLANE PLANKS
SAND PLANKS
SAW PLANKS TO SPECIFICATIONS
PUT PLANKS TOGETHER TO MAKE DOOR
```

- **Communicational cohesion:** The activities are also related to each other by the data the module uses but the sequence is not important. Each instruction in this module acts on the same input data or is concerned with the same output data.

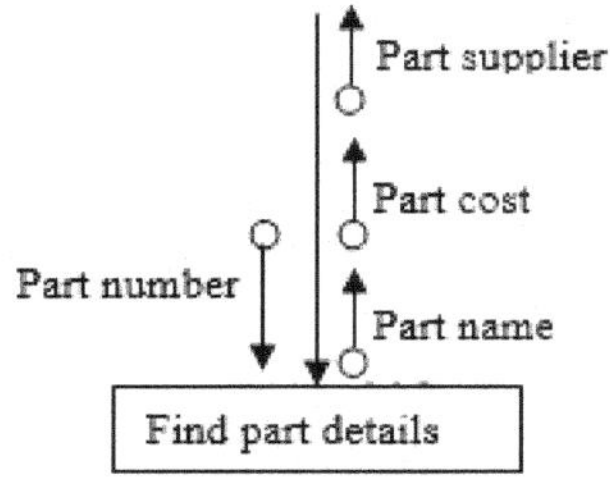

Figure 6.2: *Example of communicational cohesion*

Figure 6.3 shows the part details on input:

Using Part number
find part_name
find part_name
find part_cost
find part_supplier

Figure 6.3: *Part details on input*

The module finds the part detail shown in *Figure 6.2* is so **ambiguous** that it tips you off to the module as not being functionally cohesive. The module is designed to use part numbers as input to find a part's name, cost, and supplier (*Figure 6.3*). The sequence is not important as it does not matter whether name, cost, or supplier are found first or last.

A communicational cohesive module is easier to understand and maintain if it is split into two functionally cohesive modules, as shown in *Figure 6.4*:

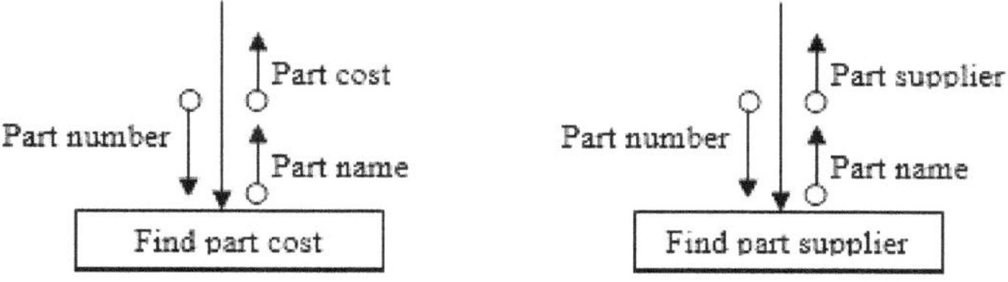

Figure 6.4: Splitting into two functional modules

- **Procedural cohesion**: Modules exhibiting these kinds of cohesion become more and more difficult to maintain. Here, the instructions in a module are related to each other through the flow of control. Instructions in a procedurally cohesive module are generally related to sequence activities.

  Following is an example:

  ```
  PICK UP THE NEWSPAPER
  CHECK MAILBOX FOR YESTERDAY'S MAIL
  PUT NEWSPAPER AND MAIL IN BOX
  WATER PLANTS
  CHECK ON WATER AND FOOD FOR DOGS
  MAKE SURE DOORS ARE LOCKED BEFORE LEAVING
  ```

  You might leave a set of instructions like this for someone who is watching your house while you are away on vacation. Although it might seem that the order of some of the instructions can be interchanged, there is logic to the order as presented. The instructions are written in the order they would be followed.

- **Temporal cohesion:** The instructions are related to each other through the flow of control, but the sequence does not matter. The only reasons the instructions are in the module occur at about the same point of time, hence the name **temporal**. The classic example is one that contains instructions for initializing a whole host of variables, counters, switches, and so on, throughout the system. Such a module is related to several other modules, making it very difficult to change the timing of a particular initialization step without affecting other modules that rely on the other instructions in the initialization module.

- **Logical cohesion:** The instructions are hardly related to each other. This consists of several sets of instructions, but the particular set being executed is determined from outside the module. Typically, a flag that specifies what is to be done is passed in from the outside. A non-system example is:

  ```
  EAT AT RESTAURANT
  EAT AT YOUR DESK
  EAT AT HOME
  SKIP LUNCH
  ```

People write logically cohesive modules to develop parts of functions that have some lines of code or the same buffers, but maintenance is very difficult.

- **Coincidental cohesion:** It is the worst type because the instructions have no relationship to each other at all. These are the result of haphazard factoring, and attempts to save time in design. Modules that suffer from this are rare. A decision tree that helps to distinguish the types of cohesion is given in *Figure 6.5*:

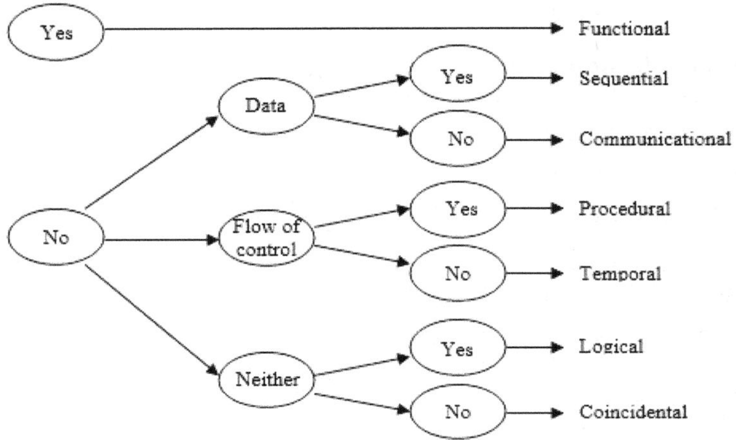

***Figure 6.5:** Cohesion in the form of a decision tree*

Coupling

The extent to which modules are interdependent is called **coupling**. Ideally, you want to minimize interdependence among modules. More dependency among modules causes more errors. The programmer, while modifying the IS, has more difficulty if the code inside one module is dependent on the code in other modules. Changing the code in one module may then cause unwanted or unexpected changes in other modules that are dependent. The more the modules are independent, the easier life is for the programmer and makes a better IS.

Data coupling

Neither module has any idea about what goes on inside the other module. The super-ordinate module has no idea of what goes on inside to calculate the new balance. Similarly, the sub-ordinate module does not need to know what goes on inside the super-ordinate module. It only needs to know what data it requires and what data it returns. The data coupling is shown in *Figure 6.6*:

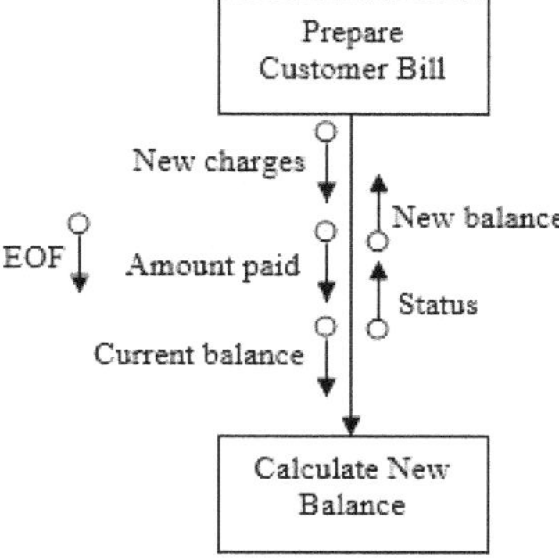

Figure 6.6: Data coupling

Stamp coupling

Data are passed in the form of data structures or entire records. It is not quite as good as data coupling because using data records instead of data elements makes the system more complicated. Changes in data structure will affect all modules that use it. This stamp coupling in *Figure 6.7* makes the modules more dependent on each other to avoid errors. This coupling exposes modules to more data than they need.

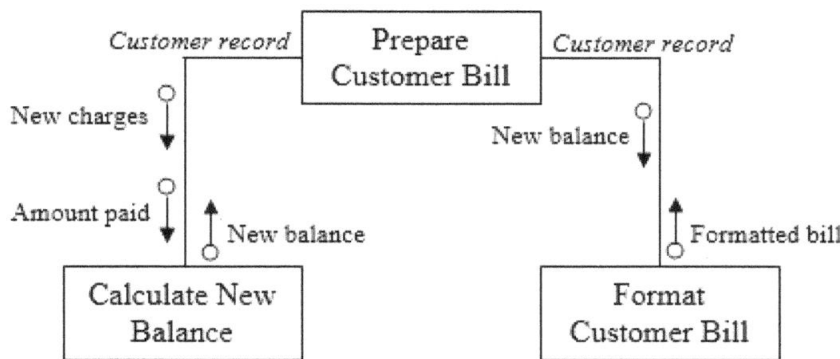

Figure 6.7: Passing records through stamp coupling

Control coupling

When one module passes control information to another module, the two are said to be control-coupled. The sending module must know a great deal about the inner workings of the receiving module. This is shown in *Figure 6.8*:

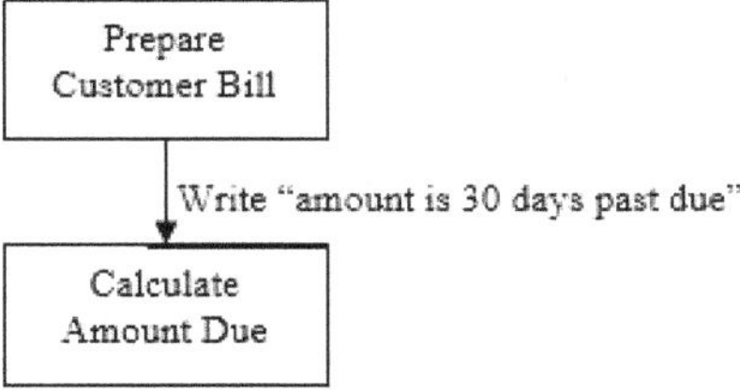

Figure 6.8: Control coupling

Common coupling

When two modules refer to the same global data area, they are commonly coupled. Global data areas are possible in many computer languages like **FORTRAN** (common block) and **COBOL** (data division). This coupling is undesirable because of the tremendous opportunity for errors to spread throughout the system. An error in any module using the global data area can show up in any other module using the same area. The level of module interdependence becomes quite high.

Content coupling

So far it is the worst type of coupling. It involves one module directly referring to the inner working of another module. For example, one module may alter data in a second module or change a statement coded into another module. Modules are tightly intertwined. There is no semblance of independence. Higher-level languages, fortunately, have no provisions for creating content coupling.

Software design approach

In the context of software engineering, the software design approach refers to the structured process of defining the architecture, components, interfaces, and data for a software system to meet specified requirements. It serves as a blueprint for developers, ensuring that the system is constructed in a way that is both efficient and maintainable. The design approach typically involves two levels: high-level design, which focuses on the overall system architecture and its major components, and low-level design, which provides detailed guidance on how individual components are implemented. By following a systematic design approach, software engineers can create scalable, flexible, and robust systems that align with user needs and business objectives. This phase is crucial as it bridges the gap between requirements specification and actual coding, helping to prevent issues later in the development lifecycle.

Top down design

It is the most widely used approach. It attempts to gain a broad understanding of the information needs of the entire organization. It begins by conducting an extensive analysis of the organization's mission, objectives, and strategy and then determining the information requirements needed to meet each objective. The problem is broken down into the major tasks. Each of the tasks is further broken down into sub-tasks, and so on, until each task is sufficiently simple to be a self-contained module. The program then consists of a series of simple modules.

Initially, describe the problem at the highest and most general level. The description of the problem should be what must be done but not how it must be done. The initial description is at a higher level and is very complex. All the operations are taken at this level and individually break them down into simpler steps that will describe how to do the tasks. When the steps are represented as acceptable algorithmic steps, no further refinement is required. **If not, a second step refinement is initiated**. The stepwise refinement continues till the highest-level operation is described in terms of acceptable shortest statements.

This method is used throughout the system analysis and design phases. It starts from a general level to gain an understanding of the system and gradually moves down to levels of greater detail. In moving from top to bottom, each component is exploded into finer detail.

To summarize, the problem is broken down into major components and then further broken into smaller steps until they are simple to write the code. Therefore, the process involves working from the most general to the most specific.

Following are the advantages:

- **Broader perspective**: If not viewed from the top, the **information system (IS)** may be implemented without first understanding the business from the general management viewpoint.
- **Improved integration**: If not viewed from the top, the new management information system may be implemented rather than planning and designing how to evolve the existing system.
- **Improved management support**: If not viewed from the top, planners may lack sufficient management acceptance of the role of IS in helping them to achieve business objectives.
- **Better understanding**: If not viewed from the top, planners and designers may lack the understanding necessary to implement IS across the entire business rather than simply to individual operating units.

In the stepwise refinement, we expand and define each of these separate sub-tasks until the problem is solved. Each sub-task is tested and verified before it is expanded further. It helps in:

- Increased intellectual manageability and comprehension.
- Abstraction of unnecessary lower-level details.
- Delayed decisions on algorithms and data structures until they are needed.
- Reduced debugging time.

Bottom up design

It requires the identification of business problems and opportunities which are used to define projects. When the problem is too large and complex, it may be very difficult to decompose. It may be easier to attack parts of the problem individually, taking the easier aspects first and thereby gaining the insight and experience to tackle the more difficult tasks, and finally bolt them all together to form the complete solution. Using a bottom-up approach for creating IS plans can be faster and less costly to develop than using a top-down approach and can also have the advantage of identifying pressing organizational problems. Yet the bottom-up approach often fails to view the informational needs of the entire organization. This can result in the creation of disparate IS and databases that are redundant or not easily integrated without a substantial network.

Following are the disadvantages:

- It suffers from the disadvantage that the parts of the program may not fit together very easily.
- There may be a lack of consistency between modules, and considerable reprogramming may have to be done.

Software specification tools

There are a variety of tools and techniques used in developing and representing software specifications. Practitioners use them with great success. The tools are used in developing software requirements specification, and other related specifications. Though the tools are enough to completely develop a successful product they affect a successful software product.

Decision support tools

A decision tool is required when one alternative has been chosen from several possible alternatives. The software engineer can make an objective decision based on all the information and wisdom available at the time of the decision required. A decision has to be taken when required. A decision process should say why one alternative is better than others. It helps eliminate subjectivity and solves the problem with a quantitative approach. There are some tools used in software design are discussed in detail in subsequent sections.

Decision table

A decision table is appropriate when a large number of conditions are to be checked in arriving at a set of actions. Decision tables have many other advantages for computer processing. The decision table is not programming language-oriented. It is oriented towards the specifications of what is to be done in a process. The specification is non-procedural, used for communicating and documenting complex decision procedures. Consider an example, give a discount of 5% if the customer pays in advance, or if the purchase is for Rs 10,000 or more, and the customer is a regular one. Refer to the following table:

		Rule-1	Rule-2	Rule-3	Rule-4
Conditions	Advance payment made?	Y	N	N	N
	Purchase amount > 10,000?	-	Y	Y	N
	Regular Customer?	-	Y	N	-
Actions	Give 5% discount	X	X	-	-
	No discount	-	-	X	X

***Table 6.1:** Decision table of discount decision*

Table 6.1 is interpreted as:

- **Rule 1:** If an advance payment is made:
    - Then give a 5% discount
- **Rule 2:** If no advance payment is made and if the purchase amount is more than 10,000 and a regular customer:
    - Then give a 5% discount
- **Rule 3:** If no advance payment is made, and if the purchase amount is more than 10,000, and the customer is not regular:
    - Then give no discount
- **Rule 4:** If no advance payment is made and if the purchase amount is not more than 10,000:
    - Then give no discount

For example, a university has the following rules for a student to qualify for a degree with physics as the main subject and mathematics as the subsidiary. (a) Marks should be 50% or more in physics and 40% or more in mathematics. (b) If marks in physics are less than 50%, then marks in mathematics must be 50% or more. However, physics marks must be at least 40%. (c) If marks in mathematics are less than 40% but those in physics are 60% or more, then only the examination in mathematics has to be repeated, and (d) In all other cases, the student fails.

		Rule-1	Rule-2	Rule-3	Rule-4
Conditions	Physics marks	>50%	>40%	>60%	Else
	Mathematics marks	>40%	>50%	<40%	
Actions	Pass candidate	X	X	-	-
	Repeat mathematics	-	-	X	-
	Fail candidates	-	-	-	X

***Table 6.2:** Decision table for university problem*

Table 6.2 is interpreted as:

- **Rule 1:** If physics marks more than 50% and mathematics marks more than 40%
  - o Then pass candidate
- **Rule 2:** If physics marks more than 40% and mathematics marks more than 50%
  - o Then pass candidate
- **Rule 3:** If physics marks more than 60% and mathematics marks less than 40%
  - o Then, repeat the mathematics examination
- **Rule 4:** In all other cases, fail the candidate (that is, if none of the rules 1, 2, 3 is true), then the rule marked else holds.

Decision tree

Let us consider an example. Bookstores get a trade discount of 25% for orders, from libraries and individuals, 5% allowed on orders of 6 to 19 copies per book title, 10% on orders for 20 to 49 copies per book title, 15% on orders for copies or more on book title.

A policy statement like this can be time-consuming to describe and confusing to implement. The analyst needs to use tools to portray the logic of the policy. The first such tool is the decision tree. As shown in *Figure 6.9*, a decision tree has many branches as there are logical alternatives. It simply sketches the logical structure based on the stated policy. In this respect, it is an excellent tool. It is easy to construct, easy to read, and easy to update. It shows only the skeletal aspects of the policy, however, in the sense that it does not lend itself to calculations or show logic as a set of instructions for action.

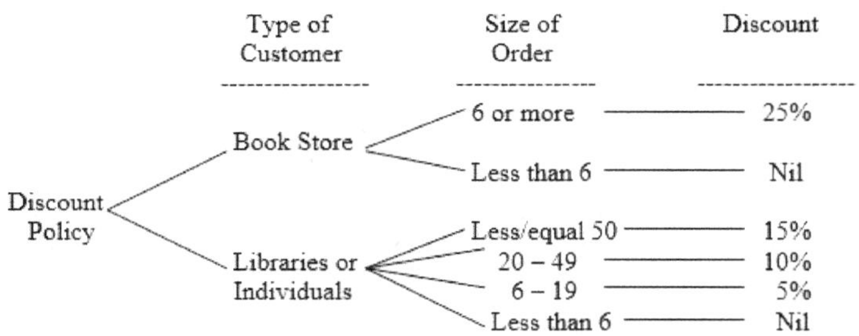

Figure 6.9: *Decision tree*

Structured english

It borrows heavily from structured programming; it uses logical construction and imperative sentences designed to carry out instructions for action. Decisions are made through **IF, THEN, ELSE**, and **SO** statements. The structured English for our publisher's discount policy, discussed in *Chapter 5, Project Scheduling through PERT or CPM* is shown in the following example:

Note: The correlation between the decision tree and structured English.

For **COMPUTE_DISCOUNT**:

- Add up the number of copies per book title
    - If the order is from a bookstore
- If the order is for six copies or more per book title.
    - Then give a discount is 25%
- If the order is for less than six copies per book title
    - Then no discount is allowed
- If the order is from libraries or individual customers.
    - If the order is for 50 copies or more per book title
        - Discount is 15%
    - If the order is for 20 to 49 copies per book title
        - Discount is 10%
    - If the order is for 6 to 19 copies per book title
        - Discount is 5%
    - If the order is for less than six copies per book title
        - So, no discount is allowed

The process **ORDER** may have the data elements **ORDER_SIZE**, which defines the four values:

- **MINIMUM**: 5 or fewer copies per book title
- **SMALL**: 6 to 19 copies
- **MEDIUM**: 20 to 49 copies
- **LARGE**: 50 or more copies

Using the values, the structured English example as above would read as shown in the following example with data dictionary values:

Structured english using data dictionary values.

For **COMPUTE_DISCOUNT**:

- Add up the number of copies per book title
- If the order is from bookstore:
    - If the **ORDER_SIZE** is **SMALL**
        - Then the discount is 25%

    - If the **ORDER_SIZE** is **MINIMUM**:
        - Then no discount is allowed
- If the order is from libraries or individuals:
    - If the **ORDER_SIZE** is **LARGE**
        - Then the discount is 5%
    - If the **ORDER_SIZE** is **MEDIUM**
        - Then the discount is 10%
    - If the **ORDER_SIZE** is **SMALL**:
        - Then the discount is 5%
    - If the **ORDER_SIZE** is **MINIMUM**
        - Then no discount is allowed

From these examples, we see that when logic is written out in English sentences using capitalization and multilevel indentation, it is structured English. Structures are indented to reflect the logical hierarchy. Sentences should also be clear in wording and meaning.

In structured English, the syntax rules are not very strict. The aim is to allow easy readability, which aids documentation and maintenance, and, at the same time, ensures some discipline in process description, which will help the programmer. Some guidelines for using structured English are given in the following:

- **Imperative sentences**: They consist of an imperative verb followed by operations to be performed on variables. It is important to use precise verbs.

  Following are the examples:
    - Multiply the gross price by the discount rate.
    - Store results in rebate.
    - Subtract rebate from gross price and obtain net price
- **Arithmetic and relational operations**: Common symbols used in mathematics are used in structured English descriptions. The symbols are as follows:
    - + add, - subtract, * multiply, / divide, and = equal
    - Relations like >, <, <, >, not equal
    - Logical operations and, or, not
    - Symbols used as keywords if, then, else, repeat, until, while, do, case, for, of, end

  For example, receive a **store issue note**:
    - Select the item issued record from the **store issue note**.
    - Cost of issued item = *quantity * price of item*.

- Balance in account = *balance in account – the cost of the issued item.*

- **Decision structures:** Branch in and branch out conditions are considered here.

If-then-else:

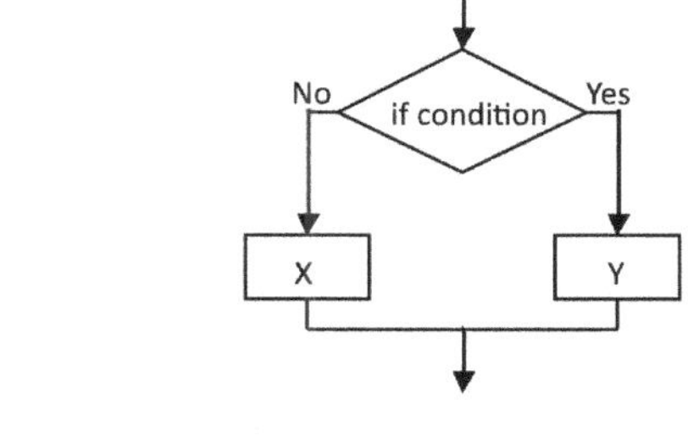

- if the condition
  - Then:
    - group Y statements

Else

- group X statements

Endif

Case

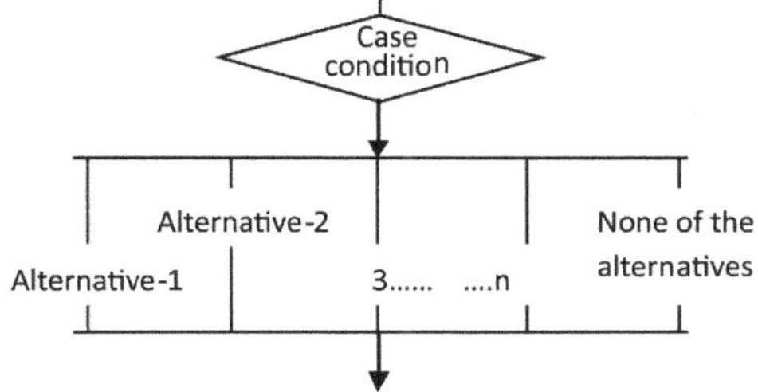

- case (variable)
  - (variable = P): statement for alt.P
  - (variable = Q): statement for alt.Q
- none of the above:
  - statement for default case
  - endcase

For example, a company makes three products which are codified as class A, class B, and class C. For class A items for purchase above Rs 5,000, a 10% discount is given. For class B, for a purchase above Rs 8,000, a discount of 5% is given. On class C, for a purchase of Rs 10,000 and above, 4% discount is given. Convert to structured English.

Case (Product class):

- (Product class = A)
  - *{if purchase > 5,000 then discount = 10%}*
- (Product class = B)
  - *{if purchase > 8,000 then discount = 5%}*
- (Product class = C)
  - *{if purchase > 10,000, then discount = 4%}*
- None of the above
  - *Discount = 0, endcase*

- **Repetition**: A sequence of operations is carried out many times. The number of repetitions to take place is governed by the type of structure used in the description. If the repetition is fixed, use it for structure.

  For example, *total marks = 0, for subject = 1 to subject = 5*

Do the following:

- o *total marks = total marks + marks(subject),*
- o *write students, roll number, total marks*

For example, while there are more student records.

Do the following:

- o Read student record
- o Total marks = 0
- o For subject = 1 to subject = 5 do
- o Total marks = total marks + marks(subject);
- o Write students, roll number, total marks

endfor

endfor

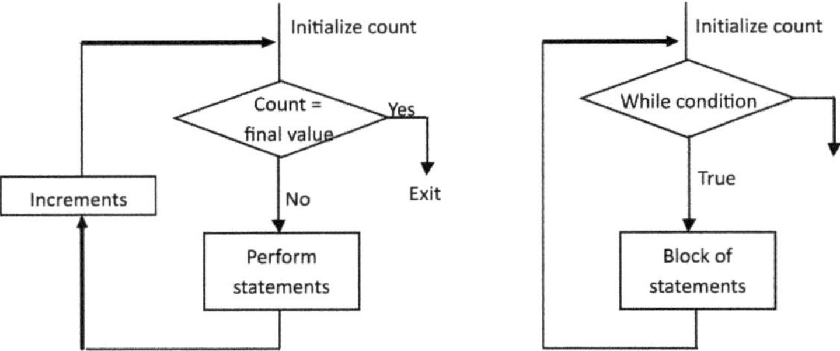

Figure 6.10: *Looping*

Data structure

This is to specify the name of each data structure and the elements it represents, provided they are defined elsewhere in the data dictionary. Some elements are mandatory, whereas others are optional. The data element of the data structure is as shown in *Table 6.4*:

		Mandatory	**Optional**
Data structure	BOOK_DETAILS		
Data elements	AUTHOR_NAME	X	
	BOOK_TITLE	X	
	EDITION	X	
	ISBN (International Standard Book No.)		X

		Mandatory	Optional
	LOCN (Library of Congress Number)		X
	PUBLISHER_NAME	X	
	QUANTITY_ORDERED	X	

Table 6.3: *Data structure of a book*

Data dictionary

It is an important tool in the software development process. It is a comprehensive definition of all of the data elements in a given software system. In a data dictionary, one will find a clear and complete definition of each data item. The data dictionary often becomes a source document for the specification and design of input processing, files, data structures, processing algorithms, and output processing. The information required to design a module to process inputs must include a description of protocols, scaling, encryption, maximum, minimum, or average values, timings, etc. The design of files and records requires detailed knowledge of both static and dynamic data elements. Production of structure charts, data flow diagrams, and process specifications are also depending heavily on the data dictionary. Data dictionary features within a CASE repository are especially valuable for the system analyst when cross-referencing data items. Cross-referencing enables us to describe the data item to be stored and accessed by all individuals so that a single definition for a data item is established and used.

Format of a data dictionary

A data dictionary is organized into five sections:

- Data elements
- Data flows
- Data stores
- Processes
- External entities

Data dictionary lists all the data elements, data flow, data stores, and processes of the system under consideration. It gives the details about each item listed in a prescribed format. The format may contain the following:

- **Data type**: Data element, data flow, data store.
- **Data name**: Name of the data element, data flow, data store.
- **Data aliases**: Alternative names used for the convenience of multiple users.
- **Data description**: A short example of data.
- **Data characteristics**: Frequency of use, data length, range of data values, etc.

- **Data composition**: Various data elements contained in a data store or data flow.
- **Data control information**: Source of data, the user or access authorization, etc. In the case of data flow, the process from which data flow is coming and the process to which data flow is going should be indicated. In the case of data stores, incoming and outgoing data flow needs to be indicated.
- **Physical location of data**: This is indicated in terms of record, file, or database.
- **Sample data dictionary for data element**: `Emp_code`
  - **DATA ELEMENT**: `Emp_code`
  - **DESCRIPTION**: A unique permanent code is assigned to each employee.
  - **TYPE**: char
  - **LENGTH**: 4
  - **ALIASES**: EC, `E_code`
  - **RANGE**: 0001 to 9999
  - **DATA STORES**: Employee table, current payroll table.
- **Sample data dictionary for data structure**: Pay slip

  It is a data flow as well as a data structure:
  - **DATA STRUCTURE**: Payslip
  - **DESCRIPTION**: Gives the pay details of the employee for the month.
  - **CONTENT**: `Emp_code`, `name`, `grade`, `Basic_Pay`, `deductions`
  - **VOLUME**: 200 per month
  - **USED IN PROCESS**: 2.2
  - **DATA FLOW**: Print `Pay_Register` and `Pay_Slip`
  - **DATA STORES**: Current payroll table.

Data flow diagram

Data flow diagrams (**DFDs**) provide a logical model of the system and show the flow of data and the flow of logic involved. A DFD has the following characteristics:

- They show the movement of data through the system.
- They emphasize the processes that transform incoming data flows (input) into outgoing data flows (outputs).
- The processes that perform the transformation of new data and the use of data.
- The entities send and receive data flows in the system.
- DFD supports a top-down approach for analysis by breaking a higher level into many lower-level diagrams to cover the details of the system.

- It is also called a bubble-chart.

Symbols used in data flow diagrams

DFDs consist of 4 symbols, which are joined with lines. There may be a single DFD for the system or it may be exploded into several levels named **Level 1, Level 2, and Level 3**, etc. The top-level diagram is often called a **context diagram** consisting of a single process that shows the overall view of the system. The symbols used in drawing the dataflow diagram (*Figure 6.10*) are:

- **Entities**: Sometimes, these are called **source** or **sink** (destinations) of the diagram. This is a noun represented by a rectangle. An entity may be a people, place, customer, program, or organization. Other entities can interact with the system.
- **Data flow**: This shows the movement of data from one point to another in the diagram. The flow is shown with an arrow headline to give the direction of flow. The data flow is given a simple and meaningful name, such as a library book deposit or booking a ticket. The data flows from entity to process or process to process.
- **Processes**: Processes show the transformation of input data flows to output data flows. It is also known as **bubbles** or **transform**. A circle denotes a process. All the processes are numbered from left to right for identification. The name of the process describes what happens to data as it flows into the system. The name should consist of a single strong verb or a singular object like `calculate_net_pay`, `compute_balance`, etc.
- **Data store**: A data store is basically a database or repository. This may be a database file or transaction file. Processes may store or retrieve data from a data store. An arrow pointing to a data store indicates writing, and from a data, store indicates reading the data. A double-headed arrow indicates both the operations of reading and writing data in the data store. The examples are `master_file`, `pending_documents`, etc. *Figure 6.10* shows symbols used in DFDs:

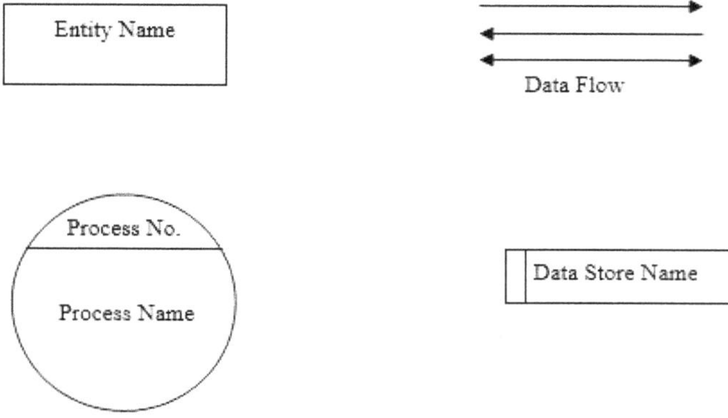

***Figure 6.11:** Symbols used in DFDs*

Construction of data flow diagram

The following steps may be followed to construct a DFD:

1. Processes should be named and numbered for easy identification.
2. The direction of flow is from top to bottom and left to right.
3. Data flow from the upper left corner source to the lower right corner destination.
4. The names of data stores, sources, and destinations are written with the first letter being capitalized.

To start with, a context diagram is made. A context diagram should have a single process. It is to understand the current system with boundaries shown in *Figure 6.12*:

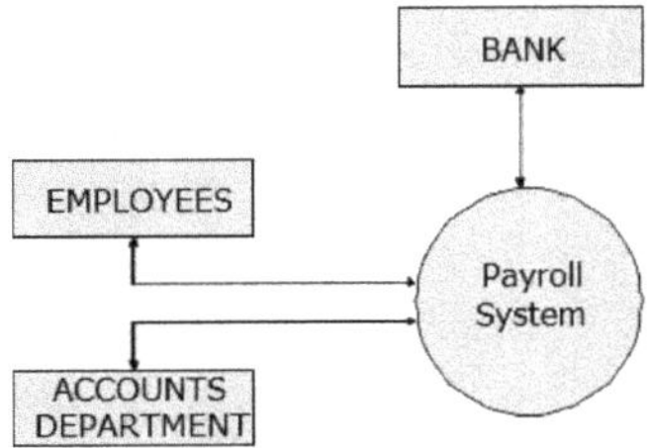

Figure 6.12: *Context diagram*

The main process given in the context diagram is exploded into sub-processes, which cover the total process. The sub-processes are one level lower than the parent process.

Developing zero level data flow diagram

The description of the payroll system in the context diagram is very brief. Hence, the next step is to describe the system at level zero, linking to sub-processes like prepare attendance and leave record, prepare payroll register, prepare bank statements and deduction reports, etc. in *Figure 6.13*:

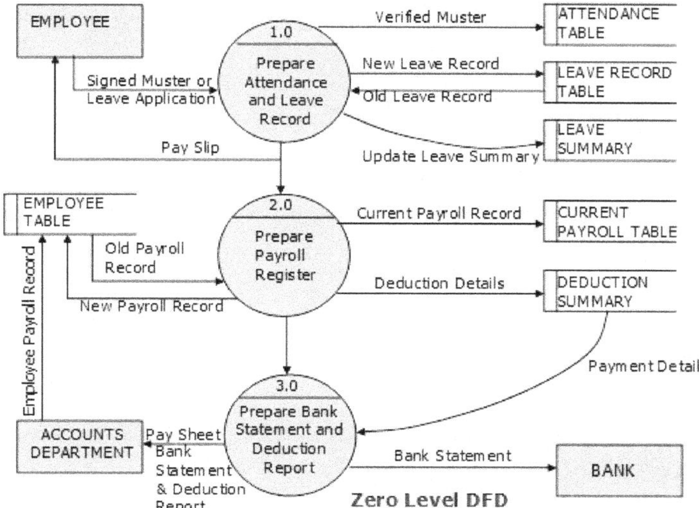

Figure 6.13: *Zero level DFD for a payroll system*

Figure 6.14 shows the level 1 DFD for process 1.0:

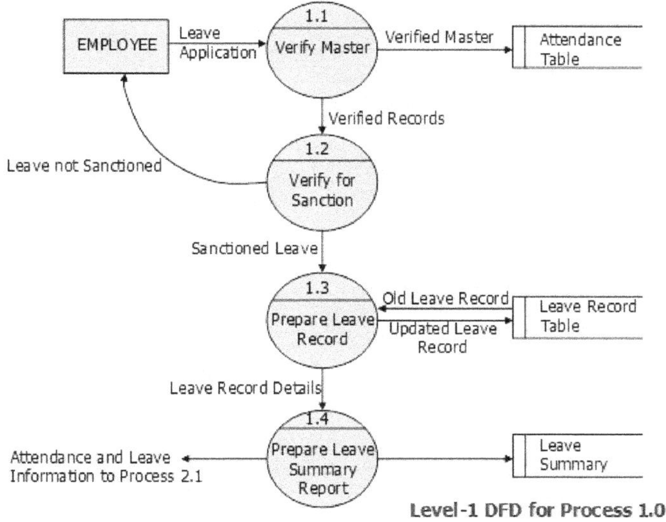

Figure 6.14: *Level 1 DFD for Process 1.0*

Now, the question is how far the explosions be carried out and how many levels of diagrams are needed depending upon the nature and complexity of the particular system under consideration. Generally, we should go as far as necessary to understand the details of the system and the way it functions. However, DFD must be drawn only after adequate interactions with the users of the system. Normally, the explosion is done when the process has multiple tasks each requiring data flow.

Explanation of level one DFD for payroll system

The process of preparing attendance and leave statements, shown in *Figure 6.13* can be broken into the following parts, shown in *Figure 6.14:*

1. Verify muster
2. Verify and sanction leave
3. Prepare leave record
4. Prepare leave summary report

Similarly, the process to prepare the payroll register in *Figure 6.12* can be broken into the following parts in *Figure 6.15*:

1. Calculate current pay
2. Print the pay register and Payslip
3. Prepare salary summary book

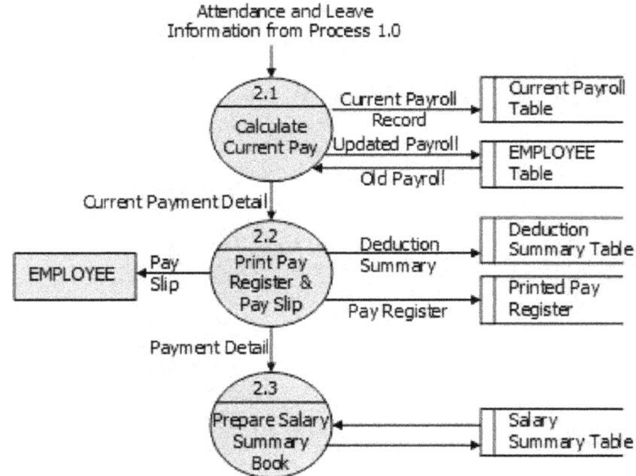

Figure 6.15: *Level 1 DFD for process 2.0*

Similarly, the third process, to prepare bank statements and deduction reports, can be further broken into (*Figure 6.16*):

1. Print payment sheet and deduction report
2. Prepare arrears payment sheet

The Level 0 DFD cannot be initiated unless the leave record is available. This is necessary because the employee concerned might have gone on medical leave, long leave, maternity leave, etc. Pay has to be adjusted accordingly. Hence, the input for 2.1 is the attendance and leave information record. The old payroll record from the employee, master is needed to know the basic pay, dearness allowance, house rent allowance, city compensatory allowance, and deductions. This has to be worked out with the current payroll record to prepare an updated payroll record. The current payment details flow from Level 0 DFD to Level 3.0 DFD for printing the payroll register and pay-slips.

A deduction summary file is prepared to consolidate and send the accrued amounts to various agencies like the Provident Fund Office, LIC, Income Tax departments, and so on. In sub-process 2.3, a salary summary book is prepared to account for the government grants utilized.

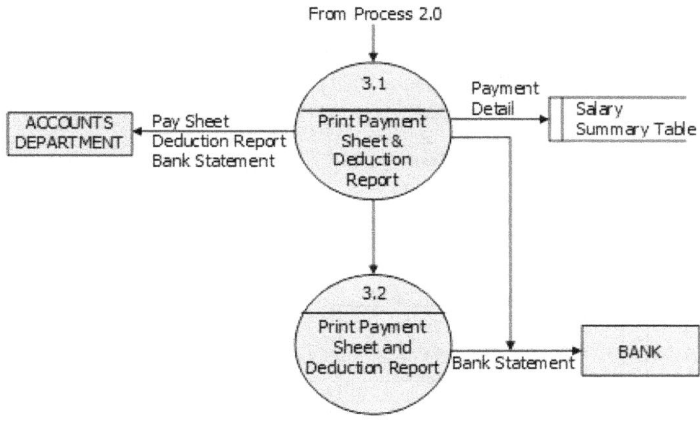

Figure 6.16: *Level 1 DFD for process 3.0*

Data flow-oriented design

Data flow-oriented design is a key approach in software engineering that focuses on the movement of data within a system and how various components process that data. This design methodology emphasizes identifying and modeling the flow of information, ensuring that data inputs, transformations, and outputs are clearly defined and logically organized. In data flow-oriented design, the system is typically broken down into smaller modules or functions, each responsible for specific operations on the data as it moves through the system. This approach enables developers to better understand the system's overall functionality, simplifies complex systems into manageable components, and supports modularity and reusability. By mapping out DFDs, developers can ensure that the system processes data efficiently and meets user requirements while maintaining clarity in design and implementation.

Transaction centered design

In a **transaction-centered system**, the system's primary function is to send data to their proper destinations within a more general system. Data come into the central module of the system, the transaction center, and they are dispatched to their proper locations based on their data type. An example of a transaction-centered system is a system designed to process banking transactions such as check deposits, savings deposits, check withdrawals, withdrawals from savings, car loan payments, and so on. Within the transaction center, the data are evaluated and dispatched, depending on their type. Deposits to checking would take one path, withdrawals from checking another path, and car loan payments yet another path. Each path leads to modules designed for processing that particular type of transaction. For on-line systems, each path is a menu choice leading to the part of the system handling that type of transaction. Processes along a transaction path often have user interactions. *Figure 6.17* shows the transaction diagram:

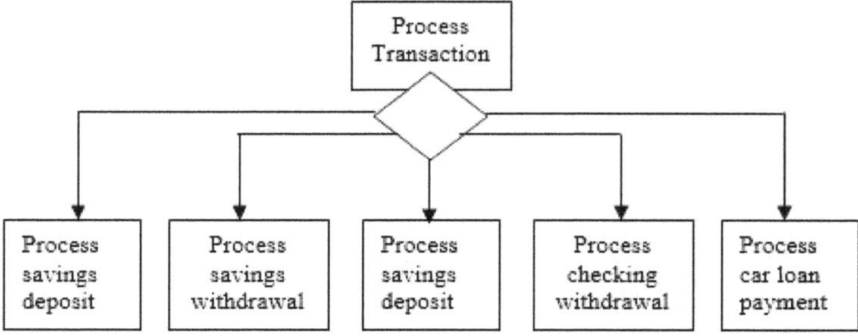

Figure 6.17: *Transaction diagram*

Transform centered design

Information systems (or a part of the information system) are typically either transaction-centered or transform-centered.

A **transform-centered system** has its central function the derivation of new data values from existing data values. An example is converting students' grades and class hours to grade point averages. The other example is calculating the loan payment from an interest rate, loan period, and principal amount. The transform-centered systems, the derivation of new data, or the transformation, tends to be the core of the system. The transformation of data is often transparent to the users. The modules that represent the core, in this case, calculate interest, are called the **central transform**. The modules that perform the task of bringing data into the system are called **afferent modules**. Afferent modules are arranged in groups referred to as afferent branches. The modules that perform tasks associated with the output of the transformed data are called **afferent modules**, which are arranged in efferent branches. Refer to *Figure 6.18*:

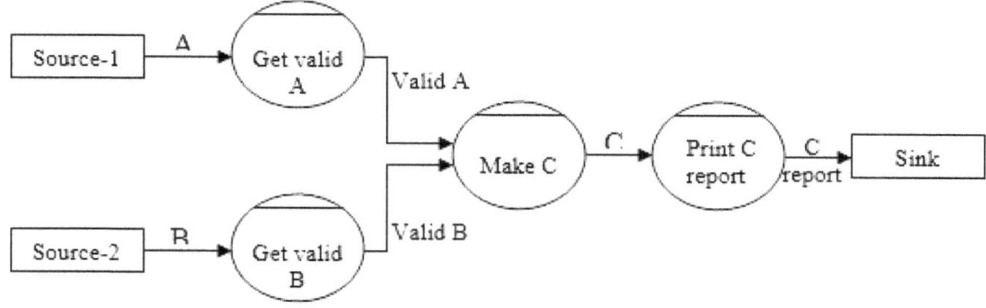

Figure 6.18: Transform centered system

Case studies

In software engineering, effective system design is crucial for building scalable, maintainable, and high-performing applications. Case studies based on real-world scenarios highlight the importance of fundamental design principles such as abstraction, refinement, modularity, and information hiding. By analyzing software architecture, control hierarchies, and structural partitioning, organizations can develop robust systems that align with business objectives. This case-study-driven approach ensures that design decisions lead to efficient data structures, optimized software procedures, and seamless integration of modules, ultimately enhancing system reliability and performance.

Reservation system

For example, a railway reservation system functions as follows:

- The passengers fill in a reservation form giving his or her particulars like starting point, destination, number of berths, sex, date of journey, train code, etc.
- The counter clerk checks the availability of berths from the reservation database. If the required berths are available, the clerk prints the ticket, computes the charges for the ticket and a booking statement is composed. If the required berths are not available, the form is returned to the passenger.
- One copy of the booking statement for the day is retained as an office copy, one copy is pasted on the compartment and the last copy is given to the train conductor.
- A cash statement is prepared at the end of each shift.

Prepare a DFD for the above system:

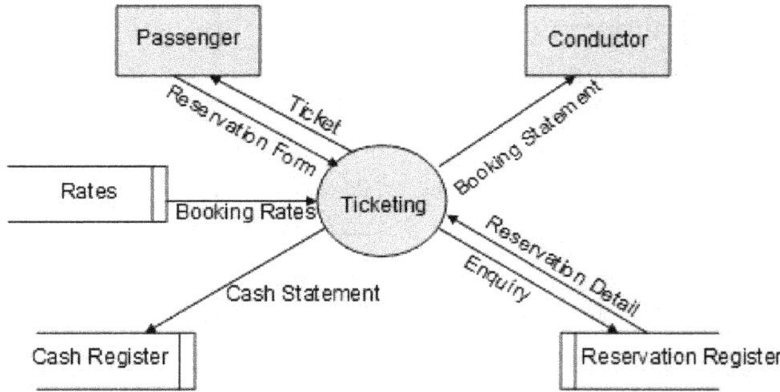

Figure 6.19: *Context diagram*

Figure 6.20 shows first level DFD:

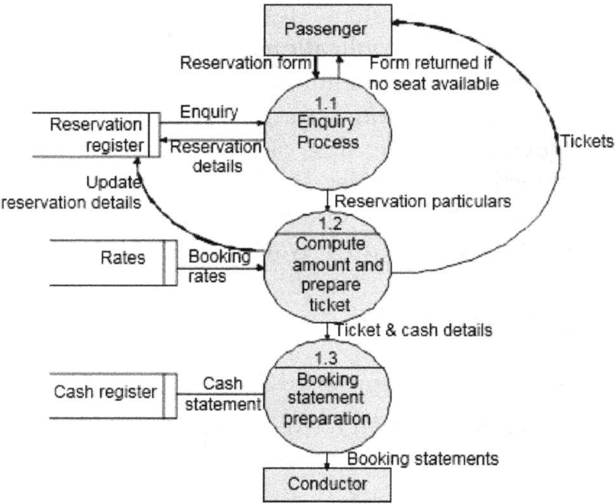

Figure 6.20: *First level DFD*

Inventory control

Inventory control is a critical component of supply chain management, focusing on the regulation and management of stock levels to meet customer demand while minimizing holding costs. To represent the system's overall flow, a **context diagram** can be used to provide a high-level overview of how the inventory control system interacts with external entities, such as suppliers and reporting systems. In *Figure 6.21*, the **inventory system** manages stock levels by processing inputs such as orders from suppliers and providing outputs like inventory reports and stock-in-hand details to relevant stakeholders. Payments and invoices are exchanged with suppliers to maintain financial accuracy.

In a **Level 0 DFD**, the system is broken down into core processes, such as **Receive Order**, **Process Payments**, **Update Inventory**, and **Generate Reports**. Each process manages specific tasks in controlling inventory, ensuring the system operates efficiently and keeps stock levels in balance. This systematic approach through DFD modeling provides a clear and structured understanding of how data flows through the inventory control system and helps optimize operations:

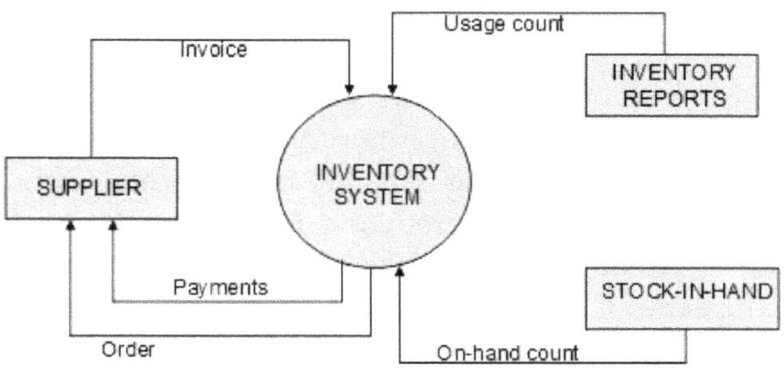

Figure 6.21: *Context diagram*

Figure 6.22 shows Level-0 DFD:

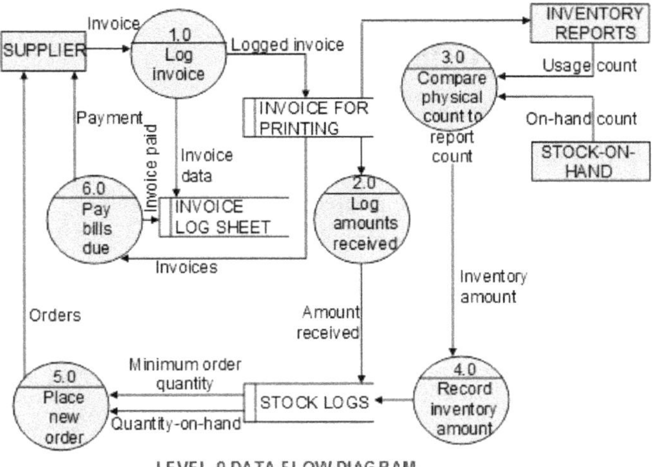

Figure 6.22: *Level-0 data flow diagram*

Conclusion

Preparing the right specification is the most important activity in software development. After planning, a set of well-defined specification documents will drive the successful completion of a software product. The SRS is the most critical one that plays the role of blueprint for the system. Categorization of the project requirement will be helpful during the development process, especially when there is a strong correlation between a specific requirement and development cost or schedule. Categorizing the requirements may help clients to prioritize requirements in light of cost and schedule implications. In a large software system, keeping track of changes, documenting the changes, and tracing the requirements to their origin is very difficult. These may be easy when the SRS is well written.

In the next chapter, Object-Oriented Analysis and Design (OOAD), readers will explore the fundamental principles of object-oriented software development. This chapter will cover key concepts such as encapsulation, inheritance, polymorphism, and abstraction, which form the foundation of designing scalable and maintainable software systems. Readers will learn how to analyze requirements using object-oriented methodologies, model real-world entities as objects and classes, and design software solutions using **Unified Modeling Language (UML)** diagrams. Additionally, the chapter will delve into best practices for creating modular, reusable, and efficient software architectures, ensuring that systems are both flexible and easy to maintain.

Exercises

To solidify your understanding of the concepts covered in this chapter, try the following exercises.

Multiple choice questions

1. **What is the primary objective of software project analysis?**
   a. To develop the software directly
   b. To define and understand the project requirements
   c. To write the program code
   d. To test the software

2. **In software design, which of the following ensures that the system components interact efficiently?**
   a. Modularity
   b. Integration testing
   c. Cohesion
   d. Coupling

3. **Which of the following is a key aspect of software design that helps reduce complexity?**
   a. Prototyping
   b. Abstraction

c. Deployment

d. Debugging

4. **During project analysis, what is the main tool used to visually represent data flow within the system?**
   a. Class diagram
   b. Entity-relationship diagram (ERD)
   c. Data flow diagram (DFD)
   d. Gantt chart

5. **What is the purpose of using design patterns in software design?**
   a. To identify bugs in the code
   b. To provide reusable solutions to common design problems
   c. To ensure faster coding
   d. To automate software testing

6. **Which software design principle aims to reduce the interdependence between modules?**
   a. Coupling
   b. Inheritance
   c. Polymorphism
   d. Encapsulation

7. **In the software design process, what does the acronym UML stands for?**
   a. Unified Model Layout
   b. Universal Modeling Logic
   c. Unified Modeling Language
   d. User Model Library

Short question

1. What is cohesion? Name different types of cohesion.
2. Define coupling. Name the different types of coupling.
3. What are the steps in the design process?
4. What are the advantages of modular programming?
5. Differentiate between system analysis and system design.
6. Define design. Name some characteristics of a good design.
7. List some design principles.

8. When a system design is complete?
9. What are the advantages of DFD?
10. What factors contribute to good design?
11. What is data design?
12. What guidelines need to be considered during the analysis phase?
13. Define system development.
14. What is software construction?
15. Construct a decision table for the following problem. Applications for admission to an extension course are screened using the rules as stated. For admission, a candidate should be sponsored by his employer, and he should possess a prescribed minimum academic qualification. If his fee is also paid, then he is sent a letter of admission. If the fee is not paid, then a letter of provisional admission is sent. In all other cases, a letter of regret is sent.
16. A policy to be followed in a store inventory system is stated as follows:
    a. If the quantity of an item ordered by a customer is available in the store, then it is shipped. The quantity of the specified item remaining in the store is checked against the order level. If it is below the reorder level then a reorder procedure is initiated.
    b. If the quantity ordered by the customer is greater than the stock, he is asked whether he would be willing to accept a partial shipment. If he is willing, then the available quantity is shipped, a reorder is initiated, and the quantity in stock is set to zero. The quantity to be shipped later is entered in a back-order file. If the customer does not accept partial shipment, then nothing is shipped, and the entire order is entered in the back-order file, and reorder is initiated. Draw a decision table.
17. Extended entry decision tables. There are a number of problems in which a question can have multiple answers, and it is clearly and concisely expressed with the questions being extended into the concerned entry part of the decision table.
18. What are the disadvantages of modular programming?
19. What is software scope?
20. How do you develop a design model?
21. Describe how the modules interact in specific cases.
22. What is software construction?
23. What guidelines need to be considered during the analysis phase?
24. What are the advantages and disadvantages of a flow chart?
25. What are the advantages and disadvantages of pseudo code?

Essay question

1. A bank has the following policy on deposits: On deposits of Rs 5.000 and above and for 3 years and above the interest is 12%. On the same deposit for a period less than 3 years it is 10%. On deposits below Rs 5,000 the interest rate id 8% regardless of the period of deposit. Write the above process using (i) structured English, (ii) a decision table.
2. An offshore gas company bills its customers according to the following rate schedule:
   a. First up to 500 liters Rs 10 (flat)
   b. Next 300 liters Rs 1.25 per 100 liters
   c. Next 30,000 liters Rs 1.20 per 100 liters
   d. Next 1,00,000 liters Rs 1.10 per 100 liters
   e. Above this Re 1.00 per 100 liters

   The input record has customer identification, name and address, meter reading past and present. Write a structured English procedure to obtain a bill for the customer.
3. Explain why accuracy is an important attribute for a data dictionary.
4. Use a DFD to characterize a complete credit card processing system. Give the specification for customer service part of the system using any tool.
5. Describe your university or college as a system. What is the input, output, and boundaries? What are the components, their relationships, constraints, the purpose, and interfaces? Draw a diagram of the system.
6. A car is a system with several subsystems, including the braking subsystem, the electrical subsystem, the engine, the fuel subsystem, climate control subsystem, and the passenger subsystem. Draw a diagram of a car as a system and label all of its system characteristics.
7. Define each of the following terms.
   a. System
   b. Interface
   c. Boundary
   d. Purpose
   e. Modularity
8. What is decomposition? Coupling? Cohesion?

Multiple choice answers

1. b
2. a
3. b
4. c
5. b
6. a
7. c

CHAPTER 7
Object Oriented Analysis and Design

Introduction

Object-oriented analysis and design (OOAD) is a methodology used in software development that focuses on defining software solutions through the concepts of objects, classes, and their interactions. In **object-oriented analysis (OOA)**, the system is examined to understand and model its structure, behavior, and requirements, using real-world objects and relationships. The goal is to capture the system's functionality by identifying objects, their attributes, and the actions they perform. **Object-oriented design (OOD)**, on the other hand, takes this analysis and transforms it into a blueprint for implementation, specifying how the identified objects will interact within the system. OOAD promotes modularity, reusability, and maintainability, allowing for more structured, scalable, and efficient software development. This approach is widely adopted in modern software engineering for building complex and robust systems.

Structure

In this chapter we will be discussing the following topics:

- Introduction to UML
- Object oriented design
- Object oriented paradigm
- Object oriented analysis

Objectives

The main objective of this chapter is to introduce the **object-oriented (OO)** methodologies and their applications in the software design process. The OO terminologies are described. The concepts and principles underlying the OO approach are discussed. The process of object identifications and class identifications is introduced in this chapter. You will also learn in this chapter how analysis and design activities are blended into the OO approach. The techniques and associated notations are incorporated into a standard OO language called the **unified modeling language (UML)**. The various static and dynamic models are described using UML with examples.

Introduction to UML

A more recent approach to system development, which is becoming more and more popular, is OOAD. OOAD is often called the third approach to systems development, after the process-oriented and data-oriented approaches. The object-oriented approach combines data and processes (call methods) into a single entity called an object. Objects usually correspond to the real things, an information system deals with, such as customers, suppliers, contracts, and rental agreements. Putting data and processes together in one place recognizes the fact that there is a limited number of operations for any given data structure. Putting data and processes together makes sense even though typical system development keeps data and processes independent of each other.

An **object-oriented** system is made up of interacting objects that maintain their local state and provide operations on that state. The representation of the state is private and cannot be accessed directly from outside the object. OOD processes involve designing object classes and the relationships between these classes. These classes define the objects in the system and their interactions. When the design is realized as an executing program, the objects are created dynamically from these class definitions.

OOD is part of object-oriented development where an object-oriented strategy is used throughout the development process:

- OOA is concerned with developing an object-oriented model of the application domain. The objects, in that model, reflect the entities and operations associated with the problem to be solved.
- OOD is concerned with developing an object-oriented model of a software system to implement the identified requirements. The objects in an OOD are related to the solution of the problem. There may be a close relationship between some problem objects and some solution objects, but the designer inevitably has to add new objects and transform problem objects to implement the solution.
- **Object-oriented programming** is concerned with realizing a software design using an object-oriented programming language such as Java. An object-oriented

programming language provides constructs to define object classes and a run-time system to create objects from these classes.

Unified modeling language

The UML is the brainchild of *Grady Brooch, James Rum Baugh,* and *Invar Jacobson*. Dubbed *The Three Amigos,* these gentlemen worked in separate organizations through the 1980s and early 1990s, each devising his methodology for OOAD. Their methodologies achieved preeminence over those of numerous competitors. By the mid-1990s, they began to borrow ideas from each other, so they decided to evolve their work together.

In 1994, *Rum Baugh* joined Rational Software Corporation, where *Brooch* was already working. Jacobson enlisted at Rational a year later.

The rest, as they say, is history. Draft versions of the UML began to circulate throughout the software industry, and the resulting feedback brought substantial changes. This is because, many corporations felt the UML would serve their strategic purposes, and the UML consortium sprung up. Members included *Digital Equipment Corporation (DEC), Hewlett-Packard, Intellicorp, Microsoft, Oracle, Texas Instruments, Rational,* and others. In 1997, the consortium produced version 1.0 of the UML and submitted it to the **Object Management Group (OMG)** in response to the OMG's request for a proposal for a standard modeling language.

The consortium expanded, generated version 1.1, and submitted it to the OMG, who adopted it in late 1997. The OMG took over the maintenance of the UML and produced two more revisions in 1998. The UML has become a de facto standard in the software industry, and it continues to evolve. Versions 1.3, 1.4, and 1.5 have come into being, and OMG recently put its stamp of approval on version 2.0. The earlier versions, referred to generically as version 1.x, have been the basis of most models.

Object orientation

Object -orientation has taken the software world by storm, and rightfully so. As a way of creating programs, it has a number of advantages. It fosters a component-based approach to software development, so that, you first create a system by creating a set of classes. Then, you can expand the system by adding capabilities to components that you have already built or by components. Finally, you can reuse the classes that you have created when you build a new down substantially on system development time.

Class

First and foremost, an object is an instance of a class (a category). For example, you and I are instances of the **`person`** class. An object has structure. That is, it has attributes (properties) and behavior or operations. We also perform these operations: eat, sleep, read, write, talk, go to work, and more (**`objectspeak`**, **`eat()`**, **`sleep()`**, **`read()`**, **`write()`**, **`talk()`**, and **goToWork()**). An object's behavior consists of the operations it carries out. Attributes and operations taken together are called **features**. *Figure 7.1*, a washing machine, is an example of an object having attributes and behavior.

The concept of a class is best understood with an analogy. Out of several objects in a room, let us talk about the pictures on the wall. There is a class, which we can call the class of **pictures**, of which the picture on the wall is an **instance** (meaning an example). The room belongs to the class of pictures, which consists of all the pictures in the world.

A class is a category or group of things that have the same attributes and the same behaviors. For example, anything in the class **washing machines** has attributes such as brand name, model, serial number, and capacity. Behaviors for things in this class include the operations **accept clothes**, **accept detergent**, **turn on**, and **turn off**. *Figure 7.1*, shows an example of the UML notation that captures these attributes and behaviors of a washing machine. A rectangle is an icon that represents the class. It is divided into three areas. The uppermost area contains the name, the middle area holds the attributes, and the lowest area holds the operations.

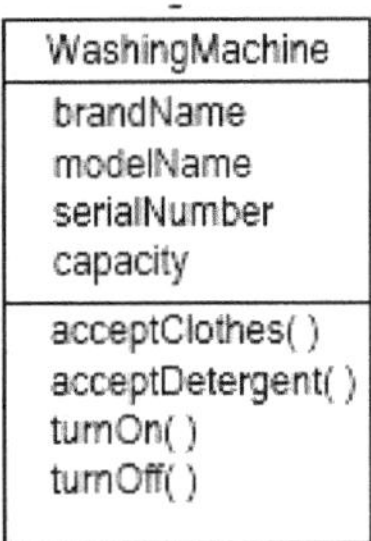

Figure 7.1: *The UML class icon*

Another example is a **chair** on which a person is sitting. They can call it **my chair**. The chair across the room is also an object. We can call this second chair **her chair**. Both these objects share certain common characteristics or attributes (associated actions that enable them to be recognized or classified as belonging to a single chair class). Thus, my chair and her chair are two examples (instances) of the chair class, but they exist independently of each other, and the values of their characteristics or attributes differ. For example, they occupy different positions in the room, and their colors are different. Thus, the chair is a class, but my chair and her chair are objects or instances of chair class.

As objects in the **person** class, **you** and **I** each have these attributes: height, weight, and age. Each person is unique because of the specific values that each of them has for those attributes. We, also, perform these operations: eat, sleep, read, write, talk, go to work, and more. The operations or functions in object **eat()**, **sleep()**, **read()**, **write()**, **talk()**, and **goToWork()**. If we were to create a system that deals with information on people, say, a payroll system or a system for a human resources department, we would likely incorporate some of these attributes and some of these operations in our software.

If we specify that the **WashingMachine** class has the attributes **brandName**, **modelName**, **serialNumber**, and capacity, along with the operations **acceptClothes()**, **acceptDetergent()**, **turnOn()**, and **turnOff()** as shown in *Figure 7.2*. You have a mechanism for turning out new instances of the **WashingMachine** class. That is, you can create new objects based on this class.

The more attributes and behaviors you take into account, the more your model will be in tune with reality. In the washing machine example, you will have a potentially more accurate model if you include the attributes **drumVolume**, **trap**, **motor**, and **motorSpeed**. You might also increase the accuracy of the model if you include operations like **acceptBleach()** and **controlWaterLevel()**, as shown in *Figure 7.2*:

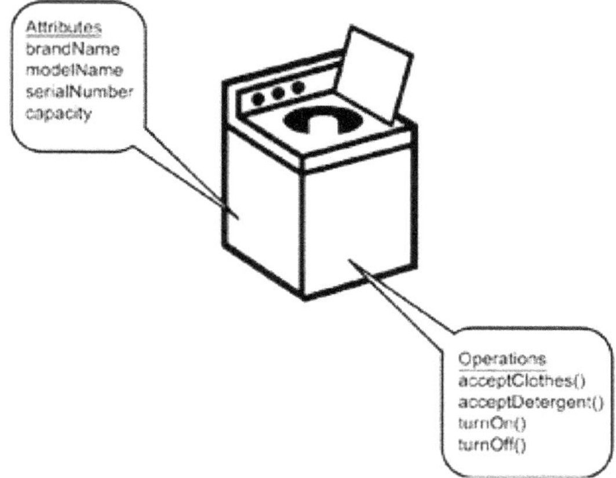

Figure 7.2: *The washing machine class (template for creating new washing machines instances)*

If we specify that the washing machine class has the attributes such as **brandName**, **modelName**, **serialNumber**, and capacity, along with the operations like **acceptClothes()**, **acceptDetergent()**, **turnOn()**, and **turnOff()**. You have a mechanism for turning out new instances of the washing machine class. That is, you can create new objects based on this class, as in *Figure 7.3*.

Object oriented paradigm

Object-oriented programming (OOP) is a programming paradigm that uses objects and their interactions to design applications and computer programs. Object-orientation goes beyond just modeling attributes and behavior. It considers other aspects of objects as well. These aspects are called modularity, abstraction, inheritance, polymorphism, and encapsulation. Three other important parts of object-orientation are message sending, association, or aggregation. It was not commonly used in mainstream software application development until the 1990s. Many modern programming languages now support OOP. Let us examine each of these concepts.

Abstraction

Abstraction means, simply filtering out an object's properties and operations until just the ones you need are left. What does **just the ones you need** mean? Different types of problems require different amounts of information, even if those problems are in the same general area. In the second pass at building a washing machine class, more attributes and operations emerged than in the first pass. *Figure 7.3* shows adding attributes and operations brings the model closer to reality:

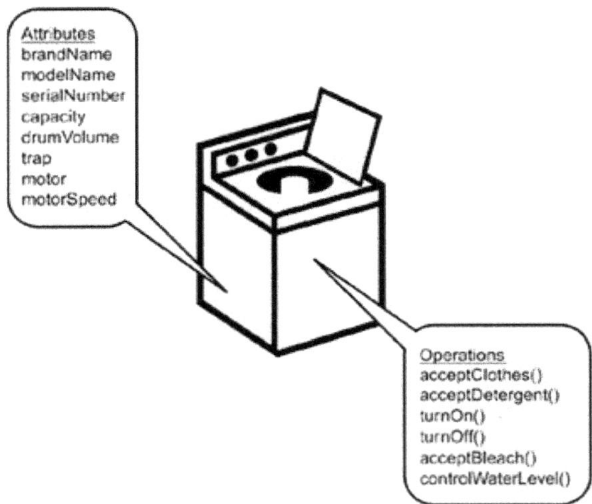

Figure 7.3: *Adding attributes and operations brings the model closer to reality*

If you are part of a development team that is ultimately going to create a computer program that simulates exactly how a washing machine does what it does, then it's worth it. A computer program like that (which might be useful to design engineers who are building a washing machine) has to have enough in it to make accurate predictions about what will happen when the washing machine is built, fully functioning, and washing clothes. For this kind of program, you can filter out the serial Number attribute because it is probably not going to be very helpful.

What if, on the other hand, you are going to create software to track the transactions in a laundry that has several washing machines? In this program, you probably will not need all the detailed attributes and operations mentioned. You might, however, want to include the `serialNumber` of each washing machine object.

In any case, what you are left with after you have made your decisions about what to include and exclude, is an abstraction of the washing machine.

Encapsulation

An object is said to encapsulate (hide) data and program. The user cannot see the inside of the object but can use the object by calling the program part of the object. For example, you drive a car without knowing much of the internal details. That is, the engine, gear, fuel injection system, etc., of the car are encapsulated, and the driver does not need to know the details.

In a TV commercial that aired a few years ago, two people discuss all the money they will save only if they dial a particular seven-digit prefix before dialing a long-distance phone call.

One of them asks, incredulously, **How does that work**?

The other replies, **How does popcorn pop? Who cares?**

That is the essence of encapsulation. When an object carries out its operations, those operations are hidden (see *Figure 7.4*). When most people watch a television show, they usually do not know or care about the complex electronic components that sit in the back of the TV screen and all the many operations that have to occur to paint the image on the screen. The TV does what it does and hides the process from us. Most other appliances work that way, too. Why is this important? In the software world, encapsulation helps cut down on the potential for bad things to happen. In a system that consists of objects, the objects depend on each other in various ways. If one of them happens to malfunction and software engineers have to change it in some way, hiding its operations from other objects means that it probably will not be necessary to change those other objects.

The TV hides
its operations
from the person
watching it.

Figure 7.4: *Objects encapsulate what they do*

Turning from software to reality, you see the importance of encapsulation in the objects you work with, too. Your computer monitor, in a sense, hides its operations from your computer's CPU. When something goes wrong with your monitor, you either fix the monitor or replace it. You probably will not have to fix or replace the CPU along with it.

While we are on the subject, here is a related concept. This is because encapsulation means that an object hides what it does from other objects and the outside world, encapsulation is also called **information hiding**. However, an object does have to present a **face** to the outside world, so you can initiate those operations. The TV, for example, has a set of buttons either on the TV itself or on a remote. A washing machine has a set of dials that enable you to set temperature and water level. The TV's buttons and the washing machine's dials are called interfaces.

Inheritance

Inheritance is defined as the property of objects by which instances of a class can have access to data and programs contained in a previously defined class. Classes are linked together in a hierarchy. They form a tree whose root is the **class** of objects. Each class (except the root class) will have a **superclass** (a class above it in the hierarchy) and possibly **subclasses**. A class can inherit (acquire) methods from its superclass and, in turn, can pass methods on to its subclasses.

Washing machines, refrigerators, microwave ovens, toasters, dishwashers, radios, waffle makers, blenders, and irons are all appliances. In the world of object-orientation, we would say that each one is a subclass of the **`Appliance`** class. Another way to say this is, that, **`Appliance`** is a superclass of all those others. **`Appliance`** is a class that has the attributes **`onOffSwitch`** and **`electricWire`**, and the operations **`turnOn()`** and **`turnOff()`**. Thus, if you know something is an appliance, you know immediately that it has the **`Appliance`** class's attributes and operations.

Figure 7.5 shows that appliances inherit the attributes and operations of the **`Appliance`** class. Each one is a subclass of the **`Appliance`** class. The **`Appliance`** class is a superclass of each subclass. Superclasses can also be subclasses and inherit from other superclasses. The **`Appliance`** superclass can also be a subclass of **`Householditem`** class, as shown in *Figure 7.6*.

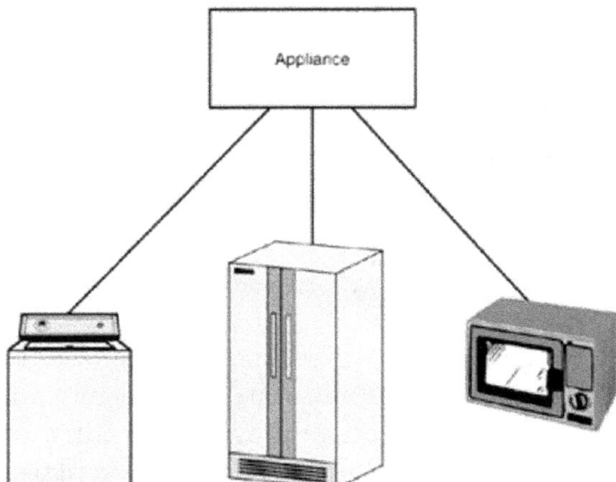

***Figure 7.5:** Appliances inherit the attributes and operations of the appliance class*

Inheritance is always transitive. A class can inherit features from super-classes many levels away. For example, if dog is a subclass of class mammal, and class mammal, in turn, a subclass of class animal, dog will inherit attributes both from mammal and from animal. The characteristics of mammals and animals are automatically included in dogs.

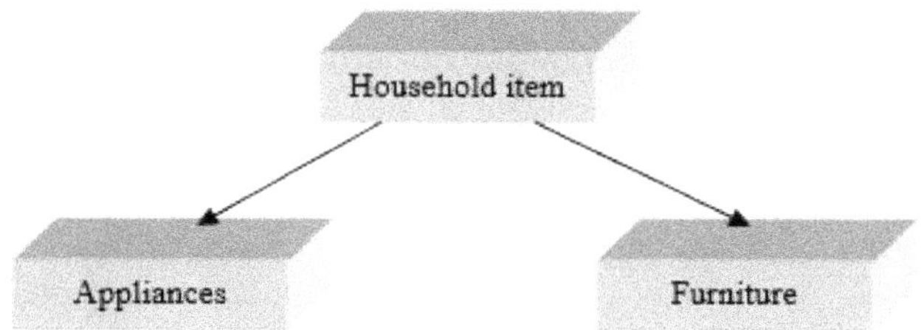

Figure 7.6: *Superclass can be a subclass and inherit from other superclass*

The concept of inheritance is also known as **generalization** or **specialization**. The supertype class is known as generalization, and the subtype class is known as specialization class. For example, furniture is referred to as a generalization class, whereas chairs, tables, and cupboards are specialization classes.

Polymorphism

Sometimes, an operation has the same name in different classes. For example, you can open a door, you can open a window, and you can open a newspaper, a presentation packet, a bank account, or a conversation. In each case, you are performing a different operation. In object-orientation, each class knows how that operation is supposed to take place. This is called **polymorphism** (see *Figure 7.7*). Polymorphism includes the ability to use the same message to objects of different classes and have them behave differently.

Figure 7.7: *Open, as polymorphism*

Thus, we could define the message + for both the addition of numbers and the concatenation (joining) of characters or strings, even though, both of these operations are completely different. For example, although, all window objects exhibit the same behavior, that is open and close, but all windows do not open and close in the same manner. Some windows **swing shut** while others **slide downwards**. Thus, polymorphism provides the ability to use the same word to invoke different methods, according to the similarity of meaning.

Messages

In a system, objects work together. They do this by sending messages to one another. One object sends another a message, a request to operate, and the receiving object performs that operation. A TV and a remote present a nice, intuitive example (*Figure 7.8*). When you want to watch a TV show, you hunt around for the remote, settle into your favorite chair, and push the **On** button. The remote object sends a message to the TV object to turn itself on. The TV object receives this message, knows how to perform the turn-on operation, and turns itself on. When you want to watch a different channel, you click the appropriate button on the remote, and the remote-object sends a different message, **change the channel**, to the TV object. The remote can also communicate with the TV via other messages to change the volume, mute the volume, and set up closed captioning.

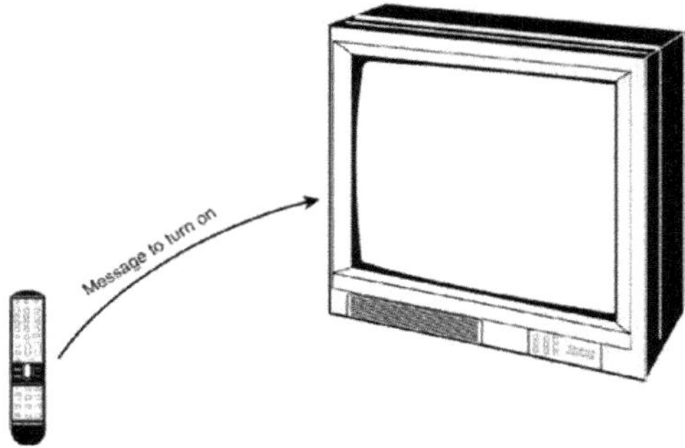

Figure 7.8: *Object sending a message to another object and vice versa*

The above figure is an example of a message sent from one object to another. The remote object sends a message to the TV object to turn itself on. The TV object receives the message through its interface, an infrared receiver.

Association

Another common occurrence is that objects are typically related to one another in some fashion. For example, when you turn on your TV, in object-oriented terms, you are in an association with your TV. The **turn-on** association is unidirectional (one-way), as in *Figure 7.9*. That is, you turn your TV on. Unless you watch way too much television, however, it does not return the favor. Other associations, like **is married to**, are bidirectional.

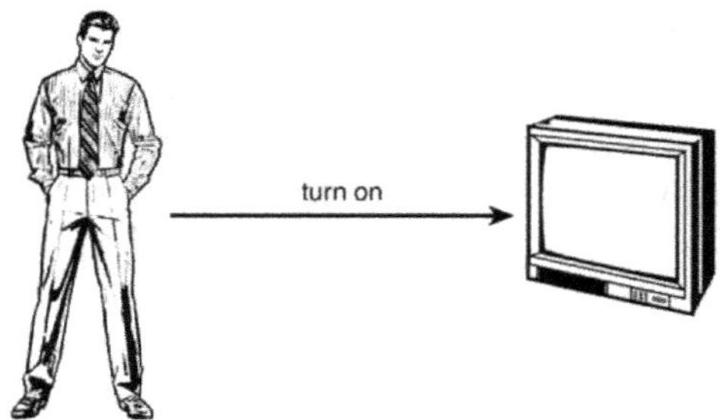

Figure 7.9: *Unidirectional association*

Objects are often associated with each other in some way. When you turn on your TV, you are in a unidirectional association with it. Sometimes, an object might be associated with another in more than one way. If you and your coworker are friends, that is an example. You are in an **is the friend of** association, as well as an is **the coworker of** association, as shown in *Figure 7.10*:

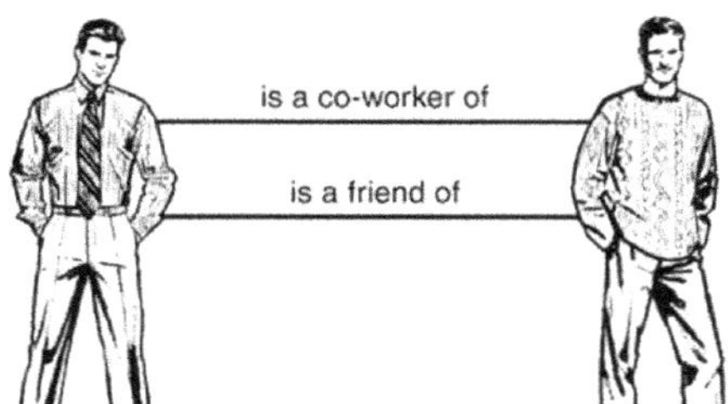

***Figure 7.10:** Association between objects in more than one way*

A class can associate with more than one other class. A person can ride in a car, and a person can also ride in a bus (see *Figure 7.11*). **Multiplicity** is an important aspect of associations among objects. It tells the number of objects in one class that relate to a single object of the associated class. For example, in a typical college course, the course is taught by a single instructor. The course and the instructor are in a one-to-one association. In a pro-seminar, however, several instructors might teach the course throughout the semester. In that case, the course and the instructor are in a one-to-many association. You can find all kinds of multiplicities if you look hard enough. A bicycle rides on two tires (one-to-two multiplicity), a tricycle rides on three, and an 18-wheeler on 18.

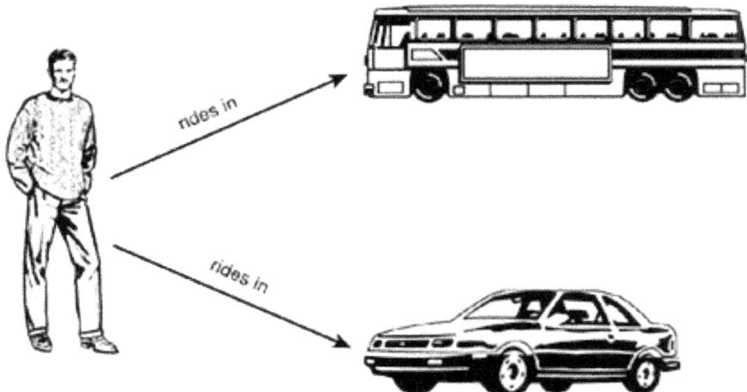

***Figure 7.11:** Association of one class with more than one other class*

Diagrammatically, the associations between the two objects can be shown as in *Figure 7.12*. Let us examine one, the association between a player and a team. You can characterize this association with the phrase **a player plays on a team**. You visualize the association as a line connecting the two classes, with the name of the association (**Plays on**) just above the line.

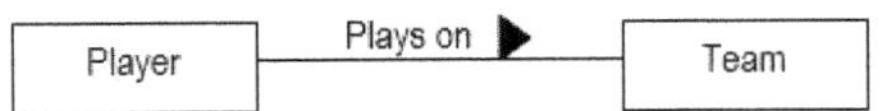

Figure 7.12: *An association between a player and a team*

Class associates with one another, and each one usually plays a role within that association. You can show each class's role by writing it near the line next to the class. Let us examine the association between a player and a team, if the team is professional, it is an employer, and the player is an employee. *Figure 7.13* shows how to represent these roles:

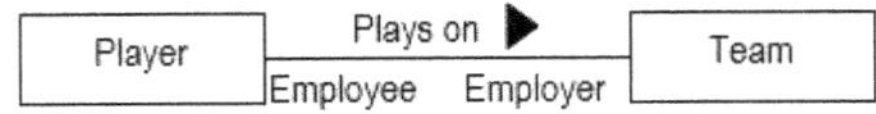

Figure 7.13: *In an association, each class typically plays a role*

You can imagine an association that you could read in the other direction: A team employs players. You can show both associations in the same diagram, with a filled triangle indicating how to read each association in *Figure 7.14*:

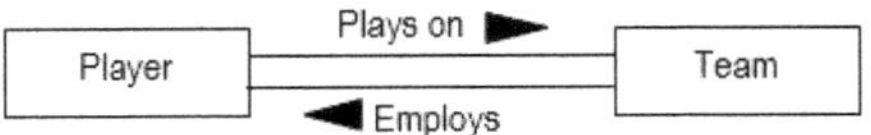

Figure 7.14: *Two associations between classes*

Associations may be more complex than just one class connected to another. Several classes can connect to one class. If you consider guards, forwards, and centers, and their associations with the **`Team`** class, you'll have the diagram in *Figure 7.15*:

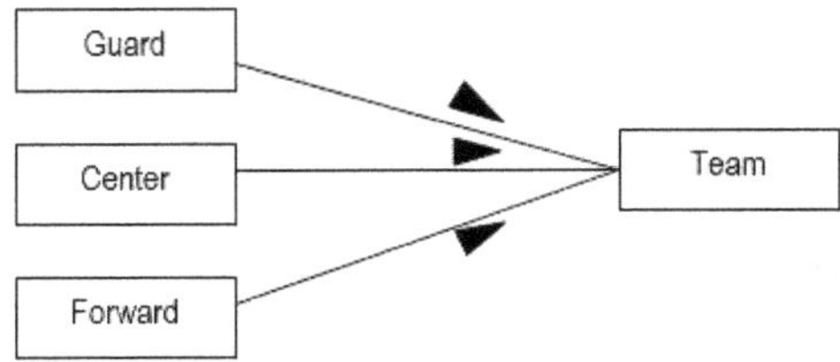

Figure 7.15: *Association of many classes with a particular class*

Sometimes, an association between two classes has to follow a rule. You indicate that rule by putting a constraint near the association line. For example, a Bank teller serves a customer, but each customer is served in the order in which he or she appears in line. You capture this in the model by putting the word ordered inside curly brackets (to indicate the constraint) near the **`Customer`** class, as in *Figure 7.16*:

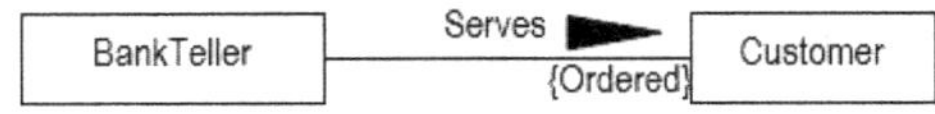

Figure 7.16: *Constraint on an association*

In this example, the serves association is constrained to have the Bank teller serve the customer in the order. The association drawn so far between player and team suggests that the two classes are in a **one-to-one** relationship. Common sense tells you that this isn't the case, however. A basketball team has five players (not counting substitutes). The Has association must take this into account. In the other direction, a player can play for just one team, and the plays on association must account for that can relate to one object of an associated class.

These specifications are examples of multiplicity, the number of objects from one class that relate to a single object in an associated class. To represent these numbers in the figure, you place them near the appropriate class, as in *Figure 7.17*.

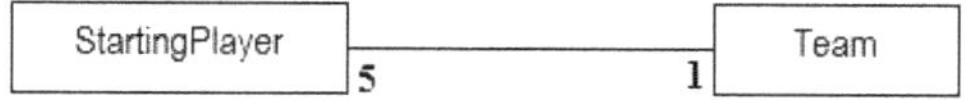

Figure 7.17: *Multiplicity shows the number of objects in one class*

The UML uses an asterisk (*) to represent more and to represent many. In one context, **or** is represented by two dots, as in 1. * (**one or more**). In another context, **or** is represented by a comma, as in 5, 10 (**5 or 10**). *Figure 7.18* shows, how to visualize possible multiplicities:

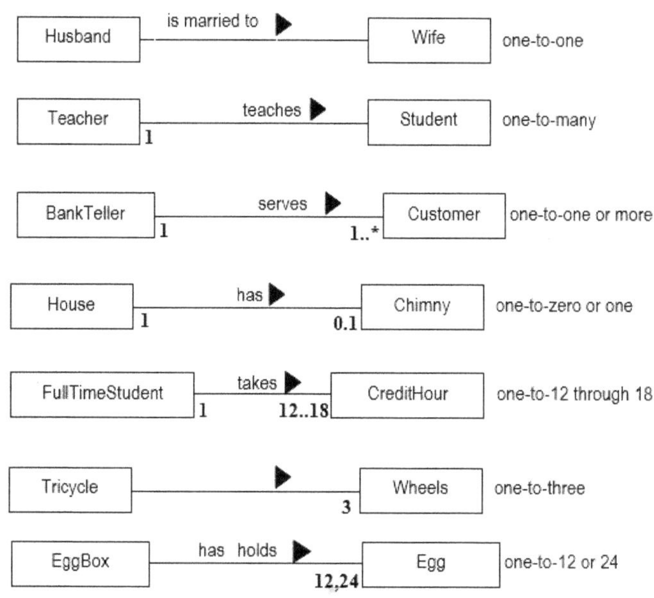

Figure 7.18: *Possible multiplicities and representation in the UML*

Aggregation

Think about your computer system. It consists of a CPU box, a keyboard, a mouse, a monitor, a CD-ROM drive, one or more hard drives, a modem, a disk drive, a printer, and possibly some speakers. Inside the CPU box, along with the aforementioned drives, you have a CPU, a graphics card, a sound card, and some other elements you would undoubtedly find hard to live without. Your computer is an aggregation, another kind of association among objects. Like many other things worth having, the computer is made from several different types of components (see *Figure 7.19*). You can probably come up with numerous examples of aggregations:

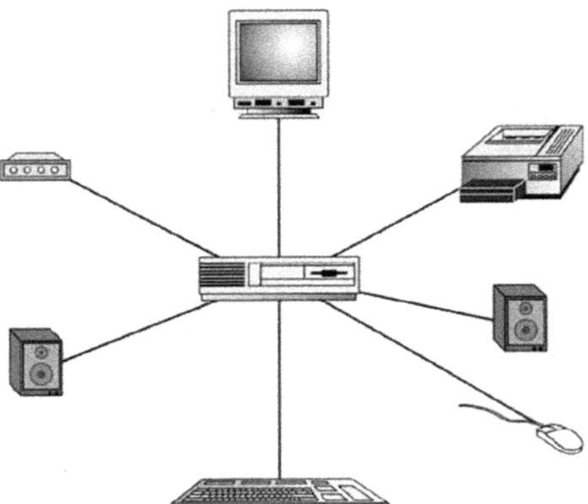

Figure 7.19: *Computer system object is made up of a combination of a number of different types of objects*

One form of aggregation involves a strong relationship between an aggregate object and its component objects. This is called **composition**. The key to composition is that the component exists as a component only within the composite object. For example, a shirt is a composite of a body, a collar, sleeves, buttons, buttonholes, and cuffs. Do away with the shirt and the collar becomes useless.

Sometimes, a component in a composite does not last as long as the composite itself. The leaves on a tree can die out before the tree does. If you destroy the tree, the leaves also die. On the destruction of the composite, the component is destroyed (see *Figure 7.20*):

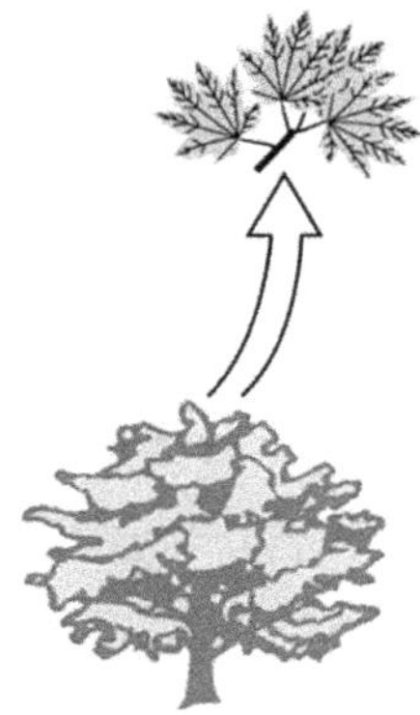

Figure 7.20: *In a composition, a component can sometimes die out before the composite does*

Object oriented analysis

OOA looks at the problem domain to produce a conceptual model of the information that exists in the area being analyzed. Analysis models do not consider any implementation constraints that might exist, such as concurrency, distribution, persistence, or how the system is to be built. Implementation constraints are dealt with during OOD. An analysis is done before the design.

The sources for the analysis can be a written requirements statement, a formal vision document, and interviews with stakeholders or other interested parties. A system may be divided into multiple domains, representing the different business, technological, or other areas of interest, each of which is analyzed separately.

The result of the OOA is a description of what the system is functionally required to do, in the form of a conceptual model. That will typically be presented as a set of use cases, one or more UML class diagrams, and a number of interaction diagrams. It may also include some kind of user interface mock-up.

Object oriented design

Objects and frames share the property that they bring descriptive and behavioral features closely together. This shared feature, phrased from the programming angle, means that the storage structures and the procedural components that operate on them are tightly coupled. The responsibilities of frames go beyond those of objects. Frames are supposed to support complex cognitive operations, including reasoning, planning, natural language understanding, and generation. In contrast, objects for software development are most often used to realize better-understood operations.

On the programming side, the Simula programming language is another, even older, historical root of objects. Unsurprisingly, Simula was aimed at supporting simulation activities. Procedures could be attached to a type (a class in Simula's terminology) to represent the behavior of an instance. Simula supported parallelism, in the approximation of co-routines, allowing for many interacting entities in a simulation.

Simula objects share the close coupling of data and procedures. The concurrency in Simula was lost in Smalltalk, Eiffel, Objective-C, C++, and other popular OO programming languages. However, parallelism has reentered the OO paradigm via OO analysis methods and distributed designs. Modeling reality with **active** objects requires giving them a large degree of autonomy.

The notion of whether objects have parallel connotations or not is currently a major difference between OO analysis and OO programming. Since, we expect OO programming languages to evolve to support the implementation of distributed, parallel systems, we expect this difference to decrease. The parallel OO paradigm is well-positioned to meet these upcoming demands.

Before 1975, most software organizations used no specific techniques. Each individual worked in his or her own way. The breakthrough was made between approximately 1975 and 1985, with the development of the so-called structured or classical paradigm. This included structured programming and structured testing. As time passed, this proved to be less successful and less acceptable because of the following:

- The technique was unable to cope with the increasing size of software products. The classical technique was adequate for small-scale software products up to 5000 lines of code. Today, large-scale products of 5,00,000 lines of code are relatively common. Even products of 5 million or more lines of code are not considered unusual. Classical techniques frequently could not scale up to handle such large products.

  Delivering large object-oriented software systems routinely and cost-effectively is still a significant challenge. To quote:

  A system composed of 100,000 lines of C++ is not to be sneezed at, but we don't have that much trouble developing 100,000 lines of COBOL today. The real test of OOP will come when systems of 1 to 10 million lines of code are developed.

  — *Ed Yourdon*

  To be fair and accurate, systems of 1,00,000 lines of C++ and those of 10,00,000 lines of **Common Business-Oriented Language (COBOL)** are often of the same order of magnitude in complexity.

- The classical paradigm did not live up to earlier expectations during post-delivery maintenance. In the classical paradigm, the cost of post-delivery maintenance used to be about two-third of the software budget. Many organizations still spend 70 to 80 percent or more of their time and effort on post-delivery maintenance [*Yourdon, 1992; Hatton, 1998*].

A major reason for the limited success of the classical approach is that classical techniques are either operation-oriented or attribute (data) oriented, but not both. In contrast, the object-oriented approach considers both attributes and operations to be equally important. An object may look like a unified software artifact that incorporates both attribute and operation (an artifact is a component of a software product that may be a specification document, a code module, or a manual).

A **class diagram** shows the static structure of an object-oriented model. The object classes, their internal structure, and the relationship in which they participate. In UML, a class is represented by a rectangle with three compartments separated by horizontal lines. The class name appears on the top compartment, the list of attributes is in the middle, and the list of operations is at the bottom compartment of the box. *Figure 7.21* shows two classes, **`Student`** and **`Course`**, along with their attributes and operations:

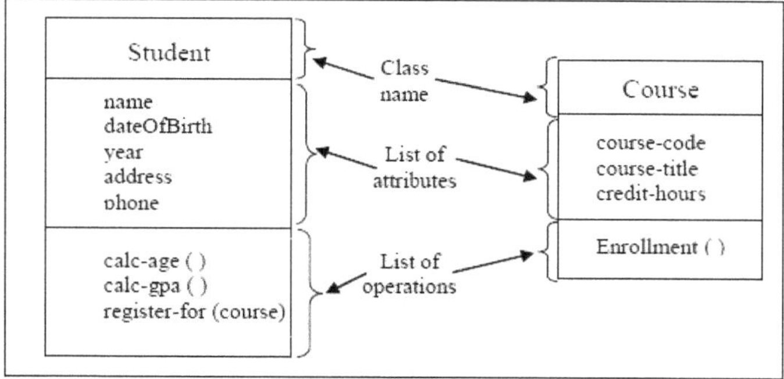

Figure 7.21: *Class diagram showing two classes*

A class provides a template or schema for its instance. Each object knows that it belongs to the **`Student`** class. An object diagram, also known as an **instance diagram**, is a graph of instances that are compatible with a given class diagram. In *Figure 7.22*, we have shown object diagrams with two instances. A static object diagram is an instance of a class diagram. In an object diagram, an object is represented as a rectangle with two compartments. The names of the project and its class are underlined and shown in the top compartment using the following syntax **`objectname: classname`**. The object's attributes and their values are shown in the second compartment.

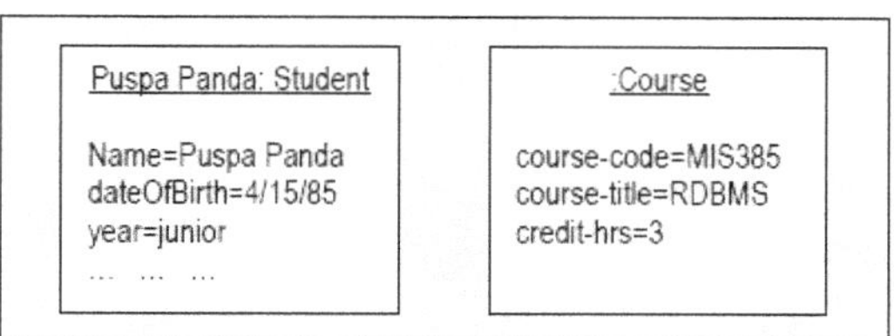

Figure 7.22: *Object diagram with two instances*

An **operation**, such as **`calc-gpa ( )`**, of student class in *Figure 7.22* is a function or a service that is provided by all instances of a class. It is only through such operations that other objects can access or manipulate the information stored in an object. It provides an external interface to a class without showing the internal structure or how its operations are implemented. The technique of hiding the internal implementation details of an object from its external view is known as encapsulation or information hiding [*Booch, 1994; Rumbaug, et al., 1991*].

Objects play a central role in all stages of project development. The entire development project becomes evolutionary in nature. A graphical representation of the project-oriented version of the software development life-cycle containing overlap and feedback is shown in *Figure 7.23*. This figure model shows that the development reaches a higher level only to fall back to a previous level and then again climb up till completion of the project. Finally, these objects at each stage may need modifications to get the final results to fulfill the aim of the project:

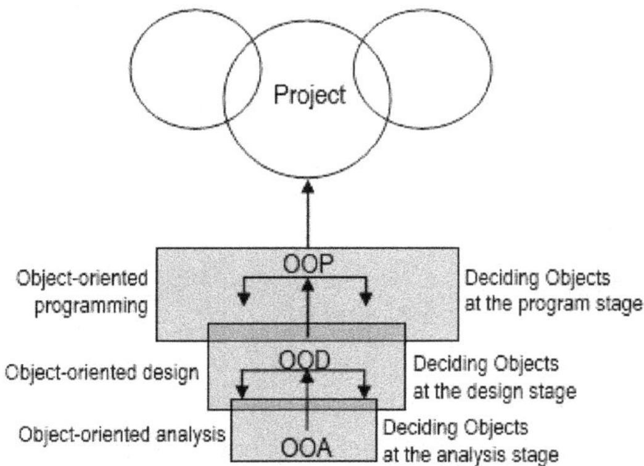

***Figure 7.23:** Series of stages in project development*

The project goes through an evolutionary development life cycle containing objects decided at three different stages, namely:

1. Objects decided at the stage of OOA.
2. Objects decided at the stage of OOD.
3. Objects finalized at the stage of final programming (OOP).

In OOA, we decide the objects, their behavior, and their interactions, meeting the requirements of the project. In OOD, we draw hierarchies from which the objects can be created. Finally, in an OOP, we implement the programs in C++ or any other OOP language using objects.

A well-defined project statement will help in deciding the objects at the analysis stage. Further refinements of the objects may need to be added at the implementation stage. At the implementation stage, the objects may have to be further modified so that each object properly fits in to give the result.

In the OO method, all three stages work more closely because of the commonality of the object model. In one stage, the problem domain objects are identified, while in the next stage, additional objects required for a particular solution are decided. The design process is repeated for these implementation-level objects.

The **object-oriented development life cycle** (**OODLC**), as shown above, consists of progressively developing an object representation through three phases such as analysis, design, and implementation, which is similar to the heart of the systems development LC. In contrast to the **software development life cycle (SDLC)**, the OODLC is more like an onion than a waterfall. In the early stages (or core) of development, the model you build is abstract, focusing on the external qualities of the application system. As the model evolves, it becomes more and more detailed, shifting the focus to how the system will be built and how it should function-system architecture, data structure, and algorithms. Like any information system, the system developer must generate code and database access routines. The emphasis in modeling should be on analysis and design, focusing on front-end conceptual issues, rather than backend implementation issues, which unnecessarily restrict design choices.

The OO development life cycle is shown in *Figure 7.24*. The different components are shown in the diagram, namely object analysis, object design, and object implementation are explained in the following subsections:

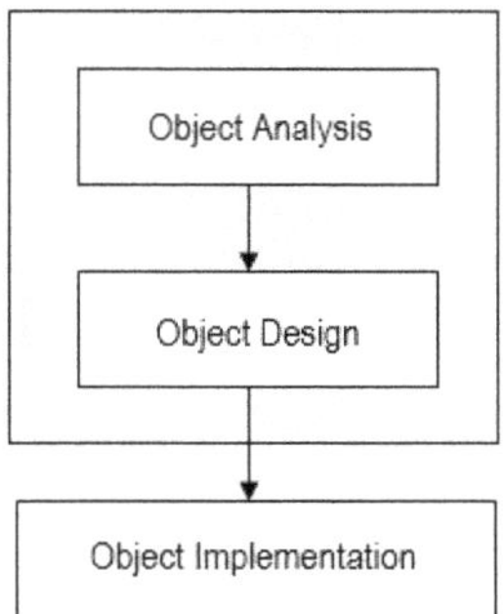

Figure 7.24: *Object-oriented life cycles*

Object analysis

In OOA, we identify objects, which are the building blocks of the project to be developed. We perform analysis using these objects. In the module-oriented approach which we studied in previous chapters, we thought in terms of building one large system. In the OOA, we identify objects as independent entities with their own local goals. These independent objects are then unified to achieve the global goal of the large system. In OOA, we consider the following points:

1. Understand the requirements of the project.
2. Write the specifications of the requirements of the user and the software.
3. Decide the objects and their attributes.
4. Establish the services that each object is expected to provide. In other words, it is called the **interface**.
5. Determine interconnections among the objects in terms of services required and the services rendered.

All the above-mentioned steps are illustrated in *Figure 7.25*.

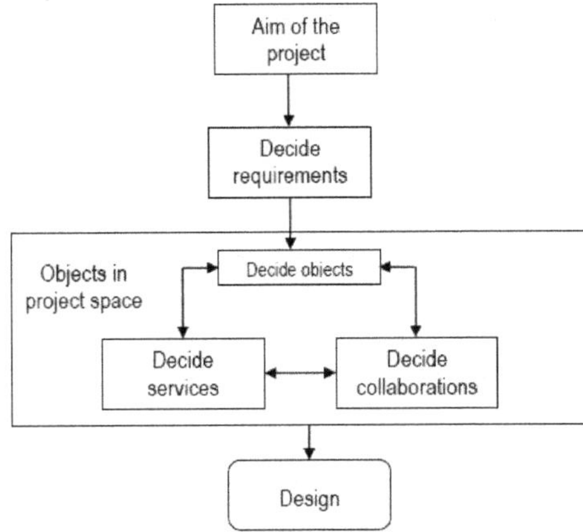

Figure 7.25: Actions of object-oriented analysis

Note: The steps 4, 5, and 6, need not be in the order in which they are mentioned above, as they are interdependent.

In object-oriented project analysis, one of the important requirements is to identify the objects. Following are the criteria for identifying objects in a system:

- An object must perform some service in the system. In other words, we should be able to assign specific responsibilities to various objects in the system.
- An object must have attributes whose values are examined and used in performing the service assigned to it. There must be several relevant attributes.
- An object must be essential for the functioning of the system. This is judged by examining whether it is essential to remember information about the object.
- There must be a common set of attributes and operations, which are necessary for all occurrences of the object.

Shlaer and Mellor suggest classes and objects usually come from one of the following sources:

- **Tangible things** (for example, cars, telemetry data, pressure sensors)
- **Roles** (for example, mother, teacher, politician)
- **Events** (for example, landing, interrupt, request)
- **Interactions** (for example, loan, meeting, depositing form)

For example, in a financial management system, we may identify objects like investments, accounts, and transactions, so on. Each of these will be operating with independent responsibilities.

Once the required objects are identified, we may identify their general properties and specialize them. For example, there are many kinds of investments such as investment in real estate, investment in shares, etc. All investments have some features in common, like an evaluation of returns on investment, as well as some features, which are specific to each.

The next step is to determine the responsibilities of each object, that is, operations it can carry out on its own. Thereafter, determine the operations, which will be performed by multiple objects in collaboration.

Thus, we can model the system as a collection of independent objects and allow these objects to communicate with each other. Communication among objects is done through the transfer of messages. A client object sends a message requesting a service from the server object. A message activates a process or method in the receiving object. The message causes the execution of the method program, which will carry out the required processing and return the response. Thus, OOA techniques are used to do the following three main activities:

- Study existing objects to see if they can be reused in the new system.
- Define new or modified objects that will be combined with the existing objects to develop the system.
- Define responsibilities or operations for each object.

Object design

In object design, we are required to specify the components of each object. There are different ways of accomplishing this. One way is to extend the **entity-relationship (ER)** model. The other way is to use the new modeling techniques specially devised for designing objects. Parallel to the definition of a relationship for the ER model, an association is a relationship among object classes. As in the ER model, the degree of an association may be one (unary), two (binary), three (ternary), or higher (n-ary).

Object oriented entity relationship model

In the **object-oriented entity-relationship (OOER)** model, we represent each entity as an object. The attributes form the object properties. Methods are also added to the OOER model. These methods, also called services, can change object properties or perform some computations.

Object diagram is similar to the ER diagram. It represents object properties.

Functional model shows the changes in the object properties. It is modeled similar to **data flow diagram (DFD)**.

Dynamic model represents the states of an object.

Object design includes the following steps:

1. Refining the objects identified in the analysis phase, so that they can be implemented in the real environment.
2. Modeling the interactions among objects and their behavior.
3. Updating the object model to reflect the implementation environment.

Object implementation

Other implementations of the systems require that the system be developed as a set of objects, using either object-oriented languages such as C++ or object-oriented database management systems, such as **Oracle 8i** and above. The implementation is independent of the analysis or design technique followed. Thus, it is possible to perform object implementation of a system that was analyzed using DFDs and ER diagrams.

Unified development process

Following are the unifies development process:

- **OO development life cycle and modeling:** It is a recent approach to systems development that is becoming popular. OOAD is often called the third approach to system development, after the process-oriented and data-oriented approaches. The object-oriented approach combines data and processes (cell methods) into single entities called objects. Objects usually correspond to the real things an information system deals with, such as customers, suppliers, contracts, and rental agreements. Putting data and processes together in one place recognizes the fact that there are a limited number of operations for any given data structure. The goal of OOAD is to make system elements more reusable, thus improving system quality and productivity of systems analysis and design.

A software development project can be viewed as a collection of objects that interact together to accomplish certain objectives. Objects may represent data files and functions. In an OO design of a project, we need to decide the objects that encapsulate data and procedures.

The object is an entity that has a well-defined role in the application domain and has a state, behavior, and identity. The state of an object encompasses its properties (attributes and relationships) and the values those properties have, and its behavior represents how an object acts and reacts [*Booch, 1994*]. All objects have an identity; that is, no two objects are the same. If there are two student instances with the same name and date of birth, they are essentially two different objects. Even if those two instances have identical values for all the attributes, the objects maintain their separate identities. You can use object instance to refer to an individual object, and object class (or simply class) to refer to a set of objects that share a common structure and common behavior.

Object modeling using a unified modeling language

UML is used to create diagrams describing the various aspects and uses of your application before you start coding, to ensure that you have everything covered. Millions of programmers in all languages have found UML to be an invaluable asset to their craft. UML consists of several graphical elements that combine to form diagrams. This is because UML is a language, it has rules for combining these elements. Expert author *Joe Schmuller* takes you through step-by-step lessons designed to ensure your understanding of UML diagrams and syntax. This updated edition includes the new features of UML 2.0, which are designed to make UML an even better modeling tool for modern object-oriented and component-based programming. UML is not a system design or development methodology. It can only be used to document OOAD.

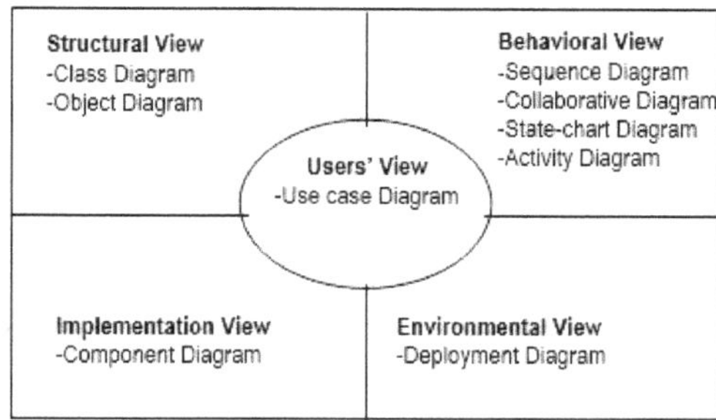

Figure 7.26: *Different types of diagrams and views supported in UML*

Figure 7.26 above shows the various UML diagrams with their respective views. These are used for OOAD. The diagram shows some of the important views which are used for system development. The different views of a system are used for development by using UML (*R Mall, 2003*):

- **User's view**: It defines the functionalities (facilities) made available by the system to its users. It is a black box where the internal structure, the dynamic behavior of system components, the implementation is not visible. This can be considered as the central view and all other views are expected to conform to this view.
- **Structural view**: It defines the kinds of objects (classes) important to the understanding of the working of a system and its implementation. It also captures the relationship among classes (objects). It is a static model since the structures of a system do not change with time.
- **Behavioral view**: It captures how objects interact with each other to realize the system behavior that captures the time-dependent (dynamic) behavior of the system.
- **Implementation view**: It captures the important components of the system and its dependencies.

- **Environmental view**: This view models how the different components are implemented on different pieces of hardware.

Do not use all UML diagrams and modeling elements while modeling a system [*Rosenberge, 2000*].

Why is it necessary to have numerous views of a system? Typically, a system has several different stakeholders such as people who have interests in different aspects of the system. Let us return to the washing machine example. If you are designing a washing machine's motor, you have one view of the system. If you are writing the operating instructions, you have another. If you are designing the machine's overall shape, you see the system differently if you just want to wash your clothes.

Conscientious system design involves all the possible viewpoints, and each UML diagram gives you a way of incorporating a particular view. The objective is to communicate clearly with every type of stakeholder.

Modeling using unified modeling language

UML offers several diagrams to model a system. Each UML diagram depicts a different aspect of the system. We will first show how to develop a use-case model during the requirement analysis phase. Next, we will show how to model the static structure of the system using class and object diagrams. Then we shall capture the dynamic aspects using state and interaction diagrams. Finally, we will provide a brief description of the component and deployment diagrams, which are generated during the design and implementation phases. The various UML diagrams are discussed in the following section.

Perform the detailed design

Figure 7.27 is constructed from the state chart of *Figure 7.28*. For example, the event button pushed and button unlit are implemented by two nested if statements, at the beginning, *Figure 7.27*. The two operations of the state are as follows:

```
void elevatorEventLoop (void)
{
   while (TRUE)
    {
       if (a button has been pressed)
           if (button is not on)
           {
   updateRequests;
   button::turnOnButton;
            }
            else if (elevator is moving up)
            {
```

```
if (there is no request to stop at floor f)
    elevator::moveUpOneFloor;
else
{
    stop elevator by not sending a message to move;
    elevatorDoors::openDoors;
    startTimer;
    if (elevatorButton is on)
   elevatorButton::turnOffButton;
    updateRequest;
}
          }
          else if (elevator is moving down)
    [similar to up case]
          else if (elevator is stopped and request is pending)
          {
  elevatorDoors::closeDoors;
  determine direction of next request;
  if (appropriate floorButton is on)
      floorButton::turnOffButton;
  elevator::moveUp/DownOneFloor;
}
else if (elevator is at rest and not (request is pending))
   elevatorDoors::closeDoors;
else
   there is no requests, elevator is stopped with
elevatorDoors closed, so do nothing;
             }
          }
```

Figure 7.27: The detailed design of the method elevator event loop

Static and dynamic modeling

A **static model** describes the layout of data or arrangement of stored data (that is, data structure), but it does not show what happens to the various parts of the system. The ER model described earlier is a static model. In contrast, the dynamic model represents the states of an object. *Figure 7.28* exemplifies the states that an object can assume in its lifetime and the transition between the states.

Dynamic modeling

Figure 7.28 is an application (object) for sanction of a personal loan in the bank that may be received, in which case it is a received application. It is then checked, and it becomes a checked application. Next, the application may be either approved or rejected. In the former case, it becomes an approved application, and in the latter case, it becomes a rejected application. Thus, the application object goes through several states, namely the received application state, the checked application state, the approved application state, and finally, the accepted application state. The movement from one state to another is known as a state transition.

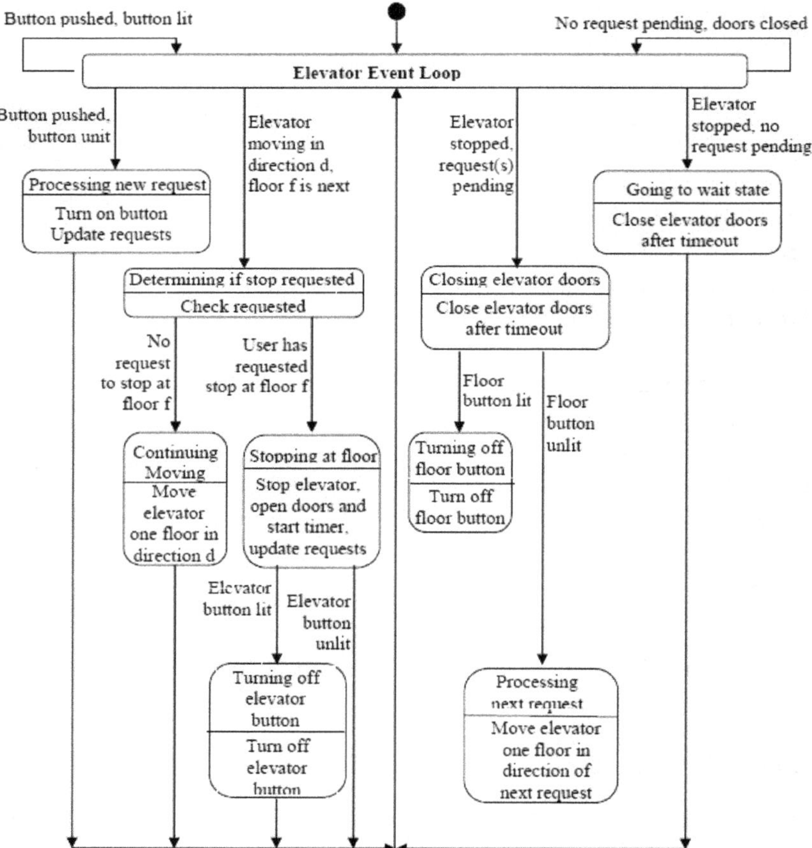

Figure 7.28: *The first iteration of the state chart for the elevator controller class*

Figure 7.28 is a dynamic model. Each state transition is activated by an internal event or by a message from another object. Each arrow in *Figure 7.28* would become a method in the application object. Hence, methods for the application object would be to receive an application, check the application, approve the application, etc. The check application method causes a state transition from the received application state to the checked application state. The transition from the checked application state depends on the result of the methods, that is, accept application or reject application.

The elevator problem case study states that, dynamic modeling aims to produce a state chart, a description of the target product similar to a finite state machine, for each class. First, consider the elevator controller class. The relevant state chart is in *Figure 7.29*. The state transition diagrams are not a complete representation of the product to be built.

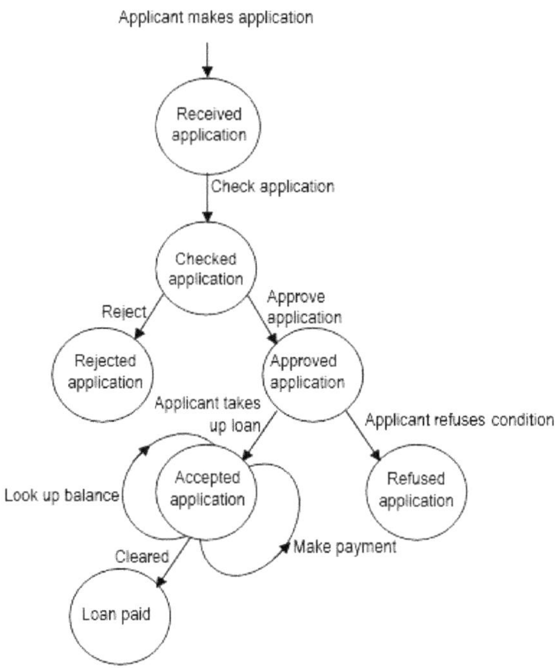

Figure 7.29: *State diagram for personal loan application in bank*

Current state, event and predicate, next state

The three aspects of a state machine (**state, event, and predicate**) are distributed over the UML diagram. For example, if the state is going to wait for the state, in *Figure 7.28*, is entered, if the present state is an elevator event loop and the event elevator stops, no requests pending are true. When the wait state has been entered, the operation of closing elevator doors after timeout is to be carried out. The solid circle denotes the start state, which takes the system into the state elevator event loop. The arrows represent the events that trigger the object to change from one state to another. The state diagram depicts the life cycle of a single object. State diagrams are not required for all objects. One simpler bank loan application is shown through a UML state diagram in *Figure 7.29*.

Dynamic modeling sequence diagram

A **sequence diagram** depicts the interactions among objects during a certain period. The pattern of interactions varies from one use case to another, and each sequence diagram shows only the interactions pertinent to a specific use case. It shows the participating objects by their lifelines, and the interactions among those objects arranged in time sequence by exchanging messages with one another.

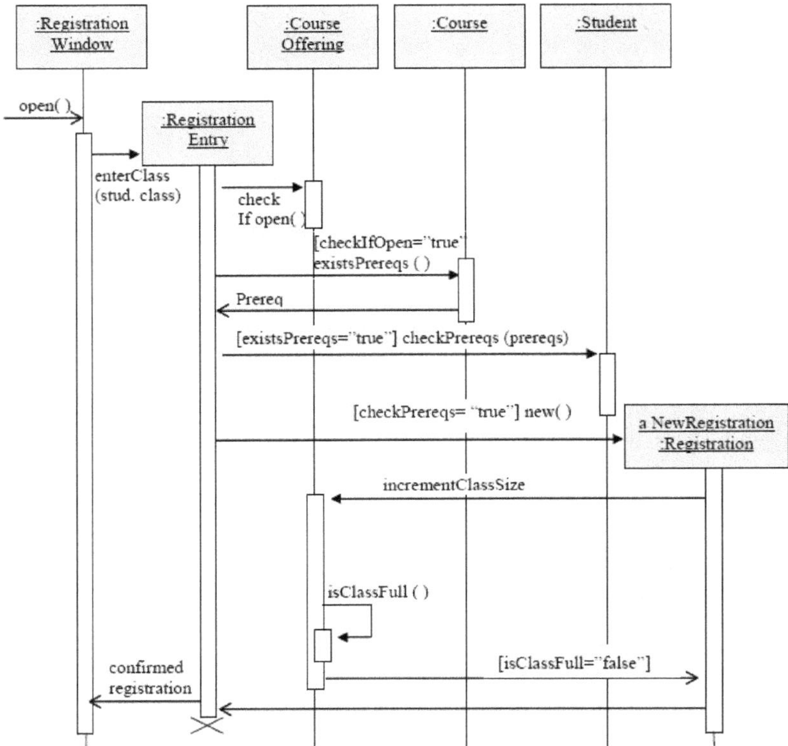

Figure 7.30: *Sequence diagram for a class registration scenario*

A **sequence diagram** may be presented in a generic form or an instance form. The generic form shows all possible sequences of interactions, that is, the sequences corresponding to all scenarios of a use case. For example, a generic sequence diagram for the class registration use case (see *Figure 7.30*) would capture the sequence interactions for every valid scenario of that use case. The instance form, on the other hand, shows the sequence for only one scenario. A scenario in UML refers to a single path, among possibly many different paths, through a use case [*Fowler, 1997*]. In *Figure 7.30,* we have shown a sequence diagram, in instance form, for a scenario where a student registers for a course that specifies one or more prerequisite courses as requirements.

The vertical axis of the diagram represents time, and the boxes represent the participating objects. Time increases as we go down the vertical axes. The diagram in *Figure 7.30* has six objects, from an instance of registration window on the left, to an instance of **Registration** called a **New Registration** on the right. The sequence of objects does not follow any rule. However, one should try to arrange the objects in such a way that the diagram is easy to read and understand. Each object has a vertical dashed line called a **lifeline**. The lifeline represents the object's existence over a certain period. An object symbol is a box with the object's name underlined and placed at the head of each lifeline.

A thin rectangle, superimposed on the lifeline of an object, represents an **activation** of the object. Activation shows the period during which the object operates. Objects communicate with one another by sending messages. A message is shown as a solid arrow from sending the object to the receiving object. For example, the **`checkOpen`** message is represented by an arrow from the registration entry object to the course offering object. Normally, the arrow is drawn horizontally, but in some situations (in the case of branching) you may draw a sloping message line.

The **synchronous message**, shown as a full, solid arrowhead, is one where the caller has to wait for the receiving object to complete executing the called **operation** before it can resume execution. The synchronous message always has an associated return message. The message may provide the caller with some return value(s), or simply acknowledge to the caller that the operation called has been completed. An example of a synchronous message is **`checkOpen`**. When a registration entry object sends this message to a course offering object, the latter responds by executing an operation called **`checkIfOpen`** (same name as the message). After the execution of this operation is completed, control is transferred back to the calling operation within the registration entry with a return value, **true** or **false**. We have not shown the return for the **`checkIfOpen`** message; it is implicit. We have explicitly shown the return for the **`existsPrereq`** message from registration entry to the course.

A simple message simply transfers control from the sender to the recipient without describing the details of the communication. In a diagram, the arrowhead for a simple message is drawn as a transverse tick mark. As we have seen, the return of the synchronous message is a simple message. The **open** message in *Figure 7.30* is also simple, it simply transfers control to the registration window object.

An asynchronous message, shown as a half arrowhead in a sequence diagram, is one where the sender does not have to wait for the recipient to handle the message. The sender can continue executing immediately after sending the message. Asynchronous messages are common in concurrent, real-time systems, where several objects operate in parallel.

Conclusion

OOAD plays a pivotal role in modern software engineering by promoting a structured and scalable approach to system development. Through its focus on encapsulation, inheritance, polymorphism, and abstraction, OOAD allows developers to create modular, maintainable, and reusable systems. The principles of OOAD help align software design with real-world problems, enabling clearer communication among stakeholders and facilitating iterative improvements throughout the development lifecycle. As software systems grow in complexity, the importance of robust OOD methods becomes even more crucial, ensuring the creation of reliable, adaptable, and efficient software solutions that meet user needs and technological advancements.

In the next chapter, readers will learn about *Use Case Diagrams*, a fundamental tool in software engineering for modeling system functionality from a user's perspective. These diagrams visually represent the interactions between actors (users or external systems) and use cases (specific functions or services the system provides). By defining the relationships and flows between users and system components, Use Case Diagrams help in capturing functional requirements, improving communication among stakeholders, and laying a strong foundation for system design. Understanding this concept is crucial for developers, architects, and business analysts to ensure a user-centered approach to software development.

Exercises

To solidify your understanding of the concepts covered in this chapter, try the following exercises.

Multiple choice questions

1. **What does UML stand for?**
   a. Unified Markup Language
   b. Unified Modeling Language
   c. Universal Modeling Language
   d. Universal Markup Language

2. **Which of the following is a key concept of Object-Oriented Programming?**
   a. Functions
   b. Modules
   c. Encapsulation
   d. Data Tables

3. **In UML, a class is represented as:**
   a. A rectangle
   b. A circle
   c. A diamond
   d. A triangle

4. **Which of the following describes an object in object-oriented analysis?**
   a. A blueprint of data types
   b. An instance of a class
   c. A method in a class
   d. A function to manage data
5. **Which of these is not a characteristic of the object-oriented paradigm?**
   a. Inheritance
   b. Polymorphism
   c. Procedural Abstraction
   d. Encapsulation
6. **UML primarily helps in:**
   a. Coding
   b. Modeling
   c. Debugging
   d. Testing
7. **The process of object-oriented analysis focuses on:**
   a. Identifying the objects and their interactions
   b. Creating detailed algorithms
   c. Testing software modules
   d. Designing user interfaces
8. **Which of the following is not a UML diagram type?**
   a. Use Case Diagram
   b. Flowchart Diagram
   c. Class Diagram
   d. Sequence Diagram
9. **In object-oriented design, inheritance is used to:**
   a. Eliminate redundant code
   b. Enhance program security
   c. Create new objects
   d. Store program state

10. **The Object-Oriented Paradigm emphasizes:**
    a. Data over behavior
    b. Behavior over data
    c. The interaction between objects
    d. The use of conditional statements

Short questions

1. What is UML, and why is it important in software engineering?
2. Define a class and an object in the context of object-oriented programming.
3. What are the key principles of object-oriented analysis?
4. Explain the concept of encapsulation with an example.
5. How does inheritance contribute to software reuse in object-oriented design?

Essay type questions

1. Discuss the importance of UML in the software development process. Explain how different UML diagrams assist in system design and analysis.
2. Compare the object-oriented paradigm with the procedural paradigm. Highlight the benefits and limitations of each.
3. Describe the role of object-oriented analysis in identifying system requirements and how it improves communication between stakeholders during software development.
4. Explain the key concepts of object-oriented programming, such as encapsulation, inheritance, and polymorphism, and discuss how they contribute to creating efficient software systems.

Multiple choice answers

1. b
2. c
3. a
4. b
5. c
6. b
7. a
8. b
9. a
10. c

CHAPTER 8
Use Case Diagram

Introduction

A **use case** is a description of a system's behavior from a user's standpoint. For system developers, the use case is a valuable tool. It is a tried-and-true technique for gathering system requirements from a user's point of view. Obtaining information from the user's point of view is important if the goal is to build a system that real people (and not just computer files) can use.

Structure

The following topics are discussed in the chapter:

- Use case modeling
- Class diagram
- Class modeling
- State-chart diagram
- Conceptual sample project

Objectives

A use case diagram is a visual representation of a system's functionality from the perspective of its users. In software engineering, it plays a crucial role in capturing the interactions between various external actors (users, systems, or devices) and the system under development. This diagram helps to outline the functional requirements, highlighting the relationships between the actors and the use cases that define the tasks they perform. By providing a high-level view of the system's behavior, a use case diagram assists both technical and non-technical stakeholders in understanding system interactions and aids developers in designing and implementing effective solutions.

Use case modeling

Use-case modeling is done in the early stages of system development to help developers gain a clear understanding of the functional requirements of the system. A use-case model consists of actors and use cases. An actor is an external entity that interacts with the system. A use case represents a sequence of related actions initiated by an actor. There is a difference between an actor and a user. A user is anyone who uses the system. An actor, on the other hand, represents a role that a user can play. The actor's name should indicate the role. An actor is a type or class of users. A user is a specific instance of an actor class playing the actor's role. The same user can play multiple roles.

A university registration system has a use case for class registration and another for student billing. In **unified modeling language (UML)**, a use-case model is depicted diagrammatically, as in *Figure 8.1*.

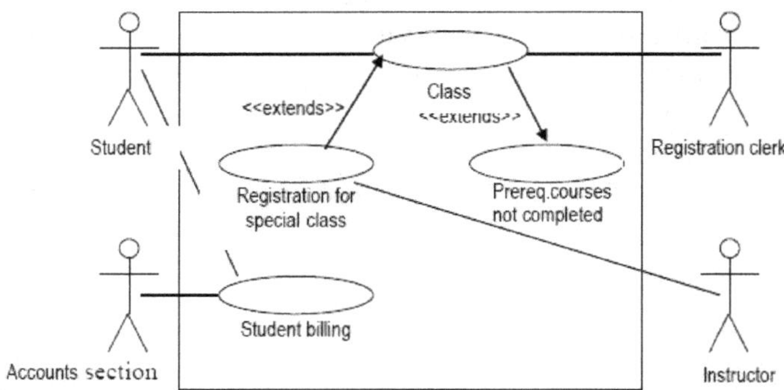

Figure 8.1: *Use-case diagram for a university registration*

This use-case diagram is for a university registration system, which is shown in a box. Outside the box are four actors, such as the student, registration clerk, instructor, and accounts officer, who interact with the system. An actor is shown using a stickman symbol, and its name is below. Inside the box are four use-cases, class registration, Registration for a special class, prerequisite courses not completed, and student billing. These are shown as ellipses with the name below. These use cases are performed by the actor outside the system. An actor does not necessarily have to be a human user. It could be anything (another system or a hardware device) with which the system interacts or exchanges information.

This use case performs a series of related actions when registering a student for a class. It represents complete functionality. Two actions are performed by the student user, submitting the registration form as the action of the class registration use case, and paying tuition as one of the actions of the student billing use case. Therefore, a use case is a complete sequence of related actions performed by an actor and the system during a dialog. An extended relationship, shown as a line with an arrowhead pointing toward the extended use case and labeled with the <<extend>> symbol, extends a use case by adding new behavior or actions. The registration for special class use case extends the class registration use case by capturing additional actions that need to be performed in registering a student for a special class.

Figure 8.2 represents a sample use case diagram of an ordering system:

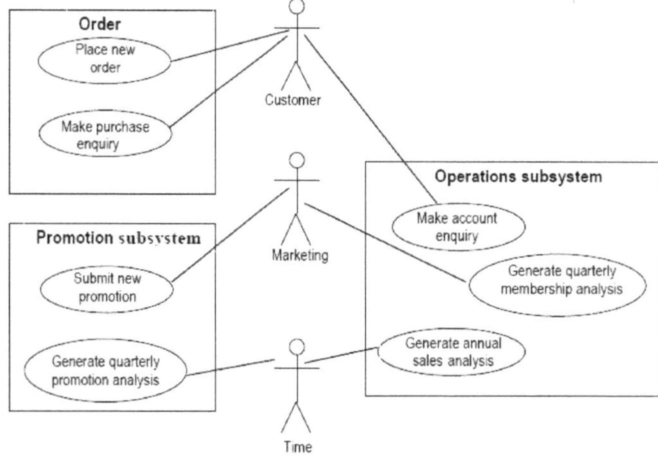

Figure 8.2: *A Sample use case diagram of an ordering system*

The little stick figure that corresponds to the customer, marketing, or time user is called an actor. The ellipse represents the use case.

Note: The actor, the entity that initiates the use case, can be a person or another system. The use case is inside a rectangle that represents the system, and the actor is outside the rectangle.

Class diagram

Think about the things in the world around you. The things that surround you have attributes (properties) and they behave in certain ways. We can think of these behaviors as a set of operations. You will also see that things naturally fall into categories (automobiles, furniture, washing machines.). We refer to these categories as **classes**. A **class** is a category or group of things that have the same attributes and the same behaviors. For example, anything in the class of washing machines has attributes such as brand name, model, serial number, and capacity. Behaviors for things in this class include the operations **accept clothes, accept detergent, turn on**, and **turn off**, behaviors of a washing machine. A rectangle is an icon that represents the class (see *Figure 8.3*). It is divided into three areas. The uppermost area contains the name, the middle area holds the attributes, and the lowermost area holds the operations.

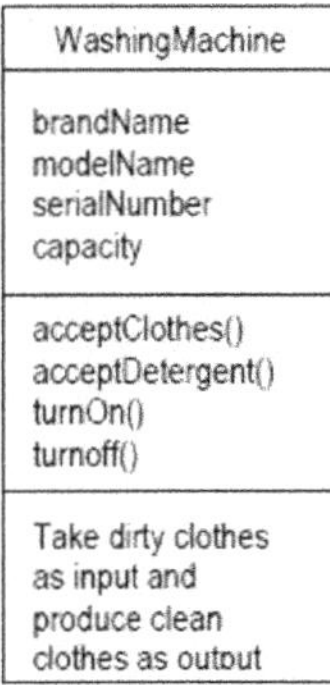

***Figure 8.3 (a)**: Representation of class icons of washing machine,*

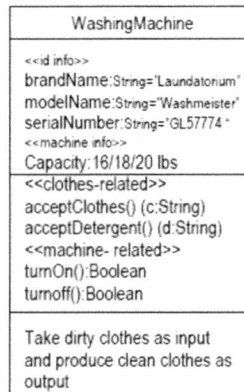

WashingMachine
<<id info>>
brandName:String='Laundatorium'
modelName:String='Washmeister'
serialNumber:String='GL57774'
<<machine info>>
Capacity:16/18/20 lbs
<<clothes-related>>
acceptClothes() (c:String)
acceptDetergent() (d:String)
<<machine- related>>
turnOn():Boolean
turnoff():Boolean
Take dirty clothes as input
and produce clean clothes as
output

***(b)**: An attribute can show its types and default values.*

Class modeling

Class modeling in software engineering is a technique used to represent the structure and relationships of objects within a system. It focuses on defining **classes**, which represent real-world entities or concepts, along with their **attributes** (data) and **methods** (functions). Through class models, developers capture the blueprint of a system's components, illustrating how different classes interact and depend on one another. Class modeling is a foundational concept in object-oriented design, enabling developers to create modular, reusable, and scalable software by organizing the system's functionality around well-defined objects. The details of a class diagram are already discussed in the previous section. In this section, we shall handle a case study to understand more about it.

Case study of an elevator

A product is to be installed to control **n** elevators in a building with **m** floors. The problem concerns the logic required to move elevators between floors according to the following constraints:

- Each elevator has a set of **m** buttons, one for each floor. These illuminate when pressed and cause the elevator to visit the corresponding floor. The illumination is canceled when the corresponding floor is visited by the elevator.
- Each floor, except the first floor and the top floor, has two buttons, one to request an up-elevator and one to request a down-elevator. These buttons illuminate when pressed. The illumination is canceled when an elevator visits the floor and then moves in the desired direction.
- When the elevator has no requests, it remains on its current floor with doors closed.

The first step in OOA is to model the use cases. A use case describes the interaction between the product to be constructed and the actors, that is, the external users of that product. The only interactions possible between a user and an elevator are the user pressing an elevator button to call an elevator or the user pressing a floor button to request the elevator to stop at a specific floor. Hence, two use cases, **Press an elevator button**, and **Press a floor button**. The two use cases are shown in the use-case diagram of *Figure 8.4*:

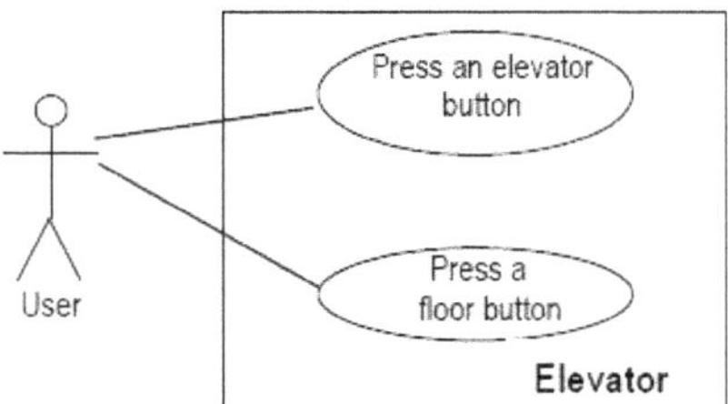

Figure 8.4: *Use-case diagrams for the elevator case study*

A use case provides a generic description of overall functionality. A scenario is a specific instantiation of a use case, just as an instantiation of a class. In general, there are a large number of scenarios, each representing one specific set of interactions. *Table 8.1* depicts a normal scenario, that is, a set of interactions between users and elevators that corresponds to the way we understand elevators should be used. *Table 8.1* is constructed by considering different users interacting with elevators (more precisely, with elevator buttons and floor buttons). The 15 numbered event describes in detail the two interactions between User A and the buttons of the elevator system (event 1 and event 6) and the operations performed by the components of the elevator system (events 1 through 5 and events 7 through 15). Two items, User A enters the elevator and User A exits from the elevator, are unnumbered. Such items essentially are comments.

In contrast, *Table 8.2* is an exception scenario. It depicts what happens when a user presses the Up button on floor three but wants to go down to floor one. This scenario, too, was constructed by observing the actions of many users in elevator. It is unlikely that someone who has never used an elevator would realize that users, sometimes, press the wrong button.

The scenarios of *Table 8.1 and 8.2,* plus innumerable others, are specific instances of the use cases, as shown in *Figure 8.4*. Sufficient scenarios should be studied to give the OOA team a comprehensive insight into the system behavior being modeled.

Entity class modeling

The first step is to extract the entity classes and their attributes to be represented in a UML class diagram. The attributes of an entity class are determined in OOA. The methods are assigned to the classes during OOD:

1	User A presses the Up-floor button on floor 3 to request an elevator. User A wishes to go to floor 7.
2	The Up-floor button is turned on.
3	An elevator arrives at floor 3. It contains User B, who entered the elevator at floor 1 and pressed the elevator button for floor 9.
4	The elevator doors open.
5	The time starts.
User A enters the elevator	
6	User A presses the elevator button for floor 7.
7	The elevator button for floor 7 is turned on.
8	The elevator doors close after a time out.
9	The Up-floor button is turned off.
10	The elevator travels to floor 7.
11	The elevator button for floor 7 is turned off.
12	The elevator doors open to allow User A to exit from the elevator.
13	The time starts.
User A exits from the elevator	
14	The elevator doors close after a time out.
15	The elevator proceeds to floor 9 with User B.

***Table 8.1**: The first iteration of a normal scenario*

Table 8.2 shows an exception scenario:

1	User A presses the Up-floor button at floor 3 to request an elevator. User A wishes to go to floor 1.
2	The Up-floor button is turned on.
3	An elevator arrives at floor 3. It contains User B, who entered the elevator at floor 1 and pressed the elevator button for floor 9.
4	The elevator doors open.
5	The time starts.
User A enters the elevator	
6	User A presses the elevator button for floor 1.
7	The elevator button for floor 1 is turned on.
8	The elevator doors close after a time out.
9	The Up-floor button is turned off.
10	The elevator travels to floor 9.
11	The elevator button for floor 9 is turned off.
12	The elevator doors open to allow User B to exit from the elevator.
13	The time starts.
User B exits from the elevator	
14	The elevator doors close after a time out.
15	The elevator proceeds to floor 1 with User A.

Table 8.2: *An exception scenario*

One method of determining the entity classes is to deduce them from the use cases. The developers carefully study the scenarios, both normal and exception, and identify the components that play a role in the use case. From the scenarios of *Tables 8.1 and 8.2*, candidate entity classes are elevator buttons, floor buttons, elevators, doors, and timers. These candidate entity classes are close to the actual classes extracted during entity class modeling. An experienced developer may be able to determine the candidate entity classes from the scenarios.

Another approach is to use noun extraction. The developers with no domain or expertise can use two-stage noun extraction methods to extract candidate entity classes and then refine the solution:

1. **Describe the software product in a single paragraph**: The elevator problem can be written as:

   Buttons in an elevator and on the floors control the movement of **n** elevators in a building with **m** floors. Buttons illuminate when pressed to request the elevator to stop at a specific floor; the illumination is canceled when the request has been satisfied. When an elevator has no requests, it remains on its current floor with its doors closed.

2. **Identify the nouns:** Identify the nouns in the informal strategy (excluding those that are outside the problem boundary, and then use these nouns as candidate entity classes.

   Buttons in the elevator and on the floors control the movement of **n** elevators in a building with **m** floors. Buttons illuminate when pressed to request the elevator to stop at a specific floor; the illumination is canceled when the request has been satisfied. When an elevator has no requests, it remains on its current floor with its doors closed. *Figure 8.5* shows the first iteration of the class diagram:

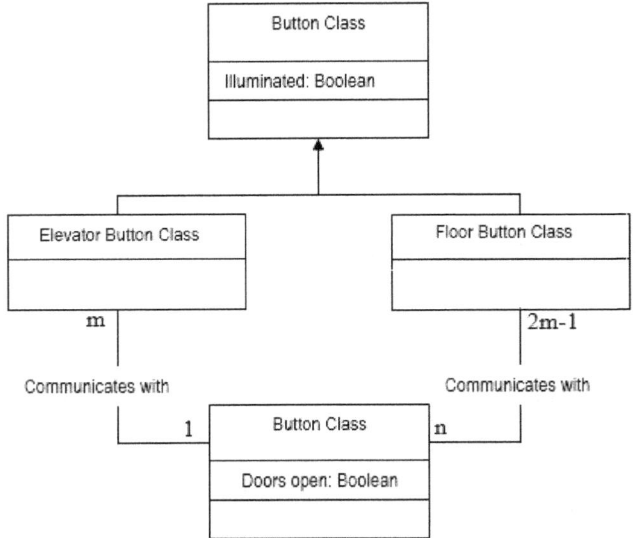

***Figure 8.5:** The first iteration of the class diagram*

There are eight different nouns, **button, elevator, floor, movement, building, illumination, request, and door**. The floor, building, and door lie outside the problem boundary and, therefore, may be ignored. Three of the remaining nouns, **movement, illumination, and request, are abstract nouns,** whose identity has no physical existence. A thumb rule is that abstract nouns rarely end up corresponding to classes. Instead, they frequently are attributes of classes. For example, illumination is an attribute of a button. This leaves two nouns and, therefore, two candidate classes, **Elevator Class** and **Button Class:**

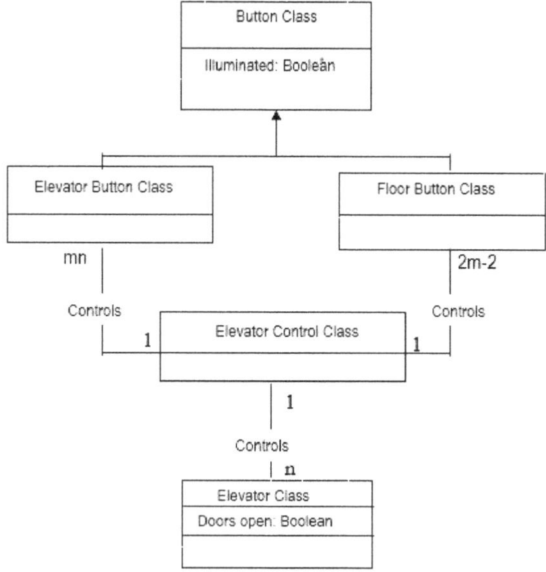

***Figure 8.6:** The second iteration of the class diagram*

In a real elevator, the buttons do not directly communicate with the elevator. An elevator controller is needed only to decide which elevator to dispatch in response to a particular request. Adding the **Elevator Control Class** to. There are now one-to-many relationships in *Figure 8.6* , as opposed to the *Figure 8.7* having a many-to-many relationship.

It, therefore, seems reasonable to go on to step 3 at this point, bearing in mind that it is possible to return to entity class modeling at any time, even as late as the implementation workflow.

Complete class diagram

Two additional operations (methods) are added (*Figure 8.7*) as they were in the Java implementation, adding two more classes. **Elevator Application Class** corresponds to the **C++ main function**, and **Elevator Utilities Class** contains Java routines that correspond to the C++ functions declared external to the C++ classes. The methods **closeDoor** and **openDoor** are assigned to the **Elevator Door Class**. That is, a client of the **Elevator Door Class** sends a message to an object of the elevator door class to close or open the doors of the elevator, and that request is then carried out by the relevant method.

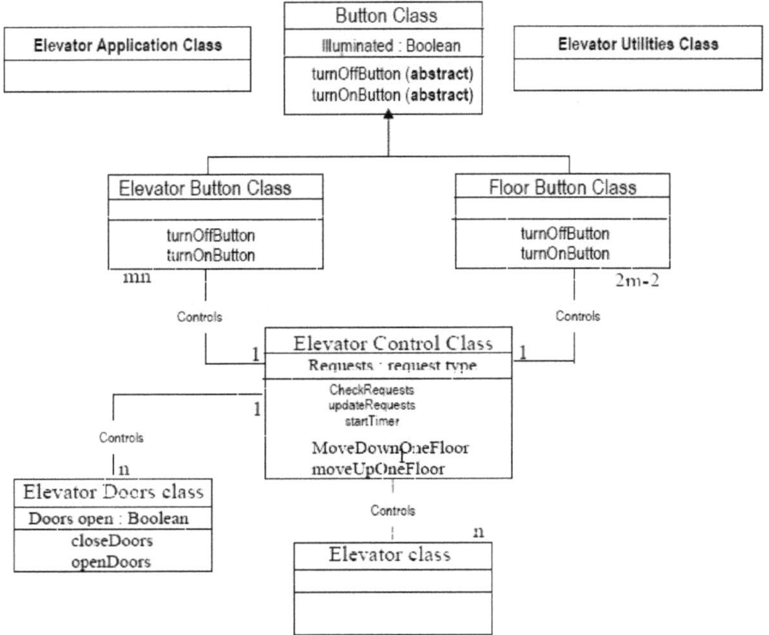

Figure 8.7: The detailed class diagram of the elevator problem

Every aspect of those two methods is encapsulated within the **Elevator Doors Class**. Also, information hiding results in a truly independent **Elevator Doors Class**, instances of which can undergo detailed design and implementation independently and be reused later in other products. The same two design principles are applied to methods **`moveDownOneFloor`**, and they are assigned to the **Elevator Class**. Finally, methods **`turnOnButton`** and **`turnOffButton`** are assigned to both **Elevator Button Class** and **Floor Button Class**. The reasoning here is the same as for the methods assigned to **Elevator Door Class** and **Elevator Class**.

State chart diagram

A **state chart diagram** in software engineering is a visual representation of an object's states and the transitions between those states in response to events. It is used to model the dynamic behavior of a system or object, showing how an object reacts to different events and how its state changes over time. Each state represents a specific condition of the object, and transitions illustrate how the system moves from one state to another based on specific triggers or conditions. State chart diagrams are particularly useful in modeling systems with complex life cycles, such as real-time or embedded systems.

State diagram

At any given time, an object is in a particular state. A person can be a newborn, infant, child, adolescent, teenager, or adult. An elevator is either moving or stationary. A washing machine can be either in the soaking, washing, rinsing, spinning, or off state. The UML state diagram shown in *Figure 8.8* captures this bit of reality. The figure shows that the washing machine transitions from one state to the next. The symbol at the top of the figure represents the start state, and the symbol at the bottom represents the end state:

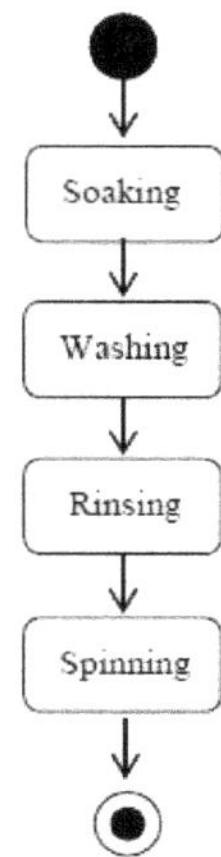

Figure 8.8: *The UML state diagram*

Interaction diagram or sequence diagram

Class diagrams and object diagrams represent static information. In a functioning system, however, objects interact with one another, and these interactions occur over time. The UML sequence diagram shows the time-based dynamics of the interaction. Continuing with the washing machine example, the components of the machine include a timer, a water pipe (for fresh water input), and a drum (the part that holds the clothes and the water). These, of course, are also objects (as you will see, an object can consist of other objects). UML creates diagrams describing the various aspects and uses of your application before you start coding, to ensure that you have everything. What happens when you invoke the **wash clothes** use case? Assuming you have completed the covered, **add clothes**, **add_detergent**, and **turn_on** operations, the sequence of steps goes something like the following:

1. At the beginning of **Soaking**, water enters the drum via the water pipe.
2. Remains stationary for five minutes.
3. At the end of **Soaking**, water stops entering the drum.
4. At the beginning of **Washing**, the drum rotates back and forth and continues doing this for 15 minutes.
5. At the end of **Washing**, the drum pumps out the soapy water.

6. The drum stops rotating.
7. At the beginning of **Rinsing**, water entry restarts.
8. The drum rotates back and forth.
9. After 15 minutes of water, entry stops.
10. At the end of **Rinsing**, the drum pumps out the rinse water.
11. The drum stops rotating.
12. At the beginning of **Spinning**, the drum rotates clockwise and continues for 5 minutes.
13. At the end of **Spinning**, the drum rotation stops.
14. The wash is done.

Imagine that the timer, the water pipe, and the drum are objects. Assume each object has one or more operations. The objects work together by sending messages to each other. Each message is a request from the sender-object to the receiver-object. The request asks the receiver to complete one of its (the receiver's) operations.

Let us get specific about the operations.

The timer can:

- Time the soaking
- Time the washing
- Time the rinsing
- Time the spinning

The water pipe can:

- Start a flow
- Stop a flow

The drum can:

- Store water
- Rotate back and forth
- Rotate clockwise
- Stop rotating
- Pump water

Figure 8.9 shows how to use these operations to create a sequence diagram that captures the timer, water pipe, drum, and drain represented as anonymous objects at the top of the diagram. Each arrow represents a message that goes from one object to another. Time, in this diagram, proceeds from top to bottom. So, the first message is **`timeSoak()`**, which the timer sends to itself. The second message is **`sendWater()`**, which the timer sends to the water pipe. The final message, **`stopRotating()`**, goes from the timer to the drum.

Collaboration diagram or communication diagram

A collaboration diagram has both properties of structural and behavioral views. Within a collaboration diagram, the example objects are shown in icons. As on a sequence diagram, arrows indicate the messages within the given use case. In this case, the sequence is indicated by numbering the messages. Numbering the messages makes it more difficult to see the sequence than putting the lines down the page. In this diagram, an object is also called a **collaborator**. The behavioral aspect is described by a set of messages exchanged among different collaborators. You can see, how the objects are linked together with solid lines to send messages between two objects. You can see the various forms of UML's object naming scheme (*Figure 8.9*). This takes the form `objectName:ClassName`, where the object name or the class name may be omitted.

Note: If you omit the object name, you must retain the colon, so that it is clear that it is the class name and not the object name.

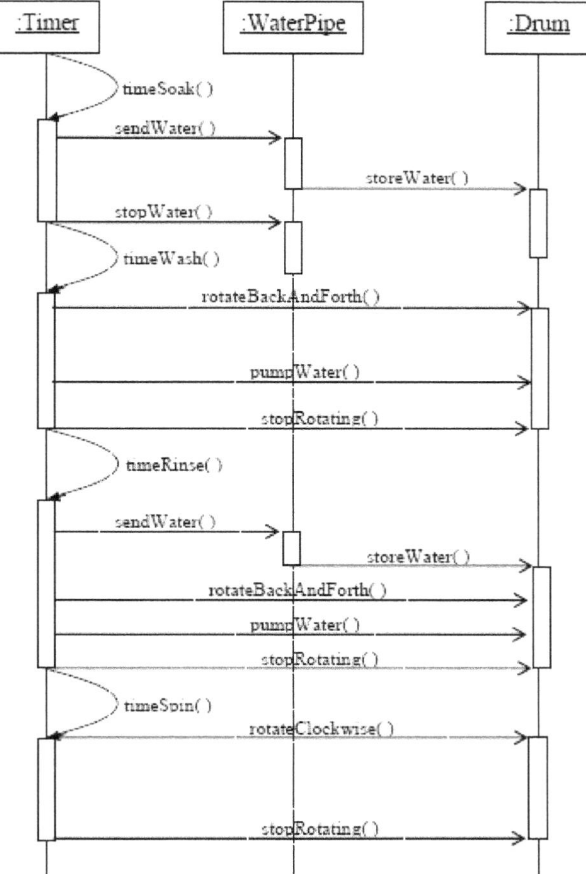

***Figure 8.9:** The UML sequence diagram*

Figure 8.10 shows the collaboration diagram for book renewal use case:

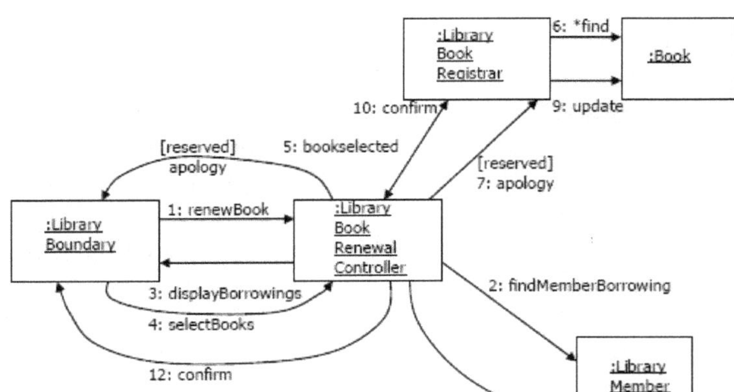

***Figure 8.10:** Collaboration diagram for book renewal use case*

Communication diagram

The elements of a system work together to accomplish the system's objectives, and a modeling language must have a way of representing this. The aforementioned sequence diagram does this. The UML communication diagram shown in *Figure 8.11* also does this but in a slightly different way. Rather than show you the communication diagram that is equivalent to the sequence diagram in *Figure 8.10, Figure 8.11* shows you one that captures just the first few messages among the timer, the water pipe, and the drum. Rather than represent time in the vertical dimension, this diagram shows the order of messages by attaching a number to the message label:

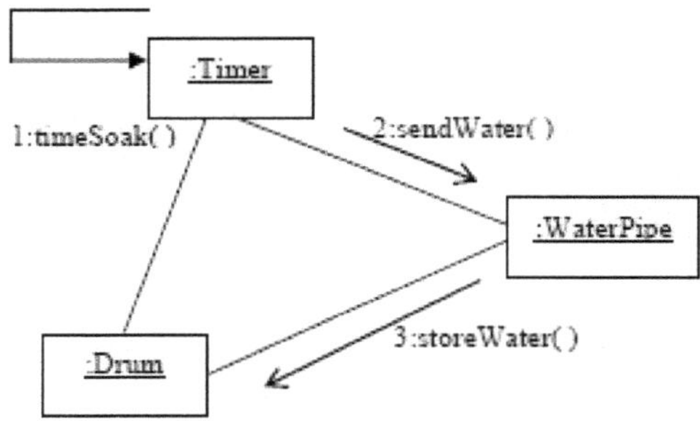

***Figure 8.11:** The UML communication diagram*

The **communication diagram** shows the interaction among objects, but it does so in a way that is slightly different from the sequence diagram. In the sequence diagram, the communication diagram shows how objects interact. It shows the objects along with the messages that travel from one object to another. So, now you may be asking yourself, *If the sequence diagram does that, why does the UML need another gram? Do they not do the same thing? Is this just overkill?*

The two types of diagrams are similar. In fact, they are semantically equivalent. That is, they present the same information, and you can turn a sequence diagram into an equivalent communication diagram and vice versa.

As it turns out, it is helpful to have both forms. The sequence diagram emphasizes the time ordering of interactions. The communication diagram emphasizes the context and overall of the objects that interact. Here is another way to look at the distinction, the sequence diagram is arranged according to time, and the communication diagram is according to space. Both deal with interactions among objects, and for that reason, each one is a type of interaction diagram.

Communication diagram

An **object diagram** shows objects and their relationships with one another. A **communication diagram** is an extension of the object diagram. In addition to the links among objects, the communication diagram shows the messages, the objects send each other. You usually omit the names of the links because they would add clutter.

One way to think of the relationship between the object diagram and the communication diagram is to imagine the difference between a snapshot and a movie. The object diagram is the snapshot, it shows how instances of classes are linked together in an instant of time (**Instants and instances**). The communication diagram is the movie, it shows interactions among those instances over time.

To represent a message, you draw an arrow near the link between two objects. The arrow points to the receiving object. A label near the arrow shows what the message is. The message typically tells the receiving object to execute one of its (the receiver's) operations. Arrowheads have the same meaning as in the sequence diagram shown in the following figure:

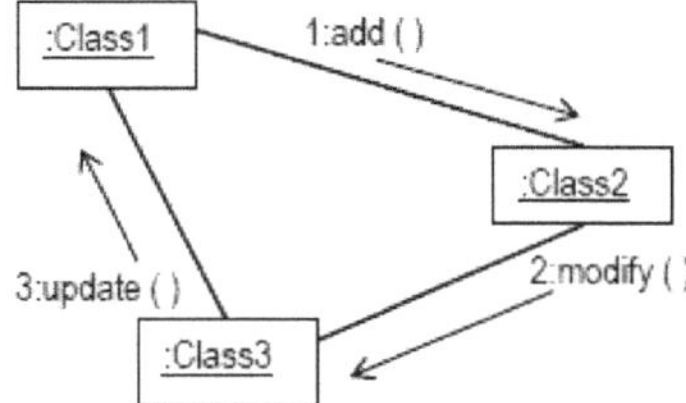

Figure 8.12: *The symbol set for the communication diagram*

To represent a message, you can turn any sequence diagram into a communication diagram, and vice versa. Thus, you have to be able to represent sequential information in a communication diagram. To do this, you add a number to the label of a message, with the number and uses of your application before you start coding, to ensure that you have everything corresponding to the message's order in the sequence. A colon separates the number from the message.

You might be familiar with the kind of car key that allows you to remotely lock and unlock a car. It also lets you open the car's trunk. If you have one of these keys, you know what happens when you push the **lock** button. The car locks itself, and then it blinks its lights and beeps to let you know it is finished locking its doors.

Let us capture all this in a class diagram. *Figure 8.13* shows the relationships among the **CarOwner**, **Car**, and **CarKey** classes, as well as some other concepts. The car processes a message from the key and causes the appropriate behavior to take place.

Notice a couple of things about this diagram. In the **CarKey** class, it shows the signature of **getButtonPress()**. This operation works with a button name (**lock**, **unlock**, or **openTrunk**). The idea is that the **Car** receives a message from the **CarKey**, processes that message, and implements the operation corresponding to the name of the pressed button.

The figure also shows the two signals, **BlinkLights** and **Beep**. You model a signal as a class with the keyword **«signal»** added. The dependency arrows between **Car** and each signal show that the **Car** sends these signals. Once again, the UML has no symbol for sending, so you add the keyword **«send»** to the dependency arrow.

Note: The CarOwner class shows something you have not seen before in a class icon, the two occurrences of the «signal» keyword. These show you that CarOwner is capable of receiving these signals. The signals do not request the CarOwner to do anything. This is because the Car (the sender) is not making a request when it sends those signals, it certainly is not waiting for the CarOwner to do anything. Hence, the sequence diagram uses the asynchronous message symbol to model signals.

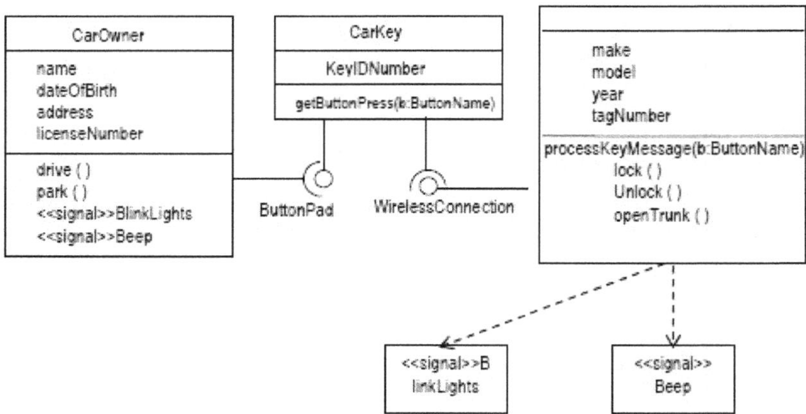

Figure 8.13: The relationship among CarOwner, CarKey and Car

A **communication diagram** in software engineering is a type of interaction diagram that visually represents how objects in a system interact through message exchanges. It emphasizes the flow of communication between objects and the order in which messages are passed, helping developers understand the dynamic behavior of a system during runtime. This diagram is useful for analyzing and designing object interactions in a clear and structured manner.

This diagram appears in *Figure 8.14* and is the foundation for a communication diagram:

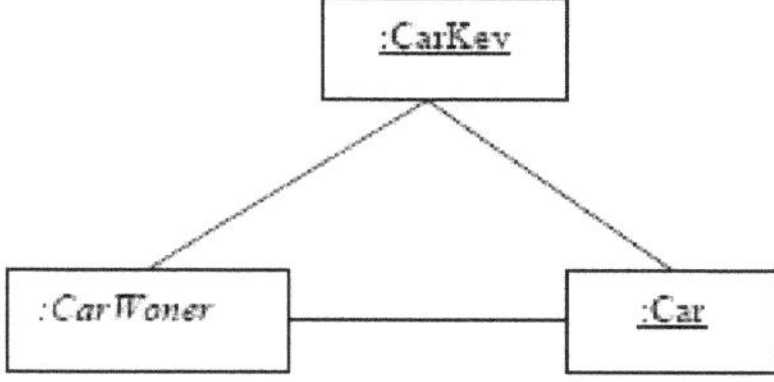

Figure 8.14: *An object diagram that models instances of the classes*

Now, you can add messages to *Figure 8.14*. *Figure 8.15* shows one way of dealing with multiple messages that pass between two objects. As you can see, messages 4 and 5 are signals that go from the `Car` to the `CarOwner`. They have separate labels but not separate arrows.

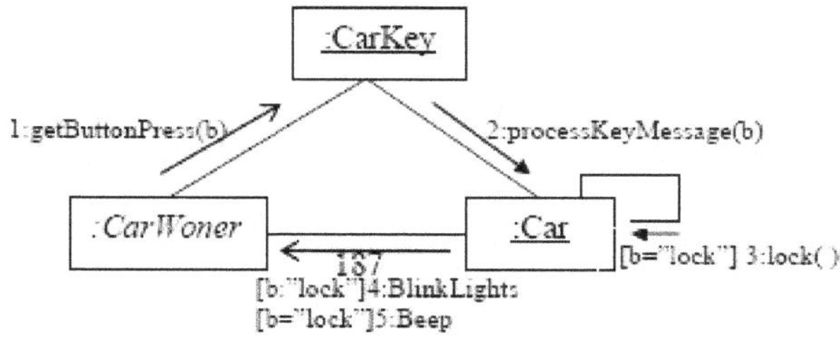

Figure 8.15: *Communication diagram with messages between objects*

The corresponding sequence diagram is shown in *Figure 8.16*, where the messages are sent from lifeline to lifeline. The first message (the one highest in the vertical dimension) is a request from `CarOwner` to `CarKey`. The request is for `CarKey` to implement its `getKeyPress()` operation, registering the button the `CarOwner` has pressed (generically referred to as b). The stick arrowhead indicates that `CarOwner` is transferring control to `CarKey`. `CarKey` then sends a message to the car, calling on the car to implement its `processKeyMessage()` operation, depending on the specified button. After it processes the message from `CarKey`, `Car` sends itself a message to implement the operation that corresponds to the pressed button.

Note: The expression in the bracket, that is a guard condition. It is the UML's way of saying "if". So, if the pressed button is "locked", the car sends itself a request to carry out the `lock ()` operation. Then the car sends a message to `CarOwner` to blink the lights or beep the light. The first message and the signals are examples of the two usages of the stick arrowhead.

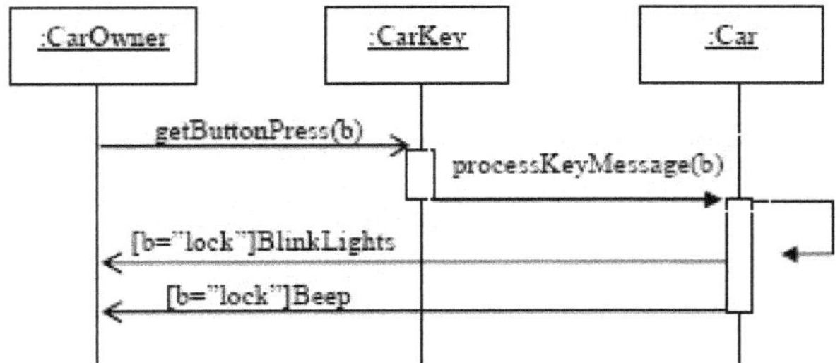

Figure 8.16: The equivalent sequence diagram

Changing states and nesting messages

Suppose, the car has an attribute, locked, whose values are either true or false. Thinking that, **working with state diagrams**, you can imagine two states, locked and unlocked for the car, as shown in *Figure 8.17:*

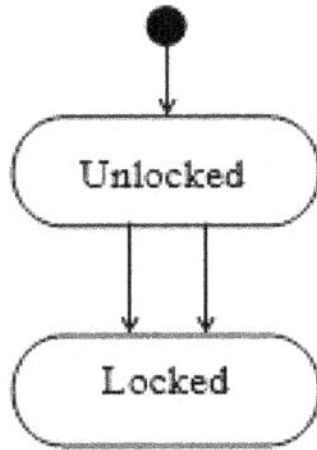

Figure 8.17: Modeling the unlocked and locked states of a car

You can show a change of state in a communication diagram. To do that in this example, *Figure 8.18,* you show the value of **locked** in the car object. Then, you duplicate the car object with the new value of locked. Connect the two, and then show a message going from the first to the second. Label the message with the keyword **<<become>>**:

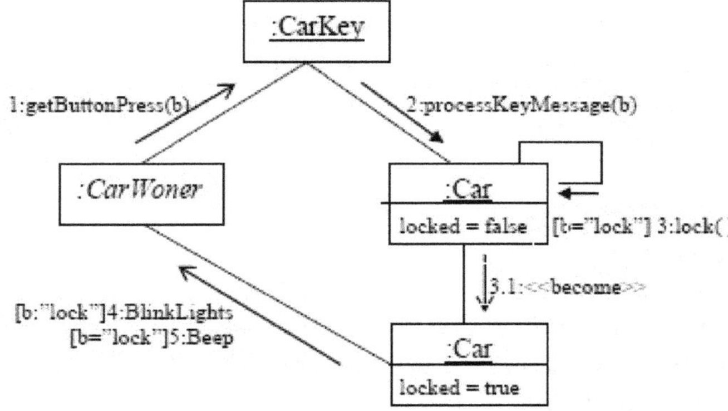

Figure 8.18: Modeling state changes in a communication diagram

Activity diagram

The activities that occur within a use case or an object's behavior typically occur in a sequence, as in the steps listed in the preceding subsection. *Figure 8.19* shows how the UML activity diagram represents the steps of that sequence:

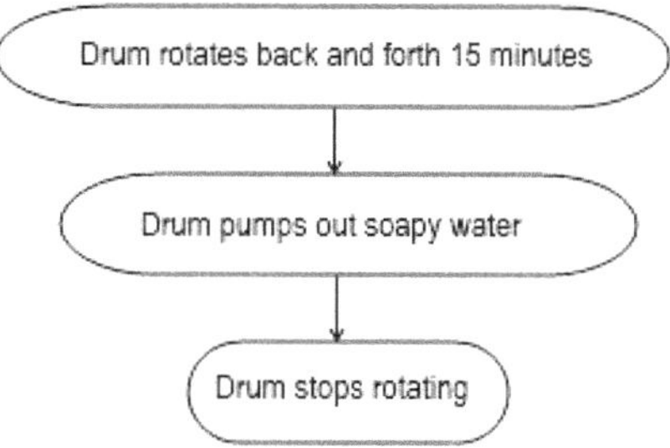

Figure 8.19: *The UML activity diagram*

A **UML activity diagram** is a behavioral diagram in software engineering that visually represents the flow of activities or tasks within a system. It models dynamic aspects such as workflows, processes, and the sequence of operations, providing a clear view of how the system behaves from start to finish. This helps in understanding complex logic and improving process clarity in system design:

- **Activity diagram:** UML activity diagram, *Figure 8.19* is much like the flowcharts of old. It includes steps (called, appropriately enough, activities) as well as decision points and branches. It is useful for showing what happens in a business process or operation. You will find it an integral part of system analysis. First and foremost, an activity diagram is designed to be a simplified look at what happens during an operation or a process.

  Each activity is represented by a rounded rectangle, narrower and more oval, shaped than the state icon you saw in *working with state diagrams*. The processing within an activity goes to completion, and then an automatic transmission to the next activity occurs. An arrow represents the transition from one activity to the next. Like the state diagram, the activity diagram is a starting point represented by a filled-in circle and an endpoint represented by a bull's eye shown in *Figure 8.20*:

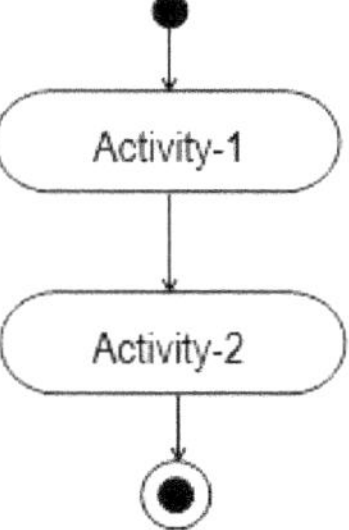

Figure 8.20: *Transitioning from one activity to another*

A sequence of activities almost always comes to a point where a decision has to take place. One set of conditions leads to one path, another set of conditions to another path, and the two paths are mutually exclusive.

You can represent a decision point in either of two ways, one way is to show the possible paths coming directly out of an activity, and the other is to have the activity transition to a small diamond, reminiscent of the decision symbol in a flowchart, and have the possible paths flow out of the diamond. Either way, you indicate the condition with a bracketed condition statement near the appropriate path. *Figure 8.21* shows you the possibilities:

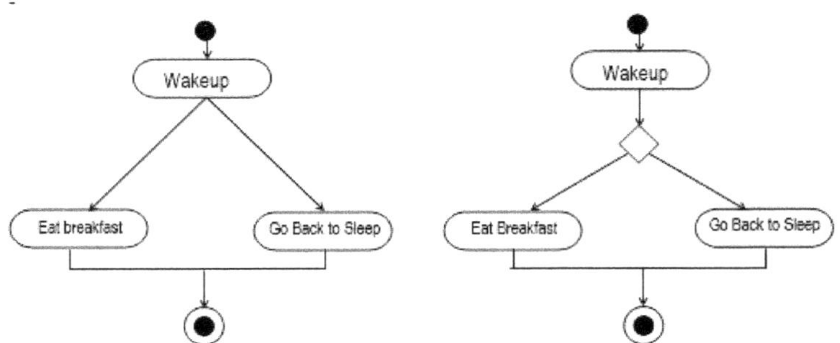

Figure 8.21: *The two ways of showing a decision*

- **Concurrent paths**: As you model activities, you will occasionally have to separate a transition into two separate paths that run at the same time (that is, concurrently) and then come together. To represent split, you use a solid bold line perpendicular to the transition and show the paths coming out of the line. To represent the merge, show the paths pointing at another solid bold line (see *Figure 8.22*):

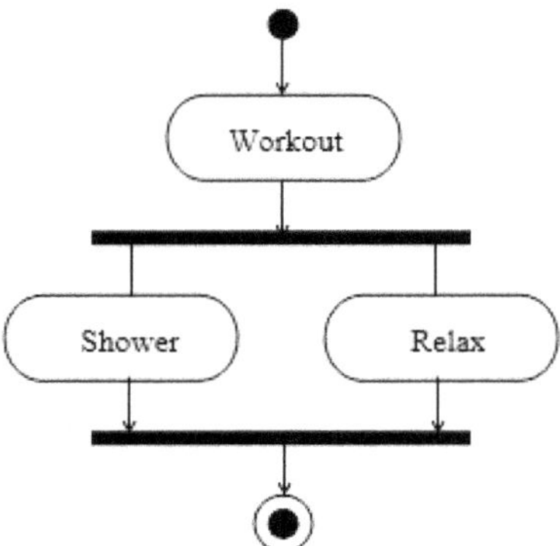

Figure 8.22: *Representing a transition split into two paths that run concurrently and then come together*

- **Signals:** During a sequence of activities, it is possible to send a signal. When received, the signal causes an activity to take place. The symbol for sending a signal is a convex polygon, and the symbol for receiving a signal is a concave polygon. *Figure 8.23* will clarify this:

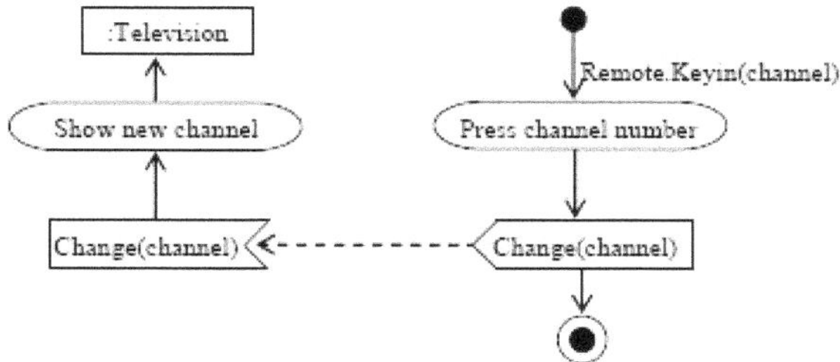

Figure 8.23: *Sending and receiving a signal*

Figure 8.24 shows an activity diagram for the process of creating a document.

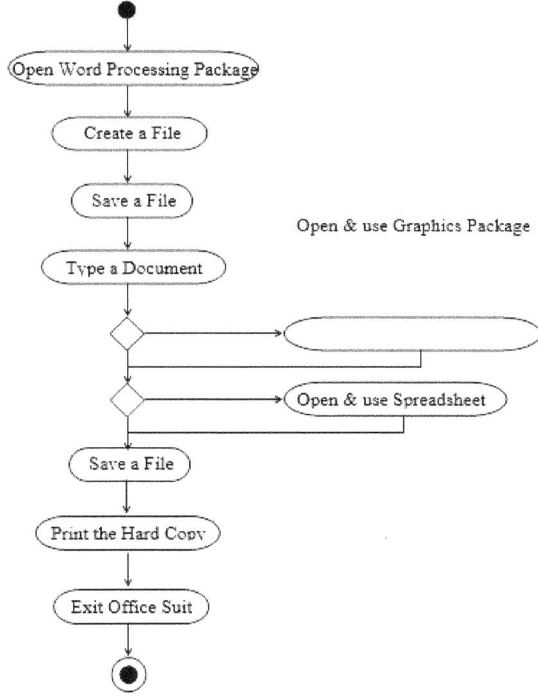

Figure 8.24: *An activity diagram for the process of creating a document*

During a sequence of activities, it is possible to send a signal. When received, the signal causes an activity to take place. The symbol for sending a signal is a convex polygon, and the symbol for receiving a signal is a concave polygon. *Figure 8.23* will clarify this. In UML terms, the convex polygon symbolizes an output event; the concave polygon symbolizes an input event.

Applying activity diagrams

Let us look at an example that uses an activity diagram to model a process.

A process for creating a document:

1. Open the word processing package.
2. Create a file.
3. Save the file under a unique name within its directory.
4. Type the document.
5. If graphics are necessary, open the graphics package, create the graphics, and paste the graphics into the document.
6. If a spreadsheet is necessary, open the spreadsheet package, create a spreadsheet, and paste the spreadsheet into the document.
7. Save the file.
8. Print the hard copy of the document.
9. Exit the office suit.

The **activity diagram** for this sequence is in *Figure 8.24*.

Component diagram

This diagram and the next one move away from the world of washing machines because the **component diagram** and the **deployment diagram** are geared expressly toward computer systems. Modern software development proceeds via components, which is particularly important in team-based development efforts. Without elaborating too much at this point, *Figure 8.25* shows how the **UML version 1.x** represents a software component:

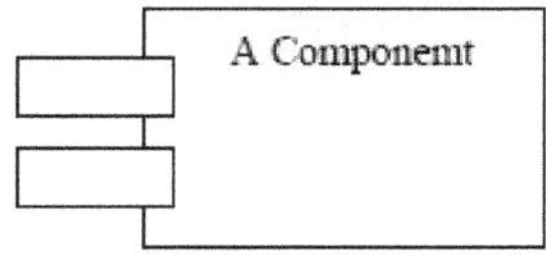

Figure 8.25: *The software component icon in UML 1.x.*

The **UML 2.0** makes an entry here. In response to the many modelers who felt this symbol as awkward, UML 2.0 provides a revised symbol. *Figure 8.26* shows the new way to represent a software component.

A software component is a modular part of a system. This is because it is the software implementation of one or more classes, a component resides in a computer, not in the mind of an analyst. A component provides interfaces to other components.

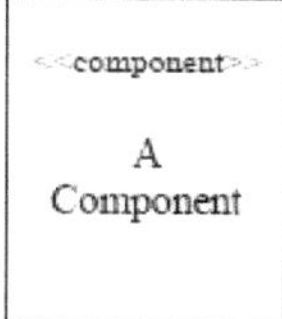

Figure 8.26: The software component icon in UML 2.0

In **UML 1.x**, data files, tables, executables, documents, and dynamic link libraries were defined as components. Modelers are used to classify these kinds of items as deployment components, work product components, and execution components. UML 2.0 refers to them instead as artifacts, pieces of information that a system uses or produces.

A component, by contrast, defines a system's functionality. When you deal with components, you have to deal with their interfaces. The object has to present a **face** to the outside world so that other objects (including, potentially, humans) can ask the object to execute its operations. This face is the object's interface.

In UML 1.x, the component diagram's main icon is a rectangle that has two rectangles overlaid on its left side. Many modelers found the 1.x symbol too cumbersome, particularly when they had to show a connection to the left side. For this reason, UML 2.0 provides a new component icon. In UML 2.0, the icon is a rectangle with the keyword **«component»** near the top. For continuity over the near-term, you can include the 1.x icon inside the 2.0 icon. *Figure 8.27* shows these icons:

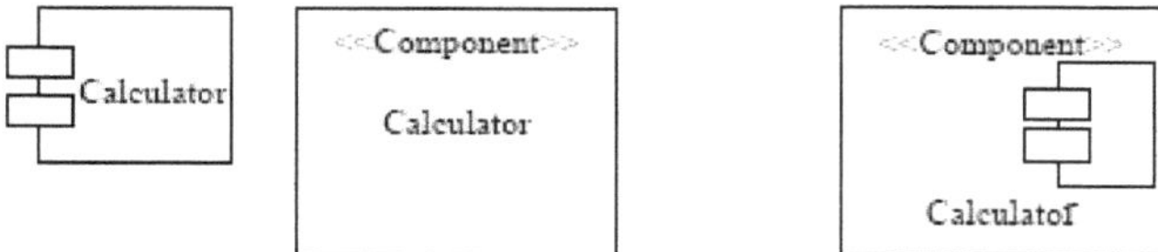

***Figure 8.27:** The component icon in UML 1.x and the two versions of the component icon in UML 2.0*

A **component diagram** contains, appropriately enough, components, along with interfaces and relationships. Other types of symbols that you have already seen can also appear in a component diagram. *Figure 8.28* shows that if the component is a member of a package, you can prefix the component's name with the name of the package. You can also show the component's operations in a separate panel.

Speaking of artifacts, *Figure 8.29* shows a couple of ways to represent them, and it also shows how to model the relationship between a particular kind of artifact (an executable) and the component it implements. As you can see, you can place a notation symbol in the artifact on, analogous to the UML 1.x component symbol in the component icon, and use your application before you start coding, to ensure that you have everything covered.

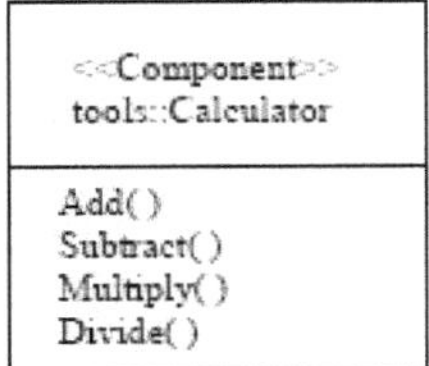

Figure 8.28: *Adding information to the component icon*

Figure 8.29 shows modeling the relationship between an artifact and a component:

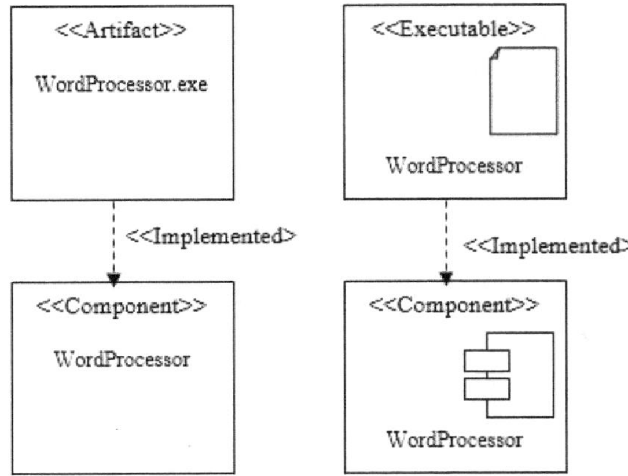

Figure ***8.29****: Modeling the relationship between an artifact and a component*

A **component** and the **interface,** of its realization can be represented in two ways. The first shows the interface as a rectangle that contains interface-related information. It is connected to the component by the dashed line and large open triangle that indicate realization. (See *Figure 8.30*)

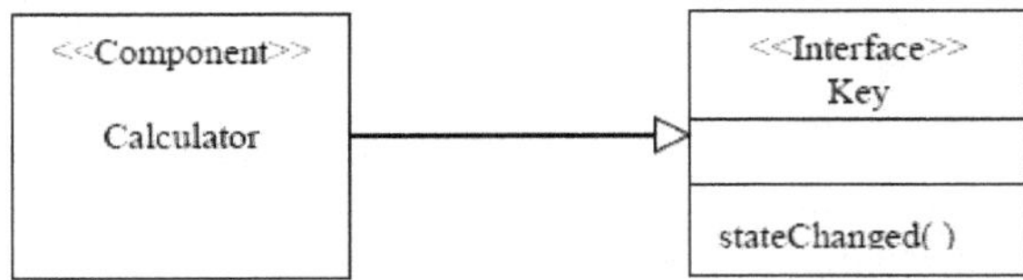

Figure 8.30: *Interface as a rectangle*

Figure 8.31 shows the second way. It is ironic that you represent the interface as a small circle connected to the component by a solid line.

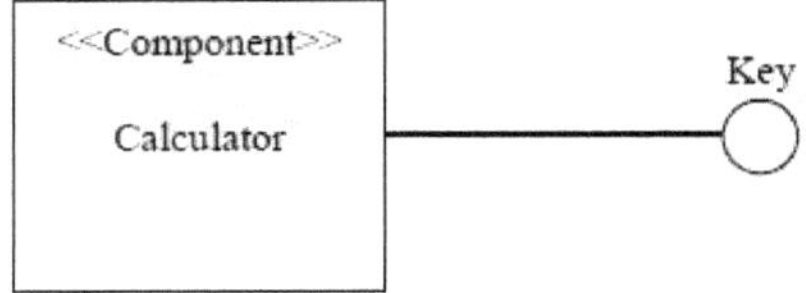

Figure 8.31: *You can represent an interface as a small circle connected to the component by a solid line*

In addition to realization, you can represent dependency. The relationship between a component and an interface through which it accesses another component. As you will recall, the dependency is visualized as a dashed line with an arrowhead. You can show realization and dependency on the same figure, as shown in *Figure 8.32*. The figure shows the equivalent ball-and-socket notation. The **ball** represents a provided interface, and the **socket** represents a required interface:

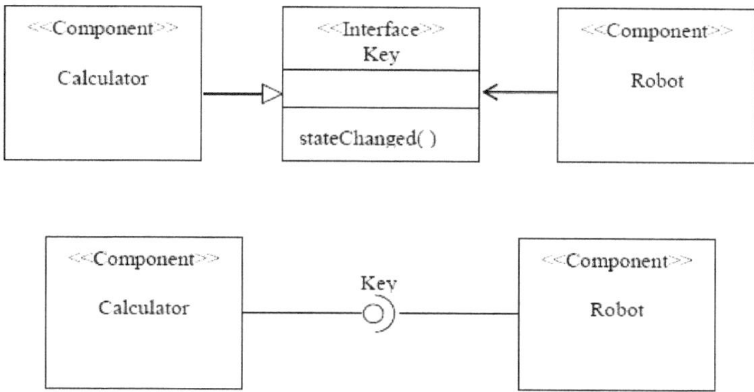

Figure 8.32: *Two ways of showing realization and dependency in the same diagram*

When you model a component's interfaces, as in *Figure 8.32*, you show what UML calls an external, or **black box**, view. You also have the option of showing an internal, or **white box**, view. This view shows interfaces listed inside the component icon and organized by keywords. *Figure 8.33* shows a white box view of the components in *Figure 8.32*:

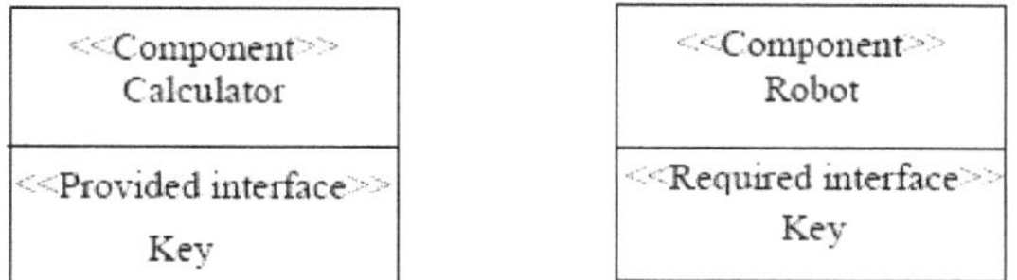

Figure 8.33: *A white box view of the components*

Deployment diagram

The UML deployment diagram shows the physical architecture of a computer-based system. It can depict the computers, show their connections with one another, and show the software that sits on each machine. Each computer is represented as a cube, with interconnections between computers drawn as lines connecting the cubes. *Figure 8.34* presents an example:

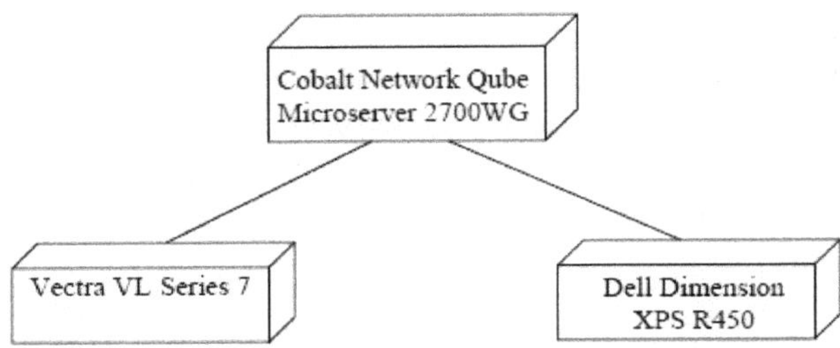

***Figure 8.34:** The UML deployment diagram*

A deployment diagram shows how artifacts (which you met in **working with component diagrams**) are deployed on system hardware, and how the pieces of hardware connect. The main hardware item is a node, a generic name for a computing.

In **UML 1.x**, many modelers (including me) distinguished between two types of nodes, a **processor** (a node that can execute a component) and a **device** (a peripheral piece of hardware that does not execute components but typically interfaces in some way with the outside world). Although that distinction was not formalized in UML 1.x, it was useful.

UML 2.0, now, formally defines a device as a node that executes artifacts (an executable is now classified as an artifact). In UML 2 .0, a cube represents a node (as was the case in UML 1.x). You supply a name for the node, and you can add the keyword **«Device»**, although it is usually not necessary. It is a good idea to distinguish between devices and peripherals, as you will see. *Figure 8.35* shows a node:

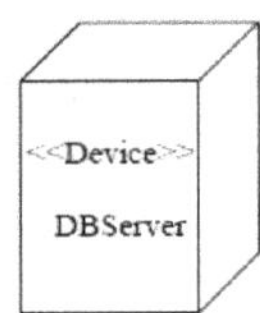

***Figure 8.35:** Representing a node in the UML*

Figure 8.36 shows three ways to model the artifacts deployed on a node:

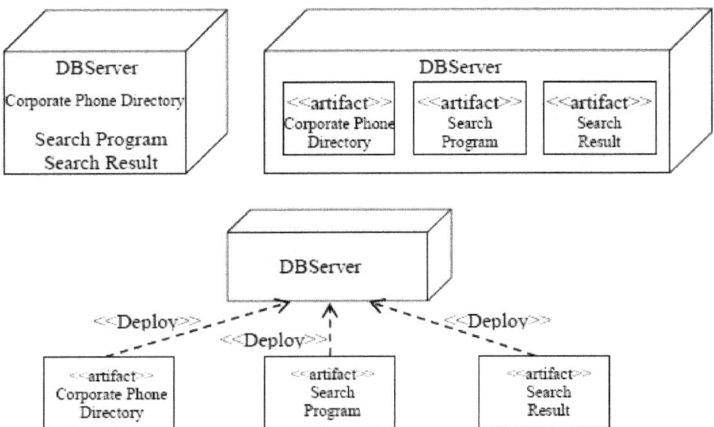

***Figure 8.36:** Three ways to model the deployment of artifacts on a node*

A line joining two cubes represents a connection between two nodes. Bear in mind that a connection is not necessarily a piece of wire or cable. You can also represent wireless connections, such as infrared and satellite. *Figure 8.37* shows an example of an inter-node connection:

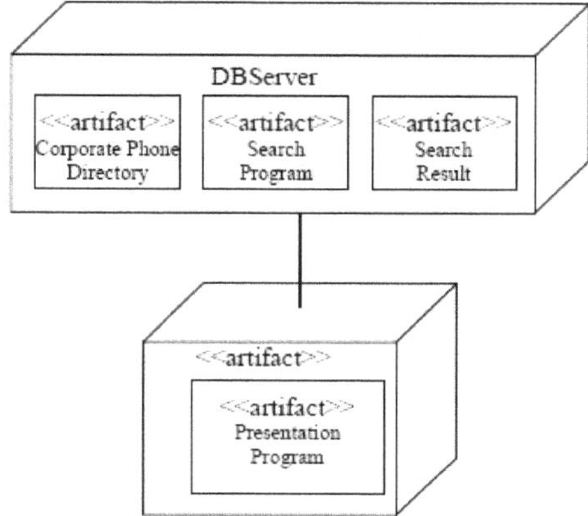

***Figure 8.37:** Representing the connection between nodes*

UML 2.0's emphasis on artifacts brings a set of new artifact-related concepts. One of these concepts is the deployment specification, an artifact that provides parameters for another artifact. A good example of this is the initialization command that some modem connections require. This is a string of characters that sets values for certain characteristics of the modem. *Figure 8.38* shows how to model a deployment specification:

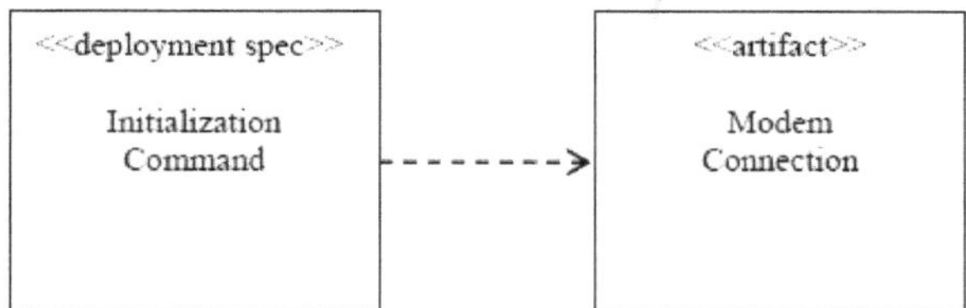

***Figure 8.38:** Representing a deployment specification and its relationship with an artifact it parameterizes*

For clarity, one could add the keyword **«parameterize»** to the arrow, although this keyword does not come with UML 2.0, it is not part of the UML specification.

Conceptual sample project

In modern food service businesses, online food ordering systems have become essential for restaurants to manage orders efficiently. This case study presents a structured approach to designing a **Use Case Diagram** for an **Online Food Ordering System**, demonstrating how different users interact with the system to perform various tasks.

1. **Project specification**

   The **Online Food Ordering System** allows customers to **browse menus, place orders, make payments, and track deliveries** while enabling restaurant administrators to **manage menus, process orders, and oversee deliveries**. The goal is to streamline the order management process, ensure customer satisfaction, and provide a seamless user experience.

2. **Project analysis**

   The system consists of different types of users, each with distinct roles and interactions:

   - **Customer**: Can **browse the menu, add items to the cart, place an order, make a payment, track the order**, and provide feedback.
   - **Restaurant Admin**: Manages the **menu, updates prices, processes orders, and oversees order status**.
   - **Delivery partner**: Accepts assigned deliveries, updates delivery status, and completes order handovers.
   - **System**: Sends real-time **notifications, payment confirmations, and order status updates**.

   The key **functional use cases** identified are:

   - **User authentication**: Customers, admins, and delivery partners must log in to access functionalities.
   - **Menu management**: Admins update food items, categories, and pricing.
   - **Order processing**: Customers place orders, and admins confirm and prepare them.
   - **Payment handling**: The system supports multiple payment options like credit/debit cards, UPI, and wallets.
   - **Delivery management**: Orders are assigned to delivery partners for tracking and fulfillment.

3. **Project Design (Use Case Diagram)**

   The **Use Case Diagram** visually represents user interactions with the system. It consists of **actors (users)**, **use cases (functions)**, and their relationships.

   Key Components of the use case diagram

   - **Actors**:
     - Customer
     - Restaurant admin
     - Delivery partner
     - Payment system (External system)

- **Use cases**:
  - **Customer actions**: Register or Login, Browse Menu, Add to Cart, Place Order, Make Payment, Track Order, Provide Feedback.
  - **Restaurant admin Actions**: Manage Menu, Update Prices, Process Orders, Assign Delivery.
  - **Delivery partner actions**: Accept Delivery, Update Status, Confirm Order Delivery.
  - **System actions**: Send Notifications, Process Payments.

If certain **design constraints** arise (e.g., customers requesting order modifications after placement), the system needs to accommodate such changes through an **order modification** use case.

4. **Project Implementation**

   Once the **use case interactions** are finalized, the development team starts implementing each functionality.

   - The **customer interface (mobile app or website)** is developed using frameworks like **React, Angular**, or **Flutter**.
   - The **backend system (Spring Boot, Node.js, or Django)** handles user authentication, order processing, and menu management.
   - The **database (PostgreSQL or MongoDB)** stores user details, orders, and payments.
   - The **payment gateway (Stripe, PayPal, Razorpay, etc.)** is integrated to process transactions securely.

   During testing, if an issue is detected—such as a payment failure not updating the order status—modifications are made to improve system reliability.

5. **Maintenance**

   Once the system is deployed, continuous monitoring ensures smooth operation. If a restaurant introduces **dynamic pricing** (e.g., discounts during non-peak hours), modifications to the **menu management use case** are needed. Regular updates include **UI enhancements, security patches, and feature expansions** based on customer feedback.

Table 8.3 gives a comparative study of the **object-oriented (OO)** approach and **module-oriented** (MO) approach:

	Object-oriented approach	Module-oriented approach
1	In this approach, a system is seen as a collection of objects, each with a functional purpose. These objects are interconnected to achieve a common objective.	In this approach, a system is seen as a set of functions, data and processes and their interrelationship.
2	It facilitates easy maintenance of the system and at a low cost. This is because a change in algorithms used by an object does not affect other objects.	Maintenance is a costlier affair in this approach. Proper and detailed documentation is needed for modification of the system.
3	Repairing faults in the system is much easier in this approach.	Repairing faults may require changes in more than one module. Also, fault identification is difficult.
4	Since objects can be reused in different applications, it promotes reuse of code in large systems.	The reuse of code is limited and infrequent.
5	It is simpler to implement in distributed systems since independent objects communicate through messages. One object can invoke methods of some other object located on a remote computer.	Difficult to implement in distributed systems.
6	Ideal for fully exploiting object technologies like C++, Java, CORBA, GUI, COM, DCOM, etc.	Not as efficient as OO tools and techniques in implementing new technologies.
7	This leads to systems that are more flexible to change.	Leads to less flexible systems.
8	Performance and start-up costs are greater. This is because the cost is involved in sending a message from one object to another. Developers have to start from scratch in the initial stage of OO system development.	Initial costs and overheads are not so high. Trained manpower is available at a cheaper price.
9	Ideal for large systems.	Ideal for small systems.

Table 8.3: *Comparison of the OO and MO approach for system design*

Conclusion

The object-oriented modeling approach is becoming more and more popular since it allows you to model a real-world application, both in terms of data and process, using a common underlying representation. The seamless nature of the transitions that an object-oriented model undergoes from analysis to design to implementation has been discussed. We have discussed the concept of object-oriented programming with different terminology. How to use different types of UML models has been discussed. The requirement analysis model is developed using use-case diagrams. The use-case diagram shows the interaction between external actors and actions performed within the system. How to model the static structure of objects in the problem domain using class diagrams is discussed. Objects having both states (conditions) and behavior (operations) are encapsulated. Associations exist between objects, like entity relationships, which are discussed. A state diagram for capturing the dynamic state transitions in an object is discussed. State transitions occur when events trigger changes in an object. Also, a detailed elaboration has been made on how to develop a dynamic model of interactions among objects using a sequence diagram. A sequence diagram shows the passing of messages between objects. Messages activate operations within objects, causing the system to perform the desired functions.

In the next chapter, readers will explore the principles and best practices for designing user interfaces and dialogues, ensuring intuitive and user-friendly interactions within a system. They will also delve into database design, learning how to structure data efficiently to support system performance, integrity, and scalability. This chapter will cover key aspects such as interface usability, dialogue structuring, normalization techniques, and database modeling, providing a comprehensive understanding of how front-end design and data management work together to create seamless and efficient software systems.

Exercises

To solidify your understanding of the concepts covered in this chapter, try the following exercises.

Multiple choice questions

1. **Objects are:**
    a. Tangible entities
    b. Intangible entities
    c. None of these
    d. Both (a) and (b)
2. **A class is a:**
    a. Group of objects
    b. Template for objects of a particular type
    c. Class of objects
    d. Classification of objects

3. In object-oriented design:

a. Operations and methods are identical

b. Methods specify algorithms, whereas operations only state what is to be done

c. Methods do not change the values of attributes

d. Methods and constructors are the same

4. By encapsulation, we mean:

a. Encapsulating data and programs

b. Hiding attributes of an object from users

c. Hiding operations on an object from users

d. Hiding implementation details of methods from users of objects

5. Encapsulation in object modeling is useful as:

a. It allows improving methods of an object independent of other parts of the system

b. It hides implementation details of methods

c. It allows easy designing

d. Encapsulates attributes and operations of an object

6. An object is selected for modeling, if:

a. Its attributes are invariant during the operation of the system

b. Its attributes change during the operation of the system

c. It has numerous attributes

d. It has no attributes relevant to the system

7. Inheritance in object modeling can be used to:

a. Generalize classes

b. Specialize classes

c. Generalize and specialize classes

d. Create new classes

8. Objects may be viewed as

a. Clients in a system

b. Servers in a system

c. As both clients and servers in a system

d. Neither as both clients nor as servers in a system

9. The advantages of object-oriented modeling are claimed by some like the following:

a. It allows easy integration of sub-systems

b. It promotes the reuse of code

c. It allows the modification of some objects by other objects

d. It allows data structures in objects to be modified by other objects.

10. In the UML diagram of a class:

a. State of an object cannot be represented

b. State is irrelevant

c. The state is represented as an attribute

d. The state is represented as a result of the operation

Short questions

1. What is information hiding?
2. What are off-the-self components?
3. What are data objects?
4. What is an attribute?
5. What is cardinality?
6. What is procedural abstraction?
7. What is data abstraction?
8. What is the operation? Name different types of operations.
9. What is an object-oriented analysis?
10. Define modeling.
11. What are the characteristics according to which classes can be categorized?
12. What is unified modeling language?
13. What is the class diagram?
14. Define association. Name two types of associations.
15. What are the primary benefits of object-oriented architecture?
16. What is a component system?
17. Define façade.
18. List the diagrams supported by UML.

Essay questions

1. List the different programming paradigms.
2. Illustrate the role of CASE tools in system analysis and design.
3. Compare and contrast the module-oriented and object-oriented approach to system analysis and design.
4. Define the terms inheritance and polymorphism. Give suitable examples.
5. Define object modeling.

Multiple choice answers

1. d
2. b
3. b
4. d
5. a
6. b
7. c
8. c
9. a
10. c

CHAPTER 9

Designing Interfaces and Dialogues and Database Design

Introduction

Designing interfaces and dialogues and **database design** are critical components in software engineering, shaping the user experience and ensuring data integrity. The design of interfaces and dialogues focuses on how users interact with a system, emphasizing usability, accessibility, and intuitive navigation. A well-designed interface improves user satisfaction and system efficiency by providing clear, logical pathways for interaction. Dialogue design ensures effective communication between the user and the system, making tasks easier to complete. On the other hand, database design deals with organizing and structuring data to support efficient storage, retrieval, and management. A robust database design ensures data consistency, integrity, and scalability, enabling systems to handle large volumes of information without performance degradation. It involves the creation of entity-relationship models, normalization of data, and defining relationships between data entities. Together, interface design and database design contribute to the overall functionality, user experience, and long-term sustainability of software systems.

Structure

- User interface design
- Interaction method and devices
- Interface design

- Database design
- Entity-relation diagram

Objectives

This chapter aims to explore the essential aspects of designing effective interfaces, dialogues, and databases in software systems. It examines how information is provided to and captured from users, ensuring seamless interaction between the user and the system. The chapter delves into the sequences of interface displays and the logical flow required for an intuitive user experience. Additionally, it outlines key rules for designing user-friendly interfaces and dialogues, emphasizing clarity and efficiency. Furthermore, it covers navigation between forms and reports, highlighting the deliverables necessary for smooth transitions. The chapter also addresses the system's data requirements while using interfaces, databases, forms, and reports, focusing on how to structure and manage this data effectively. **Entity relationship** (**ER**) diagrams, along with graphical notations, will be used to visually represent the relationships and interactions between data entities within the system. Through these concepts, this chapter aims to equip readers with the knowledge needed to design efficient, user-centric software systems. The ER data models represent a conceptual view of the organizational data independence of any particular database processing technology. We will learn about structuring the description of data through logical data modeling.

The purpose of logical data modeling is to create a stable structure that does not change over time and has minimal redundancy. Database to be simple, efficient, and less susceptible to problems, to develop logical data modeling, which will help build a physical database. The database discussed in this chapter is a relational database. We will discuss the basic principles of the relational data models from ER models. The aim is to develop a data model, which will reflect the actual data requirement, which exists in the forms and reports of an information system.

User interface design

The design of forms and reports is the design of the human-computer interface. The logical design of system files and databases is required for interfaces. Designing the forms, reports, interfaces, dialogues, or databases are to be critically viewed. These activities can be developed in parallel.

Process of designing interfaces and dialogues

Similar to designing forms and reports, the process of designing interfaces and dialogues is a user-focused activity. Follow a prototyping methodology of iteratively collecting information, constructing a prototype, assessing usability, and making refinements. To design usable interfaces and dialogues, one must answer who, what, when, where, and how; questions used to guide the design of forms and reports.

Deliverables and outcomes

The deliverables and outcome from a system interface and dialogue design are the creation of a design specification. The specification is similar to the specification produced for form and report designs. The sections are the following:

- Narrative overview
- Sample design
- Testing and usability assessment

For interface and dialogue designs, one additional subsection is included, which is:

- A section outlining the dialogue sequence;
- The way a user can move from one display to another.

The sequence can be shown by using a dialogue diagram and a state transition diagram. An outline for a design specification for interface and dialogue is shown in *Figure 9.1*:

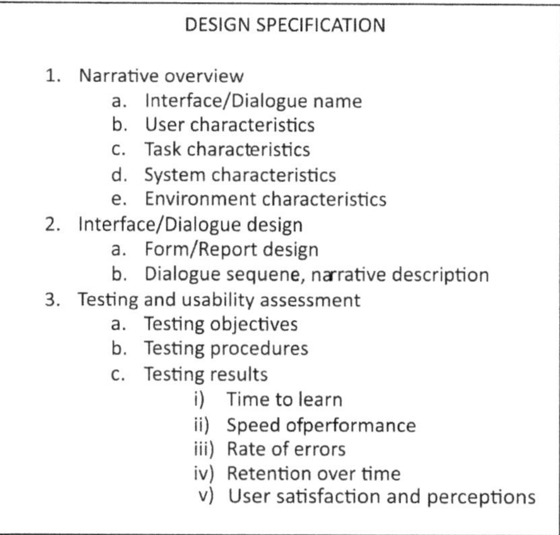
DESIGN SPECIFICATION

1. Narrative overview
   a. Interface/Dialogue name
   b. User characteristics
   c. Task characteristics
   d. System characteristics
   e. Environment characteristics
2. Interface/Dialogue design
   a. Form/Report design
   b. Dialogue sequene, narrative description
3. Testing and usability assessment
   a. Testing objectives
   b. Testing procedures
   c. Testing results
      i) Time to learn
      ii) Speed ofperformance
      iii) Rate of errors
      iv) Retention over time
      v) User satisfaction and perceptions

Figure 9.1: *Specification outline design for interface and dialogue*

Interaction methods and devices

The **human-computer** interface defines the way in which users interact with an information system. All human-computer interfaces must have an interaction style and use some hardware devices to support this interaction. Various interaction methods and guidelines for designing usable interfaces are described.

When designing the user interface, the most fundamental decision is made that relates to methods used to interact with the system. There are numerous approaches for designing the interactions, basics of five widely used styles are command language, menu, form, object, and natural language.

Command language interaction

In **command language interaction**, the user enters explicit statements to invoke operations within a system. This type of interaction requires users to remember the command syntax and semantics. Example: COPY C: LETTER.DOC A: LETTERNEW.DOC.

Command language interaction places a substantial burden on the user to remember names, syntax, and operations.

Menu interaction

Menu Interaction is a means by which many designers have accomplished ease of use and understandability. **A menu is simply a list of options, which, when selected by the user, a specific command is invoked, or another menu is activated**. Menus have become the most widely used interface method because the user only needs to understand simple signposts and route options to effectively navigate through the system. To develop a menu system, complexity in design is encountered. The development environment, the skill of the developer, and the size of complexity are the main factors for developing a menu-based system. For large and complex systems, the menu hierarchy provides a navigation between menus.

In a **pop-up-menu** (dialogue box), menus are displayed near the current cursor position, so the user does not have to move the cursor. A pop-up-menu shows a list of commands relevant to the current cursor position (delete, clear, copy, and so on.). In a list of possible values, one can select the desired one by navigating and clicking the mouse. In a drop-down menu, menus drop down from the top line of the display. **Drop-down** menu has become very popular as it provides consistency in menu location and operation.

Form interaction

Form interaction allows the users to fill in the blanks when working with a system. Form interaction is effective for both input and presentation of information. A well-designed form includes a self-explanatory title and field headings organized into logical groups and distinct boundaries. Form interaction is the most commonly used method for data entry and retrieval in business-based systems.

Object based interaction

Object-based interaction is the most common method for implementing through the use of icons. Icons are the graphic symbols that look like the processing option they are meant to represent. Users select operations by pointing to the appropriate icon with some type of pointing device. The primary advantage of using an icon is that it takes a little space and is easily understood by the user. An icon may also look like a button, when selected or pressed, causes the system to take an action. For example, save, edit a record, cancel, and so on.

Natural language interaction

A branch of artificial intelligence research studies techniques for allowing systems to accept inputs and produce outputs in a conventional language like English. This method of interaction is referred to as natural language interaction. Natural language interaction is being applied within both the keyboard and voice entry systems.

Hardware option for system interaction

There is also a growing number of hardware devices employed to support interaction. The most fundamental and widely used is the keyboard, which is the mainstay of most computer-based applications for the entry of alphanumeric information. The growth of graphical user environments has facilitated the use of pointing devices such as, mice, joystick, trackballs, and so on. The creation of notebook and pen-based computers has got this type of device to interface.

Interface design

To ease the job of the data recording, a standard format for computer-based forms and reports similar to paper-based forms and reports is essential. The form should have the following:

- Header information
- Sequence and time-related information
- Instruction or formatting information
- Body or data details
- Totals or data summary
- Authorization or signatures
- Comments

When designing the layouts to record or display information, one should try to make it similar to with paper-based forms. The data entry displays should be consistently formatted across applications to speed up the data entry and reduce errors.

The navigation between fields, while designing the layout, should be considered. Standard screen navigation should flow from left to right and top to bottom as one works on paper. If necessary, data fields should be grouped into logical categories with labels added. In the design process, the navigation procedures should have flexibility and consistency to move forward and backward. The data should not be permanently saved by the system until the user makes an explicit request to do so. A functional and consistent interface is required to move the cursor to different places on the form, edit characters, and fields, move among form displays, and obtain help. These functions may be provided by keystrokes, mouse clicks, menu selection, or button activation. A good form layout design also provides data validation and verification.

Structuring data entry

To minimize data entry errors, never allow the user to enter data, which are available in the system. The unit of measurement of a value need not be entered. This should be provided on the screen. The data entered into the form should automatically justify in a standard format (for example, date, time, money, or phone number).

Control input data

In designing the interface, care must be taken to reduce the data entry errors. Steps must be taken to ensure the data's validity. Avoid, detect, and correct data entry mistakes. Data errors, during appending (adding additional characters to a field), truncating (losing characters from a field), transcripting (entering invalid data into a field), and transposing (reversing the sequence of one or more characters in a field), are to be handled at the time of data entry.

Provide feedback

While designing the system interfaces, provide appropriate feedback to the user from time to time to make the user's job more enjoyable. The feedback should be relevant to the process, like status information, prompting cues, errors, or warning messages. Not providing the feedback information to the user is frustrating.

Providing help

Providing the help feature during the interface is very important. The user may face problems, which should be answered immediately without abandoning the screen. The help message should be short and simple. The help message needs to be organized and easily absorbed by the user. After leaving the help screen, users should always return back to the original screen from where the request was initiated.

Controlling user access

When the data is very sensitive and vulnerable to unwanted access, some restrictions are to be imposed at the interface stage. Several techniques are available to control user access, which are as follows:

- **Views**: This is one form of user access control for a system interface, which is used to provide a customized version of the system data to the user. A view is a subset of the database that is presented to one or more users. Views promote security by restricting user access to limited data. Views are not adequate security measures, as unauthorized persons gain knowledge of or access to a particular view. Many may read the data, but few can update it.

- **Authentication rules**: Controls are incorporated into the system that restrict access to data and actions that people may take on accessed data. Using user **identification (ID)** and password authenticates a user's use of the computer.
- **Encryption procedure**: For very sensitive data, such as data related to defense and finance, encryption can be used. The encrypted data cannot be read by human beings. Special software and hardware are used along with an algorithm to convert the data into encrypted one. The encryption routines automatically encode the data. The encryption facility provides complementary routines to decode the data. This method provides adequate security.

The human-computer interfaces and dialogs are important for the software design process. Understanding various characteristics of interaction methods is a fundamental skill you should master. The techniques for structuring and controlling the data entry were presented along with guidelines for providing feedback, prompting, and error messages.

Database design

The database design is at a conceptual level before the physical database is made. This is basically a logical design, which concerns the specifications of major data features of the system that would meet the objectives. The logical design can be called the **blueprint** of the database. A conceptual data model is a representation of organizational data. The purpose is to show as many rules about the meaning and inter-relationships among data as possible. The data information is gathered through interviews, questionnaires, and **joint application development (JAD)** sessions. After this, the team members work in coordination and share the project dictionary or repository. The repository is often maintained by a common CASE tool.

Database models

Database models are of three types. Although **relational databases** are ruling the Information Technology, it is worthwhile to know about other models. Almost all data administrators know about **the database management system well,** but they have little knowledge about the **data centers**. The different database models are as follows:

- **Hierarchical model:** A hierarchical model is created to eliminate redundancy and is used with smaller components, which are added to a larger one until all components are together. Its structure resembles an upside-down tree. A hierarchy of segments (nodes) is similar to record types. Layers of segments include root, parent, children, leaves, and so on. Each parent can have many children, but each child must have only one parent. It follows a sequence method beginning with a root and going down the leftmost side of a segment, proceeding right until all segments are visited.

Following are the advantages:

- o Database can be shared easily.
- o Security is enforced.
- o Creates an environment for data independence.
- o Database integrity is promoted by the link between parent and child segments.
- o Very efficient for large amounts of data using fixed relationships.
- o The installed base is large.

Following are the disadvantages:

- o Requires knowledge of the physical level of storage.
- o Difficult to implement many-to-many relationships.
- o Multiple parent conditions occur in the real world.
- o Complex to manage, not very flexible.
- o Requires extensive application programming, not user friendly.
- o Support tools must be invoked separately.
- o No common standard.

- **Network model:** A network data model has been created to represent complex data relationships more efficiently than in a hierarchical model, improve database performance, and impose database standards. A 3-level architecture originated with this model, **Data Definition Language (DDL)**, and **Data Manipulation Language (DML)** are introduced. They are as follows:
  - o **Subschema**: External view description (view of application programmer)
  - o **Schema**: Conceptual view (as viewed by database administrator)
  - o **Data storage definition language**: Specified internal models and physical details of storage

  DML characteristics, data, and data structures, and provides a way to manipulate the data. **Data Base Task Group (DBTG)** uses sets to express relationships (owner: member) **1: M**. A set consists of an owner record (parent) and a member (child). One major difference here is that a member can have two parents (owners).

  A network is a directed graph of nodes connected by links or directed arcs, nodes correspond to record types and link to pointers. The network database has record types described in the schema and has data items (fields), which are the smallest units of data. Each data item has a specific type and relates to an attribute as the record corresponds to an entity.

  Following are the advantages:

- o Many-to-many relationships and easier to implement than the hierarchical model.
- o More flexible and better data access method.
- o Data integrity is enforced because the owner record is defined first and then the member.
- o Achieves data independence by isolating the program from physical details.

Following are the disadvantages:

- o Difficult to design and use since an in-depth understanding of the record is needed.
- o Difficult to make changes because it is not structurally independent.
- o Complex structure from a program point of view.
- o Provides navigational data access like the hierarchical model.

- **Relational model:** In the relational model, the relationships between the entities in a database are considered. Relationships are the glue that holds various components together. A relationship is an association between the instances of one or more entity types that are of interest to the organization. An association usually means an event that has occurred due to the natural linkage between entity instances. This model is widely used and is more popular than other models.

  Following are the advantages:

  - o Data and structural independence.
  - o Single data repository whose contents are easier to manage.
  - o Powerful yet flexible query capability, especially for ad-hoc queries.
  - o **Structured Query Language (SQL)** requires less programming and is standard.
  - o The system's physical complexity is hidden from the designer and end user.

  Following are the disadvantages:

  - o Substantial amount of hardware and software overhead slows the system.
  - o Large databases may slow down the system with certain operations like JOIN and so on.

Entity relation diagram

P.P. Chen introduced the ER models and the corresponding diagrams. The overall logic structure of a database can be expressed graphically by an ER diagram. While drawing the ER diagram, entity names are represented by a rectangle, relationships are represented by a diamond and oval shapes are used for representing attributes.

Entity relationship analysis

It involves capturing and analyzing as much possible details on the data required for building an information system for an organization. ER modeling is concerned with the structure of data. The structure of data involves details on the following:

- Data entities
- Relationships
- Associated attributes

ER model is expressed in terms of entities in the business environment, the associations among those entities, and the attributes or properties of both entities and their relationships.

ER analysis involves the following:

- Determining what type of people, places, things, and materials interact with the business and which objects the data must be maintained. These objects form entities.
- Determining different characteristics (attributes) of each entity. This involves identifying only those characteristics, which are of interest to the organization and for which the system is being built.
- Determining what unique features, such as the primary key, can be used to identify an entity in an entity list.
- Determining the associations (relationship) among identified objects.

Entity

An entity is a person, location, object, or event about which the organization wishes to maintain data. An entity has its own identity, which distinguishes it from other entities. Following are the examples:

- **Person**: EMPLOYEE, STUDENT, PATIENT
- **Place**: STATE, REGION, COUNTRY, BRANCH
- **Object**: MACHINE, BUILDING, AUTOMOBILE
- **Event**: SALE, REGISTRATION, RENEWAL
- **Concept**: ACCOUNTING, COURSE, WORKCENTRE

Entity type

Entity type is a collection of entities that share common properties or characteristics. Each entity type in an ER model is given a name, it is an object, and uses capital letters in naming. It is placed inside a rectangle representing an entity.

Entity instance

Entity instance is a single occurrence of an entity type. An entity type with one instance is described in a data model, while many instances of that entity type may be represented by data stored in the database. Consider an example, there is one **EMPLOYEE** entity type in most organizations, but there may be hundreds (or even thousands) of instances of this entity type stored in the database.

Basic symbols

Following are the symbols shown in the figure:

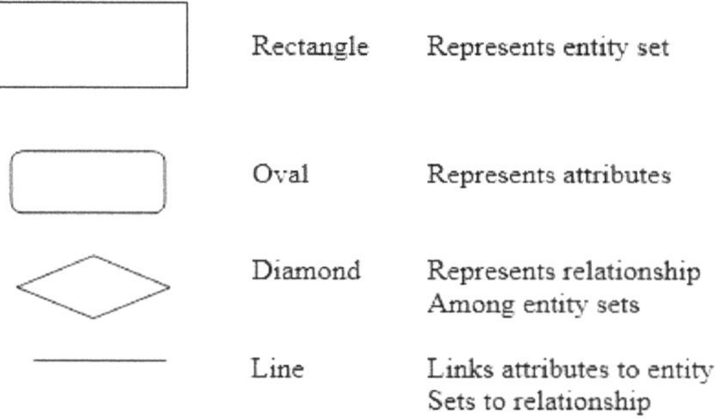

Rectangle
Represents entity set
Oval
Represents attributes
Diamond
Represents relationship
Among entity sets
Line
Links attributes to entity
Sets to relationship

Figure 9.2: *Basic symbols*

Attributes

An attribute is a property or characteristic of an entity which is of interest to the organization. An entity has a set of attributes associated with it. Following are examples:

- STUDENT: **Student_id, Stud_nm, Addr, Ph_no, Major**
- AUTOMOBILE: **Vehicle_id, colour, Weight, HP**
- EMPLOYEE: **Emp_id, Emp_name, Address, Skill**

While naming an entity, make the first letter a capital followed by lowercase letters, and use nouns in naming an attribute. An attribute is placed inside an ellipse with a line connecting to the associated entity. The attributes of an entity are listed in the repository, then each attribute may be separately defined as another object in the repository.

Candidate key and identifiers

A candidate key is an attribute (or combination of attributes) that uniquely identifies each instance of an entity type. A candidate key for a STUDENT entity type might be **Student_id**.

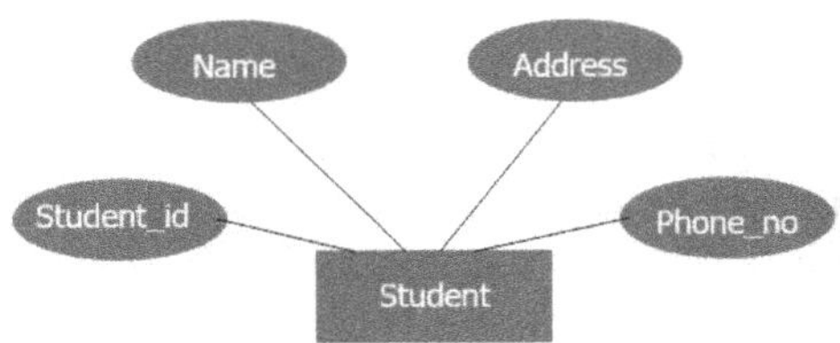

Figure 9.3: Candidate key for a student

Multi-valued attribute

Multi-valued attributes may take more than one value for each entity instance. Suppose skill is one of the attributes of an **EMPLOYEE**. Each employee can have more than one skill, therefore, **Skill** is a multi-valued attribute, as shown in the figure:

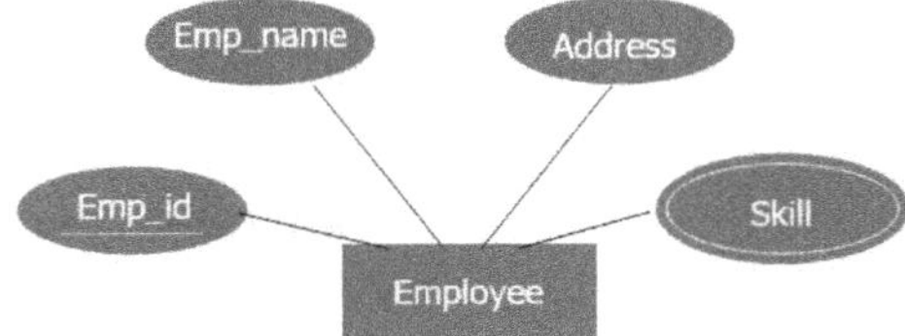

Figure 9.4: Multi-valued attribute of an employee

Attribute entity

An **attribute** is a characteristic or property that provides additional information about an entity within a system, helping to describe its specific details or features. An **entity** represents a real-world object or concept in a database or system that holds relevant data. Attributes define the values or qualities associated with entities, contributing to their complete definition and functionality within a system.

Degree of a relationship

An association among entities leads to a relationship. The degree of a relationship is the number of entity types that participate in that relationship. There are two types entities in a 2-degree relationship.

Crow foot notation is used to show the association between the entities. They are as follows:

- One-to-one (1:1)
- One-to-many (1:M)
- Many-to-many (M:M)

Following are the relationships:

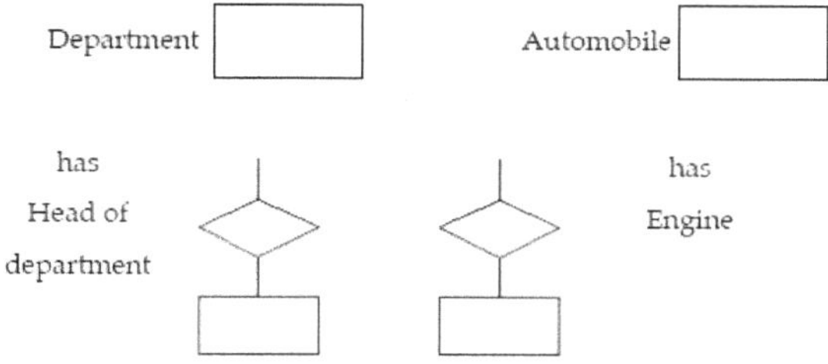

Figure 9.5: *One-to-one (1:1)*

Following is 1:M relationship:

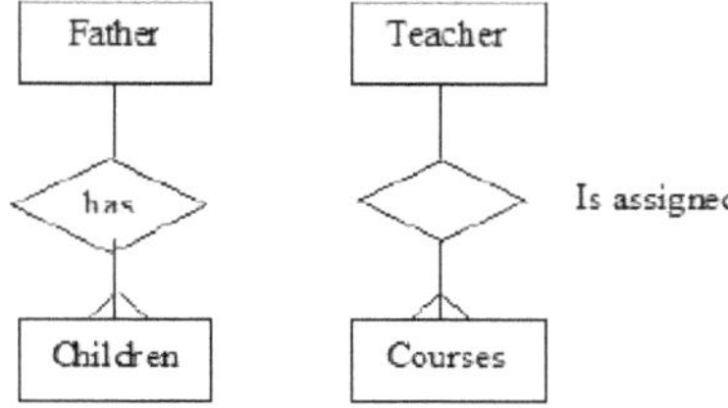

Figure 9.6: *One-to-many(1:M)*

Following is M:M relationship:

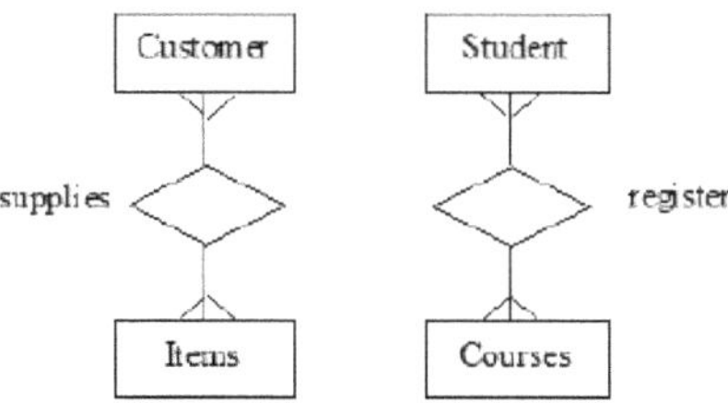

Figure 9.7: *Many to many (M:M)*

Data normalization

In software engineering, **data normalization** is the process of structuring and transforming data to eliminate redundancy, improve consistency, and optimize storage efficiency. It is commonly used in database design, where normalization involves organizing tables and relationships to minimize data duplication and ensure data integrity. Techniques such as decomposing tables into **normal forms (1NF, 2NF, 3NF, etc.)** help maintain consistency and improve query performance. In other contexts, such as machine learning and data processing, normalization scales numerical data to a standard range (for example, 0 to 1) to enhance model accuracy and comparability.

- **Concepts of normalization**: Normalization is a process of simplifying the relationship among the data elements in a record. By normalization, a collection of data in a record structure is replaced by simpler records that are more predictable and manageable.
    - Convert the ER model into **tables** or **relations**.
    - Examine the tables for redundancy and, if necessary, change them to non-redundant forms.

  This non-redundant model is then converted to a database definition, which achieves the objective of the database **design phase**.

  The goal of database design is to generate a set of schemes, which allow us to store information without redundant data and to retrieve information easily and efficiently. The design schemes are in an appropriate form, known as **normalization**.
- **Need for normalization**: Redundancy is the unnecessary repetition of data. It can cause problems with the storage and retrieval of data. Normalization reduces redundancy. Redundant can lead to the following:
    - **Inconsistencies**: errors are more likely to occur when facts are repeated.
    - **Update anomalies**: inserting, modifying, and deleting data may cause inconsistencies. While updating and deleting data in one relation, you may forget to make corresponding changes in other relations.

  Normalization helps to simplify the structure of tables. A fully normalized record consists of the following:
    - A primary key that identifies the entities.
    - A set of attributes that describes the entity.
- **1st normal form (1NF):** The repeating columns or fields in an un-normalized *Table 9.1* are removed and put into separate tables. The key to these tables must be a part of the parent table so that the parent tables and derived tables (*Table 9.2*) can be related to each other. Isolate repeating groups from an entity because they are easier to process separately.

Salesperson						
Emp_no	Emp_name	Store_Br.	Department	Item_no	Item_desc.	Sale_Price
201	Anand K	Delhi	Production	TR10	Router	35.00
				SA51	Saw	19.00
				PT6	Drill	21.00
				A16	Lawnmower	245.00
301	Zadoo S	Noida	Research	TT01	Humidfier	114.00
				DO10	Dishwasher	262.00
419	Balwant	Gurgaon	Accounts	C16	New tire	85.00

Salesperson						
				AT146	Alternator	65.00
				BH90	Battery	49.50
612	Bhagwan	Faridabad	Marketing	S10	Suit	215.00

Table 9.1: *Unnormalized File 2nd normal form*

A table is in the **second normal form** if all its non-key fields are fully dependent on the whole key. It means that each field in a table must depend upon the entire key. Those fields, which do not depend upon the combination key, are moved to another table on whose key they depend. Structures, which do not contain combination keys are automatically in the 2NF.

Non-key attributes that do not meet this condition are split into simpler entities. To solve the problem, we create a new independent entity for **item description** and **sales price**. In one file, we create the item description attribute with item number keys from the salesperson item file. The remaining attributes (employee number, item number, and sales price) become the second relation or file. (*Table 9.3*):

*Emp_no	Emp_name	Store_Br	Dept
201	Anand K	Delhi	Production
301	Zadoo S	Noida	Research
419	Balwant	Gurgaon	Accounts
612	Bhagwan	Faidabad	Marketing

*Emp_no	*Item_no	Item_des	Sale_Price
201	TR10	Router	35.00
201	SA51	Saw	19.00
201	PT6	Drill	21.00
201	A16	Lawnmowr	245.00
301	TT01	Humidfier	114.00
301	DO10	Dishwasher	262.00
419	C16	Snow tire	85.00
419	AT146	Alternator	65.00
419	BH90	Battery	49.50
612	S10	Suit	215.00

* **Key**

Table 9.2: *First normalized file*

Table 9.3 shows second normalization:

Sales Person Data File			
***Emp_no**	**Emp_name**	**Store_Br**	**Dept**
201	Anand K	Delhi	Production
301	Zadoo S	Noida	Research
419	Balwant	Gurgaon	Accounts
612	Bhagwan	Faridabad	Marketing

Salesperson item file			Item file	
***Emp_no**	***Item_no**	**Sale_Price**	***Item_no**	**Item_des**
201	TR10	35.00	TR10	Router
201	SA51	19.00	SA51	Saw
201	PT6	21.00	PT6	Drill
201	A16	245.00	A16	Lawnmower
301	TT01	114.00	TT01	Humidifier
301	DO10	262.00	DO10	Dishwasher
419	C16	85.00	C16	New tire
419	AT146	65.00	AT146	Alternator
419	BH90	49.50	BH90	Battery
612	S10	215.00	S10	Suit

Table 9.3: *Second normalization*

- **3rd normal form (3NF)**: A table is said to be in the **third normal form**, if all the non-key fields of the table are independent of all other non-key fields of the same fields. A relation is in the third normal form provided it is in the second normal form, and no non-prime attribute is functionally dependent on other prime attributes.

  We find further room for improvement. In the salesperson data file, the attribute **stores branch** is tagged to the primary key **employee number**, while the attribute **department** is related to **store branch**, which is a non-key attribute. Making a **store branch**, as a key attribute, requires isolating the **department** and the **store branch** in a new relationship. With the third normalization, we can store branch information independent of the salespersons in the branch. We can make changes in the **department** without having to update the employee's record.

  For store branches, the system goes through three steps:

  1. Computes total sales for each salesperson from the salesperson item file.
  2. Goes to the employee data file to look up the store branch to which the salesperson is assigned.
  3. Accumulate each salesperson's sale in a specified field (*Table 9.4*):

Salesperson Data File		
***Emp_no**	**Emp_name**	**Store_Br**
201	Anand K	Delhi
301	Zadoo S	Noida
419	Balwant	Gurgaon
612	Bhagwan	Faridabad

Store Branch File	
Store_Br	**Dept**
Delhi	Hardware
Noida	Home Appliance
Gurgaon	Auto parts
Faridabad	Men's clothing

Salesperson item file		
***Espino**	***Item_no**	**Sale_Price**
201	TR10	35.00
201	SA51	19.00
201	PT6	21.00
201	A16	245.00
301	TT01	114.00
301	DO10	262.00
419	C16	85.00
419	AT146	65.00
419	BH90	49.50
612	S10	215.00

Item file	
***Item_no**	**Item_des**
TR10	Router
SA51	Saw
PT6	Drill
A16	Lawnmower
TT01	Humidifier
DO10	Dishwasher
C16	New tire
AT146	Alternator
BH90	Battery
S10	Suit

Table 9.4: *Third normalization*

This procedure is repeated for each salesperson in the file. *Table 9.5* illustrates the processing cycle for salesperson 201:

Emp_no	Emp_name	Store_Br
201	Anand K	Delhi
301	Zadoo S	Noida
419	Balwant	Gurgaon
612	Bhagwan	Faridabad

*Store_Br	Dept	Total Sales
Delhi	Hardware	320.00
Noida	Home Appliance	376.00
Gurgaon	Auto parts	199.00
Faridabad	Men's clothing	215.00

*Emp no	*Item no	Sale Price	
201	TR10	35.00	} 320
201	SA51	19.00	
201	PT6	21.00	
201	A16	245.00	
301	TT01	114.00	
301	D010	262.00	
419	C16	85.00	
419	AT146	65.00	
419	BH90	49.50	
612	$10	215.00	

*Item no	Item des
TR10	Router
SA51	Saw
PT6	Drill
A16	Lawnmower
TT01	Humidfier
DO10	Dishwasher
C16	New tire
AT146	Alternator
BH90	Battery
$10	Suit

Table 9.5: *Processing cycle*

Conclusion

Physical file and database design take, as input, the normalized relations from logical data modeling as well as other models that explain how data in files and databases will be accessed. Physical file and database design involves designing fields, records, files, and databases. Designing a field includes selecting a data type, coding, and compression methods to reduce the storage space and improve data accuracy, the format for primary keys, and data integrity control to ease data entry and reduce errors. Designing physical records involves grouping fields together based on a shared primary key and an affinity of usage. Records are also designed to minimize the wasted space in secondary memory storage units called pages. CASE tools can help in physical and database design by storing the results of file and database design in a CASE repository, generating file, or database definition code, reverse engineering existing file and database definitions for elements of current systems that will be reused in the new application.

In the next chapter, readers will explore the critical phases of coding and debugging, which are essential steps in the software development process. The chapter will cover how to translate design specifications into functional code using programming languages, focusing on writing clean, efficient, and maintainable code. It will also delve into the importance of debugging, a process used to identify, analyze, and resolve errors or bugs that occur during coding. Readers will learn various debugging techniques, tools, and best practices to ensure that the software runs smoothly and meets the specified requirements. Through this chapter, readers will gain insights into how to develop high-quality, error-free software systems.

Exercises

To solidify your understanding of the concepts covered in this chapter, try the following exercises.

Multiple choice questions

1. **What is the primary goal of user interface (UI) design?**
   a. To create complex algorithms
   b. To enhance user experience
   c. To minimize hardware costs
   d. To improve database security

2. **Which of the following is an interaction method?**
   a. Keyboard and mouse
   b. SQL Queries
   c. Encryption
   d. Cloud computing

3. **In database design, what does an entity-relationship diagram (ERD) represent?**
   a. The flow of data in a system
   b. The relationships between users and interfaces
   c. The structure of a database with entities and their relationships
   d. The physical design of hardware
4. **Which of the following is NOT an interaction device?**
   a. Touchscreen
   b. Microphone
   c. Relational database
   d. Trackpad
5. **What is the purpose of database normalization?**
   a. To improve the aesthetics of the UI
   b. To reduce data redundancy
   c. To increase user interaction
   d. To create ER diagrams
6. **A well-designed user interface should:**
   a. Be complex and detailed
   b. Require minimal training for users
   c. Be hardware-dependent
   d. Focus solely on aesthetic appeal
7. **Which of these is a key element of database design?**
   a. Screen resolution
   b. Data integrity
   c. User interaction
   d. Device drivers
8. **In an ER diagram, a relationship is represented by:**
   a. A rectangle
   b. A diamond
   c. A triangle
   d. A circle
9. **Which of the following devices allows for direct user interaction?**
   a. Web server
   b. Touchscreen
   c. Firewall
   d. Database schema

10. **The process of designing interfaces and dialogues in a system involves:**
    a. Establishing how users interact with the system
    b. Configuring the backend database
    c. Installing operating systems
    d. Managing server security

Short questions

1. What are the main principles of user interface (UI) design?
2. Describe the role of interaction methods and devices in user interface design.
3. What is an entity-relationship diagram (ERD) and what are its components?
4. How does database normalization improve the efficiency of a database?
5. Explain the difference between a primary key and a foreign key in database design.

Essay type questions

1. Discuss the importance of designing user interfaces and dialogues in software systems. How do these designs impact the overall user experience?
2. Explain the significance of interaction methods and devices in modern user interface design. How have advancements in technology influenced user interaction?
3. Describe the steps involved in database design, including the use of entity-relationship diagrams (ERDs). Discuss the role of normalization in ensuring an efficient database structure.
4. Compare and contrast different types of user interaction devices (e.g., mouse, keyboard, touchscreen). How do these devices influence the design of user interfaces?

Multiple choice answers

1. b
2. a
3. c
4. c
5. b
6. b
7. b
8. b
9. b
10. a

CHAPTER 10
Coding and Debugging

Introduction

In a software development life cycle, the product takes the least time in comparison to other phases. A well-structured code will help in reducing the testing and integration time, maintaining a good documentation and improving the maintainability of the software product after implementation.

The maintenance phase of the product life is the highest of all. In order to have a very smooth operation during the software maintenance phase, we should not compromise the cost, time, and size of the software code. The coding phase of a software development cycle represents only about 10% to 15% of total software cost. A 20% increase in the cost coding will increase the total cost by 2% to 3% of total development cost (*Ali Behforooz*). If this additional effort results in a better-structured, better-documented, and more readable code, the benefits that occur during test, integration, implementation, and operational phase will be more than the additional cost during coding. The criteria for deciding the quality of a software program are the size, **kilo lines of code (KLOC),** memory utilization, readability, execution time, cyclomatic complexity, and algorithmic complexity.

Structure

In this chapter, we are going to discuss:

- Programming language characteristics

- Fundamentals of computer language
- Computer languages
- Art of debugging
- Debugging process
- Debugging tools

Objectives

By the end of the chapter, it will provide a comprehensive understanding of the coding phase in software engineering and the critical role of debugging in ensuring software quality. This chapter aims to equip readers with the knowledge of best practices in writing clean, efficient code and the techniques to systematically identify, analyze, and fix errors. Readers will learn how proper debugging approaches contribute to software stability, reliability, and performance. Additionally, the chapter will emphasize the importance of using tools and methodologies that streamline the coding and debugging processes, enhancing overall project success.

Programming language characteristics

The followings are the indication of the extent of language support for the characteristics. Programs written in a particular language will vary widely with respect to these characteristics, depending on the support provided by language, skill, and discipline of the programmers:

- **Clarity of source code**: The extent to which inherent language features support source code which is readable and understandable and that clearly reflects the underlying logical structure of the program.

  Most of the life cycle cost of a software system (usually between 60% and 80%) will come during the time after its initial development has been completed [*Schach*] [*Sommerville*]. This includes all the efforts to change the software, whether it is to fix the problems or to add new capabilities. Regardless of the purpose, changing the software implies that a significant cost will be associated with understanding the program and its structure. This is the first step before any changes can be made. Although it is always possible to use techniques to make a program easier to understand. Language support for source code clarity can facilitate this process considerably.

Note: Clarity is a readability issue. It is not unusual for languages with good readability to be somewhat more verbose than less readable languages.

- **Complexity management (architecture support):** The extent to which inherent language features support the management of system complexity, in terms of addressing issues of data, algorithm, interface, and architectural complexity.

The more complex a system get, the more important its complexity to be managed. Properly structuring a system from beginning, as well as using appropriate supporting tools, is essential. However, complexity management is always difficult, and it is very helpful if the language can facilitate this goal.

- **Concurrency support**: The extent to which inherent language features support the construction of code with multiple threads of control (also known as parallel processing).

  For many types of applications, multiple threads of control are very useful. This is particularly true for real-time systems and those running on hardware with multiple processors. Concurrency is rarely directly supported by a language, and, in fact, the philosophy of some languages is that it should be a separate issue for the operating system to deal with. However, the language support can make concurrent processing more straightforward and understandable, and it can also provide the programmer with more control over how it is implemented.

- **Distributed system support**: The extent to which inherent language features support the construction of code to be distributed across multiple platforms on a network.

  It is becoming more and more common for the software components of systems, particularly for a very large software system, to be distributed across multiple platforms on a network. In this networked configuration, each platform performs some portion of the system functions. This makes sense for various reasons, with performance right at the top of the list. However, distribution creates many new problems, not the least of which is that the multiple platforms are generally heterogeneous (different hardware and operating systems). The problems of the distribution can be dealt with by tools rather than language. Some newer languages also address the issues of distribution.

- **Maintainability**: The extent to which inherent language features support the construction of code that can be readily modified to satisfy the new requirements or to correct the deficiencies.

  Support for clarity has been mentioned above as one type of support for maintainability. Maintainability is facilitated by many of the language characteristics, those which make it easier to understand and then change the software. The structure of the code also has a significant impact on how easy the code is to change. The technique of encapsulating units and limiting their access through well-defined interfaces greatly facilitates the maintainability. Hence, language features which facilitate encapsulation can be very beneficial.

- **Mixed language support**: The extent to which inherent language features support interfacing to other languages.

  This should not be confused with the complementary product support that provides calling interfaces (bindings) for specific languages. Binding is the product characteristic tool support for interfacing with other languages. Mixed language support, from the perspective of the language, means the provision of specific capabilities to interface with other languages. This type of support can have a significant impact on the reliability of the data that is exchanged between languages. Without specific language support, no checking may be done on the form, or even the existence, of data exchanged on a call between units of different languages, and the potential for unreliability is high. Specific language support can provide the expected reliability.

- **Object-oriented programming support**: The extent to which inherent language features support the construction of object-oriented code.

  There is general agreement that object-oriented programming support means specific language support for the creation of code with encapsulated classes and objects, inheritance, and polymorphism. This form of programming is associated with the software that has good maintainability characteristics because of the encapsulation of classes and objects. It also facilitates the creation of reusable software because it encourages well-structured software with well-defined interfaces, and existing abstractions. There are two different ways a language can provide object-oriented programming support. Some languages are strictly object-oriented and do not support any other form of programming. Other languages provide object-oriented capabilities along with more conventional programming capabilities, and the programmer determines whether or not the language is used to create object-oriented software. For this language characteristic, the specific mechanism for providing the capability is not the issue but the extent of support.

- **Portability**: The extent to which inherent language features support the transfer of a program from one hardware and software platform to another.

  To make software readily portable, it must be written using non-system-dependent constructs except where system dependencies are encapsulated. The system dependent parts, if any, must be re-accomplished for the new platform, but if those parts of the software are encapsulated, a relatively small amount of new code is required to run the software on the new platform. Language support for portability comes from support for encapsulation, and it can also come from support for expressing constructs in a non-system-dependent manner. Language standardization has a significant impact on the portability because non-standard language constructs can only be ported to systems that support the same non-standard constructs. Consider an example, if both systems have compilers from the same vendor. In some circles, the issue of existing compatible support products, including compilers, on many different platforms is considered in the concept of portability.

Note: A language's portability characteristics can be severely compromised by poor programming practices.

- **Real-time support**: The extent to which inherent language features support the construction of a real-time system.

  Real-time systems have mandatory time constraints, and often space constraints, that must be met. These will usually tax both the software and the hardware of the system, and system performance predictability becomes an important issue. Language can support real-time systems in two ways. A language can provide specific constructs for specifying the time and space constraints of a system. It can also support streamlined ways to express the program instructions. For example, real-time systems often have unique requirements in areas such as device control and interrupt handling, and a language can support managing these in a straightforward, predictable manner. Since many real-time systems are concurrent systems, real-time support, and concurrency support are closely related.

- **Reliability**: The extent to which inherent language features support the construction of components that can be expected to perform their intended functions in a satisfactory manner throughout the expected lifetime of the product.

  Reliability is concerned with making a system failure free, and thus is concerned with all possible errors. System reliability is suspected when software is being stressed to its capacity limits or when it is interfacing with resources outside the system, particularly when receiving input from such resources. One way that interfacing with outside resources occurs is when users operate the system. Reliability problems often surface when novices use the system, because they can provide unexpected input that was not tested. Interfacing with outside resources also occurs when the system is interfacing with devices or other software systems. Language can provide support for this potential reliability problem through consistency checking of data exchanged. Language can also provide the support for robustness with features facilitating the construction of independent (encapsulated) components which do not communicate with the other parts of the software except through well-defined interfaces. Language may also provide support for reliability by supporting explicit mechanisms for dealing with problems that are detected when the system is in operation (exception handling).

Note: Poor reliability in a safety-oriented portion of the software also becomes a safety issue.

- **Reusability**: The extent to which inherent language features support the adaptation of code for use in another application.

  Code is reusable when it is independent of other code except for communication through well-defined interfaces. This type of construction can occur at many levels. It is very common, for example, to reuse common data structures, such as stacks, queues, and trees. When these have been defined with common operations on the structures, these abstract data types are easy to reuse. When reusing larger portions of code, the biggest issue for reusability is whether the interfaces defined for the code to be reused are compatible with the interfaces defined for the system being created. This is facilitated by the definition of software architecture for the domain of the system under construction. If those defining the components to be reused are aware of the architecture definition, then they can follow the standard interfaces defined in the architecture to ensure the code is reusable for other systems by using the same architecture. Reusing at any level can be facilitated by language features that make it easy to write independent (encapsulated) modules with well-defined interfaces.

- **Safety**: The extent to which inherent language features support the construction of safety-critical systems, yielding systems that are fault-tolerant, fail-safe, or robust in the face of the system failure.

  Safety is related to reliability, but it is of great importance. The more reliable a system is, the more it does what is expected. A system is safe if it protects against the physical danger to people, as well as against loss or damage to other physical resources, such as equipment. This implies that the system must always do what is expected from it and be able to recover from any situation that might lead to a mishap or actual system hazard. Thus, safety tries to ensure that any failures that occur are minor consequences, and even potentially dangerous failures are handled in a fail-safe fashion. Language can facilitate this through such features as a rigorous computational model, built-in consistency checking, and exception handling.

- **Standardization**: The extent to which inherent language definition has been formally standardized (by recognized bodies such as ANSI and ISO) and the extent to which it can be reasonably expected that this standard will be followed in a language translator.

  Most popular languages are standardized through **American National Standards Institute (ANSI)** and **International Organization for Standardization (ISO),** but an important issue here is that the language definition that is supported by a compiler product may not be that which is standardized. Most languages have evolved in a manner that has produced a proliferation of different dialects before the language was standardized, and the result has been that most compiler products support non-standard features from these dialects in addition to the standard language. Some of these products also support a mode that enforces the use of the standard language constructs, but programmer discipline is still required to use this mode.

- **Support for modern engineering methods**: The extent to which inherent language features support the expression of source code that enforces good software engineering principles.

Support for modern software engineering methods is to encourage the use of good engineering practices and discourages poor practices. Hence, support for code clarity, encapsulation, and all forms of consistency checking are Language features that provide this support. Also, support for complexity management and construction of large systems and subsystems support software engineering tenets.

Fundamentals of computer language

The first computer codes were specialized for the applications. In the first decades of the twentieth century, numerical calculations were based on the decimal numbers. Eventually, it was realized that logic could be represented with numbers, as well as with words. For example, Alonzo Church was able to express the lambda calculus in a formulaic way.

Like many **firsts** in history, the first modern programming language is hard to identify. From the start, the restrictions of the hardware defined the language. Punch cards allowed 80 columns, but some of the columns had to be used for sorting numbers on each card. **FORTRAN** included some keywords which were the same as English words, such as **IF**, **GOTO** (go to) and **CONTINUE**. To some people, the answer depends on how much power and human-readability is required before the status of **programming language** is granted. Jacquard looms and Charles Babbage's difference engine both had simple, extremely limited languages for describing the actions that these machines should perform.

In the 1940s the first recognizably modern, electrically powered computers were created. The limited speed and memory capacity forced programmers to write hand tuned assembly language programs. It was soon discovered that programming in assembly language required a great deal of intellectual effort and was error-prone.

In the 1950s, the first three modern programming languages whose descendants are still in widespread use today were designed:

- **Formula translator (FORTRAN)** (1955), invented by *John W. Backus et al.*
- **List processor (LISP)**, invented by *John McCarthy et al.*
- **Common business oriented language (COBOL)**, created by the Short Range Committee, heavily influenced by *Grace Hopper*.

Another milestone in the late 1950s was the publication, by a committee of American and European computer scientists, of **a new language for algorithms**; the Algol 60 Report (the **algorithmic language**). This report consolidated many ideas circulating at the time and featured two key language innovations:

- **Arbitrarily nested block structure**: meaningful chunks of code could be grouped into statement blocks without having to be turned into separate, explicitly named procedures.
- **Lexical scoping**: a block could have its own variables that code outside the chunk cannot access, let alone manipulate.

Another innovation, related to this, was in how the language was described:

A mathematically exact notation, **Backus-Naur Form (BNF)**, was used to describe the language's syntax. Nearly all subsequent programming languages have used a variant of BNF to describe the context-free portion of their syntax.

Algol 60 was particularly influential in the design of later languages, some of which soon became more popular. The Burroughs large systems were designed to be programmed in an extended subset of Algol.

Algol 68's many little-used language features (concurrent and parallel blocks) and its complex system of syntactic shortcuts and automatic type coercions made it unpopular with implementers and gained it a reputation of being difficult. *Niklaus Wirth* actually walked out of the design committee to create the simpler Pascal language.

The period from the late 1960s to the late 1970s brought a major flowering of programming languages. Most of the major language paradigms now in use were invented in this period:

- **Simula**, invented in the late 1960s by *Nygaard* and *Dahl* as a superset of Algol 60, was the first language designed to support object-oriented programming.
- **C**, an early systems programming language, was developed by *Dennis Ritchie* and *Ken Thompson* at Bell Labs between 1969 and 1973.
- **Smalltalk** (mid 1970s) provided a complete ground-up design of an object-oriented language.
- **Prolog**, designed in 1972 by *Colmerauer, Roussel, and Kowalski,* was the first logic programming language.
- **ML** built a polymorphic type system (invented by *Robin Milner* in 1973) on top of Lisp, pioneering statically typed functional programming languages.

Each of these languages spawned an entire family of descendants, and most modern languages count at least one of them in their ancestry.

The 1960s and 1970s also saw considerable debate over the merits of **structured programming**, which essentially meant programming without the use of **GOTO**. This debate was closely related to language design: some languages did not include GOTO, which forced structured programming on the programmer. Although the debate raged hotly at the time, nearly all programmers now agree that, even in languages that provide GOTO, it is bad style to use it except in rare circumstances. As a result, later generations of language designers have found the structured programming debate tedious and even bewildering.

The 1980s was the year of relative consolidation. C++ combined object-oriented and systems programming. The United States government standardized Ada, a systems programming language intended for use by defense contractors. In Japan and elsewhere, vast sums were spent investigating so-called **fifth generation** languages that incorporated logic programming constructs. The functional languages community moved to standardize ML and Lisp. Rather than inventing new paradigms, all of these movements elaborated upon the ideas invented in the previous decade.

However, one new important new trend in language design was an increased focus on programming for large-scale systems through the use of modules, or large-scale organizational units of code. Modula, Ada, and ML all developed notable module systems in the 1980s. Module systems were often wedded to generic programming constructs such as generics being, in essence, parameterized modules.

Although major new paradigms for programming languages did not appear, many researchers expanded their ideas of prior languages and adapted them to new contexts. For example, the languages of the Argus and Emerald systems adapted object-oriented programming to distributed systems.

The 1980s also brought advances in programming language implementation. The **reduced instruction set computing (RISC)** movement in computer architecture postulated that hardware should be designed for compilers rather than for human assembly programmers. Aided by processor speed improvements that enabled increasingly aggressive compilation techniques, the RISC movement sparked greater interest in compilation technology for high-level languages.

The 1990s saw no fundamental novelty, but much recombination as well as maturation of old ideas. A big driving philosophy was programmer productivity. Many **rapid application development (RAD)** languages emerged, which usually came with an **integrated development environment (IDE)**, garbage collection, and were descendants of older languages. All such languages were object-oriented. These included Object Pascal, Visual Basic, and C#. Java was a more conservative language that also featured garbage collection and received much attention. More radical and innovative than the RAD languages were the new scripting languages. These did not directly descend from other languages and featured new syntaxes and more liberal incorporation of features. Many consider these scripting languages to be more productive than even the RAD languages, but often because of choices that make small programs simpler but large programs more difficult to write and maintain. Nevertheless, scripting languages came to be the most prominent ones used in connection with the web.

Haskell (1990). Python (1991), Java (1991), Ruby (1993), Lua (1993), ANSI Common Lisp (1994), JavaScript (1995), PHP (1995), C# (2000), and JavaFX Script (2008) are some of the languages in use.

Programming language evolution continues, in both industry and research. Some of the current trends include:

- Mechanisms for adding security and reliability verification to the language such as extended static checking, information flow control, and static thread safety.
- Alternative mechanisms for modularity such as mixins, delegates, aspects.
- Component-oriented software development.
- Meta-programming, reflection, or access to the abstract syntax tree.
- Increased emphasis on distribution and mobility.
- Integration with databases, including **Extensible Markup Language (XML)** and relational databases.

- Support for Unicode so that source code (program text) is not restricted to those characters contained in the **American Standard Code for Information Interchange (ASCII)** character set; allowing, for example, use of non-Latin-based scripts or extended punctuation.
- XML for graphical interface (XUL, XAML).

Computer languages

Around more than 250 languages have been used till today. Computer languages can be categorized as procedural, nonprocedural, imperative, declarative, functional, logic, object oriented, fourth generation, and fifth generation. Some of the categories overlap, and some languages belong to more than one category.

Categories of computer languages

Following are the categories of computer language:

- **Procedural languages**: The programmer can precisely define each step to perform a task. Through the language, the programmer can give a step-by-step instruction on how the task is going to be accomplished. The programmer can specify language statements to perform a sequence of algorithmic steps. To find the average of three numbers, the procedural language will direct the computer through language statements to add the three numbers by adding the first two, then adding the third one to the result and then dividing the sum by three to obtain the average of the three numbers. Such languages are Ada, Algol, BASIC, C, C++, COBOL, FORTRAN, Pascal, and so on.
- **Nonprocedural languages**: The programmer tells the computer through language, what must be done, but leaves the details of how to perform the task to the language itself. To compute the average of three numbers, a nonprocedural language will require the programmer to state: Compute average of X, Y, Z. Some of the nonprocedural languages are SQL, dBase, and Paradox. Fourth generation languages are nonprocedural.
- **Imperative languages**: In this the expressions are computed and results are stored as variables. Language control statements direct the computer to execute an exact sequence of statements. Most of the procedural languages are high-level languages. Some of the imperative languages are COBOL, FORTRAN, BASIC, Pascal, C, C++, and Ada.
- **Declarative languages**: Most logic programming languages are considered as declarative languages. The semantic definitions in declarative languages are called declarative semantics. In an imperative language, the programmer is required to keep track of many elements that may be distributed throughout the program. For example, type definition, data structure definition, and scoping. Whereas

in a declarative semantic, the meaning of an expression is contained within the expression itself.

- **Functional languages**: In functional languages, every entity is a function. A function in functional language has the same meaning as a function in mathematics. In mathematics, a function has a name and one or more arguments. So, it is with a functional programming language. LISP is one of the oldest and most widely used functional languages. Other functional programming languages are FP, Miranda, ML, and FQL. Both functional and imperative languages are mainly procedural languages.
- **Logic languages**: The design of the logic programming languages is based on mathematical propositions to define the objects and operations on objects. The language is designed around mathematical logic, predicate calculus, and lambda calculus. Languages used for logic programming are usually declarative languages. Prolog is a widely used logic programming language. Other languages are **Simple Authentication and Security Layer (SASL)**, and **Logic and Lisp (LOGLISP)**.
- **Object-oriented languages**: Smalltalk is the first truly object-oriented programming language. The object-oriented languages define and use classes, inheritance and polymorphism. Ada95, C++, JAVA are some of the most widely used languages among many available products today. One of the goals of object-oriented programming language is to achieve both reusability and evolvability.
- **Visual languages**: This has got a wide acceptability by the users due to its graphic user interface capability. The languages under this category are Visual Basic, Visual C++, Visual FoxPro, and Visual Pascal. Its graphic interactive communication with user made it popular.
- **Fourth-generation languages (4GL)**: In early 1980s many such languages were developed. These are very easy to learn and use. The main goal was to develop a nonprocedural language. These languages were put into a new category called **fourth generation languages**. The main emphasis was to give novice users the capability to define, design, and develop application software without involving a professional programmer. The combination of 4GLs and databases created a powerful database management system. Microsoft and Oracle have developed such languages and become popular. Languages of this category are **application development framework (ADF), automated data systems (ADS), a programming language (APL), document management system (DMS), Focus, Intellect, Natural,** and **Structured Query Language (SQL).** Many of these languages are available on PC platforms.
- **Fifth-generation languages**: Till today there is no such distinct language available on computer. Some of the 4GLs showed an extended capability. The 5GLs are supposed to make communications with computers as easy as like human communicate with each other and possibly with the same tools through voice and vision.

Some important languages

The chronological evolution of programming language was discussed in the previous section. The details of some of the important languages are:

- **Machine language** refers to the **ones and zeroes** that digital processors use as instructions. Give it one pattern of bits (11001001) and it will add two numbers, give it a different pattern (11001010), it will instead subtract one from the other in as little as a billionth of a second. The instruction sets within a CPU family are usually compatible, but not between product lines. For example, Intel's x86/ Pentium language and Motorola's PPC/Gx language are completely incompatible. Machine language is painfully difficult to work with, and almost never worth the effort anymore. Instead, programmers use the higher-level languages, which are either compiled or interpreted into machine language by the computer itself with the help of a compiler or an interpreter.
- **Assembly language** is as close as you can come to writing in machine language, but has the advantage that it is also human-readable, using a small vocabulary of words with one syllable. Each written instruction (such as MOV A, B) typically corresponds to a single machine-language instruction (such as 11001001). An assembler makes the translation before the program is executed. Back when CPU speed was measured in Kilo-Hertz and storage space was measured in Kilo-Bytes, assembly language was the most cost-efficient way to implement a program. It is used less often now (with all those kilos replaced by megas or gigas, and even teras on the horizon, it seems no one cares anymore about efficiency), but if you need speed and compactness above all else, assembly language is the solution.
- **C** [successor to the language **B**] offers an elegant compromise between the efficiency of coding in assembly language and the convenience and portability of writing in a structured, high-level language. By keeping many of its commands and syntax analogous to those of common machine languages, and with several generations of optimizing compilers behind it, C makes it easy to write fast code without necessarily sacrificing readability. However, it still tempts you to write code that only a machine can follow, which can be a problem when it comes time to debug it or make changes. Free and commercial tools (most of which now also support C++) are available from various sources for just about every operating system.
- **C++** [**C** with the C instruction to **increment**] is probably the most widely-supported language today, and most commercial software is written in C++. The name reflects why: when it was introduced, it took all the benefits of the then-reigning development language (C) and incrementally added the next set of features programmers were looking for (**object-oriented programming (OOP)**). So, programmers did not have to throw anything out and re-do it; but they could add those techniques to their repertoire as needed. OO purists hate the results, but it is difficult to argue with that success. Free and commercial tools are available

from various sources for just about every operating system. Objective-C is an alternate approach to adding OO characteristics to C (borrowing directly from SmallTalk), which has not attracted a large community of users.

- **C#** [**C++** with the plus signs overlapping, pronounced **C sharp**] is actually Microsoft's answer to Java. They originally tried to release **Java** development tools that would produce applications that were not truly portable. You could only use them on Windows, but this violated their licensing agreement with Sun (creators of Java), who successfully put a stop to that. So, Microsoft turned around and produced a language with similar features that effectively is tied to Windows. Although they are submitting the language to a standard-setting body, for all practical purposes it is just a proprietary variant of C++ whose specs they will dictate, available only from Microsoft, and practical only for Windows.
- **Java** [slang for **coffee**] is kind of a streamlined version of C++, designed for portability. Its key advantage is that the Java programs can be run on any operating system for which a Java **virtual environment** is available. (Programs in most other languages have to be modified and recompiled to go from one operating system to another.) The language is defined by Sun and widely licensed to other companies, making it possible to run Java applications in web browsers, portable phones, desktop computers, web servers, and so on. It is not as fast as applications written in a compiled language like C++. However, free, and commercial tools are available from various sources for most current operating systems. Although Microsoft is removing support for Java from the default setup of new versions of Windows, it can easily be added back in.
- **Pascal** [mathematician or philosopher Blaise Pascal] was designed primarily as a tool for teaching good programming skills, but largely to the availability of Borland's inexpensive Pascal compiler for the early IBM PC. It has become popular outside of the classroom. Unlike many languages, Pascal requires a fairly structured approach, which prevents the kinds of indecipherable **spaghetti code** and easily-overlooked mistakes that plague programmers using languages such as Fortran or C. Free and commercial tools are available from various sources for DOS, Windows, Mac, OS/2, AmigaOS, and Unix-like systems. The web site editor BBEdit is written in Pascal.
- **Delphi** [home of the Greek oracle Pythia] is a non-standard, object-oriented version of Pascal developed by Borland for their rapid application development tool of the same name. The Delphi environment was designed to compete with Microsoft's Visual Basic tools, freeing the programmer from having to write all the code for the user interface by letting her drag and drop objects and attach functions to various buttons and other on-screen elements. Its ability to manipulate databases is another strength. Commercial tools are available from Borland for Windows and Linux.
- **Beginner's All-purpose Symbolic Instruction Code (BASIC)** is the first language that most early microcomputer users learned. The BASIC interpreters on those

machines were not very sophisticated or fast, largely due to the memory and speed limitations of the hardware, and the language encouraged sloppy coding. **BASIC is to computer languages what Roman numerals are to arithmetic**. Modern versions of BASIC are more structured. They often include compilers for greater speed. Free and commercial tools are available from various sources for DOS, Windows, Mac, and Unix-like systems.

- **Visual Basic** [a version of **BASIC** for graphical environments] is Microsoft's Jack of all Trades language. It is a cross between BASIC, the various macro languages of Microsoft Office, and some rapid application development tools. The idea was to get people started writing macros using **Visual Basic for Applications (VBA)**, then sell them the whole VB programming tool when they run into the limits of that approach. Unfortunately, VB applications are impossible to port to other environments, and you are at the mercy of Microsoft's changing specs for the language. Programs written in VB6 or earlier will not run properly in VB.NET. It is available only from Microsoft and runs in Windows.
- **SmallTalk [easy conversation]** is object-oriented. Graphical Smalltalk development environment is what inspired *Steve Jobs* and later *Bill Gates* to **invent** the Mac OS and Windows interfaces. Focusing on the superficial aspects of it (windows and mice) they missed the real gem: the language.
- **Squeak** [the sound a mouse makes] is a variant of SmallTalk, created by alumni of the Xerox PARC (where SmallTalk and the computer mouse were invented) and of Apple, who are now working at Disney (home of a famous mouse). It is a deliberately open system, with even the Squeak interpreter itself written in Squeak. This makes it highly portable, and it is available for Mac OS, Windows (95 and later), WinCE, Unix-like systems, BeOS, OS/2, and RISC OS. Squeak makes it possible for a programmer to modify the language itself. The interpreter, optional compiler, and everything else are free.
- **Practical Extraction and Report Language (PERL)** is often treated as synonymous with **CGI scripting**. In fact, Perl is even older than the web itself. It got its nose into the web-scripting tent and thrived due to its strong text-processing abilities, incredible flexibility (its creator likens it to duct tape), portability (it is available for nearly every modern operating system), and price (free). The Internet Movie Database and Yahoo both run on it.
- **Ruby** [the birthstone for July (following **PERL** for June)] combines some of the best features of several other languages, leaving behind many of their shortcomings. It is a pure object-oriented language like SmallTalk, but with clearer syntax (inspired by Eiffel). It has powerful text-handling like Perl, but is better structured and more consistent. It borrows ideas (but not the parentheses) from Lisp. Those who have tried it seem to love it, and rarely switch back to their previous languages. A free interpreter is available for Windows, Unix-like, Mac, OS/2, and BeOS systems.
- **Python** [comedy troupe *Monty Python*] is an open-source, interpreted object-oriented language developed for Unix and now available for everything from

DOS to Mac OS to OS/2 to Windows to Unix-like systems. It shares many positive attributes with Ruby, and adds the ability to run it on any machine that supports Java. It is often criticized, however, for not being as purely object-oriented as other languages.

- **Macromedia Director** and **Flash** are the de facto tools of choice for developing web sites featuring dynamic media. They are not really **languages**, though both include a bit of their own scripting. Instead they are GUI development environments for producing **source code** modules containing both data and instructions, which can in turn be **compiled** into executable programs. As tools for creating snazzy graphical user interfaces, they are top-notch, but they require some separate back-end programming for anything that will require processing or manipulating data.
- **List processing (LISP)** is **a programmable programming language**, built on the concept of recursion and highly adaptable to vague specifications. Avoid it if you find parentheses unappealing (its syntax tends toward a proliferation of nested parentheses), but its ability to handle problems that other languages cannot is one of the reasons that this more than year-old language is still in use. There is an entire cross-platform web server written in it.
- **Programming in logic (PROLOG)** is an independent study project in college, written a Prolog application which evaluated and proved (if possible) arguments in propositional logic (example, *A implies B, and A is true, therefore B is true*) a task which would have been much more difficult using a procedural language.
- **ToonTalk** is a highly-visual environment designed to teach children the principles of programming. Rather than typing instructions, the programmer manipulates various objects (LEGO-looking toy items that come to life when used) to define how the system is supposed to work. Unlike **educational** puzzle-solving computer games, ToonTalk encourages its users to create their own puzzles. Experienced C++ programmers will hate it, but then, most 4th-graders would not care for C++. It is available for Windows only.
- **Common Business-Oriented Language (COBOL)** is the language which modern programmers love to hate and ridicule. Although it is nearly as old as commercial computing itself, improperly blamed for Y2K issues, and its imminent extinction is frequently predicted, it is still in widespread use due to its usefulness for traditional business uses of processing data and producing reports. A version with object-oriented tools has been created, with an inexpensive IDE for Linux and Windows available. It is very verbose, designed so that its commands would describe in English exactly what it was doing. Example, **Add shipping-charge to invoice-subtotal**.
- **Formula translation (FORTRAN)** is the oldest language but still in general use, dating back to 1957, the year the space age began. It excels at the first task computers were called on for, such as number-crunching. This is the language that literally put a man on the moon, and some of the features it developed in the

process of that project (and other less glamorous ones) have yet to be duplicated in other, more **modern** languages.

- **DataBASE (DBASE)** (renamed **Xbase** to avoid trademark issues) was the command language for Ashton-Tate's ground-breaking database management program (the first such tool for microcomputers). As the program grew, so did the language, until it became an application development tool in its own right. At its zenith, various competing implementations and compilers were available and the language became standardized. Xbase did not make the transition to Windows very well, but it is still being used and supported (kind of the COBOL of the microcomputer age).

Coding style

The following are some rules and guidelines that will lead to a better programming style:

- The identifiers should be as simple as possible and meaningful, which does not need to be explained. Use as many comment lines as possible for proper understanding. Avoid using identifiers like *SUB1, SUB2, TOTAL_1, or TOTAL_2,* and so on. These may cause typographical errors to mistype SUB2 for SUB1, which may not be noticed during compilation or execution.
- Same names not to be used for two different variables. Same name for both global and local variables may cause disasters and confusion in debugging. Use more local definitions, data types, and identifiers. Do not clutter with more global variables to save a few lines of code.
- Use simple key elements for a successful completion of a program. Shortcuts, tricky code, and complicated algorithms will conceal errors, and reduce readability.
- Function should be simple and should compute one value. Use the function that returns a value and the function that returns no value (void) appropriately. The function in mathematics has one or more than one argument and produces one value and does not redefine or change the value of its arguments during computation. Function arguments should not be used to return values to the calling program. Avoid using a function without an argument
- Use a procedure subprogram to perform a simple task, as we know the procedure is task-oriented and a function is value-oriented. At the beginning of each subprogram, define the arguments and their initial values. Also, for those arguments that return values to the calling program, define the value they must return.
- For control structures, the program control pointer must enter the structure at its entry point and leave it at its exit point. Do not create a conditional jump from the middle of a control structure to a point outside the structure. This shortcut may save execution time but it may also result in the loss of readability, understandability, and comprehension. If necessary to use nested control structures, limit the direct

nesting to no more than three levels. Nested loops and if-then-else statements reduce the readability of the program. Too many nested subprograms make it extremely difficult to follow the program logic.

- Use of *GOTO, a BREAK, or EXIT* statements can clarify a control structure or divide a long control structure into smaller ones. Limit the use of GOTO statements to only these kinds of situations.
- Avoid defining subprograms whose execution may create confusion. Try to describe it clearly. Limit the number of arguments in a subprogram up to five. Too many arguments reduce clarity and readability.
- A better program is simple, clear, easy to understand, and maintain. The fastest program is not necessarily the shortest program. Therefore, while developing a program, avoid using difficult and tricky statements to shorten the program.
- Use abstraction in the design and coding programs only to the extent program readability is preserved. The use of abstraction helps to create reusable code.
- While writing code, use more indentation for better clarity and readability.
- To improve the portability of the program, use minimum system utilities.
- Effective use of comment statements strategically located in the code can enhance program understanding greatly.

Coding quality

The coding consumes a small fraction (10% to 15%) of the entire software development cost and schedule. A poorly written program can have very bad effect at the time of testing and maintenance. A good program has certain measurable attributes. These attributes can be specified in the **software requirements specification (SRS)** and tested during test and integration phases. Subsequently, these attributes can become quality assurance parameters for the program. The attributes include:

- **Readability, understandability, and comprehensibility (RUC):** The most important characteristics of a program are smooth readability and following the logic and its structure. RUC refers to all these features and assists in debugging and maintenance of a program.
- **Logical structure**: Application of structured programming rules help to create a logically and structurally sound coding. A well designed and structured program will have low level of coupling and high level of cohesion among its subprograms and will not allow multiple entry and exit points in subprograms. A logically designed program will become stronger and long lasting.
- **Physical layout**: It refers to the actual listing of the source code of a program. Good use of indentation, separation of key words from identifiers, use of meaningful identifiers, extensive use of comment statements, minimum use of explanatory comment statements, proper beginning, and end of each block are some of the features of physical layout of a good programming.

- **Robustness**: It means how well a program can withstand the time of handling incorrect input data. A software product must be protected against the misuse and be designed to deal with bad input data. On encountering bad input data, the execution should not stop, and sufficient warning should be given on validation, or self-correcting capability should be provided. This attribute should be specified in user manual, operation manual, and SRS.
- **Memory and execution efficiency**: This refer how fast the program works and how much computer memory is used. A program must use fast and efficient algorithms. Appropriate file, data structures, and access methods should be used. Since the memory of a computer is very expensive, care must be taken to minimize the use of memory without sacrificing the execution efficiency.
- **Complexity**: Both algorithmic complexity and cyclomatic or structural complexity will make the program difficult to understand and implement. Less complexity with less branching of program needs to be used for a good coding.
- **Human factors**: Proper care must be given in developing the human-to-computer interface. For example, an input screen that is hard to read, has more fields than a person can easily comprehend, is not laid out properly, and is not robust with regard to human error will be rejected by the users. This effect will be an economic failure of the software product.
- **Reusable code**: Segments of code are available in the libraries or market. In order to reduce the cost of the software product and make it available in shortest possible time these segments are used in different parts of the program. Hence, the reusability attribute of a program segment could be a measure of segment quality.

Art of debugging

Art of Debugging is a process of locating and correcting the causes of known errors. Commonly used debugging methods include induction, deduction, and backtracking.

Debugging by **induction** method involves the following steps:

1. Collect the available information. Enumerate known facts about the observed failure and known facts concerning successful test cases. What are the observed symptoms? When did the error occur? How does the failure case differ from successful cases?
2. Look for patterns. Examine the collected information for conditions that differentiate the failure case from successful cases.
3. Form one or more hypotheses. Derive one or more hypotheses from the observed relationships. If no hypotheses are apparent, re-examine the available information and collect additional information. If several hypotheses emerge, rank them in order of most likely to least likely.

4. Prove or disapprove each hypothesis. Re-examine the available information to determine whether the hypotheses explain all aspects of the observed problem. Do not proceed to steps until step-4 is completed.
5. Implement appropriate corrections. Make the corrections to back up your copy of the code in case the modifications are not correct.
6. Verify the correction. Rerun the failure case to be sure that the fix corrects the observed symptom. If the fix is not successful, then go to step a.

Debugging by **deduction** method proceeds as follows:

1. List possible causes for the observed failure.
2. Use the available information to eliminate various hypotheses.
3. Elaborate the remaining hypotheses.
4. Prove or disapprove each hypothesis.
5. Determine the appropriate correctness.
6. Verify the corrections.

Debugging by **backtracking** involves working backward in the source code from the point where the error was observed in an attempt to identify the exact point where the error occurred.

Traditional debugging

Traditional debugging techniques utilize:

- **Diagnostic output statements**: These can be embedded in the source code as specially formatted comment statements that are activated using a special translator option.
- **Snap shot dumps**: A snapshot dump is a machine level representation of the partial or total program state at a particular point in the execution sequence.
- **Trace facility**: A trace facility lists changes in selected state components.
- **Traditional breakpoint**: This facility interrupts program execution and transfers control to the programmer's terminal when execution reaches a specified break instruction in the source code.

Modern debugging

Modern debugging tools utilize:

- **Assertion-driven debugging**: Assertions are logical predicates written in the source code level to describe relationships among the components of the current program state and relationships between program states. An assertion violation can alter the execution sequence. Assertion violation that transfers control to the programmer's terminal are called conditional break points. They become unconditional break points under assertion such as 0 = 1 or false. Conditional break points are state dependent while unconditional break points are instruction dependent.

For example, for an assertion-driven debugging and unit testing tool, the **Assembly Language Assertiòn Driven Debugging Interpreter (AL ADD IN)**

- **Execution histories**: An execution history is a record of execution events collected from an executing program. The history is typically stored in a database for post-mortem examination after the program has terminated execution. A trace back facility uses the execution history to trace the control flow and data flow both forward and backward in execution time.

In this approach, only changes in execution state are recorded as the program executes. This approach is use to reduce the unreasonable overhead in execution time and memory space that would be required to maintain a complete copy of the execution state at each step in the execution sequence. **Executable debugging and monitoring system (EXDAMS)** and **interactive semantic modeling system (ISMS)** are the examples for this approach.

Debugging process

Debugging is done when a failure occurs during the execution of a software program. The failure symptoms are examined through a debugging process. Testing and debugging are two different activities with different objectives. In testing, the primary objective is to produce failures due to the software faults. The testing team finds a way to make the software fail. The objective of debugging is to locate and remove the identified fault in a module. The debugging process consists of six steps:

1. Information gathering
2. Fault location
3. Confirmation
4. Documentation
5. Fault removal
6. Retesting

For the failure the related data and information should be collected. The fault must be localized within a small segment of the software like a function, a procedure, or a small block of code. The fault must be uncovered that is causing failure. The debugging process and remedial actions taken must be documented.

Information gathering

The software engineer, during debugging, tries to collect as much information as it can on the failure. They may refer to test logs, test anomaly report, hearsay, and eyewitness accounts, and so on. Frequent feedback from debugging will help in improving the quality of the software. The debugging activity is supported by the test log and anomaly reports. To debug a software, it is essential to learn more about it so that the debugging process is easier and smoother.

Fault isolation

It is necessary to isolate the failure to a specific statement, a block of statements, a control structure, and so on. There are different types of approaches to isolate failure. The first approach is a **binary approach** by which an attempt is made to bracket the statements or control structures that are the sources of failure. The second approach is the **structured question and answer approach** where a set of questions is posed and answered. The third approach is based on **inducing other people into failure analysis**. The fourth approach relies on the **development of new test cases** specifically designed to isolate the known faults.

Fault confirmation

Once the fault isolation process identifies a function, a procedure, a control structure, a block of statements, or a single statement as fault, the error must be confirmed. Using additional special testing, desk checking, reviews, walk-through, and other methods, the cause of failure must be fully verified. The fault must be confirmed as the sole cause of failure.

Documentation

A proper documentation is required on every correction, updating, modification, and addition. The abnormal behavior of the program under new test cases must be recorded. A structured documentation of the debugging process helps in the testing process. A large program may run perfectly at the test site but may not run properly at the operation site. In such cases, the embedded software is blamed for the problems. Therefore, based on the documentation, all the system engineers, software engineers, hardware engineers, and testers must work together to sort out the problem.

Fixing the fault

On confirmation of the fault with its exact nature, location, remedial action can be initiated. Changing one part of the program may influence other part immediately or remain latent for the future. The software must be evaluated carefully. The best way is to re-run the selected portion of the program during acceptance test.

Test after correction

After each modification, change, or correction in the module the full software needs to be tested. Change in a specific path may cause failures in another place. Execute new test cases to ensure the affected area is working without any further failure. The test and integration team must work together to ensure the correctness of the unexecuted portion.

Debugging tools

The debugging tools are generally embedded with the compiler, which helps the software engineer to locate the logical errors in the program. This helps in identifying and removing the errors effectively. The debugging tools facilitate a structured walk through, while the program is in execution mode. There are a variety of debuggers that work differently with different levels of sophistication. The debuggers show the errors on the screen in the form of a visual trace of execution. The programmer is able to see the statement with an indication of the error. The statement under execution will show all types of errors directly or indirectly. An experienced programmer can use the debugger to reduce the debugging time effectively. The debugger is especially helpful in isolating the source of the reported error.

Conclusion

This chapter describes the evolution of coding language and different languages widely used for writing a program. The chapter has also discussed the characteristics of a language that can be used in coding effectively. The difference in testing and debugging can be realized here. The debugging process is discussed here, and the steps involved are investigating the different errors thoroughly to isolate the failure causing faults, confirming the identified faults by additional tests, correcting the faults with the same degree of discipline and control as in the original development process, and performing the regression testing on the software product. This ensures that the program is fully corrected and bug free.

In the next chapter, readers will explore **software testing**, a critical phase in the software development lifecycle that ensures the quality, reliability, and functionality of a system. Testing helps identify defects, validate requirements, and improve software performance before deployment. This chapter will cover key testing methodologies, including **manual and automated testing**, as well as different levels such as **unit testing, integration testing, system testing, and acceptance testing**. Readers will also learn about testing strategies, tools, and best practices to enhance software robustness. Understanding software testing is essential for delivering high-quality applications that meet user expectations and industry standards.

Exercises

To solidify your understanding of the concepts covered in this chapter, try the following exercises.

Multiple choice questions

1. **What is the primary goal of coding in software engineering?**
   a. To write complex programs
   b. To implement user requirements efficiently
   c. To create errors for debugging
   d. To document the project
2. **Which of the following is a key practice in writing maintainable code?**
   a. Using long variable names
   b. Avoiding comments
   c. Following coding standards
   d. Using global variables frequently
3. **Which tool is commonly used for debugging in software development?**
   a. Git
   b. Compiler
   c. IDE with debugger
   d. UML diagram
4. **What is the first step in debugging a program?**
   a. Writing more code
   b. Re-running the program repeatedly
   c. Identifying the bug or error
   d. Deleting the program and starting over
5. **Which type of error occurs due to improper logic implementation?**
   a. Syntax error
   b. Runtime error
   c. Logic error
   d. Compilation error
6. **What does debugging refer to in software engineering?**
   a. Writing code
   b. Removing errors from code
   c. Writing documentation
   d. Optimizing performance
7. **Which of the following is a debugging technique?**
   a. Unit testing
   b. Code commenting

c. Binary search
d. Rubber duck debugging

Short answer questions

1. What is debugging?
2. What are the outcomes of debugging process?
3. What are the categories of debugging?
4. Brute force, backtracking, cause elimination.
5. Define defect removal efficiency.
6. List some categories of faults.
7. Define software error, software fault and software failure.
8. What is error tracking?

Essay type questions

1. **Take a newly written program of around 1000 lines and perform the following steps:**
   a. Identify the faults, if any, in the program.
   b. Isolate the cause of each fault using a debugger.
   c. Remove the failure causing code by replacing a new statement.
   d. At the time of isolating the faults and correcting them, other failures may occur. Make a report of them.
2. **While performing the tasks in the above problem, collect the data as below:**
   a. Number of faults
   b. Number of errors
   c. The number of failures causing errors found during debugging
   d. Density of faults per 100 lines of code.
   e. Test time spent debugging the program

Multiple choice answers

1. b
2. c
3. c
4. c
5. c
6. b
7. d

CHAPTER 11
Software Testing

Introduction

The system development phases involve many activities where chances for the occurrence of human errors are enormous. Logical error, carelessness, improper communication, the need to hurry through the whole process of software development due to time constraint, cost constraint, and so on; provide ways for errors to creep in. The system must be tested thoroughly so that such errors are detected and corrected as early as possible. A successful test is the one that uncovers every possible error.

The analyst prepares system specifications that are passed to programmers for coding. The coding takes considerable effort and skill of the programmer to convert the charts, tables, and instructions into program statements. These need to be tested at various intervals. Testing software begins earlier in the systems development life cycle, even though many of the actual testing activities are carried out during implementation. During analysis, a master test plan is developed. The indicative test plan is shown in *Table 11.1*. During design, you develop a unit test plan, an integration test plan, and a system test plan. During implementation, these various plans are put into effect, and the actual testing is performed.

Structure

In this chapter, we are going to discuss:

- Test plan
- Static testing
- Dynamic testing
- Various testing strategies
- Guidelines for module testing

Objectives

The objectives of testing a system are to identify all defects existing in software, remove them, and achieve error-free operation under stated conditions for a stated period of time. Testing is vital to the success of a system. System testing makes a logical assumption that if all the parts of the system are correct, the goal will be successfully achieved. Inadequate testing or non-testing leads to errors, which may not appear until months later. This creates two problems; the time lag between the cause and the appearance of the problem (the longer the time interval, the more complicated the problem has become) and the effect of the system errors on files and records within the system.

Small system error can conceivably explode into a much larger problem. Effective testing early in the process translates directly into long-term cost savings from a reduced number of errors.

Another objective of system testing is its utility as a **user-oriented** vehicle before implementation. The best program is worthless if it does not meet user needs. Unfortunately, the user's demands are often compromised by the efforts to facilitate program or design efficiency in terms of processing time or memory utilization. Often the computer technician and the user have communication barriers due to different backgrounds, interests, priorities, and languages. The system tester (designer, programmer, or user) who has developed some computer mastery can bridge this barrier.

In **software development life cycle (SWDLC),** testing is the most important phase. The testing is carried out along with system integration. All types of issues found are unresolved during the requirement analysis, design, and coding stage. Many unforeseen problems are handled.

The testing activity is described here as a part of the system development.

Test plan

The purpose of the written test plans is to improve the communication among all the people involved in testing application software. The plan specifies each person's role during testing. The test plan also serves as a checklist, which you can use to determine whether the entire master test plan has been completed or not. The master test plan is not just a single document but a collection of documents. A master test plan is a project within the overall system development project. The overall plan and testing requirements sections are like a baseline project plan for testing, with a schedule of events, resource requirements, and standards of practice outlined. Procedure control explains how testing to be conducted, how to fix errors will be documented.

Testing managers are responsible for developing test plans, establishing testing standards, integrating testing, and development activities in the life cycle, and ensuring the test plans are completed. Testing specialists help in developing test plans, create test cases, and scenarios, execute the actual tests, and analyze report test results.

1		**Introduction**	4		**Procedure control**
	a	Description of the system to be tested		a	Test initiation
	b	Objective of the test plan		b	Test execution
	c	Method of testing		c	Test failure
	d	Supporting documents		d	Access or change control
2		**Overall Plan**		e	Document control
	a	Mile stone, schedule & locations	5		**Test specific or component test plans**
	b	Test material		a	Objectives
		1. Test plans		b	Software description
		2. Test cases		c	Method
		3. Test scenario		d	Milestone, schedule, location
		4. Test log		e	Requirements
3		**Testing requirements**		f	Criteria for passing tests
	a	Hardware		g	Resulting test material
	b	Software		h	Execution control
	c	Personnel		i	Attachments

Table: 11.1: *Table of content of a master test plan*

Software application testing is an umbrella term that covers several types of tests. *Mosley (1993)* organizes the types of tests according to whether they employ static or dynamic techniques and whether the test is automated or manual. Static testing means that the code being tested is not executed. The results of running the code are not an issue for that particular test. Dynamic testing, on the other hand, involves the execution of code. Automated testing means the computer conducts the test, while manual testing means that people do. Using this framework, we can categorize the type of tests as shown in *Table 11.2*:

	Manual	Automated
Static	Inspections	Syntax checking
Dynamic	Walkthrough	Unit test
	Desk checking	Integration test
		System test

Table: 11.2: Categorization of test types

Inspections

Inspections are a formal group of activities where participants manually examine the code for the occurrences of well-known errors. Syntax, grammar, and some other routine errors can be checked by automated inspection software, so manual inspection checks are used for more subtle errors. This detects 60 to 90 percent of all software defects and provides feedback to the programmers with the feedback that enables them to avoid making the same type of errors in future work. It is a testing technique in which participants examine the program code for predictable language-specific errors.

Walkthrough

Walkthrough, in a structured manner, is a very effective method of detecting errors in code. A structured walkthrough is used to review many system development deliverables, including logical and physical design specifications as well as code. The specification walkthrough tends to be formal reviews, and code walkthroughs tend to be informal. According to *Yourdon (1989)*, code walkthroughs should be done frequently when the pieces of work reviewed are relatively small and before the work is formally tested. Different organizations conduct the walkthrough differently. There is a basic structure you can follow, that works well.

Guidelines for conducting a code walkthrough:

- Have the review meeting chaired by the project manager or chief programmer, who is also responsible for scheduling the meeting, reserving a room, setting the agenda, inviting participants, and so on.
- The programmer presents his or her work to the reviewers. Discussion should be general during the presentation.
- Following the general discussion, the programmer walks through the code in detail, focusing on the logic of the code rather than on specific test cases.
- Reviewers ask to walk through specific cases.
- The chair resolves disagreement if the review team cannot reach an agreement among themselves and assigns duties, usually to the programmer, for making specific changes.
- A second walkthrough is then scheduled if needed.

Desk checking

Walkthrough is another testing technique in which the program code is sequentially executed manually by the reviewer. What the code does is also important in desk checking, an informal process where the programmer or someone else, who understands the logic of the program, works through the code with a paper and pencil. The programmer executes each instruction by using test cases that may or may not be written down. In one sense, the reviewer acts as the computer, mentally checking each step, and its results for the entire set of computer instructions.

Among the list of automated checking in *Table 11.2*, there is only one static technique, which checks syntax. Syntax checking is typically done by a compiler. Errors in syntax are uncovered but the code is not executed. For the other three automated techniques, the code is executed.

Unit testing

Unit testing, sometimes called **module testing** is an automated technique. In unit testing, each module is tested alone in an attempt to discover any error that may exist in the module's code. Since modules coexist and work with other modules in programs and systems, they must be tested together in large groups. *Figure 11.1* shows the testing process:

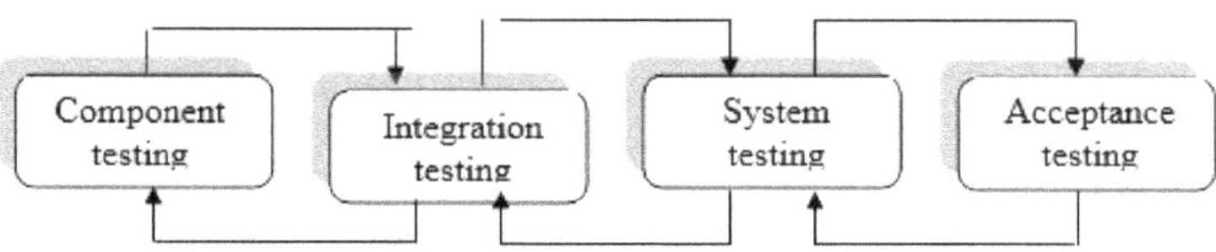

Figure 11.1: *Testing process*

Except for small programs, system should not be tested as a single, monolithic unit. *Figure 11.1* shows a four-stage testing process where system components are tested, the integrated system is tested and, finally system is tested with the customer's data. On completion of acceptance testing the sign-on procedure takes place between the developer and customer where the handing over of the application system takes place.

Integration testing

Integration testing is done by combining the modules and testing them together. Integration testing is gradual. The integration plan is guided by the module dependency graph of the structure chart. The structure chart shows the chronological arrangement of various modules calling each other. Hence, by examining the structure chart, the integration plan is developed. The structure chart is shown in *Figure 11.2*. First, you test the coordinating module (the root module in a structure chart tree) and only one of its subordinate modules. After the first test, you add one or two other subordinate modules from the same level. Once the program has been tested with the coordinating module and all of its immediately subordinate modules, you add modules from the next level and then test the program. The modules are typically integrated in a top-down, incremental order. You continue this procedure until the entire program has been tested as a unit. Some of the popular methods are used in making an integrated test plan.

Top-down approach

It starts with the root module and one or two sub modules followed by testing. After the top-level modules are tested, the immediate module is combined and become ready for testing. It is suitable for small systems. It causes problem for testing if there are no lower level routines which may be called by top level one.

Bottom-up approach

In the **bottom-up** approach, all the sub-modules are tested separately, and finally, the full system is tested. The purpose of testing each sub-module is to test the interfaces among them. In this situation, control and data interfaces between modules are tested. Lower-level subsystems are tested and are combined with the higher-level modules for further testing. The advantage is that many subsystems, having no dependency, can be tested simultaneously. The disadvantage is that during the testing of a number of sub-systems, the situation becomes complex. This extreme condition calls for a big bang approach. *Figure 11.2* shows the structure chart of a program:

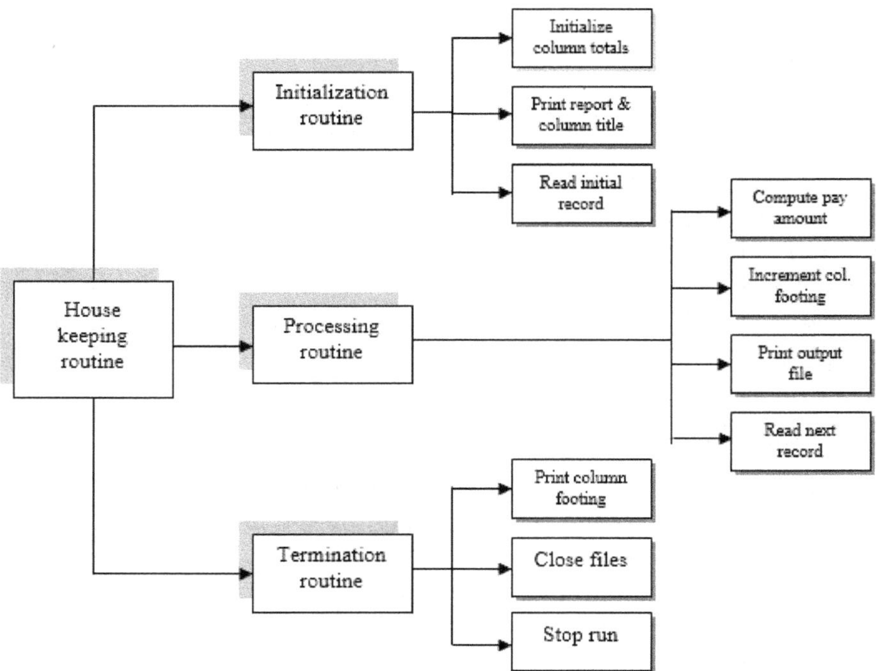

Figure 11.2: *Structure chart of a program*

Big-bang approach

All the sub-modules are integrated in a single step and tested together. This approach is convenient for a small system where, in one go, the errors are fixed. The disadvantage is that it is difficult to spot the error found in the exact module during integration testing. To remove the error during integration testing is costly and time-consuming.

Mixed approach

Mixed approach is a combination of both top-down and bottom-up approaches. The disadvantages of both the approaches are reduced to a great extent. The testing is possible from both top and bottom level, wherever the modules are available. This is common approach for integration testing.

System testing

System testing is a similar process, but instead of integrating modules into programs for testing, you integrate programs into systems. System testing follows the same incremental logic that is used in integration testing. Programs are typically integrated in top-down, incremental fashion. Under both integration and system testing, the individual modules and programs get tested many times, as well as the interfaces between modules and programs also get tested. Considering the testing location and data, two types of testing are conducted.

Alpha testing

Tests performed at the developer's site before the system is finally installed in the real working environment (user's site) are known as **alpha testing**. It involves testing the system with live data supplied by the organization rather than by the test data used by the system designer and is also called as **acceptance testing**.

Beta testing

In beta testing, the system is delivered to a number of potential users who agree to use that system and provide feedback to the designers. Testing should be repeated if any modification is done based on the feedback given by the users, and it is also called as **regression testing**.

Stub testing

Stub testing is a technique used in testing modules, where modules are written and tested in a top-down fashion, where a few lines of code are used to substitute the subordinate modules. Under a top-down approach, the coordinating module is written first. Then, the modules at the next level in the structure chart are written, followed by the modules at the next level, and so on, until all the modules in the system are done. Each module is tested as it is written. Since top-level modules contain many calls to subordinate modules, you may wonder how they can be tested if the lower-level modules have not been written yet. The answer is stub testing, which is two to three lines of code written by a programmer to stand for the missing modules. During the testing, the coordinating module calls the stub instead of the subordinate module. The stub accepts control and then returns it to the coordinating module.

Acceptance testing

Acceptance testing is the final stage in the testing process before the system is accepted for operational use by the client. The system is tested with data supplied by the user rather than with simulated data. Acceptance testing may reveal errors and omissions in the system requirement definition because real data exercises the system in different ways from the test data. Acceptance testing may also reveal requirements problems where the system's facilities do not really meet the user's needs, or the system performance is not acceptable. Refer to *Figure 11.3*:

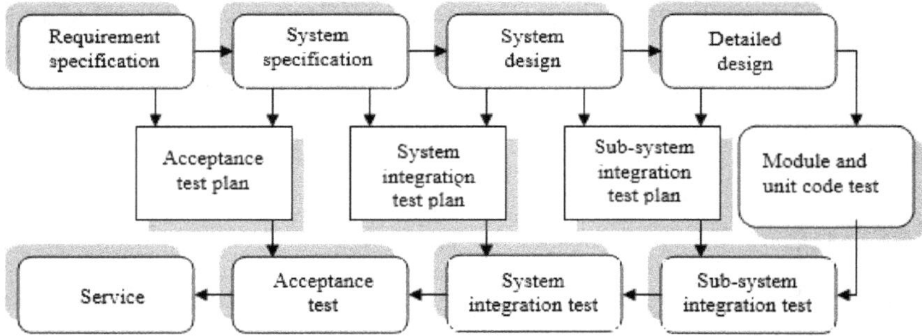

Figure 11.3: *Testing phases in the software process*

Normally, component (unit) development and testing are interleaved. Programmers make up their own test data and incrementally test the code as it is developed. This is an economically sensible approach, as the programmer knows the component best and is, therefore, the best person to generate test cases.

Static testing

The static testing refers to **non-executable files** like requirement analysis, audits, desk checks, inspections, and walkthroughs. It is employed to verify the correctness of requirements, designs, and code before execution of the test cases.

The static testing functions are performed in code auditing, consistency checking, cross referencing, interface analysis, input, and output specification analysis, data flow analysis, error checking, type analysis, unit analysis, walkthroughs, and clean-room correctness verification.

Dynamic testing

Dynamic testing is used to describe the development and execution of test cases, test procedures, structures, use of test logs, and so on. The two common ways to perform dynamic testing are **black box and white box testing**. Both the methods require a set of well-developed and well-structured test cases. The dynamic testing cannot prove the absolute correctness of a software product unless it is performed in an exhaustive manner. The exhaustive testing takes a lot of time to cover all the possible module paths, combinations of paths, and combinations of inputs.

The exhaustive testing of a small system is not practical. For example, suppose one is required to test an integer addition algorithm by employing an exhaustive testing approach. It will include approximately 2^{64} test executions (assuming integers are stored in 32 bits). For a computer that performs 2^{24} operations per second, it will take 2^{40} seconds or approximately 35,000 years to complete an exhaustive test of the addition algorithm. Hence an exhaustive testing is not a viable approach.

Test data for unit testing can be constructed systematically in two basic ways. The first is to **test to specifications**. The technique also is called black-box, behavioral, data-driven, functional, and input or output-driven testing. In this approach, the code itself is ignored. The only information used in drawing up test cases is the specification document. The other extreme is to test the code and to ignore the specification document when selecting test cases. Other names for this technique are **glass-box, white-box, structural, logic-driven, and path-oriented testing.**

Black box testing

Black-box testing is concerned with the proper execution of the program specification. In this testing, each function or sub-program used in the main program is first identified. For example, in a payroll system, `Calc_grosspay( )` and `Print_payslips( )` may be the functions used to calculate the gross pay and printing of pay slips. Test cases are devised to test each function or sub-program separately. Test-cases are decided solely on the basis of the requirements or specifications of the program and not on the basis of the coding (data structure used) of the modules.

Black-box testing is complementary to **white-box** technique. It uncovers a different class of errors which are not discovered by white-box methods. This type of testing attempts to find the following errors:

- Interface error
- Incorrect or missing functions
- Errors in external database access
- Performance errors
- Initialization and termination errors

Feasibility of black box

For example, suppose that the specifications for a certain data-processing product state that five types of commission and seven types of discount must be incorporated. Testing every possible combination of just commission and discount requires 35 test cases. It is no use in saying that commission and discount are computed in two entirely separate code artifacts, and hence, may be tested independently. On the contrary, in black-box testing, the product is treated as a black box, and its internal structure therefore is completely irrelevant.

This example contains only two factors, commission, and discount, taking on five and seven different values, respectively. Any realistic product has hundreds, if not thousands, of different factors. Even if there are only 20 factors, each taking on only four different values, a total of 4^{20} or 1.1×10^{12} different test cases must be examined. To see the implication of over a trillion test cases, consider how long it would take to test them all. If a team of programmers could be found that could generate, run, and examine the test cases at an average rate of one every 30 seconds, then it would take more than a million years to test the product exhaustively. Therefore, exhaustive testing to specifications is impossible in practice because of the combinatorial explosion. There are simply too many test cases to consider.

Black box unit-testing techniques

Exhaustive black-box testing generally requires billions and billions of test cases. The art of testing is to devise a small, manageable set of test cases to maximize the chances of detecting a fault while minimizing the chances of wasting a set of case by having the same fault detected by more than one test case. Every test case must be chosen to detect a previously undetected fault. One such black-box technique is **equivalence testing** combined with **boundary value analysis**.

Equivalence testing and boundary value analysis

Suppose the specification for a database product states that the product must be able to handle any number of records from 1 through 16,383 (2^{14}–1). If the product can handle 34 records and 14,870 records, then the chances are good that it will work fine. In fact, the chances of detecting a fault, if present, are likely to be equally good if any test case from 1 to 16,383 records is selected. Conversely, if the product works correctly for any one test case in the range from 1 through 16,383, then it probably will work for any other test case in the range. The range from 1 to 16,383 constitutes an equivalence class, that is, a set of test cases such that any one member of the class is as good a test case as any other. To be more precise, the specified range of numbers of records that the product must be able to handle defines three equivalence classes:

- Equivalence class 1= Less than 1 record.
- Equivalence class 2= From 1 to 16,383 records.
- Equivalence class 3= More than 16,383 records.

Testing the database product by using the technique of equivalence classes requires that one test case from each equivalence class is selected. The test case from equivalence class 2 should be handled correctly, whereas error messages should be printed for the test cases from class 1 and class 3. A successful test case detects a previously undetected fault. To maximize the chances of finding such a fault, a high-payoff technique is **boundary value analysis**. Experience has shown that, when a test case on or just to one side of the boundary of an equivalence class is selected, the probability of detecting a fault increases. Therefore, when testing the database product, seven test cases should be selected.

- **Test case 1= 0 record**: Member of equivalence class 1 and adjacent to boundary value.
- **Test case 2= 1 record**: Boundary value.
- **Test case 3= 2 records**: Adjacent to boundary value.
- **Test case 4= 723 records**: Member of equivalence class 2.
- **Test case 5= 16,383 records**: Adjacent to boundary value.
- **Test case 6= 16,383 records**: Boundary value.
- **Test case 7= 16,383 records**: Member of equivalence class 3 and adjacent to boundary values.

For each range (R_1, R_2) listed in either the input or the output specifications, five test cases should be selected, corresponding to values less than R_1, equal to R_1, greater than R_1 but less than R_2, equal to R_2, and greater than R_2. Where it is specified that an item has to be a member of a certain set, two equivalence classes must be tested, which are a member of the specified set and a non-member of the set. The use of equivalence classes, together with boundary value analysis, to test both the input specifications and the output specifications is a valuable technique for generating a relatively small set of test data with the potential of uncovering a number of faults that might well remain hidden if less powerful techniques for test data selection were used.

Functional testing

An alternative form of black-box testing is to base the test data on the functionality of a code artifact. In functional testing [*Howden, 1987*], each item of functionality or function implemented in a code artifact is identified. Typical functions in a classical module for a computerized warehouse product might be `get_next_ database_ record` or determine whether `quantity_on_hand` is below the reorder point. In a weapon control system, a module might include the function `compute_trajectory`. In a module of an operating system, one function might be `determine_whether_file_is_` empty.

After determining all the functions of a code artifact, test data are devised to test each function separately. Now, the functional testing is taken a step further. If the code artifact consists of a hierarchy of power-level functions, connected by control structures of structured programming, then functional testing proceeds recursively. For example, if a higher-level function is of the form:

```
<higher-level function> :: =      if <conditional expression>
                               <lower-level function 1>;
                           else
                                <lower-level function 2>;
```

Then, because **<conditional expression>**, **<lower-level function 1>**, and **<lower-level function 2>** have been subjected to functional testing, **<higher-level function>** can be tested, by using branch coverage, which is a glass-box technique.

Note: This form of structural testing is a hybrid technique, where the lower-level functions are tested using a glass-box technique.

In practice, however, higher-level functions are not constructed in such a structured fashion as lower-level functions. Instead, the lower-level functions usually are intertwined in some way. To determine faults in this situation, **functional analysis** is required, a somewhat complex procedure.

White box testing

White-box testing is concerned with the implementation of the program. In this type of testing different programming structures and data structures used in the program are tested for proper operations. This test concentrates on the examination of the coding. The system software engineers and programmers coin test-cases and test-data. The system designer creates test-cases that have likelihood of finding out the possible errors.

Feasibility of white box testing

The most common form of testing code requires that each path through code artifact be executed at least once. Consider the code fragment of *Figure 11.4*. The corresponding flowchart is shown in *Figure 11.5*. Even though the flowchart appears to be almost trivial, it has over 10^{12} different paths. There are five possible paths through the central group of six shaded boxes, and the total number of possible paths through the flowchart therefore is:

$$5^1 + 5^2 + 5^3 + \cdots + 5^{18} = \frac{5X(5^{18}-1)}{(5-1)} = 4.77X10^{12}$$

If there can be these many paths through a simple flowchart containing a single loop, it is not difficult to imagine the total number of different paths in a code artifact of reasonable size and complexity. In short, the huge number of possible paths renders exhaustive testing to code as infeasible as exhaustive testing to specifications:

```
read(kmax)      //kmax is an integer between 1 and 18
                for (k=0; k < kmax; k++) do
                {
                    read(myChar) //myChar is the character A, B, or C
                    switch(myChar)
                    {
                        case 'A':
                         blockA;
                         if(cond1) blockC
                         break;
                        case 'B':
                         blockB;
                         if(cond2) blockC
                         break;
                        case 'C':
                         blockC;
                         break;
                    }
                                    blockD;
                            }
```

Figure 11.4: *A code fragment*

Figure 11.5 shows a flowchart with over 10^{12} possible paths:

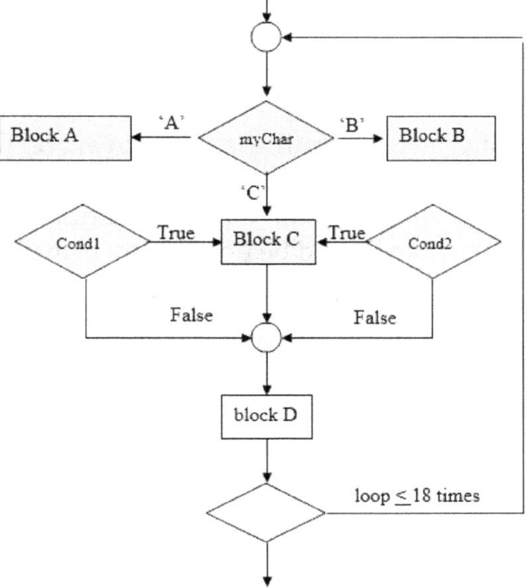

Figure 11.5: *A flowchart with over 10^{12} possible paths*

White box unit testing techniques

In white-box or glass-box techniques, test cases are selected on the basis of examination of the code rather than the specifications. There are a number of different forms of glass-box testing, including statement, branch, and path coverage.

Structural testing

Statement coverage is the simplest form of glass-box testing, in which a series of test cases is run during which every statement is executed at least once. To keep track of which statements are still to be executed, a **CASE tool** keeps a record of how many times each statement has been executed over the series of tests.

A weakness of this approach is that there is no guarantee that all outcomes of branches are properly tested. To see this, consider the code fragment of *Figure 11.6*. The programmers made a mistake; the compound conditional *s | 1 && t = = 0* should read *s | 1 | | t = 0*. The test data shown in *Figure 11.6* allow the statement *x = 9* to be executed without the fault being highlighted:

```
if (s > 1 && t = = 0)
        X=9;
Test case:       s = 2, t = 0.
```

Figure 11.6: *Code fragment with test data*

An improvement over statement coverage **is branch coverage**, that is, running a series of tests to ensure that all branches are tested at least once. Again, a tool usually is needed to help the tester to keep the track of which branches have or have not been tested. **Generic coverage tool (GCT)** is an example of a branch coverage tool for C programs. Techniques such as statement or branch coverage are termed structural tests.

The most powerful form of structural testing is **path coverage**, which is testing all paths. As shown previously, in a product with loops, the number of paths can be very large. The researchers have been investigating ways of reducing the number of paths to be examined while uncovering more faults than would be possible by using branch coverage.

When using structural testing, the tester simply might not come up with a test case that exercises a specific statement, branch, or path. What may have happened is that an infeasible path (dead code) is in the code artifact, that is, a path that cannot be possibly executed for any input data. *Figure 11.7* shows two examples of infeasible paths. In *Figure 11.7(a)* the programmer omitted a minus sign. If k is less than 2, then k cannot possibly be greater than 3, so the statement $x = x * k$ cannot be reached.

```
if (k < 2)
{
If (k > 3) // should be k > -3
x = x * k;
}
```

Figure 11.7(a): 1st example of infeasible path

Similarly, in **Figure 11.7(b)**, j is never less than 0, so the statement total = total + value[j] can never be reached. The programmer had intended the test to be *j < 10*, but made a typing mistake. A tester using statement coverage would soon realize that neither statement could be reached, and the fault would be found.

```
for (j = 0; j < 0; j+ +)          // should be j < 10
    total = total + value [ j];
```

Figure 11.7(b): 2nd example of infeasible path

Complexity metrics

Complexity metrics are another glass-box unit approach being used in the quality assurance viewpoint. Suppose a manager is told that code artifact m1 is more complex than code artifact m2. Irrespective of the precise way in which the term complex is defined, the manager intuitively believes that m1 is likely to have more faults than m2. Following this idea, computer scientists have developed a number of metrics of software complexity as an aid in determining which code artifacts are most likely to have faults. If the complexity of a code artifact is found to be reasonably high, a manager may direct that the artifact be redesigned and re-implemented on the ground that it is less costly and faster to start from scratch than to attempt to debug a fault-prone code artifact.

A simple metric for predicting a number of faults is the number of lines of code. The underlying assumption is that there is a constant probability (p), that a line of code contains a fault. If a tester believes that, on average, a line of code has a 2% chance of containing a fault, and the artifact under test is 100 lines long, then it implies that the artifact is expected to contain two faults, and an artifact that is twice as long is likely to have four faults.

Attempts have been made to find more sophisticated predictors of fault based on the measures of product complexity. McCabe's *cyclomatic complexity* is a measure through a number of binary decisions (predicates) plus 1. The cyclomatic complexity essentially is the number of branches in the code artifact. Accordingly, cyclomatic complexity can be used as a metrics for the number of test cases needed for branch coverage of a code artifact. This is the basis for so-called **structured testing**.

McCabe's metrics can be computed almost as easily as lines of code. In some cases, it has been shown to be a good metric for predicting faults; the higher the value of **M**, the greater the chance that a code artifact contains a fault. However, the validity of McCabe's metric has been questioned seriously on both theoretical and experimental grounds.

Various testing strategies

Let us first understand what we test for. The first test of a system is to see whether it produces the correct output or not. Follow the given steps to see a variety of other tests which are conducted:

- **Online response:** Online systems have a response time that will not cause a hardship to the user. One way to test this is to input the transactions on as many input screens as would normally be used in peak hours and time the response to each online function to establish a true performance level.
- **Volume:** In this test, we create as many records as would normally be introduced to verify that the hardware and software will function correctly. The user is usually asked to provide test data for volume testing.
- **Stress testing:** The purpose of stress testing is to prove that the candidate system does not malfunction under the peak loads. Unlike volume testing, where time is not a factor, we subject the system to a high volume of data over a short time period. This simulates an online environment where a high volume of activities occurs in spurts.
- **Recovery and security:** A forced system failure is induced to test a backup recovery procedure for file integrity. Inaccurate data are entered to see how the system responds in terms of error detection and protection. Related to file integrity is a test to demonstrate that data and programs are secure from unauthorized access.
- **Usability documentation and procedure:** The usability test verifies the user-friendly nature of the system. This relates to normal operating and error-handling procedures. Consider an example, one aspect of user friendliness is accurate and complete documentation. The user is asked to use only the documentation and procedures as a guide to determine whether the system can be run smoothly.

Nature of test data

The proper choice of test data is as important as the test itself. If test data as input are not valid or representative of the data to be provided by the user, then the reliability of the output is suspected. Test data may be artificial or live. Properly created artificial test data should provide all combinations of values and formats and make it possible to test all logic and transaction path subroutines.

Test strategy

The first step in system testing is to check out the strategy and prepare a plan that will test all the aspects of the system in a way that promotes its credibility among potential users. There is a psychology in testing:

- Programmers usually do a better job in unit testing because they are expected to document and report on the method and extent of their testing.
- Users are involved, which means communication is improved between users and the designer group.
- Programmers are involved when they become aware of user problems and expectations. The user also becomes more aware of the complexity of programming and testing. The outcome of all this is a more realistic and cooperative user for successful testing.

Activity network for system testing

A test strategy entails the following activities *(Figure 11.8)*:

- Prepare a test plan.
- Specify conditions for user acceptance testing.
- Prepare test data for program testing.
- Prepare test data for transaction path testing.
- Plan user training.
- Compile or assemble programs.
- Prepare job performance aids.
- Prepare operational documents.

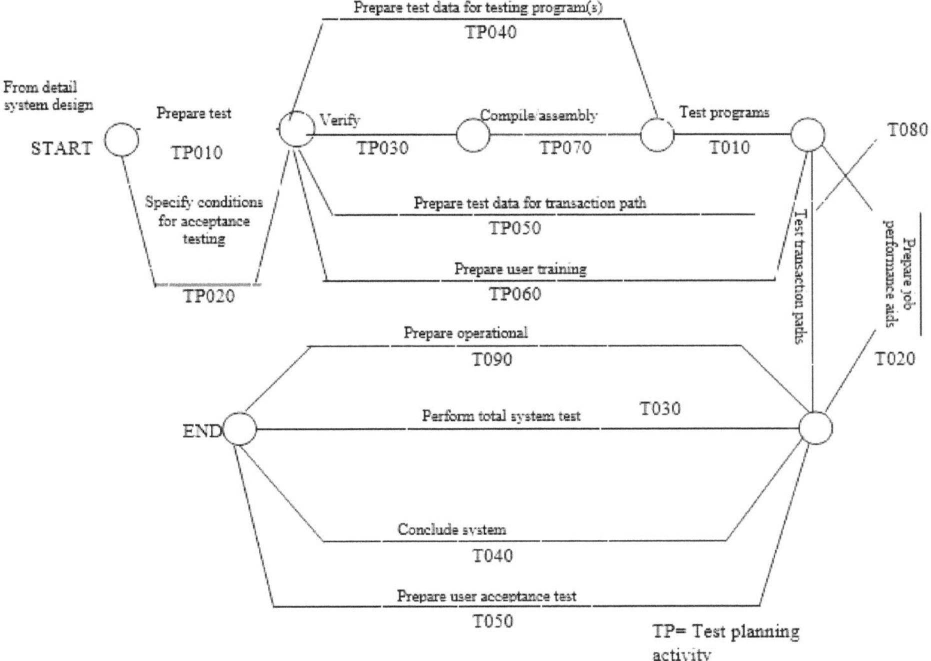

Figure 11.8: *Activity network for system testing*

Prepare test strategies

A workable test strategy must be prepared in accordance with the established design specifications. It includes:

- Outputs expected from the system
- Criteria for evaluating outputs
- A volume of test data
- Procedure for using test data
- Personnel and training requirements

Prepare test plan

A workable test plan must be prepared in accordance with the established design specifications. It includes:

- Outputs expected from the system
- Criteria for evaluating outputs
- A volume of test data
- Procedure for using test data
- Personnel and training requirements

Specify conditions for user acceptance testing

Planning for user acceptance testing calls for the analyst and the user to agree on the conditions for the test. Many of these conditions may be derived from the test plan. Others are an agreement on the test schedule, the test duration, and the persons designated for the test. The start and termination dates for the test should also be specified in advance.

Prepare test data for program testing

As each program is coded, test data are prepared and documented to ensure that all aspects of the program are properly tested. After the testing, the data are filed for future reference.

Prepare test data for transition path testing

This activity develops the data required for testing every condition and transaction to be introduced into the system. The path of each transaction from origin to destination is carefully tested for reliable results. The test verifies that the test data are virtually comparable to live data used after conversion.

Plan for user training

User training is designed to prepare the user for testing and converting the system. User involvement and training take place parallel with programming for three reasons:

- The system group has time available to spend on training while the programs are being written.
- Initiating a user-training program gives the systems group a clearer image of the user's interest in the new system.
- A trained user participates more effectively in system testing.

For user training, preparation of a checklist is useful which is shown in *Figure 11.9*. The provisions for developing training materials and other document to complete the training activity are included. In effect, the checklist calls for a commitment of personnel, facilities, and efforts for implementing the candidate system.

The training plan is followed by the preparation of the user training manual and other text materials. Facility requirements and the necessary hardware are specified and documented. A common procedure is to train the supervisors and department heads who, in turn, train their staff. The reasons are:

- User supervisors are knowledgeable about the capabilities of their staff and the overall preparation.
- Staff members usually respond more favorably and accept instructions better from supervisors than from outsiders.
- Familiarity of users with their particular problems (bugs) makes them better candidates for handling user training than the system analyst. The analyst gets the feedback to ensure that proper training is provided.

Company---------------------------					**Analyst-----------------------**	
Project Name----------------------						**Date --/--/----**
	Activity	**Start date**	**End date**	**Staff in-charge**	**Department in-charge**	**Comments**
1	Notification	mm/dd	mm/dd			
	Announcement to the officers	10/06	10/20	P K Mohanty	Sr. Vice. Prez	
	Announcement to the employees	10/06	10/20	R C Munde	Auditing	
	Coordinated customer activities	10/06	10/29	Shanket Paul	Casier	
	Coordinate computer service	10/06	10/29	Trina Dwivedi	PersonnelMgr.	
2	Procedures					
	Inter-departmental	10/14	11/01	Arjun Sethy	Auditing	
	Inter-departmental	10/14	11/01	Amit Raina	Systems	
3	Forms					
	Design	11/01	11/14	Madan Pai	Systems	
	Printing	11/01	11/20	P V Srinivas	Systems	

Company----------------------------					Analyst------------------------	
Project Name-----------------------					Date --/--/----	
	Activity	**Start date**	**End date**	**Staff in-charge**	**Department in-charge**	**Comments**
4	Equipment					
	P Cs, Printers, UPS & network	11/01	12/15	S K Mishra	HW engineer	
5	Training & Orientation					
	Manuals	12/01	12/16	Sudhir Sen	Systems	
	Training aids	12/01	12/16	Bikash Jain	Systems	
	Special workshops	12/10	12/14	Sweta Sudha	Systems	
6	Lobby Layout	12/10	12/30	S K Bebortha	President	
7	Supplies	12/10	12/15	Ranjan Sahoo	Purchase mgr.	
8	Personnel					
	Transfers	12/10	12/12	Naresh Jha	PersonnelMgr.	
	New hires	12/12	12/30	M Anthony	PersonnelMgr.	

Figure 11.9: *A check list for user training*

Compile or assemble program

All programs have to be compiled or assembled for testing. Earlier to this, a complete program description should be available. Program and system flowcharts of the project should be available. Before actual program testing, the run order schedule and test schemes are finalized. A run order schedule specifies the transactions to test and the order in which they should be tested. The bottom-up (linking small-scale modules to higher-level modules) or top-down (after testing the general program and then adding one lower-level program) approaches can be used.

Prepare job performance aids

In this activity the materials to be used by personnel to run the system are specified and scheduled. This includes a display of materials such as program codes, a list of input codes attached to the computer screen, and a posted instruction schedule to load to the disk drive or to a help menu. These aids reduce the training time and employ personnel at lower level.

Prepare operational documents

During the test plan stage, all the operational documents are finalized, including copies of the operational formats required by the candidate system. During operational documentation of the new system operation, the personnel with proper experience, training, and educational qualification are to be involved.

During the system testing, some of the performance criteria that need to be used are planned in advance. A substandard performance or service interruptions may cause system failure and are checked during the test. Some of the performance criteria being used during testing are:

- **Turnaround time** is the elapsed time between the receipt of the input and the availability of the output. In an online system, high priority processing is handled during the peak hours, while low priority processing is done later. The objective is to decide on and evaluate all the factors that might have bearing on the turnaround time for handling all applications.
- **Backup** relates to procedures to be used when the system is down. Backup plans might call for the use of another computer. The software for the candidate system must be tested for compatibility with a backup computer. Many times, a server with a **Redundant Array of Independent Disks (RAID)** control system can be tested for backups in case the main hard disk drive fails.
- **File protection** pertains to storing files in a separate area for protection against fire, flood, or natural disaster. Strategy should be established for reconstructing files through a hardware malfunction. Fortress, cold backup, warm backup, mutual backup approaches can be planned to meet the disaster recovery.
- The **human factor** applies to the personnel involved in the candidate system. During system testing, lighting, air conditioning, noise, and other environmental factors are evaluated. Hardware should be designed to match human comfort with consideration of agronomy.

Guidelines for module testing

To emphasize the importance and applicability of module testing, the following guidelines are to be followed:

- Try to design module tests so that failure to pass one test case will not move to the next test case.
- Under stressful loads and conditions, test the modules at their performance limit and beyond.
- The performance characteristics like throughput accuracy, input and output capacities, and timings should be measured for each module.
- A log book may be maintained to provide information to debug a failure.
- Concurrently, many problems should not be solved. They should be handled one after the other so that the source of error can be traced easily.
- Conduct a critical analysis after each module test to ensure that you are doing better next time.

Conclusion

Software testing is done to ensure that it runs correctly, including hardware and other software linked to it. Planning, discipline, control, and documentation are very important factors for successful software testing. Software testing is the most important phase in the SDLC. Planning for the test phase should begin early in the development life cycle and should be a constant concern throughout the development cycle. The activity network or flow graphs should be prepared to determine the distinct and independent paths through the program module. Executing every line in the program and performing black-box tests on each path are necessary. When a program module is tested, it is important to test for all required internal and external interfaces.

In the next chapter, readers will explore **System Implementation and Maintenance**, a crucial phase in the software development lifecycle. Implementation involves deploying the developed software into a live environment, ensuring smooth integration with existing systems, and conducting user training. This phase also includes final testing to validate performance and functionality. However, software development does not end at deployment—**maintenance** plays a critical role in ensuring long-term reliability and adaptability. Through corrective, adaptive, perfective, and preventive maintenance strategies, teams address bugs, improve performance, and adapt to evolving requirements. Understanding these processes is essential for sustaining software quality and user satisfaction over time.

Exercises

To solidify your understanding of the concepts covered in this chapter, try the following exercises.

Multiple choice questions

1. **What is the primary objective of software testing?**
   a. To improve software design
   b. To identify and fix bugs
   c. To document the code
   d. To develop new features

2. **Which type of testing is performed without executing the program?**
   a. Unit testing
   b. Static testing
   c. Integration testing
   d. Load testing

3. **Which of the following is a black-box testing technique?**
   a. Code review
   b. Boundary value analysis
   c. Code coverage
   d. Static analysis

4. **What does unit testing primarily focus on?**
   a. Testing the complete system
   b. Testing individual components or functions
   c. Testing system performance under load
   d. Testing integration between components
5. **Which testing ensures that new code does not adversely affect existing functionality?**
   a. System testing
   b. Regression testing
   c. Alpha testing
   d. Smoke testing
6. **What type of testing evaluates the software's ability to handle large volumes of data or users?**
   a. Functional testing
   b. Unit testing
   c. Load testing
   d. Smoke testing
7. **Which of the following is a goal of integration testing?**
   a. Ensure modules work together correctly
   b. Verify user acceptance
   c. Test performance under stress
   d. Evaluate overall system security
8. **Which testing is typically performed by end users to confirm the system meets their requirements?**
   a. Integration testing
   b. Unit testing
   c. Acceptance testing
   d. Load testing

Short answer questions

1. What is a software error, software fault, and software failure?
2. What are the types of failure cost?
3. Why do error removal costs increase as a project progress?
4. What is the difference between verification and validation?
5. What is a system acceptance test? What are the levels of acceptance testing?
6. Who are the role players in the system testing?
7. Define system testing.
8. What is security testing?
9. Define stress testing.

10. Define performance testing.
11. What is debugging?
12. What is the goal of the software tester?
13. What errors are found during black-box testing?
14. Define loop testing.
15. Name the different categories of system testing.
16. When to stop testing?
17. Why is it impossible to test a program completely?
18. Can a software tester perform white box testing on a specification?
19. You can perform dynamic black box testing without a product specification or requirement document. True or False.
20. It is unfair to perform stress testing at the same time as you are performing load testing. True or False.
21. Name several advantages of performing static white box testing.
22. White box testing can find missing items as well as problems. True or False.
23. What is the difference between dynamic white box testing and debugging?
24. Why a testing in big-bang software development model is nearly impossible?
25. What is Ad Hoc testing?
26. Who are the role players in the system testing process?

Essay questions

1. Distinguish between system testing and system acceptance testing.
2. Discuss how both the white box and black box testing can be used together.
3. Discuss the difference between black box (functional) and white box (structural) testing models.
4. Why a real time software system that has been tested in a simulated environment is not always reliable?
5. What are the deliverables from coding, testing, and installation?
6. What are structured walkthroughs for code? What is their purpose? How are they conducted?
7. What are activities take place in a testing process?
8. What is cyclomatic complexity? Where it is used?

Multiple choice answers

1. b
2. b
3. b
4. b
5. b
6. c
7. a
8. c

CHAPTER 12
System Implementation and Maintenance

Introduction

Once the application modules are coded with **high-level languages**, the next step is to assemble them into a computer software system. This is known as **software system implementation**. The successful implementation of the new software package is the most important part of the **system development life cycle**. We have to buy the equipment, plan individual sub-system, and hire people to implement the whole system. The implementation depends on the available resources and the type of hardware equipment available. It can be more complex, because equipment may be shared among multiple systems. One has to do a lot of planning before implementing a system.

Structure

In this chapter, we are going to discuss:

- Implementation procedures
- Implementation techniques
- System acceptance
- Maintenance, reliability and availability
- Maintenance
- Reverse engineering

- Re-engineering
- Business process reengineering

Objectives

This chapter provides a comprehensive understanding of the critical final stages in the software development lifecycle. In this chapter, we will explore the key processes involved in implementing a software system into its operational environment, including deployment strategies, user training, and system configuration. Additionally, we will delve into the importance of ongoing maintenance to ensure the software remains functional, secure, and up-to-date with evolving requirements. The chapter aims to equip readers with the knowledge of best practices for ensuring smooth system implementation and long-term sustainability through effective maintenance strategies. This chapter deals with both system implementation and maintenance.

Implementation procedures

The process of ensuring that the information system is operational and then allowing users to take its operation for use and evaluation is called **system implementation**. Implementation includes all those activities that take place to convert from the old system to the new one. The new system may be totally new, replacing an existing manual, or automatic system, or it may be a major modification in the existing system. In either case, proper implementation is essential to provide a reliable system to meet the organizational requirements. Successful implementation may not guarantee improvement in the organization by using the new system, but improper installation will prevent it. There are four aspects of implementation:

- Equipment installation
- Training the personnel
- Conversion procedures
- Post-implementation evaluation

Equipment installation

The hardware required to support the new system is selected prior to the implementation phase. The necessary hardware should be ordered in time to allow for the installation and testing of equipment during the implementation phase. An installation checklist should be developed at this time with operating advice from the vendor and system development team. In those installations where people are experienced in the installation of same or similar equipment, adequate time should be scheduled to allow the completion of the following activities:

- **Site preparation**: An appropriate location must be found to provide an operating environment for the equipment that will meet the vendor's temperature, humidity, and dust control specifications. It is very important to lay down a proper procedure for acquiring and planning space layout in the system's implementation. It would be foolish to be stingy on layout expenses and the human environment when so much is spent on system analysis, design, and development. A bad layout can not only drastically reduce the productivity of the data processing department but also that of the entire organization as a whole.

  If the system is a small computer, little layout and site preparation work is needed. However, the electric lines should be checked to ensure that they are free of static or power fluctuation. It will be better to install a dedicated line that is not shared by other equipment. In case of a medium or large mainframe computer, the project manager should prepare a rough layout, make cost estimates, and get budget approval from top management. Layout planning must be done in advance in order to permit the acquisition of long lead-time items like air conditioning equipment, electrical earthing, fire or smoke detection systems, and so on. The following factors should be taken into consideration for space planning:

  - Space occupied by equipment
  - Space occupied by people
  - Movement of equipment and people

  The site layout should allow ample space for moving the equipment in and setting it for normal operation. Vendors will provide clearance requirements for performing service, maintenance, and air circulation. These requirements must be strictly adhered. Otherwise, warranties may become void and maintenance discontinued until specifications are met. Carpets should be avoided whenever possible in computer rooms because they catch dust and create static power, which may damage the data stored in a magnetic medium. Highly waxed floors may cause the same type of effects. It is best to have the site preparation completed prior to the delivery of the equipment, since many vendors are reluctant to deliver equipment when construction work is still in progress.

- **Equipment installation**: The equipment must be physically installed by the manufacturer, connected to the power source, and wired to communication lines if required.

- **Equipment checks out**: The equipment must be turned on for testing under normal operating conditions. Not only should the routine diagnostic tests be run by the vendor, but also the implementation team should devise and run extensive tests of its own to ensure that the equipment is in proper working condition.

Training the personnel

A system can succeed or fail depending on the way it is operated and used. The quality of training received by the personnel involved with the system in various capacities, helps to hinder the successful implementation of the information system. Thus, training is becoming a major component of system implementation. When a new system is acquired, which often involves new hardware and software, both users and computer professionals generally need some type of training. Often, this is imparted through classes, which are organized by vendors, and through hands-on learning techniques.

- **Training the systems operators**: Many systems depend on the computer-centre personnel, who are responsible for keeping the equipment running and for providing the necessary support services. Their training must ensure that they are able to handle all the possible operations, both routine and extraordinary. Operator training must also involve the data entry personnel if the system calls for the installation of new equipment like computers, printers, special terminals for data entry equipment, and so on. The operator training should include such fundamentals as how to turn the equipment on and use it with the knowledge of normal operation. The operators should also be instructed in what common malfunctioning may occur, how to recognize them, and what steps to take when they arise. As a part of their training, operators should be given both a troubleshooting list that identifies possible problems and remedies for them, as well as the names and telephone numbers of the contact persons in case of unexpected or unusual problems arising. Training also involves familiarization with run procedures, which involve working through the sequence of activities needed to use a new system on an ongoing basis.
- **User training**: User training may involve the equipment use, particularly in the case where a personal computer is in use, and the individual involved is both operator and user. In these cases, the user must be instructed to operate the equipment. User training must also instruct individuals involved in troubleshooting the system, determining whether the problem is caused by the equipment or software or something they have done in using the system. Most user training deals with the operation of the system itself. Training in data coding emphasizes the methods to be followed in capturing data from transactions or preparing data for decision activities. Users should be trained in data handling activities such as handling input or output screens, editing data, formulating inquiries (finding specific records or getting responses to questions), and deleting records of data. From time to time, users will have to prepare disks, load papers into printers, or change cartridges or ribbons on printers. Some training time should be devoted to such system maintenance activities.

Training is often seen as a necessary evil by managers. While reorganizing its importance, many managers have to release employees from their regular job activities so that they can be trained. When managers are actively involved in determining training needs, they are usually more supportive of training efforts. It is common to have managers directly involved in evaluating the effectiveness of training activities because training deficiencies can translate into reduced user productivity levels.

Conversion from manual to computerized system

Conversion or changeover is the process of changing from the old system (manual system) to the new system. It requires careful planning to establish the basic approach to be used in the actual changeover. There are many conversion strategies available to the analyst, regarding who has to consider several organizational variables in deciding which conversion strategy to use. There is no single best way to proceed with conversion. It may be noted that adequate planning and scheduling of conversion, as well as adequate security, are more important for a successful changeover:

- **Conversion strategies**: There are five strategies for converting from the old system to the new system:
    - **Direct changeover**: Conversion by direct changeover means that on a specified date, the old system is dropped, and the new system is put into use. Direct changeover can only be successful if extensive testing is done beforehand. An advantage of the direct changeover is that users have no possibility of using the old system other than the new adaptation.

      Direct changeover is considered a risky approach to conversion, and disadvantages are numerous. For instance, long delays might ensure if errors occur, since there is no other way to accomplish processing. Additionally, users may resent being forced into using an unfamiliar system without recourse. Finally, there is no adequate way to compare new results with old ones.
    - **Parallel conversion**: This refers to running the old system at the same time, in parallel. This is the most frequently used conversion approach, but its popularity may be in decline because it works best when a computerized system replaces a manual one. Both systems are run simultaneously for a specified period of time, and the reliability of results is examined. When the same results are gained over time, the new system is put into use and the old system is ceased.

      The advantage of running both systems in parallel includes the possibility of checking new data against old data in order to catch any errors in processing the new system. Parallel processing also offers a feeling of security to users, who are not forced to make an abrupt change to the new system.

      There are many disadvantages to parallel conversion. These include the cost of running two systems at the same time, and the burden on employees of virtually doubling their workload during conversion. Another disadvantage is that unless the system being replaced is a manual one, it is difficult to make a comparison between the output of the new system and the old one. Supposedly, the new system was created to improve on the old one. Therefore, outputs from the system should differ. Finally, it is understandable that employees who are faced with a choice between two systems will continue using the old one because of their familiarity with it.

- **Gradual conversion**: Gradual conversion attempts to combine the best features of the earlier two plans, without incurring the risks. In this plan, the volume of transaction is gradually increased as the system is phased in. The disadvantages include allowing users to get involved with the system gradually and the possibility of detecting and recovering from errors without a lot of downtime. Disadvantages of gradual conversion include taking too long to get the new system in place and its inappropriateness for conversion of small, uncomplicated systems.
- **Modular prototype conversion**: This approach to conversion uses the building of modular, operational prototype to change from old system to new in a gradual manner. As each module is modified and accepted, it is put into use. One advantage is that each module is thoroughly tested before being used. Another advantage is that users are familiar with each module as it becomes operational.

  The fact that many times a prototype is not feasible and automatically rules out this approach for many conversions. Another disadvantage is that special attention must be paid to interfaces so that the modules being built actually work as a system.
- **Distributed conversion**: This refers to a situation in which many installations of the same system are contemplated, like in banking or in franchises such as restaurants or clothing stores. One entire conversion is done (with any of the four approaches considered already) at one site. When that conversion is successfully completed, other conversions are done for other sites.

  An advantage of the distributed conversion is that problems can be detected (and contained) rather than inflicting them, in succession, on all sites. A disadvantage is that even when one conversion is successful, each site will have its own peculiarities to work through, and these must be handled.

- **Activities involved in conversion**: Conversion includes all those activities which must be completed to successfully convert from the previous system to the new information system. Fundamentally, these activities can be classified as follows:
  - **Procedure conversion**: Operating procedure should be completely documented for the new system. This applies to both computer operations and functional area operations. Before any parallel or conversion activities

can start, operating procedures must be clearly spelled out for personnel in the functional areas undergoing changes. Information on input, data files, methods, procedures, output, and internal control must be presented in clear, concise, and understandable terms for the average reader. Written operating procedures must be supplemented by oral communication during the training sessions on the system change.

Despite many hours of training, many questions will have to be answered during the conversion activities. Brief meetings must be held when changes are taking place in order to inform all operating employees of any change initiated. Qualified system personnel must be in the conversion area to communicate and coordinate new developments as they occur. Likewise, revisions to operating procedures should be issued as quickly as possible. These efforts enhance the chances of successful conversion.

Once the new system is completely operational, the system implementation group should spend several days checking with all supervisory personnel about their respective areas. As with every new installation, minor adjustments should be expected. Channels of communication should be open between the systems development team members and all the supervisory personnel so that necessary changes can be initiated as conditions change. There is no need to get locked into a rigid system when it would be beneficial for the organization to make necessary changes. Thus, the proper machinery for making changes must be set in place.

- **File conversion**: In this phase, many large files of information are going to be converted from one medium to another. Therefore, programming and testing are to be completed long before. The cost and related problems of file conversion are significant whether they involve online files or offline files. Present manual files are likely to be inaccurate and incomplete, where deviations from the accepted format are common. These files suffer from the shortcomings of inexperienced and, at times, indifferent personnel whose jobs are to maintain them. Computer-generated files tend to be more accurate and consistent. If the existing system is operating on a computer but of different configurations, the formats of the present computer files are generally unacceptable for the new system.

  Besides the need to provide a compatible format, there are several other reasons for file conversion. The files may require character translation that is acceptable to the character set of the new computer system. Data from one magnetic storage to another media is to be placed in order to construct an online common database. Also, the rearrangement of certain data fields for more efficient programming may be desired.

In order for the conversion to be as accurate as possible, file conversion programs must be thoroughly tested. Adequate control, such as record counts and control totals, should be required for the output of the conversion program. The existing computer files should be kept for a period of time until sufficient files are accumulated for backup. This is necessary in case the files must be reconstructed from scratch after a bug is discovered later in the conversion routine.

- **System conversion**: After the files have been converted and the reliability has been confirmed for a functional area, daily processing can be shifted from the existing information system to the new one. A cut-point is established so that the database and other data requirements can be updated to the cut-off point. All transactions initiated after this time are processed on the new system. System development team members should be present to assist and answer any questions that might develop. Consideration should be given to the old system for some more time to permit checking and balancing the total results of both systems. All differences must be reconciled. If necessary, appropriate changes are made to the new system and its computer programs. The old system can be dropped as soon as the data processing group is satisfied with the new system's performance.
- **Scheduling personnel and equipment**: Scheduling data processing operations of a new information system for the first time is a difficult task for the system manager. As users become more familiar with the new system, the job becomes more routine. Before the new design project is complete, it is necessary to schedule the new equipment. Some programs will be operational while others will be in various stages of compiling and testing. Since production runs tend to push aside new program testing, the system manager must assign ample time for all individuals involved. This generally means second shift for those working on programs.

  Schedules should be set up by the system manager in conjunction with the department of operational units serviced by the equipment. The master schedule for next month should provide sufficient computer time to handle all the required processing. Daily schedules should be prepared in accordance with the master schedule and should include time necessary for reruns, program testing, special non-recurring reports and other necessary runs. Hence, the schedule should be as realistic as possible.

  Just as the equipment must be scheduled for its maximum utilization, so must be personnel who operate the equipment. It is also imperative that personnel who enter input data and handle output data be included in the data processing schedule. Otherwise, data will not be available when the equipment needs it for processing. It is essential that each person follow the methods and procedures set forth by the management. Non-compliance with established norms will have an adverse effect on the entire system.

Implementation techniques

Software system implementation can be carried out using two primary approaches: the traditional approach and the incremental approach. In the traditional approach, also known as the **big bang** or **waterfall method**, the entire system is developed and tested in a single phase before being deployed in its entirety. This method is suitable for well-defined projects but can be risky if any major issues arise late in the process. On the other hand, the incremental approach involves deploying the software system in smaller, manageable parts or modules over time. Each module is implemented, tested, and refined before moving on to the next, allowing for continuous feedback, risk mitigation, and faster delivery of functional components. This approach is more flexible and adaptive to changes, making it popular in modern agile development practices. Implementation of software systems can be done in the following two ways:

- Traditional approach
- Incremental approach

Traditional approach

In the traditional approach, the following sequence is followed:

- Each module or small group of modules is coded, tested, and debugged.
- After all the modules of the whole system are debugged, these modules are grouped into sub-systems.
- Subsequently, each sub-system is tested and debugged.
- Next, the sub-systems are combined to form the whole system. This is known as system integration.
- Finally, the whole system is tested and debugged.

The traditional system is not very popular these days, as the system as a whole is tested very late in the project. By then, there would be little time left to correct the problems, which are sure to occur. Therefore, the development team is unable to meet the project deadline. The team continues to get stuck until the problems are over. Such problems occur because of the reluctance of implementers to begin the testing as soon as possible. When the project deadline approaches, the team hurriedly tests the module. This leads to a lack of resources for testing. Due to the lack of time the team decides to perform testing without using all the required resources. This leads to major defects going undetected. Major faults are known only when the system as a whole is tested, wherein the bug passes from one module to another.

Incremental approach

In the incremental approach to implementation, the first module is first coded, tested, and debugged. Subsequently, further modules are added to it one by one or in small groups. In this approach, the system begins as a small unit but eventually, with additions, builds into a complete system. The system is implemented from bottom to top. One can incrementally implement a system from top to bottom, from bottom to top, from left to right, or from right to left. Such a system provides enough time for major changes.

System acceptance

System testing is done after all programs are completed. Acceptance testing puts the system through a procedure design to convince the user that the system will meet the stated requirement. Acceptance testing is technically similar to system testing, but politically it is different. In system testing, bugs are found and corrected. Acceptance testing is conducted in the presence of the user, audit representative, or the entire staff.

Both system testing and acceptance testing may share test cases; system testing may be viewed as a dress rehearsal for the acceptance test. The criteria or plan for acceptance should be available in the structured specification.

System evaluation and performance

Application systems may be evaluated in terms of measures of system value. These may also be compared with the reports of technical, operational, and economic feasibility where they were originally and initially justified:

- **Evaluation of system value:**
    - Significant task relevance
    - Willingness to pay
    - System usage
    - User information satisfaction
- **Technical evaluation:**
    - Data transmission is fast to handle data.
    - Sufficient secondary storage to hold data.
    - CPU responds well to all requests.
- **Operational evaluation**: Operational considerations relate to whether the input data is properly provided and the output is usable and used appropriately. Evaluation of applications should examine how well they operate with special reference to input, error rates, timeliness of output, and utilization of reports.

- **Economic evaluation**: Actual costs are compared with actual benefits. It is easy to calculate costs but not benefits. Hence, we may make estimates to evaluate. It may aid future decision making to identify the cost of applications for which an economic return was not expected. It shows the **return-on-investment (ROI)**. An economic analysis is required to decide whether or not to drop the application uses.
- **Evaluation by use of performance monitors:**
  - **Hardware monitors**: Use of a sensor to measure the time of the CPU in a wait state. Read or write time in **floppy or hard disk**.
  - **Software monitors**: They reside in main memory and require execution time; they interrupt the program being executed to record data about the execution. These can identify particular program or programs modules within the operating system environment.
- **Evaluation by the use of system logs and observations:** Small installations maintain simple logs of jobs and job times. An analysis of the system may indicate problems with returns, variations in job running times, or excessive machine failures. The log may be used to develop a distribution of jobs by time required. Observations of computer operations are useful in detecting inefficient scheduling of resource use and inefficient applications.

System acceptance criteria

A system must possess some basic desirable features for acceptance. In the following, we will be discussing these qualities:

- **Correctness**: Correctness means that the system meets the organizational desired goals. In other words, correctness is the degree to which the system performs required functions. The most common measure for correctness is defects per thousand lines of code (KLOC), where the defect is defined as a lack of conformance to requirements.
- **Reliability**: A system is reliable if the user can trust the results given by the system. Reliability is defined as the probability of failure-free operation of a system in a specified environment for a specified time. For example, if we say that program **A** has a reliability of 0.90 over 10 hours, it means that when the program runs 100 times, it will work without failure 90 times in 10 hours of execution time. A simple measure of reliability is:

  $$MTBF = MTTF + MTTR$$

  Where:

  - **MTBF** is mean time between failures
  - **MTTF** is mean time to failure
  - **MTTR** is mean time to repair

- **Robustness**: A system is said to be robust if it can adapt to an unanticipated change in the environment such as disk crash or incorrect input data. For example, a system is said to be robust if it provides some standby (duplicate data file in the backup hard disk) to recover from hard disk failure.
- **Performance**: The performance of a system is measured in terms of the following parameters:
    - o Processing speed
    - o Response time
    - o Resource consumption
    - o Throughput and efficiency

  If a system is too slow it reduces the productivity. If a computer-based system uses too much disk space it may be very expensive to run. Also, it may affect other applications. Hence, performance parameters are important from system's function point of view.
- **User friendliness**: If a system is not user-friendly, it is sure to lose the support of the user. User friendliness can be measured in terms of:
    - o The physical and/or intellectual skill required to learn the system.
    - o The time required to become moderately efficient in using the system.
    - o Measure of user's attitude towards a system.

  The user interface is an important component of the user-friendliness. A software system that presents the novice user with a Windows interface and a mouse is friendly than one requires the user to use a set of textual commands.
- **Maintainability**: Maintainability of a system is measured as a function of the effort required to locate and fix an error in the system. A system is maintainable if it allows corrections of its defects with a limited amount of work. Maintenance involves corrective, adaptive, and perfective practices.
- **Testability**: Testability is a measure of effort required to test the system in order to ensure its accurate performance.
- **Reusability**: Reusability is the creation and reuse of the system building blocks. As in the automobile industry, the engine specification and design are reused in different models. The same software modules can be used for the development of other modules. This saves production costs, time, and labor. The reuse of a system can be considered at a number of different levels, like system reuse, sub-system reuse, object, or module reuse, and function reuse.
- **Interoperability**: Interoperability refers to the ability of the system to co-exist and co-operate with other systems. For example, a word processing software can incorporate a chart produced by a spreadsheet package. Interoperability has become a key characteristic of many systems. New systems must communicate with the existing old system.

Maintenance, reliability, and availability

The software production was viewed, in seventies, as consisting of two distinct activities which are performed sequentially:

- Development
- Maintenance

From the starting, the software product was developed, and then installed on the client's computer. Any change to the software after installation on the client's computer and acceptance by the client, whether to fix a residual fault or extend the functionality, constituted classical maintenance. Hence, the way that software was developed classically can be described as the development-then-maintenance model. The post-delivery maintenance refers to the 1990 IEEE definition of maintenance as any change to the software after it has been delivered and installed on the client's computer. The modern maintenance or just maintenance refers to the 1995 ISO/IEC definition of corrective, perfective, or adaptive activities performed at any time. Post-delivery maintenance is therefore a subset of (modern) maintenance.

System availability and **reliability** are closely related properties that can be expressed as a numerical probability. The reliability of a system is the probability that the system's services will be correctly delivered as specified. The availability of a system will be up and running to deliver these services to users when they request them.

So, system reliability is the probability of failure-free operation over a specified time in a given environment for a specific purpose. System availability is the probability that a system, at a point of time, will be operational and able to deliver the requested service.

Maintenance

Maintenance means restoring something to its original condition. It covers a wide range of activities, including correcting coding, design errors, updating documentation, test data, and upgrading user support. Many activities are classified as maintenance are actually enhancements. Enhancement means adding, modifying, or redeveloping the code to support the changes in specifications. It is necessary to keep up with changing user needs and operational environment.

Although software does not wear out like a piece of hardware, it ages and eventually fails to perform because of cumulative maintenance. Over the time, the integrity of the program, test data, and documentation degenerates as a result of modifications. Eventually, it takes more effort to maintain the application than to rewrite it.

Characteristics

The obsolescence of hardware is very fast as compared to the software. The user wants to see the existing software is running smoothly on the new hardware platform. If the software performs a low-level function, maintenance is necessary. The software product needs re-work to cope with new interface. Therefore, every software product continues to evolve after its development through the maintenance efforts.

Types of software maintenance

There are several types of maintenance that one can perform on an information system. By maintenance, we mean fixing or enhancing an information system:

- **Corrective maintenance** refers to the changes made to repair defects in the design, coding, or implementation of the system. Most corrective maintenance problems surface soon after installation. When corrective maintenance problems surface, they are typically urgent and need to be resolved to curtail possible interruptions in normal business activities. Of all types of maintenance, corrective accounts for as much as 75% of all maintenance activity (*Andrews and Leventhal, 1993*). This is unfortunate because corrective maintenance adds little or no value to the organization. It simply focuses on removing defects from an existing system without adding new functionality.
- **Adaptive maintenance** involves making changes to an information system to evolve its functionality to changing business needs or to migrate to a different operating environment. Adaptive maintenance is usually less urgent than corrective maintenance because business and technical changes typically occur over some period of time. Contrary to corrective maintenance, adaptive maintenance is generally a small part of an organization's maintenance effort but does add value to the organization.
- **Perfective maintenance** involves making enhancements to improve processing performance, interface usability, or to add desired but not necessarily required, system failures (**bells and whistles**). For example, perfect maintenance would be adding a new room to our home. Many system professionals feel that perfect maintenance is not really maintenance but new development.
- **Preventive maintenance** involves changes made to a system to reduce the chance of future system failure. An example of preventive maintenance might be to increase the number of records that a system can process far beyond what is currently needed or to generalize how a system sends report information to a printer so that the system can easily adapt to changes in printer technology. Consider an example, in a home, the preventive maintenance could be painting the exterior to protect the home from severe weather conditions. As with adaptive maintenance, both perfective and preventive maintenance are of much lower priority than

corrective maintenance. Over the life of a system, corrective maintenance is most likely to occur after initial system installation or after major system changes. This means that adaptive, perfective, and preventive maintenance activities can lead to corrective maintenance activities if not carefully designed and implemented. (*Table 12.1*)

Type	Description
Corrective	Repair design and programming errors.
Adaptive	Modify the system for environmental changes. Changes made to a system to evolve its functionality to changing business needs or technologies.
Perfective	Evolve system to solve new problems or take advantage of new opportunities. Changes made to a system to add new features or to improve performance.
Preventive	Safeguard the system from future problems. Changes made to a system to avoid possible future problems.

Table 12.1: *Types of maintenance*

Maintenance tasks

There is always a required plan to solve the ever-growing problem of software maintenance. Many organizations have done this through a maintenance reduction task. They are as follows:

- **Maintenance management audit**, which is done through interviews and questionnaires. It evaluates the quality of maintenance effort. Some of the questions asked are:
    - Are maintenance requests logged in?
    - What percent of total hours are spent on error correction, additions, changes, deletions, and improvements?
    - Does your organization currently have a well-defined maintenance reduction program?
    - The data gathered are used to develop a diagnostic study to provide the management with an assessment of the software maintenance function.
- **Software system audit**, which entails:
    - An overall view of the system documentation and an assessment of the quality of data files, databases, and system maintainability, reliability, and efficiency.
    - Functional information gathered on all the programs in the system to determine how well they do the job. Each program is assigned a preliminary ranking value.

 - A detailed program audit, which considers the ranking value, **mean time between failure (MTBF)**, and size of the maintenance backlog. MTBF determines system availability to users.
- **Software modification**, which consists of the following steps:
  - Program rewrites, which include logic simplification, documentation updates, and error correction.
  - System level update, which completes system level documentation, brings up to date the data flow diagrams or system flowcharts, and cross-reference programs.
  - Re-audit of low-ranking programs to make sure that the errors have been corrected.

Side effects

The effect of such maintenance reduction tasks is that a system is a more reliable software, a reduced maintenance backlog, improved response time in correcting errors, improved user satisfaction, higher morale among maintenance staff. The maintenance demands more orientation and training than any other programming activities, especially for entry-level programmers.

Measuring maintenance effectiveness

The measurement of maintenance activities is fundamental to understanding the quality of development and maintenance efforts. To measure the effectiveness, you must measure these factors:

- Number of failures
- Time between each failure
- Type of failure

Measuring the number and time between failures will provide you the basis to calculate a widely used measure of system quality. This metric is referred to as the MTBF. As its name implies, the MTBF measures the average length of time between the identification of one system failure and the next. Over time, you should expect the MTBF value to rapidly increase after a few months of use (corrective maintenance) of the system. If the MTBF does not rapidly increase over time, it will be a signal to management that major problems exist within the system that are not being adequately resolved through the maintenance process.

A more revealing method of measurement is to examine the failures that are occurring. Over time, logging the types of failures will provide a very clear picture of where, when, and how failures occur. For example, knowing that a system repeatedly fails to log new account information to the database when a particular customer is using the system can provide invaluable information to the maintenance personnel.

Tracking these failures also provides important management information for future projects. If a higher frequency of errors occurs when a particular development environment is used, such information can help to guide personnel assignments, training courses, or the avoidance of a particular package or language during future development.

Reverse engineering

Reverse engineering is the process of creating design specifications for a system or program module from program code and data definitions. For example, **computer aided software engineering (CASE)** tools that support reverse engineering read program sources as input, perform analysis, and extract information such as program control structures, data structures, logic, and data flow. Once a program is represented at a design level by using both graphical and textual representations, the system analyst can more effectively restructure the code according to the current business needs or programming practices. This tool provides analysts with a powerful method to quickly explore and understand a system. The tool many times shows a mapping between the variables and program procedures. This high-level view of a program allows the programmers to see more quickly the interrelationships and structure of a program, thus making it easier to understand and maintain. As with many legacy systems, only the source code may exist, yet additional documentation is necessary to make program maintenance productive. *Reverse engineering is an automated tool that reads program source code as input and creates graphical and textual representations of program design-level information such as program control structures, logical flow, and data flow.*

Reengineering

Reengineering tools are similar to reverse engineering tools but include analysis features that can automatically or interactively with a system analyst, alter an existing system in an effort to improve its quality or performance. Although most organizations may have numerous systems that are candidates for reverse engineering or reengineering, the complexity, and effort in using these tools have limited their widespread use. Additionally, most CASE environments do not yet have reverse or reengineering capabilities. However, as automated development environments evolve to support these features, CASE should evolve to have a greater impact beyond what the technology has experienced, so far.

The critical distinction between reengineering and new software development is the starting point for the development. Rather than starting with a written specification, the old system acts as a specification for the new system. *Chikofsky and Cross call conventional development* forward engineering to distinguish it from software reengineering. **Forward engineering** starts with a system specification and involves the design and implementation of a new system. **Reengineering** starts with an existing system and the development process for the replacement, which is based on understanding and transforming the original system.

Figure 12.1 illustrates the reengineering process. The input to the process is a legacy program and the output is a structured, and the modularized version of the same program. During program reengineering, the data for the system may also be reengineered.

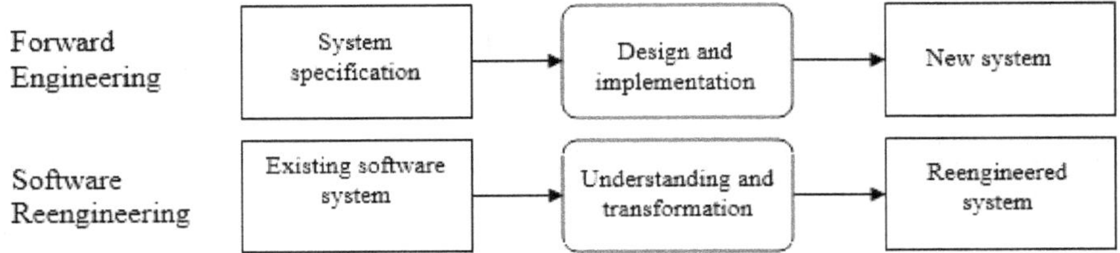

Figure 12.1: *Forward and re-engineering processes*

Figure 12.2 shows the reengineering process:

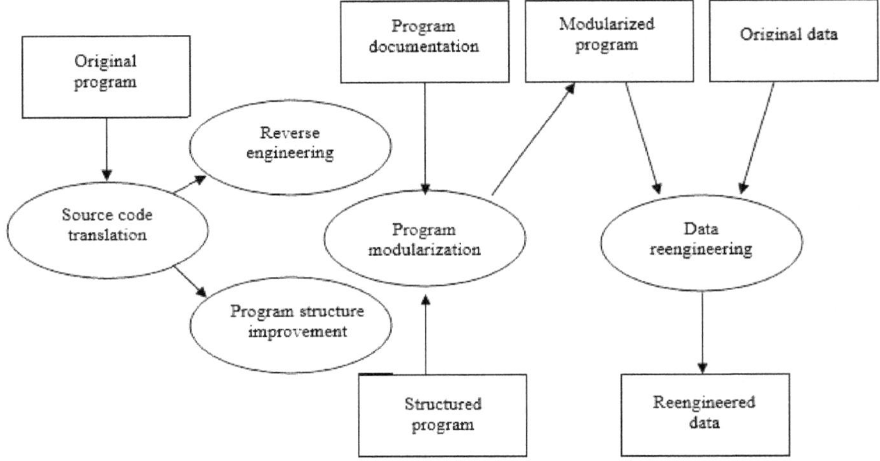

Figure 12.2: *Reengineering process*

The activities in this reengineering process are:

- **Source code translation**: The program is converted from an old programming language to a more modern version of the same language or to a different language.
- **Reverse engineering**: The program is analyzed and information extracted from it. This helps to document its organization and functionality.
- **Program structure improvement**: The control structure of the program is analyzed and modified to make it easier to read and understand.
- **Program modularization**: Related parts of the program are grouped together and, where appropriate the redundancy is removed. In some cases, this stage may involve architectural transformation where a centralized system intended for a single computer is modified to run on a distributed platform.

- **Data reengineering**: The data processes by the program are changed to reflect program changes.

To summarize, reengineering is the automated tool (*Figure 12.2*) that read program source code as input, perform an analysis of the program's data, and logic, and then automatically, or interactively with a system analyst, alter an existing system in an effort to improve its quality or performance.

Business process reengineering

Sometimes it is understood that a system reengineering and a **business process reengineering (BPR)** are synonyms. To make the organization more profitable or systematic the BPR is initiated. Along with the BPR, the system reengineering is automatically invoked. The BPR is the popular term for re-optimization of organizational processes and structures following the introduction of new information technology into an organization.

There are *seven principles of reengineering* suggested by *Michael Hammer and James Champy* to streamline the work-process and thereby achieve significant levels of improvement in quality, time management, and cost:

- Organize around outcomes and cost.
- Identify all the processes in an organization and prioritize them in order of redesign urgency.
- Integrate information processing work into the real work that produces the information.
- Treat geographically dispersed resources as they were centralized.
- Link parallel activities in workflow instead of just integrating their results.
- Put the decision point where the work is performed, and build control into the process.
- Capture information once and catch the source for improvement.

Conclusion

In conclusion, system implementation and maintenance are crucial stages in the software development lifecycle that ensure the smooth deployment and long-term sustainability of a system. Whether through the traditional or incremental approach, effective implementation, combined with ongoing maintenance, helps maintain the system's performance, security, and adaptability to evolving requirements. By understanding these processes, software engineers can ensure a successful transition from development to operation.

In the next chapter, we will explore **software reliability**, where we will discuss the importance of building dependable and fault-tolerant systems. You will learn about the factors influencing software reliability and the techniques used to measure, enhance, and maintain high standards of reliability throughout the software lifecycle.

Exercises

To solidify your understanding of the concepts covered in this chapter, try the following exercises.

Multiple choice questions

1. **Which of the following is a key stage in system implementation?**
   a. Requirement gathering
   b. Code refactoring
   c. Deployment
   d. User feedback analysis
2. **What is a significant advantage of the incremental approach in system implementation?**
   a. Faster full-system deployment
   b. Easier rollback
   c. Reduced need for maintenance
   d. Continuous feedback and risk mitigation
3. **In the traditional approach to system implementation, when is the system fully deployed?**
   a. After completing each module
   b. Once the entire system is developed and tested
   c. In phases based on user feedback
   d. Immediately after the design phase
4. **Which of the following best describes the purpose of system maintenance?**
   a. To implement new features continuously
   b. To ensure long-term performance and security of the software
   c. To revert the system back to the initial version
   d. To test the system under real-world conditions
5. **Which of the following is NOT typically involved in system implementation?**
   a. Training users
   b. Code debugging
   c. System deployment
   d. Data migration

6. **What is the main drawback of the traditional approach to software implementation?**
   a. It is not suitable for small projects
   b. Delays are difficult to manage as all features are implemented at once
   c. It does not allow for large-scale projects
   d. It provides continuous user feedback
7. **Which of the following is a key activity during the maintenance phase?**
   a. Conducting system design
   b. Updating software based on bug reports
   c. Gathering requirements from stakeholders
   d. Creating initial prototypes
8. **In incremental implementation, what happens after a module is implemented?**
   a. The system is fully deployed
   b. The next module is developed after feedback and testing
   c. The system is returned to the design phase
   d. The system is left as-is without further updates

Short answer questions

1. Define maintainability.
2. Discuss the two main implementation techniques
3. Discuss the different steps which should be followed while converting from old system to a new system.
4. What is a system acceptance test? What are the three levels of acceptance testing?
5. Discuss the human psychological factors that can hamper the system implementation process.

Essay questions

1. Write a short note on planning for system implementation.
2. Explain briefly the parallel running (or conversion) in implementation.
3. Would you like to have a career for yourself in software maintenance? Describe the career path.
4. Develop a means to quantify and measure the maintainability attribute of a software product.
5. What is the appropriate set of tools and documents required to maintain a large software product?

6. If a software product or part of it spends 60% of its operational life cycle in maintenance, why do you pay so little attention to maintainability during design phase?
7. Is it practical to specify maintainability in the SRS? How would you specify it?
8. What is the conventional wisdom about implementation success?
9. What are the different types of maintenance and how do they differ?
10. What types of measurements must be taken to gain an understanding of the effectiveness of maintenance? Why is tracking MTBFs an important measurement?
11. What is the difference between reverse engineering and re-engineering CASE tools?

Multiple choice answers

1. c
2. d
3. b
4. b
5. b
6. b
7. b
8. b

CHAPTER 13
Reliability

Introduction

Reliability is defined as the probability of a software system performing its specified functions correctly over a long period of time or for different input sets under the usage environment similar to that of its input target customers (*Goel, 1985; Musa et al, 1987, Titan,1995*). **Software reliability engineering (SRE)** is the branch of software engineering that studies the issues related to the measurement, modeling, and improvement of software reliability. Reliability is a measure of the frequency and criticality of product failure. A failure is an unacceptable effect or behavior, under permissible operating conditions, that occurs as a consequence of a fault. The product must be stable.

Structure

In this chapter, we are going to discuss the following topics:

- Reliability
- Myth of stable requirements
- Concepts
- Errors
- Reliability models
- Availability

Objectives

In this chapter, we are going to discuss the reliability required while developing a software package used by public, need of the reliability for the developers to apply the concept for a smooth running of the product and the important properties of good reliability models for software measurement.

Reliability

Reliability may be defined as:

- The idea that something is fit for the purpose with respect to time.
- The capacity of a device or system to perform as designed.
- The resistance to failure of a device or system.
- The ability of a device or a system to perform a required function under the stated conditions for a specified period of time.
- The probability that a functional unit will perform its required function for a specified interval of time under stated conditions.

It is a paradox that more effort is given to increase hardware reliability, but it is ignored in the case of software. A failure in software may cause more damage than a hardware failure. The characteristics of a product failure take the shape of a bath tub shown in *Figure 13.1*. When the product is launched, it fails more frequently at the initial stage, while correcting the fault, it slowly stabilizes with a constant failure rate. At the end of the product life cycle, due to wear and tear, aging effect, and technology obsolescence, the product encounters more failures and needs rejuvenation.

The major goal of reliability and quality assurance is to identify all the possible influences on failure rates and take an appropriate step to reduce and eliminate those influences.

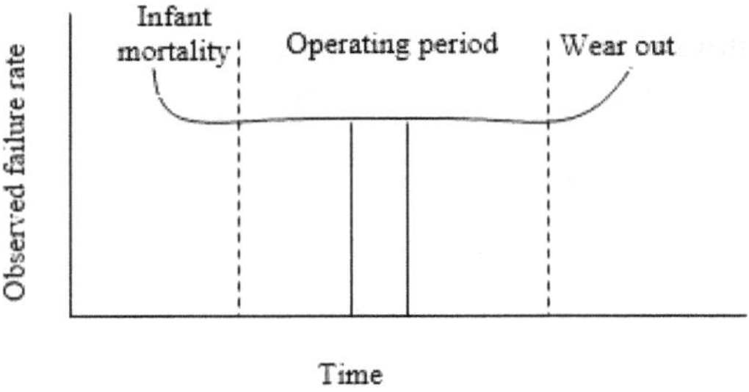

Figure 13.1: *Bath tub curve on failure*

Myth of stable requirements

Stable requirements are the holy grail of software development. With stable requirements, a project can proceed from architecture to design to coding to testing in a way that is orderly, predictable, and calm. You have predictable expenses, and you never have to worry about a feature costing 100 times as much to implement as it would otherwise because your user did not think of it until you were finished **debugging**. It is fine to hope that once your customer has accepted a requirements document, no changes will be needed. On a typical project, however, the customer cannot reliably describe what is needed before the code is written. The problem is not that the customers are a lower life-form. Just as the more you work with the project, the better you understand it, the more they work with it, the better they understand it.

Concepts

Reliability is defined as the **probability** that a device will perform its intended function during a specified period of time under the stated conditions. If the reliability of a system or device is 0.95 for a 100-hour operating period, the device will operate successfully for 100 hours with a probability of 0.95. If in an experiment employing 100 such devices, at the end of 100 hours, it is expected that 5 of the 100 devices will experience a failure. We sometimes say that the device has a 95 percent chance of surviving 100 hours of operation.

Reliability, R(t), is defined as the probability that a device, component, unit, module, or system will function correctly for a specified period of time in a specified operating environment. If T is a continuous random variable representing the specified failure-free service life, then the reliability as a function of the length of any operating time t is defined by:

$$R(t) = P(T>t)$$

The probability that the successful operating time will be greater than the specified service life, T, is often referred to as the probability of survival. The function R(t) is a decreasing function of time:

$$0 < R(t) < 1$$

$$R(0) = 1 \text{ and } R(\infty) = 0$$

The unreliability or probability of failure, F(t), is obtained as:

$$F(t) = 1 - R(t) = P(T<t)$$

F(t) is an increasing function of time and is often referred to as the **cumulative distribution** function of the service life, T. The derivative of F(t) with respect to t is:

$$f(t) = \frac{dF(t)}{dt}$$

It is the probability density function of the continuous random variable T, service life.

Any product, in service, may fail from time to time. It is necessary to know how often the product fails, the **mean time between failures (MTBF),** and how bad the effects of that failure can be. When a product fails, an important issue is how long it takes to repair it, the

mean time to repair (MTTR). It is important to know how long it takes to repair the result of the failure. This last point is frequently overlooked. Suppose that the software running on a communication front fails, on average, only once every 6 months. When it fails, it completely wipes out a database. At best, the database can be re-initialized to its status when the last checkpoint dump was taken, and the audit trail can then be used to put the database into a state that is virtually up to date. However, this recovery process takes two days, during which time the database and communication front end are inoperative. In this case, the reliability of the product is low, notwithstanding that the MTBF is six months:

$$Probability\ of\ failure = F(t) = 1 - R(t)$$

Where, R(t) is the probability of failure-free operation in time period t, that is the reliability. The reliability function, R(t), and the probability density function, f(t), can be expressed explicitly in terms of hazard function Z(t). Differentiating *F(t) = 1 - R(t)* with respect to t yields:

$$\frac{dF(t)}{dt} = \frac{-dR(t)}{dt}$$

Or;

$$F'(t) = -R'(t)$$

On the other hand, we had *Z(t) = F'(t)/R'(t)*. Substituting for *F'(t)* we get

$$Z(t) = \frac{R'(t)}{R(t)}$$

Integrating this equation with respect to t we obtain:

$$\int Z(t)dt = -\int \frac{R'(t)}{R(t)}dt = -\ln R(t)$$

From this we have:

$$R(t) = e^{-\int_0^1 Z(u)du}$$

$$\text{and } f(t) = Z(t)R(t) = Z(t)e^{-\int_0^1 Z(u)du}$$

Z(t) for hardware failure can be closely approximated by a constant failure rate. A constant failure rate model has been used quite successfully in the system and subsystem reliability work, including computer hardware reliability. Substituting in the just above equation for Z(t) the constant λ, have:

$$R(t) = e^{-\int_0^1 \lambda du}$$

Since:

$$\int_0^1 \lambda du = \lambda t$$

We conclude that:

$$R(t)=e -\lambda t$$

Therefore,

$$f(t)= \lambda e^{-\lambda t}$$

Where λ is the mean failure rate.

At the time of system failure, there is a cost associated with the software, which is dependent on the probability of failure. The equation is:

$$C_f = c_f \cdot p_f$$

C_f is the total failure cost and c_f is the average single failure cost. In order to minimize C_f, one has to minimize either c_f or p_f.

c_f is determined by the nature of software applications and overall environment, the software is used. More cannot be done to reduce c_f. To minimize p_f, one has to improve the reliability. This needs additional development cost, additional testing time, and the use of additional quality assurance techniques.

Reliability design begins with the development of a model. Reliability models use *block diagrams* and *fault trees* to provide a graphical means of evaluating the relationships between the different parts of the system. These models incorporate predictions based on the parts-count failure rates, which are taken from the historical data. While the predictions are not often accurate in an absolute sense, they are valuable to assess relative differences in design alternatives.

One of the most important design techniques is *redundancy*. This means that if one part of the system fails, there is an alternate success path, such as a backup system. An automobile brake light might use two light bulbs. If one bulb fails, the brake light still operates using the other bulb. Redundancy significantly increases system reliability, and is often the only viable means of doing so. However, redundancy is difficult and expensive, and is therefore limited to critical parts of the system. Another design technique, *physics of failure*, relies on understanding the physical processes of stress, strength, and failure at a very detailed level. Then the material or component can be re-designed to reduce the probability of failure.

Errors

While writing the program or handling data, various errors are committed and they are encountered during the software testing or running the system. When designing the system interfaces, try to provide an appropriate feedback on encountering errors. The system feedback can consist of three types:

- Status information
- Prompting cues
- Error or warning messages

Providing *status information* is a simple technique for keeping users informed of what is going on within a system. For example, relevant status information, such as displaying the current customer name or time, placing appropriate titles on a menu or screen, identifying the number of screens following the current one, and so on; are the feedbacks needed by the user. The second feedback method is to display *prompting cues*. When prompting the user for information or action, it is useful to be specific in your request. For example, suppose a system prompted users with the following request:

READY FOR INPUT: ____________________

With such a prompt, the designer assumes that the user knows exactly what to enter. A better design would be specific in its request, possibly providing an example, default value, or formatting information. A final method available to the user for providing system feedback is using *error and warning messages*. Practical experience has found that a few simple guidelines can greatly improve their usefulness.

Error tolerance

Error tolerance property can be considered as a part of usability and reflects the extent to which the system has been designed so that user input error is avoided and tolerated. When user errors occur, the system should, as far as possible, detect these errors and either fixes them automatically or request the user to re-input their data.

Error processing

Error processing is turning out to be one of the thorniest problems of modern computer science, and you cannot afford to deal with it haphazardly. Some people have estimated that as much as 90 percent of a program's code is written for exceptional, error-processing cases or housekeeping, implying that only 10 percent is written for nominal cases (*Shaw in Bentley 1982*). With so much code dedicated to handling errors, a strategy for handling them consistently should be spelled out in the architecture.

Error handling is often treated as a **coding-convention-level** issue, if it is treated at all. However, because it has system-wide implications, it is best treated at the architectural level. Following are some questions to consider:

- **Is error detection active or passive?** The system can actively anticipate errors or example, by checking user input for validity, or it can passively respond to them only when it cannot avoid them. For example, when a combination of user input produces a numeric overflow. It can clear the way or clean up the mess. Again, in either case, the choice has user interface implications.

- **How does the program propagate errors?** Once it detects an error, it can immediately discard the data that caused the error, it can treat the error as an error and enter an error-processing state, or it can wait until all processing is complete and notify the user that errors were detected (somewhere).
- **What are the conventions for handling error messages?** If the architecture does not specify a single, consistent strategy, the user interface will appear to be a confusing macaroni-and-dried-bean collage of different interfaces in different parts of the program. To avoid such an appearance, the architecture should establish conventions for error messages.
- **Is error processing corrective or merely detective?** If corrective, the program can attempt to recover from errors. If it is merely detective, the program can continue processing as if nothing had happened, or it can quit. In either case, it should notify the user that it detected an error.
- **Inside the program, at what level are errors handled?** You can handle them at the point of detection, pass them off to an error-handling class, or pass them up the call chain.
- **Is error detection active passive?** The system can actively anticipate errors, for example, by checking user input for validity, or it can passively respond to them only when it cannot avoid them. For example, when a combination of user input produces a numeric overflow. It can clear the way or clean up the mess. Again, in either case, the choice has user-interface implications.
- **How does the program propagate errors?** Once it detects an error, it can immediately discard the data that caused the error, it can treat the error as an error and enter an error-processing state, or it can wait until all the processing is complete and notify the user that errors were detected (somewhere).
- **What are the conventions for handling error messages?** If the architecture does not specify a single, consistent strategy, the user interface will appear to be a confusing macaroni-and-dried-bean collage of different interfaces in different parts of the program. To avoid such an appearance, the architecture should establish conventions for error messages.
- **What is the level of responsibility of each class for validating its input data?** Is each class being responsible for validating its own data, or is there a group of classes responsible for validating the system's data? Can classes at any level assume that the data they are receiving is clean?
- **Do you want to use your environment's built-in exception handling mechanism, or build your own?** The fact that an environment has a particular error handling approach does not mean that it is the best approach for your requirements.

System faults

It is a characteristic of a software system that can lead to a system error. For example, failure to initialize a variable could lead to that variable having the wrong value when it is used. A **fault** is injected into the software when a human makes a mistake. One mistake on the part of the software professional may cause several faults; conversely, various mistakes may cause identical faults. A **failure** is the observed incorrect behavior of the software product as a consequence of a fault, and the **error** is the amount by which a result is incorrect.

The distinction between the terms helps us to identify three complementary approaches that are used to improve the reliability of a system, are:

- **Fault avoidance:** Development techniques are used that either minimize the possibility or mistakes and/or that trap the mistakes before they result in the introduction of system faults. Examples of such techniques include avoiding error-prone programming language constructs such as pointers and the use of static analysis to detect the program anomalies.
- **Fault detection and removal:** The use of verification and validation techniques that increase the chances that faults will be detected and removed before the system is used. Systematic system testing and debugging is an example of a fault-detection technique.
- **Fault tolerance:** Techniques that ensure faults in a system do not result in system errors or that ensure system errors do not result in system failures. The incorporation of self-checking facilities in a system and use of redundant system modules are the example of fault tolerance techniques.

Fault tolerance

The architecture should indicate the kind of fault tolerance expected. Fault tolerance is a collection of techniques that increase a system's reliability by detecting errors, recovering from them if possible, and containing their bad effects if not.

There are four aspects of fault tolerance:

- **Fault detection**: The system must detect a fault that could lead to a system failure. Generally, this involves checking that the system state is consistent.
- **Damage assessment**: The parts of the system state that have been affected by the fault must be detected.
- **Fault recovery**: The system must restore its state to a known safe state. This may be achieved by correcting the damaged state (forward error recovery) or by restoring the system to a known safe state (backward error recovery).
- **Fault repair**: This involves modifying the system so that the fault does not recur. However, many software faults manifest themselves as transient states. They are due to a peculiar combination of system inputs. No repair is necessary and normal processing can resume immediately after fault recovery.

You might think that fault-tolerance facilities are unnecessary in systems that have been developed by using techniques that avoid the introduction of faults. If there are no faults in the system, there would not seem to be any chance of system failure.

For example, a system could make the computation of the square root of a number fault tolerant in any of several ways:

- The system might back up and try again when it detects a fault. If the first answer is wrong, it would back up to a point at which it knew everything was all right and continue from there.
- The system might have an auxiliary code to use if it detects a fault in the primary code. In the example, if the first answer appears to be wrong, the system switches over to an alternative square-root routine and uses it instead.
- The system might use a voting algorithm. It might have three square-root classes that each use a different method. Each class computes the square root, and then the system compares the results. Depending on the kind of fault tolerance built into the system, it then uses the mean, the median, or the mode of the three results.
- The system might replace the erroneous value with a phony value that it knows to have a benign effect on the rest of the system.
- Other fault-tolerance approaches include having the system change to a state of partial operation or a state of degraded functionality when it detects an error. It can shut itself down or automatically restart itself. These examples are necessarily simplistic. Fault tolerance is a fascinating and complex subject.

Reliability models

A model is required to predict the future behavior of a system accurately. The model is a representation of a real-world problem based on mathematical equations with one or more measurable parameters. The model takes the observation data and then analyzes it to predict future behavior. The model is either confirmed or modified to better match the reality by comparing both the actual observed performance and the predicted performance. Some desirable model characteristics include the following:

- **Simplicity**: The model may be simple to understand, easily interpret the observed data, and explain the analyzed output. The important parameters responsible to measure the performance are included in the model.
- **Completeness**: The parameters those are important to performance are identified and include in the model. The constraints and limitations are clearly stated and observed.
- **Accuracy**: Matching the performance of real-world problems with the desired accuracy level.
- **Utility**: The model may predict the desired future behavior accurately with the better understanding of reality. It may be as close to reality during experiment.

- **Validity**: Model performance is confirmed through exhaustive testing and constraints carefully defined to limit the model application to the area where the model is valid.

The software reliability is yet to catch up with the hardware reliability. Much to be learned about software reliability. While hardware reliability models have been predicted on an observed constant failure rate. Software reliability have been based more on logically or analytically derived failure rate. *Figure 13.2* shows a cumulative software failure rate.

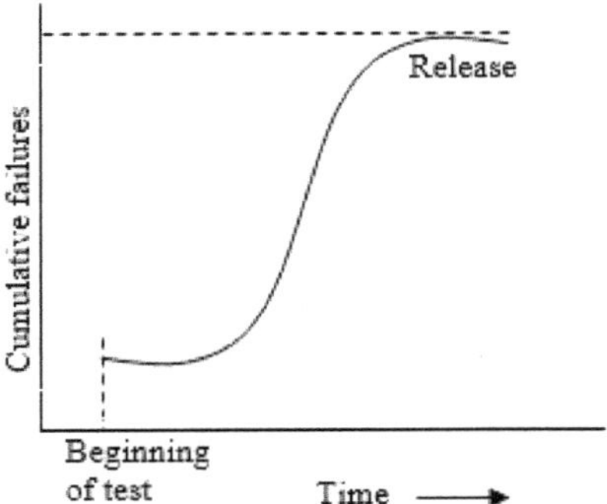

Figure 13.2: *Cumulative software failure rate*

The figure shows that initially, when a software product is introduced to the system test environment, reported failure rates are low because the testers are not familiar with the product and have difficulty separating failures from test operator errors, errors in test cases, and sources other than the test objects. The period is followed by a test period in which failure rates are initially high but decline as testing continues and faults are removed. The failure rate declines until the software product is released. The failure rate behavior is a learning curve for the testers. Once the testers become familiar with the product, the resident faults in the software product are more easily detected. Software products are released when failure rates reach some established threshold. Shortly after the release, the failure rate increases due to more users, different environments, and different test cases. The scenario is followed by a declining failure rate. The following equation:

$$R(t) = e^{-\int_0^1 Z(u)du}$$

represents a family of software reliability modules, in which Z(u) is the hazard function. The simplest Z(u) is when Z(u) is a constant value equal to an average software failure rate. This will result in a reliability model represented by the following equation:

$$R(t)=e^{-\lambda t}$$

Reliability systems

Reliability models are basically computed with a series or parallel system. The parallel systems are called **redundant systems**. The cost of a redundant system is greater than the cost of a simplex system. Reliability modeling for redundant systems is a straightforward application of probability theory. The total reliability of a string of n subsystems or components connected in a series (*Figure 13.3*) configuration. In the series model, a failure in any one of the components results in loss of the entire system's capability, and the reliability is determined by the product of the n individual subsystem reliability.

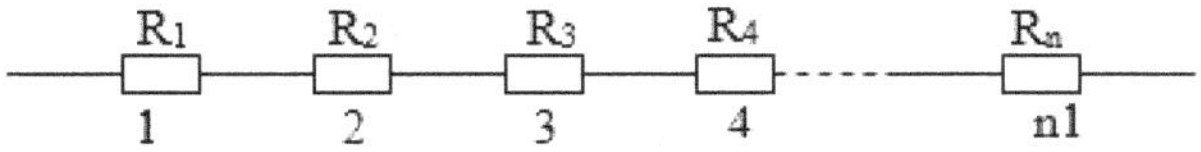

R1 R2 R3 R4 Rn
1 2 3 4 n1

Figure 13.3: *Components are in series*

The reliability of the system where the components are in series is:

$$R(t) = \prod_{i=1}^{i=n} R_i$$

When two subsystems are connected in parallel shown in *Figure 13.4,* the total reliability of this redundant system is represented as union of R_1 and R_2.

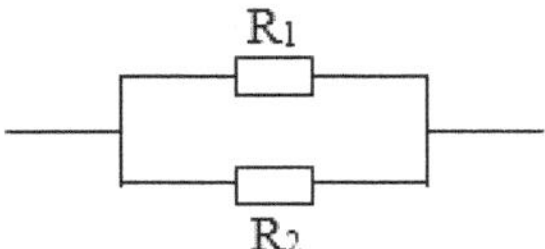

Figure 13.4: *A parallel system with two components*

The total reliability of the parallel system is $R(t) = R_1 + (1 - R_1) * R_2$

Another configuration having both serial and parallel connections of components, which has a complex nature, is given in *Figure 13.5.* In the figure, the configuration shows two parallel configurations connected in series:

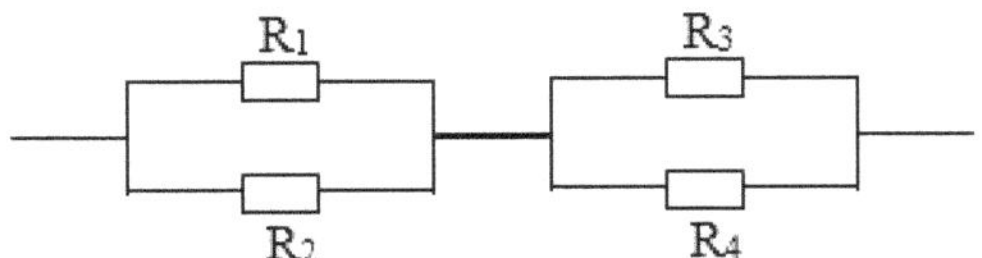

Figure 13.5: *A combined configuration*

The reliability of this configuration is given by:

$$R(t) = (R_1 + (1 - R_1) * R_2) * (R_3 + (1 - R_3) * R_4)$$

Systematic application of elementary series and parallel results can be used to reduce the complex configuration and obtain a single reliability value for the entire configuration.

Availability

Another parameter of reliability is **availability,** which is a more meaningful performance parameter. Availability is the ability to repair a system and restore it to operating condition. It is the probability that a system is fit for operation at a time t. This can be stated as the amount of expected downtime over a specified time interval. The availability has two terms, MTTF and MTTR. If R(t) is the reliability function for the system, then:

$$MTTF = \int_0^\infty R(t)dt$$

If it is known that there have been n failures occurring at times t_1, t_2....,t_n, then we have:

$$MTTF = \frac{1}{n}\sum_{i=1}^{i=n} t_i$$

The reciprocal of MTTF is called **hazard function**. For example, if R(t) is as shown in the previous equation, then MTTF is $1/\lambda = 1/Z$.

MTTR is defined as the **average time** required to affect a maintenance action. Its reciprocal $r(t)$, is called the **repaired hazard**. Therefore,

$$MTTF = \frac{1}{Z(t)}$$

$$\text{and } MTTR = \frac{1}{r(t)}$$

The probability that the system is operational, p(t), is the desired availability expression. As t increases, the first term dominates and eventually a steady state availability is reached at this point:

$$p(t) = \frac{r(t)}{Z(t) + r(t)}$$

Or, in terms of MTTF and MTTR, we have

$$p(t) = A = \frac{MTTF}{MTTF + MTTR}$$

Where A is the availability, the probability that the system is in service.

Example 1

One can respond to combined reliability and availability specification, assume that an availability of 0.999 per year (2000 hours of operation) in system service is acceptable, which translates into an availability.

$$A = \frac{r}{Z + r} = 0.999$$

Or,

$$r = 999 * Z$$

There are many combinations of failure rate and repair hazards that can meet this requirement. However, if a reasonable system reliability for one year, 2000 hours of operation, is set to be 0.9, and the hazard functions considered to be a constant failure rate, λ, then failure rate of 5.3E-5 is obtained form equation $R(t)=e^{-\lambda t}$

$$0.9 = R(t)=e^{-\lambda 2000}$$

$$\lambda = \frac{-\ln 0.9}{2000} = 0.000053 = 5.3E-5$$

To compute r from $r = 999 * Z$

$$r = 999 * 5.3E\text{-}5$$

$$= 5.3E\text{-}2 = 0.053$$

Therefore, MTTR is approximately 19 hours (18.1). MTTR and mean time to failure values can be traded to achieve realistic design goal. The availability based on the combination of a MTTR of 19 hours and a reliability for one year of 0.9 yields a probability of the system being in service of 99.9%.

Example 2

A requirement for a 0.975 probability of no interruption of service greater than ten seconds might be imposed on certain air traffic control functions. To meet this requirement with hardware/software reliability of say 0.37 for one year of a period of continuous operation (8766 hours) implies an availability of 0.999999842 and a MTTR of approximately five seconds. The five second MTTR is needed to assure that 97.5% of the interruption will not exceed ten seconds. The following computations confirm these numbers.

$$R(t) = e^{-\lambda t}$$

$$R(t) = 0.37$$

$$T = 8766$$

$$0.37 = e^{-\lambda 8766}$$

$$Z(t) = \lambda = 0.000113421$$

$$MTTF = 1/Z(t) = 8816.676002 \text{ hours}$$

$$A = \frac{MTTF}{MTTF + MTTR}$$

Since the probability of no service interruption over a full year of continuous service is 0.975, we must have an MTTR of five to six seconds to guarantee that 97.5% of the time the repair takes less than ten seconds. With the assumption we have:

$$A = \frac{8816.676002}{8816.676002 + \frac{5}{3600}} = 0.999999842$$

Redundancy offers a way to improve both reliability and availability. In the air traffic control system, the need to make repairs in less than five seconds implies automatic error detection and correction for both hardware and software failures.

Conclusion

In conclusion, software reliability is a critical aspect of software engineering, ensuring that systems perform consistently under expected conditions without failure. By focusing on reliability, software engineers can build systems that users can trust, reducing the risk of errors, downtime, and failures that can disrupt operations. Techniques such as fault tolerance, redundancy, and rigorous testing are essential in enhancing the reliability of software systems throughout their lifecycle. Achieving high software reliability not only improves user satisfaction but also increases the overall success of the project.

In the next chapter, we will dive into **software quality**, where we will examine the key attributes that define a high-quality software system. You will learn about various quality assurance processes, testing techniques, and standards that ensure software meets both user expectations and business requirements.

Exercises

To solidify your understanding of the concepts covered in this chapter, try the following exercises.

Multiple choice questions

1. **What does software reliability primarily refer to?**
   a. The performance of the software under stress conditions
   b. The ability of the software to perform its required functions without failure
   c. The adaptability of the software to new environments
   d. The ease of maintaining and updating the software

2. **Which of the following techniques is commonly used to enhance software reliability?**
   a. Modular programming
   b. Fault tolerance
   c. User feedback sessions
   d. Agile development

3. **In software reliability, what is the purpose of redundancy?**
   a. To reduce the complexity of the software
   b. To ensure continuous operation even if one component fails

c. To speed up the development process
d. To avoid software upgrades

4. **Which of the following is a key factor in measuring software reliability?**
   a. Time taken to develop the software
   b. Number of lines of code
   c. Mean time between failures (MTBF)
   d. User interface design

5. **What is the main goal of performing rigorous software testing?**
   a. To enhance the software's graphical user interface
   b. To ensure the software meets reliability and performance expectations
   c. To reduce the software's overall development cost
   d. To increase the number of features

6. **Which method helps software continue functioning correctly after a fault has occurred?**
   a. System refactoring
   b. Fault tolerance
   c. Design prototyping
   d. Software debugging

7. **Which of the following is NOT a direct indicator of software reliability?**
   a. Frequency of system crashes
   b. Response time of the software
   c. User satisfaction level
   d. Mean time to failure (MTTF)

8. **Why is software reliability important in mission-critical systems?**
   a. It ensures faster system updates
   b. Any software failure could result in significant damage or loss
   c. It reduces hardware costs
   d. It simplifies the software's architecture

Short answer questions

1. Define MTTF.
2. Define MTBF.
3. Define availability.

Essay questions

1. Ten units are placed in a test environment. Failures and failure times are recorded. The results are as follows:

Failure number	1	2	3	4	5	6	7	8	9	10
Operating time	8	20	34	46	63	86	111	141	186	266

   Using the tables as raw data, plot failure density and hazard rate as a function of time. Also plot failure distribution and reliability as a function of time.

2. A four-hour computation process involving a computer operating system, and an application software product must run from initialization to completion with a very low probability of error. Describe in detail the you would follow to allocate failure rates to individual subsystems. List the questions you would ask and the issues that would need resolution in order to complete the allocation process. Where would you expect to get your answer?

3. Determine the required MTTR for a system with an availability requirement of 99.9% and a mean time to failure of 5000 hours. What observation would you make?

4. Compute the end-to-end reliability (A to B) for the configuration in the following. Assume the probability of failure detection, switchover, and recovery is unity.

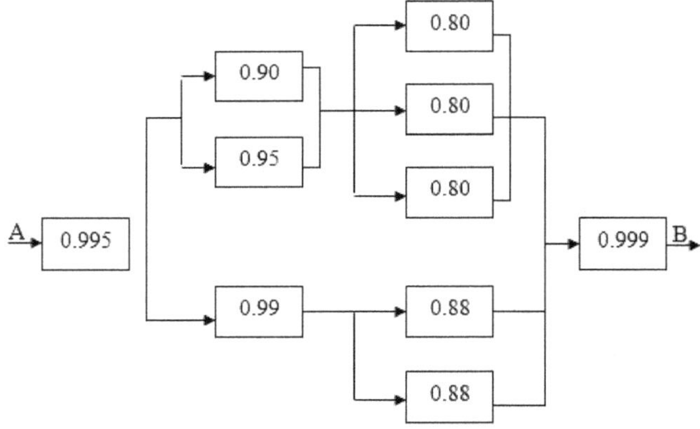

Multiple choice answers

1. b
2. b
3. b
4. c
5. b
6. b
7. b
8. b

CHAPTER 14
Software Quality

Introduction

Software quality is a critical aspect of software engineering, focusing on the degree to which a software product meets its requirements and satisfies the expectations of its users. It encompasses various attributes such as functionality, reliability, efficiency, maintainability, and usability, all of which contribute to the overall performance and value of the software. Ensuring high-quality software is essential to prevent errors, reduce risks, and improve customer satisfaction. In the field of software engineering, the pursuit of quality is an ongoing process that spans the entire software development life cycle, from initial design to final deployment, requiring continuous testing, evaluation, and refinement.

Structure

In this chapter, we are going to discuss:

- Software quality
- Metrics
- Software quality engineering program
- Techniques and tools
- Characteristics of software quality
- Techniques for improving software quality

- Software quality assurance
- Quality assurance in maintenance processes
- ISO-9001
- Certification
- Auditing
- Advantages
- Problems
- Quality planning for software
- Software development and design
- Document and data control
- SEI CMM
- Capability maturity model
- Six Sigmas in software engineering
- Promises

Objectives

The objective of this chapter is to provide a detailed understanding of software quality in software engineering. It will cover key areas such as metrics for assessing quality, software quality engineering programs, and tools and techniques to enhance software quality. The chapter will explore **software quality assurance (SQA)** practices in development and maintenance, ISO-9001 certification, auditing processes, and the advantages and challenges of maintaining quality. Additionally, topics like SEI CMM, CMM, Six Sigma, and quality planning will be discussed, highlighting their role in improving software development and design. The chapter concludes with insights into the future of software quality initiatives. What is software quality? The question is bound to generate many different answers, depending on whom you ask, under what circumstances, for what kind of software systems, and so on.

Concept

The different views of quality in a systematic manner, based on the different roles, responsibilities, and quality expectations of different people, are laid down here. A small set of views and related properties are discussed.

Five major views, according to *P Fleeger et al., 2002,* are transcendental, user, manufacturing, product, and value-based views, which are as follows:

- In the transcendental view, quality is hard to define or describe in abstract terms, but can be recognized if it is present. It is generally associated with some intangible properties that delight users.

- In the user view, quality is fitness for the purpose of meeting the user's needs.
- In the manufacturing view, quality means conformance to the process standards.
- In the product view, the focus is on the inherent characteristics in the product itself in the hope that controlling these internal quality indicators (product-internal metrics) will result in improved external product behavior (quality in use).
- In the value-based view, quality is the customers' willingness to pay for software.

Following is the roles and expectations that shape software quality:

- **People's roles and responsibilities**: When software quality is concerned, different people would have different views and expectations based on their roles and responsibilities. With the **quality assurance** (**QA**) and quality engineering focus of this book, we can divide the people into two broad groups:
    - Consumers of software products or services, including customers and users, either internally or externally. Sometimes, we also make the distinction between the customers, who are responsible for the acquisition of software products or services, and the users, who use the software products or services for various purposes, although the dual roles of customers and users are quite common. We can also extend the concept of users to include such non-human or **invisible** users as other software, embedded hardware, and the overall operational environment that the software operates under and interacts with (*Whittaker, 2001*).
    - Producers of software products, or anyone involved with the development, management, maintenance, marketing, and service of software products. We adopt a broad definition of producers, which also includes third-party participants who may be involved in add-on products and services, software packaging, software certification, fulfilling **independent verification and validation (IV and V)** responsibilities, and so on.
- **Quality expectations on the consumer side:** The basic quality expectations of a user are that a software system performs useful functions as it is specified. There are two basic elements to this expectation:
    - It performs the right functions as specified, which, hopefully, fits the user's needs.
    - It performs these specified functions correctly over repeated use or over a long period of time, or performs its functions reliably.

  These two elements are related to the validation and verification aspects of QA.
- **Quality in software engineering**: Within software engineering, quality has been one of the most important factors, including cost, schedule, and functionality, which have been studied by researchers and practitioners. These factors determine the success or failure of a software product in evolving market environments, but

may have varying importance for different time periods and different market segments.

In *Musa and Everett (1990)*, these varying primary concerns were conveniently used to divide software engineering into four progressive stages:

- In the functional stage, the focus was on providing automated functions to replace what had been done manually before.
- In the schedule stage, the focus was on introducing the important features and new systems on a timely and orderly basis to satisfy the urgent user needs.
- In the cost stage, the focus was on reducing the price to stay competitive, accompanied by the widespread use of personal computers.
- In the reliability stage, the focus was managing users' quality expectations under the increased dependency on software and high cost or severe damages associated with software failures.

We can see a gradual increase in the importance of quality within software engineering. This general characterization is in agreement with what we have discussed so far, namely, the importance of focusing on correctness-centered quality attributes in our software QA effort for modern software systems.

The **software quality engineering (SQE)** is a process that evaluates, assesses, and improves the quality of software. Software quality is often defined as the degree to which software meets requirements for reliability, maintainability, transportability, and so on, as contrasted with functional, performance, and interface requirements that are satisfied as a result of software engineering.

Quality must be built into a software product during its development to satisfy the quality requirements as established for it. SQE ensures that the process of incorporating quality in the software is done properly, and that the resulting software product meets the quality requirements and is usually determined by analysis while functional requirements are demonstrated by testing. SQE performs a function complementary to software development engineering. Their common goal is to ensure that a safe, reliable, and quality-engineered software product is developed.

Software qualities

Qualities for which an SQE evaluation is to be done must first be selected and then the requirements are set for them. Some commonly used qualities are:

- **Reliability**: Hardware reliability is often defined in terms of the **mean-time-to-failure (MTTF)** of a given set of equipment. An analogous notion is useful for software, although the failure mechanisms are different, and the mathematical predictions used for hardware have not yet been usefully applied to software. Software reliability is often defined as the extent to which a program can be expected to perform intended functions with the required precision over a given period of time. Software reliability engineering is concerned with the detection and correction of errors in the software; even more, it is concerned with the techniques to compensate for unknown software errors and for problems in the hardware and data environments in which the software must operate.

- **Maintainability**: Software maintainability is defined as the ease of finding and correcting errors in the software. It is analogous to the hardware quality of **mean-time-to-repair (MTTR)**. While there is as yet no way to directly measure or predict software maintainability, there is a significant body of knowledge about software attributes that make software easier to maintain. These include modularity, self (internal) documentation, code readability, and structured coding techniques. These same attributes also improve sustainability and the ability to make improvements to the software.
- **Transportability**: Transportability is defined as the ease of transporting a given set of software to a new hardware and/or operating system environment.
- **Interoperability**: Software interoperability is the ability of two or more software systems used to exchange information and to mutually use the exchanged information.
- **Efficiency**: Efficiency is the extent to which software uses the minimum hardware resources to perform its functions.

Some of the software quality requirements one would look for are outlined in the following:

- **Specific non-functional (quality) requirements:**
    - Is the expected response time, from the user's point of view, specified for all necessary operations?
    - Are other timing considerations specified, such as processing time, data-transfer rate, and system throughput?
    - Is the level of security specified?
    - Is the reliability specified, including the consequences of software failure, the vital information that needs to be protected from failure, and the strategy for error detection and recovery?
    - Is maximum memory specified?
    - Is the maximum storage specified?
    - Is the maintainability of the system specified, including its ability to adapt to changes in specific functionality, changes in the operating environment, and changes in its interfaces with other software?
    - Is the definition of success included? Of failure?

- **Requirements quality:**
    - o Are the requirements written in the user's language? Do the users think so?
    - o Does each requirement avoid conflicts with other requirements?
    - o Are acceptable trade-offs are there between competing attributes specified, for example, between robustness and correctness?
    - o Do the requirements avoid specifying the design?
    - o Are the requirements at a fairly consistent level of detail? Should any requirement be specified in more detail? Should any requirement be specified in less detail?
    - o Are the requirements clear enough to be turned over to an independent group for construction and still be understood?
    - o Is each item relevant to the problem and its solution? Can each item be traced to its origin in the problem environment?
    - o Is each requirement testable? Will it be possible for independent testing to determine whether each requirement has been satisfied?
    - o Are all possible changes to the requirements specified, including the likelihood of each change?

There are many other software qualities. Some of them are not important to a specific software system, thus no activities will be performed to assess or improve them. Maximizing some qualities may cause others to be decreased. For example, increasing the efficiency of a piece of software may require writing parts of it in assembly language. This will decrease the transportability and maintainability of the software.

Metrics

Metrics are the quantitative values, usually computed from the design or code, that measure the quality in question, or some attribute of the software related to the quality. Many metrics have been invented, and a number of them have been successfully used in specific environments, but none have gained widespread acceptance.

Software quality engineering program

The two software qualities which command the most attention are reliability and maintainability. Some practical programs and techniques have been developed to improve the reliability and maintainability of the software, even if they are not measurable or predictable. The types of activities that might be included in an SQE program are described in terms of these two qualities. These activities could be used as a model for the SQE activities for additional qualities:

- **Qualities and attributes:**
  - An initial step in laying out an SQE program is to select the qualities that are important in the context of the use of the software that is being developed. For example, the highest priority qualities for flight software are usually reliability and efficiency. If revised flight software can be up-linked during flight, maintainability may be of interest, but considerations like transportability will not drive the design or implementation. On the other hand, the use of science analysis software might require ease of change and maintainability, with reliability a concern and efficiency not a driver at all.
  - After the software qualities are selected and ranked, specific attributes of the software which help to increase those qualities should be identified. For example, modularity is an attribute that tends to increase both reliability and maintainability. Modular software is designed to result in code that is apportioned into small, self-contained, functionally unique components, or units. Modular code is easier to maintain, because the interactions between units of code are easily understood, and low-level functions are contained in a few units of code. Modular code is also more reliable, because it is easier to completely test a small, self-contained unit.
  - Not all software qualities are simply related to measurable design and code attributes, and no quality is so simple that it can be easily measured. The idea is to select or devise measurable, analyzable, or testable design and code attributes that will increase the desired qualities. Attributes like information hiding, strength, cohesion, and coupling should be considered.
- **Quality evaluations:**
  - Once some decisions have been made about the quality objectives and software attributes, quality evaluations can be done. The intent in an evaluation is to measure the effectiveness of a standard or procedure in promoting the desired attributes of the software product. Consider an example, the design and coding standards should undergo a quality evaluation. If modularity is desired, the standards should clearly say so and should set standards for the size of units or components. Since internal documentation is linked to maintainability, the documentation standards should be clear and require good internal documentation.
  - Quality of designs and code should also be evaluated. This can be done as a part of the walkthrough or inspection process, or a quality audit can be done. In either case, the implementation is evaluated against the standard, and the evaluator's knowledge of good software engineering practices and examples of poor quality in the product are identified for possible correction.

- **Nonconformance analysis**: One very useful SQE activity is an analysis of a project's nonconformance records. The nonconformance should be analyzed for unexpectedly high numbers of events in specific sections or modules of code. If areas of code are found that have had an unusually high error count (assuming it is not because the code in question has been tested more thoroughly), then the code should be examined. The high error count may be due to poor quality code, an inappropriate design, or requirements that are not well understood or defined. In any case, the analysis may indicate changes and rework that can improve the reliability of the completed software. In addition to code problems, the analysis may also reveal software development or maintenance processes that allow or cause a high proportion of errors to be introduced into the software. If so, an audit may discover that the procedures are not being followed.
- **Fault tolerance engineering**: For software that must be of high reliability, a fault tolerance activity should be established. It should identify the software which provides and accomplishes critical functions and requirements. For this software, the engineering activity should determine and develop techniques which will ensure that the needed reliability or fault tolerance will be attained. Some of the techniques that have been developed for high reliability environments include:
    - Quality of designs and code should also be evaluated. This can be done as a part of the walkthrough or inspection process, or a quality audit can be done. In either case the implementation is evaluated against the standard and the evaluator's knowledge of good software engineering practices and example of poor quality in the product are identified for possible correction.
    - Input data checking and error tolerance, consider an example, if out-of-range or missing input data can affect reliability, then sophisticated error checking and data interpolation or extrapolation schemes may significantly improve the reliability.
    - For limited amounts of code, formal **proof of correctness** methods may be able to demonstrate that no errors exist.
    - **N-item voting** is a design and implementation scheme where a number of independent sets of software and hardware operate on the same input. Some comparison (voting) scheme is used to determine which output to use. This is especially effective where subtle timing or hardware errors may be present.
    - **Independent development**: In this scheme, more or more of the N-items are independently developed units of software. This helps to prevent the simultaneous failure of all items due to a common coding error.

Techniques and tools

Standard statistical techniques can be used to manipulate nonconformance data. In addition, there is considerable experimentation with the **failure modes and effect analysis (FMEA)** technique adapted from hardware reliability engineering. In particular, the FMEA can be used to identify the failure modes or other assemblies (hardware) system states, which can then lead the quality engineer to an analysis of the software that controls the system as it assumes those states.

There are also tools that are useful for quality engineering. They include system and software simulators, which allow the modeling of system behavior, dynamic analyzers, which detect the portions of the code that are used most intensively, software tools that are used to compute metrics from code or designs; and a host of special purpose tools that can, for example, detect all system calls to help decide on portability limits.

Characteristics of software quality

The software has both external and internal quality characteristics. External characteristics are the characteristics that a user of the software product is aware of, and they include the following:

- **Correctness**: The degree to which a system is free from faults in its specification, design, and implementation.
- **Usability**: The ease with which users can learn and use a system.
- **Efficiency**: Minimal use of system resources, including memory, and execution time.
- **Reliability**: The ability of a system to perform its required functions under stated conditions whenever required, which is having a long mean time between failures.
- **Integrity**: The degree to which a system prevents unauthorized or improper access to its programs and its data. The idea of integrity includes restricting unauthorized user accesses as well as ensuring that data is accessed properly, that is, that tables with parallel data are modified in parallel, that date fields contain only valid dates, and so on.
- **Adaptability**: The extent to which a system can be used, without modification, in applications or environments other than those for which it was specifically designed.
- **Accuracy**: The degree to which a system built is free from error, especially with respect to quantitative outputs. Accuracy differs from correctness, it is a determination of how well a system does the job it is built for rather than whether it was built correctly.
- **Robustness**: The degree to which a system continues to function in the presence of invalid inputs or stressful environmental conditions.

Some of these characteristics overlap, but all have different shades of meaning that are applicable more in some cases, less in others.

External characteristics of quality are the only kind of software characteristics that users care about. Users care about whether the software is easy to use, or whether it is easy for you to modify. They care about whether the software works correctly, not about whether the code is readable or well structured.

Programmers care about the internal characteristics of the software as well as the external ones. We try here to be code-centered, therefore, it focuses on the internal quality characteristics. They include the following:

- **Maintainability**: The ease with which you can modify a software system to change or add capabilities, improve performance, or correct defects.
- **Flexibility**: The extent to which you can modify a system for use or environments other than those for which it was specifically designed.
- **Portability**: The ease with which you can modify a system to operate in an environment different from that for which it was specifically designed.
- **Reusability**: The extent to which and the ease with which you can use parts of a system in other systems.
- **Readability**: The ease with which you can read and understand the source code of a system, especially at the detailed-statement level.
- **Testability**: The degree to which you can unit-test and system-test a system, the degree to which you can verify that the system meets its requirements.
- **Understandability**: The ease with which you can comprehend a system at both the system-organizational and detailed-statement levels. Understandability has to do with the coherence of the system at a more general level than readability does.

As in the list of external quality characteristics, some of these internal characteristics overlap, but they too each have different shades of meaning that are valuable.

The internal aspects of system quality are the main subject. The difference between internal and external characteristics is not completely clear-cut because at some level, internal characteristics affect external ones. Software that is not internally understandable or maintainable impairs your ability to correct defects, which in turn affects the external characteristics of correctness and reliability. Software that is not flexible cannot be enhanced in response to user requests, which in turn affects the external characteristic of usability. The point is that some quality characteristics are emphasized to make life easier for the user, and some are emphasized to make life easier for the programmer.

The attempt to maximize certain characteristics invariably conflicts with the attempt to maximize others. Finding an optimal solution from a set of competing objectives is one activity that makes software development a true engineering discipline. These kinds of relationships can be found among the internal characteristics of software quality.

The most interesting aspect of this chart is that it focuses on a specific characteristic that does not always mean a trade-off with another characteristic. Sometimes one hurts another, sometimes one helps another, and sometimes one neither hurts nor helps another. For example, correctness is the characteristic of functioning exactly to specification. Robustness is the ability to continue functioning even under the unanticipated conditions. Sometimes focusing on correctness hurts robustness of the software and vice versa. In contrast, focusing on adaptability helps robustness and vice versa.

Techniques for improving software quality

SQA is a planned and systematic program of activities designed to ensure that a system has the desired characteristics. Although it might seem that the best way to develop a high-quality product would be to focus on the product itself, in SQA the best place is on the process. Following are some of the elements of a software quality program:

- **Software quality objectives**: One powerful technique for improving software quality is setting explicit quality objectives from among the external characteristics described in the last section. Without explicit goals, programmers can work to maximize characteristics different from the ones you expect them to maximize. The power of setting explicit goals is discussed in more detail later in this section.
- **Explicit quality-assurance activity**: One common problem in assuring quality is that quality is perceived as a secondary goal. Indeed, in some organizations, quick and dirty programming is the rule rather than the exception. Programmers who litter their code with defects and **complete** their programs quickly, are rewarded more than programmers who write excellent programs and make sure that they are usable before releasing them. In such organizations, it shouldn't be surprising that programmers do not make quality their first priority. The organization must show programmers that quality is a priority. Making the quality-assurance activity independent makes the priority clear, and programmers will respond accordingly.
- **Testing strategy**: Execution testing can provide a detailed assessment of product reliability. Developers on many projects rely on testing as the primary method of both quality assessment and quality improvement. Testing does have a role in the construction of high-quality software, however, and part of QA is developing a test strategy in conjunction with the product requirements, the architecture, and the design.
- **Software-engineering guidelines**: These are the guidelines that control the technical character of the software as it is developed. Such guidelines apply to all software development activities including problem definition, requirements development, architecture, construction, and system testing. The guidelines in this book are, in one sense, a set of software engineering guidelines for construction (detailed design, coding, unit testing, and integration).

- **Informal technical reviews**: Many software developers review their work before turning it over for formal review. Informal reviews include desk-checking the design or the code, or walking through the code with a few peers.
- **Formal technical reviews**: One part of managing a software-engineering process is catching problems at the **lowest-value** stage, that is, at the stage in which problems cost the least to correct. To achieve such a goal, developers on most software engineering projects use **quality gates**, periodic tests that determine whether the quality of the product at one stage is sufficient to support moving on to the next. Quality gates are usually used to transition between requirements development, architecture, detailed design, and construction, and system testing. The **gate** can be a peer review, a customer review, an inspection, a walkthrough, or an audit.

  A gate does not mean that architecture or requirements need to be 100 percent complete or frozen; it does mean that you will use the gate to determine whether the requirements or architecture are good enough to support downstream development. **Good enough** might mean that you have sketched out the most critical 20 percent of the requirements or architecture, or it might mean you have specified 95 percent in excruciating detail. Which end of the scale should you aim for, depending on the nature of your specific project?
- **External audits**: An external audit is a specific kind of technical review used to determine the status of a project or the quality of a product being developed. An audit team is brought in from outside the organization and reports its findings to whoever commissioned the audit, usually management.
- **Development process**: Each of the elements mentioned so far has something to do explicitly with assuring software quality and implicitly with the process of software development. Development efforts that include quality-assurance activities produce better software than those that do not. Other processes that aren't explicitly quality-assurance activities also affect software quality
- **Change-control procedures**: One big obstacle to achieving software quality is uncontrolled changes. Uncontrolled requirements changes can result in disruption to design and coding. Uncontrolled changes in architecture or design can result in code that does not agree with its design, inconsistencies in the code, or the use of more time in modifying code to meet the changing design than in moving the project forward. Uncontrolled changes in the code itself can result in internal inconsistencies and uncertainties about which code has been fully reviewed and tested and which has not. Uncontrolled changes in requirements, architecture, design, or code can have all of these effects. Consequently, handling changes effectively is a key to effective product development.
- **Measurement of results**: Unless the results of a quality-assurance plan are measured, you will have no way of knowing whether the plan is working. Measurement tells you whether your plan is a success or a failure and also allows you to vary your process in a controlled way to see whether it can be improved.

Measurement has a second motivational effect. People pay attention to whatever is measured, assuming that it is used to evaluate them. Choose what you measure carefully. People tend to focus on work that is measured and ignore work that is not.

- **Prototyping**: Prototyping is the development of realistic models of a system's key functions. A developer can prototype parts of a user interface to determine usability, critical calculations to determine execution time, or typical data sets to determine the memory requirements. A survey of 16 published and eight unpublished case studies compared prototyping to traditional and specification-development methods. The comparison revealed that prototyping can lead to better designs, better matches with user needs, and improved maintainability (*Gordon and Bieman 1991*).
- **Setting objectives**: Explicitly setting quality objectives is a simple, obvious step in achieving quality software, but it is easy to overlook. You might wonder whether, if you set quality objectives, programmers will actually work to achieve them. The answer is, yes, they will, if they know what the objectives are and the objectives are reasonable. Programmers cannot respond to a set of objectives that change daily or those that are impossible to meet.

Software quality assurance

SQA consists of a means of monitoring the software engineering processes and methods used to ensure the quality. It does this by means of audits of the quality management system under which the software system is created. The audits are backed by one or more standards, usually **ISO 9000** series.

It is distinct from software **quality control** (**QC**), which includes reviewing requirements documents, and software testing. SQA encompasses the entire software development process, which includes processes such as software design, coding, source code control, code reviews, change management, configuration management, and release management. Whereas software QC is a control of products, SQA is a control of processes.

SQA is related to the practice of QA in product manufacturing. There are, however, some notable differences between software and a manufactured product. These differences stem from the fact that the manufactured product is physical and can be seen, whereas the software product is not visible. Therefore, its function, benefit, and costs are not as easily measured. What is more, when a manufactured product rolls off the assembly line, it is essentially a complete, finished product, whereas software is never finished. Software lives, grows, evolves, and metamorphoses, unlike its tangible counterparts. Therefore, the processes and methods to manage, monitor, and measure its ongoing quality are as fluid and sometimes elusive as the defects that they are meant to keep in check.

The quality system has undergone four stages of evolution, as shown in *Figure 14.1*. Inspection used to be carried out earlier with the finished product. The process is used to ensure quality products by eliminating the defective ones. Inspection was done after the jobs were produced. The rejection of defective products used to be a costly affair for the organization. The initial product inspection method gave way to QC. The QC detects the defective products and eliminates them, and at the same time, it is able to determine the cause of defects. The process is called error **detection**. The cause of the defect in the production process was removed to produce good products thereafter. The QC method was found to be a better solution than inspection.

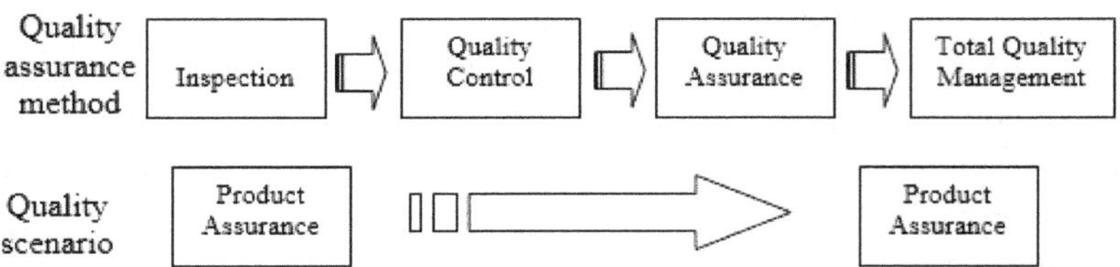

Figure 14.1: *Evolution of quality concept and quality paradigm*

The next breakthrough in quality systems was QA. The process of QA was to give more emphasis on the production process to prevent errors. If the process is good and closely monitored, the products being processed are bound to be non-defective and of good quality. The process is called **error prevention**. This modern quality procedure includes the procedures for recognizing, defining, analyzing, and improving the production process. From the organizational viewpoint, **total quality management (TQM)** was adopted instead of process control. This would ensure organizational improvement as a whole by achieving continuous process improvement.

Inspection is most commonly applied to code, but it could also be applied to requirement specifications, designs, test plans, test cases, user manuals, and other documents or software artifacts. Therefore, inspection can be used throughout the development process, particularly early in the software development, before anything can be tested. Consequently, inspection can be an effective and economical QA alternative because of the much-increased cost of fixing late defects as compared to fixing early ones. These causal analysis results can be used to guide defect prevention activities by removing identified error sources or correcting identified missing or incorrect human actions.

According to the different ways different QA alternatives deal with defects, they can be classified into three general categories:

- Defect prevention through error source elimination and error blocking activities, such as education and training, formal specification and verification, and proper selection and application of appropriate technologies, tools, processes, or standards.
- Defect reduction through inspection, testing, and other static analyses or dynamic activities, to detect and remove faults from software. One of the most important and widely used alternatives, is testing.

- Defect containment through fault tolerance, failure prevention, or failure impact minimization, to assure the software reliability and safety. Existing software quality literature generally covers defect reduction techniques such as testing and inspection in more detail than defect prevention activities, while largely ignoring the role of defect containment in QA.

Quality assurance in the maintenance process

In the software maintenance process, the focus of QA is on defect handling to make sure that each problem reported by customers from field operations is logged, analyzed, and resolved, and a complete tracking record is kept so that we can learn from past problems for future quality improvement. In addition, such defect information can be used as additional input in planning for future releases of the same product or for replacement products. Among the different QA activities, defect containment activities play an important role in post-release product operations and maintenance support.

QA in the waterfall process

In the most commonly used waterfall process for large software projects, development activities are typically grouped into different sequential stages to form a waterfall, although overlaps are common among successive pairs of stages (*Zelkowitz, 1988*). A typical sequence includes, in chronological order, product planning, requirement analysis, specification, design, coding, testing, release, and post-release product support. As a central part of QA activities, testing is an integral part of the waterfall development process, forming an important link in the overall development chain. Other QA activities, although not explicitly stated in the description process, can be carried out throughout other phases and in the transition from one phase to another. Consider an example, part of the criteria to move on from each phase to the next is quality, typically in the form of checking to see if certain quality plans or standards have been completed or followed, as demonstrated by the results from various forms or reviews or inspections.

Various defect prevention activities are typically concentrated in the earlier phases of software development before actual faults have been injected into the software systems. There are several important reasons for this focus on early development phases:

- The error sources are typically associated with activities in these early phases, such as conceptual mistakes by designers and programmers, unfamiliarity with the product domain, inexperience with the specific development methodologies, and so on. Therefore, error source removal, a primary method of defect prevention, is closely associated with these early development phases.
- Although some faults could be injected into the software systems during testing and other late development phases, the experience tells us that the vast majority of faults are injected in the early development phases, particularly in the detailed design and implementation phases. Therefore, effective defect prevention through error blocking needs to be carried out during these phases.

This is because of the possibilities of defect propagations and the increasing cost over time or successive development phases to fix the defects once they are injected into the system, we need to reduce the number of faults in software systems by the combination of defect prevention and application of QA techniques that can help to remove software faults early. Some defect detection and removal techniques, such as inspection, can be applied to early phases, such as inspecting requirement documents, product specifications, and different levels of product designs. On the other hand, there are practical obstacles to the early fixing of injected defects. For example, dynamic problems may only become apparent during execution, and inter-dependency only becomes apparent with the implementation of related components or modules. This is because of these reasons, other fault detection and removal activities, such as testing, are typically concentrated in the middle to late phases of software development.

Finally, failure prevention and containment activities, such as fault tolerance and safety assurance, typically focus on the operational phases. However, their planning, design, and implementation need to be carried out throughout the software development process. In some sense, they are equivalent to adding some necessary functions or features into the existing product to make them safe or fault tolerant.

Figure 14.2 illustrates how the different QA activities fit into the waterfall process:

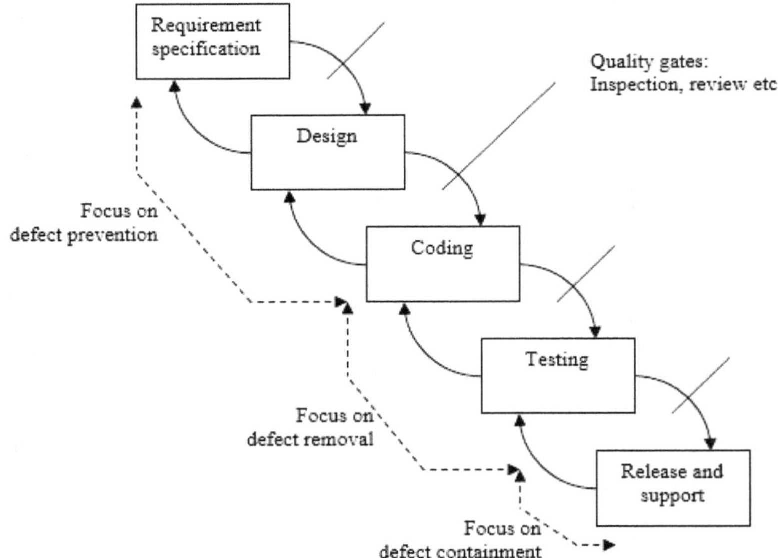

Figure 14.2: *Quality assurance activities on a waterfall model*

Three key characteristics of this activity distribution are illustrated:

- The phase with QA as the focus, such as the **testing** phase.
- QA activities, typically include inspections and reviews, carried out at the transitions from one phase to the next, are shown as barriers or gates to pass. The

exception to this is between testing and release, where the reviews are typically accompanied by the acceptance testing.

- Other QA activities scattered over other development phases, such as the general distribution scope is shown by the dotted bracket, with a focus on defect prevention in the early phases, a focus on defect removal during coding and testing phases, and a focus on defect containment in operational support.

ISO-9001

ISO 9001 is an internationally recognized standard for **quality management systems (QMS)**, applicable across various industries, including software engineering. In the context of software development, ISO 9001 provides a framework for ensuring that software products and services meet customer requirements and comply with regulatory standards. The standard emphasizes continuous improvement, risk management, and customer satisfaction, guiding software engineering organizations in establishing efficient processes, maintaining high-quality standards, and enhancing overall product reliability. By adhering to ISO 9001, software development teams can improve operational efficiency, ensure consistency in product quality, and foster trust with clients and stakeholders.

History of ISO 9000

During World War II, there were quality problems in many British industries, such as munitions, where bombs were exploding in factories during assembly. The adopted solution was to require factories to document their manufacturing procedures and to prove by record-keeping that the procedures were being followed. The name of the standard was **BS 5750**, and it was known as a management standard because it specified not what to manufacture, but how the manufacturing process was to be managed. According to Seddon, *In 1987, the British Government persuaded the International Organization for Standardization to adopt BS 5750 as an international standard. BS 5750 became ISO 9000.*

ISO 9000

ISO 9000 is a family of standards for QMS. ISO 9000 is maintained by **International Organization for Standardization (ISO)**, and is administered by accreditation and certification bodies. It published its 9000 series of standards in 1987. ISO is a consortium of around 100 exporting countries established to formulate and foster standardization. The ISO 9000 standards have been adopted by many countries, including all members of the European Community, Canada, Mexico, the United States, Australia, New Zealand, and the Pacific Rim. Countries in Latin and South America have also shown interest in the standards.

After adopting the standards, a country typically permits only ISO-registered companies to supply goods and services to government agencies and public utilities. Telecommunication equipment and medical devices are examples of product categories that must be supplied by ISO-registered companies. In turn, manufacturers of these products often require their suppliers to become registered. Private companies such as automobile and computer manufacturers frequently require their suppliers to be ISO-registered as well.

To register to one of the QA system models contained in ISO 9000, a company's quality system and operations are scrutinized by third party auditors for compliance to the standard and for effective operation. Upon successful registration, a company issued a certificate from a registration body represented by the auditors. Semi-annual surveillance audits ensure continued compliance to the standard.

ISO 9000 describes the elements of a QA system in general terms. These elements include the organizational structure, procedures, processes, and resources needed to implement quality planning, QC, QA, and quality improvement. However, ISO 9000 does not describe how an organization should implement these quality system elements. Consequently, the challenge lies in designing and implementing a QA system that meets the standard and fits the company's products, services, and culture.

Requirements of ISO 9001

Some of the requirements in ISO 9001 (which is one of the standards in the ISO 9000 family) include:

- A set of procedures that cover all the key processes in the business
- Monitoring processes to ensure they are effective
- Keeping adequate records
- Checking output for defects, with appropriate and corrective action where necessary
- Regularly reviewing individual processes and the quality system itself for effectiveness, and
- Facilitating continual improvement

A company or organization that has been independently audited and certified to be in conformance with ISO 9001 may publicly state that it is **ISO 9001 certified** or **ISO 9001 registered**. Certification to an ISO 9000 standard does not guarantee the compliance (and therefore the quality) of end products and services; rather, it certifies that consistent business processes are being applied. Indeed, some companies enter the ISO 9001 certification as a marketing tool.

Although the standards originated in manufacturing, they are now employed across a wide range of other types of organizations. A **product**, in ISO vocabulary, can mean a physical object, service, or software. In fact, according to ISO in 2004, *service sectors now account by far for the highest number of ISO 9001:2000 certificates - about 31% of the total.*

ISO 9001:2000 QMS, such as **requirements,** are intended for use in any organization that designs, develops, manufactures, installs, and/or services any product or provides any form of service. It provides a number of requirements, which an organization needs to fulfill if it is to achieve customer satisfaction through consistent products and services, which meet customer expectations. It includes a requirement for the continual (such as planned) improvement of the quality management system, for which ISO 9004:2000 provides many hints. This is the only implementation for which third-party auditors may grant certification.

Note that the previous members of the ISO 9000 family, 9001, 9002, and 9003, have all been integrated into 9001. In most cases, an organization claiming to be "ISO 9000 registered" is referring to ISO 9001.

ISO 9000:1987 version

ISO 9000:1987 had the same structure as the UK Standard BS 5750, with three **models** for QMS, the selection of which was based on the scope of activities of the organization:

- **ISO 9001:1987** model for QA in design, development, production, installation, and servicing was for companies and organizations whose activities included the creation of new products.
- **ISO 9002:1987** model for QA in production, installation, and servicing had basically the same material as ISO 9001 but without covering the creation of new products.
- **ISO 9003:1987** model for QA in final inspection and test covered only the final inspection of the finished product, with no concern for how the product was produced.

ISO 9000:1987 was also influenced by existing U.S. and other defense standards (**MIL SPECS**), and so was well-suited to manufacturing. The emphasis tended to be placed on conformance with procedures rather than the overall process of management, which was likely the actual intent.

ISO 9000:1994 version

ISO 9000:1994 emphasized QA via preventive actions, instead of just checking final product, and continued to require evidence of compliance with documented procedures. As with the first edition, the down-side was that companies tended to implement its requirements by creating shelf-loads of procedure manuals, and becoming burdened with an ISO bureaucracy. In some companies, adapting and improving processes could actually be impeded by the quality system.

ISO 9000:2000 version

ISO 9001:2000 combines the three standards **9001**, **9002**, and **9003,** into one, now called **9001**. Design and development procedures are required only if a company does, in fact, engage in the creation of new products. The 2000 version sought to make a radical change in thinking by actually placing the concept of process management front and center (**Process management** was the monitoring and optimizing of a company's tasks and activities, instead of just inspecting the final product). The 2000 version also demands the involvement of upper executives, in order to integrate quality into the business system and avoid delegation of quality functions to junior administrators. Another goal is to improve effectiveness via process performance metrics and numerical measurement of the effectiveness of tasks and activities. Expectations of continual process improvement and tracking customer satisfaction were made explicit.

ISO 9000:2008 version

The ISO 9001 technical committee reviewed the next version of ISO 9001, which will in all likelihood, be termed the ISO 9001:2008 standard, assuming its planned release date of 2008 is met. Early reports are that the standard will not be substantially changed from its 2000 version. As with the release of previous versions, organizations registered to ISO 9001 will be given a substantial period to transition to the new version of the standard, assuming changes are needed. Organizations registered to 9001:1994 had until December 2003 to undergo upgrade audits.

Certification

ISO does not itself certify organizations. Many countries have formed accreditation bodies to authorize certification bodies, which audit organizations applying for ISO 9001 compliance certification. Although commonly referred to as **ISO 9000:2000** certifications, the actual standard to which an organization's quality management can be certified is ISO 9001:2000. Both the accreditation bodies and the certification bodies charge fees for their services. The various accreditation bodies have mutual agreements with each other to ensure that certificates issued by one of the **Accredited Certification Bodies (ACB)** are accepted world-wide.

The applying organization is assessed based on an extensive sample of its sites, functions, products, services, and processes; a list of problems (**action requests** or **non-compliances**) is made known to the management. If there are no major problems on this list, the certification body will issue an **ISO 9001** certificate for each geographical site it has visited, once it receives a satisfactory improvement plan from the management showing how any problems will be resolved.

An ISO certificate is not a once-and-for-all award, but must be renewed at regular intervals recommended by the certification body, usually around three years. In contrast to the **capability maturity model** (**CMM**), there are no grades of competence within ISO 9001.

Auditing

Two types of auditing are required to become registered to the standard:

- Auditing by an external certification body (external audit)
- Audits by internal staff trained for this process (internal audits)

The aim is a continual process of review and assessment, to verify that the system is working as it is supposed to, find out where it can improve, and correct or prevent problems identified. It is considered healthier for internal auditors to audit outside their usual management line, so as to bring a degree of independence to their judgments.

Under the 1994 standard, the auditing process could be adequately addressed by performing **compliance auditing**. The 2000 standard uses the process approach. While auditors perform similar functions, they are expected to go beyond mere auditing for **compliance** by focusing on risk, status, and importance. This means they are expected to make more judgments on what is effective, rather than merely adhering to what is formally prescribed.

Under the 1994 version, the question was *Are you doing what the manual says you should be doing?", whereas under the 2000 version, the question is "Will this process help you achieve your stated objectives? Is it a good process or is there a way to do it better?*

The ISO 19011 standard for auditing applies to ISO 9001 besides other management systems like EMS (ISO 14001), FSMS (ISO 22000), and so on.

Advantages

It is widely acknowledged that proper quality management improves business, often having a positive effect on investment, market share, sales growth, sales margins, competitive advantage, and avoidance of litigation. The quality principles in **ISO 9000:2000** are also sound. ISO 9000 guidelines provide a comprehensive model for QMS that can make any company competitive [*Wade and Barnes*]. According to the Providence Business News, implementing ISO often gives the following advantages:

- Create a more efficient, effective operation
- Increase customer satisfaction and retention
- Reduce audits
- Enhance marketing
- Improve employee motivation, awareness, and morale
- Promote international trade
- Increases profit
- Reduce waste and increase productivity

In today's service-sector driven economy, more and more companies are using ISO 9000 as a business tool. Through the use of properly stated quality objectives, customer satisfaction surveys and a well-defined continual improvement program companies are using ISO 9000 processes to increase their efficiency and profitability.

Problems

A common criticism of ISO 9001 is the amount of money, time, and paperwork required for registration. Opponents claim that it is only for documentation. Proponents believe that if a company has documented its quality systems, then most of the paperwork has already been completed [*Barnes*].

ISO 9001 promotes specification, control, and procedures rather than understanding and improvement [*Seddon*]. Wade argues that ISO 9000 is effective as a guideline, but that promoting it as a standard helps to mislead companies into thinking that certification means better quality. An organization needs to set its own quality standards. Blind reliance on the specifications of ISO 9001 does not guarantee a successful quality system.

The standard is seen as especially prone to failure when a company is interested in certification before quality. Certifications are in fact often based on customer contractual requirements rather than a desire to actually improve quality. *If you just want the certificate on the wall, chances are, you will create a paper system that doesn't have much to do with the way you actually run your business.* Certification by an independent auditor is often seen as the problem area, and has become a vehicle to increase consulting services. In fact, ISO itself advises that ISO 9001 can be implemented without certification, simply for the quality benefits that can be achieved. Another problem reported is the competition among the numerous certifying bodies, leading to a softer approach to the defects noticed in the operation of the quality system of a firm.

Quality planning for software

Develop quality plans to control your software development projects.

- The quality plans should control project implementation, project schedules, project resources, project approvals, project phases (the beginning and end).
- Your quality plans should define the quality requirements, responsibilities, authorities, life cycle model, review methods, testing methods, verification methods, and validation methods.
- Develop detailed quality plans and procedures and define specific responsibilities and authorities to control the configuration management, product verification, product validation, nonconforming products, and corrective actions.
- Your quality plans may include or refer to generic or special project, product, or contract procedures.

- Your quality plan can be a separate document or it can be part of another larger document. Or, it can be made up of several specific documents.
- Your quality plan should be updated and refined as your software development plan is implemented.
- Make sure that all participating groups and organizations get a chance to review and approve the quality plan before it is implemented.

Contract review

Develop and document procedures to coordinate the review of software development contracts. Develop procedures to coordinate the review of contracts that the software will be developed for a customer, for a market sector, or for your internal use, or the software will be embedded in a hardware product. The contract review procedures should ensure that all contractual requirements are acceptable before you agree to provide products to your customers. Specifically, your procedures should make sure that the data and facilities to be provided by the customer, to carry out the joint product development, life cycle processes to be imposed by the customer, deployment of software product, the changes to be handled during software development and software maintenance, handling of software problems after acceptance and training of users, and so on.

Software development and design

Software development and design are foundational aspects of software engineering, focusing on creating efficient, reliable, and scalable software solutions. This process involves a series of structured activities, from understanding user requirements to crafting the architecture and designing the system's components. The design phase ensures that the software is built with the right balance of functionality, performance, and maintainability. Throughout development, various methodologies such as agile, waterfall, and DevOps are employed to manage tasks, foster collaboration, and deliver high-quality results. Effective software development and design are crucial for meeting business goals and providing users with a seamless, robust experience. Develop and document procedures to control the product design and development process. These procedures must ensure that all requirements are being met.

Software development

Control your software development project and make sure that it is executed in a disciplined manner. Use one or more life cycle models to organize your software development project. Develop and document your software development procedures. These procedures should ensure that:

- Software products meet all requirements.
- Software development follows your:

- o Quality plan.
- o Development plan.

Software design

Control your software design process and make sure that it is performed in a systematic way. Use a suitable software design method. Study previous software design projects to avoid repeating old mistakes. Design software that is easy to test, install, use, and maintain. Develop and document rules to control the coding activities, naming conventions, commentary practices, and programming languages. Apply configuration management techniques to document, and control the use and review of all analysis tools, design techniques, compilers, and assemblers. Train personnel in the use of such tools and techniques.

Design and development planning

Create design and development planning procedures. The product planning procedures should ensure that plans are prepared for each design activity. Responsibility for implementing each plan, activity, or phase is properly defined. Qualified personnel are assigned to the product design and development process. Adequate resources are allocated to the product design and development process. Plans are updated, and circulated to the appropriate participants, as designs change.

Software design and development planning

Prepare a software development plan. Your plan should be documented and approved before it is implemented. Your plan should control:

- Technical activities like requirements analyses, design processes, coding activities, integration methods, testing techniques, installation work, and acceptance testing.
- Management activities like project supervision, progress reviews, and reporting requirements.

Your software development plan should define your project, identify related plans and projects, list your project objectives, and define project inputs and outputs.

Software design input

Design input requirements should be specified by the customer. However, sometimes the customer will expect you to develop the design input specification. In this case, you should:

- Prepare procedures that you can use to develop the design input specification. These procedures should be documented and explain how interviews, surveys, studies, prototypes, and demonstrations will be used to develop your design-input specification. How you and your customer will formally agree to accept the official specification, and to accept changes to the official specification. The method to change of specification, evaluation of product demonstration, and input requirements to be met through the use of hardware, software, and interface technologies are to be laid down. The procedures of review, evaluation, and discussions need to be recorded.

- Work closely with your customer in order to avoid misunderstandings and to ensure that the specification meets the customer's needs.
- Express your specifications by using terms that will make it easy to validate during product acceptance.
- Ask your customer to formally approve the resulting design input specification.

Your design input specification may address the following kinds of characteristics or requirements like functionality, reliability, usability, efficiency, maintainability, portability, and hardware or software interfaces.

Your design input specification may also need to address the following kinds of requirements:

- Operational requirements
- Safety requirements
- Security requirements
- Statutory requirements

Design output

Develop procedures to control design outputs.

- Design outputs are usually documents. It includes drawings, parts lists, process specifications, servicing procedures, and storage instructions. These types of documents are used for purchasing, production, installation, inspection, testing, and servicing.
- Design outputs must be expressed in terms that allow them to be compared with design input requirements.
- Design output documents must identify those aspects of the product that are crucial to its safe and effective operation. These aspects include operating, storage, handling, maintenance, and disposal requirements.
- Design output documents must be reviewed and approved before they are distributed.
- Design outputs must be accepted only if they meet official acceptance criteria.

Software design output

Following is the software design output:

- Prepare design output documents by using standardized methods and make sure that your documents are correct and complete.
- Software design outputs can include design specifications, source code, user guides, and so on.

Design review

Following are about the design review:

- Develop procedures that specify how design reviews should be planned and performed.
- Plan and perform design reviews for software development projects.
- Develop and document design review procedures.
- Define the methods that should be used to ensure that all rules and conventions are being followed.
- Define what needs to be done to prepare for a design review.
- Allow design activities to continue only if all deficiencies and nonconformities have been addressed and risks and consequences have been assessed.

Design verification

Develop procedures that specify how design outputs, at every stage of the product design, and development process, should be verified. Verify design outputs by performing design reviews, performing demonstrations, and performing tests.

Design validation

Develop procedures that validate the assumption that your newly designed products will meet customer needs. Develop design validation procedures to confirm that your new product performs properly under all real-world operating conditions. It should also confirm that your new product will meet every legitimate customer need and expectation. Ensure that validations are carried out early in the design process, whenever this will help to meet the customer's needs.

Document and data control

Develop procedures to control all the documents and data related to your quality system. These procedures should control internal and external documents with data, electronic, or hardcopy documents with data. Therefore, identify all internal and external documents and data that must be controlled. Develop procedures to control documents and data by using configuration management procedures.

Use the procedures to control the quality of documents and data by adopting proper communications, specifications, requirements, descriptions, instructions, procedures, contracts, standards, manuals, reports, and plans. The procedures should control documents and data connected with customer interactions, periodic evaluations, and progress reviews.

SEI CMM

Since 1984, the *Carnegie Mellon* **Software Engineering Institute (SEI)** has served as a federally funded research and development center. The SEI staff has advanced software engineering principles and practices and has served as a national resource in software engineering, computer security, and process improvement. As a part of *Carnegie Mellon University*, Pittsburgh, which is well known for its highly rated programs in computer science and engineering, the SEI operates at the leading edge of technical innovation.

The SEI works closely with defense and government organizations, industry, and academia to continually improve our software-intensive systems. To accomplish this, the SEI:

- Performs research to explore promising solutions to software engineering problems
- Identifies and codifies technological and methodological solutions
- Tests and refines the solutions through pilot programs that help industry and government solve their problems
- Widely disseminates proven solutions through training, licensing, and publication of best practices

The SEI's core purpose is to help an organization improve their software engineering capabilities and to develop or acquire the right software, defect free, within budget and on time, every time.

Capability maturity model

The CMM is a process CMM which aids in the definition and understanding of an organization's processes. The CMM was first described in a book *Managing the Software Process* by *Watts Humphrey* and hence was also known as **Humphrey's CMM**. Active development of this model by the SEI (US Dept. of Defense Software Engineering Institute) began in 1986.

The CMM was originally intended as a tool for objectively assessing the ability of government contractors' processes to perform a contracted software project. Though it comes from the area of software development, it can be applied as a generally applicable model to assist in understanding the process capability maturity of organizations in diverse areas. For example, software engineering, system engineering, project management, software maintenance, risk management, system acquisition, **information technology (IT)**, and personnel management. It has been used extensively for avionics software and government projects around the world.

The CMM has been superseded by a variant, the **capability maturity model integration (CMMI)**. The old CMM was renamed to **Software Engineering CMM (SE-CMM)**, and organizations' accreditations based on SE-CMM expired on 31 December 2007. Maturity models have been internationally standardized as part of ISO 15504.

Maturity model

A maturity model can be described as a **structured collection** of elements that describe certain aspects of maturity in an organization. A maturity model provides:

- A place to start
- The benefits of a community's prior experiences
- A common language and a shared vision
- A framework for prioritizing actions
- A way to define what improvement means for your organization

A maturity model can be used as a benchmark for comparison and as an aid to understanding, for example, a comparative assessment of different organizations where there is something in common that can be used as a basis for comparison. In the case of the CMM, for example, the basis for comparison would be the organization's software development processes.

Structure of capability maturity model

The CMM involves the following aspects:

- **Maturity levels**: A number of levels culminating in the discipline needed to engage in continuous process improvement and optimization.
- **Key process areas**: A **key process area (KPA)** identifies a cluster of related activities that, when performed collectively, achieve a set of goals considered important.
- **Goals**: The goals of a KPA summarize the states that must exist for that KPA to have been implemented in an effective and lasting way. The extent to which the goals have been accomplished is an indicator of how much capability the organization has established at that maturity level. The goals signify the scope, boundaries, and intent of each KPA.
- **Common features**: Common features include practices that implement and institutionalize a KPA. There are five types of common features: Commitment to perform, ability to perform, activities performed, measurement and analysis, and verifying implementation.

- **Key practices**: The key practices describe the elements of infrastructure and practice that contribute most effectively to the implementation and institutionalization of the KPAs.

Levels of the capability maturity model

There are five levels defined along the continuum of the CMM, and, according to the SEI, *Predictability, effectiveness, and control of an organization's software processes are believed to improve as the organization moves up these five levels. While not rigorous, the empirical evidence to date supports this belief.*

Following are the levels of the CMM:

- **Level 1, Ad hoc (Chaotic):** Level 1-Ad hoc (Chaotic) is characteristic of processes at this level that are (typically) undocumented and in a state of dynamic change, tending to be driven in an ad hoc, uncontrolled, and reactive manner by users or events. This provides a chaotic or unstable environment for the processes.

  Following are the organizational implications:

  - This is because institutional knowledge tends to be scattered (there being a limited structured approach to knowledge management) in such environments, not all of the stakeholders or participants in the processes may know or understand all of the components that make up the processes. Since the software production processes are not defined, different professionals follow their own processes and methods, and as a result, the development effort becomes chaotic. As a result, process performance in such organizations is likely to be variable (inconsistent) and depend heavily on the institutional knowledge, competence, or the heroic efforts of relatively few people or small groups.
  - Despite the chaos, such organizations manage to produce products and services. However, in doing so, there is a significant risk that will tend to exceed any estimated budgets or schedules for their projects. It is difficult to estimate what a process will do when you do not fully understand the process in the first place and cannot, therefore, control it or manage it effectively.
  - Due to the lack of structure and formality, organizations at this level, may over-commit, or abandon processes during a crisis, and be unable to repeat past successes. There tends to be limited planning, limited executive commitment, or buy-in to projects, and limited acceptance of processes.

- **Level 2, Repeatable:** It is characteristic of processes at this level that some processes are repeatable, possibly with consistent results. The processes may not repeat for all the projects in the organization. The organization may use some basic project management to track cost and schedule. Size and cost estimation techniques such as function point analysis, **Constructive Cost Estimation Model (COCOMO)**, and so on are used.

Process discipline is unlikely to be rigorous, but where it exists, it may help to ensure that existing practices are retained during times of stress. When these practices are in place, projects are performed and managed according to their documented plans.

Following are the organizational implications:

- Project status and the delivery of services are visible to management at defined points. For example, at major milestones and at the completion of major tasks and activities.
- Basic project management processes are established to track cost, schedule, and functionality. The minimum process discipline is in place to repeat earlier successes on projects with similar applications and scope. There is still a significant risk of exceeding cost and time estimates.

- **Level 3, Defined** is characteristic of processes at this level that there are sets of defined and documented standard processes established and subject to some degree of improvement over time. The processes for both management and development activities are defined and documented. These standard processes are in place (like, they are the AS-IS processes) and used to establish consistency of process performance across the organization. Projects establish their defined processes by applying the organization's set of standard processes, tailored, if necessary, within similarly standardized guidelines.

  Following is the organizational implications:

  - The organization's management establishes and mandates process objectives for the organization, has a set of standard processes, and ensures that these objectives are appropriately addressed.

- **Level 4, Managed**: It is characteristic of processes at this level that, using process metrics, management can effectively control the AS-IS process (e.g., for software development). In particular, management can identify ways to adjust and adapt the process to particular projects without measurable losses of quality or deviations from specifications. Process capability is established from this level. The process metrics reflect the effectiveness of the process being used, like average defect correction time, productivity, the average number of defects found per hour of inspection, and the average number of failures detected during testing per **line of code (LOC)**.

  Following are the organizational implications:

  - Quantitative quality goals tend to set for process output. For example, software or software maintenance. The quantitative quality goals are set for products.
  - Using quantitative or statistical techniques, process performance is measured and monitored, and process performance is thus generally predictable and

controllable. Tools like Pareto charts, fishbone diagrams are used to measure the product and process quality.

- **Level 5, Optimized:** It is characteristic of processes at this level that the focus is on continually improving process performance through both incremental and innovative technological changes or improvements. The process and product measurement data are analyzed for continuous process improvement. The lessons learned from specific projects are incorporated into the process. Continuous process improvement is achieved both by carefully analyzing the quantitative feedback from the process measurements and by the application of innovative ideas and technologies.

  Each maturity level is characterized by several KPAs that indicate what the organization should focus on to improve its software process to the next level. The focus and KPAs of each level is indicated in the *Table 14.1*.

  SEI CMM provides a list of key areas on which to focus to take an organization from one level of maturity to the next. It provides a way for gradual quality improvement over several stages. Each stage is carefully designed such that one stage enhances the capability already built up. The major problem faced by an organization adopting CMM based process improvement initiative that they understand what is needed to be improved, but they need more guidance about how to improve it.

CMM level	Focus	Key process area
Ad-hoc	Competent people	Nil
Repeatable	Project management	Software project planning Software configuration management
Defined	Definition of process	Process definition, Training program, Peer reviews
Managed	Product and process quality	Quantitative process metrics Software quality management
Optimizing	Continuous process improvement	Defect prevention Process change management Technology change management

Table14.1: *Level wise focus and KPA*

Six Sigmas in software engineering

It is concerned with reducing the defects in the process of production or engineering. It cannot be applied to engineering activities. Six Sigmas originated in Motorola in the early 1980s in response to achieving a 10X reduction in product failure levels in 5 years. Engineer *Bill Smith* invented Six Sigma, but died of a heart attack in the Motorola cafeteria in 1993, never knowing the scope of the craze and controversy he had touched off. Six Sigma is based on various quality management theories (for example, Deming, Juran). (*Table 14.3*)

Six Sigma is a business-driven, multi-dimensional structured approach to improving processes, lowering defects, reducing process variability, reducing costs, and increasing customer satisfaction, and profits. (*Figure 14.3*)

Six Sigma dimensions

Six Sigma dimensions in software engineering refer to the set of key characteristics that define the quality and performance of a software system. Six Sigma, a methodology focused on process improvement and defect reduction, emphasizes measuring and enhancing software quality across various dimensions, such as reliability, efficiency, and maintainability. These dimensions are critical in ensuring that software development processes meet high standards and deliver products that are free from defects and aligned with user expectations. By applying Six Sigma principles, software engineers can systematically identify areas of improvement, reduce variation, and optimize processes to achieve near-perfect performance and quality in their software systems. *Figure 14.3* shows the Six Sigma dimension:

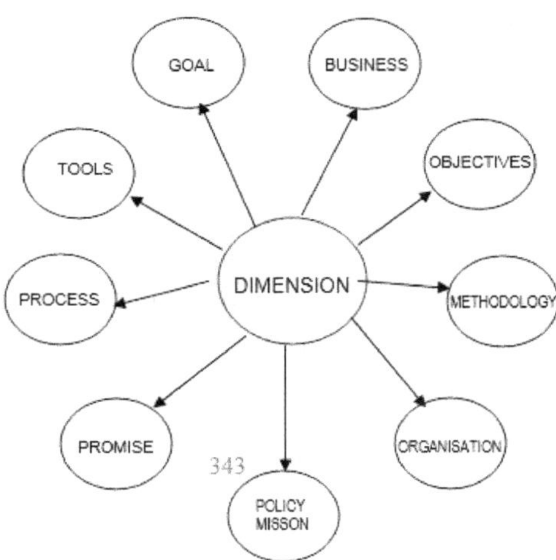

Figure 14.3: *Six Sigma dimension*

Mission or policy

The mission or policy of the organization is to do business smarter and increase profitability. Six Sigma shall be instituted throughout the organization. All employees shall be Six Sigma trained. Provide innovative solutions for the attainment of business goals and objectives. Processes shall be at their highest Sigma level. (*Figure 14.4, 14.5*):

Specification Limit	Percentage
+ 1σ	30.23%
+ 2σ	69.13%
+ 3σ	93.32%
+ 4σ	99.3790%
+ 5σ	99.97670%
+ 3σ	99.999660%

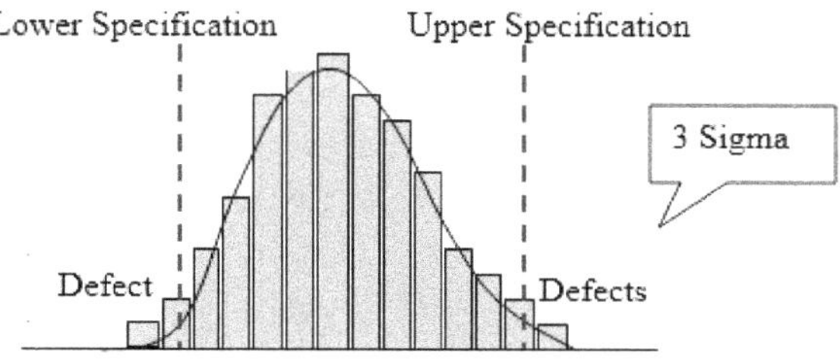

Figure 14.4: Distribution of 3 Sigma

In software engineering, **Distribution in Six Sigma** refers to the statistical analysis of data to identify variations in a software process and its outcomes. By understanding the distribution of data, Six Sigma aims to reduce defects and improve the quality of software products, ensuring they meet user expectations and business requirements. This approach helps in identifying areas of improvement and optimizing processes for greater efficiency and consistency.

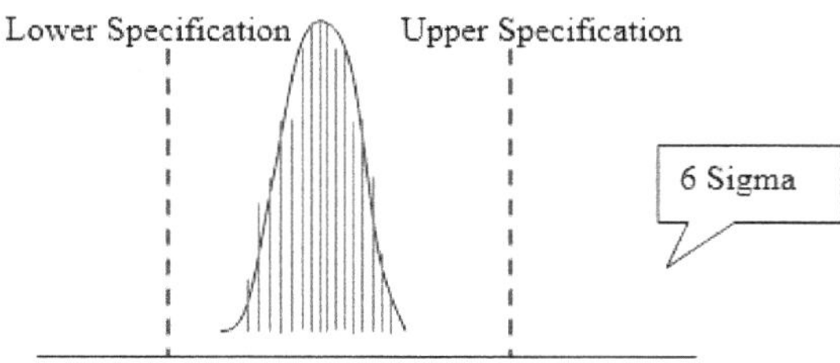

Figure 14.5: Distribution in 6 Sigma

Table 14.3 shows the nature of Six Sigma quality:

3σ (93.32%)	6σ (99.9997%)
20,000 lost articles of mail per hour	1 per hour
Unsafe drinking water for 15 minutes per day	1 minute every 4 years
5,000 incorrect surgical operations per week	1 per month
2 long/short landings at most major airports each day	1 in 28 years
200,000 wrong drug prescriptions each year	10 each year
No electricity for 7 hours each month	1 minute every 4 years

Table 14.3: The Nature of Six Sigma Quality

Goal

The goal of Six Sigma is to realize the organization's financial objectives of increasing profits. The initial fundamental goal is to reduce the process output variation to ±6 Sigma and attain three to four defects per million opportunities (DPMO). A Six Sigma defect is defined as anything outside of customer specifications. A Six Sigma opportunity is the total quantity of chances for a defect.

Objectives of Six Sigma

The objectives of Six Sigma, are the implementation of a measurement-based data or fact-driven approach that focuses on continuous process improvement with defect & variation reduction. As the process sigma value increases from zero to six, the variation also decreases to zero. It generates customer satisfaction and increases savings or profitability.

Organization

Following are the organizations:

- **Green belt**: As the Six Sigma quality program evolves, employees include Six Sigma methodology in their daily activities. Employees who are trained in Six Sigma and spend 10% to 50% portion of their time completing projects, but maintain their regular work roles and responsibilities.
- **Black belt**: The black belts coach green belts on their projects, lead quality projects, and work full-time until they are complete. They are the heart and soul of the Six Sigma quality initiative and are referred to as *change agents*.
- **Master black belt**: Master black belt works with process owners and ensures that objectives and targets are set, plans are determined, progress is tracked, and education is provided. He is assigned to a specific area or function of a business or organization.
- **Process owner**: Process owners are responsible individuals for a specific process. The process owners are found at all levels of the organization.
- **Champions**: Champions are integrated into the business and help to deploy Six Sigma, remove roadblocks, select projects, adjust, and take responsibility for implementation. Champions diminish deployment risks.
- **Quality leader or manager**: Quality leader or manager represent the needs of the customer and improve the operational effectiveness of the organization. The quality manager sits on the CEO or President's staff, and has equal authority to all other direct reports.

Methodology

Objectives are accomplished through 6σ projects by following one of three defined processes:

- **DMAIC**: Define–Measure–Analyze–Improve–Control
- **DMADV**: Define–Measure–Analyze–Design–Verify
- **DFSS**: Define–Identify–Design–Optimize–Verify

DMAIC versus DMADV

The main differences between DMAIC and DMADV are:

- DMAIC looks at improving existing processes. DMADV looks at designing new or existing processes.
- DMADV is used when there is no defined process. Incremental changes are not sufficient and the entire process needs to be changed.

DMAIC versus DMADV versus DFSS

DMAIC and DMADV are used in improving process capability, DFSS primarily focused on the design of the product whose purposes is to increase the product quality by increasing reliability, responding to customer's needs. This increases the profit margin.

Promises

Six Sigma technique can reduce costs by 50% or more. It can reduce defects to six Sigma, increases profitability, increase understanding of customer requirements, and improve delivery and quality performance. According to Six Sigma Academy, Black Belts save @$230,000/project and can complete four to six projects per year. *General Electric*, has estimated benefits on the order of $10 billion during the first five years of implementation.

Conclusion

Software QC is better than software coding inspection. SQA is a better approach than software QC. The QA is applied to each step-in software process. It enforces the procedure for the effective applications of methods and tools, formal technical reviews, testing strategies and techniques, procedures for change control, procedures for assuring compliance to standards, and measurement and reporting mechanism. Software review is one of the most important QA activities. It streamlines the software process and removes error. The ability to ensure quality is a measure of mature engineering discipline.

In the next chapter, readers will explore Case Studies and Reusability, focusing on how real-world software engineering projects demonstrate best practices, challenges, and solutions. Case studies provide valuable insights into design decisions, development methodologies, and problem-solving approaches used in successful software systems. Additionally, the concept of reusability—a fundamental principle in software engineering—will be examined in detail. This includes understanding how modular design, code reuse, software libraries, and design patterns contribute to efficiency, maintainability, and scalability. By studying practical examples, readers will gain a deeper understanding of how to build robust, adaptable, and cost-effective software solutions.

Exercises

To solidify your understanding of the concepts covered in this chapter, try the following exercises.

Multiple choice questions

1. **Which of the following is NOT a characteristic of software quality?**
   a. Functionality
   b. Efficiency
   c. Color scheme
   d. Usability
2. **What is the main objective of SQA?**
   a. To reduce the cost of software development
   b. To ensure software meets the required standards
   c. To speed up software development
   d. To introduce new features in software
3. **Which of the following tools is commonly used in SQA?**
   a. Version control systems
   b. Debuggers
   c. Test automation tools
   d. Code editors
4. **What does ISO-9001 certification ensure in software development?**
   a. The software meets security standards
   b. The development process follows quality management principles
   c. The software is user-friendly
   d. The software is optimized for performance
5. **Which technique focuses on eliminating defects in software processes to achieve near-perfect quality?**
   a. CMM
   b. Six Sigma
   c. Agile development
   d. Waterfall model
6. **What is the purpose of quality metrics in software engineering?**
   a. To measure the performance of hardware
   b. To track the number of users
   c. To assess and quantify software quality attributes
   d. To calculate the cost of development

7. **Which model focuses on improving processes in software development?**
   a. ISO-9001
   b. CMM
   c. Agile
   d. Six Sigma
8. **What is the primary advantage of software auditing?**
   a. It increases software development speed
   b. It ensures compliance with quality standards
   c. It reduces the software's functionality
   d. It improves user interface design
9. **Which of the following is a common problem in ensuring software quality?**
   a. Clear documentation
   b. Limited testing
   c. Effective collaboration
   d. Automated tools
10. **What is the role of SEI CMM in software quality?**
   a. To improve communication between developers
   b. To guide the improvement of software development processes
   c. To design user interfaces
   d. To focus on hardware integration

Short answer questions

1. What is software quality management?
2. What is defect prevention?
3. What is quality of conformance?
4. Define quality control.
5. What is quality cost?
6. Define software quality.
7. Name some characteristics of software product quality.
8. What do you mean by formal technical reviews (FTR) and what are the objectives of FTR?
9. What are the different forms of FTR?
10. What are the guidelines for conducting FTR?
11. What are the factors involved in prevention cost?
12. Define clean room engineering.
13. What processes are involved in clean room technology?
14. What is software quality assurance (QA)?

15. Define a quality assurance system.
16. What are the requirements of a quality assurance system?
17. Mention McCall's quality factors.
18. Define correctness.
19. Define accuracy.
20. Define maintainability.
21. How do you assess quality factors?
22. Define integrity
23. Define the term maturity.
24. What is CMM?
25. Name the different categories of CMM.

Essay questions

1. Quality and reliability are related concepts but are fundamentally different in many ways. Discuss them.
2. Can a program be correct and still not reliable? Explain.
3. Can a program be correct and still not exhibit quality? Explain.
4. Given the responsibility to improve the quality of the software in your organization, what are the steps you will follow?
5. What do you understand by repeatable software development? At which level does SEI CMM achieve repeatable software development?
6. What are the factors considered for a quality software product?
7. What are the merits of ISO 9001 and SEI CMM certification?
8. What is Six Sigma quality? What are its organizational structures?

Multiple choice answers

1. c
2. b
3. c
4. b
5. b
6. c
7. b
8. b
9. b
10. b

CHAPTER 15

CASE Studies and Reusability

Introduction

A good workshop for any craftsperson, whether a mechanic, carpenter, or software engineer, has three primary characteristics: a collection of useful tools that assist in every step of building a product, an organized layout that allows tools to be easily found and used efficiently, and a skilled artisan who knows how to effectively utilize those tools. Software engineers now recognize that they need more and varied tools along with an organized and efficient workshop to place the tools. The software development needs an engineering type discipline. The goal is to concentrate on developing a common technique, standard methodologies, and automated tools in a manner similar to the traditional engineering field. The evolution of using automated tools to support the information system development process became **computer aided software engineering (CASE)**.

Structure

In this chapter, the following topics will be discussed:

- Taxonomy of CASE tools
- Components of CASE tool
- Integrated CASE environment
- CASE repository

- Component model of software development
- Software reuse
- Types of reuse

Objectives

CASE tools are utilized to automate and support the system development process, with the primary objective of enhancing productivity and improving the overall quality of the system. These tools offer software engineers the capability to automate manual tasks while improving engineering insight. Many organizations implement CASE tools with specific goals in mind, such as improving the quality of developed systems, speeding up system design and development, easing and improving the testing process through automated checks, and enhancing the integration of development activities by employing common methodologies. Additionally, CASE tools contribute to better documentation quality and completeness, help standardize the development process, improve project management, simplify program maintenance, and promote the reusability of both modules and documentation.

Taxonomy of CASE tools

A number of risks are inherent whenever we attempt to categorize CASE tools. There is a subtle implication that to create an effective CASE environment, one must implement all the categories of tools, is simply not true. Confusion (or antagonism) can be created by placing a specific tool within one category when others might believe that it belongs to another category. It is necessary to create a taxonomy of CASE tools, to better understand the breadth of CASE and to better appreciate where such tools can be applied in the software engineering process.

CASE tools can be classified as:

- By function
- By their role as instruments for managers or technical people
- By their use in the various steps of the software engineering process
- By the environment architecture (hardware and software) that supports them
- By their origin or cost

The taxonomy presented here uses function as a primary criterion.

In the taxonomy of CASE tools, categorizing tools based on their functionality provides a clear and structured approach to understanding their roles in the software development process. The taxonomy presented here uses function as the primary criterion, allowing for efficient classification of tools according to the specific tasks they perform, from design and coding to testing and maintenance. This functional perspective helps in identifying and selecting the right tools to enhance productivity and streamline software engineering workflows:

- **Business process engineering tools:** By modeling the strategic information requirements of an organization, business process engineering tools provide a **meta-model** from which specific information systems are derived. Rather than focusing on the requirements of a specific application, business information is modeled as it moves between various organizational entities within a company. The primary objective for tools in this category is to represent the business data objects, their relationships, and how these data objects flow between different business areas within a company.
- **Process modeling and management tools:** If an organization works to improve a business (software) process, it must first understand it. Process modeling tools (process technology tools) are used to represent the key elements of a process so that it can be better understood. Such tools can also provide links to process descriptions that help those involved in the process to understand the work tasks that are required to perform it. Process management tools provide links to other tools that support defined process activities.
- **Project planning tools:** Tools in this category focus on two primary areas:
    - software project effort
    - cost estimation and project scheduling

  Estimation tools compute estimated effort, project duration, and recommended number of people for a project. Project scheduling tools enable the manager to define all project tasks (the work breakdown structure), create a task network (usually using graphical input to represent task interdependencies, and model the amount of parallelism possible for the project.
- **Risk analysis tools**: Identifying potential risks and developing a plan to mitigate, monitor, and manage them is of paramount importance in large projects. Risk analysis tools enable a project manager to build a risk table by providing detailed guidance in the identification and analysis of risks.
- **Project management tools**: The project schedule and project plan must be tracked and monitored on a continuing basis. In addition, a manager should use tools to collect the metrics that will ultimately provide an indication of software product quality. Tools in the category are often extensions to project planning tools.
- **Requirements tracing tools**: When large systems are developed, things *fall into the cracks*. That is, the delivered system does not fully meet customer specified requirements. The objective of requirements tracing tools is to provide a systematic approach to the isolation of requirements, beginning with the customer's request for a proposal or specification. The typical requirements tracing tool combines human interactive text evaluation with a database management system that stores and categorizes each system requirement.

- **Metrics and management tools**: Software metrics improve a manager's ability to control and coordinate the software engineering process and a practitioner's ability to improve the quality of the software that is produced. Today's metrics or measurement tools focus on the process and product characteristics. Management-oriented tools capture project specific metrics, such as example: **line of code (LOC)/ person-month (pm)**, defects per function point that provide an overall indication of productivity or quality. Technically oriented tools determine the technical metrics that provide greater insight into the quality of design or code.
- **Documentation tools**: This is also called a document generator. Document production and desktop publishing tools support nearly every aspect of software engineering and represent a substantial **leverage** opportunity for all software developers. Most software development organizations spend a substantial amount of time developing documents, and in many cases, the documentation process itself is quite inefficient. It is not unusual for a software development organization to spend as much as 20 or 30 percent of all software development effort on documentation. For this reason, documentation tools provide an important opportunity to improve productivity. This helps to produce both technical and user documentation in standard formats.
- **System software tools**: CASE is a workstation technology. Therefore, the CASE environment must accommodate high-quality network system software, object management services, distributed component support, electronic mail, bulletin boards, and quality assurance tools. The majority of CASE tools that claim to focus on quality assurance are actually metrics tools that audit source code to determine compliance with language standards.
- **Database management tools**: Database management software serves as a foundation for the establishment of a CASE database (repository) that we have called the project database. Given the emphasis on configuration objects, database management tools for CASE are evolving from relational database management systems to **object oriented** (**OO**) database management systems. It enables the integrated storage of specification, diagrams, reports, and project management information.
- **Software configuration management tools**: Software configuration management lies at the kernel of every CASE environment. Tools can assist in all five major SCM tasks, which are:
    - Identification
    - Version control
    - Change control
    - Auditing
    - Status accounting

The CASE database provides a mechanism for identifying each configuration item and relating it to other items; the change control process can be implemented with the aid of specialized tools; easy access to individual configuration items facilitates the auditing process; and CASE communication tools can greatly improve status accounting.

- **Analysis and design tools**: Analysis and design tools enable a software engineer to create models of the system to be built. The models contain a representation of data, function, and behavior (at the analysis level) and characterizations of data, architectural, component-level, and interface design. By performing consistency and validity checking on the models, analysis, and design tools provides a software engineer with some degree of insight into the analysis representation and helps to eliminate the errors before they propagate into the design or, worse, into the implementation itself. It automatically checks for incomplete, inconsistent, or incorrect specifications in diagrams, forms, and reports.
- **Diagramming tools**: This enables the system process, data, and control structures to be represented graphically.
- **PRO and SIM tools**: **Prototyping and simulation (PRO and SIM)** tools provide the software engineer with the ability to predict the behavior of a real-time system prior to the time that it is built. In addition, these tools enable the software engineer to develop mock-ups of the real-time system, allowing the customer to gain insight into the function, operation, and response prior to actual implementation.
- **Interface design and development tools**: Interface design and development tools are actually a tool kit of software components (classes) such as menus, buttons, window structures, icons, scrolling mechanisms, device drivers, and so forth. However, these tool kits are being replaced by interface prototyping tools that enable rapid onscreen creation of sophisticated user interfaces that conform to the interfacing standard that has been adopted for the software.
- **Prototyping tools**: A variety of different prototyping tools can be used. Screen painters enable software engineers to define screen layouts rapidly for interactive applications. More sophisticated CASE prototyping tools enable the creation of a data design, coupled with both screen and report layouts. Many analysis and design tool have extensions that provide a prototyping option. PRO and SIM tools generate skeleton Ada and C source code for engineering (real-time) applications. Finally, a variety of fourth generation tools have prototyping features.
- **Programming tools**: The programming tools category encompasses the compilers, editors, and debuggers that are available to support most conventional programming languages. In addition, object-oriented programming environments, fourth-generation languages, graphical programming environments, application generators, and database query languages also reside within this category. The code generators enable the automatic generation of program and database definition code directly from the design document, diagrams, forms, and reports.

- **Computer display and report generator**: The tool helps prototype how systems look and feel to users. Display (or form) and report generators also make it easier for the system analyst to identify data requirements and relationships.
- **Web development tools**: The activities associated with Web engineering are supported by a variety of tools for web application development. These include tools that assist in the generation of text, graphics, forms, scripts, applets, and other elements of a web page.
- **Integration and testing tools**: In their directory of software testing tools, software quality engineering defines the following testing tools categories:
    - **Data acquisition:** Tools that acquire data to be used during testing.
    - **Static measurement:** Tools that analyze source code without executing test cases.
    - **Dynamic measurement:** Tools that analyze source code during execution.
    - **Simulation:** Tools that simulate the function of hardware or other externals.
    - **Test management:** Tools that assist in the planning, development, and control of testing.
    - **Cross-functional tools:** Tools that cross the bounds of the preceding categories.

Note: Many testing tools have features that span two or more of the categories.

- **Static analysis tools**: Static testing tools assist the software engineer in deriving test cases. Three different types of static testing tools are used in the industry:
    - Code-based testing tools accept source code or **program design language (PDL)** as input and perform a number of analyses that result in the generation of test cases.
    - Specialized testing languages (**Abbreviated Test Language for All Systems (ATLAS)**) enable a software engineer to write detailed test specifications that describe each test case and the logistics for its execution.
    - Requirements-based testing tools isolate specific user requirements and suggest test cases (or classes of tests) that will exercise the requirements.
- **Dynamic analysis tools:** Dynamic testing tools interact with an executing program, checking path coverage, testing assertions about the value of specific variables, and otherwise initiating the execution flow of the program. Dynamic tools can be either intrusive or non-intrusive. An intrusive tool changes the software to be tested by inserting probes (extra instructions) that perform the activities just mentioned. Non-intrusive testing tools use a separate hardware processor that runs in parallel with the processor containing the program that is being tested.
- **Test management tools:** Test management tools are used to control and coordinate software testing for each of the major testing steps. Tools in this category manage

and coordinate regression testing, perform comparisons that ascertain differences between actual and expected output, and conduct batch testing of programs with an interactive human or computer interface. In addition to the functions noted, many test management tools also serve as generic test drivers. A test driver reads one or more test cases from a testing file, formats the test data to conform to the needs of the software under test, and then invokes the software to be tested.

- **Client or server testing tools:** The client or server environment demands specialized testing tools that exercise the graphical user interface and the network communications requirements for the client and server.
- **Reengineering tools:** Tools for legacy software address a set of maintenance activities that currently absorb a significant percentage of all software-related effort. The reengineering tools category can be subdivided into the following functions:
  - **Reverse engineering** to specification tools take source code as input and generate graphical structured analysis and design models, where-used lists, and other design information.
  - **Code restructuring and analysis tools** analyze program syntax, generate a control flow graph, and automatically generate a structured program.
  - **On-line system reengineering tools** are used to modify on-line database systems (for example, convert DB2 files into entity-relationship format).

These tools are limited to a specific programming language (although most major languages are addressed) and require some degree of interaction with the software engineer. Many organizations do not use CASE tools to support all phases of SDLC. Some organizations may extensively use the diagramming features but not use code generators. *Table 15.1* summarizes how CASE is commonly used within the SDLC phase:

SDLC phase	Key activities	CASE tool usage
Project identification and selection	Display and structure high-level organizational information	Diagramming and matrix tools to create and structure information
Project initiation and planning	Develop project scope and feasibility	Repository and documentation generators to develop project plans
Analysis	Determine structure system requirements	Diagramming to create process, logic, and data models
Logical and physical designs	Create new system designs	Form and report generators to prototype designs, analysis, and documentation generators to define specifications

SDLC phase	Key activities	CASE tool usage
Implementation	Translate designs into an information system	Code generators and analysis, form, and report generators to develop system; document generators to develop system and user documentation
Maintenance	Evolve information system	All tools are used (repeat life cycle)

Table 15.1: *Examples of CASE usage within the SDLC*

In traditional system development, much of the time is spent on coding and testing. When software changes are approved, the code is first changed and then tested. Once the functionality of the code is assured, the documentation, and the specification documents are updated to reflect the system changes.

Components of CASE tools

Case tools are used to support a wide variety of SDLC activities. CASE tools can be used to help in the project identification and selection, project initiation, and planning, analysis, and design phases (upper CASE) and/or in the implementation and maintenance phases (lower CASE) of the SDLC (*Figure 15.1*). A third category of CASE, cross life cycle CASE, is tools used to support activities that occur across multiple phases of SDLC.

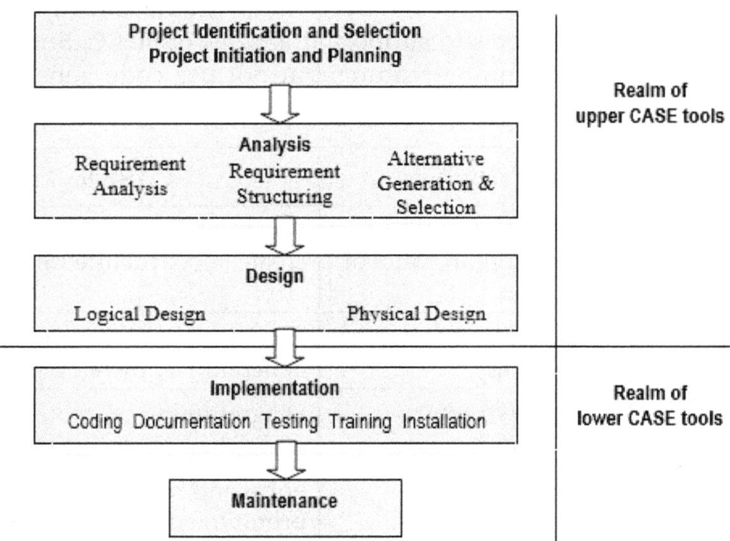

Figure 15.1: *Relationship between CASE tools and SDLC*

CASE documentation generator tools

Each phase of the SDLC produces documentation. The types of documentation that flow from one phase to the next vary depending upon the organization, methodologies employed, and type of system being built. Documentation generator modules can create standard reports based on the contents of the repository. Typically, SDLC documentation includes textual description needs, solution trade-offs, diagrams of data and processes, prototype forms and reports, program specifications, and user documentation, including application, and reference materials. A system that does not have adequate documentation is virtually impossible to use and maintain.

Documentation generators within a CASE environment provide a method for managing the vast amounts of documentation created during the SDLC. Documentation generators allow the creation of master templates that can be used to verify the documentation created for each SDLC phase conforms to a standard and that all required documents have been produced.

CASE code generator tools

Code generators are automated systems that produce high-level source code from diagrams and forms that are used to represent the system. As target environments vary on several dimensions, such as hardware and operating system platforms, many code generators are designed to be the special-purpose system that produces source code for a particular environment in a particular programming language. Most CASE tools that generate source code take a more flexible approach by producing standard source code and database definitions. Using standard language conventions, CASE-generated code can typically be compiled and executed on numerous hardware and operating system platforms with no, or very minor changes.

Integrated CASE environment

Although benefits can be derived from individual CASE tools that address separate software engineering activities, the real power of CASE can be achieved only through integration. The benefits of **Integrated CASE (I-CASE)** are:

- Smooth transfer of information (models, programs, documents, data) from one tool to another and one software engineering step to the next
- A reduction in the effort required to perform umbrella activities such as software configuration management, quality assurance, and document production
- An increase in project control that is achieved through better planning, monitoring, and communication
- Improved coordination among staff members who are working on a large software project

I-CASE also poses significant challenges. Integration demands consistent representations of software engineering information, standardized interfaces between tools, a homogeneous mechanism for communication between the software engineer and each tool, and an effective approach that will enable I-CASE to move among various hardware platforms and operating systems. Comprehensive I-CASE environments have emerged more slowly than originally expected. However, integrated environments do exist and are becoming more powerful as the years pass.

The term integration implies both combination and closure. I-CASE combines a variety of different tools and a spectrum of information in a way that enables closure of communication among tools, between people, and across the software process. Tools are integrated so that software engineering information is available to each tool that needs it, usage is integrated so that a common look and feel is provided for all tools, a development philosophy is integrated, implying a standardized software engineering approach that applies modern practice and proven methods. To define integration in the context of the software engineering process, it is necessary to establish a set of requirements for I-CASE. An I-CASE environment should:

- Provide a mechanism for sharing software engineering information among all tools contained in the environment.
- Enable a change to one item of information to be tracked to other related information items.
- Provide version control and overall configuration management for all software engineering information.
- Allow direct, non-sequential access to any tool contained in the environment.
- Establish automated support for the software process model that has been chosen, integrating CASE tools and **software configuration items (SCIs)** into a standard work breakdown structure.
- Enable the users of each tool to experience a consistent look and feel at the human or computer interface.
- Support communication among software engineers.
- Collect both management and technical metrics that can be used to improve the process and the product.

To achieve these requirements, each of the building blocks of a CASE architecture (*Figure 15.2*) must fit together in a seamless fashion. The foundation building blocks, including environment architecture, hardware platform, and operating system, must be **joined** through a set of portability services to an integration framework that achieves these requirements.

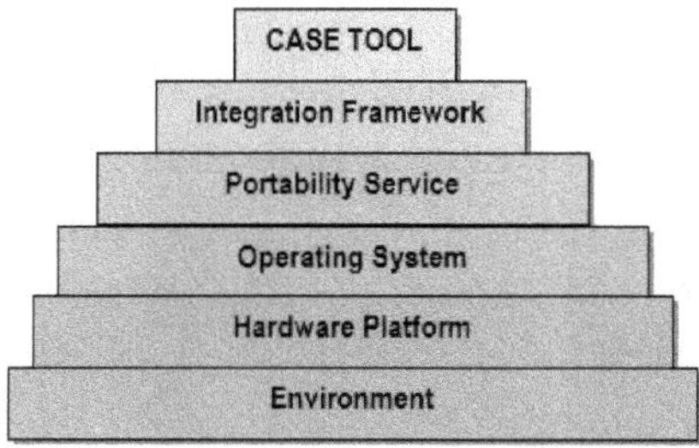

Figure 15.2: *CASE building blocks*

Integration architecture

A software engineering team uses CASE tools, corresponding methods, and a process framework to create a pool of software engineering information. The integration framework facilitates the transfer of information into and out of the pool. To accomplish this, the following architectural components must exist. A database must be created to store the information; an object management system must be built to manage changes to the information; a tools control mechanism must be constructed to coordinate the use of CASE tools; a user interface must provide a consistent pathway between actions made by the user and the tools contained in the environment. The user interface layer (*Figure 15.3*) incorporates a standardized interface tool kit with a common presentation protocol:

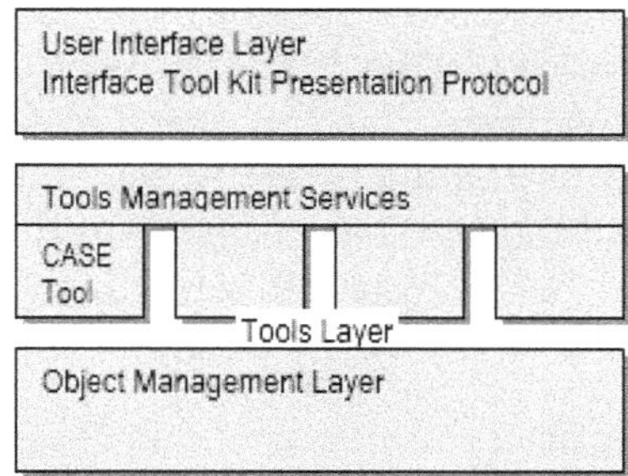

Figure 15.3: *User interface layer*

The interface tool kit contains software for human or computer interface management and a library of display objects. Both provide a consistent mechanism for communication between the interface and individual CASE tools. The presentation protocol is the set of guidelines that gives all CASE tools the same look and feel. Screen layout conventions, menu names and organization, icons, object names, the use of the keyboard and mouse, and the mechanism for tool access are all defined as part of the presentation protocol. The tools layer incorporates a set of **tools management services** (**TMS**) with the CASE tools themselves. TMS control the behavior of tools within the environment. If multitasking is used during the execution of one or more tools, TMS performs multitask synchronization and communication, coordinates the flow of information from the repository and object management system into the tools, accomplishes security and auditing functions, and collects metrics on tool usage. The **object management layer (OML)** performs the configuration management functions. In essence, software in this layer of the framework architecture provides the mechanism for tool integration. Every CASE tool is **plugged into** the OML. Working in conjunction with the CASE repository, the OML provides integration services, a set of standard modules that couple tools with the repository. In addition, the OML provides configuration management services by enabling the identification of all configuration objects, performing version control, and providing support for change control, audits, and status accounting. The shared repository layer is the CASE database and the access control functions that enable the OML to interact with the database. Data integration is achieved by the object management and shared repository layers.

CASE repository

The word repository is *anything or a person thought of as a center of accumulation or storage.* During the early history of software development, the repository was indeed a person, the programmer who had to remember the location of all information relevant to the software project, who had to recall information that was never written down and reconstruct information that had been lost. Sadly, using a person as *the center for accumulation and storage,* does not work very well. Today, the repository is a database that acts as the center for both the accumulation and storage of software engineering information. The role of the person (the software engineer) is to interact with the repository by using CASE tools that are integrated with it. The repository holds the complete information needed to create, modify, and evolve a software system from project initiation and planning to code generation and maintenance (*Figure 15.4*) In this book, a number of different terms have been used to refer to the storage place for software engineering information: CASE database, project database, **Integrated Project Support Environment (IPSE)** database, requirements dictionary (a limited database), and repository. Although there are subtle differences between some of these terms, all refer to the center for accumulation and storage. (*Figure 15.4*):

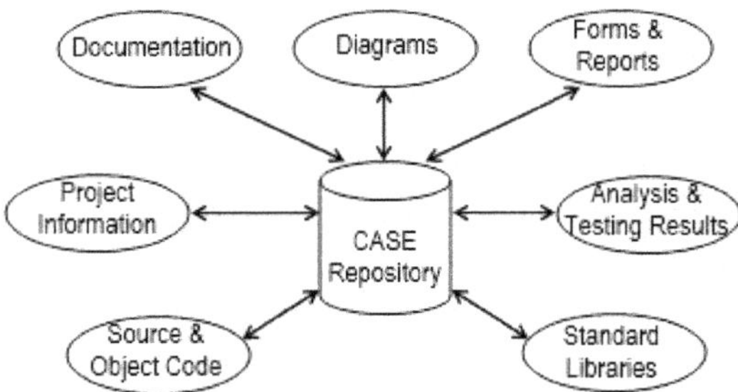

Figure 15.4: *System development items stored in the CASE repository*

For years, common development repositories have been used to create information systems independent of CASE. *Figure 15.5* reflects the common components of a comprehensive CASE repository. The application development environment is one in which either information specialists or end users use CASE tools, high-level languages, and other tools to develop new applications. The production environment is one in which these same people use applications to build databases, keep the data current, and extract data from databases.

The **data dictionary** is a computer software tool used to manage and control access to the information repository. It provides facilities for recording, storing, and processing descriptions of an organization's significant data and data processing resources. Data dictionary features within a CASE repository are especially valuable for the system analyst when cross-referencing data items. Cross-referencing enables one description of a data item to be stored and accessed by all individuals (system analysts and end users) so that a single definition for a data item is established and used. Such a description helps to avoid data duplication and makes systems development and maintenance more efficient.

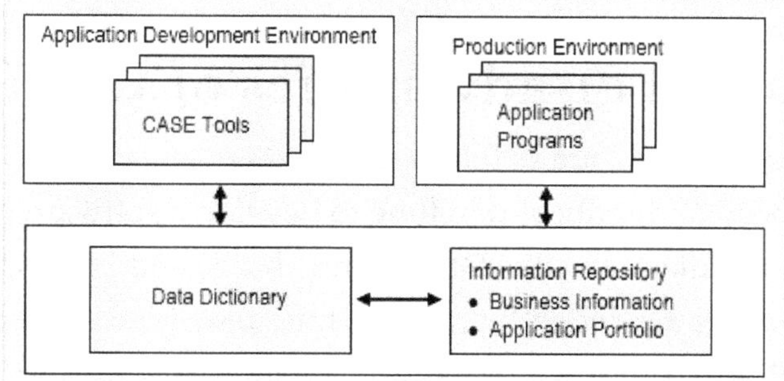

Figure 15.5: *Common components of a comprehensive CASE repository*

Role of the repository in integrated CASE

The repository for an I-CASE environment is the set of mechanisms and data structures that achieve data or tool and data or data integration. It provides the obvious functions of a database management system, but in addition, the repository performs or precipitates the following functions:

- Data integrity includes functions to validate entries to the repository, ensure consistency among the related objects, and automatically perform **cascading** modifications when a change to one object demands some change to objects.
- Information sharing provides a mechanism for sharing information among multiple developers and between the multiple tools, manages and controls multi user access to data and locks or unlocks objects so that changes are not inadvertently overlaid on one another.
- Data or tool integration establishes a data model that can be accessed by all tools in the I-CASE environment, controls access to the data, and performs appropriate configuration management functions.
- Data or data integration is the database management system that relates data objects so that other functions can be achieved.
- Methodology enforcement defines an entity-relationship model stored in the repository that implies a specific paradigm for software engineering; at a minimum, the relationships and objects define a set of steps that must be conducted to build the contents of the repository.
- Document standardization is the definition of objects in the database that leads directly to a standard approach for the creation of software engineering documents.

To achieve these functions, the repository is defined in terms of a meta-model. The meta-model determines how the information is stored in the repository, how data can be accessed by tools and viewed by software engineers, how well data security and integrity can be maintained, and how easily the existing model can be extended to accommodate new needs.

Advantages and disadvantages of CASE tools

The advantages of a CASE tool are as follows:

- Improved speed and reduction in time to develop a software product.
- Development of diagrams like DFD, Gantt charts, and PERT charts.
- When procedures are coded by a CASE tool, they give a consistent look. It helps in creating a uniform user interface, messaging schemes, standard layouts, and documentation plans.
- In addition to enforcement of consistency, the CASE tool ensures completeness.
- Generation of code out of specifications and standardization of program structure to help in maintaining and reducing errors.
- It facilitates prototyping as it makes it easy to change and adjust specifications in handling screen and report layout with the least effort and less time.
- Use of CASE tools increases the user requirements since CASE tools reduce development time by eliminating users long waiting time. More powerful systems can be developed in much shorter time.

The limitations of CASE tools are as follows:

- Most CASE tools support structured methods for software development. Many software organizations use a mixture of structured approach, modular approach, and object-oriented approach in developing systems.
- There is no standardization between available CASE tools in the market.
- The CASE tools do not generate narrative kind of documentation.
- Different CASE tools have their individual strengths in the area of design, analysis, code generation, documentation, security, and maintenance. No CASE tool is strong in all the areas.
- CASE tools have limited scope since none of the CASE tools support requirement analysis, feasibility study that require human intellect.
- A novice driver cannot be an expert driver by using a sophisticated car. Similarly, a bad analyst or designer can never become a good professional by just using sophisticated CASE tools. A CASE tool provides assistance in modeling, verification, clerical data management, and housekeeping that improves efficiency and productivity if they are used by a skilled and intelligent developer.

A software development platform includes three categories of tools.

- The essential tools include operating systems, programming languages, assemblers, and compilers.
- Very useful tools include editors, linkers, program generators, debuggers, and program definition languages.
- The primary tools classified as useful tools are known as CASE tools. There are two types of useful tools:
    - Workbench
    - I-CASE tools

Functional CASE tools are designed to assist software engineers in a specific phase of the **software development life cycle (SWDLC)**. I-CASE tools cover the entire SWDLC.

A CASE repository is a large database containing huge amounts of descriptive or numeric information about the details of the software product. The information is kept in a CASE repository helps to build and verify the data dictionary for the software product. It also serves as a cross-reference between the data dictionary and other documents required by the software product.

Though there are some limitations in costing and scheduling, the most benefit of CASE tool is discipline and predefined procedures for the software development process.

Component model of software development

Modern software systems become more and more large-scale, complex, and uneasily controlled, resulting in high development costs, low productivity, unmanageable software quality, and a high risk to move to new technology. Consequently, there is a growing demand of searching for a new, efficient, and cost-effective software development paradigm.

One of the most promising solutions today is the component-based software development approach. This approach is based on the idea that software systems can be developed by selecting appropriate off-the-shelf components and then assembling them with well-defined software architecture. This new software development approach is very different from the traditional approach in which software systems can only be implemented from scratch. These **commercial off-the shelf (COTS)** components can be developed by different developers using different languages and different platforms. This can be shown in *Figure15.6*, where COTS components can be checked out from a component repository, and assembled into a target software system:

COTS components

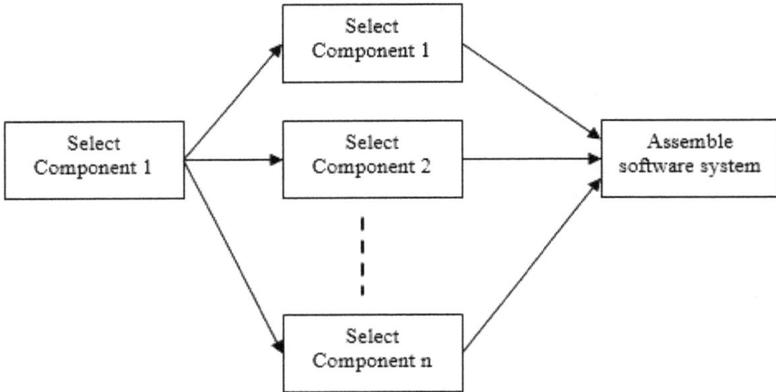

Figure 15.6: *Component-based software development*

Component-based software development (CBSD) can significantly reduce development costs and time-to-market, improving maintainability, reliability, and overall quality of software systems. This approach has raised a tremendous amount of interest both in the research community and in the software industry. The life cycle and software engineering model of CBSD is much different from that of the traditional ones. This is what the **component-based software engineering (CBSE)** is focused on.

Up to now, software component technologies are emerging technology, which is far from being mature.

Current component technologies

Some approaches, such as **Visual Basic Controls (VBX),** ActiveX controls, class libraries, and JavaBeans, make it possible for their related languages, such as Visual Basic, C++, Java, and the supporting tools to share and distribute application pieces. However, all of these approaches rely on certain underlying services to provide the communication and coordination necessary for the application. The infrastructure of components (a component model) acts as the **plumbing** that allows communication among components. Among the component infrastructure technologies that have been developed, the following have become somewhat standardized:

- **Object Management Group's Common Object Request Broker Architecture (OMG's CORBA)**
- Microsoft's **component object model (COM)**
- **Distributed COM (DCOM)**
- Sun's JavaBeans
- Enterprise JavaBeans

Life cycle of component-based software systems

Component-based software systems are developed by selecting the various components and assembling them together rather than programming an overall system from scratch, thus the life cycle of component-based software systems is different from that of the traditional software systems. The life cycle of component-based software:

- Requirements analysis
- Software architecture selection
- Component identification and customization
- System integration

Software reuse

Although computing power and network bandwidth have increased dramatically in recent years, the design, and implementation of networked applications remain expensive and error-prone. Much of the cost and effort stems from the continual re-discovery and re-invention of the core patterns and framework components throughout the software industry. The heterogeneity of hardware architectures, the diversity of OS and network platforms, and stiff global competition are making it increasingly infeasible, however, to build networked applications from scratch with the following qualities:

- Portability, to reduce the effort required to support applications across heterogeneous OS platforms, programming languages, and compilers
- Flexibility, to support a growing range of multimedia datatypes, traffic patterns, and end-to-end **quality of service (QoS)** requirements
- Extensibility, to support succession of quick updates and additions to take advantage of new requirements and emerging markets
- Predictability and efficiency, to provide low latency to delay-sensitive real-time applications and high performance to bandwidth-intensive applications and
- Reliability, to ensure that applications are robust, fault tolerant, and highly available

Developing software that achieves these qualities is hard, systematically developing high-quality reusable software components and frameworks is even harder [*Douglas C. Schmidt*]. Reusable components and frameworks are inherently abstract, which makes it hard to engineer their quality and manage their production. Moreover, the skills required to develop, deploy, and support reusable software have traditionally been a **black art**, locked in the heads of expert developers. When these technical impediments to reuse are combined with common non-technical organizational, economical, administrative, political, and psychological impediments, achieving significant levels of software reuse throughout an organization becomes decidedly non-trivial.

Software reuse assets

Software reuse (code reuse) is the use of existing software, or software knowledge, to build new software. Ad hoc reuse has been practiced from the earliest days of programming. Programmers have always reused sections of code, templates, functions, and procedures. Software reuse is a recognized area of study in software engineering, however, it dates only from 1968 when *Douglas McIlroy* of *Bell Laboratories* proposed basing the software industry on reusable components.

Reusable software, or software knowledge items, are called **reusable assets**. Assets may be designs, requirements, test cases, architectures, knowledge, and so on.

Perhaps the most well-known reusable asset is code. Code reuse is the idea that a partial or complete computer program is written at one time can be, should be, or is being used in another program written at a later time. The reuse of programming code is a common technique which attempts to save time and energy by reducing redundant work.

Usage of software reuse

The software library is a good example of abstraction. Programmers may decide to create internal abstractions so that certain parts of their program can be re-used or may create custom libraries for their own use. Some characteristics that make software more easily reusable are modularity, loose coupling, high cohesion, information hiding, and separation of concerns.

Many common operations, such as converting information among different well-known formats, accessing external storage, interfacing with external programs, or manipulating information (numbers, words, names, locations, dates, and so on.) in common ways, are needed by many different programs. Authors of new programs can use the code in a software library to perform these tasks, instead of re-inventing the wheel, by writing fully new code directly in a program to perform an operation. Library implementations often have the benefit of being well-tested and covering unusual or arcane cases. Disadvantages include the inability to tweak details, which may affect performance or the desired output, and the time and cost of acquiring, learning, and configuring the library.

For newly written code to use a piece of existing code, some kind of interface, or means of communication, must be defined. These commonly include a **call** or use of a subroutine, object, class, or prototype. In organizations, such practices are formalized and standardized by software product line engineering.

The general practice of using a prior version of an extant program as a starting point for the next version is also a form of software reuse.

Software reuse involves simply copying some or all of the code from an existing program into a new one. While organizations can realize time to market benefits for a new product with this approach, they can subsequently be saddled with many of the same code duplication problems caused by cut and paste programming.

Many researchers have worked to make reuse faster, easier, more systematic, and an integral part of the normal process of programming. These are some of the main goals behind the invention of object-oriented programming, which became one of the most common forms of formalized reuse. A somewhat later invention is generic programming.

Another, newer means is to use software **generators**, programs that can create new programs of a certain type, based on a set of parameters that users choose. Fields of study about such systems are generative programming and metaprogramming.

Reusing of software has failed historically

Reuse has been a popular topic of debate and discussion for over 30 years in the software community. Many developers have successfully applied reuse opportunistically, for example, by cutting and pasting code snippets from existing programs into new programs. Opportunistic reuse works fine in a limited way for individual programmers or small groups. However, it does not scale up across business units or enterprises to provide systematic software reuse. Systematic software reuse is a promising means to reduce development cycle time and cost, improve software quality, and leverage existing effort by constructing, and applying multi-use assets like architectures, patterns, components, and frameworks.

Like many other promising techniques in the history of software, systematic reuse of software has not universally delivered significant improvements in quality and productivity. There have certainly been successes, for example, sophisticated frameworks of reusable components are now available in OO languages running on many OS platforms. In general, however, these frameworks have focused on a relatively small number of domains, such as graphical user-interfaces, or C++ container libraries like STL. Moreover, component reuse is often limited in practice to third-party libraries and tools, rather than being an integral part of an organization's software development processes.

In theory, organizations recognize the value of systematic reuse and reward internal reuse efforts. In practice, many factors conspire to make systematic software reuse hard, particularly in companies with a large installed base of legacy software and developers.

Impediments to reuse

There are a number of impediments to reuse:

- **Not invented here**: All too many software professionals would rather rewrite a routine from scratch than reuse a routine written by someone else, the implication being that a routine cannot be any good unless they wrote it themselves. It is **not invented here (NIH)** syndrome [*Griss 1993*]. NIH is a management issue. Application developers may also perceive top-down reuse efforts as an indication that management lacks confidence in their technical abilities. If management is aware of the problem, it can be solved, usually by offering financial incentives to promote reuse.

- **No exhaustive testing**: Many developers would be willing to reuse a routine provided they could be sure that the routine in question would not introduce faults to the product. This attitude towards software quality is perfectly easy to understand. After all, every software professional has faulty software written by others. The solution is to subject potentially reusable routines to exhaustive testing before making them available for reuse.
- **High-degree storage or retrieval problem**: A large organization may have hundreds of thousands of potentially useful components. It is hard to catalog, archive, and retrieve reusable assets across multiple business units within large organizations. Although it is common to scavenge small classes or functions opportunistically from existing programs, developers often find it hard to locate suitable reusable assets outside of their immediate workgroups.
- **Reuse is expensive**: In reuse, three costs are involved in it. They are the cost of making something reusable, the cost of reusing it, the cost of defining and implementing a reuse process. Supporting corporate-wide reusable assets requires an economic investment, particularly if reuse groups operate as cost-centers.
- **Political impediments**: Groups that develop reusable middleware platforms are often viewed with suspicion by application developers, who resent the fact that they may no longer be empowered to make key architectural decisions. Likewise, internecine rivalries among business units may stifle reuse of assets developed by other internal product groups, which are perceived as a threat to job security or corporate influence.
- **Violation of legal issues**: It may arise with contract software. In terms of the type of contract usually drawn up between a client and a software development organization, the software product belongs to the client. If the software developer reuses a component of one client's product in a new product for a different client, this essentially constitutes a violation of the first client's copyright. For internal software, that is, when the developers and client members of the same organization, this problem does not arise.
- **Inefficient COTS component**: Another impediment arises when a **Commercial Off-the-Self (COTS)** component is reused. The developers are given a COTS component that is used in the software and has limited extensibility and modifiability.

The first five impediments can be overcome, at least in principle. Other than the last two impediments essentially no major impediments prevent implementing reuse within a software organization.

Strive for successful systematic reuse

A systematic software reuse is most effective when the following prerequisites are met:

- **The market is competitive**: In a competitive business environment, such as financial services or wireless networking, time-to-market is crucial. It is therefore essential to leverage the existing software to reduce development effort and cycle time. When a market is not competitive, however, organizations tend to reinvent, rather than reuse, software.

- **The application domain is complex**: Components that are relatively easy to develop, such as generic linked lists, stacks, or queues, are often rewritten from scratch rather than reused. In contrast, developers working in highly complex domains, such as distributed, real-time systems, are often willing to reuse components, such as dynamic scheduling frameworks, when building equivalent solutions from scratch proves too error-prone, costly, or time-consuming.
- **The corporate culture and development process are supportive**: Not only is it hard to develop high-quality reusable components and frameworks, but it is even harder to reap the benefits of reuse immediately. Significant investment must be expended up-front to produce efficient, flexible, and well-documented reusable software assets before they can be leveraged in subsequent generations of a product line. Therefore, organizations must support an appropriate software development process that allows systematic reuse to flourish.
- **Attractive reuse magnets exist**: To attract systematic reuse, it is crucial to develop and support **reuse magnets**, such as well-documented frameworks and component repositories. These repositories must be well-maintained so that the application developers will have confidence in their quality and assurance that any defects they encounter will be fixed promptly. Likewise, framework and component repositories must be well-supported so that developers can gain experience through hands-on training and mentoring programs.

  The open-source development processes are an effective process for creating attractive reuse magnets [*Schmidt*]. Open-source processes have yielded many widely used software tools and frameworks, such as Linux, Apache, **GNU's Not Unix (GNU), Adaptive Communication Environment (ACE),** and **The ACE ORB (TAO)**. The open-source model allows users and developers to participate together in evolving software assets. One of the key strengths of this model is that it scales well to large user communities, where application developers and end-users can assist with much of the quality assurance, documentation, and support.
- **Strong leadership and empowerment of skilled architects and developers**: It is observed that the ability of companies and projects to succeed with reuse is highly correlated with the quality and quantity of experienced developers and effective leaders. Conversely, reuse projects that lack a critical mass of developers with the necessarily technical and leadership skills rarely succeed, regardless of the level of managerial and organizational support.

Unfortunately, many organizations lack the five prerequisites as described above. As a result, these organizations often fall victim to the not-invented-here syndrome and redevelop many software components from scratch. However, deregulation, global competition, and the general dearth of experienced application, and middleware developers is making it increasingly hard to succeed by building complex networked applications from the ground up.

Types of reuse

The types of reuses are:

- **Opportunistic reuse:** While getting ready to begin a project, the team realizes that there are existing components that they can reuse.
- **Planned reuse:** A team strategically designs components so that they'll be reusable in future projects.

Opportunistic reuse can be categorized further:

- **Internal reuse**: A team reuses its own components. This may be a business decision, since the team may want to control a component critical to the project.
- **External reuse:** A team may choose to buy a third-party component. Buying a third-party component typically costs the team 1 to 20 percent of what it would cost to develop internally [*McConnell 1996*]. The team must also consider the time it takes to find, learn, and integrate the component.

Conclusion

Software reuse and automated software synthesis are the two concepts that have been employed to reduce the development cost and time. Both of these methods follow the waterfall model in development but take advantage of either software product, which is already developed and used to automate many of the waterfall SWDLC steps. Software reuse, while on the surface sounds like an idea that would lead to substantial cost savings, should be approached skeptically. A software product or element already written, tested, and used cannot be plugged directly into a new application without some analysis to ensure that the product meets the actual requirements. Some effort to document requirements and document the reused software product is needed, new interfaces must be confirmed, and the reused product must be tested in its new configuration and in its new operational environment.

In the next chapter, the reader will learn about recent trends and developments in software engineering, exploring how emerging technologies and methodologies are shaping the industry. From the rise of AI-driven development and low-code/no-code platforms to the growing influence of DevOps, cloud-native architectures, and microservices, this chapter delves into the innovations driving modern software engineering. Readers will also gain insights into the impact of cybersecurity advancements, the role of blockchain in secure software solutions, and the increasing adoption of Agile and CI/CD practices. By understanding these trends, software engineers and technology enthusiasts can stay ahead of the curve and adapt to the rapidly evolving landscape of software development.

Exercises

To solidify your understanding of the concepts covered in this chapter, try the following exercises.

Multiple choice questions

1. **What is the primary goal of CASE tools?**
   a. To enhance system security
   b. To automate and support system development
   c. To reduce system costs
   d. To increase system downtime
2. **PDL, often used in software development, stands for:**
   a. Program design language
   b. Process data language
   c. Performance development language
   d. Project development loop
3. **What does CORBA in OMG's CORBA stand for?**
   a. Common Object Request Broadcast Architecture
   b. Component Object Runtime and Broker Architecture
   c. Common Object Request Broker Architecture
   d. Centralized Object Request Builder Architecture
4. **GNU is a widely known project. What does GNU stand for?**
   a. GNU's New Utility
   b. General Network Utility
   c. GNU's Not Unix
   d. General Non-User
5. **ACE, used in software systems, refers to:**
   a. Advanced Computing Environment
   b. Adaptive Communication Environment
   c. Automated Control Engine
   d. Advanced Code Editor
6. **TAO is built on the ACE framework and is primarily used as:**
   a. A database management System
   b. A real-time CORBA implementation

c. A network security tool
d. A software version control system

7. **Which of the following is NOT an objective of using CASE tools in software development?**
   a. Simplifying program maintenance
   b. Increasing the speed of system design
   c. Promoting module reusability
   d. Reducing internet bandwidth usage

Short answers questions

1. What are the contents of a CASE repository?
2. What is a component-based software engineering (CBSE)?
3. What are the CBSE framework activities?
4. How do we certify a software component?
5. List some CASE tools.
6. List the functions of a repository.
7. What is a repository and what are the kinds of repository?
8. What is a meta-model?

Essay questions

1. Illustrate the role of CASE tools in system analysis and design. What are its advantages and disadvantages?
2. What is reusability of software? Explain the reuse benefits.
3. What are the hindrances one faces during reuse of software code?
4. What are the merits and demerits of a component-based software system?
5. Why I-CASE environment is mostly favored by the software developer?

Multiple choice answers

1. b
2. a
3. c
4. c
5. b
6. b
7. d

CHAPTER 16
Recent Trends and Developments in Software Engineering

Introduction

Advances in sensor technologies, wireless communications, and mobile devices have resulted in software applications, usually known as ubiquitous, that can be used anywhere and everywhere. These applications are sensible to the context in which they operate, which makes them adaptable and responsive to users' profiles and personal requirements. Context-awareness is increasingly featured in many instances of application domains such as e-commerce, e-learning, e-healthcare, and so on. Despite this recent flurry of interest in context-awareness, modeling, capturing, and processing contextual information pose a new set of challenges, resulting in high application development overheads. Sensing, localizing, recognizing, profiling, provisioning, discovering, and dealing with the uncertainty and privacy of, contextual information are typical processes associated with such application development overheads. Traditional software engineering and tools have already shown their limitations, which calls for new techniques and tools.

According to *Barry Boehm,* the software engineering future trend in 2014 will look towards, the increasing integration of software engineering and system engineering, an increased emphasis on users and end value, increasing criticality and need for dependability and security, increasing rapid change, increasing SIS globalization and the need for interoperability, increasingly complex systems of systems, increasing needs for **Commercial Off-The-Shelf (COTS)**, reuse, and legacy SIS integration and computational plenty.

This is the second of several levels on the future of software engineering. The first level focused on trends in application programming, particularly related to quality. This level reviews data on programmer staffing and then covers application programming skills. Future levels deal with the trends in system programming and implications of these trends for software engineering and software engineers.

Structure

In this chapter, we will be discussing the following topics:

- Current trends in software engineering
- Adopting SE trends in artificial intelligence
- Research advancement in SE
- Hypertext support for software maintenance
- Empirical software engineering
- Data modelling
- Ontology
- Data mining in software engineering
- Facts

Objectives

The objective of this chapter is to explore the recent trends shaping the field of software engineering. It will delve into current advancements in software engineering practices, highlighting the growing integration of **artificial intelligence** (**AI**) to enhance development processes and improve automation. The chapter will also focus on research advancements that are driving innovation in the industry, with a particular emphasis on empirical software engineering, which relies on data-driven insights to refine methodologies. Additionally, the chapter will cover emerging areas such as data modeling and its role in managing complex data structures, as well as the use of ontology to provide a structured understanding of knowledge representation in software systems. These topics collectively aim to provide a comprehensive overview of how modern trends are influencing the evolution of software engineering.

Current trends in software engineering

Software engineering is a young discipline, and is still developing. The directions in which software engineering is developing include:

- **Aspects**: Aspects help software engineers to deal with the abilities by providing tools to add or remove boilerplate code from many areas in the source code. Aspects describe how all objects or functions should behave in a particular circumstance.

For example, aspects can add debugging, logging, or locking control into all objects of the particular types. Researchers are currently working to understand how to use aspects to design general-purpose code. Related concepts include generative programming and templates.

- **Agile**: Agile software development guides software development projects that evolve rapidly with changing expectations and competitive markets. Proponents of this method believe that heavy document driven processes (TickIT, **Capability Maturity Model (CMM), International Organization for Standardization (ISO)** 9000) are fading in importance. Some people believe that companies and agencies export many of the jobs that can be guided by heavy-weight processes. Related concepts include extreme programming and lean software.
- **Experimental**: Experimental software engineering is a branch of software engineering interested in devising experiments on software, collecting data from the experiments, and devising laws and theories from this data. A proponent of this method advocates that the nature of software is such that we can advance the knowledge of software through experiments only.
- **Model-driven**: Model driven software development uses both textual and graphical models as primary development artifacts. By means of model transformation and code generation, a part or complete application is generated.
- **Software product lines**: A software product line is a systematic way to produce families of software systems instead of creating a succession of completely individual products. This method emphasizes extensive, systematic, formal code reuse to try to industrialize the software development process.
- **Embedded software**: Embedded software increases the variability, configurability, extendibility, and changeability of every product. It allows for a greater variety of functions. In the future, embedded software will be in everything like automated homes, intelligent automobiles, communication infrastructures, medical instruments and implants, and ubiquitous control systems. The new energy-related technologies that increase the efficiency of electrical current transmission will provide immediate, effective ways to address the energy and climate demands. The embedded system is no longer defined by the computing hardware being used. Rather, they will be designed to do any function to achieve multiple and changing objectives, whether on a microcontroller, a microprocessor, a signal processor, a biological assembly, or any other programmable logic device. The more quality of life we desire, the higher living standards we want to establish across the planet, and the more we demand security and safety, the more we need embedded software [*Christol Ebert & Jürgen Salecker*]. Our task is to evolve embedded software engineering to master these grand challenges.

The **Future of Software Engineering Conference (FOSE),** held at ICSE 2000, documented the state of the art of SE in 2000 and listed many problems to be solved over the next decade. The FOSE tracks at the ICSE 2000 and the ICSE 2007 conferences to identify the state of the art in software engineering.

Adopting SE trends in artificial intelligence

Designing and developing reliable, robust, well-architected, and easy-to-extend software applications or tools in any field requires conformance to sound principles and rules of software engineering. Intelligent systems, especially AI development tools, are no exception. However, AI has always been a wellspring of ideas that software engineering has later adopted, most of its gems remain buried in laboratories, available only to a few AI practitioners.

We can integrate the AI development environment with model-driven architecture to familiarize the mainstream software technologies and expand them with new functionalities. This integrated environment provides a general modeling and meta-modeling infrastructure for AI systems analysis, system design, and system development.

Software engineering trends

Keeping an eye on current software engineering developments and trends can help us design more stable AI tools. Some SE trends are general and span many fields and application domains. The specific SE trends, such as agent-oriented SE.

A relatively new, generally applicable SE trend involves application development based on model driven architecture, which has received intensive support from the **Object Management Group (OMG)**.

Model Driven Architecture (MDA) interests AI developers because it has much in common with ontology modeling and development. Essentially, MDA defines the following levels of abstraction in system modeling:

- The computation-independent model corresponds to the system's domain model and resembles the domain ontology. It does not show details of the system structure.
- The platform-independent model is computationally dependent but unaware of specific computer platform details.

Knowledge based SE vs. application of inductive methods in SE

The application of AI technology to software engineering is known as **Knowledge Based Software Engineering (KBSE)** [*Lowry and Duran 1989 p.243*]. While this definition is fairly broad, most KBSE systems explicitly encode the knowledge that they employ [*McCartney 1991 p. xix*]. KBSE systems are designed to assist software engineers in low-level everyday maintenance tasks and have the potential of representing and deducing the relations among components of a software system at the expense of requiring a fairly extensive body of knowledge and employing, sometimes computationally demanding, deductions, and other algorithms. In other words, such systems are fairly knowledge rich. KBSE systems tend to employ expert systems or knowledge bases as their underlying technology.

While there has been a fair body of work that has applied deductive methods to different aspects of software engineering, the application of inductive methods (machine learning) in software engineering has received far less attention.

It has been argued that learning systems have the potential to go beyond the performance of an expert so as to find new relations among concepts by examining examples of successfully solved cases. In effect, this could allow the incorporation of knowledge into a system without the need for a knowledge engineer. In other words, using inductive methods to extract the knowledge that helps a software engineer understand a software system is an alternative to more traditional KBSE techniques. We should point out that this does not mean that one cannot incorporate expert knowledge in the process. On the contrary, it is believed that such a contribution can increase the potential gain obtained by using inductive methods [*Weiss and Kulikowski 1991 p. 3*]. Unlike KBSE systems, expert knowledge is not coded in the form of a large knowledge base.

Research advancement in SE

The conducted research focused on software engineering. Software engineering aims to systematically support the different phases of software production. Software engineering includes automated software engineering and empirical software engineering. The scientific research interests include automated and empirical aspects of software engineering as related to software maintenance and evolution. Software maintenance is the last part of the software life cycle. Generally, maintenance is defined as starting when the software product has first been delivered to its customers. Software maintenance and evolution is the most expensive and time-consuming phase of the life cycle. The sub-areas of maintenance that have traditionally been studied include the technical aspects of software and also the effects of the attributes of the persons maintaining software. Other areas have traditionally been less studied. In the actual maintenance, changing of source code is a central task. Self-evidently, the size and complexity of the programs to be maintained correlate positively with the problems. Also, problems with the documentation (such as non-existent, insufficient, and misleading documentation) complicate maintenance. Problems related to software maintenance can be alleviated in various ways. Proper allocation of resources for achieving a sufficient level of software quality (and its sub-factors, most importantly maintainability, and comprehensibility) during the initial development of the software is one strategy. In principle, all changes should be made such that no negative side effects emerge. In principle, this goal could be approached via complete regression testing. In the case of large software, however, complete testing is not possible. Therefore, test cases have to be selected wisely. Reading and interpreting large programs and comprehending their structure, operation, and purpose is a central, problematic, and time-consuming sub-task. Proper comprehension of the relevant issues is a necessary condition for the successful fulfillment of maintenance tasks.

Automated software engineering

In case of maintaining poorly documented, large or otherwise hard-to-manipulate software, supporting techniques and tools are needed. These include reverse engineering, reengineering, restructuring, re-documentation, modernization, renovation, and re-factoring. Specific techniques include static and dynamic program analysis, program slicing, simulation, and systematic configuration management. There also exist multiple tools for these purposes.

Hypertext support for software maintenance

Automated **hypertext support for software maintenance (Hyper Soft)**, software maintainers have situation-dependent information needs while maintaining the software. Hyper Soft is an automated approach for satisfying these needs. Hyper Soft applies static program analysis and transient hypertext representation. Program comprehension is supported by the formed **Transient Hyper Textual Access Structures (THASs)**. THASs support nonlinear browsing of the source code. HyperSoft applies linear, hypertextual, hierarchical, and graphical views. Potentially cross-linked graphs are also linked to source code. Hypertext has earlier been applied both to manual cross-document linkage and to automated intra-modular linkage in so-called software hypertext systems. HyperSoft's specialties include transient, fully automated cross-module linkage and automated formation of abstracted graphs with hypertextual links to source code. Some of the keywords being used are software maintenance, program comprehension, reverse engineering, legacy systems, hypertext representation, software hypertext systems, program slicing, and impact analysis.

Program slicing

Program slicing can be used to support various tasks of software maintenance. The two main variants of slicing are backward slicing and forward slicing. Backward slicing is useful in debugging, and forward slicing is in impact analysis. The efficiency of slicing is improved by using program dependence graphs as a way to store the needed program information. Some of the keywords being used are program slicing, program dependence graphs, forward slicing, static analysis, impact analysis, Java, and Visual Basic.

Open source software maintenance support

Open source software development has specific characteristics in terms of maintenance, and therefore, specific reverse engineering capabilities are needed. These characteristics include software licensing. Keywords such as open source software, reverse engineering, and software licenses.

SwMaster

SwMaster is a **program comprehension tool**. SwMaster applies symbolic analysis and program simulation to program comprehension support, reverse engineering, and reengineering. The keywords are software maintenance, program comprehension, reverse engineering, legacy systems, symbolic analysis, program simulation, reengineering.

Data mining

Data mining means nontrivial extraction of implicit, previously unknown, and potentially useful information from data. Research in the intersection of data mining and reverse engineering clearly has good future potential as a basis for sophisticated reverse engineering tools.

Empirical software engineering

Empirical software engineering is a field that focuses on the study and analysis of software engineering practices through empirical methods such as experiments, case studies, and surveys. It involves collecting real-world data from software development processes and products to understand how different practices, tools, and methods impact software quality, productivity, and efficiency. By using evidence-based approaches, empirical software engineering helps improve decision-making in software development, leading to more reliable and effective software systems. It bridges the gap between theoretical research and practical application in the software industry.

Evaluation of software modernizations

Extending the life-time of information systems (ELTIS) studies decision-making support related to large-scale software evolution choices. Generally, the proportion of software maintenance and evolution activities is 50-75% of the total software life-cycle costs, and there seems to be a slightly increasing trend. Nowadays, the proportion can sometimes be the case of successful systems with long lifetimes, but poor maintainability can be even as high as 90%. Since the proportion of the maintenance costs is large, it is important to estimate the induced needed effort and costs of maintenance and modernization activities. There is also a need to evaluate software evolution alternatives. Successful systems with long life-times are often problematic in the sense of insufficient maintainability and thus modifiability. They are called legacy systems. Being large investments with poor flexibility, their complete discard is often undesirable, but radical modernizations are hard to implement successfully. Main general-level evolution options include continued conventional maintenance, reduced maintenance, modernization, and replacement. Continued conventional maintenance is a viable option while both the economic and technical values of the system are high. Reduced maintenance is lucrative while the technical value is sufficient, but the economic value is low. Modernization is the prime option while the economic value is high, but the technical value is low. Finally, replacement is suggested while both the economic and technical values of the system are low. Industrial decision-making processes related to the evaluation of software evolution alternatives should be supported by empirically based methods. ELTIS includes theoretical comparative studies, empirical industrial case studies, and method development and validation activities. Some of the keywords being used are software evolution, software maintenance, legacy systems, modernization, software benefits, software costs, and **return on investment (ROI)**.

Software inspections

Software inspections mean peer reviews of software artifacts. Software inspections can be applied to increase the quality of software already prior to testing, therefore reducing the needed corrective effort. Both the technical and organizational aspects of inspections have been studied in the scientific literature since the 1980s. The studies include different kinds of inspection techniques and some reverse engineering tools for supporting the inspections. We have conducted both the literature survey and empirical industrial case studies related to software inspections.

Software metrics

Software metrics mean measures of some properties of a piece of software or its specifications. Software metrics cover many quality aspects. They are needed as a basis for the software evolution evaluation methods. We have gathered empirical data concerning open-source software systems and studied the relations between internal and external quality attributes statistically.

Software engineering education

Software maintenance education (SME) is a conducted research focused on software maintenance and evolution, especially on the effects and factors affecting software maintenance seminars. Despite its importance, maintenance rarely deserves proper treatment in software engineering education. One reason for this is the tradition of covering other subject areas, which have been established earlier, instead of maintenance in the past and even current educational curricula. Another related reason is that the general software engineering books deal with software maintenance and evolution only at a shallow level, having typically only 5-10% text coverage as compared to the 50-90% cost proportion. Seminars, on the other hand, allow motivating interactivity and cover a wide range of scientifically relevant and new theoretical advances. Students need that sort of knowledge in order to become mature enough to commit themselves to large applicative SME work projects. Therefore, seminars and other similar forms of teaching are needed, and they should also be studied scientifically.

Decision making support

Decision support systems are computer-based information systems that support decision making activities. In addition to the here summarized two branches of specific novel applications, general decision-making theories, and surveys, the earlier described ELTIS-project has extensively studied decision-making support in the context of software evolution.

Fluid Soft (Fluidity in Software Systems) refers to the concept of applying fluid-like information representations and data transformations within the context of software engineering. The goal is to introduce flexibility and adaptability in how data is managed and processed in software systems.

Data modelling

Data modelling is the way to make an information display for the information to be put away in a database. This information display is a theoretical portrayal of:

- Data objects
- The relationship between various information objects
- The rules

Data modeling helps in the visual portrayal of information and implements business rules, administrative compliances, and government approaches to the information. Data models guarantee consistency in naming traditions, default esteems, semantics, and security while guaranteeing the nature of the information.

Information shows accentuate what information is required and how it ought to be sorted out rather than what tasks should be performed on the information. An information model resembles an architect's building plan, which fabricates a reasonable model and sets the connection between information things.

The two sorts of data model methods are as follows:

- **Entity Relationship (E-R)** model
- **Unified Modeling Language (UML)**

Objectives of utilizing data models

The essential objectives of utilizing data models are as follows:

- Ensures that all information objects required by the database are precisely spoken to. Oversight of information will prompt the making of faulty reports and deliver erroneous outcomes.
- An information demonstrates to plan the database at the calculated, physical, and legitimate dimensions.

- Data model structure characterizes the social tables, essential, and outside keys, and put-away strategies.
- It gives a reasonable image of the base information and can be utilized by database engineers to make a physical database.
- It is additionally useful to distinguish absent and excess information.
- Though the underlying making of the information shown is work and tedious, over the long haul, it makes the IT framework overhaul.

Types of data models

There are principally three distinct kinds of information models:

- **Conceptual**: Conceptual data model characterizes **WHAT** the framework contains. This model is normally made by business partners and data architects. The reason for existing is to sort out, scope, and characterize business ideas and standards.
- **Logical**: Defines **HOW** the framework ought to be actualized paying little respect to the **Data Base Management System (DBMS)**. This model is regularly made by data architects and business analysts. The reason for existing is to create a specialized guide of tenets and information structures.
- **Physical**: The physical data model portrays **HOW** the framework will be executed by utilizing a particular DBMS framework. This model is ordinarily made by DBA and engineers. The object is a genuine execution of the database. (*Figure 16.1*):

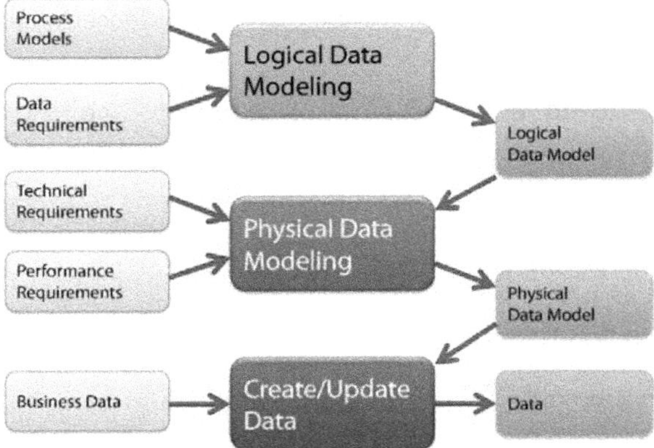

***Figure 16.1:** Data model types*

Conceptual model

The primary goal of this model is to build up the substances, their traits, and their connections. In this data demonstrating level, there is no detail accessible of the real database structure.

The three fundamental occupants of the data model are as follows:

- **Entity:** A genuine thing
- **Attribute:** Characteristics or properties of a substance
- **Relationship:** Dependency or relationship between two substances

For instance:

- Customer and product are two substances. Client number and name are the properties of customer substances.
- Product name and cost are the properties of the item substance.
- Sale is the connection between the client and the item. (*Figure 16.2*):

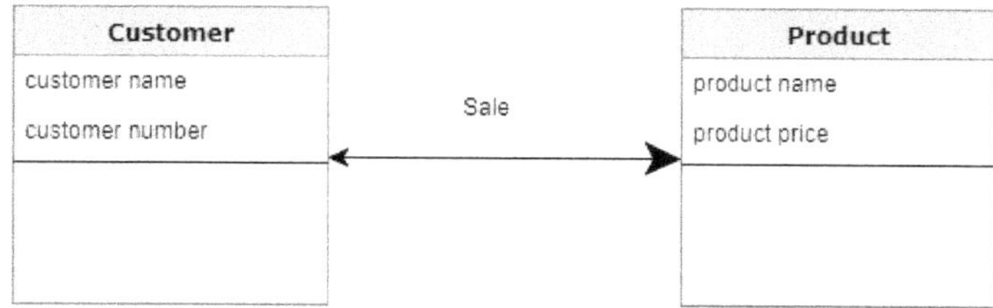

***Figure 16.2:** Conceptual model*

Following are the attributes of a reasonable information display:

- Offers organization-wide inclusion of business ideas.
- This sort of data model is planned and created for a business group of onlookers.
- The applied model is created autonomously of equipment details like information stockpiling limit, area, or programming particulars like DBMS merchant and innovation. The center is to speak to information as a client will see it in **this present reality**.

Reasonable information models, known as **domain models,** make a typical vocabulary for all partners by setting up essential ideas and degrees.

Logical data model

Logical data models add additional data to the reasonable model components. It characterizes the structure of the information components and sets the connections between them. (*Figure 16.3*)

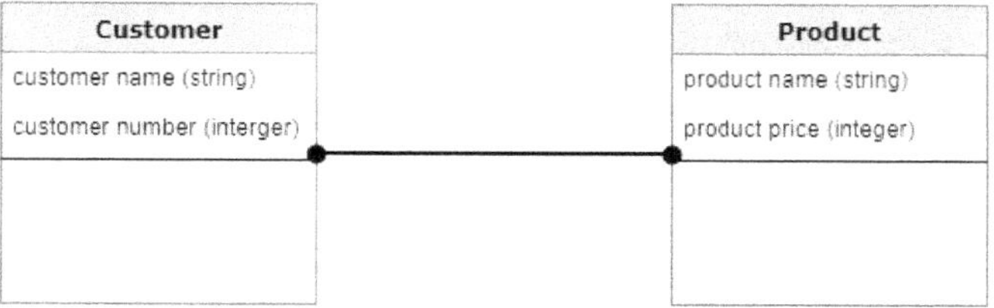

***Figure 16.3:** Logical Data Model*

The benefit of the logical information is to frame the base for the physical model. In any case, the demonstrating structure stays conventional. At this data modeling level, no essential or optional key is characterized. At this data demonstrating level, you have to check and change the connector subtitle that was set before the connections.

The following are the attributes of a logical information display

- Portrays information requirements for a solitary task yet could be incorporated with other legitimate information models depending on the extent of the venture.
- Planned and grew autonomously from the DBMS.
- Information characteristics will have datatypes with correct precisions and length.
- Standardization procedures to the model are connected normally till 3NF.

Physical data model

A physical data model depicts the database's explicit execution of the information. It offers a reflection of the database and produces the diagram. This is a direct result of the lavishness of meta-information offered by a physical data model. This kind of data demonstrates the database structure. It displays database section keys, imperatives, files, triggers, and different RDBMS highlights. (*Figure 16.4*)

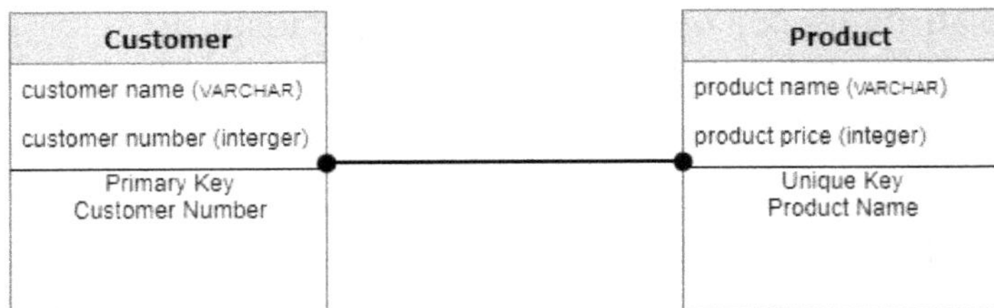

Figure 16.4 *Physical data model*

The following are the qualities of a physical information display:

- The physical information portrays information requirements for a solitary venture or application however it might be incorporated with other physical information model's dependent on the task scope.
- Information model contains connections between tables, which tends to cardinality and nullability of the connections.
- Produced for a particular adaptation of a DBMS, area, information stockpiling, or innovation to be utilized in the task.
- Segments ought to have correct datatypes, lengths allocated, and default esteems.
- Essential and foreign keys, views, indexes, get-to profiles, approvals, and so forth are characterized.

Advantages and disadvantages of data model

The following are the advantages of the data model:

- The fundamental objective of structuring information is to verify that information objects offered by the practical group are spoken precisely.
- The information model ought to be point by point enough to be utilized for building the physical database.
- The data in the information model can be utilized for characterizing the connection between tables, essential-outside keys, and put away strategies.
- Data model causes business to convey the inside and crosswise over associations.
- Data display serves to archive information mappings in the **extract, transform, load (ETL)** process.
- Help to perceive the right wellsprings of information to populate the model.

The following are the disadvantages of the data model:

- To designer data show one should realize physical information by putting away the qualities.
- This is a navigational framework that produces complex application improvement, the board. Consequently, it requires information on the true to life truth.
- Even smaller changes made in structure require an alteration in the whole application.
- There is no set information control dialect in DBMS.

Ontology

Ontologies are utilized for the formal portrayal of domain information. Learning based applications use ontologies for information sharing, which shapes the essential utilization of ontologies. Ontologies improvement is to a great extent gone for AI specialists with learning of different systems starting from the field of AI. This learning is anyway obscure to a vast area of the product business. To overcome any issues between the learning of software engineering professionals and AI strategies, a few propositions have been made recommending the utilization of ontologies in the field of software engineering. Recommendations incorporate the utilization of UML graphs in the advancement of ontologies. Indeed, the *Protégé Software* created by Stanford University has a tab that remarkably characterizes the utilization of UML charts in ontology advancement. This usefulness can be utilized to build up a UML graph from the ontology created. In any case, it can likewise be seen, that product building approaches themselves do not empower the portrayal of cosmology ideas got from depiction rationales and different ideas incorporated into the **Semantic Web Languages**.

Tools for ontology development

A few important ways to deal with applying programming designing systems to ontology advancement lead to UML-based instruments that empower the improvement of ontologies utilizing software engineering languages. The list is as follows:

- **Protégé**: Protégé is one of the main ontological designing tools. It is an open source. Protégé is known to have a critical design which can additionally be broadened utilizing plug-ins. numerous segments giving interfaces to other learning-based apparatuses (Jess, Argenon, OIL, PAL Constraint, and so forth.) have been actualized and coordinated into Protégé. This meta-model is extensible and versatile. This implies Protégé can be adjusted to help another ontology language by including new meta-classes and meta-openings to the Protégé philosophy. The presentation of these new meta-modeling ideas empowers clients to include the vital metaphysics primitives.
- **DUET**: DUET empowers the bringing of DAML ontologies into **International Business Machines (IBM)** Rational Rose and ArgoUML and the trading of UML models into the DAML ontology language. The apparatus is really actualized as an include for IBM Rational Rose and as a module for ArgoUML. Like Protégé it is openly accessible. DUET has a straightforward UML profile that contains generalizations for demonstrating ontologies (in light of a UML bundle) and properties (in light of a UML class). DUET was the first UML device expansion that empowers sharing of ontologies between an ontology language (such as, DAML) and a UML apparatus in the two headings.
- **XPetal**: Ontology tools that change IBM Rational Rose models from the mdl configuration to **Resource Description Framework (RDF)** and **Resource Description Framework Schema (RDFS)** ontologies have been created, better known as XPetal. The device has been actualized in Java.
- **Visual Ontology Modeler (VOM):** The VOM is an after effect of collective work between *Sandpiper Software Inc.* and the *Knowledge System Laboratory* at Stanford University. This instrument was utilized to expand IBM Rational Rose and empower ontology advancement with easy to understand wizards that mechanize the making of a consistent model and related graphs. The apparatus depends on a UML profile for ontology improvement that is firmly identified with Protégé's metamodel for ontologies.

Data mining in software engineering

Data mining for programming building comprises gathering programming designing information, removing some learning from it, and, if conceivable, utilize this information to enhance the product designing procedure, at the end of the day, **operationalize** the mined learning. For example, analysts have removed used patterns from a large number of lines of code of the Linux kernel so as to discover bugs.

Generally, information digging for programming building can deteriorate along three tomahawks: the objective, the info information utilized, and the mining method utilized. For instance, the objective might be to enhance the code finish frameworks:

- **The objective:** Program building comprises numerous errands, from particular, structure, improvement, checking at runtime, and so on. Each undertaking deteriorates into numerous smaller-scale errands. Consider an example, a designer always switches between assignments, such as exploring code, perusing documentation, composing code, troubleshooting, and so forth. In the recent decade, it has appeared that most programming designing assignments can make a profit by information mining approaches, the errands being whether specialized or more individuals arranged. Moreover, the network, in spite of the fact that favoring solid commitments, likewise delivers exploratory outcomes, elucidating marvels seen in programming designing information.
- **The information:** The product building process completely controls a wide range of information. Obviously, one considers code. However, there are likewise many composed records (particulars, documentation), plan archives (charts, equations), runtime reports (logs), and so forth. A large portion of them can be formed utilizing a version control system (for example, **Concurrent Versions System (CVS), Subversion(SVN)**, Git). Contingent upon the focused-on objective, a few curios are pretty much suitable, and mixed methodologies are conceivable (utilizing various types of programming designing ancient rarities related). Additionally, there is typically a decent lot of pre-preparing that is explicit to the relics under thought: characteristic language handling for composed records, static examinations for code, and so forth.
- **The systems:** These days, there is an abundance of information mining and machine learning procedures. They exist; however, developed usage is accessible, and incredible equipment empowers strategies to scale to extensive datasets. To control programming building information, no one estimate fits all arrangement. From managed to unsupervised methodologies, numerical or all out, bunch or on the web, numerous systems have been utilized. There are activities, for example, that bring together datasets and challenges to empower logical correlations of propriety and execution.

Facts

The demand for software engineers is at an all-time high and continues to increase. The data shows that the number of programmers in the USA doubled from 1986 to 1996. While good data are sparse for such an important field, the demand for programmers has clearly increased in the past ten years, and it is likely to continue increasing in the future. Most of the professionals in the fields of engineering and science now write at least some software to do their jobs, the number of people who write, modify, fix, and support software must be very large. If growth trends implied by census data apply to the entire population of casual and full-time programmers, the demand for new programmers in the next ten years is likely to run into millions.

Viewing the latest trends shows that every industrial organization will need more people with software application programming skills and that most programming groups will be seriously understaffed. Since many software groups are already understaffed for onshore-offshore projects, the current university graduation rate of software professionals is higher. So, there is an ample scope of job opportunities.

Obtaining more software-skilled immigrants into the US and other developed countries is an attractive alternative. India alone produces graduates about 1,00,000 English-speaking software professionals a year. However, the US has tight visa restrictions, and many other groups also have claims on the available slots. Since the demand for software skills is increasing rapidly in India, and since many Indian professionals can now find attractive opportunities at home, the available numbers of Indian immigrants will likely be limited in the future.

The packaged applications are now gaining popularity. Companies are starting to market packaged applications much like those offered by **Systems, Applications, and Products (SAP)** in data processing and Oracle. They produce essentially prepackaged application systems that can be configured in prescribed ways. Rather than custom-designing each application, the industry will increasingly develop families of tolerable application systems. By tailoring the system, the users adjust their business procedures to fit the available facilities of the system.

Conclusion

There are many software becoming popular, and many are going out of the market because of their individual efficiency in the development of systems and maintenance. The systems developed in the specific languages have merits and demerits that a software developer or user should judge carefully. Users of lightweight J2EE (spring) are becoming more for developing open jobs. The relative growth of Groovy, Ruby, and Scala over the past years is very impressive as they are growing very fast. Is it hype, or are these programming languages of tomorrow? Maybe you ask yourself which computer language you should learn next. Should you learn Groovy, Ruby, Scala, or take a look at Microsoft .NET? According to indeed.com, Java is the most wanted programming language on the market. We can see the growing cloud computing trend even better if we view the percentage growth. What about the web framework? JSP and Struts still rock the world. JSP and Struts developers are still most wanted. JBoss is the only open-source application server used in production. What about Java Application Servers? Oracle Application Server is the most wanted, but JBoss is growing fast. Now, Tomcat is the dominating web container in comparison to Java web container. Similarly, Flash dominates the web and the job market. Though Silverlight is growing, its growth in the market is impressive.

According to indeed.com, you are currently the most valuable IT resource if you are a Java Developer with Spring and Hibernet knowledge. You should know how to develop web applications with JSP, Struts, or Web Flow and how to deploy them on Tomcat or Oracle Application Servers. If you are a rich client developer, you should be able to develop with Swing or Flash. If you want to be the elite of the future, you should take a look at cloud computing, Groovy, Spring, JPA, GlassFish, Jetty, ActiveMQ, and Silverlight.

The next chapter, **integration of AI with SDLC**, is to explore how AI can be seamlessly incorporated into the SDLC to enhance efficiency, quality, and decision-making. This chapter will focus on examining the various stages of SDLC, such as planning, design, coding, testing, and maintenance, and how AI technologies, including machine learning and natural language processing, can optimize each phase. By integrating AI into SDLC, organizations can achieve better automation, predictive analytics, and improved problem-solving capabilities, ultimately leading to faster development cycles and more reliable software products.

Exercises

To solidify your understanding of the concepts covered in this chapter, try the following exercises.

Multiple choice questions

1. **Which of the following is a recent trend in software engineering?**
   a. Manual coding
   b. AI integration in SDLC
   c. Use of paper documentation
   d. Waterfall model adoption

2. **What is one of the key developments in modern software engineering?**
   a. Use of monolithic architectures
   b. Cloud computing and DevOps
   c. Manual testing
   d. Reducing automation

3. **Which methodology is being increasingly adopted for agile software development?**
   a. V-Model
   b. Scrum
   c. Waterfall
   d. Spiral

4. **What does CI/CD stand for in modern software development practices?**
    a. Continuous Integration / Continuous Deployment
    b. Continuous Innovation / Continuous Delivery
    c. Critical Integration / Critical Deployment
    d. Centralized Integration / Centralized Delivery
5. **Which technology is driving automation in modern software engineering?**
    a. Blockchain
    b. Artificial intelligence
    c. Microservices
    d. Mainframe systems

Short questions

1. What is AI's role in recent developments in software engineering?
2. Name one key development in software engineering in the last decade.
3. What is the purpose of Agile methodologies in software development?
4. What is the benefit of using cloud computing in software engineering?

Essay questions

1. Explain the role of Agile methodologies in modern software engineering and how it has transformed traditional development practices.
2. Describe how AI is being integrated into the **software development life cycle (SDLC)** and its impact on the development process.
3. What are the benefits and challenges of adopting DevOps practices in modern software engineering, and how do these practices contribute to software quality and faster delivery?
4. Discuss the significance of cloud computing in software engineering and how it has reshaped development practices in recent years.

Multiple choice answers

1. b
2. b
3. b
4. a
5. b

Chapter 17
Artificial Intelligence Integration with SDLC

Introduction

This chapter explores the integration of **artificial intelligence** (AI) into the **software development life cycle** (**SDLC**) and how it is reshaping the way software is designed, developed, tested, deployed, and maintained. Traditionally, the SDLC has relied heavily on manual processes, but with the advent of AI, many aspects of software development can now be automated, streamlined, and optimized. AI tools and techniques bring significant improvements in efficiency, accuracy, and decision-making, enabling faster development cycles and more reliable software. This chapter focuses into how AI enhances each phase of the SDLC, from planning and design to testing and maintenance, while also addressing the challenges and opportunities that arise from this integration. By understanding the role of AI in SDLC, developers and teams can harness its potential to create high-quality software in a more efficient and scalable manner.

Structure

In this chapter, we will cover the following:

- Introduction to AI in SDCL
- AI integration in SDLC phases
- Benefits and challenges of AI in SDLC

- AI tools and platforms for SDLC
- Future trends and innovations

Objectives

The chapter aims to provide an in-depth understanding of how AI technologies can be integrated into various phases of the SDLC to improve efficiency, accuracy, and quality in software development. By exploring AI's role in phases such as planning, design, development, testing, deployment, and maintenance, this chapter highlights the transformative potential of AI in automating repetitive tasks, optimizing system architectures, predicting failures, and enhancing decision-making. Students will learn about AI-powered tools and techniques that assist in generating code, automating test cases, predicting system failures through predictive maintenance, and managing continuous integration and deployment pipelines. The chapter also discusses challenges associated with AI integration, such as data quality, model transparency, and the complexity of integrating AI into legacy systems. Through practical examples and case studies, students will gain a clearer understanding of how AI can be leveraged to build more reliable, scalable, and high-performing software systems, while addressing the key obstacles in adopting AI in modern SDLC processes.

Introduction to AI in SDLC

AI is transforming the SDLC by introducing automation, efficiency, and enhanced decision-making into every phase. Traditionally, software development involved manual processes, from planning and design to coding, testing, deployment, and maintenance. With the integration of AI, many of these processes can be streamlined, reducing human effort while improving accuracy and speed. In the SDLC, AI can automate repetitive tasks, optimize system designs, detect bugs earlier, and predict potential failures before they occur. By leveraging machine learning models and predictive analytics, AI can help teams make data-driven decisions, ensuring better resource allocation, accurate timelines, and proactive maintenance. This transformation allows development teams to focus more on creativity and innovation while AI handles much of the operational complexity, resulting in faster, more reliable, and cost-effective software development.

Overview of artificial intelligence

AI refers to the ability of machines to mimic human intelligence and perform tasks like problem-solving, learning, and understanding language. AI systems use algorithms and models to analyze data, recognize patterns, and make decisions, often with a high degree of accuracy. These capabilities make AI suitable for a wide range of applications, from everyday tasks like voice assistants to complex fields like medical diagnosis.

One of the foundational concepts of AI is **machine learning** (**ML**). ML involves training algorithms to identify patterns in data, allowing computers to improve their performance over time without being explicitly programmed. For example, in spam detection for emails, ML models analyze the characteristics of spam emails (like certain words or phrases) and learn to identify new spam messages. Another common use of ML is in recommendation systems, such as those used by Netflix or Amazon, where the algorithms learn users' preferences over time to suggest movies or products they might like.

A more advanced subset of ML is **deep learning** (**DL**), which involves using neural networks that mimic the structure of the human brain. DL is especially powerful for processing large amounts of complex data, such as images, audio, and text. For example, DL is used in image recognition systems that power features like facial recognition in smartphones or automatic tagging of photos on social media platforms. It is also used in autonomous vehicles, where DL models process inputs from cameras, lidar, and sensors to understand the environment and make driving decisions.

Natural language processing (**NLP**) is another critical area of AI that focuses on enabling machines to understand, interpret, and generate human language. NLP is used in chatbots and virtual assistants like Siri, Alexa, and Google Assistant, which can understand user commands and respond accordingly. It also powers language translation services like Google Translate, which can convert text or speech from one language to another with a high degree of accuracy. NLP is also used in sentiment analysis, where algorithms analyze social media posts, reviews, or feedback to determine the sentiment behind them, such as whether a review is positive, negative, or neutral.

AI also includes computer vision, where machines learn to interpret visual information from the world around them. This is used in applications like medical imaging, where AI models help doctors detect diseases in X-rays or MRIs by identifying patterns that might be missed by the human eye. Another example is quality inspection in manufacturing, where AI-powered cameras can identify defects in products on a production line, ensuring consistency and reducing waste.

Another key area is reinforcement learning, where an AI system learns to make decisions through trial and error, optimizing for long-term rewards. This approach is often used in game-playing AI, such as the system that defeated the world champion in the game of Go. It is also used in robotics, where robots learn how to navigate complex environments by continuously improving their movements and strategies based on feedback from their surroundings. Overall, AI encompasses a diverse set of techniques and technologies, all aimed at making machines more capable and intelligent. These capabilities allow AI to automate repetitive tasks, make data-driven decisions, and interact with users in a natural way, making it an essential tool across various industries.

Rationale for AI integration with SDLC

Integrating AI with the SDLC is changing the way software is developed, making the process more efficient, accurate, and adaptive. AI can automate repetitive tasks, enhance decision-making, and improve error detection. By streamlining processes, AI allows development teams to focus more on innovation rather than manual work. This not only speeds up the development process but also improves the accuracy of results, leading to better quality software. Here are some real-world examples of how AI is being applied within the different phases of SDLC:

- **Automating repetitive tasks in code development:** AI tools like GitHub Copilot and TabNine use advanced ML models to suggest code snippets and complete lines of code based on the context of what the developer is writing. This helps developers save time and reduces the effort spent on writing boilerplate code. For instance, when a developer is working on building APIs or implementing standard functions like user authentication, these AI tools can automatically generate the code structure, allowing the developer to focus on more complex logic. This integration of AI can significantly accelerate the development phase by reducing manual coding tasks.
- **Enhancing decision-making in project planning:** AI-powered analytics tools, such as Microsoft's Azure Machine Learning, can analyze past project data and provide insights into project timelines, resource allocation, and potential risks. For example, AI can predict how long it will take to complete a particular software module by analyzing the team's previous performance data. This helps project managers create more accurate timelines and allocate resources efficiently. For example, a software firm might use AI to assess which team members have the best track record in completing certain types of tasks, helping to assign the right people to the right roles, thus improving project outcomes.
- **Automating bug detection and code review:** AI systems like DeepCode or SonarQube use ML models to review codebases and identify potential bugs, security vulnerabilities, or code smells before the code is even tested. For instance, a large-scale financial software company can use such tools to review complex algorithms for data processing, ensuring that any potential issues are flagged before they reach production. This proactive approach minimizes the number of bugs that reach the testing phase and enhances software security, especially in projects that handle sensitive user data.
- **AI in testing automation:** Traditional software testing can be time-consuming, especially when a project involves frequent changes. AI-powered testing tools like Testim and Applitools automate the generation of test cases and adapt to changes in the **user interface** (**UI**). For example, an e-commerce company that frequently updates its website design can use AI-based visual testing tools to automatically validate that the visual elements render correctly on different devices and screen

sizes. This reduces the manual effort required in regression testing and ensures that new features do not break existing functionalities.

- **AI for predictive maintenance in the maintenance phase:** After deployment, software often needs updates and bug fixes to ensure smooth operation. AI helps in predictive maintenance by analyzing log data to predict potential system failures before they happen. For example, AI-powered monitoring tools like Dynatrace or Splunk can detect unusual patterns in server logs, such as slow response times or unexpected traffic spikes, and alert developers to potential issues before they cause system outages. This is especially important for **Software as a Service** (**SaaS**) companies that need to maintain high uptime for their customers. By preventing issues before they impact users, AI helps maintain a reliable software experience.
- **AI-driven DevOps for faster releases:** DevOps is all about speeding up the development-to-deployment process through automation, and AI is playing a significant role in this area. Tools like Jenkins combined with AI models can optimize **continuous integration** and **continuous deployment** (**CI/CD**) pipelines, making the release process smoother and more efficient. For instance, AI can analyze past deployment logs to identify the optimal time for rolling out a new software update, reducing the risk of deployment failures during peak user hours. A cloud service provider, for example, could use this approach to ensure that new features are deployed when user activity is low, minimizing disruption and improving user satisfaction.
- **Risk management and quality analysis:** AI can also play a crucial role in identifying risks and assessing software quality during the development process. AI-driven platforms like IBM's Watson AI can analyze the codebase and assess the complexity and maintainability of the software. This helps developers identify areas of the code that may become problematic over time, such as highly complex modules that could be difficult to modify. For example, a banking software project might use AI to assess the quality of code related to transaction processing, ensuring that the code is robust enough to handle millions of transactions without errors. This kind of insight helps in making informed decisions about code refactoring and optimization.

The integration of AI into the SDLC has a direct impact on the speed and quality of software development. It allows teams to work smarter by providing them with the tools and insights needed to develop software that is both reliable and efficient. AI-driven automation and predictive analytics help reduce development time and minimize errors, ensuring that software projects are delivered on time and meet the required quality standards. This transformation is especially valuable in today's competitive tech landscape, where rapid delivery and high quality are essential for success. These real-time implementations of AI in various SDLC phases demonstrate the value it brings to the software development process. By leveraging AI, development teams can better predict project timelines, reduce errors during coding, and identify potential risks, ultimately resulting in software that is not only built faster but is also more reliable and user-friendly.

AI integration in SDLC phases

The integration of AI in the SDLC is transforming how software is designed, developed, tested, and maintained. In the **planning and requirement analysis** phase, AI-driven tools can analyze user needs, predict project risks, and optimize resource allocation. During **design**, AI assists in generating efficient architectures, detecting potential flaws, and automating UI/UX improvements. In the **development phase**, AI-powered code generators, such as GitHub Copilot, enhance productivity by suggesting optimized code snippets and reducing errors. AI-based **testing** tools perform automated test case generation, bug detection, and predictive analytics to improve software quality. In the **deployment** phase, AI optimizes CI/CD pipelines, automates infrastructure provisioning, and ensures seamless rollout with minimal downtime. Lastly, in **maintenance and monitoring**, AI-driven observability tools predict system failures, detect security vulnerabilities, and provide self-healing mechanisms. By integrating AI across SDLC phases, organizations can enhance efficiency, reduce development time, and improve software reliability.

AI integration in the SDLC enhances each phase by automating tasks, improving accuracy, and speeding up processes. From planning to maintenance, AI brings intelligent solutions that assist in decision-making, optimize designs, and predict potential issues. This section explores how AI is applied at different stages of the SDLC, including planning, design, development, testing, deployment, and maintenance, providing real-world examples of its impact. Through AI, development teams can streamline workflows, reduce human error, and deliver more efficient, reliable software.

Planning phase

In the planning phase, AI can play a critical role in project estimation, resource allocation, and scope definition. Traditionally, project planning relies on manual assessments and the experience of project managers to estimate timelines and resource needs. However, AI algorithms can analyze data from past projects, learning from patterns in project duration, team performance, and resource consumption to provide more accurate predictions for new projects. This allows development teams to set realistic timelines and budgets that align with the project's complexity and scope.

For instance, AI-powered project management tools like *JIRA Align* or *Monday.com* can leverage AI to analyze historical project data and provide insights into the estimated time for different tasks. If a software development team has previously built a customer management system, the AI tool can analyze the data from that project—such as the time taken for each development phase, challenges faced, and resources used—and use that information to predict the time and resources needed for building a similar system. This way, the team can avoid underestimating or overestimating the time required, which often leads to project delays or unnecessary resource allocation. AI also helps in identifying potential risks during the planning stage by analyzing data from similar projects. For example, if a software company is planning to develop a mobile app, the AI system can compare this project with past mobile app projects to identify common risks, such as compatibility issues with different devices or performance bottlenecks. By identifying these risks early, the team can prepare strategies to mitigate them, such as planning for extra testing time or allocating additional resources for device compatibility checks.

Following is an example of an AI-assisted requirement analysis

A practical example of AI in the planning phase is the use of NLP in tools like IBM's Watson for requirement analysis. When a company gathers requirements from clients through documents or meeting notes, AI can analyze these texts to highlight ambiguities or inconsistencies in the requirements. For instance, if a client says they need a **fast and secure payment system**, the AI tool can flag **fast** and **secure** as ambiguous terms, prompting the team to clarify what speed is expected and what specific security measures are required. This ensures that all parties have a clear understanding of the project's goals from the beginning.

In one real-world scenario, a financial services company used an AI tool to analyze client requirements for a new banking app. The AI system processed the requirement documents and identified that terms like **user-friendly** and **secure data storage** needed further clarification. It also suggested questions like, **What specific encryption standards should be used for data storage? What user experience metrics are most important for the client?** This allowed the development team to have a more detailed discussion with the client, resulting in a clearer, more precise project plan. By using AI to review requirements and identify potential gaps or unclear terms, the planning process becomes more thorough and reduces the risk of misunderstandings later in the development cycle. This ensures that the project starts with well-defined goals and a realistic roadmap, which is crucial for the overall success of the project.

Design Phase

During the design phase of the **SDLC**, AI can play a transformative role in optimizing system architecture, recommending design patterns, and even automating parts of the design process. By analyzing data from similar projects, AI tools can suggest architectural patterns that are best suited for the current project's needs, helping developers choose the most effective approach. This is particularly useful when dealing with complex software systems where selecting the right design patterns can have a significant impact on performance, scalability, and maintainability.

AI-assisted architecture selection

AI-based design tools can analyze the requirements of a new project and suggest architectures that have worked well for similar projects. For example, if a company is designing a microservices-based architecture for a new e-commerce platform, AI tools like AWS Architecture Advisor or Microsoft Azure Machine Learning Studio can analyze the needs—such as expected user load, data handling capacity, and security requirements—

and suggest a scalable microservices architecture. The AI can recommend using specific patterns like API Gateway, Service Registry, and Circuit Breaker patterns, which are common in microservices architectures, to improve resilience and manageability.

Following is an example of an AI-based UI design suggestions:

AI tools can also be invaluable when it comes to designing UIs. For instance, platforms like Adobe XD with AI-powered plugins or Figma's AI design assistants can suggest UI layouts based on user behavior data. If a team is building a mobile app for a retail store, the AI can analyze successful UI patterns from similar e-commerce apps and recommend design elements like button placements, color schemes, or navigation structures that have proven to increase user engagement. This helps in creating intuitive and user-friendly interfaces without starting from scratch. A tool like UIzard can even transform rough sketches into fully realized UI components by understanding the structure and translating it into design elements. For example, a designer might upload a sketch of a login screen, and the AI can generate the following codes for a basic login form:

```
<form action="/login" method="POST">
    <div class="form-group">
        <label for="username">Username:</label>
       <input type="text" id="username" name="username" class="form-control"
required>
    </div>
    <div class="form-group">
        <label for="password">Password:</label>
          <input type="password" id="password" name="password" class="form-
control" required>
    </div>
    <button type="submit" class="btn btn-primary">Login</button>
</form>
```

The preceding code snippet could be generated by an AI tool that converts a simple hand-drawn sketch into HTML, saving time for developers and designers while maintaining consistency in the UI.

Development phase

AI plays a crucial role in the development phase of the SDLC, making coding faster, more efficient, and less error prone. By leveraging AI-powered tools, developers can receive real-time assistance while writing code, reducing the time and effort required for certain tasks. These tools can suggest code snippets, auto-complete functions, and even generate entire sections of code based on plain language instructions, allowing developers to focus more on solving complex problems. Additionally, AI is instrumental in detecting bugs and potential issues early, leading to cleaner and more reliable code.

AI-powered code suggestion and auto-completion

One of the most common uses of AI in the development phase is code suggestion and auto-completion. Tools like GitHub Copilot, developed by OpenAI, use ML models to analyze the context of the code that a developer is writing and provide real-time suggestions. For example, if a developer is writing a function to calculate the sum of an array in Python, GitHub Copilot can automatically suggest the complete code for the function.

```
def calculate_sum(numbers);
return sum(numbers)
```

In this scenario, the developer only needs to type the function signature (**`def calculate_sum(numbers):`**), and the AI tool can complete the function by suggesting the use of Python's built-in **`sum()`** function. This not only saves time but also helps new developers learn standard approaches and best practices.

Generating code from plain language instructions

Some AI tools, like OpenAI's Codex and Replit's Ghostwriter, can go a step further by generating code directly from plain language instructions. This means that developers can describe what they want in simple English, and the AI will write the corresponding code. For example, if a developer wants to create a function that returns the square of a number in JavaScript, they could type a prompt like, **Write a function that returns the square of a number**, and the AI would generate the code:

```
function square(num) {
return num * num;
}
```

This is particularly useful for beginners who might not yet be familiar with the syntax of a specific programming language. It helps them translate their logical ideas into working code more easily. It also speeds up development for experienced programmers by allowing them to focus on more complex parts of the application.

AI for bug detection and code quality improvement

AI is also valuable in detecting bugs and improving code quality. Tools like *SonarQube*, *DeepCode* (acquired by *Snyk*), and *PyCharm* with AI-powered plugins analyze the codebase and identify potential issues such as security vulnerabilities, code smells (areas that could be optimized), and common mistakes. For instance, if a developer accidentally creates a loop that might result in infinite execution, the AI-powered tool can flag this issue before it becomes a problem during testing. Consider a scenario where a developer writes a Python function to process user data.

Following is an example of an AI-based bug detection in Python code:

```
def process_user_data(users):
    for user in users:
        if user['active']:
            print(f"Processing user: {user['name']}")
            # Code to process active users
```

In this code, if the dictionary **user** is missing the **'name'** key, it could cause a runtime error. An AI-powered tool could automatically detect this potential issue and suggest adding a safe check. Following is an example of an AI-based bug detection in Python code 1:

```
def process_user_data(users):
    for user in users:
        if user['active']:
            name = user.get('name', 'Unknown')
            print(f"Processing user: {name}")
            # Code to process active users
```

In this revised version, the AI suggests using the **get()** method to safely access the **'name'** key, providing a default value of **Unknown** if the key is missing. This makes the code more robust and prevents errors during execution. Such real-time feedback is particularly valuable for beginners, as it helps them learn how to write more error-resistant code.

```
# Original version
def filter_even_numbers(numbers):
    result = []
    for number in numbers:
        if number % 2 == 0:
            result.append(number)
    return result

# AI-suggested refactored version
def filter_even_numbers(numbers):
    return [number for number in numbers if number % 2 == 0]
```

Testing phase

The testing phase is a crucial part of the SDLC, ensuring that software functions as expected and is free from defects before being released to users. However, testing can be time-consuming, especially for large projects with many features and edge cases. AI plays a significant role in automating and optimizing this phase, making testing faster, more thorough, and more effective. By using AI-powered tools, development teams can automatically generate test cases, prioritize them, and even predict potential bugs, resulting in higher-quality software with fewer errors.

AI for automated test case generation

One of the key areas where AI can help in the testing phase is **automated test case generation**. Traditionally, writing test cases is a manual process where testers define inputs and expected outputs for different parts of the code. AI changes this by analyzing the source code and user requirements to automatically generate relevant test cases. This ensures that a wide range of scenarios are covered, including edge cases that might be overlooked by human testers. For example, tools like *Testim* and *Applitools* use ML to understand the structure of the application and generate test cases for various user interactions. If a team is developing an online shopping platform, the AI tool can automatically create test cases for common user actions like adding items to the cart, proceeding to checkout, and applying discount codes. These AI-generated tests can be run on different browsers and devices to ensure consistent behavior across all environments, which is especially valuable for web applications. Following is a basic example of what an AI-generated test case might look like using *Selenium* (a popular testing tool) with an AI-powered plugin:

```
# Example of a test case generated for adding an item to the cart using Selenium
from selenium import webdriver
# Set up the web driver
driver = webdriver.Chrome()
# Open the online store
driver.get("https://example-online-store.com")
# AI-generated actions
# Find the search bar and search for a product
driver.find_element_by_id("search").send_keys("laptop")
driver.find_element_by_id("search-button").click()
# Add the first product to the cart
driver.find_element_by_css_selector(".product-item:first-child .add-to-cart").click()
# Verify that the cart now contains the product
assert "laptop" in driver.find_element_by_id("cart-items").text
# Close the browser
driver.quit()
```

In this example, the AI tool suggests interactions with the web application based on its analysis of the site's structure, creating a test case that verifies the functionality of adding a product to the shopping cart. This helps the testing team ensure that the cart feature is working as expected without writing every test case manually.

Prioritizing test cases using machine learning

In large software projects, it is often impractical to run every single test case for every new update, as it can take a considerable amount of time. AI can assist by using **ML models** to prioritize test cases, focusing on those that are more likely to uncover bugs. By analyzing past test results and patterns in the codebase, AI can identify areas that have historically been more error-prone and give them higher priority during testing. For instance, if an AI tool analyzes a web application and finds that a particular module, like the payment gateway, frequently has bugs after updates, it can ensure that test cases for this module are run first whenever new changes are made. This targeted testing approach helps testers catch critical issues early, improving the stability of the software.

Following is an example of an AI for test case prioritization in continuous integration pipelines:

Let us say a team uses Jenkins as their CI tool for a project. The team integrates an AI-powered testing tool like *Diffblue Cover*, which automatically writes and prioritizes Java unit tests. When a developer makes changes to the codebase, the AI tool analyzes those changes and prioritizes test cases that are most likely to be affected by the recent updates. This ensures that tests related to newly modified code run first, minimizing the time needed for regression testing and allowing developers to get quicker feedback. Following is an example of a Jenkins CI configuration with AI test prioritization:

```
# Example of a Jenkins CI configuration with AI test prioritization
pipeline {
    agent any
    stages {
        stage('Build') {
            steps {
                echo 'Building the application...'
                sh 'mvn clean install'
            }
        }
        stage('AI-Driven Test Execution') {
            steps {
                echo 'Running AI-prioritized tests...'
                sh 'diffblue-test-prioritizer run'
            }
        }
        stage('Deploy') {
            steps {
                echo 'Deploying the application...'
```

```
                sh 'mvn deploy'
            }
        }
    }
}
```

In this example, the Jenkins pipeline uses an AI tool to prioritize tests, ensuring that the most critical tests are run first. This helps the development team quickly identify and fix issues before the code is deployed to production, reducing the risk of introducing bugs into the live system.

AI for predictive bug detection

AI is also effective in **predicting bugs** before they become serious issues. By analyzing historical data from past projects, such as bug reports, commit histories, and test outcomes, AI tools can identify patterns that typically lead to bugs. For example, if certain coding practices or specific areas of a codebase are often associated with bugs, AI can alert developers or testers to pay special attention to these areas. A practical example is the use of **bug prediction models** in AI tools like *DeepCode* or *CodeGuru* by AWS. These tools analyze the code and provide predictions about potential vulnerabilities or logic errors based on past data. For example, if a developer introduces a new loop in the code that could potentially result in a memory leak or performance issues, the AI might flag this and suggest alternatives before the code even reaches the testing phase:

```
# AI identifies potential issue with an infinite loop
def process_data(data):
    while len(data) > 0:
        # Process each item
        item = data.pop(0)
       # AI recommendation: Check if data size is changing to avoid infinite
loop
```

AI-driven visual testing

For applications with **graphical user interfaces (GUIs)**, **visual testing** is essential to ensure that the UI renders correctly across different devices and screen sizes. AI tools like **Applitools Eyes** use computer vision to compare screenshots of the UI before and after changes, automatically identifying any differences. This allows testers to ensure that updates to the software do not inadvertently break the design or layout of the application. For example, if a web application undergoes a redesign, Applitools can automatically capture screenshots of each page and compare them to a baseline, highlighting any unexpected visual changes such as misplaced buttons or incorrect font sizes. This approach is much faster than manual visual testing, where testers would have to manually check each page.

AI transforms the testing phase by automating test case generation, prioritizing tests, predicting potential bugs, and ensuring that UIs remain consistent. These capabilities reduce the time and effort required for testing, allowing testers to focus on more critical issues while maintaining high standards of quality. By incorporating AI into the testing phase, development teams can identify problems earlier, address them before they reach end-users, and deliver more reliable and polished software. This is especially beneficial for students who are learning about testing, as it provides them with modern tools and techniques that improve efficiency and accuracy.

Deployment phase

The deployment phase is a critical part of the SDLC where the software is made available to users, either as a new release or an update to an existing application. This phase involves activities like configuring servers, setting up environments, and ensuring that the software works smoothly in its live environment. AI plays a significant role in making the deployment process faster, more efficient, and less prone to errors by automating various tasks and optimizing the timing of releases. By using AI-powered tools, development teams can reduce manual effort, minimize disruptions for users, and maintain high software quality even when frequent changes are made.

Optimizing the timing of software releases

AI can also help determine the best time to release updates based on user activity patterns and server loads. For example, by analyzing historical data, AI can identify periods when user activity is low, such as late at night or during weekends, making these times ideal for deploying updates with minimal disruption to users. This helps ensure that users are less likely to experience downtime or slow performance during the update process.

AI for environment configuration and management

Deploying software often involves setting up the right environments, such as development, staging, and production. Each environment needs to be configured with specific settings like database connections, API keys, and server parameters. AI can automate these configurations, reducing the chances of human error and speeding up the deployment process. Tools like **Terraform** combined with **AI-based configuration management** can automatically set up cloud resources, scaling them according to the application's needs.

Following is an example of an AI-driven environment configuration for a SaaS application:

Imagine a team working on a **Software as a Service (SaaS)** application that needs to scale up during peak usage times, such as during a product launch. An AI tool integrated with **Terraform** can automatically detect an increase in user load and adjust the cloud infrastructure by adding more servers or increasing database capacity. It can also ensure that all configurations, such as load balancer settings and security group adjustments, are applied consistently across development, testing, and production environments.

The AI system can predict usage patterns based on historical data, ensuring that resources are scaled up in anticipation of traffic spikes. For example, if a company plans to launch a marketing campaign, AI can analyze similar past campaigns and adjust server capacity automatically, reducing the risk of servers becoming overwhelmed by increased traffic:

```
# Example GitLab CI/CD configuration for automatic deployment
stages:
  - test
  - deploy

test:
  script:
    - echo "Running AI-enhanced tests..."
    - python run_tests.py  # AI tool runs tests and provides insights
    - if [ $? -eq 0 ]; then echo "Tests passed"; else echo "Tests failed";
exit 1; fi

deploy:
  script:
    - echo "Deploying to production..."
    - ./deploy_to_cloud.sh
  when: on_success
```

AI greatly improves the deployment phase by automating software releases, optimizing the timing of updates, and managing environment configurations. By leveraging AI, development teams can deploy software with minimal manual intervention, ensuring a smooth user experience and reducing the risk of issues during updates. AI-driven tools help manage the complexity of deployments, allowing teams to focus on delivering new features and improvements rather than dealing with deployment logistics. For students, understanding how AI can assist in the deployment phase provides insight into modern software development practices that prioritize speed, stability, and user satisfaction.

Maintenance phase

After software is deployed, it enters the **maintenance phase**, where ongoing updates, bug fixes, and performance optimizations are necessary to ensure smooth operation over time. This phase is critical because it ensures that the software continues to meet user needs, adapts to changes in the environment, and remains secure. AI plays a pivotal role in making maintenance more efficient through techniques like **predictive maintenance**, **automated log analysis**, and **self-healing systems**. These AI-powered approaches help development teams identify and resolve issues before they impact users, reducing downtime and improving user satisfaction.

AI for predictive maintenance

Predictive maintenance uses AI to analyze data from the software's runtime environment and predict potential failures before they occur. By continuously monitoring log data, performance metrics, and user behavior, AI can identify patterns that indicate when a problem might arise. For example, if an AI system detects a gradual increase in memory usage over time, it might predict that the application could run out of memory in the near future. The development team can then address the memory leak before it crashes the system, ensuring a seamless experience for users.

Following is an example of AI-powered predictive maintenance in a banking application

Imagine a banking application that must process thousands of transactions every minute. Downtime or failures in such a system could lead to financial losses and unhappy customers. By using AI-powered tools like **Splunk** or **Datadog**, the development team can monitor metrics such as **CPU usage**, **database response times**, and **network latency** in real time. The AI analyzes these metrics and learns what **normal** behavior looks like for the system.

If the AI detects a significant deviation from normal behavior, such as a sudden spike in database query times or an increase in failed transactions, it can send an alert to the maintenance team. The team can then investigate and resolve the issue before it leads to a system outage. This predictive maintenance approach is especially useful in industries like banking, where even a few minutes of downtime can have serious consequences.

Automated log analysis with AI

Log files are a crucial source of information for understanding the behavior of software after deployment. Logs contain details about user interactions, system errors, and performance data. However, manually analyzing log data can be time-consuming, especially in large systems that generate thousands of log entries every second. AI can automate this process by using **NLP** and **ML** to sift through log data and identify patterns that might indicate problems.

Following is an example of using an AI to analyze server logs in a social media app:

Consider a social media app with millions of daily users. The server logs for such an app might include information about user logins, image uploads, messaging activity, and more. Using an AI tool like **Elasticsearch with Kibana and ML plugins**, the development team can automatically analyze these logs to detect anomalies. For example, if there is a sudden increase in *500 Internal Server Error* messages in the logs, the AI might identify this as a sign of a potential issue with a backend API. It could then generate an alert for the maintenance team, who can investigate the root cause before users start to notice the problem. This proactive approach means that issues are resolved quickly, and the time spent on manual log analysis is greatly reduced. Following is a simple Python code example using **log analysis with NLP** to illustrate how AI might process logs:

```
from sklearn.feature_extraction.text import CountVectorizer
from sklearn.cluster import KMeans

# Sample log data
logs = [
    "Error: Database connection failed at 10:05 AM",
    "User login successful at 10:06 AM",
    "Warning: High memory usage detected at 10:07 AM",
    "Error: Timeout while processing request at 10:08 AM",
    "User uploaded image at 10:09 AM"
]

# Vectorize log data to analyze text patterns
vectorizer = CountVectorizer()
X = vectorizer.fit_transform(logs)

# Use KMeans clustering to identify similar patterns
kmeans = KMeans(n_clusters=2)
kmeans.fit(X)

# Display identified clusters of logs
for i, log in enumerate(logs):
    print(f"Log: {log} - Cluster: {kmeans.labels_[i]}")
```

In this example, the code uses KMeans clustering to group similar log entries. This could help identify patterns, such as clustering together logs that mention **Error** or **Warning**. AI tools use more advanced versions of such techniques to automatically categorize logs and detect unusual patterns, making it easier for maintenance teams to focus on critical issues.

Self-healing systems with AI

AI can also enable self-healing capabilities in software systems, where the system automatically takes corrective actions when an issue is detected. For example, if an AI system monitoring a web application notices that one of the servers has become unresponsive, it can automatically restart the server or shift the load to other servers to maintain service continuity. This minimizes the impact on users and reduces the need for manual intervention.

Following is an example of an AI-enabled self-healing in cloud environments:

Let us consider a cloud-based video streaming platform that needs to maintain high availability, especially during peak viewing times like a major sports event. By using AI-powered tools like **AWS Auto Scaling** with **AI-driven anomaly detection**, the platform can monitor the health of its servers. If one of the servers starts showing signs of degradation, such as a slow response time or a high error rate, the AI system can automatically spin up additional servers to balance the load or replace the failing server with a new one. This self-healing capability ensures that users do not experience buffering or interruptions during their viewing experience. It also helps the operations team by reducing the need for manual monitoring and intervention, allowing them to focus on optimizing the platform's performance rather than responding to individual server failures.

AI for performance optimization

In addition to fixing issues, AI can help optimize the performance of software applications over time. By analyzing user interactions and system metrics, AI can suggest changes that improve the efficiency of the application. For example, it might identify that certain queries in a database are taking too long and suggest optimizations like adding indexes or restructuring the database schema.

Example: AI-assisted database tuning for an e-commerce platform

Consider an e-commerce platform that needs to maintain a fast and responsive search feature for users. If the database queries that power the product search start slowing down, an AI tool like *Oracle Autonomous Database* can automatically analyze the queries and recommend changes, such as creating new indexes or rewriting the SQL statements for better performance. This ensures that the search feature remains fast and responsive, even as the number of products and users grows over time. For example, the AI tool might analyze a query that takes several seconds to execute:

```
-- Original query without optimization
SELECT * FROM products WHERE category = 'electronics' AND price < 1000;
```

The AI might suggest creating an index on the **category** and **price** columns to speed up the search:

```
-- AI-suggested index for optimization
CREATE INDEX idx_category_price ON products (category, price);
```

By implementing this suggestion, the query becomes significantly faster, improving the user experience when searching for products. This kind of AI-driven performance tuning helps the maintenance team keep the application running smoothly even as the data grows. AI significantly enhances the maintenance phase of software development by predicting failures before they occur, automating log analysis, enabling self-healing capabilities, and optimizing performance. By taking a proactive approach, AI helps maintenance teams identify and address issues before they impact users, reducing downtime and improving overall software reliability. For students, understanding how AI can be used in the maintenance phase provides valuable insights into modern techniques that keep software systems efficient and user-friendly long after they have been deployed.

Benefits and challenges of AI in SDLC

Let us look at the various benefits and challenges of AI in SDLC:

Benefits of AI integration

Integrating AI into the SDLC offers numerous benefits. It enhances productivity by automating routine tasks, allowing developers to focus on more complex work. AI-driven insights help in making data-driven decisions, ensuring that project timelines and resources are used efficiently. AI also reduces human errors by automating testing and bug detection, leading to higher-quality software. With AI, software development becomes faster, more accurate, and more aligned with user needs.

Challenges and risks

Despite the advantages, there are challenges in using AI in SDLC. AI models require a large amount of data for training, and if the data is of poor quality, the AI might make incorrect predictions. There are also ethical issues, such as biases in AI algorithms, which can affect decision-making. Integrating AI tools with existing SDLC processes can be complex, requiring time and expertise. Additionally, the cost of implementing AI solutions can be high, especially for smaller organizations.

Data quality and availability

AI systems require large volumes of high-quality data for training and accurate predictions. If the available data is incomplete, inconsistent, or biased, the AI models might produce inaccurate results. In many cases, gathering sufficient data to train AI models can be time-consuming and costly.

Complexity of AI model integration

Integrating AI models into existing SDLC processes can be complex. AI algorithms often require specialized infrastructure, such as GPUs for DL models, and integration can require a high level of expertise. Additionally, adapting traditional SDLC processes to accommodate AI workflows may require significant changes in tools and methodologies.

High initial costs

Implementing AI solutions in the SDLC can require a significant initial investment in terms of software, hardware, and skilled personnel. This can be a barrier, especially for **small to medium-sized enterprises** (**SMEs**) that may not have the budget to invest in AI infrastructure and training.

Explainability and transparency of AI models

Many AI models, particularly those based on DL, are often considered "black boxes" because it is difficult to understand how they arrive at their conclusions. This lack of transparency can make it challenging for developers and stakeholders to trust the AI's decisions, especially when the AI flags certain code as buggy or suggests specific architectural changes.

Integration with legacy systems

Many organizations have legacy systems that were not designed with AI integration in mind. Incorporating AI tools into these older systems can be difficult, as they may lack the APIs, data structures, or processing power required to interact with modern AI algorithms.

Bias in AI algorithms

AI models can inadvertently learn biases from the training data they are provided with. If the data used to train an AI model contains biases, such as overlooking certain edge cases or prioritizing specific types of errors, the AI system may perpetuate these biases in its predictions or recommendations. Example: Suppose an AI model is trained to prioritize certain types of bugs in a software project based on past bug reports. If the training data contains mostly bugs related to UI issues but lacks sufficient data on performance-related bugs, the AI might fail to identify performance bottlenecks in future projects. This could lead to a system that is visually functional but struggles with speed and scalability.

Ethical and privacy concerns

AI systems that collect and analyze data as part of the SDLC may face challenges related to data privacy and compliance with regulations like **General Data Protection Regulation** (**GDPR**) or **California Consumer Privacy Act** (**CCPA**). Ensuring that user data is protected while still providing enough information for the AI to function is a delicate balance.

Continuous model maintenance

AI models require regular updates and retraining to remain accurate, especially when the underlying data changes over time. This means that AI models used in the SDLC must be continuously monitored and updated to adapt to new codebases, software updates, or changing user requirements.

Resistance to change and lack of AI expertise

Integrating AI into the SDLC often requires changes to existing workflows and processes, which can face resistance from development teams who are used to traditional methods. Additionally, there may be a lack of expertise in AI among team members, making it difficult to implement and manage AI-based solutions.

Ensuring AI reliability in real-world scenarios

While AI models can perform well in controlled environments or with well-structured training data, their performance may degrade in real-world scenarios where data is noisy or unpredictable. This makes it challenging to ensure that the AI will perform reliably when integrated into a live software development environment.

Using AI in the SDLC offers many advantages, but it also comes with challenges like data quality, integration complexity, high costs, and the need for continuous maintenance. Addressing these challenges requires careful planning, investment in AI expertise, and ongoing adjustments to workflows. Despite the hurdles, successfully integrating AI into the SDLC can result in more efficient software development processes and higher-quality software products, making it a worthwhile endeavor for organizations willing to navigate the complexities involved.

Strategies to overcome challenges

To overcome these challenges, teams need to focus on data quality and ensure that their AI models are trained with diverse datasets. Establishing clear guidelines for AI ethics can help address biases. It is also important to involve AI experts who can ensure that the integration process is smooth. Adopting a phased approach, where AI is gradually introduced into SDLC processes, can help manage costs and complexities. Cross-functional teams that combine AI expertise with development skills can make the integration more successful.

AI tools and platforms for SDLC

AI tools and platforms are revolutionizing the SDLC by automating repetitive tasks, enhancing decision-making, and improving overall software quality. From planning and design to testing and deployment, AI-powered solutions streamline processes, reduce human error, and accelerate development timelines. These tools can analyze large datasets, predict project outcomes, and recommend optimized solutions, making the development process more efficient and adaptable. As the demand for faster and more reliable software grows, integrating AI into SDLC has become crucial for modern software engineering, driving innovation and boosting productivity.

Overview of popular AI tools in SDLC

There are many AI tools that can be used throughout the SDLC. For example, GitHub Copilot helps developers by suggesting code as they type, making coding faster. TensorFlow is widely used for building AI models that can be integrated into various phases of the development process. JIRA automation with AI helps in project management by automating tasks like assigning issues and tracking progress. These tools streamline processes and help developers focus on creative problem-solving.

AI platforms for software development

Several cloud-based AI platforms support software development. AWS AI, Google AI Platform, and Microsoft Azure AI provide services like ML models, data analysis, and NLP. These platforms allow teams to integrate AI without needing to build everything from scratch. They offer pre-built models and APIs, which can be customized for specific project needs. By using these platforms, development teams can quickly adopt AI technologies and scale their applications.

Future trends and innovations

The future of AI in the SDLC promises even greater innovations, with AI-driven automation continuing to enhance efficiency. Emerging trends include AI-powered CI/CD pipelines, adaptive models that optimize development in real-time, and hyper-automation that streamlines complex tasks. Innovations like AI-driven DevSecOps and predictive analytics will improve security and project planning, enabling smarter and more resilient software systems. This section explores these upcoming trends and the transformative impact AI will have on the SDLC, driving faster, more scalable development processes.

Emerging trends in AI and SDLC integration

The future of AI in SDLC looks promising, with trends like hyper-automation, where AI automates even complex decision-making tasks. AI Ops (AI for IT Operations) is another trend, using AI to improve system performance and predict issues before they occur. AI is also becoming crucial in adaptive software development, where it helps software automatically adjust to changing user needs.

The role of AI in next-generation SDLC

Next-generation SDLC will rely heavily on predictive analytics, using AI to anticipate user needs and system performance issues. AI is also playing a bigger role in DevSecOps, ensuring that security is integrated into the development process from the start. This helps teams build secure software more efficiently, reducing the risk of vulnerabilities in production.

Challenges and opportunities for future research

While AI has many benefits, there are still areas where further research is needed. For example, improving AI's ability to understand complex user requirements is a key challenge. Researchers are also exploring ways to make AI models more transparent, so that their decision-making processes are easier to understand. Collaboration between academic institutions and industry can help address these challenges and drive new innovations in AI integration with SDLC.

Conclusion

This chapter explored how AI can be integrated into each phase of the SDLC. From automating coding tasks to enhancing testing and deployment, AI transforms software development into a faster and more efficient process. It also highlighted the challenges that come with AI integration, such as data quality and ethical concerns. AI is reshaping the way software is developed, offering opportunities to improve quality and speed. As AI tools continue to evolve, developers have a chance to build smarter, more adaptive software. Embracing AI in the SDLC can help teams stay competitive and deliver better software solutions for their users.

In the next chapter, the reader will learn about the integration of machine learning in the SDLC process, exploring how ML-driven solutions are transforming traditional software engineering practices. This chapter will cover how ML enhances various SDLC phases, from automating requirement analysis and optimizing system design to improving code generation and debugging. Readers will discover how ML-powered testing frameworks can detect vulnerabilities and predict defects, while intelligent deployment strategies leverage ML for efficient resource allocation and performance monitoring. Additionally, the chapter will discuss the role of ML in predictive maintenance, anomaly detection, and automated software optimization. By understanding these advancements, software engineers can harness ML to increase productivity, improve software quality, and streamline development workflows.

Exercises

To solidify your understanding of the concepts covered in this chapter, try the following exercises:

Multiple choice questions

1. **Which phase of the SDLC can benefit from AI through automated test case generation?**
   a. Design Phase
   b. Development Phase
   c. Testing Phase
   d. Deployment Phase
2. **What is the primary advantage of using AI for predictive maintenance in software systems?**
   a. Reducing development time
   b. Optimizing database queries
   c. Identifying system failures before they occur
   d. Enhancing user interface design
3. **Which of the following is a challenge when integrating AI into the SDLC?**
   a. Availability of high-quality data
   b. Increased manual testing effort
   c. Improved code readability
   d. Reduced software costs
4. **AI-based canary release during the deployment phase is primarily used to:**
   a. Roll out a feature to all users simultaneously
   b. Gradually release a new feature to a subset of users for testing
   c. Automatically revert to a previous software version
   d. Analyze log data for performance metrics
5. **Which AI tool is commonly used for code suggestions and auto-completion?**
   a. JIRA
   b. Selenium
   c. GitHub Copilot
   d. Applitools

Short answer questions

1. Explain how AI can assist in the development phase of the SDLC with an example.
2. What is predictive maintenance in the context of AI and the SDLC, and why is it important?

3. List two challenges faced when integrating AI into the SDLC and briefly describe each.
4. How does AI optimize the deployment phase of software development?
5. Describe how AI can be used for automated log analysis during the maintenance phase, with an example.

Essay questions

1. Discuss the role of AI in the design phase of the SDLC. Provide examples of how AI can recommend design patterns and optimize system architecture.
2. Analyze the benefits and challenges of using AI in the testing phase of the SDLC. Include examples such as automated test case generation and test case prioritization.
3. Explain the process of using AI for self-healing systems in the maintenance phase. How does this approach help in minimizing system downtime?
4. Describe the impact of AI on the CI/CD pipeline. How does AI enhance the process of releasing software updates?
5. What are some ethical and privacy concerns associated with using AI in the SDLC? Provide examples of how these challenges might manifest in real-world projects.
6. A company is developing a video streaming service. How might AI be used in the deployment phase to ensure smooth release of new features?
7. Imagine you are a part of a team that is using AI for code refactoring. How would AI suggest improvements for a piece of code? Provide an example.
8. Suppose a banking application is using AI for predictive maintenance. What types of metrics might the AI monitor, and how could it help prevent potential system failures?
9. How can AI-based bug detection improve the development phase of a project? Give an example of how an AI tool might identify a potential issue in a codebase.
10. A software development team is facing difficulties with the integration of AI into their legacy system. What challenges might they encounter, and how could they address these challenges?
11. Read the following scenario: A team is developing a mobile banking app and is using AI to automatically generate test cases for new features. Discuss how AI can ensure comprehensive testing in this context. What are the possible limitations of relying on AI-generated tests?
12. Consider a scenario where a cloud-based e-commerce platform uses AI for real-time server monitoring. How can AI be used to detect anomalies in user behavior or system performance? How does this improve the maintenance process?
13. A software company wants to use AI to assist with canary releases for a new chat feature in their messaging app. Explain how AI can help in monitoring the release and deciding when to proceed with the full deployment.

14. Analyze the following problem:
15. A startup is struggling with high initial costs associated with implementing AI in their SDLC. What strategies could they use to manage these costs while still benefiting from AI technologies?
16. A healthcare application uses AI for log analysis to identify potential security breaches in real-time. How might AI analyze log data for this purpose, and what advantages does this offer compared to traditional methods?

Multiple choice answers

1. c
2. c
3. a
4. b
5. c

Join our book's Discord space

Join the book's Discord Workspace for Latest updates, Offers, Tech happenings around the world, New Release and Sessions with the Authors:

https://discord.bpbonline.com

CHAPTER 18

Integration of Machine Learning in SDLC Process

Introduction

Integrating **machine learning (ML)** into the **software development life cycle (SDLC)** is changing how software is built. Traditionally, the SDLC follows clear steps such as planning, design, coding, testing, deployment, and maintenance. With ML, these steps are becoming faster and more efficient. ML can help automate tasks like predicting project timelines, finding bugs during testing, or improving code. This reduces human errors and speeds up the process. ML also helps teams make better decisions by analyzing large amounts of data. As a result, software can be developed with fewer risks and higher quality. Companies that use ML in their development process are gaining an edge by creating smarter, more reliable software.

Structure

In this chapter, we will learn the following:

- Overview of the SDLC
- Introduction to ML and its growing influence in software engineering
- Importance of integrating ML into SDLC process
- Traditional SDCL process
- Understanding ML in the context of SDCL

- Role of ML in enhancing software process
- ML integration at different SDCL phases
- Challenges of integrating ML in SDCL
- Best practices for ML integration in SDLC
- Future trends and emerging technologies

Objectives

This chapter is to explore how ML can be integrated into the SDLC to improve efficiency, accuracy, and decision-making. It aims to highlight key areas where ML can automate processes, reduce human error, and enhance the quality of software products. Additionally, this chapter will examine the benefits of incorporating ML into various SDLC stages, helping organizations optimize their development workflows and deliver smarter, more reliable software solutions.

Overview of the software development life cycle

The SDLC is a structured process used by software developers to design, develop, test, and deploy software systems. It provides a clear step-by-step approach, helping teams to manage complex software projects efficiently. SDLC helps ensure that software meets user needs, is built within time and budget, and is reliable and maintainable. SDLC typically follows several key phases:

- **Requirement analysis**: In this phase, developers gather the needs and expectations of the users or clients. This helps in defining what the software will do.
- **Design**: Once the requirements are clear, developers plan the architecture of the software. They decide how different components will interact with each other.
- **Implementation (coding):** The actual writing of code happens here. Developers turn the design into a working software application.
- **Testing**: Before releasing the software, it is tested to ensure that it works as expected. Bugs or issues are identified and fixed.
- **Deployment**: After successful testing, the software is delivered to users. It becomes operational in the real-world environment.
- **Maintenance**: After deployment, the software may need updates or fixes. Maintenance ensures it continues to function well over time.

  For example, a mobile banking app goes through SDLC to ensure it is secure, easy to use and delivers the features customers need. From analyzing what customers want, designing the app's look, coding its functions, and testing for errors to maintaining it with updates. All these steps follow the SDLC process.

Introduction to ML and its growing influence in SE

ML is a subset of **artificial intelligence (AI)** that enables computers to learn from data and make decisions without being explicitly programmed for `every task. In traditional programming, developers manually write specific instructions to achieve a result. However, with ML, the computer learns from experience, meaning it becomes better as it processes more data. This ability to learn and improve over time makes ML particularly useful in solving complex problems where it is difficult or inefficient to define clear-cut rules.

Difference between ML and traditional programming

In traditional programming, developers follow a rigid structure. They provide input data into a program, the program processes the data according to predefined rules, and the result is output based on those fixed instructions. With ML, the process is different; the developers input both the data and the desired outcome (in many cases), and the ML model analyzes the data and figures out patterns that relate to the outcome over time as more data is fed into the system, The ML model adjusts its internal rules (or weights) to improve its predictions. ML's ability to automatically evolve and enhance its decision-making process without ongoing manual intervention is what makes it particularly valuable in the fast-paced world of software development.

Growing role of ML in software engineering

In software engineering, ML is being integrated into multiple stages of the SDLC. This is primarily because ML can analyze large amounts of data, detect hidden patterns, and predict outcomes more accurately and efficiently than manual methods. ML is used to streamline workflows, enhance productivity, and improve software quality. Following is how ML is transforming software engineering:

- **Bug detection**: ML models can automatically scan code for common errors or issues, significantly speeding up the debugging process. Instead of developers manually searching for bugs, ML algorithms can point out likely areas where bugs exist.
- **Performance optimization:** ML tools can monitor software performance over time, detecting areas where improvements are needed. For example, ML can identify performance bottlenecks by analyzing system logs and usage data.
- **Predictive maintenance**: ML can be used to predict future problems by analyzing trends and anomalies in software behavior. This allows developers to preemptively address issues before they impact users, reducing downtime.

Key concepts in machine learning

Algorithms are the core of any ML system. They are mathematical models or formulas that the system uses to process data and make decisions. There are many types of ML algorithms, each designed for different tasks. Following are the examples:

- **Classification algorithms**: Used to categorize data into predefined classes (for example, classifying emails as spam or not).
- **Regression algorithms**: Used to predict continuous outcomes (for example, predicting future stock prices).
- **Clustering algorithms:** Used to group similar data points together (for example, customer segmentation in marketing).

  The choice of algorithm depends on the problem being solved. For example, if you want to predict future sales based on past data, a regression algorithm would be suitable.

Data is the fuel that powers any ML model. ML systems need large amounts of data to learn effectively. The data can be structured (like rows and columns in a database) or unstructured (like images or text). The more diverse and accurate the data, the better the ML model will perform. Without sufficient and high-quality data, even the best algorithm will struggle to make accurate predictions.

There are two primary types of data used in ML:

- **Training data**: This is the data the model learns from. It contains both the input data and the correct answers (labels) from which the ML model can be learned.
- **Test data:** Once the model has been trained, test data is used to see how well the model performs on unseen data.

For example, in email spam filtering, the training data would consist of past emails labeled as **spam** or **not spam**. The ML model analyzes this data to learn the patterns that differentiate spam from legitimate emails.

Models an ML model is the result of applying an algorithm to the data. It represents the system's understanding of the patterns in the data. After the model is trained on a dataset, it can be used to make predictions on new data. The accuracy of an ML model depends on the following several factors:

- The quality of the data it was trained on.
- The choice of algorithm.
- How well the model was fine-tuned (a process known as hyperparameter tuning).

Once trained, the model can generalize its learning to new situations. For instance, a model trained to recognize email spam can analyze new, incoming emails and predict whether they are spam or not. For example, suppose an ML model is trained to recognize handwritten digits (like those from 0 to 9). After processing thousands of images of handwritten numbers, the model learns what each digit typically looks like. Now, when it is shown a new image of a handwritten number, it can predict what digit it is, even if the handwriting is slightly different from what it has seen before.

Example for email spam filtering using ML

One of the most common uses of ML is email spam filtering. Following is how it works:

- **Training data:** A large collection of emails, some labeled as **spam** and others as **not spam**, is used to train the model.
- **Algorithm**: A classification algorithm is used, which learns patterns in the email content, sender information, and other features that distinguish spam from legitimate emails.
- **Model**: Once trained, the model can analyze incoming emails and decide whether they are likely to be spam.
- **Improvement over time**: As the model processes more emails, it continuously learns and becomes better at filtering spam. The more data it processes, the more accurately it identifies new patterns in spam emails.

For instance, early spam filters relied on manually created rules like flagging emails with certain words. ML-based spam filters, however, analyze entire email datasets and automatically learn to spot even subtle indicators of spam, such as unusual formatting, sender behavior, or context. ML is becoming an essential tool in modern software engineering. Its ability to analyze large datasets, find hidden patterns, and make accurate predictions is transforming traditional development processes. As software continues to evolve, ML will play a crucial role in automating and enhancing each step of the SDLC, from design and coding to testing and maintenance. Whether it is predicting system failures or detecting security threats, ML's potential is vast, and its influence will continue to grow.

Importance of integrating ML in the SDLC process

Integrating ML into the SDLC is transforming how software is developed, tested, and maintained. Traditional software development processes can be time-consuming, repetitive, and prone to human error. With ML, these challenges can be addressed by automating many tasks and enhancing accuracy. ML helps developers focus on complex problem-solving rather than repetitive manual work, and as a result, it increases the overall efficiency of the software development process.

Efficiency

One of the biggest advantages of integrating ML into SDLC is the ability to automate repetitive and mundane tasks. In traditional development, tasks like code reviews, bug detection, and test case generation can take significant time and manual effort. With ML, these tasks can be automated, speeding up the development process and freeing up time for developers to focus on more creative and strategic aspects of the project.

- **Automated bug detection**: ML models can analyze the codebase and automatically flag potential bugs, making the detection process faster and more reliable. Unlike static rule-based analysis, ML-driven tools learn from historical bug patterns and evolve over time, becoming better at identifying critical issues as more code is analyzed.
- **Code reviews**: Instead of having developers manually review every line of code, ML can assist by scanning through the code and highlighting areas that need attention. It can identify coding patterns that often lead to bugs, such as security vulnerabilities or inefficient algorithms. This not only speeds up the review process but also ensures a more thorough evaluation.

For example, Facebook uses ML in its code review system to catch potential bugs before the code is merged. The system uses past bug data to predict which lines of code are likely to cause issues, reducing manual review times and improving software reliability.

Accuracy

ML models have the capability to identify patterns and trends in data that humans may not easily recognize. This ability makes ML particularly useful in ensuring higher accuracy in software development. By analyzing historical data, ML can predict potential failures, identify risky areas in the code, and suggest optimizations before the software reaches users:

- **Predicting failures:** Based on past data, ML models can predict when and where a system is likely to fail. For instance, if a particular module has a history of causing problems, an ML model can flag it early in the development cycle, allowing developers to fix it before it becomes a bigger issue. This predictive capability helps reduce the number of bugs that make it into production, improving software quality.
- **Pattern recognition:** ML can spot anomalies or unexpected behaviors that human developers might miss. For example, in large codebases, patterns of inefficient or error-prone code can go unnoticed. ML models, trained on large datasets, can quickly identify these patterns and recommend changes that lead to more robust software.

For example, Google's ML models analyze vast amounts of log data to predict system failures in data centers. This allows their engineers to fix issues before they impact customers, ensuring higher uptime and reliability.

Improved testing

Testing is a crucial part of the SDLC, and ML can significantly improve this phase by automating test case generation, predicting which parts of the code are most likely to fail, and running tests more efficiently. ML-based testing tools ensure that potential issues are caught earlier in the development process, reducing the likelihood of costly fixes later on in the SDLC cycle such as:

- **Automated test case generation**: ML models can generate test cases automatically by analyzing the code structure and identifying areas that need to be tested. This saves developers time and ensures comprehensive testing coverage, as the model can create test cases based on patterns it identifies in the code, including edge cases that developers might overlook.
- **Fault prediction:** ML models can predict which parts of the software are most likely to contain defects. This allows testing efforts to be focused on the riskiest areas, improving the efficiency of the testing process. By prioritizing tests for the most vulnerable parts of the code, development teams can catch critical bugs earlier.

For example, Microsoft uses ML to prioritize test cases in its software development. The ML model predicts which features or areas of the code are most likely to contain bugs, allowing testers to focus on those areas, improving overall software quality and reducing testing time.

Continuous improvement

After software is deployed, it continues to run in real-world environments, where new issues and challenges can emerge. ML models can continuously monitor software performance, detect anomalies, and suggest improvements. This capability makes it easier for development teams to maintain and enhance the software over time without waiting for user-reported bugs or performance issues:

- **Real-time monitoring**: ML can analyze system logs, user behavior, and performance metrics to detect anomalies that might indicate an issue. For instance, if a sudden increase in server response time is detected, an ML model could alert developers to investigate potential causes. This proactive approach helps reduce downtime and ensures smooth operations.
- **Predictive maintenance**: ML can predict when certain parts of the system might fail or need maintenance, allowing developers to take preventive measures. By analyzing patterns in system behavior, such as resource usage or error rates, ML models can anticipate future issues and recommend fixes before they affect users.

For example, Netflix uses ML to continuously monitor its streaming services. The system detects potential disruptions in video quality or playback performance, allowing engineers to make adjustments in real-time, ensuring a seamless experience for users. The integration of ML into the SDLC brings a new level of efficiency, accuracy, and continuous improvement to the software development process. By automating repetitive tasks, improving testing accuracy, predicting potential failures, and continuously monitoring deployed software, ML helps development teams build better, more reliable software faster. As more tools and platforms adopt ML, its influence on the SDLC will continue to grow, making software development smarter and more adaptive.

Traditional SDLC process

SDLC is the process that guides the creation of software applications. It is a structured approach, breaking down software development into manageable stages. Let us look at the key stages of the traditional SDLC process and common methodologies used before ML became a part of it.

Overview of methodologies

Several methodologies are used to execute the SDLC stages. Following are the most common ones:

- **Waterfall methodology**: The waterfall model is a linear approach where each stage must be completed before moving on to the next. It is simple and easy to manage but has limited flexibility. For example, a project following the waterfall model would complete all the requirements and design before any coding begins. If any changes arise during implementation, it would be hard to go back and modify previous stages.
- **Agile methodology:** Agile is an iterative and flexible model where the development process is broken into smaller cycles called sprints. Teams work on small chunks of the project, test them, and get feedback before moving forward. For example, in agile, developers might release an early version of the banking app with basic features like viewing the account balance. In later sprints, they would add more complex features like transactions. Agile is popular for its ability to adapt to changes quickly.
- **DevOps methodology**: DevOps is a methodology that emphasizes collaboration between development and operations teams. It focuses on continuous integration, testing, and deployment, ensuring faster and more reliable releases. For example, in a DevOps environment, the banking app would undergo automatic testing and deployment processes, reducing the time to go from coding to deployment.

Limitations of traditional SDLC without ML integration

While traditional SDLC processes are reliable, they face several limitations in today's fast-paced and data-driven world:

- **Manual requirement analysis**: Traditional SDLC relies heavily on manual efforts to gather and analyze requirements. Human errors or misunderstandings can lead to incomplete or incorrect specifications. For example, in a large-scale e-commerce project, manual analysis may miss subtle trends in user behavior, leading to a misalignment between the features developed and customer needs.
- **Inefficient testing processes**: Manual and predefined testing approaches may not cover all possible edge cases. As software grows more complex, traditional testing may not be able to handle it efficiently. For example, testing for a complex AI-based recommendation system would require a more dynamic testing process, which traditional methods struggle to provide.
- **Delayed feedback and updates**: In waterfall and other traditional models, feedback is often delayed until late in the development cycle, making it harder to correct mistakes. For example, in large projects, developers may finish coding only to discover in testing that critical user experience issues were missed, requiring major rewrites.
- **Lack of predictive capabilities**: Traditional SDLC does not have predictive insights, meaning it cannot foresee future issues or bottlenecks based on historical data. For example, a large web application may experience a spike in traffic post-launch, but traditional SDLC models lack the tools to predict and prepare for such scenarios.

In traditional software development, the SDLC follows a manual process involving planning, designing, coding, testing, deploying, and maintaining software. Each phase relies on the expertise of developers and project managers, but this approach often leads to time-consuming tasks, human errors, and challenges in managing complex systems. To highlight these limitations, examining real-world examples is useful:

- **E-commerce website development**: A company developing an e-commerce website using the waterfall model spends months gathering requirements, designing, and building the site. When it finally launches, they discover that customer behavior has shifted, and key features are no longer as relevant. Without ML, the company missed out on predictive insights that could have adapted the product in real-time.
- **Mobile banking application**: A traditional SDLC approach was used for a mobile banking app, where requirements were manually collected, and testing followed predefined cases. Post-launch, users faced unexpected errors when trying to perform certain transactions during high traffic periods. Without ML, the testing phase failed to account for these edge cases that could have been predicted by analyzing historical traffic data.

The traditional SDLC process, while effective, shows limitations in today's complex software environments. ML can address many of these limitations by adding intelligence, automation, and predictive insights throughout the lifecycle. As we move forward, the integration of ML in SDLC helps overcome these challenges and significantly enhances the development process.

Understanding ML in the context of SDLC

ML is the branch of AI that enables systems to learn and improve from data without being explicitly programmed. To understand its integration into the SDLC, we need to first grasp its key concepts, such as algorithms, models, and data processing:

- **Algorithms**: Algorithms in ML are a set of rules or instructions a machine follows to perform tasks. These algorithms analyze patterns in data to make predictions or decisions. Examples of ML algorithms include decision trees, neural networks, and support vector machines. For instance, in software testing, a decision tree algorithm can help predict the most likely sources of code bugs based on past data.
- **Models:** ML models are created by training algorithms on data. A model is essentially the output generated after an algorithm processes the training data. The model is then used to make predictions on new, unseen data. In the context of SDLC, an ML model could be trained to optimize resource allocation during software design or detect code anomalies during testing.
- **Data processing:** Data is the core of any ML system. Before algorithms can learn from data, it must be cleaned and prepared. This process involves handling missing values, normalizing data, and selecting the right features. For example, in defect prediction, historical bug data needs to be properly processed before being fed into a model. Poor data quality can lead to inaccurate predictions, which could harm the entire software development process.

Role of ML in enhancing software processes

Integrating ML into the SDLC helps enhance the overall efficiency and quality of the software development process. Following is how ML plays a significant role:

- **Automation**: ML can automate repetitive tasks. For example, in the testing phase, ML can automatically generate test cases based on previous bugs, reducing manual work and speeding up the process.
- **Predictive analytics**: ML models can predict potential issues early. For instance, an ML model could analyze historical project data to predict if a project will be delayed, allowing teams to take preventive measures.
- **Improved decision making:** ML helps developers make better decisions by providing insights from large datasets. A recommendation engine can suggest the best software design patterns based on historical projects.

Types of ML algorithms applicable in SDLC

There are three main types of ML algorithms that can be applied at different stages of the SDLC. They are as follows:

- **Supervised learning**: Supervised learning algorithms are trained using labeled data, meaning the outcome is known in advance. The algorithm learns the relationship between the input data and the known output. For example, in code review, a supervised learning model could predict whether a piece of code will likely cause a bug based on past labeled code errors. For example, a supervised learning algorithm is trained on historical data where code changes are labeled as **bug-free** or **buggy**. The trained model can then analyze new code and predict the likelihood of errors.
- **Unsupervised learning**: Unsupervised learning works with unlabeled data. The algorithm tries to find hidden patterns or structures in the data without any prior knowledge of outcomes. In the SDLC, unsupervised learning can be used to group similar user stories or feature requests, helping teams identify trends in requirements. For example, an unsupervised learning algorithm clusters user feedback into groups. This helps developers identify common issues or feature requests from users without needing to manually go through hundreds of feedback entries.
- **Reinforcement learning:** Reinforcement learning is based on a system of rewards and penalties. The algorithm learns by interacting with the environment and receiving feedback. In the context of SDLC, reinforcement learning can be applied to optimize system performance during the deployment phase. The model adjusts parameters to maximize system performance based on feedback from real-time performance data. For example, in the deployment phase, reinforcement learning could be used to tune server configurations. The algorithm learns from previous configurations and adjusts settings to improve system performance under different workloads.

Case studies

- **Case study 1**: Predicting software defects using ML. A software company integrated ML into its testing phase to predict software defects. By using historical bug data, the company trained a supervised learning model to predict the likelihood of defects in new code. This helped the company focus its testing efforts on the most critical areas, reducing testing time by 30%.
- **Case study 2**: Automating code review with ML. Another organization used ML to automate the code review process. An unsupervised learning model was applied to analyze coding patterns and flag potential code smells or inefficiencies. This saved the company significant time in manual code reviews while also improving code quality.
- **Case study 3:** Resource allocation with reinforcement learning. In the deployment phase, a company used reinforcement learning to allocate cloud resources efficiently. The algorithm learned from previous deployment data and adjusted the resource allocation dynamically. This led to a 20% cost saving in cloud resource usage while maintaining performance.

These examples highlight how ML, when integrated into the SDLC, can significantly enhance software processes, leading to faster development, reduced costs, and better-quality software. By leveraging supervised, unsupervised, and reinforcement learning techniques, software development teams can automate and optimize various phases of the SDLC, making the process more efficient and intelligent.

ML integration at different SDLC phases

ML has a transformative effect on each phase of the SDLC. It automates processes, predicts outcomes, and improves overall efficiency. Let us look at how ML can be integrated into different phases of SDLC:

- **Planning phase**: The planning stage of a conventional waterfall SDLC includes project initiation, project scope definition, resource allocation, timeline and milestones, budgeting and cost estimation, risk management planning, quality assurance planning, project schedule development, and project plan finalization.

  Whereas, ML-based SDLC involves project initiation, project scope definition, resource allocation, timeline and milestones, budgeting and cost estimation, risk management, quality assurance planning, data management planning, model development planning, evaluation metrics definition, and project plan finalization in its planning phase. *Figure 18.1* shows the time is reduced by transferring the knowledge of some components from similar ML-based SDLC in the same domain or task:

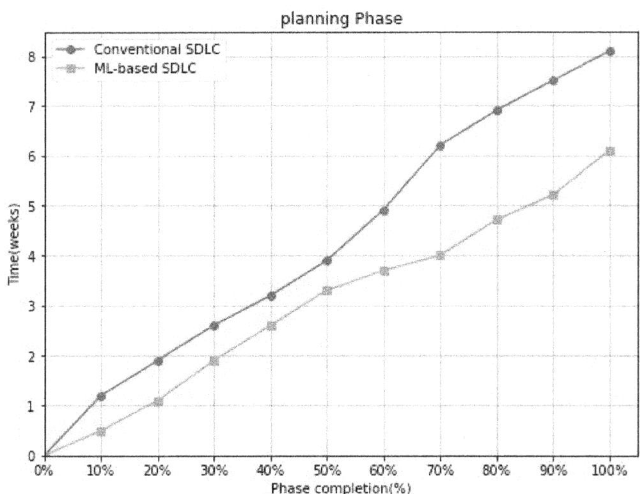

***Figure 18.1:** Comparative analysis of planning phase performance between SDLC and ML-SDLC*

- **Requirement analysis:**
  - **Predicting customer needs and analyzing historical data:** ML helps in predicting customer needs by analyzing past project data, user feedback, and

market trends. Using **natural language processing (NLP)**, ML can sift through customer feedback and identify patterns or frequent requests. These insights can then shape the project's requirements, ensuring that customer needs are met. For example, an e-commerce company might use ML to analyze historical purchasing behavior. The model identifies that customers often request faster payment processing. This insight leads to a feature request for a quicker, more efficient checkout process. The comparative analysis of requirement analysis phase performance between SDLC and ML-SDLC is shown in the *Figure 18.2:*

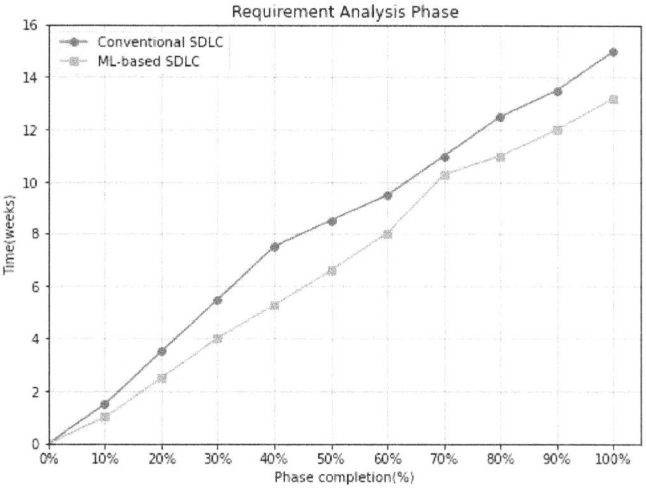

Figure 18.2: *Comparative analysis of requirement analysis phase performance between SDLC and ML-SDLC*

- **Tools and techniques for automating requirement gathering:** ML tools like chatbots can interact with clients to gather and clarify requirements. These bots can automatically categorize and prioritize requirements based on customer feedback. Other techniques include using ML algorithms to extract key requirements from large datasets of customer reviews or bug reports. For example, a chatbot could ask users questions about their desired software features. Based on their responses, the bot generates a prioritized list of features for developers to consider, speeding up the requirement-gathering process.

- **Design and architecture:**
  - **Optimizing software design and predicting performance bottlenecks:** ML can predict how certain software designs will perform under stress. By learning from historical data, ML models can suggest optimized designs that avoid known bottlenecks, such as inefficient memory use or slow processing in large systems. This helps teams design better architectures from the start. For example, a cloud-based software company uses ML to predict the performance of different architectures. By simulating high-traffic conditions, ML models

suggest design changes that prevent performance degradation, like adjusting server load balancing strategies.

- o **Predictive modeling for system architecture:** ML models can predict how architectural decisions will impact software scalability and performance. Using data from previous projects, predictive models can foresee challenges like scalability issues or integration failures, helping architects create more robust designs. For example, a predictive model analyzes previous software systems built for similar industries. It highlights potential scaling issues in the chosen architecture, suggesting adjustments to ensure the system can handle expected user growth. *Figure 18.3* presents the comparative analysis of the design phase performance between SDLC and ML-SDLC:

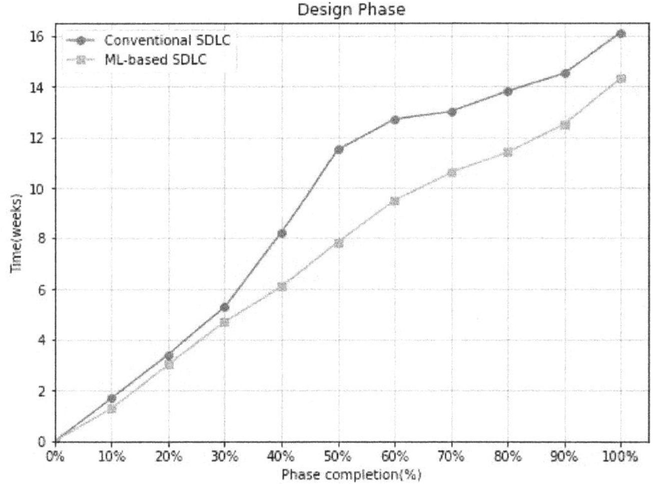

***Figure 18.3:** Comparative analysis of design phase performance between SDLC and ML-SDLC*

- **Implementation and coding:**
  - o **ML for code suggestion and auto-generation**: Tools like GitHub Copilot and Microsoft IntelliCode use ML to suggest code snippets as developers write. These models have been trained on vast amounts of code and can predict the next line or function a developer might need. This speeds up development by reducing the need for manual coding. For example, a developer working on a ML algorithm uses GitHub Copilot. As the developer begins typing, Copilot automatically suggests the next few lines of code to complete the function, saving time and reducing errors.

- **Enhancing code quality through ML-driven linting and static analysis:** ML-driven tools analyze code in real time, detecting issues like code smells, bugs, or inefficiencies. These tools provide real-time feedback, helping developers fix problems early in the coding phase. Static analysis powered by ML ensures that the code is cleaner and less prone to errors. For example, a static analysis tool powered by ML flags potential memory leaks in a developer's code. The developer can fix the issue before it becomes a significant problem during testing. *Figure 18.4* presents the comparative analysis of implementation/coding phase performance between SDLC and ML-SDLC:

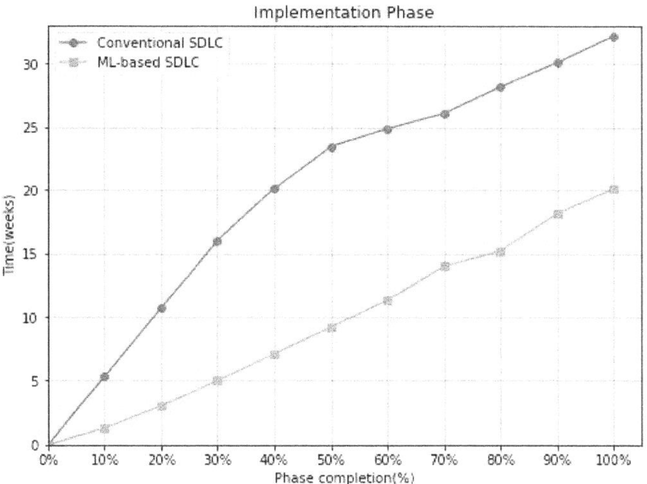

***Figure 18.4**: Comparative analysis of implementation/coding phase performance between SDLC and ML-SDLC*

- **Testing and quality assurance:**
  - **Predictive testing using ML to identify critical test cases**: ML models can analyze previous testing data to identify the most critical test cases that are likely to fail. This reduces the need for exhaustive testing and ensures that testing resources are focused on high-risk areas. For example, a software team uses an ML model to predict which test cases are most likely to find defects. The model prioritizes these test cases, helping the team focus on the most critical issues and speeding up the testing process. *Figure 18.5* presents the comparative analysis of testing phase performance between SDLC and ML-SDLC:

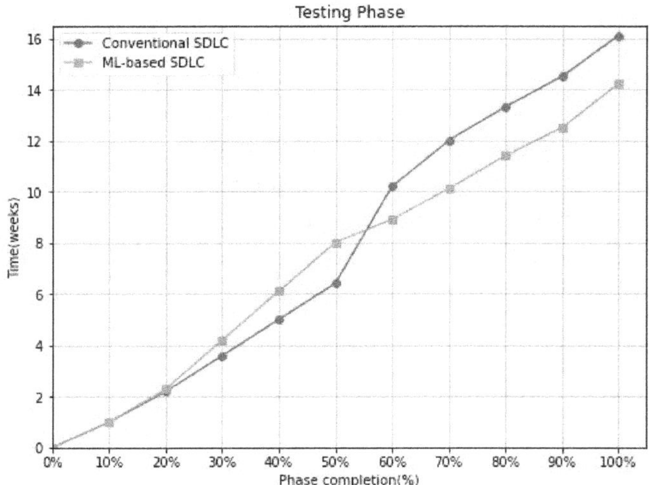

Figure 18.5: *Comparative analysis of testing phase performance between SDLC and ML-SDLC*

- **Automated testing and defect detection:** ML models can automate the testing process by generating test cases and running them automatically. ML can also detect defects in real-time by comparing new software builds against known patterns of bugs. This ensures higher accuracy in defect detection and faster bug resolution. For example, an automated testing tool powered by ML identifies a recurring bug in the login system of an app. The model recognizes the issue from previous patterns and flags it before the app is deployed to production.

- **Deployment:**
  - **Smart deployment strategies using ML**: ML can predict the best deployment strategies by analyzing traffic patterns and system usage data. It can adjust deployment plans in real-time, using predictive scaling to handle incoming traffic or rolling back faulty deployments automatically. For example, a video streaming platform uses ML to monitor system traffic during deployments. The ML model predicts a surge in traffic due to a new release and automatically scales up server resources to prevent downtime.
  - **DevOps tools powered by ML:** DevOps tools use ML to streamline the deployment process. These tools can predict deployment failures, optimize resource usage, and automate the rollback process when issues arise. Continuous integration and delivery pipelines can be made smarter with the help of ML. For example, an ML-powered DevOps tool detects a failure during deployment and triggers an automatic rollback. The system then identifies the root cause of the failure and suggests fixes to prevent it in future deployments.

- **Maintenance and monitoring:**
  - **Anomaly detection in production systems using ML:** ML models continuously monitor production systems for unusual patterns. These models can detect anomalies such as performance drops, security breaches, or unexpected user behavior. By catching these anomalies early, teams can prevent major system failures. For example, an e-commerce platform uses ML to monitor its payment system. The ML model detects unusual traffic patterns indicating a possible security breach and sends an alert to the development team, allowing them to respond before any data is compromised. The comparative analysis of maintenance phase performance between SDLC and ML-SDLC is shown in *Figure 18.6:*

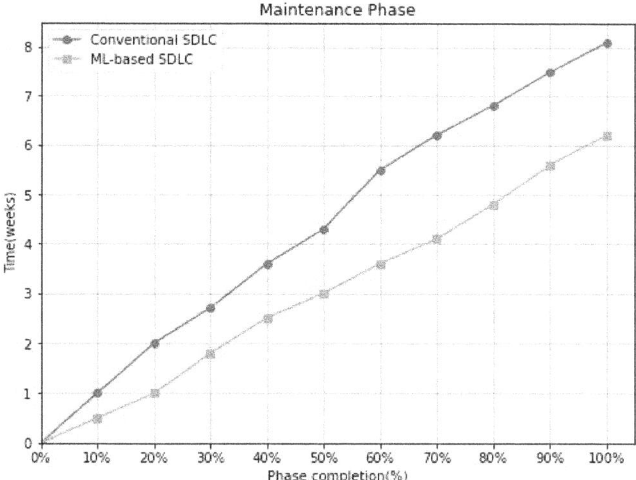

***Figure 18.6:** Comparative analysis of maintenance phase performance between SDLC and ML-SDLC*

  - **Predictive maintenance with ML**: ML can analyze historical system data to predict when maintenance will be required. This predictive maintenance prevents unexpected downtime by identifying issues before they escalate. ML models can also predict hardware failures based on sensor data, allowing for timely repairs. For example, a large-scale web hosting service uses ML to predict server failures. Based on temperature and usage data from the servers, the ML model alerts the team when a server is likely to fail, allowing them to replace it before it causes downtime.

Challenges of integrating ML in SDLC

Integrating ML into the SDLC offers numerous benefits, but it also comes with its own set of challenges. These challenges can arise from data handling, model understanding, scalability, security, and human factors. Let us explore these in detail.

Data collection and preparation challenges

In an ML-integrated SDLC model, data collection and preparation present significant challenges. ML systems rely heavily on large, high-quality datasets, but gathering accurate and relevant data can be difficult. Often, data comes from multiple sources and may be incomplete, inconsistent, or unstructured. This requires extensive preprocessing, such as cleaning, formatting, and normalizing the data, which can be time-consuming and complex. Additionally, ensuring data privacy and compliance with regulations like GDPR adds another layer of difficulty. Inaccurate or biased data can lead to flawed models, making it essential to carefully manage the data collection and preparation process to ensure the effectiveness of ML algorithms in the SDLC:

- **Data availability**: ML models rely heavily on data to learn and make accurate predictions. However, gathering the right amount and quality of data is often challenging. For instance, a project might not have enough historical data to train an ML model effectively. Lack of relevant data can result in poor model performance. For example, in a bug prediction system, if the historical data on bugs is incomplete or scattered across different systems, the ML model will struggle to predict future bugs accurately.
- **Data quality**: Even when data is available, it might not always be clean or consistent. Data often has missing values, incorrect entries, or outliers. Preparing this data for an ML model involves cleaning, filtering, and transforming it. This process can be time-consuming and prone to errors. For example, a team working on a recommendation system for e-commerce must ensure that customer data (example, purchase history) is free from duplicates or incorrect entries. If this step is not done properly, the ML model might recommend irrelevant products.
- **Data privacy and ethical concerns**: When using customer or user data, privacy becomes a significant concern. Collecting and using data without proper consent can lead to legal and ethical issues. Organizations must comply with data privacy regulations like **General Data Protection Regulation (GDPR)** to avoid legal penalties. For example, a healthcare company using ML to predict patient health outcomes must ensure that all patient data is anonymized and collected in compliance with data privacy laws.

Model interpretability and trust issues

In an ML-integrated SDLC model, ensuring model interpretability and addressing trust issues is critical. ML models, particularly complex ones like deep learning, often operate as "black boxes," making it difficult for developers and stakeholders to understand how decisions are made. This lack of transparency can lead to trust issues, especially when the models are used in high-stakes applications like healthcare, finance, or legal systems:

- **Black-box nature of ML models**: Many ML models, especially complex ones like deep neural networks, are often considered **black-box** models. This means their internal workings are difficult to understand, even for experts. This lack of transparency can cause trust issues, especially in critical software where human developers need to understand how decisions are made. For example, in an autonomous driving system, if an ML model suggests a sudden change in the driving route, developers may struggle to explain why the model made that decision, leading to hesitation in deploying such models in real-world applications.

- **Bias in ML models**: ML models can sometimes inherit biases from the data they are trained on. If the training data is biased, the model's predictions will reflect that bias, leading to unfair or inaccurate outcomes. This is particularly critical in applications like hiring or loan approval systems. For example: If an ML model used to screen job applicants is trained on biased data (example, historical hiring patterns that favor a certain demographic), it may continue to exhibit this bias, leading to unfair hiring practices.
- **Explainability tools:** Developers are working on tools and techniques to make ML models more interpretable. Explainability tools, like **Local Interpretable Model-agnostic Explanations (LIME)**, help developers understand why a model made a specific decision. However, these tools are still evolving and may not always provide complete transparency. For example, using an explainability tool, a company can better understand why an ML model recommended a certain software design change, helping developers trust the model's suggestions.

Scalability and computational resource challenges

In an ML-integrated SDLC model, scalability and computational resource challenges arise due to the high demand for processing large datasets and running complex algorithms. This strain is particularly felt during testing and deployment, requiring powerful infrastructure like cloud services or computing clusters. Efficiently scaling ML models while managing resource demands is crucial to ensure system performance and cost-effectiveness as projects grow:

- **Scalability of ML models:** As software systems grow, ML models must scale to handle increasing data volumes and complexity. However, many ML models struggle with scalability, especially when they rely on large datasets or complex algorithms. This can slow down the entire SDLC process. For example, a company using ML to monitor website traffic might find that as the website grows in popularity, the ML model takes longer to process data, causing delays in performance monitoring.
- **High computational resource demand:** Training and deploying ML models, especially deep learning models, require significant computational resources. High-end servers, GPUs, and cloud infrastructure are often needed. This can be costly and may not be feasible for smaller companies with limited resources. For example, a small startup using ML to automate its software testing finds that training its model requires expensive cloud services, adding to their operational costs.

- **Optimization techniques:** To address scalability and resource issues, developers use optimization techniques like model pruning (removing unnecessary parts of a model) or using lightweight ML models designed for faster computation. However, these techniques may reduce model accuracy. Example: A company opts to prune its ML model used in defect detection, reducing computational costs but also slightly lowering the accuracy of the model.

Security concerns in ML enhanced software systems

The integration of ML into the SDLC introduces unique security concerns that need to be addressed at each stage. From data collection and preprocessing to model training and deployment, ensuring the integrity and privacy of sensitive information is critical. Threats such as adversarial attacks, model inversion, and data poisoning can compromise the reliability of ML models, making robust security measures essential. Additionally, continuous monitoring and vulnerability assessments are required to safeguard against evolving threats in production environment:

- **Data security:** ML models are often trained on sensitive data, making data security a top concern. If the training data or model itself is compromised, it can lead to security breaches. Attackers can also use techniques like model inversion to extract sensitive information from the model. For example, an attacker could use model inversion techniques to reconstruct user data from an ML model trained on private user information, potentially leading to a data breach.
- **Adversarial attacks:** ML models are vulnerable to adversarial attacks, where attackers manipulate the input data to fool the model into making incorrect predictions. These attacks can be dangerous, especially in security-critical applications like fraud detection or autonomous vehicles. For example, a self-driving car's ML system could be tricked into misinterpreting a stop sign by adding small, imperceptible changes to the image, potentially causing a dangerous situation.
- **Model poisoning:** In some cases, attackers can manipulate the training data itself, leading to model poisoning. This corrupts the model's learning process, making it unreliable. For example, in a financial software system, an attacker could introduce false data into the model's training set, causing it to make incorrect financial predictions, and harming the company's operations.

Human factors

In an ML-integrated SDLC, human factors like skill gaps and change management are crucial for development teams' success. The adoption of ML models requires teams to acquire new skills in data science and ML frameworks, often leading to skill gaps that necessitate ongoing learning. Change management is equally important, as integrating ML into existing workflows can cause resistance. Effective strategies, including clear communication and training, help teams adapt to these changes, ensuring smooth collaboration and successful project outcomes:

- **Skills gap in development teams**: Integrating ML into the SDLC requires specific skills that traditional software developers may not have. This skills gap can slow down the process and lead to inefficient ML implementation. Developers need to learn new tools, frameworks, and languages specific to ML. For example, a team of software developers with expertise in traditional programming languages like Java and Python may struggle to implement ML algorithms, leading to delays in the development process.
- **Change management:** The integration of ML into the SDLC often requires a shift in how teams work. Traditional development workflows may need to adapt to include data scientists and ML engineers. Resistance to this change can cause friction within teams, slowing down the adoption of ML. For example, a company introducing ML-based testing tools faces resistance from its manual testers, who are unfamiliar with the new tools and skeptical about how it will affect their roles.
- **Collaboration between developers and data scientists**: Successful integration of ML in SDLC requires collaboration between software developers and data scientists. These two groups often have different workflows and goals, which can lead to communication issues. Establishing clear lines of collaboration is essential to make the process smooth. For example, in an ML-driven software project, developers and data scientists struggle to coordinate on model deployment. Developers need to understand how the model works, while data scientists need insights into the system architecture, causing delays without proper collaboration.

Best practices for ML integration in SDLC

Integrating ML into the SDLC can transform how software is designed, developed, and deployed. However, to ensure that ML delivers its full potential, certain best practices should be followed. These practices focus on model selection, data management, collaboration, and the use of appropriate tools. Let us explore these best practices in detail.

Selecting the right ML model for different SDLC phases

Selecting the right ML model for each SDLC phase involves matching model capabilities to specific needs. In the requirements phase, data analysis models help define goals, while design benefits from simulation or optimization models. For implementation, supervised models automate tasks, and unsupervised models aid in feature extraction. Testing uses anomaly detection models, and deployment benefits from real-time decision-making models, ensuring smooth ML integration throughout the SDLC:

- **Understanding the problem:** The first step in selecting the right ML model is to understand the problem you are trying to solve. Each phase of the SDLC may have different requirements. For example, in the testing phase, you might need a classification model to predict defects, while during design, a regression model could help predict performance bottlenecks. For example, during requirement analysis, a company might use a clustering algorithm to group similar customer feedback, helping prioritize new features. In the coding phase, they could opt for a code-suggestion model, like GitHub Copilot, which uses language models to assist developers.
- **Matching models to phases**:
  - **Requirement analysis**: Use unsupervised learning models (For example, clustering) to identify trends in customer needs.
  - **Design and architecture:** Regression models can predict the impact of design choices on system performance.
  - **Testing and quality assurance:** Classification models are ideal for predicting defects or determining high-risk test cases.
  - **Maintenance and monitoring**: Anomaly detection models help monitor production systems and detect unusual patterns.

  For example, for retail software, the team chooses a supervised learning model for the testing phase to predict where bugs are likely to occur based on historical bug data.
- **Consider complexity and resource requirements:** Simpler models, like decision trees, may be more appropriate for early stages, while deep learning models may offer better performance but require more computational power, especially during maintenance and deployment. For example, a startup with limited resources selects a decision tree model for requirement analysis, which provides enough accuracy without overwhelming its systems.

Effective data management strategies for ML applications

Effective data management strategies for ML applications involve several key practices. First, data collection should focus on high-quality, relevant, and diverse datasets to ensure robust model training. Data preprocessing, including cleaning, normalization, and feature selection, helps improve model accuracy. Proper data labeling is essential for supervised learning tasks. Storing data in a structured and scalable manner, using tools like databases or data lakes, ensures easy access and management. Implementing data security and privacy measures protects sensitive information, while continuous monitoring and updating of datasets are crucial for maintaining model performance over time. Efficient data management ultimately supports the development of reliable and effective ML applications:

- **Data collection and preparation:** Quality data is the foundation of any ML model. Ensuring you collect accurate, clean, and relevant data is critical. Establishing pipelines for data collection, cleaning, and labeling saves time and increases model effectiveness. For example, a company developing a recommendation system gathers user interaction data (for example, clicks and searches), cleans the dataset to remove duplicates, and ensures proper labeling to train the model effectively.
- **Data versioning**: Just like versioning is essential in software development, it is crucial to version datasets. This ensures that you can trace which version of data was used to train a model, making it easier to debug and refine models over time. For example, a development team working on an ML model for fraud detection keeps versions of their training data so that they can roll back to previous datasets if new data leads to a drop in performance.
- **Handling data bias**: Ensuring your data is balanced and representative is essential to prevent biased models. Bias in data can lead to unfair outcomes and reduce the overall trust in the software system. For example, in a hiring system, the team makes sure their data is balanced across gender and ethnicity to avoid biased hiring recommendations by the ML model.

Model training, validation, and deployment pipelines

Model training, validation, and deployment pipelines streamline ML development. The training pipeline involves data preprocessing and model training. Validation tunes hyperparameters and ensures generalizability using separate datasets. The deployment pipeline focuses on moving the validated model to production for real-time predictions, with continuous monitoring and updates to maintain accuracy. These pipelines ensure smooth model development and optimization:

- **Automating model pipelines**: Creating automated pipelines for model training, validation, and deployment helps reduce manual effort and errors. A typical pipeline involves feeding in the data, training the model, validating it with test data, and then deploying it into production. For example, a software company sets up an automated pipeline using MLflow to continuously train and validate models during the development phase. This ensures that the models are always updated and tested with the latest data.
- **Validation and testing of ML models**: It is important to validate ML models before deploying them. Cross-validation techniques, such as k-fold validation, are commonly used to assess how well a model will perform on unseen data. This helps avoid overfitting and ensures that the model generalizes well. For example, a fraud detection team uses k-fold validation to ensure their model does not just

work well on their training data but also performs accurately on new, unseen transactions.

- **Continuous monitoring and updating models**: After deployment, ML models must be continuously monitored. If the real-world data changes, the model might become less accurate over time. Regular retraining and updating of the model are necessary to maintain its performance. For example, an e-commerce platform continuously monitors its recommendation engine's performance. If the recommendation accuracy drops due to changing user behavior, the team retrains the model using more recent data.

Cross functional collaboration

Cross-functional collaboration between data scientists and software developers is essential for successful ML project execution. Data scientists bring expertise in model building, data analysis, and algorithm development, while software developers focus on integrating models into scalable, efficient applications. Effective collaboration ensures that data scientists' models are optimized for deployment, and developers understand the technical requirements for model integration. Regular communication, shared goals, and collaborative tools foster innovation, streamline workflows, and address challenges, ultimately leading to robust, production-ready ML systems:

- **Bridging the gap between data science and development**: ML integration into SDLC often requires close collaboration between software developers and data scientists. Developers bring expertise in coding and system architecture, while data scientists focus on the model. These teams must work together to ensure that the model fits into the software system. For example, in a project to integrate ML-driven customer support chatbots, developers handle the chatbot architecture, while data scientists develop the model to understand and respond to user queries. Effective communication between these teams ensures smooth integration.
- **Clear communication of goals and expectations:** Both teams must have a shared understanding of the project goals. Data scientists should explain how the model works, while developers must clarify how the model will be used in the overall system. This ensures that the ML model is both accurate and practical for the software system. For example, a data science team developing a predictive maintenance model works closely with the development team to ensure the model's predictions can be easily integrated into the software's dashboard for real-time alerts.
- **Shared tools and platforms**: Using shared tools, such as ML platforms or version control systems, helps streamline collaboration. Platforms like MLflow allow both data scientists and developers to track model development and changes. For example, a team uses MLflow to keep track of all versions of the ML models being tested and deployed, allowing both developers and data scientists to collaborate more effectively on the project.

Tools and platforms to streamline ML integration

Tools and platforms that streamline ML integration are essential for efficient deployment and scaling. They automate key stages of the ML lifecycle, from data preprocessing to model deployment. Cloud services like Google AI Platform and AWS SageMaker, along with frameworks such as TensorFlow, PyTorch, and tools like MLflow and Kubeflow, help enhance collaboration, improve model performance, and ensure scalability in production environments:

- **TensorFlow**: TensorFlow is one of the most popular ML platforms, offering a comprehensive suite of tools for developing, training, and deploying ML models. It supports both deep learning and traditional ML, making it versatile for different phases of SDLC. For example, a software team uses TensorFlow to develop a facial recognition feature in their application, leveraging its ability to handle image data and train complex models.
- **MLflow**: MLflow simplifies the management of ML experiments, allowing teams to track models, compare results, and deploy them easily. It integrates well with existing DevOps practices, making it easier to bring ML models into production. For example, an MLflow setup helps a development team track the performance of various models they are testing for defect prediction, making it easy to identify which model works best.
- **Azure Machine Learning and AWS SageMaker:** Cloud platforms like Azure ML and AWS SageMaker offer pre-built environments for developing, training, and deploying ML models. These platforms allow for scalability and integrate well with cloud infrastructure, making them ideal for production-level ML applications. For example, a team using AWS SageMaker trains and deploys a real-time recommendation engine for an online marketplace, leveraging its scalable cloud infrastructure.
- **Scikit-learn**: For simpler applications, Scikit-learn is an easy-to-use tool for traditional ML algorithms like classification, regression, and clustering. It is ideal for smaller projects or quick iterations during the early SDLC phases. For example, a company developing an internal tool for automatic email categorization uses Scikit-learn to quickly build a prototype, as it does not require heavy computational resources.

Future trends and emerging technologies

The landscape of software engineering is rapidly evolving, especially with the integration of ML in the SDLC. As technology advances, new trends and tools are emerging that will further transform how software is developed, deployed, and maintained. Here, we explore the future trends in ML and software engineering, including **Machine learning Operations (MLOps)**, AI-driven SDLC, and upcoming technologies.

Evolving role of ML in software engineering and SDLC

The evolving role of ML in software engineering and the SDLC is transforming development practices. ML automates tasks like bug detection, code generation, and performance optimization, improving efficiency and accuracy. It also enhances decision-making, predicts system behavior, and enables continuous learning, leading to smarter, more efficient software development:

- **Increased automation**: ML is set to play a critical role in automating various tasks within the SDLC. As ML algorithms become more sophisticated, they will be able to handle repetitive tasks such as code reviews, bug detection, and even feature suggestions. For example, a software development team might implement an ML model that automatically reviews code for potential bugs, suggesting corrections based on historical data from previous projects. This saves time and reduces the burden on developers.
- **Enhanced decision-making**: ML will increasingly provide insights that enhance decision-making throughout the SDLC. By analyzing historical project data, ML can predict project risks, suggest optimal resource allocations, and even recommend the best design patterns for specific projects. For example, in a large-scale application development, an ML model analyzes past projects and predicts the likelihood of feature success. This data helps project managers decide which features to prioritize.
- **Personalized development experiences**: Future tools will leverage ML to create personalized experiences for developers. By learning from individual coding patterns, preferences, and strengths, ML can suggest relevant resources, tutorials, and tools tailored to each developer's unique style. For example, a developer using an **integrated development environment (IDE)** could receive personalized suggestions for code snippets and libraries based on their past projects and coding habits.

Rise of MLOps and its integration with DevOps

MLOps is the emerging practice of integrating ML workflows with DevOps principles to streamline the deployment, monitoring, and management of ML models. By combining DevOps' focus on automation, continuous integration, and collaboration with ML's need for data management, mode:

The training, and evaluation, MLOps ensures faster, more reliable model deployment. This integration helps organizations scale their ML efforts, maintain model performance over time, and bridge the gap between data science and operations teams for seamless production environments.

- **Streamlining ML deployment**: MLOps is a set of practices that combines ML and DevOps. It aims to streamline the deployment and management of ML models in production environments. This integration ensures that models are updated regularly and perform optimally. For example, a company implementing MLOps might create a **continuous integration or continuous deployment (CI or CD)** pipeline for ML models. This allows for frequent updates and testing, ensuring that the model adapts to new data over time.
- **Improved collaboration:** MLOps fosters collaboration between data scientists and DevOps engineers. This collaboration helps bridge the gap between model development and deployment, allowing teams to work together more effectively. For example, a data scientist and a DevOps engineer collaborate on a project to create a real-time fraud detection system. The MLOps practices ensure that the model is regularly monitored and updated, allowing for better fraud detection over time.
- **Monitoring and maintenance**: With MLOps, ongoing monitoring of ML models becomes a standard practice. This includes tracking model performance, data drift, and anomalies in predictions. Regular maintenance helps prevent model degradation and ensures high-quality outcomes. For example, an e-commerce company uses MLOps to monitor their recommendation engine. If the engine's accuracy drops, the team can quickly retrain the model with updated data to restore performance.

AI driven SDLC

An AI-driven SDLC evolves from automating tasks like code generation and testing to enabling autonomous development, where AI optimizes workflows and adapts to changing requirements with minimal human input. This progression leads to faster, more accurate development cycles, continuous learning, and intelligent systems that improve over time, transforming the SDLC and reducing manual intervention:

- **Automation of complex tasks**: AI will enable the automation of increasingly complex tasks within the SDLC. This goes beyond basic code generation to include automated testing, debugging, and even project management. For example, an AI-driven system could automate the entire testing process, running various test scenarios based on user behavior patterns and reporting results in real-time. This not only speeds up development but also enhances the quality of the software.
- **Autonomous development:** In the future, we may see a shift towards fully autonomous development environments. AI could take over aspects of software development, allowing it to create applications with minimal human intervention. For example, imagine a scenario where a company inputs high-level requirements into an AI system. The AI then generates a complete application, from design to deployment, with minimal human oversight, significantly reducing development time.

- **Continuous learning**: AI-driven systems will continuously learn from user interactions and feedback. This capability allows the software to evolve and improve over time, adapting to changing user needs without requiring manual updates. For example, a social media platform might utilize AI to analyze user engagement patterns. Based on this data, the platform adjusts its features and interface automatically, enhancing user experience.

New tools for ML-SDLC

Upcoming technologies like AutoML, GitHub Copilot, and MLOps platforms (for example, Kubeflow, MLflow) are set to revolutionize the SDLC. AI-driven tools for code generation, testing, and review improve efficiency and accuracy. Predictive analytics also enable data-driven decisions by forecasting project timelines and risks, streamlining software development, and model management:

- **No-code and low-code platforms:** No-code and low-code development platforms are gaining popularity. These platforms allow users with little to no coding experience to create applications. By integrating ML into these platforms, users can build intelligent applications quickly and efficiently. For example, a small business owner could use a no-code platform with built-in ML features to create a **customer relationship management (CRM)** system, leveraging ML for automated customer segmentation and communication.
- **Federated learning**: Federated learning is an emerging technology that enables ML models to be trained across decentralized devices while keeping data localized. This approach enhances privacy and security while allowing for collaborative model improvement. For example, in healthcare, hospitals can collaboratively train a model to predict patient outcomes without sharing sensitive patient data, ensuring compliance with privacy regulations.
- **AI-powered code review tools**: Future code review tools will leverage AI to analyze code quality, security vulnerabilities, and adherence to coding standards. These tools will provide real-time feedback to developers, enhancing code quality. For example, a team using an AI-powered code review tool might receive instant alerts about potential security issues or code smells, allowing them to address problems before they reach production.
- **Enhanced DevSecOps**: As security becomes a top priority, integrating security practices into the development process through ML will become standard. AI will help identify security vulnerabilities early in the development cycle. For example, an AI system scans code for security vulnerabilities as developers write it, alerting them immediately. This proactive approach significantly reduces the risk of security breaches.

Conclusion

The integration of ML into the SDLC marks a transformative shift in how software is developed, tested, and maintained. This chapter explored key insights on ML's role in enhancing various phases of the SDLC, from requirement analysis to maintenance. We discussed how ML techniques such as supervised and unsupervised learning can automate processes, improve code quality, and drive predictive testing. Practical examples, like GitHub Copilot for code generation, illustrated ML's potential to streamline software development. Challenges such as data preparation and model interpretability were also addressed, along with best practices like effective data management and fostering collaboration between data scientists and developers. The rise of AI-driven SDLC and MLOps further signals a shift toward more automated and efficient development processes.

ML's impact on software engineering is profound, enabling teams to automate repetitive tasks, make data-driven decisions, and improve collaboration. ML-driven tools help predict and prevent issues before they occur, reducing downtime and enhancing user satisfaction. Automated testing powered by ML identifies critical test cases early, improving software quality while reducing time and costs. As ML technologies evolve, it is crucial for software engineers to embrace continuous learning. Staying updated with advancements in ML will enable engineers to effectively leverage new tools and collaborate better with data scientists, fostering more innovative and integrated solutions.

In the next chapter, we will explore the integration of **large language models (LLMs)** with software engineering. This chapter will demonstrate how LLMs, such as those used in AI, can enhance various stages of software development, from code generation to documentation and bug detection. You will learn about the potential benefits and challenges of using LLMs in automating tasks, improving code quality, and streamlining development processes, ultimately leading to more efficient and intelligent software engineering practices.

Exercises

To solidify your understanding of the concepts covered in this chapter, try the following exercises.

Multiple choice questions

1. **Which of the following best describes the role of machine learning in the SDLC?**
    a. It solely focuses on coding practices.
    b. It helps automate various tasks and improves decision-making.
    c. It eliminates the need for human developers.
    d. It is only applicable in testing phases.

2. **What type of machine learning algorithm is primarily used for predicting outcomes based on labeled historical data?**
   a. Unsupervised learning
   b. Reinforcement learning
   c. Supervised learning
   d. Semi-supervised learning
3. **What is MLOps?**
   a. A programming language for machine learning.
   b. A set of practices that integrates ML and DevOps.
   c. A type of machine learning model.
   d. A software development methodology.
4. **Which of the following tools can enhance code quality through machine learning?**
   a. Microsoft Word
   b. GitHub Copilot
   c. Notepad
   d. Photoshop
5. **What is the key challenge of integrating machine learning into the SDLC?**
   a. Excessive coding required.
   b. Difficulty in collecting and preparing data.
   c. Limited communication between teams.
   d. Decreased software performance.

Short answer questions

1. Explain how machine learning can enhance requirement analysis in the SDLC. Provide an example.
2. Discuss the importance of collaboration between data scientists and software developers in the context of MLOps.
3. What are the benefits of using predictive testing in the software development process?
4. Describe two best practices for selecting the right machine learning model for different phases of the SDLC.
5. Identify and explain a future trend in software engineering related to the integration of machine learning.

Essay questions

1. Analyze the transformative impact of machine learning on software engineering practices. Discuss how it affects various phases of the SDLC.
2. Evaluate the challenges faced during the integration of machine learning in the SDLC. Discuss potential solutions to these challenges.
3. Discuss the importance of continuous learning in machine learning technologies for software engineers. How can engineers stay updated with the latest trends?
4. Consider the future of the SDLC with machine learning. What opportunities and challenges do you foresee in the next five years?
5. Reflect on the role of AI-driven systems in automating complex tasks within the SDLC. Provide examples of how these systems could enhance software development processes.

Multiple choice answers

1. b
2. c
3. b
4. b
5. b

Join our book's Discord space

Join the book's Discord Workspace for Latest updates, Offers, Tech happenings around the world, New Release and Sessions with the Authors:

https://discord.bpbonline.com

CHAPTER 19
Unlocking the LLM for SDLC Model

Introduction

Incorporating **large language models (LLMs)** into the **software development life cycle (SDLC)** represents a transformative approach to modern software engineering. LLMs, powered by advanced artificial intelligence, bring significant potential in automating various stages of the SDLC, including requirements gathering, code generation, testing, and maintenance. By understanding natural language inputs, these models can streamline processes, improve accuracy, and reduce the manual effort required for coding and documentation. As software systems become more complex, integrating LLMs in SDLC models offers a path to enhanced efficiency, better decision-making, and faster development cycles.

Structure

In this chapter, we will learn the following:

- Introduction to LLMs in SDCL
- Understanding LLM
- Ethics and limitations of LLMs in development
- LLMs integration across different SDCL models

- Integration of LLM with SDLC stages
- Challenges and future of LLMs in SDLC

Objectives

The objective of this chapter is to explore the integration of LLMs within the SDLC and analyze their impact on various phases of software development. It aims to provide a comprehensive understanding of how LLMs can automate tasks such as code generation, bug detection, and documentation, enhancing overall efficiency and productivity. Additionally, the chapter will discuss the benefits, challenges, and best practices for implementing LLMs in SDLC, offering insights into how this emerging technology can shape the future of software engineering.

Introduction to LLMs in SDLC

LLMs are AI models trained on vast amounts of text data. They can understand, generate, and refine human language with surprising accuracy. Common examples include models like GPT-4 and **Bidirectional Encoder Representations from Transformers (BERT)**. These models analyze patterns in language, allowing them to perform tasks that used to require direct human input. In software engineering, LLMs have become incredibly useful. They assist in writing, debugging, and even planning software. For example, a developer can ask an LLM to **generate a login code in Python**. The model then provides a code snippet, saving the developer time and reducing errors. By automating tasks like LLMs helps engineers focus on more complex issues, boosting productivity.

Relevance of LLMs to various stages in the SDLC process

LLMs are transforming each stage of the SDLC, from planning to maintenance. Following is a breakdown:

- **Planning and requirements gathering**: LLMs can help clarify project requirements by analyzing user feedback and predicting needed features. For example, suppose a team is building an e-commerce website. They can ask an LLM to **list essential features for an e-commerce platform.** The model might suggest a product catalog, shopping cart, checkout process, and customer review are the key features for the team to consider.
- **Design**: LLMs assist in creating design documents, diagrams, and even UI suggestions. For example, for a project's design phase, developers can ask the model and **generate a high-level design for a to-do app**. The LLM can outline an architecture with a user database, task manager, and notification system.

- **Implementation**: LLMs can write code snippets, suggest optimizations, and refactor code to improve efficiency. Example: A developer working on a JavaScript project might ask the LLM to **convert a function from synchronous to asynchronous**. The model provides a refactored function, enhancing performance without extra manual effort.
- **Testing**: LLMs support automated test generation, helping to catch bugs early. For example, for a login function, an LLM can generate test cases to check if the function correctly validates usernames and passwords.
- **Deployment**: LLMs streamline documentation and configuration, making the deployment process smoother. For example, during deployment, a team can ask, **what are common environment variables needed for deploying a Node.js app?** The model might suggest variables like PORT, DATABASE_URL, and JWT_SECRET.
- **Maintenance**: LLMs assist with bug fixing, log analysis, and suggesting updates to existing code. For example, when an error arises in production, an LLM can help diagnose the issue by analyzing log files and proposing potential fixes.

Understanding large language models

LLMs are advanced AI systems designed to understand and generate human-like text by processing vast amounts of data. Models like GPT and BERT excel at tasks such as content generation, translation, and question answering. By capturing linguistic patterns, LLMs produce coherent and meaningful text, making them valuable tools in various industries. This chapter explores their architecture, capabilities, and real-world applications, highlighting their growing impact on AI-driven communication.

Basics of large language models

LLMs are advanced AI models designed to understand and generate human-like language. They are **large** due to the vast number of parameters they contain millions or even billions of adjustable factors that the model fine-tunes during training to capture the structure and nuances of language. The following parameters allow LLMs to analyze and generate text based on complex patterns in their training data:

- **Evolution of LLMs:** Early language models, like rule-based chatbots, were limited in scope and could only complete specific tasks with predefined inputs. As AI research progressed, LLMs like OpenAI's GPT series and Google's BERT evolved, capable of more complex language tasks like summarizing articles, translating languages, or even writing coherent essays. The latest models, such as GPT-4, have advanced to the point where they can carry on conversations, write entire reports, and even assist with programming tasks.
- **Underlying principle:** LLMs learn through exposure to vast datasets comprising books, websites, scientific articles, and other textual sources. By analyzing these

data sources, the model recognizes patterns, contexts, and relationships between words and sentences. This understanding allows LLMs to make highly accurate predictions on how to complete or respond to text inputs. For example, if given the prompt `What is the impact of renewable energy on climate change?`, an LLM does not just look at the words individually. Instead, it leverages its understanding of relationships between concepts like **renewable energy** and **climate change** to generate a relevant, coherent answer.

Technical foundations

The technical foundation of LLMs is built on transformer-based architectures, which enable efficient processing of vast amounts of textual data. Transformers, introduced in the paper *Attention is All You Need*, rely on self-attention mechanisms that allow models to focus on different parts of a sentence when generating or interpreting text. This architecture supports parallel processing, making it highly scalable for large datasets. LLMs are typically pre-trained on extensive corpora using unsupervised learning, capturing linguistic structures, context, and relationships between words. After pre-training, these models are fine-tuned for specific tasks such as translation, summarization, or code generation. The combination of deep neural networks, self-attention, and vast training datasets allows LLMs to achieve state-of-the-art performance in natural language understanding and generation tasks.

A key component of LLMs lies in the intricate interplay between neural networks, training data, and model architecture. Neural networks, specifically deep learning models, form the backbone of LLMs, enabling them to learn complex patterns in language. The quality and size of the training data are crucial, as they determine the model's ability to generalize and understand diverse linguistic contexts. Additionally, the model architecture, typically based on transformers, dictates how efficiently the model processes and generates text. This synergy of neural networks, data, and architecture drives the exceptional capabilities of LLMs in natural language tasks:

- **Neural networks**: LLMs rely on a specialized form of neural networks, a type of AI that mimics the structure of the human brain. These networks consist of layers of artificial **neurons** that process input data in a step-by-step manner. Each layer of neurons extracts specific features or patterns from the data, gradually building a comprehensive understanding of the input. For example, when processing a question like, `What are the effects of pollution on health?`, the neural network's layers capture patterns related to **pollution** and **health effects**. The model analyzes these patterns to produce a meaningful response, drawing from its vast learned knowledge of environmental science and healthcare topics.
- **Training data**: The training data for LLMs consists of large volumes of text from diverse sources, including books, websites, news articles, and other publicly available information. This broad base of information helps the model learn various topics and language styles, which improves its versatility and adaptability. For example, if an LLM is trained on technical and conversational language, it

can switch easily between explaining medical procedures in a clinical tone and answering casual questions about everyday health concerns.

- **Model architecture**: Most LLMs use the transformer architecture, a powerful neural network design that introduces **attention mechanisms**. Attention allows the model to weigh the importance of each word in a sentence based on context, enabling it to focus on the most relevant information. For example, for the question, **`How does exercise improve mental health?`**, the model focuses on terms like **exercise** and **mental health**, adjusting its **attention** to emphasize these keywords. This helps it generate an accurate answer on how physical activity affects psychological well-being. It involves the ability to cope with stress, maintain healthy relationships, and achieve personal growth. *Figure 19.1* shows the LLM-SDLC architecture:

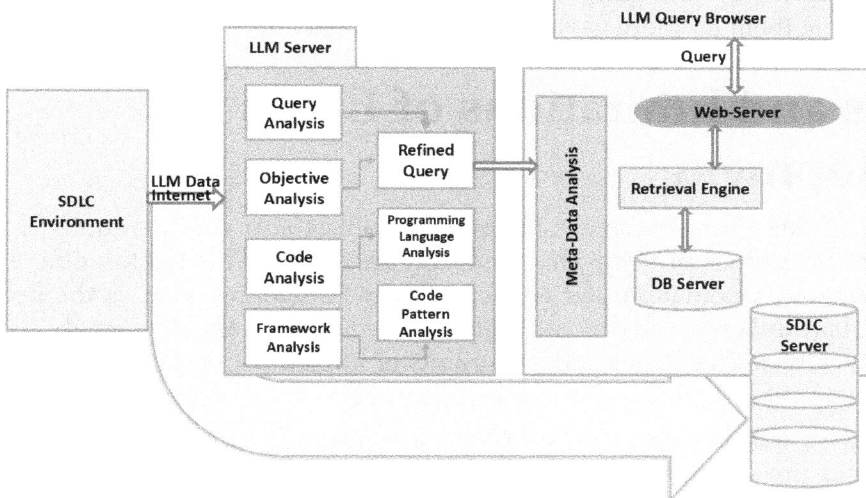

***Figure 19.1:** LLM-SDLC architecture*

Comparison with traditional models

LLM-integrated SDLC leverages the power of large-scale, data-driven models to automate tasks like code generation, testing, and documentation, offering higher efficiency and adaptability compared to traditional rule-based models. In contrast, rule-based models rely on predefined logic and small-scale models are limited by their narrow scope, making them less flexible and capable of handling complex, dynamic tasks in modern software development:

- **Rule based models**: Traditional rule-based models follow strict sets of rules or scripts and perform tasks based on predefined input patterns. They lack flexibility and struggle with unexpected variations in language or phrasing. For example, a rule-based chatbot may respond correctly to **`Hello, I need help`**, but it might fail if the user rephrases it to **`Hey, could you assist me with something?`**

Without an exact match to its programmed phrases, the rule-based system may not respond as intended. In contrast, an LLM can interpret various ways of asking for help due to its learned language understanding.

- **Small-scale models**: Small models are designed for focused, specific tasks, like spam detection or sentiment analysis. They generally have fewer parameters and lack the depth and flexibility of LLMs, so they do not possess the same level of comprehension or generation capability. For example, a small model trained for spam detection could classify an email as spam or not, but it would be unable to answer a complex question like, **`What is the history of artificial intelligence?`** Unlike an LLM, it lacks the comprehensive training and versatility needed to generate detailed responses. LLMs offer flexibility by adapting to various inputs and generating diverse outputs across different language styles, making them far more versatile than traditional models.

Ethics and limitations of LLMs in development

The use of LLMs in development raises important ethical considerations, particularly around issues of data privacy, bias, and accountability. While LLMs offer significant advancements in automation and efficiency, their limitations, such as the potential for generating harmful or biased content, highlight the need for careful oversight. This section explores the ethical challenges and constraints of implementing LLMs, emphasizing the importance of responsible usage and transparent development practices:

- **Bias in training data:** Since LLMs learn from real-world data, they inherit any biases present in their training sets. This means that if the input data is biased, the model's responses may reflect these biases, which could lead to unintended ethical issues. For example, if an LLM trained on social media posts learns biased viewpoints, it may generate biased responses. This can be problematic in applications requiring fairness and inclusion, such as hiring or education-related tools.
- **Data privacy**: Data privacy is a significant concern because LLMs may inadvertently generate outputs based on sensitive information. Developers must carefully select and anonymize training data to avoid privacy issues. For example, if an LLM is trained on healthcare data, there is a risk it might include private details unintentionally when generating responses, breaching confidentiality. Strict guidelines and anonymization processes are necessary to protect sensitive information.
- **Over-reliance and automation risks:** Relying too heavily on LLMs, especially for critical areas like legal advice or medical information, can lead to risky automation. Human oversight is essential to validate the model's outputs, as errors or misinterpretations could have serious consequences. For example, if an LLM gives

medical advice based on incomplete information, a patient might misunderstand or misuse the advice. This is why LLM-generated content in sensitive domains must be carefully monitored and verified.

- **Environmental impact**: Training LLMs requires extensive computing power, which consumes substantial energy and contributes to carbon emissions. As these models grow, so does their environmental footprint. AI companies are exploring more efficient models and green computing practices to mitigate these impacts. The ethical considerations and limitations associated with LLMs are crucial for responsible use in development. Developers need to be aware of the potential risks and implement strategies to address them, ensuring that these powerful tools are used responsibly and ethically.

LLMs integration across different SDLC models

The integration of LLMs across various SDLC models has the potential to transform the development process. These models streamline workflows, automate repetitive tasks, improve productivity, and help developers focus on more complex issues. As each SDLC model follows its unique structure and methodology, LLMs can adapt to each, providing significant benefits tailored to the needs of different development stages. Here, we will look at how LLMs fit into common SDLC models, including Waterfall, agile, DevOps, and Spiral, with detailed examples and insights into the improvements they bring.

Waterfall model with large language models

The Waterfall model is a linear, sequential approach to development where each phase is completed before moving to the next. Its well-defined structure means that requirements and design are established early, and later stages focus on coding, testing, and maintenance. LLMs can enhance each of these distinct phases through documentation, analysis, coding, and testing processes of the traditional SDLC models. **Requirements gathering**: In the Waterfall model, defining requirements early is crucial. LLMs can analyze inputs from various sources like client meetings, user surveys, and existing documentation, helping organize, summarize, and clarify requirements before moving forward. For example, for a project aimed at developing banking software, an LLM can sift through user needs like secure logins, transaction processing, and reporting. The model can categorize this data, creating a requirements document that clearly outlines each feature's functionality and security requirements:

- **System design**: LLMs can assist in generating technical specifications, flowcharts, or visual models of system architecture based on the requirements gathered. They can also suggest design patterns and provide skeleton code for core components. For example, suppose a team is building an e-commerce platform. An LLM could help outline a basic system structure that includes modules like a product catalog, payment processing, and user authentication. The model might suggest using secure APIs for payment and provide diagrams to visualize data flow between the catalog and payment modules.

- **Implementation**: LLMs can speed up the coding phase by generating initial code snippets, suggesting functions, and even flagging possible improvements or security concerns in the code. For example, a developer tasked with implementing a login module could prompt the LLM to generate initial code for encryption and secure password storage, ensuring compliance with security standards from the start. The LLM might also suggest using hashing algorithms like **bcrypt** for added security.
- **Testing:** It can be streamlined by LLMs, which can generate test cases and scripts and even assist in debugging. This phase often includes unit tests, integration tests, and system tests. For example, in an e-commerce checkout process, an LLM can create test cases that cover scenarios like adding items to the cart, calculating taxes, verifying payment methods, and completing transactions. The generated test cases ensure coverage for critical components of the checkout process.
- **Maintenance**: In the maintenance phase, LLMs can help identify and resolve bugs by analyzing error logs, understanding recurring patterns, and suggesting updates or optimizations based on new requirements. For example, for a customer feedback feature on a website, the LLM can monitor usage data, flag common issues reported by users, and recommend optimizations, such as simplifying the feedback form interface for better usability.

Agile model with large language models

The Agile model emphasizes flexibility, collaboration, and rapid delivery through iterative development. Agile projects are typically organized into short cycles or **sprints**, where small, functional software increments are developed and refined based on feedback. LLMs can support this fast-paced approach by streamlining communication, automating tasks, and enhancing the speed of each sprint. This leads to quick deliverable within short waiting time:

- **Sprint planning**: During sprint planning, LLMs assist by summarizing feedback from previous sprints, identifying high-priority tasks, and even suggesting a roadmap for upcoming sprints. For example, if a team is working on adding a chat feature to an application, the LLM can summarize user feedback from the last sprint, identifying lag or UX issues that need prioritization for the next sprint. This ensures the most relevant improvements are tackled first.
- **Daily standups and communication**: In Agile environments, efficient communication is key to staying aligned. LLMs can summarize daily standups, track progress, and provide updates, allowing team members to stay in sync without lengthy explanations. For example, after each daily standup meeting, an LLM could generate a summary of what each team member is working on,

challenges faced, and any blockers. This summary helps everyone understand project progress, identify areas for collaboration, and maintain a transparent workflow.

- **Backlog refinement**: LLMs can organize and prioritize the backlog, identifying high-impact items, technical debt, and potential improvement areas. This helps the team focus on critical features. For example, in the case of a social media app, the LLM could suggest prioritizing neglected features like content moderation, given the increased user activity. This ensures the team allocates resources to high-urgency items.
- **Testing during each iteration:** Testing is performed at the end of each sprint in Agile. LLMs can generate test cases tailored to each user story, ensuring thorough verification of each feature before release. For example, for a profile update feature, the LLM could generate tests for data validation, security checks, and cross-platform compatibility, ensuring the feature works seamlessly on all devices.

DevOps model with large language models

DevOps combines development and operations to create a CI or CD pipeline. It emphasizes collaboration, automation, and monitoring for seamless deployments. LLMs are invaluable here, offering support for deployment, testing, and monitoring, improving speed and reliability across the pipeline. In a software project, a pipeline refers to an automated sequence of processes, such as code compilation, testing, and deployment. It supports CI or CD, ensuring that code changes are quickly and reliably tested and deployed:

- **Continuous integration**: In CI or CD pipelines, LLMs analyze code changes, detect integration conflicts, and propose fixes, making the merging process more efficient. For example, if multiple developers submit code changes for an online booking system, an LLM can analyze the changes to identify conflicting updates in the booking module and suggest resolutions. This minimizes downtime and speeds up code integration.
- **Automated testing**: LLMs support automated testing by generating scripts and running tests after every code update, ensuring the application's stability. For example, for an online shopping cart, an LLM could create automated tests for various workflows, like adding items, updating quantities, and checking out. These automated tests run with each code change, ensuring the cart's functionality remains intact.
- **Continuous deployment:** LLMs assist in setting up deployment configurations for different environments, which reduces manual errors and ensures consistency across staging, production, and other environments. For example, when deploying an updated feature, an LLM could generate the necessary deployment scripts and configurations tailored for each environment, minimizing setup time and errors.
- **Monitoring and feedback:** LLMs continuously monitor logs and system performance after deployment. They identify issues like bottlenecks or server

downtimes and provide real-time feedback. For example, for a streaming service, an LLM might monitor server response times and notify the team if any lag occurs during peak hours. This proactive approach helps maintain a smooth user experience.

Spiral model with large language models

The Spiral model emphasizes iterative development with a focus on risk analysis at each stage. Each cycle in the spiral includes risk assessment, prototyping, testing, and improvements, which makes it a suitable model for high-risk projects. LLMs enhance this model by providing risk analysis, prototyping support, testing, and comprehensive documentation:

- **Risk analysis**: LLMs assess risks in each cycle by analyzing historical data and previous project outcomes, suggesting mitigation strategies, and identifying potential issues. For example, in developing a healthcare app, an LLM might flag data privacy risks related to sensitive patient information. The model could suggest measures like data encryption and secure access control to mitigate these risks.
- **Prototyping**: LLMs accelerate prototyping by generating quick designs or code samples based on risk assessment findings, allowing the team to evaluate ideas before committing fully. For example, for a recommendation engine, an LLM could quickly generate a prototype that suggests items to users based on simple inputs. This prototype enables stakeholders to assess the feature's potential before full implementation.
- **Iterative testing and improvement**: LLMs can generate test cases for each iteration, providing insights on necessary improvements and facilitating smoother transitions between cycles. For example, in each iteration of a finance app, the LLM could analyze transaction workflows and suggest optimizations for speed or accuracy, ensuring improvements align with user needs.
- **Documentation and knowledge management**: Comprehensive documentation is essential for the Spiral model, as each cycle builds on previous work. LLMs maintain up-to-date records of decisions, risks, and solutions, ensuring that knowledge is retained for future use. For example, after every iteration, the LLM could generate a summary documenting challenges, solutions, and improvements, helping new team members or stakeholders quickly understand project history.

LLMs provide valuable support across different SDLC models, from requirements gathering to deployment and maintenance. Their adaptability enables them to handle varied tasks, including documentation, coding, testing, and risk management, tailored to each SDLC model's unique demands. Integrating LLMs into SDLC processes increases productivity, reduces errors, and accelerates project timelines, enabling teams to focus on innovative solutions and delivering high-quality software.

Integration of LLM with SDLC stages

LLMs play a transformative role in the planning and requirements gathering phase of software development. This phase is crucial, as it sets the foundation for the project by identifying user needs, defining goals, and establishing project specifications. LLMs assist in this stage by analyzing requirements, automating repetitive documentation tasks, and generating insights from user data. They streamline processes and reduce human error, which helps produce clear, accurate requirements and speeds up the initial stages of development.

LLMs for requirements analysis and specification

The requirements analysis and specification stage focuses on understanding what the software needs to accomplish and translating user needs into detailed, actionable requirements. LLMs facilitate this by interpreting unstructured data, such as user feedback, and converting it into structured requirements. They provide support through detailed requirements documentation, summarization, and prioritization. Prioritization of modules in a software project involves determining the order in which features or components should be developed based on factors like business value, user needs, and technical dependencies:

- Analyzing requirements from raw data
- Defining and documenting requirements
- Requirements validation and consistency checks

Examples of automating user story generation, and feedback

LLMs excel at automating routine documentation and gathering user input, which significantly improves the efficiency of the planning stage. By generating user stories, collecting feedback, and translating insights into actionable requirements, LLMs allow teams to focus on high-priority tasks and decision-making or prioritization:

- **Automating user story generation:** User stories are short, simple descriptions of a feature from the user's perspective, essential for Agile projects. LLMs can quickly generate these user stories, converting user requirements into clear, actionable descriptions of desired functionalities. For example, for a fitness app, an LLM might generate a user story like, `As a user, I want to track my daily steps so that I can monitor my fitness progress`. The LLM can create dozens of similar stories, covering various functionalities such as goal-setting, calorie counting, and social sharing, which provide developers with a clear roadmap for feature implementation.

- **Gathering and analyzing user feedback:** User feedback is vital for identifying pain points and desired features. LLMs streamline this by analyzing feedback from sources such as surveys, reviews, and support tickets, summarizing key points, and categorizing suggestions. For example, for an e-commerce platform, an LLM could analyze customer reviews to identify frequent complaints about the checkout process. If users mention **slow checkout**, **confusing interface**, or **limited payment options**, the LLM summarizes this feedback for the development team, highlighting areas for improvement.
- **Identifying requirements from use cases**: LLMs can interpret use cases, which describe specific interactions between users and the system, to generate high-level requirements. By analyzing these scenarios, LLMs ensure that the software design aligns with real-world applications. For example, in a project to develop a hotel booking system, an LLM might review use cases like **making a reservation** and **cancelling a booking**. For each case, the LLM identifies essential requirements, such as providing room availability, processing refunds, and sending booking confirmations, which are crucial for system functionality.

Case studies on LLMs applications for planning accuracy

The integration of LLMs in requirements gathering is already yielding positive results in various industries. The following case studies demonstrate how LLMs have enhanced planning accuracy, reduced the risk of errors, and sped up the requirements-gathering phase:

- **Case study 1:** E-commerce platform enhancement
- **Case study 2:** Financial application for wealth management
- **Case study 3:** Smart healthcare system for remote patient monitoring
- **Case study 4:** Educational platform for personalized learning

Design phase using LLMs for architectural design

In the design phase of the SDLC, LLMs offer support by generating design patterns, proposing architectures, and creating initial code structures. LLMs streamline the design process by providing pre-built solutions, suggestions, and comprehensive documentation that set a strong foundation for building functional, scalable software. Here, we explore how LLMs contribute to architectural design by generating patterns, scaffolding code, designing interfaces, and offering visual aids for clarity.

Role of LLMs in generating design patterns and architectures

Design patterns and architectural decisions are essential in determining how different components of an application will interact, and LLMs can assist by offering suggestions tailored to specific project needs. These patterns serve as reusable solutions to recurring problems in software design, helping teams save time and reduce potential errors. In any software project, various potential errors can arise during development, testing, and deployment, impacting the project's quality and timeline:

- **Generating design patterns:** LLMs can recommend design patterns based on project requirements, guiding developers toward standardized solutions for common issues. By analyzing the nature of the application, such as whether it is a web application, an embedded system, or a mobile app, LLMs can suggest patterns like **Model-View-Controller (MVC)**, singleton, or factory patterns. For example, for an e-commerce platform, an LLM might recommend the MVC pattern, which separates the application into three layers such as model (data), view (UI), and controller (logic). The pattern ensures a modular design, making it easier to update one layer without affecting others.
- **Architectural style recommendations**: Besides design patterns, LLMs assist in choosing architectural styles, like microservices, monolithic, or client-server, based on scalability, performance, and maintenance needs. For example, if a team is building a large social media app, the LLM might suggest a microservices architecture. This approach separates services like user management, posts, messaging, and notifications into individual modules. Each module functions independently, allowing easy scaling and improving fault tolerance.

Examples

Once the architecture and patterns are in place, LLMs help by generating initial code scaffolding, designing user interfaces, and creating thorough documentation. This support accelerates the design process, allowing developers to move quickly from conceptualization to implementation or execution:

- **Code scaffolding**: LLMs provide a **scaffold** or basic structure for code, establishing the core framework and leaving space for customization. This foundation includes essential elements like classes, methods, and dependencies, allowing developers to focus on building out specific functionalities. For example, in a banking app, an LLM could scaffold a `UserAccount` class that includes placeholders for attributes like account balance, account number, and transaction history, as well as methods for deposit, withdrawal, and transfer. Developers then fill in the logic, saving time compared to creating these structures from scratch.
- **Interface design**: LLMs support **user interface (UI)** design by providing basic layout suggestions or generating HTML and **Cascading Style Sheets (CSS)**

code. These interfaces can be based on user-centered design principles, ensuring usability and accessibility. For example, for a fitness app, an LLM could produce an initial UI layout that includes a dashboard, activity tracker, and user profile. This layout would include placeholders for displaying user data, like step counts and calories burned, and would follow best practices to ensure the UI is easy to navigate and visually appealing.

- **Documentation generation**: Comprehensive documentation is critical in the design phase to keep all stakeholders informed about architectural decisions, design patterns, and the purpose of various modules. LLMs generate clear documentation for code scaffolding, interface specifications, and architectural choices. For example, for an educational platform, an LLM can produce documentation explaining why the MVC pattern was selected, detailing each module (for example, user profile, course catalog, progress tracker), and specifying how these modules interact. This documentation helps new developers understand the project's design and ensures consistency across the team.

Visual aids flow diagrams and example outputs for clarity

LLMs also assist in creating visual aids, like flow diagrams and sample outputs, which clarify system functionality and facilitate communication among team members. These visuals like DFD, ER-diagram serve as references for both developers and stakeholders, offering insights into how different components will interact and how users will experience the system:

- **Flow diagrams for system design**: Flow diagrams are essential in illustrating workflows, data flow, and component interactions. LLMs can produce these diagrams based on project requirements, ensuring that complex interactions are visualized and easy to understand. For example, for a hotel booking system, an LLM can create a flow diagram showing the booking process, starting from the user selecting a room to making a payment. The flow diagram would include key steps, like room selection, date verification, payment processing, and confirmation, making it clear how data moves through the system.
- **Data flow diagrams (DFD):** DFDs illustrate how information flows within the system, identifying data sources, destinations, and the processes involved in moving data. LLMs can generate these diagrams to help teams understand data interactions and dependencies. For example, in a ride-sharing app, a DFD generated by an LLM might display data flows between the driver's app, the rider's app, and a central server. Key processes, like location sharing, fare calculation, and trip history storage, would be represented, offering a clear view of how data is managed in real time.
- **Mock outputs for system behavior:** LLMs can also produce example outputs or mock-ups for critical components, helping teams visualize expected behaviors and

identify potential issues before full implementation. For example, for a financial reporting tool, an LLM could generate sample outputs of monthly spending summaries, showing line items for each transaction, a breakdown of categories (for example, **Food**, **Transport**), and total spending. This mock-up offers clarity on how data will be presented to users.

Detailed examples of LLMs in the design phase

To further illustrate the impact of LLMs on the design phase, let us explore the following practical scenarios across different software types:

- **E-commerce application:**
  - **Design pattern**: LLMs might recommend the Factory pattern for creating different product objects (for example, electronics, clothing, books) based on user selections. The Factory pattern is advantageous here as it centralizes object creation, simplifying maintenance and expansion when new product types are added.
  - **Interface design:** An LLM could create a responsive UI scaffold with placeholders for product categories, filters, and a shopping cart, adhering to best practices for usability and accessibility.
- **Educational platform:**
  - **Architecture recommendation:** An LLM might suggest a client-server architecture, where the client handles UI interactions, and the server manages data processing and storage. This structure ensures scalability and separation of concerns.
  - **Documentation**: For each module, like user profiles, course management, and progress tracking, the LLM could generate documentation that explains module functionality, interactions, and dependencies. This keeps team members aligned and reduces onboarding time for new developers.
- **Customer relationship management (CRM) system:**
  - **Code scaffolding**: LLMs could create classes for customers, sales, and support, with methods for data handling, email communications, and scheduling tasks. Each class serves as a blueprint, making the development phase faster and more organized.
  - **Flow diagram**: An LLM could generate a flow diagram that shows how customer data flows from initial contact to sale closure, illustrating interactions between sales, support, and analytics modules. This helps teams anticipate data needs and track data movement effectively.

In the design phase, LLMs simplify and enhance architectural planning, from generating design patterns to documenting system requirements. By offering reusable solutions, creating initial code structures, designing interfaces, and providing visual aids, LLMs enable development teams to move efficiently from concept to implementation. These models ensure consistency, save time, and improve clarity, allowing developers to focus on building innovative and reliable software solutions. As LLMs continue to evolve, they will play an increasingly integral role in the architectural design process, helping teams develop software that is robust, user-friendly, and scalable.

Large language models in coding and implementation

LLMs are revolutionizing coding and implementation by generating code snippets, optimizing code, and assisting developers through collaborative coding platforms. This stage of the SDLC is where ideas are brought to life through actual code, and LLMs can help make this process more efficient, collaborative, and robust. However, like any tool, they come with benefits, limitations, and considerations that must be carefully managed to ensure secure and ethical use.

Code generation and refactoring with large language models

LLMs have become valuable assets in the coding phase, where they assist developers by generating code, refactoring existing code, and automating repetitive tasks. By analyzing vast amounts of programming language data, these models understand syntax, best practices, and common structures, making them capable of delivering code for various functions and even refactoring it for efficiency in terms of outcome based on the given prompt from developers end:

- **Benefits of code generation and refactoring:** LLMs can significantly reduce coding time by auto-generating code that follows standard practices, suggesting efficient structures, and flagging potential errors early on. This automation also means that developers can focus on complex parts of the project rather than getting bogged down by routine tasks. Example: If a developer needs a function to validate email addresses, an LLM can instantly generate a code snippet using **regular expressions (Regex)** for the task. Instead of researching or writing code from scratch, the developer receives a ready-to-use function that can be directly incorporated.
- **Limitations of code generation and refactoring:** While LLMs are powerful, they lack true understanding and can sometimes produce incorrect or inefficient code, especially for highly specialized problems. They might also repeat patterns from their training data that are outdated or suboptimal. For example, when working on a machine learning project, an LLM might generate a basic model using a simple algorithm, even though the problem might require a more sophisticated approach

like neural networks. The developer would need to review and potentially modify the LLM-generated code to ensure it meets project requirements.

Incorporating LLMs in collaborative coding platforms

Collaborative coding platforms like GitHub are essential for version control and teamwork in software development, and tools like GitHub Copilot, powered by LLMs, are transforming how developers collaborate. By integrating LLMs, these platforms can provide real-time coding assistance, suggest improvements, and even catch errors early on, all within a shared environment like cloud-based projects:

- **Real-time code suggestions**: LLM-powered tools embedded in collaborative platforms suggest code completions as developers type, offering everything from single lines of code to entire functions. This boosts productivity and ensures code consistency across team members. For example, a developer working on a Python project might type **`def calculate_mean`** and receive an automatic suggestion from Copilot for the full function, complete with input checks and comments, streamlining development and maintaining code clarity.
- **Improved team collaboration and code consistency**: By using LLMs in a shared platform, developers can maintain consistent coding practices and styles. LLMs help enforce coding standards and can even suggest stylistic changes to align with project guidelines. For example, in a large team working on a web application, the LLM might suggest consistent formatting, such as indentation styles or variable naming conventions. This automated guidance ensures that the codebase remains uniform and readable, even with multiple contributors.
- **Collaborative issue tracking and error detection:** LLMs can assist in identifying and suggesting fixes for code errors in real time, reducing the number of bugs pushed into production and helping teams identify issues early. For example, while writing a complex **Structured Query Language (SQL)** query, a developer might receive a prompt from the LLM-powered tool pointing out a potential SQL injection vulnerability. The tool might then suggest a parameterized query as a secure alternative, preventing a major security risk.

Practical examples

LLMs provide numerous practical benefits by auto-generating code snippets, suggesting code optimizations, and refactoring existing code to improve readability, performance, and efficiency:

- **Auto-generating code snippets:** LLMs excel at generating reusable code snippets based on simple prompts, whether for database queries, utility functions, or API calls. Developers can simply describe the functionality they need, and the LLM generates a relevant snippet. For example, a developer working on a weather app might ask the LLM to **get the current temperature from weather API**, and it generates the code for an HTTP request to fetch and display temperature data. This shortens development time and enables quick prototyping.

- **Suggesting code optimizations:** LLMs can identify parts of the code that may not be optimized and suggest alternatives to improve efficiency. They look for repeated code, inefficient loops, or redundant logic, helping developers clean up code for faster execution and easier maintenance. For example, if a developer writes a loop to append items to a list, the LLM might suggest using list comprehension instead, improving both readability and performance. For instance, changing a for loop to [expression for item in list] where possible.
- **Refactoring legacy code**: LLMs assist in refactoring outdated code by identifying improvements that follow modern programming practices. They can update old syntax, replace deprecated functions, or reorganize complex code for readability. For example, in a web application built using older JavaScript syntax, an LLM can convert var declarations to let or const, replace callback functions with async or await for better readability, and suggest improvements that align with the latest ECMAScript standards.

Ethical and security considerations in LLM powered coding

Using LLMs for coding brings several ethical and security considerations, as these models rely on large datasets, which may include publicly available code or sensitive information. Developers must approach LLM-powered coding responsibly, especially regarding proprietary code, security vulnerabilities, and ethical practices:

- **Copyright and licensing concerns**: Since LLMs are trained on massive datasets that may include open-source or licensed code, they might inadvertently generate code snippets that resemble copyrighted code. Developers should verify that generated code adheres to project licensing terms and avoid copying proprietary patterns without modification. For example, if a developer requests a sorting algorithm from an LLM, they should double-check its origin and structure. If it resembles an algorithm from a specific software library with restrictive licensing, they may need to modify it or reference the source appropriately.
- **Data privacy and confidentiality risks:** Developers using LLMs in sensitive environments, such as healthcare or finance, should avoid inputting confidential data into these tools. Some LLM tools may log prompts, raising concerns about inadvertently storing or sharing private information. For example, a developer working on a banking application should avoid entering sensitive client data (like account details) into an LLM-powered tool to generate code or test functions. Instead, they should use generalized placeholders or test data to maintain privacy and security.
- **Security risks in generated code:** LLMs may produce code that contains vulnerabilities, such as SQL injection risks or insecure authentication methods.

It is essential to review generated code for potential security flaws and ensure compliance with best practices. For example, if an LLM generates code for logging users into an application, the developer must check that the code uses secure password handling (for example, hashing with bcrypt) instead of storing plaintext passwords, which could create security risks.

- **Bias and ethical use of automated code**: LLMs may sometimes reflect biases in their training data, which can lead to unfair or biased outcomes in generated code. For instance, certain assumptions about user roles or access permissions might inadvertently exclude some groups. Developers must remain vigilant in reviewing code for inclusivity and fairness. For example, suppose an LLM-generated user role-checking function assumes that administrators are the only ones allowed to make updates. This could unintentionally restrict authorized users from other departments. Reviewing such assumptions is critical to prevent unintended biases.

LLMs are becoming indispensable tools in the coding and implementation phase, enabling faster development, real-time collaboration, and improved code quality. Through features like auto-generated code snippets, code optimizations, and collaborative platforms, they offer robust support for developers at all experience levels. However, using LLMs in coding requires careful attention to ethical and security considerations. Developers must verify the origins and quality of LLM-generated code, safeguard sensitive information, and review outputs for potential biases or vulnerabilities. By thoughtfully integrating LLMs into their workflows, developers can leverage these tools for more efficient, secure, and collaborative coding experiences, paving the way for innovative software solutions.

Testing and quality assurance with LLM

In software development, **quality assurance** (**QA**) and testing are critical for delivering reliable, efficient, and user-friendly software. LLMs have begun transforming how testing and QA are conducted by automating test generation, enhancing bug detection, and streamlining code reviews. This section explores how LLMs can contribute across different testing stages, assist in code quality verification, and improve overall QA processes, with practical examples to illustrate their application and effectiveness.

Using LLMs for automated testing

Automated testing helps reduce the time and effort needed to verify software functionality, and LLMs play a major role here by automating test creation, suggesting test cases, and generating expected outcomes. Let us examine how LLMs fit into different testing levels:

- **Unit testing**: In unit testing, individual components or functions are tested in isolation. LLMs can assist by generating tests for each function, helping ensure that all edge cases are covered. With LLMs, developers can quickly set up test cases that verify the correctness of each small module in the application. For example, suppose a developer has written a function that calculates the total cost of items in a shopping cart, including discounts. An LLM could generate unit tests to check if the function handles various scenarios, such as no items in the cart, one item, multiple items, or items with different discount rules. This automation saves time and reduces manual errors in test creation.

- **Integration testing**: Integration testing verifies that different modules work together correctly. LLMs can suggest integration test cases by analyzing dependencies between modules and ensuring they interact as expected. LLMs help generate scenarios where components are tested in combination, such as ensuring that a user authentication module correctly integrates with a profile management module. For example, in a web application, an LLM could create integration tests to check if a login component correctly communicates with the user database. It might include tests for scenarios like successful logins, incorrect passwords, and locked accounts, all of which help confirm that user data flows properly between modules.
- **System testing:** System testing validates the entire application as a whole. LLMs can automate the creation of system-level tests, which simulate real-world usage scenarios to check end-to-end functionality. This ensures that all features work together as expected. For example, for an online booking system, an LLM could generate a test scenario where a user searches for flights, selects a seat, books a ticket, and receives a confirmation. This comprehensive approach verifies that each component is functioning correctly within the broader system.

Enhancing bug detection and code review processes with LLMs

Bug detection and code review are essential parts of maintaining code quality and ensuring the final product meets standards. LLMs assist in automating bug detection, spotting inconsistencies in the code, and suggesting improvements during the code review process.

- **Automated bug detection**: LLMs analyze code for patterns associated with common bugs, such as uninitialized variables, improper error handling, or mismatched data types. This automated bug detection is especially helpful in large codebases where human review alone might miss subtle errors. For example, while reviewing a function that processes user input, an LLM might flag a potential null reference bug, warning the developer to add checks for empty or invalid inputs. This proactive approach minimizes runtime errors and improves stability.
- **Code review assistance**: In code reviews, LLMs can flag code that deviates from best practices, suggests optimizations, and recommends improvements for readability. They can point out inconsistencies, such as mismatched naming conventions or redundant logic, enhancing the quality and maintainability of the codebase. For example, if a developer writes nested loops to perform a task, the LLM might suggest using a more efficient data structure or replacing the loop with

a more optimized algorithm. This guidance makes code reviews more thorough and less dependent on human memory and attention to detail.

- **Pattern recognition for advanced issues:** LLMs can detect advanced patterns and potential security issues that might go unnoticed, such as SQL injection risks or insecure handling of user data. This makes them valuable in identifying vulnerabilities early in the development process. For example, in a function that queries a database, the LLM could recognize that user inputs are directly included in SQL queries, leading to an SQL injection vulnerability. It might then suggest using prepared statements or parameterized queries to secure the function.

Examples of LLM based test case generation and reporting

LLMs can automate the creation of comprehensive test cases, which save developers time and ensure that critical functions are thoroughly tested. They also streamline test reporting by automatically generating readable summaries of test results.

- **Automated test case generation**: By analyzing the code's structure and functionality, LLMs generate test cases that cover a wide range of scenarios, from typical user inputs to edge cases. This reduces the need for manual test writing, ensuring that even less obvious cases are considered. For example, in an e-commerce application, an LLM could create test cases for adding items to the cart, removing items, applying a discount, and proceeding to checkout. This automation ensures that all primary user interactions are verified, reducing the chance of bugs in the production version.
- **Automated test reporting:** After executing test cases, LLMs can generate concise, understandable reports summarizing test results, highlighting passed and failed tests, and explaining potential issues. This enables quicker analysis of test outcomes and more efficient debugging. For example, if a unit test fails, the LLM might report that the `calculate_total` function did not account for a scenario where the cart is empty. The report might suggest modifying the function to handle this case, guiding the developer directly to the solution.

Potential practices to maintain accuracy and reliability

While LLMs offer powerful tools for automated testing and QA, there are challenges to consider. Awareness of these pitfalls and following best practices can help maximize the accuracy and reliability of LLM-powered QA:

- **Pitfall 1 (Over-reliance on generated tests):** LLMs can generate numerous test cases, but they may miss certain project-specific scenarios or unique requirements. Over-reliance on automated tests could result in overlooking custom business logic. The best practice is combining LLM-generated tests with manual test creation to ensure complete coverage. Manual reviews help catch scenarios that automated tools might miss.

- **Pitfall 2 (Misinterpretation of generated code):** LLM-generated code for test cases might occasionally misinterpret the intended functionality, leading to incorrect test scenarios or assumptions. The best practice is reviewing all LLM-generated tests for correctness. By inspecting each test case, developers can ensure that test parameters align with the application's requirements.
- **Pitfall 3 (Security vulnerabilities in testing):** If LLMs generate tests that directly handle sensitive data, it may introduce security risks. Testing environments should avoid using real data to prevent unintended leaks or breaches. The best practice is using dummy or anonymized data for testing. Avoid exposing sensitive information in test environments, even if the tests are generated automatically.
- **Pitfall 4 (Ensuring adaptability in test scenarios):** LLMs sometimes produce rigid test cases that don't easily adapt to changes in the codebase, which can lead to test failures when minor updates are made. The best practice is making tests adaptable by using parameterization and modular design. This way, even if the code changes, test cases can be updated with minimal adjustments.

LLMs are powerful allies in the testing and QA stages of software development, helping automate test generation, enhance bug detection, and streamline code review. Through automated testing at the unit, integration, and system levels, LLMs save developers time and contribute to a more robust and error-free application. For example, of practical applications, such as automated test case creation, test reporting, and code reviews, illustrate their potential to transform QA processes. However, careful attention to best practices and a balanced approach can help teams leverage LLMs effectively while ensuring accuracy, security, and adaptability.

Deployment and maintenance support

The final stages of the SDLC, like deployment and maintenance, are crucial for delivering, monitoring, and continuously improving software applications. LLMs can enhance these stages by streamlining deployment, aiding in monitoring and troubleshooting, and analyzing user feedback to optimize performance. This section explains how LLMs support CI or CD, improve maintenance processes through proactive troubleshooting, and enable predictive maintenance with real-world examples for clarity.

Deploying LLM assisted application

CI or CD practices are essential for modern software applications, helping developers regularly integrate new code, test it, and deploy it with minimal manual intervention. LLMs can play a role in this process by automating various CI or CD tasks, such as writing deployment scripts, suggesting pipeline optimizations, and even predicting potential issues before they impact stakeholders.

- **Automating deployment scripts:** Deployment scripts are critical in the CI or CD process, as they define how and when code is integrated, tested, and deployed. LLMs can generate or refine these scripts to align with the specific requirements of an application, which reduces manual work and minimizes errors. For example, for a web application hosted on a cloud platform, an LLM can generate scripts for setting up servers, configuring load balancers, and managing data storage. This automation ensures that deployment is consistent across different environments (development, staging, and production) and reduces the time developers spend on manual configuration.
- **Pipeline optimization:** In CI or CD, pipelines are workflows that automate steps such as code building, testing, and deployment. LLMs can analyze existing pipelines to suggest optimizations, such as identifying redundant steps or recommending tools that align with project requirements. For example, in a project with separate testing and deployment phases, an LLM might suggest merging tests to run in parallel, reducing overall pipeline time. This makes the integration and deployment process more efficient, ensuring that updates reach users faster.
- **Proactive error prediction**: LLMs can also analyze code changes to predict potential errors during deployment, such as compatibility issues or performance bottlenecks. By flagging these concerns early, LLMs help developers resolve issues before they impact end-users. For example, if a new feature might increase memory usage beyond server capacity, the LLM could suggest alternative designs or configurations to prevent failures. This foresight minimizes downtime and supports seamless deployment.

Leveraging LLMs for maintenance of software project

Once deployed, software applications require continuous monitoring and troubleshooting to ensure they perform reliably and efficiently. LLMs offer powerful tools for automating monitoring tasks, providing insights into system performance, identifying issues, and helping teams respond proactively.

- **Monitoring application health:** LLMs can be set up to monitor application logs and detect unusual patterns, such as spikes in response time, high memory usage, or increased error rates. This ongoing analysis alerts teams to potential problems before they become critical. For example, in a banking app, the LLM can monitor user login times and detect any increase in delays, which could indicate performance issues. By analyzing this data, the team can make necessary adjustments to improve speed, reducing the risk of poor user experience.
- **Automated troubleshooting:** When issues arise, LLMs can assist by generating troubleshooting steps and suggesting fixes based on similar past occurrences. This can include steps like restarting services, scaling resources, or optimizing code sections that are causing slowdowns. For example, if a high-traffic e-commerce platform experiences slow page loading, an LLM might analyze logs, identify

high-memory functions, and suggest increasing server resources or optimizing the identified code. This guidance can shorten resolution times and help maintain smooth operations during peak usage.

- **User feedback analysis**: User feedback is a valuable resource for identifying potential issues, feature requests, or areas needing improvement. LLMs can analyze user feedback from reviews, surveys, or support tickets to identify common themes, helping development teams understand user needs and prioritize updates. For example, if a social media app receives multiple complaints about slow image uploads, the LLM can categorize these issues and suggest investigating the upload functionality. This insight helps the team address user concerns promptly, improving satisfaction and engagement.

Case study LLMs in predictive maintenance for software

Predictive maintenance uses data analysis to forecast when an application or system component might fail, allowing teams to address issues before they lead to downtime. By incorporating LLMs into predictive maintenance, software teams can proactively maintain systems, reduce interruptions, and improve application reliability.

- **Scenario**: A cloud-based file-sharing service wants to ensure minimal downtime for its users, especially during file uploads and downloads. Given the volume of daily transactions, the service aims to anticipate system strain and prevent disruptions.
- **Solution**: An LLM is trained to monitor system logs, track usage patterns, and detect anomalies. It learns to recognize signs of potential issues, such as high CPU usage during file uploads or a backlog in server requests, which may indicate a need for resource scaling.
- **Predictive analysis**: Using data from previous incidents, the LLM predicts when certain services might experience high demand. For example, if the LLM detects that CPU load typically spikes during weekends, it alerts the team to preemptively allocate more resources, preventing slowdowns or system crashes.
- **Outcome**: With the help of LLM-driven predictive maintenance, the file-sharing service reduces downtime and provides a smoother experience for users. By proactively scaling resources based on the LLM's insights, the team can prevent failures, boost user satisfaction, and manage infrastructure costs more effectively.

LLMs play a transformative role in the deployment and maintenance stages of the SDLC by enhancing CI or CD processes, automating monitoring, and enabling proactive troubleshooting. By analyzing user feedback, LLMs further support continuous improvement in software applications. Through predictive maintenance, teams can anticipate system needs and address issues before they affect users. With these tools, development teams can focus on delivering reliable, responsive, and user-centered software that meets evolving demands.

Challenges and future of LLMs in SDLC

As LLMs become more integrated into the SDLC, they offer many benefits, such as automating tasks and enhancing productivity. However, they also present challenges that need to be addressed for successful implementation. Additionally, the future of LLMs in SDLC is filled with exciting trends and opportunities for research and development. This section explores the common challenges associated with LLMs, future trends in their development, and research areas that can improve their application across emerging SDLC models.

Common challenges

Following are the common challenges faces:

- **Data quality**: LLMs rely heavily on the data used to train them. If the training data is of low quality, the model's outputs will also be unreliable. Inaccurate, incomplete, or biased data can lead to poor performance and faulty recommendations. For example, if an LLM is trained primarily on outdated programming practices, it may suggest inefficient coding techniques, which could hinder software performance and security. This underlines the importance of using high-quality, relevant datasets.
- **Model biases:** Biases in training data can lead to biased outputs, affecting the fairness and effectiveness of LLMs. If the data reflects societal biases, the model may produce skewed or inappropriate suggestions. For example, in a code review context, if an LLM has been trained on a dataset that predominantly features a specific programming style or language, it may inadvertently favor those styles over others, limiting creativity and diversity in coding approaches.
- **Interpretability**: LLMs are often seen as **black boxes**, making it difficult for developers to understand how decisions are made. This lack of transparency can be problematic, especially when model recommendations lead to critical software decisions. For example, if an LLM suggests changes to a software architecture based on certain parameters, the developers may struggle to understand why those suggestions were made. This uncertainty can lead to reluctance in accepting the model's recommendations.
- **Dependency on large batasets:** Training effective LLMs often requires vast amounts of data, which can be challenging to obtain. Organizations may struggle with collecting enough high-quality data specific to their domain, leading to underperformance. For example, a company developing a niche application may not have access to the large datasets needed to train a robust LLM, limiting its ability to fully leverage the model's capabilities. This scarcity can hinder the model's adaptability to the specific context of the software being developed.

Conclusion

In summary, integrating LLMs into the SDLC offers significant advantages, such as automating tasks, enhancing communication, and improving decision-making across all stages of development. Key takeaways include the importance of high-quality training data to ensure effective model performance, the need for ongoing efforts to address biases and enhance interpretability, and the potential of LLMs to streamline processes from planning to deployment. LLMs have the power to transform software engineering by increasing efficiency and fostering innovation, enabling teams to focus more on creativity and problem-solving rather than repetitive tasks. Looking ahead, the role of AI in SDLC innovation will likely expand, paving the way for smarter tools that continuously learn and adapt to developers' needs, ultimately reshaping how software is designed, built, and maintained. As we embrace these advancements, it is crucial to balance innovation with ethical considerations to ensure that AI contributes positively to the future of software development.

Exercise

To solidify your understanding of the concepts covered in this chapter, try the following exercises.

Multiple choice questions

1. **What is the primary benefit of using LLMs in the planning phase of the SDLC?**
   a. Decreased coding time
   b. Improved requirements gathering and analysis
   c. Enhanced bug detection
   d. Simplified user interface design
2. **Which of the following is a challenge associated with integrating LLMs into software development?**
   a. Lack of programming languages
   b. High-quality data dependency
   c. Insufficient hardware resources
   d. Decreased team collaboration
3. **How can LLMs assist in the testing phase of the SDLC?**
   a. By generating marketing materials
   b. By creating automated test cases

c. By conducting user interviews

d. By coding applications

4. **What future trend involves the development of models that can learn from user interactions?**

   a. Open-source LLMs

   b. Advanced models

   c. Continuous learning

   d. Ethical AI

Short answer questions

1. Explain how LLMs can improve the coding and implementation phase of the SDLC. Provide specific examples.
2. Discuss the importance of ethical considerations when implementing LLMs in software development. What measures can developers take to mitigate biases?
3. What are the implications of using LLMs for monitoring and troubleshooting applications after deployment? Give an example of how this can be beneficial.

Essay questions

1. Analyze the impact of LLMs on the software development lifecycle. Discuss both the advantages and challenges that come with their integration, providing real-world examples where applicable.
2. Explore the future of AI in the SDLC. How might advancements in LLM technology reshape traditional software development practices? Discuss potential research areas and trends that could influence this evolution.
3. Evaluate a specific case study where LLMs were successfully implemented in the SDLC. What were the key factors that contributed to its success, and what lessons can be learned for future implementations?

Multiple choice answers

1. b
2. b
3. b
4. c

Join our book's Discord space

Join the book's Discord Workspace for Latest updates, Offers, Tech happenings around the world, New Release and Sessions with the Authors:

https://discord.bpbonline.com

CHAPTER 20
Model Questions with Answers

1. **Define software engineering.**

   Software engineering is the application of systematic, disciplined, quantifier approach. It is used for the development, operations, and maintenance of software

2. **What is the process framework?**

   Process framework is used to establish the foundation for a complete software process. By identifying a small number of framework activities that are applicable to all software projects regardless of their size and complexity

3. **What are the generic framework activities?**

   The generic framework activities are as follows:

   a. Communication
   b. Planning
   c. Modeling
   d. Construction
   e. Deployment

4. **Define Stakeholder.**

   Stakeholder are:

   a. Anyone who has a stake in the successful outcome of the project
   b. Business managers, end-users, software engineers, support people

5. **How does the process model differ from one another?**

   In the following ways, the process model differ from one another:

   a. Based on the flow of activities
   b. Interdependencies between activities
   c. Manner of quality assurance
   d. Manner of project tracking
   e. Team organization and roles
   f. Work products identify a requirement identifier

6. **What are the reasons for the failure of the waterfall model?**

   The reasons for the failure of the waterfall model are:

   a. Real projects rarely follow sequential flow. Iterations are made in an indirect manner
   b. Difficult for the customer to state all requirements explicitly
   c. Customers need more patience as working products reach only the deployment phase

7. **What are the drawbacks of the RAD model?**

   The drawbacks of RAD model are as follows:

   a. Require a sufficient number of human resources to create enough number of teams
   b. Developers and customers are not committed, system result in failure
   c. Not properly modularized building component may problematic
   d. Not applicable when there is more possibility for technical risk

8. **Why formal methods are not widely used?**

   The reasons are as follows:

   a. Quite time consuming and expensive
   b. Extensive expertise is needed for developers to apply formal methods
   c. Difficult to use as they are technically sophisticated maintenance may become risk

9. **What are cross-cutting concerns?**

   When concerns cut across multiple functions, features and information

10. **What are the different phases of unified process?**

    Different phases of unified process are as follows:

    a. Inception phase
    b. Elaboration phase
    c. Construction phase

d. Transition phase
e. Production phase

11. Define the terms:

a. Agility

Agility are dynamic, content specific, aggressively change embracing and growth oriented.

b. Agile team

The following defines an agile team:

i. Fast team

ii. Able to respond to changes

c. Agile methods

Agile methods are as follows:

i. Methods to overcome perceive and actual weakness in conventional software engineering

ii. To accommodate changes in environment, requirements and use cases

d. Agile process

Agile process focus on team structures, team communications, rapid delivery of software and it de-emphasis importance of intermediate product

12. What is the use of process technology tools?

Use of process technology tools are as follows:

a. Help software organizations
b. Analyze their current process
c. Organize a work task
d. Control and monitor progress
e. Manage technical quality

13. Define the term Scripts.

Scripts are specific process activities and other detailed work functions that are part of the team process.

14. What is the objective of the project planning process?

The objective of the project planning process is to provide a framework that enables the manager to make reasonable estimates of resources, cost, and schedule.

15. What are decomposition techniques?

Decomposition techniques are as follows:

a. Software sizing
b. Problem based estimation
c. Process based estimation

d. Estimation with use cases
e. Reconciling estimates

16. How do we compute the Expected Value for software size?

The expected value for the estimation variable(size), S, can be computed as Weighted Average of Optimistic (Sopt), most likely (Sm), and Pessimistic(Spess) estimates

S = (Sopt+4Sm+Spess)/6

17. What is an object point?

Count is determined by multiplying the original number of object instances by a weighting factor and summing to obtain total object point count

18. What is the difference between the known risks and predictable risks?

Following are the known risks:

a. That can be uncovered after careful evaluation of the project plan, the business, and technical environment in which the product is being developed
b. Example: Unrealistic delivery rate

Following are the predictable risks:

a. Extrapolated from past project experience
b. Example: Staff turnover

19. List out the basic principles of software project scheduling?

Basic principles of software project scheduling:

a. Compartmentalization
b. Interdependency
c. Time allocation
d. Effort validation
e. Defined responsibilities
f. Defined outcomes
g. Defined milestones

20. What are the classifications of system engineering?

The classifications of system engineering are as follows:

a. Business Process Engineering (BPE)
b. Product engineering

21. List out the elements in computer-based system?

Elements in computer-based system are as follows:

a. Software
b. Hardware
c. People

d. Database
e. Documentation
f. Procedures

22. What are the factors to be considered in the system model construction?

Following are the factors:

a. Assumption
b. Simplification
c. Limitation
d. Constraints
e. Preferences

23. What does a system engineering model accomplish?

The accomplishments are as follows:

a. Define processes that serve the needs of the view
b. Represent behavior of process and assumption
c. Explicitly define exogenous and endogenous input
d. Represent all linkages that enable the engineer to better understand the view.

24. What architectures are defined and developed as part of BPE?

The architectures are as follows:

a. Data architecture
b. Applications architecture
c. Technology architecture

25. What is meant by cardinality and modality?

Cardinality are:

a. The number of occurrences of one object related to the number of occurrences of another object
b. One to One [1: 1]
c. One to Many [1: N]
d. Many to Many [M: N]

Modality is whether or not a particular data object must participate in the relationship

26. What are the objectives of requirement analysis?

The objectives of the requirement analysis are:

a. Describe what the customer requires
b. Establish a basis for the creation of software design
c. Define a set of requirements that can be validated once the software design is built

27. What are the two additional features of Hayley Pirbhai model?

The two additional features are:

a. User interface processing

b. Maintenance and self-test processing

28. Define system context diagram (SCD).

Following is system context diagram:

a. Establish information boundary between System being implemented and environment which system operates.

b. Defines all external producers, external consumers, and entities that communicate through user interface.

29. Define system flow diagram (SFD).

Following is the system flow diagram:

a. Indicates information flow across SCD region

b. Used to guide system engineers in developing a system

30. What are the requirements engineering process functions?

Following are the requirements:

a. Inception

b. Elicitation

c. Elaboration

d. Negotiation

e. Specification

f. Validation

g. Management

31. What are the difficulties in elicitation?

Following are the difficulties in elicitation:

a. Problem of scope

b. Problem of understanding

c. Problem of volatility

32. List out the types of traceability tables.

Following are the types of traceability tables:

a. Features traceability table

b. Source traceability table

c. Dependency traceability table

d. Subsystem traceability table

e. Interface traceability table

33. **Define quality function deployment (QFD).**

    Following is the quality function deployment:

    a. Technique translates the needs of the customer into technical requirements

    b. Concentrates on maximizing customer satisfaction from the software engineering process

34. **What are the benefits of analysis pattern?**

    Following are the benefits of analysis pattern:

    a. Speed up development of analysis model

    b. Transformation of analysis into the design model

35. **What is system modeling?**

    The system modeling are:

    a. Important element in system engineering process

    b. Define process in each view to be constructed

    c. Represent behavior of the process

    d. Explicitly define exogenous and endogenous inputs

36. **Define CRC modeling.**

    CRC modeling is defined as:

    a. Class responsibility collaborator modeling

    b. Collection of Standard Index Card. It can be divided into three sections

       i. Name of class at top

       ii. List of class responsibilities at left

       iii. Collaborators at right

    c. Classes that cover the Information to complete its responsibilities

37. **List out the factors of data modeling.**

    Factors of data modeling are:

    a. Data objects

    b. Data attributes

    c. Relationship

    d. Cardinality and modality

38. **Define swim lane diagram.**

    The swim lane diagram is:

    a. Variation of activity diagram

    b. Allows modular to represent the flow of activities

    c. The actor responsible for the activity

39. What is the selection characteristic for classes?

Selection characteristics for classes are:

a. Retained information
b. Needed services
c. Multiple attribute
d. Common attribute
e. Common operation
f. Essential requirements

40. Define steps in behavioral model.

The steps in behavioral model are:

a. Evaluate all use cases
b. Identify events
c. Create sequence for each use cases
d. Build a state diagram
e. Review model for accuracy and consistency

41. Define the terms in software designing.

a. Abstraction

   Abstraction are:

   i. Highest level: Solution is stated in a broad term using the language of the problem environment.
   ii. Lower level: More detailed description of the solution is provided.

b. Modularity

   Software is divided into separately named and addressable components, called Modules, that are integrated to satisfy problem requirements

42. How can architectural design be represented?

Architectural design can be represented by one or more different models. They are

a. Structural models
b. Framework models
c. Dynamic models
d. Process models

43. What is the advantage of information hiding?

During the testing and maintenance phase, if changes are required that is done in a particular module without affecting another module

44. What types of classes does the designer create?

The types are as follows:

a. User interface classes

b. Business domain classes
c. Process classes
d. Persistent classes
e. System classes

45. What is coupling?

Coupling is a quantitative measure of the degree to which classes are connected to one another. It should be kept as low as possible

46. What is cohesion?

Cohesion is:

a. Indication of relative functional strength of a module
b. A natural extension of information hiding
c. Performs a single task, requiring little integration with other components

47. Define refactoring

Refactoring is changing the software system in a way that does not alter the external behavior of the code.

48. What are the five types of design classes?

Five types of design classes are:

- User interface classes
- Business domain classes
- Process classes
- Persistent classes
- System classes

49. What are the different types of design models? Explain.

Different types of design models are:

a. Process dimension: Indicate the evolution of the design model as design tasks are executed as part of the software process
b. Abstraction dimension: Represent the level of detail as each element of the analysis model is transformed into a design equivalent

50. List out the different elements of design model?

Different elements of design model are:

a. Data design elements
b. Architectural design elements
c. Interface design elements
d. Component level design elements
e. Deployment level design elements

51. **What are the types of interface design elements?**

    Types of interface design elements are:

    a. User interfaces
    b. External interfaces
    c. Internal interfaces

52. **What types of design patterns are available for the software engineer?**

    Types of design patterns are:

    a. Architectural patterns
    b. Design patterns
    c. Idioms

53. **Define framework.**

    Framework is defined as:

    a. Code skeleton that can be fleshed out with specific classes or functionality.
    b. Designed to address specifies problem at hand.

54. **What is the objective of architectural design?**

    The objective of architectural design is to model the overall software structure by representing component interfaces, dependencies, relationships, and interactions

55. **What are the important roles of conventional components within the software architecture?**

    Following are the important roles of conventional components within the software architecture

    a. Control component: that coordinates invocation of all other problem domain
    b. Problem domain component: that implement Complete or Partial function required by the customer
    c. Infrastructure component: responsible for functions that support processing required in the problem domain

56. **What are the basic design principles of class-based components?**

    Basic Design principles of class-based components are:

    a. Open-Closed Principle (OCP)
    b. Liskov Substitution Principle (LSP)
    c. Dependency Inversion Principle (DIP)
    d. Interface Segregation Principle (ISP)
    e. Release Reuse Equivalency Principle (REP)
    f. Common Closure Principle (CCP)
    g. Common Reuse Principle (CRP)

57. What should we consider when we name components?

We should consider the following:

a. Components
b. Interface
c. Dependencies and inheritance

58. What are the different types of cohesion?

Following are the different types of cohesion:

a. Functional
b. Layer
c. Communicational
d. Sequential
e. Procedural
f. Temporal
g. Utility

59. What are the different types of coupling?

Different types of coupling are:

a. Content coupling
b. Common coupling
c. Control coupling
d. Stamp coupling
e. Data coupling
f. Routine call coupling
g. Type use coupling
h. Inclusion or import coupling
i. External coupling

60. What is program design language (PDL)?

Program design language are:

a. Also called structured English or pseudocode
b. Pidgin language in that it uses the vocabulary of one language and the overall syntax of another

61. What are the basic principles of software testing?

Basic principles of software testing are:

a. Traceable to customer requirements
b. Planned long before testing begins
c. Pareto principles applied to software testing
d. Begin small and progress toward testing

e. Exhaustive testing is not possible
f. Conducted by an independent third party

62. List out the characteristics of the testability of software.

Characteristics of testability of software are:

a. Operability
b. Observability
c. Controllability
d. Decomposability
e. Simplicity
f. Stability
g. Understandability

63. List out various methods for finding cyclomatic complexity?

The various methods are:

a. Number of Regions
b. Cyclomatic Complexity V(G), for Flow Graph
   $V(G) = E - N + 2$
c. Cyclomatic Complexity V(G)
   $V(G) = P + 1$

64. Define smoke testing.

Smoke testing is described :

a. Integration testing
b. Commonly used when software products are being developed

65. What are the attributes of good test?

Attributes of good test are:

a. High probability of finding errors
b. Not Redundant
c. Best of Breed
d. Neither too simple nor too complex

66. Define white box testing.

White box testing are:

a. Also called glass box testing
b. Test case design uses the control structure of procedural
c. Design to derive test cases

67. Define basic path testing.

Basic path testing are:

a. White box testing
b. Enable test case designer to derive a logical complexity measure of a procedural design
c. Use this measure as a guide for defining a basic set of execution paths

68. Define the terms:

a. Graph matrices

To develop software tools, the data structure used is:

i. Graph matrix
ii. Square matrix
iii. Size equals the number of nodes on the flowgraph

b. Connection matrices

If link weight =1 => connection exists

If link weight =1 => connection does not exist

69. What is behavioral testing?

Behavioral testing are:

a. Also known as black box testing
b. Focuses on the functional requirement of software
c. Enables software engineer to derive a set of input conditions that fully exercises all functional requirements of software.

70. What are the benefits of conducting smoke testing?

Benefits of conducting smoke testing are:

a. Integration risk is minimized
b. The quality of the end-product is improved
c. Error diagnosis and correction are simplified
d. Progress is easy to assess

71. What errors are commonly found during unit testing?

The errors found are:

a. Misunderstood or incorrect arithmetic precedence
b. Mixed mode operations
c. Incorrect initializations
d. Precision accuracy
e. Incorrect symbolic representation of the expression

72. What problems may be encountered when top-down integration is chosen?

The problems are:

a. Delay is tested until stubs are replaced with actual modules

b. Develop stubs that perform limited functions that simulate the actual module

c. Integrate the software from the bottom of the hierarchy upward

73. What are the steps in bottom-up integration?

Steps in bottom-up integration are:

a. Low-level components are combined into clusters perform specific software subfunction

b. The driver is written to coordinate test case input and output

c. Cluster is tested

d. Drivers are removed, and clusters are combined, moving inward in the program structure.

74. What is regression testing?

Regression testing are:

a. Re-execution of some subset of tests that have already been conducted

b. To ensure changes have not propagated unintended side effects

75. What are the characteristics of the critical module?

Characteristics of the critical module are:

a. Addresses several software requirements

b. Has a high level of control

c. Complex or error prone

d. Has definite performance requirements

76. What are the properties of connection matrices?

Properties of connection matrices:

a. Probability that the link will execute.

b. Processing time expended during traversal of the link.

c. Memory required during traversal of the link.

d. Resource required during traversal of the link.

77. What is flow graph notation?

Flow graph notation is:

a. Simple notation for representing control flow

b. Draw only when the logical structure of the component is complex

78. Define cyclomatic complexity.

Cyclomatic Complexity is:

a. A software metric

b. A quantitative measure of logical complexity
c. Number of independent paths in the basic set of program

79. What is equivalence partition?

Equivalence partitions are:

a. Derives an input domain of a program into classes of data from which test cases are derived
b. A set of objects is linked by relationships as symmetric, transitive, and reflexive an equivalence class is present

80. List out the possible errors of black box testing?

Errors of black box testing are:

a. Incorrect or missing functions
b. Interface errors
c. Errors in data structures or external databases
d. Behavioral or performance errors
e. Initialization or termination errors

81. Define data objects.

Data objects are:

a. Represent composite information
b. The external entity, thin, occurrence or event, role, organizational unit, place or structure
c. Encapsulates data only

82. What are the components of the cost of quality?

Components of the cost of quality are:

a. Quality costs
b. Prevention costs
c. Appraisal costs

83. What is software quality control?

Software quality ontrol are:

a. Involves a series of inspections, reviews, and tests
b. Used throughout the software process to ensure each work product meets requirements placed upon it

84. What is software quality assurance?

Software quality assurance are:

a. Set of auditing and reporting functions
b. Assess the effectiveness and completeness of quality control activities

85. What is the objective of formal technical reviews?

The objectives of formal technical reviews are:

a. Uncover errors in function, logic, and implementation for the representation of software
b. Software represented according to a predefined standard
c. Verify that the software under review meets the requirements
d. Achieve software developed in Uniform Manner
e. Make projects more manageable

86. What steps are required to perform statistical SQA?

The steps to be followed are:

a. Information about software defects is collected and categorized
b. An attempt is made to trace each defect
c. Using the Pareto principle, isolate 20%
d. Once vital causes are identified, correct problems that cause defects

87. Define the SQA plan.

SQA plans are:

a. Provides a roadmap for instituting SQA
b. The plan serves as a template for SQA activities that are instituted for each software project

88. What are the baseline criteria in SCM?

The baseline criteria in SCM are:

a. Help to control change
b. Specification or product that has been formally
c. Reviewed and agreed upon serves as the basis for future development
d. That can be changed only through formal change control procedures

89. Define status reporting.

Status reporting is:

a. Also called configuration status reporting
b. an SCM task that answers:
    i. What happened?
    ii. Who did it?
    iii. When did it happen?
    iv. What else will be affected?

90. What is the origin of changes that are requested for software?

Origin of changes are:-

a. New business or market condition

b. New customer needs
c. Reorganization or business growth downsizing
d. Budgetary or scheduling constraints

91. List out the elements of SCM.

Elements of SCM are:

a. Component elements
b. Process elements
c. Construction elements
d. Human elements

92. What are the features supported by SCM?

Features supported by SCM are:

a. Versioning
b. Dependency tracking and change management
c. Requirements tracking
d. Configuration management
e. Audit trails

93. What are the objectives of the SCM process?

The objectives of the SCM process are:

a. Identify all items, collectively define software configuration
b. Manage changes to one or more of these items
c. Facilitate the construction of different versions of an application
d. Ensure that the software quality is maintained

94. What are the issues to be considered for developing tactics for WebApp configuration management?

The issues are as follows

a. Context
b. People
c. Scalability

95. Define CASE tools.

CASE tools is defined as:

a. Computer aided software engineering
b. It is a system software
c. Provide automated support for software process activities
d. Includes program used to support software process activities
e. Such as requirement analysis, system modeling, debugging, and testing

96. **How do we define software quality?**

Software quality is defined as:

a. Conformance to explicitly stated functional and performance requirements, explicitly documented development standards
b. Implicit characteristics, expected for professionally developed software

97. **Define the terms:**

a. Quality of design

Characteristics, designer specify for an item

b. Quality of conformance

Degree to which design specifications are followed during manufacturing

98. **What is the type of CASE tool?**

Types of CASE tools are:

a. Upper CASE tools
b. Lower CASE tools

99. **Define software reliability?**

Software reliability is the probability of failure-free operation of the computer program in a specified environment for a specified time.

100. **How the Registration process of ISO 9000 certification is done?**

The registration process of ISO 9000 certification has the following stages:

a. Application
b. Pre-assessment
c. Document review and adequacy of audit
d. Compliance audit
e. Registration
f. Continued surveillance

Short questions with answers

1. **Define software engineering**

The establishment and use of sound engineering principles in order to obtain economically software that is reliable and works efficiently on real machines.

2. **Differentiate software engineering methods, tools, and procedures.**

Following are the methods, tools, and procedures:

a. Methods: Broad array of tasks like project planning, cost estimation, etc..
b. Tools: Automated or semi-automated support for methods.
c. Procedures: Hold the methods and tools together. It enables the timely development of computer software.

3. **Write the disadvantages of the classic life cycle model.**

   Disadvantages of the classic life cycle model are:

   a. Real projects rarely follow the sequential flow. Iteration always occurs and creates
   b. problem.
   c. Difficult for the customer to state all requirements
   d. A working version of the program is not available. So the customer must have patience.

4. **What do you mean by task set in the spiral model?**

   Each of the regions in the spiral model is populated by a set of work tasks called a task set that are adapted to the characteristics of the project to be undertaken.

5. **What is the main objective of the Win-Win Spiral model?**

   The customer and the developer enter into the process of negotiation where the customer may be asked to balance functionality, performance, and other products against cost and time to market.

6. **Which of the software engineering paradigms would be most effective? Why?**

   The incremental or spiral model will be most effective.

   The reasons are as follows:

   a. It combines the linear sequential model with the iterative nature of prototyping
   b. Focuses on delivery of the product at each increment
   c. It can be planned to manage technical risks

7. **Who is called the stakeholder?**

   A stakeholder is anyone in the organization who has a direct business interest in the system or product to be built.

8. **Write the objective of project planning.**

   It is to provide a framework that enables the manager to make reasonable estimates of resources, cost, and schedule.

9. **What is boot strapping?**

   A sequence of instructions whose execution causes additional instructions to be loaded and executed until the complete program is in storage.

10. **Write a short note on the Fourth Generation Technique (4GT).**

    4GT encompasses a broad array of software tools. Each tool enables the software developer to specify some characteristics of software at a higher level.

11. **What is a Function Point (FP)? How is it used for project estimation?**

    Function Point. It is used as the estimation variable to size each element of the software. It requires considerably less detail. Estimated indirectly by estimating the number of inputs, outputs, data files, and external interfaces.

12. What is LOC? How is it used for project estimation?

LOC is used as an estimation variable to size each element of the software. It requires a considerable level of detail.

13. Write the formula to calculate the effort in person-months used in Dynamic multivariable model?

E=[LOC * B0.333/P]3 *(1/t4), where E is an effort in person-months, t is projected duration, B is a special skills factor, and P is the productivity parameter.

14. What is called object points?

It is an indirect software measure that is computed using counts of the number of screens, reports, and components.

15. What are the four different degrees of Rigor?

Four different degrees of Rigor are:

- Casual
- Structured
- Strict
- Quick reaction

16. Write about democratic teams in software development. (Egoless Team)

It is an egoless team. All team members participate in all decisions. Group leadership rotates from member to member based on tasks to be performed.

17. What are the two project scheduling methods?

The two projects are:

- Program Evaluation and Review Techniques (PERT)
- Critical Path Method (CPM)

18. What is called support risk?

The degree of uncertainty that the resultant software will be easy to correct, adapt and enhance.

19. What is RMMM?

Risk Mitigation, Monitoring and Management Plan. It is also called Risk Aversion.

20. What are the four impacts of the project risk?

Catastrophic, Critical, Marginal, Negligible.

21. List the tools or methods available for rapid prototyping.

The methods for rapid prototyping (speed) are:

a. 4GT

b. Reusable software components

c. Formal specification and prototyping environments.

22. What is the need for modularity?

The need for modularity are:

a. Easier to solve a complex problem.

b. Can achieve reusability.

c. Best effort and complexity reduction.

23. What are the five criteria that are used in modularity?

The five criteria are:

a. Modular decomposability

b. Modular composability

c. Modular understandability

d. Modular continuity

e. Modular protection

24. What is software architecture?

The overall structure of the software and the ways in which that software provides conceptual integrity for the system.

25. What are the models used for architectural design?

The models used are:

a. Structural models

b. Framework models

c. Dynamic models

d. Process models

e. Functional models

26. What is cohesion?

It is a measure of the relative functional strength of a module. (Binding)

27. What is coupling?

The measure of the relative interdependence among modules.

(Measure of interconnection among modules in a software structure.)

28. List the coupling factors.

The factors are:

a. Interface complexity between modules

b. Reference to the module

c. Data pass across the interface.

29. Define stamp coupling.

When a portion of the data structure is passed via the module interface, then it is called stamp coupling.

30. **Define common coupling.**

When a number of modules reference a global data area, then the coupling is called common coupling.

31. **Define temporal cohesion.**

When a module contains tasks that are related by the fact that all must be executed within the same span of time, then it is termed as temporal cohesion.

32. **Write a short note on structure charts.**

These are used in architectural design to document hierarchical structure, parameters, and interconnections in a system. No Decision box. The chart can be augmented with the module by module specifications of I/P and O/P parameters as well as I/P and O/P attributes.

33. **What do you mean by factoring?**

It is also called vertical partitioning. It follows a top-down strategy. We can say that there are some top-level modules and low-level modules.

a. **Top level modules:** Control functions, actual processing works

b. **Low-level modules**: Workers. Performing all input computation and output tasks.

34. **What is aesthetics?**

It is a science of art and beauty. These are fundamental to software design, whether in art or technology.

Simplicity, elegance(refinement), clarity of purpose.

35. **What do you mean by common coupling?**

When a number of modules reference a global data area, then the coupling is called common coupling.

36. **Write about real-time systems.**

It provides a specified amount of computation within fixed time intervals. RTS sense and control external devices, respond to external events and share processing time between tasks.

37. **Define distributed system.**

It consists of a collection of nearly autonomous processors that communicate to achieve a coherent computing system.

38. **Compare data flow oriented design with data structure-oriented design**

a. Data flow-oriented design: Used to represent a system or software at any level of abstraction.

b. Data Structure-oriented design: It is used for representing information hierarchy using the three constructs for sequence, selection, and repetition.

39. Define architectural design and data design.

Architectural design is to develop a modular program structure and represent the relationships between modules.

Data design isto select the logical representations of data objects, data storage and the concepts of information hiding and data abstraction.

40. What are the contents of the HIPO diagrams?

A visual table of contents, set of overview diagrams, and set of detail diagrams.

41. What are the aspects of software reuse?

The aspect are:

a. Software development with reuse
b. Software development for reuse
c. Generator based reuse
d. Application system reuse

42. Define configuration status reporting.

Configuration status reporting is defines as:

a. What happened?
b. Who did it?
c. When did it happen?
d. What else will be affected?

It is also called status accounting.

43. What is the need for baseline?

Need for baseline:

a. Basis for further development
b. Uses formal change control procedure for change
c. Helps to control change

44. Define SCM.

It is an umbrella activity that is applied throughout the software process. It has a set of tracking and control activities that begin when a software engineering project begins and terminate only when the software project is taken out of operation.

45. List the SCM activities.

The SCM activities are:

a. Identify a change
b. Control change
c. Ensure that change is being properly implemented
d. Report changes to others who may have an interest

46. **What is meant by software reusability?**

    A software component should be designed and implemented so that it can be reused in many different programs.

47. **What is computer aided software engineering**

    CASE provides the engineer with the ability to automate manual activities and improve engineering insight.

48. **Write the distinction between SCM and software support.**

    a. SCM: It has a set of tracking and control activities that begin when a software engineering project begins and terminates only when the software project is taken out of operation.

    b. Software support: It has a set of software engineering activities that occur after the software has been delivered to the customer and put into operation.

49. **What is the difference between basic objects and aggregate objects used in software configuration?**

    a. Basic objects: It represents a unit of text. For example, the section of requirement specification, Source listing for a component

    b. Aggregate objects: Collection of basic objects and other aggregate objects. For example, full design specification

50. **What is configuration audit? Has the change specified in ECO been made? Has formal technical review been conducted?**

    Software Engineering procedures for noting the change, recording it, reporting it been followed? SCI is updated?

Essay type questions

1. Explain the linear sequential model and prototyping model in detail.
2. Explain the spiral model and win-win spiral model in detail.
3. Explain incremental model in detail.
4. Discuss fourth generation techniques.
5. Explain the activities of project planning.
6. Explain the cost estimation procedure using the COCOMO model.
7. Explain the following:
    a. Delphi Cost Estimation
    b. Putnam Estimation model
    c. Decomposition approach:
8. Explain the organizational structure of software development.
9. Explain the process of risk analysis and management.

10. Explain the following:
    a. Software requirement specification.
    b. Specification review
11. Explain the types of coupling and cohesion.
12. Explain the various software design concepts
13. Explain software design documentation in detail.
14. Discuss the design procedure for Real-time and distributed system software.
15. Explain Jackson system development with an example.
16. Explain software design notations
17. Explain data flow oriented design in detail.
18. Explain programming standards in detail
19. What is software reuse? Explain the various aspects of software reuse.
20. Describe the various software configuration management tasks in detail.
21. Write notes on version control and change control.
22. What are CASE tools and their usage in software engineering? Discuss each tool in brief.
23. Explain the integrated CASE environment in detail.

    Explanations of Integrated CASE Environment, Benefits, Integration Architecture
24. Explain CASE repository in detail
25. Explain the building blocks for CASE

Model test papers

Question paper 1

Full Marks – 70 Time – 3 Hours

Question no.1 is compulsory, and do any five from the rest.

1. **Answer the following questions. (2 X 10)**
    a. Define software engineering. What is the difference between just writing software and software engineering?
    b. How cohesions and coupling are related?
    c. What makes software design different from coding?
    d. What do you mean by the term functional independence in the context of software design?
    e. Explain the difference between black box testing and white box testing.

f. What are the two most important aims of software inspection? What are the three basic input documents to any inspection?

g. Is Lines-of-Code (LOC) a useful productivity measure?

h. What is SPMP document?

i. What are the main steps that must be taken to ensure there is a high degree of reusability in a software system?

j. What is the new COCOMO-II formula for calculating project effort?

2. **Answer the following question. (5 X 2)**

a. What is the principal aim of software engineering discipline? What do you mean by the term software reverse engineering? Why is it required?

b. Do you design software when you write a program? What is a good software design?

3. **Answer the following question. (5 X 2)**

a. Explain how to select the best risk reduction technique when there are many ways of reducing risk.

b. When a software project has got seriously behind schedule it is not usually appropriate to add more staff. Explain why this is so and suggest what effective actions might be taken to best recover from the situation? Justify the actions you would take.

4. **Answer the following question. (5 X 2)**

a. Create a use case diagram for the following description:

A professor uses an office for preparing classes and carrying out research. Both activities include studying the relevant literature. The office is also used for meeting students.

b. How do we construct a black box testing plan? Who should do the testing?

5. **Answer the following question. (5 X 2)**

c. What is a user interface portion of a software product? What are the characteristics of a good user interface?

d. Define, compare, and contrast KLOC and FP metrics. What are pros and cons of each?

6. **Answer the following question. (5 X 2)**

a. Develop an activity diagram showing the following activities and their synchronization. Use concurrent activities where it is possible.

Problem description: To develop a software system, the first step is to develop the system architecture. Based on the system architecture, a system design can be developed and then implemented. The architecture can also be used for defining test cases. In addition, it can be used as a basis for the user manual. When all things are available, the system can be delivered to the customer. Then, it will be installed and beta-tested.

b. What is the purpose of the Capacity Maturity Model? Given a particular experiment and findings, assess the reliability of the findings.

7. **Answer the following question. (5 X 2)**

a. What is Lehman's law for software evaluation? What are the different problems associated with software maintenance?

b. What is the relationship between cyclometric complexity and program comprehensibility? Can you justify why such an apparent relationship exists?

8. **Answer the following question. (2.5 X 4)**

a. How do we assess the quality of software design?

b. What is the role of interfaces in a class-based component-level design?

c. Explain what is the main goal of a high level of architectural design and how it differs from the detailed design phase?

d. Define and differentiate between the Waterfall model and the Spiral model.

Question paper 2

Full Marks – 70 Time – 3 Hours

Question no.1 is compulsory and attempt any five from the rest.

1. **Answer the following questions. (2 X 10)**

a. Distinguish between a program and a software product?

b. What are the important activities that are carried out during the feasibility study phase of the classical Waterfall model?

c. Which are the two current metrics used for project size estimation? Which one is better than the other and why?

d. List the five desirable characteristics of a good Software Requirement Specification (SRS) document.

e. What is the meaning of the terms 'Coupling' in the context of software design? What problems are likely to arise if two modules have high coupling?

f. What do you understand by the term 'UML' and 'Use Case' in the context of the object-oriented design of software?

g. What are the differences between a Graphical User Interface (GUI) and a Text-Based User Interface?

h. What is the difference between coding standards and coding guidelines? List at least two coding standards.

i. What are the three levels of testing of any software product?

j. What is software reverse engineering?

2. **Answer the following question. (5 X 2)**

   a. Distinguish between control flow based design, data structure oriented design, data flow oriented design, and object-oriented design of software products?

   b. Give a brief explanation with schematic diagram the prototyping model of software development.

3. **Answer the following question. (5 X 2)**

   a. Give a brief comparison of the different life cycle models. Explain in brief the classical Waterfall model.

   b. Which life cycle model you would follow for developing extremely large software that would provide, monitor and control cellular communication among its subscribers using a set of revolving satellites. Justify your answer.

4. **Answer the following question. (5 X 2)**

   a. What is the SRS document? Who are the typical users of the SRS document?

   b. Give a broad structure of a good SRS document. Specify some characteristics of a good SRS document and some characteristics of a bad SRS document?

5. **Answer the following question. (5 X 2)**

   a. Briefly highlight the difference between Code inspection and Code Walk-through. Compare the relative merits of code inspection and code walk-through. What is the difference between verification and validation of a software product?

   b. Distinguish between unit testing, Integration testing, and system testing. Explain how unit testing is done with driver and stub modules.

6. **Answer the following question. (5 X 2)**

   a. What is Black Box testing? Explain the equivalence class partitioning and Boundary value analysis approaches with examples to designing of Black Box test cases.

   b. Explain various strategies for White Box testing. What do you understand by the statement Strategy A is stronger testing than Strategy B?

7. **Answer the following question. (5 X 2)**

   a. Write short notes on:

      i. SEI Capability Maturity Model (CMM).

      ii. ISO 9000 Certification.

b. State Lehman's first and second law in connection with software evolution. Explain with a schematic diagram the process of 'software reverse engineering'.

8. **Answer the following question. (5 X 2)**

   a. Specify different software maintenance process models and explain any one of the models with schematic diagrams. How would you select an appropriate maintenance model for a maintenance project at hand?

   b. What are the different COCOMO models used for estimating cost and effort for a software project? Which model is better? Explain in brief the Basic COCOMO model.

Question paper 3

Full Marks – 70 Time – 3 Hours

Question no.1 is compulsory, and any five from the rest.

1. **Answer the following questions. (2 X 10)**

   a. Which phases in the Waterfall life cycle model consumes the maximum effort for developing a typical software product?

   b. Which parameter (s) is/are used in COCOMO estimation model?

   c. Who is responsible for developing the SRS document?

   d. What is the difference between revision and version?

   e. What is object persistence? How a persistent object can be realized?

   f. Is the Unified Modeling Language (UML) is strictly a language? Justify your answer.

   g. What is Rapid Application Development (RAD)?

   h. What do you mean by smoke testing?

   i. What is the pattern in object-oriented analysis and design?

   j. What do you mean by Key Process Areas (KPAs) in the context of SEI CMM?

2. **Answer the following questions.**

   a. Draw a schematic diagram to represent the iterative waterfall model of software development. (6)

   b. On your diagram represent the deliverables produced at the end of each phase.

3. **Answer the following questions. (5 X 2)**

   a. What are the different categories of software development projects according to the COCOMO model?

b. What are the relative advantages of using either the LOC or the function point metric to measure the size of a software product?

4. **Answer the following questions.**

The system analysis group working on a system design project estimated the schedule of activities as given in the following:

Activity	Notation	Must Follow	Expected Time (Days)
Draw DFD	A	None	9
Draw decision tree	B	A	12
Revise tree	C	B	3
Write up report	D	C, H	7
Organize data dictionary	E	A	11
Do output prototype	F	None	8
Revise design	G	F	14
Design database	H	E, G	5

a. Draw PERT diagram based on the above-mentioned data. (6)

b. List all paths and identify the critical path. (4)

5. **Answer the following questions.**

a. What do mean by the term cohesion and coupling in the context of software design? (6)

b. Why high coupling and low cohesion in a design are preferable? (4)

6. **Explain with appropriate examples the following: (4+3+3)**

a. DFD

b. Structure chart

c. Data dictionary

7. **What do you mean by the following views of a system? (2 X 5)**

a. User's view

b. Structural view

c. Behavioral view

d. Implementation view

e. Environmental view

8. **Answer the following questions. (5 X 2)**
   a. Schematically draw the architecture of a CASE environment and explain how the different tools are integrated.
   b. What do you mean by the term Software Reengineering? Why it is required?

Question paper 4

Full Marks – 70, Time – 3 Hours

Question no.1 is compulsory, and attempt any five from the rest.

1. **Answer the following questions. (2 X 10)**
   a. What is the principal aim of software engineering? Draw the pyramid diagram for OOSE architecture.
   b. What are the three different kinds of testing associated with system testing?
   c. What are the prominent qualities in system design with the OO method?
   d. What do you mean by software process?
   e. What is the role of the data dictionary in the CASE environment?
   f. Differentiate between object-oriented analysis and object-oriented design.
   g. Define the term cohesion in the context of the object-oriented design of the system.
   h. What are the advantages of encapsulation?
   i. What is the difference between a coding standard and coding guideline?
   j. What is meant by a code walk-through?
2. **Answer the following questions. (5 X 2)**
   a. Why should a requirement analyst avoid making any design decisions during requirements analysis? Must a good programmer also be a good requirement analyst?
   b. Discuss the major advantages of object-oriented design methodologies over the data flow-oriented design methodologies.
3. **Answer the following questions. (5 X 2)**
   a. What is meant by the structural complexity of a program? Define metrics for measuring the structural complexity of a program. How this is different from the computational complexity of a program?
   b. Draw a data flow diagram for the inventory of a large medicine store.

4. **Answer the following questions. (5 X 2)**
   a. Why is it important to properly document a software product? What are the different ways of documenting a software product?
   b. What is stress testing? Why is stress testing applicable to only certain types of system?
5. **Answer the following questions. (5 X 2)**
   a. What is regression testing? Why regression testing is necessary? How is regression testing performed?
   b. Discuss the relative merits of ISO 9001 certification and SEI CMM based quality assessment?
6. **Answer the following questions. (5 X 2)**
   a. What are the different types of views that can be modeled using UML? What are the different UML diagrams which can be used to capture each of the views?
   b. What do you mean by repeatable software development? Organizations assessed at which level of SEI CMM maturity achieves repeatable software environment?
7. **Answer the following questions. (5 X 2)**
   a. Discuss how the reliability changes over the lifetime of a software product?
   b. How cohesion and couplings are related? Give an example where cohesion increases and coupling decreases.
8. **Answer the following questions. (2.5 X 4)**
   a. Define and differentiate between software engineering and software reengineering.
   b. If a module has logical cohesion, what kind of coupling is the module likely to have with others?
   c. Define the metrics to measure the software reliability.
   d. Define and differentiate between CASE roll and CASE environment.

Question paper 5

Full Marks – 70 Time – 3 Hours

Question no.1 is compulsory and attempt any five from the rest.

1. **Answer the following questions. (2 X 10)**
   a. Discuss the major advantages of OOD methodology over the data flow oriented design methodologies.
   b. Explain why the spiral life cycle model is considered to be a metamodel.

c. Define risk leverage.

d. Enumerate two different types of coupling that exist between two modules.

e. Distinguish between a DFD and a flow-chart.

f. What are the advantages of UML class diagrams?

g. What is meant by a code walkthrough?

h. How can you determine the number of latent defects in a software product during the testing phase?

i. What are the main advantages of using CASE tools?

j. What is an application generator?

2. **Answer the following questions. (5 X 2)**

   a. What are the symptoms of the present software crisis? What factors have contributed to the making of the present software crisis? What are the possible solutions to the present software crisis?

   b. What do you understand by the visibility of design and code? How does increased visibility help in systematic software development?

3. **Answer the following questions. (5 X 2)**

   a. What do you understand by the term 'phase containment of errors'? Why is phase containment of errors so important? How can phase containment of errors be achieved?

   b. Explain with suitable examples the type of product developments for which the evolutionary life cycle model is more suitable and the type of problems for which the spiral model is more suitable.

4. **Answer the following questions.**

   a. What do you mean by the term cohesion and coupling in the context of software design? How are these concepts useful arriving at a good design of a system? (6)

   b. Compare the relative advantages of the object-oriented and function-oriented approaches to software design. (4)

5. **Answer the following questions.**

   a. What are the different system views that can be modeled using UML? What are the different UML diagrams which can be used to capture each of the views? Do you need to develop all the views of a system using all the modeling diagrams supported by UML? Justify your answer. (7)

   b. What causes increased productivity when the object-oriented paradigm is adopted?

6. **Answer the following questions.**
   a. Differentiate between black-box testing and white-box testing with suitable examples. (4)
   b. What is meant by the structural complexity of a problem? Define a metric for measuring the structural complexity of a program. How is structural complexity of a program different from its computational complexity? (6)
7. **Answer the following questions.**
   a. What do you understand by key process areas (KPAs) in the context of SEI CMM? Would there be any problem if an organization tries to implement the high-level KPAs before achieving a lower level of KPAs? Justify your answer using a suitable example. (6)
   b. What is a legacy software product? Explain the problems one would encounter while maintaining a legacy product. (4)
8. **Answer the following questions. (5 X 2)**
   a. What do you mean by the term software reverse engineering? Why is it required? Explain the different activities undertaken during reverse engineering.
   b. What do you understand by the term faceted classification in the context of software reuse? How does faceted classification simplify the component search in a component store?

Question paper 6

Full Marks – 70 Time – 3 Hours

Question no.1 is compulsory and attempt any five from the rest.

1. **Answer the following questions. (2 X 10)**
   a. What do you mean by a software process?
   b. What do you mean by the term phase containment error?
   c. Which are the 7 standard software quality characteristics?
   d. Define CASE tools and CASE environment.
   e. What is stress testing?
   f. What is the use of a Use Case diagram in software design?
   g. What do you mean by the term software reverse engineering?
   h. Define and differentiate between corrective and perfective maintenance.
   i. What is the new COCOMO-II formula for calculating project effort?
   j. What do you understand by a layered software design?

2. **Answer the following questions. (5 X 2)**
   a. What is a prototype? Under what circumstance is it beneficial to construct a prototype?
   b. Who are the different users of SRS document? What are their expectations from the SRS document?
3. **Discuss how the effort spent in the different phases of the iterative Water Fall model is spread over time. (5)**
4. **Answer the following questions. (5 X 2)**
   a. Explain coupling and cohesion in the context of software design. Describe the type of coupling and cohesion.
   b. How can management organization and the systematic application of methods increase the chance that a development project will succeed?
5. **Answer the following questions. (5 X 2)**
   a. What are the features of good software design? Can quality be measured?
   b. Explain the various steps in the cost estimation procedure using COCOMO.
6. **Answer the following questions. (5 X 2)**
   a. Development methods involve building models to describe the system being investigated. What are the three kinds of the model developed during object-oriented analysis and design?
   b. Discuss the relative merits of ISO 9001 certification and SEI CMM based quality assessment.
7. **Answer the following questions. (2.5 X 4)**
   a. Differentiate between alpha and beta testing.
   b. Differentiate between software validation and verification.
   c. Differentiate between CASE environment and CASE tools.
   d. Differentiate between object oriented and function-oriented design.
8. **A system is required to maintain an inventory of the contents of a warehouse. Items are delivered for storage at any time during the day and must be allocated space. An identification label must be attached to each item before storage and some items need to be stored in a refrigerated unit. An item can be stored for any period of time but some items have an expiry date by which they must be removed from the warehouse. When items are removed, they need to be labeled, packaged for delivery and put on the correct delivery truck. The truck driver should be given a list of delivery addresses for the items. The system should be able to generate reports showing the current contents of the warehouse and the last day's deliveries and collections.**

a. Taking an object-oriented point of view, draw up a list of potential classes, attributes, and external entities using the specification above as a guide. (5)

b. Starting with the classes you have identified in part (a), generate a class diagram for the warehouse software system. Make sure each class is labeled with any key attributes or operations. (5)

Index

Symbols

A

D

E

F

G

H

I

J

K

L

M

N

O

P

Q

R

S

T

U

V

W

X

Z

www.ingramcontent.com/pod-product-compliance
Lightning Source LLC
Chambersburg PA
CBHW061737210326
41599CB00034B/6711